Official Trainer's Guide & Pokédex

The People of Kanto

Professor Oak

"I study Pokémon as a profession."

Red, Blue, and Green

"... ...!"

"Smell ya later, newbie!"

"Just show me how strong you've gotten!"

Your Character

Your Rival

"It's battle time!"

"My Pokémon are all hard as rock and have true-grit determination!"

Brock

Misty

"My sweet Pokémon are ready! Are you?"

Lt. Surge

"A Pokémon battle is war!"

Erika

"...Oh dear. I must have dozed off."

Lorelei

"No one can best me when it comes to icy Pokémon."

Bruno

"We will grind you down with our superior power!"

Agatha

"I'll show you how a real Trainer battles!"

Lance

"Well, are you ready to lose?"

Getting Started

Table of Contents

Alphabetical List of Kanto Maps

Alphabetical List of Pokémon

The Kanto Region

Pokémon Gyms

Challenge the Gym Leaders at these Gyms to collect Badges in the cities you visit.

Pokémon Centers

Visit these locations to completely heal your Pokémon for free.

Poké Marts

Buy all sorts of helpful items at these shops, such as Poké Balls and Potions.

Partner Move Tutor

Teach your partner Pokémon different unique moves at certain Pokémon Centers.

Love Checker

Talk to your rival's sister in Pallet Town to check how much your Pokémon love you.

Pokémon Day Care

At this facility on Route 5, leave a Pokémon to level up, or do some Hyper Training (p. 125).

Fortune Teller

Madam Celadon can predict the Nature of wild Pokémon you'll encounter (p. 388).

GO Park Complex

Visit this complex in Fuchsia City's Safari Zone to catch Pokémon you've sent to your game from Pokémon GO.

Move Reminder

Talk to Madam Memorial on the Indigo Plateau to remind your Pokémon of moves they forgot or to teach them moves they did not learn.

Mega Stone Seller

Purchase Mega Stones from this man who appears at the Pokémon League after you've become Champion.

Indigo Plateau

Route 23

Victory Road

Route 23

Pewter City

Route 3

Diglett's Cave (West entrance)

Viridian Forest

Route 2

Route 2

Route 17

Route 22

Viridian City

Route 1

Pallet Town

Route 21

Cinnabar Island

Route 20

Pallet Town

- Oak Pokémon Research Lab
- Love Checker

Viridian City

- Pokémon Center
- Poké Mart
- Pokémon Gym
- Trainers' School

Pewter City

- Pokémon Center
- Poké Mart
- Pokémon Gym
- Pewter Museum of Science
- Pewter Crunchies Seller

Cerulean City

- Pokémon Center
- Poké Mart
- Pokémon Gym
- Partner Move Tutor
- Cerulean Cave

Vermilion City

- Pokémon Center
- Poké Mart
- Pokémon Gym
- Vermilion Port
- S.S. Anne
- Pokémon Fan Club

Lavender Town

- Pokémon Center
- Poké Mart
- Pokémon Tower
- Pokémon House

Below is the map of the Kanto region, where you'll embark on your adventure to challenge the Pokémon League. The cities, towns, routes, caves, and other key locations are shown. Routes are labeled in **red**, while other important locations are labeled in **pink**. Information about key facilities located in each town can be found below and beside the map.

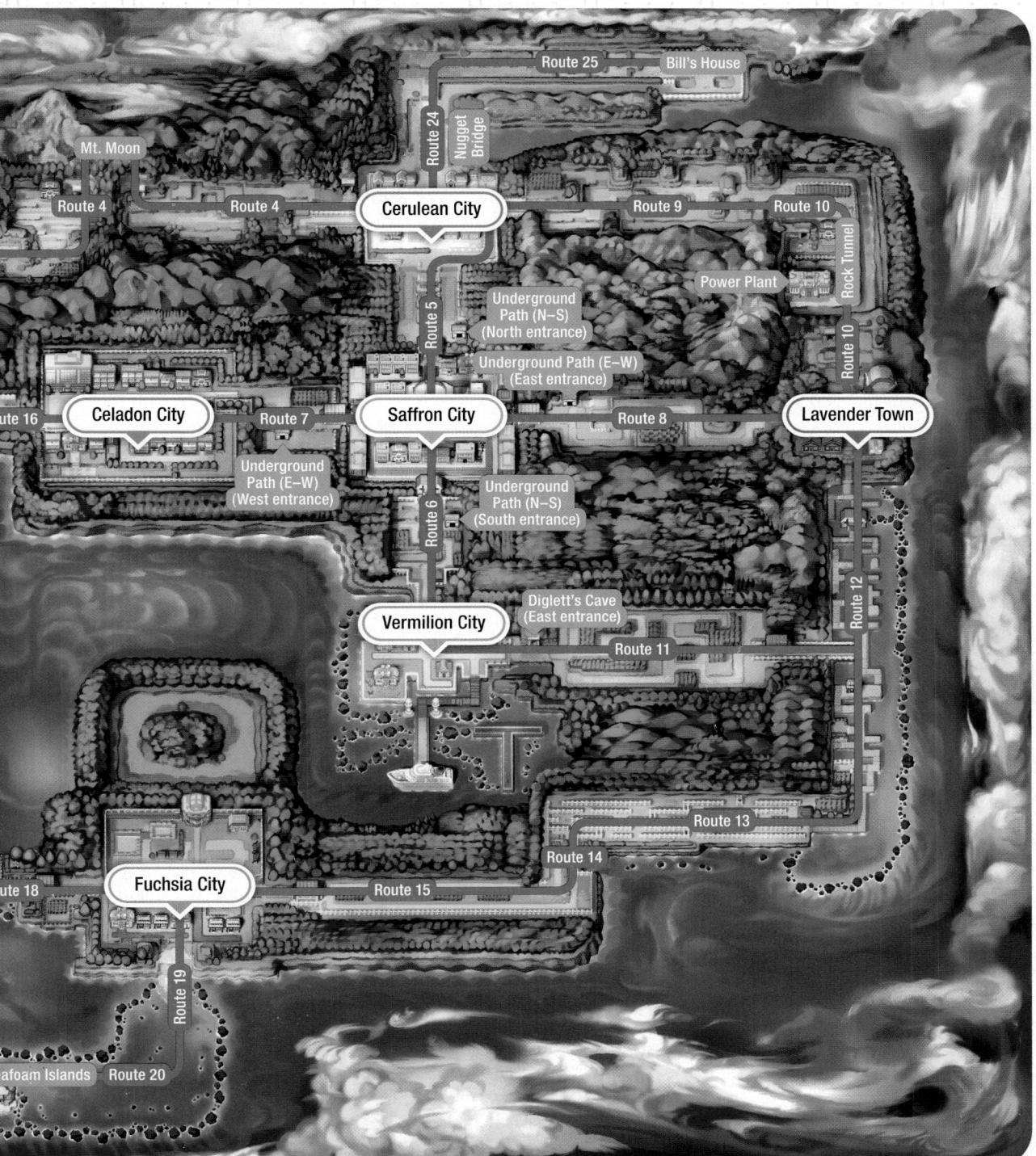

Celadon City

- Pokémon Center
- Celadon Department Store
- Pokémon Gym
- Rocket Game Corner
- Fortune Teller
- Partner Move Tutor
- GAME FREAK Office

Fuchsia City

- Pokémon Center
- Poké Mart
- Pokémon Gym
- Safari Zone
- GO Park Complex
- Burrowing Diglett
- Partner Move Tutor

Saffron City

- Pokémon Center
- Poké Mart
- Pokémon Gym
- Silph Co.
- Fighting Dojo

Cinnabar Island

- Pokémon Center
- Poké Mart
- Pokémon Gym
- Pokémon Mansion
- Cinnabar Lab

Indigo Plateau

- Pokémon Center
- Poké Mart
- Pokémon League
- Move Reminder
- Mega Stone Seller

Welcome to the World of Pokémon!

The Pokémon world is similar to ours in many ways, but it has one huge difference: the existence of creatures called Pokémon! Pokémon are found in just about every corner of this world—lush forests, vast oceans, and even rocky caves. Humans and Pokémon live together and help each other thrive.

What Is a Pokémon Trainer?

Pokémon Trainers are people who love Pokémon so much that they dedicate themselves to catching, training, and battling with them. Battling together with your Pokémon helps you better understand each other—and lets you learn and grow together. Nothing is impossible when people and Pokémon work together!

Catching Pokémon

Pokémon Trainers have the chance to catch new Pokémon whenever they meet them in the wild. Pokémon are caught in special devices called Poké Balls, which comfortably hold them. You can have up to six Pokémon in your party to use in battle. The rest will be stored in your Pokémon Box, which you can easily switch Pokémon in and out of (p. 118).

Battling with Pokémon

Pokémon seem to enjoy battling alongside their Trainers, like a sport! When Trainers meet, it almost always means they'll have a battle. Usually Pokémon battles start with each Trainer sending out one Pokémon at a time, and the Pokémon take turns using moves to try to win. Moves have many different effects, and becoming a great Trainer means learning how and when to use the right moves (p. 131).

Completing the Pokédex

The Pokédex is a high-tech device that records data about any new Pokémon you catch. New Pokémon are always being discovered, and many Trainers catch Pokémon to complete their Pokédex and learn more about these diverse and wondrous creatures. If you want to be a great Trainer, try to catch 'em all and complete your Kanto Region Pokédex (p. 119)!

Pidgey's data will be added to the Pokédex!

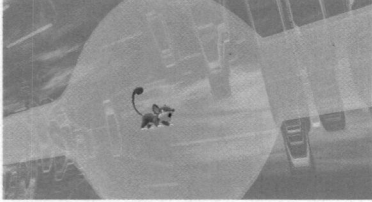

Trading Pokémon

You can also obtain new Pokémon by trading with certain characters in the game and with other players (p. 120)! Some Pokémon are exclusive to certain versions of the game (p. 20), so trading will be necessary to complete your Pokédex. Traded Pokémon also grow a bit quicker than Pokémon you catch yourself, gaining more experience after every battle.

The Pokémon League

Many Pokémon Trainers dream of challenging the Elite Four and becoming the Pokémon League Champion. To reach this lofty goal, they must prove themselves at eight Pokémon Gyms around the region. Pokémon Gyms are run by powerful Trainers known as Gym Leaders, who hand out Gym Badges to those who prove themselves worthy. Try to collect all eight Gym Badges to be able to take on the Pokémon League for yourself!

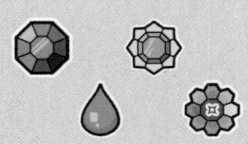

GETTING STARTED

Pokémon Basics

Every Trainer has to know what makes each Pokémon unique and how to help them grow. Read on for a quick introduction before you dive into your adventure!

Pokémon have types

Every Pokémon can have one or two of 18 possible types. These types—such as Grass, Fire, and Water—interact with each other in different ways. An easy way to think of it is like a game of rock-paper-scissors. Fire-type moves are strong against Grass-type Pokémon because fire burns up grass. However, Fire-type moves aren't very effective against Water-type Pokémon because water puts fire out! To learn more about how to be super effective with types, turn to page 123. The complete type matchup chart can be found on page 399.

Bulbasaur — Grass type **and** Poison type

Charmander — Fire type

Squirtle — Water type

Pokémon have stats

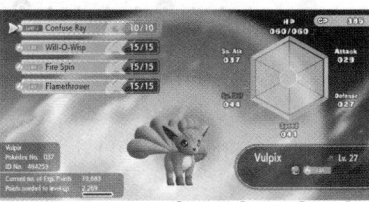

Every Pokémon has six stats: HP, Attack, Defense, Special Attack (Sp. Atk), Special Defense (Sp. Def), and Speed. These stats are a big part of how your Pokémon will do in battle. A Pokémon with higher Speed gets to move first in battle, while a Pokémon with high HP can take more hits before it faints.

Pokémon grow stronger

Mankey grew to Lv. 11!

When you catch a Pokémon, or when an opponent's Pokémon faints in battle, all of the Pokémon in your party that haven't fainted will gain experience. This experience is measured in Experience Points (Exp. Points). When a Pokémon gains enough Exp. Points, its level goes up. When a Pokémon's level goes up, its stats often increase, and it may also learn a new move—or even several at once!

 TIP All of your party will get Exp. Points after a battle, but Pokémon that actually appear in a battle will get more Exp. Points than those that don't!

Pokémon learn moves

Butterfree learned Gust!

Pokémon can learn up to four moves to be used in battle. This limited number means you'll need to think carefully about which moves you want your Pokémon to know. Most Pokémon learn moves as they level up or evolve, but they can also be taught moves through the use of items called TMs (p. 387) or even by Madam Memorial (p.131) later in the game. Your partner Pikachu or Eevee can also be taught rare moves by a character known as the Partner Move Tutor (p. 387).

The moves Pokémon can learn for battle will also be affected by your Pokémon's stats. There are three kinds of moves: physical, special, and status moves. Pokémon with high Attack deal more damage with physical moves, but Pokémon with high Defense will take less damage from those physical moves. The same is true of Sp. Atk and Sp. Def when it comes to special moves.

	Physical moves	Special moves	Status moves
What they are	Moves that deal physical damage to a Pokémon	Moves that deal special damage to a Pokémon	Moves with other effects, such as boosting stats or causing status conditions (p. 133)
Making them stronger	Use a Pokémon with a high Attack stat	Use a Pokémon with a high Sp. Atk stat	Status moves usually have fixed effects and don't get stronger
Defending against them	Use a Pokémon with a high Defense stat	Use a Pokémon with a high Sp. Def stat	Some Pokémon are immune to certain status conditions

Pokémon evolve

Once certain Pokémon reach a high enough level, they will evolve and become a new species of Pokémon. Not only does this change the way the Pokémon looks, but it also increases the Pokémon's stats greatly. It may even change the Pokémon's types. But not every Pokémon can evolve, and some Pokémon need the use of certain items or other conditions to evolve. The Kanto Region Pokédex (p. 161) has more details. Explore Kanto and see what new Pokémon you can obtain through Pokémon Evolution!

Level 7   Level 10

Weedle   Kakuna   Beedrill

> **TIP** Evolution makes your Pokémon stronger, but that doesn't always mean you'll want to evolve your Pokémon right away. Some Pokémon will lose the chance to learn certain moves after evolving. Check out the move tables in the Pokédex to decide whether you want to evolve your Pokémon or not! Press Ⓑ when a Pokémon is evolving if you want to make it stop.

Your Pokémon and You

In *Pokémon: Let's Go, Pikachu!* and *Pokémon: Let's Go, Eevee!*, you can travel together with your Pokémon in all kinds of exciting ways! You can choose a Pokémon from your team to follow you on your adventure, and you can even ride on some of these Pokémon!

Traveling together

Choose one of the Pokémon on your team and let it out of its Poké Ball to have that Pokémon travel with you on your journey! While a Pokémon is traveling with you, you can check on it to see how it's feeling about the area, your recent battles, recent Pokémon you've caught, and more. The Pokémon you're traveling with can also occasionally find helpful items, so be sure to check in on them often (p. 144)!

Squirtle seems interested in the Mankey you just caught.

Riding on Pokémon

When you let some Pokémon out of their Poké Balls, they won't follow behind you—they'll actually give you a ride! Depending on the Pokémon you choose, you may be able to move faster across the land, sail across the water to reach new places, or reach Pokémon that are flying high up in the air! Ride on Pokémon to get where you're going faster and explore new parts of Kanto! Learn more about riding on Pokémon on page 144.

 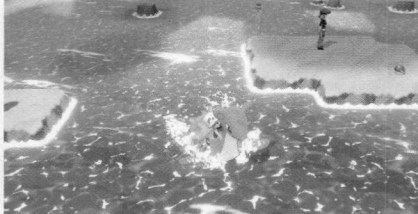 

Love

Charmander avoided the move in time via your shout!

Bulbasaur gathered all its energy to break through its paralysis so you wouldn't worry!

As you work together with your Pokémon to bring out each other's full potential, the bond of trust between you will grow stronger. This is called love. Love increases from interacting with a Pokémon while it's walking with you but also from things like making sure it doesn't faint in battle and using items on it. Pokémon with high love gain a number of benefits in battle (p. 129), so take good care of your Pokémon!

Adventuring in Kanto

The Kanto region is full of all sorts of things just waiting to be found, even if you're a Trainer who's visited the region in the past!

Finding items

As you travel across Kanto, you'll likely come across what look like Poké Balls lying on the ground. These can contain a variety of different items—maybe even several of the same item at once—but you won't know what until you pick them up! You can get anything from Potions to restore the HP of your Pokémon to TMs that can teach your Pokémon new moves. Items in the field will be shown on each area's map, and you can find a list of all the items in these games in Items, starting on page 389.

Hidden items

In addition to the regular items you can spot while on your adventure, there are also items that are on the ground but can't be seen. These hidden items can be picked up, too, but you'll have to do a little more work to find them. The trick is to watch your partner Pokémon's tail. When it starts wagging, you know an item is near—whether you can see one or not! Learn more on page 143.

Obstacles in Your Way

Adventuring as a Pokémon Trainer means going off the beaten path and traveling through forests, caves, and beyond. That also means that sometimes you're going to encounter obstacles that may stop you from reaching some parts of the game until later on. Ledges that can be hopped down but not back up, small trees that block you, and bodies of water are common obstacles you'll run into on your adventure.

GETTING STARTED

Secret Techniques

Secret Techniques are unique actions your partner Pokémon can learn. These five techniques will help you reach new areas of the world and get around easier.

Chop Down (p. 49)	Sky Dash (p. 68)	Strong Push (p. 88)	Sea Skim (p. 72)	Light Up (p. 53)
				Light Up
Clear small trees out of your way to open new paths	Instantly travel back to towns you've been to before	Push heavy blocks around	Travel across bodies of water to reach new areas	Light up pitch-black places, such as caves

Once your partner learns a Secret Technique, you can use it by interacting with certain objects in the field, such as choosing to use Chop Down after investigating trees. You can also use Sky Dash from the Town Map. Otherwise, open the main menu with ⊗ or the equivalent, then select the icon of your partner at the top of the screen. From there, choose the Secret Techniques menu to find them all!

 TIP Once your partner learns some of these Secret Techniques, it can also help other Pokémon use them. Learning Sky Dash will let you dash from place to place with other Pokémon you can ride on, too, just like learning Sea Skim will make it possible to travel across the water with Pokémon like Lapras and Gyarados.

GETTING STARTED

How to Play

Pokémon: Let's Go, Pikachu! and *Pokémon: Let's Go, Eevee!* are ready to go with you wherever you go. Choose the play mode and controller setup that works best for you.

Handheld Mode

Take your game with you wherever you go by playing in handheld mode! When your Joy-Con™ controllers are attached to your system, you'll use the buttons on both Joy-Con controllers to play your game.

Move/select	⊚	Cancel/quit	Ⓑ
Open main menu	Ⓧ	Navigate sub menus, etc.	Ⓨ/⊕/Ⓡ
Talk/confirm	Ⓐ		

> **TIP** The instructions throughout this guide use the default buttons for handheld mode, but you can use whatever button is appropriate for your controller.

Tabletop / TV Mode

If you want to take a more active approach, snap out that stand, slide off a Joy-Con, and try playing in tabletop mode. Or, by docking your Nintendo Switch™, you can enjoy *Pokémon: Let's Go, Pikachu!* and *Pokémon: Let's Go, Eevee!* on your TV screen!

When playing in either of these two modes, you have the choice of playing either with one of your Joy-Con controllers or with the Poké Ball Plus, if you have one.

Joy-Con controls

Detach either your right or left Joy-Con to play with one hand or to play with a Support Trainer (which you can read more about on the next page). The controls will depend on which Joy-Con you're playing with.

Left Joy-Con		**Right Joy-Con**	
Move/select	⊚	Move/select	⊚
Open main menu	✛	Open main menu	Ⓧ
Talk/confirm	✛	Talk/confirm	Ⓐ
Cancel/quit	✛	Cancel/quit	Ⓑ
Navigate sub menus, etc.	✛/⊖/Ⓛ	Navigate sub menus, etc.	Ⓨ/⊕/Ⓡ

Poké Ball Plus controls

The Poké Ball Plus is a special device that can be used as a controller for *Pokémon: Let's Go, Pikachu!* and *Pokémon: Let's Go, Eevee!* But that's not all it can do— you can also use it to take your Pokémon for a stroll, earning rewards and helping them grow (p. 157). If you're using it as a controller, you'll be able to control your game using the inputs shown on the right.

Move/select	⊚
Open main menu	Top Button
Talk/confirm	Press ⊚
Cancel/quit	Top Button
Navigate sub menus, etc.	Shake device

> If you try to catch Pokémon when playing in tabletop or TV mode, you can earn an extra Technique Bonus by throwing your Poké Ball with great accuracy! Learn more on page 116.

Connect your game with Pokémon GO!

You can connect your game to a Pokémon GO account belonging to you or your family to send Pokémon from the app to your game. If you're using the Poké Ball Plus to play *Pokémon: Let's Go, Pikachu!* or *Pokémon: Let's Go, Eevee!*, it can also work as a Pokémon GO Plus to play Pokémon GO! Learn more about what this device can do by turning to page 157.

Support Play

Have another player join in on your adventure with Support Play! When you see ((■)) on the screen, you can have another player join you. Use a Poké Ball Plus or detach one of your Joy-Con controllers, then hand one to them and have them shake it. Once they appear in your game, they'll be able to join the fun with you!

Travel together

A Support Trainer can run around with you, but they won't be able to trigger story events, Pokémon encounters, or battles against other Trainers in the field. They won't be able to pick up items or take you out of the current area you're in. You're still the star of this show!

Catch together

Your Support Trainer can throw Berries or Poké Balls with you when you encounter wild Pokémon. If you both throw your Poké Balls in sync, you'll be more likely to catch the wild Pokémon! Have another player help you out against Pokémon you simply can't seem to catch.

Battle together

A Support Trainer can join you in most battles you face, turning them into a 2-vs-1 matchup! They will get control of the second Pokémon in your party and will be able to choose moves for them.

 TIP Your Support Trainer will help you in less obvious ways, too! When you're playing together with another player, your Pokémon will get a little extra Exp. Points for every successful catch you make together!

Multiple Save Files

Even when you aren't playing together, your family can all enjoy *Pokémon: Let's Go, Pikachu!* and *Pokémon: Let's Go, Eevee!* You can each save your own game by saving your progress on your own user accounts. You can have up to eight user accounts on a Nintendo Switch system.

Creating new user accounts

1. Select System Settings on the HOME Menu.
2. Scroll down to find Users, then select Add User on the right side of the screen and click Next.
3. Select an icon to represent your new account, or create a Mii.
4. When prompted, enter your nickname and select OK twice to finish.
5. Choose to link an existing Nintendo Account or create a new one—or press Later to create a user without using a Nintendo Account.

Starting Your Game

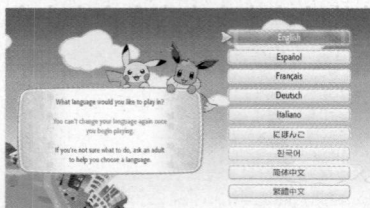

Now that you know all about what you can do in these games, it's time to get started! When you open *Pokémon: Let's Go, Pikachu!* or *Pokémon: Let's Go, Eevee!* from your HOME Menu the first time, you will need to choose a language that you wish to play in. You can choose from English, Spanish, French, German, Italian, Japanese, Korean, Simplified Chinese, or Traditional Chinese. But once you choose a language, you won't be able to change it later.

 TIP If you select a different user account and start up the game, you can choose to create a save file in a different language!

How to delete a save file

So what if you want to delete your game for any reason? You'll do that through System Settings on your Nintendo Switch. But once you delete your data for any user account, it and everything from your game will be gone forever—so think carefully before you do!

1. From the HOME Menu, select System Settings.
2. Scroll down to Data Management.
3. Select Manage Save Data/Screenshots and Videos, then select Delete Save Data.
4. Choose the game, then choose to either delete the save data linked to a specific user account or delete all save data for the software. Confirm that you really want to delete your data if you're sure!

Choosing an appearance and name

Once you start a new game and get your first introduction to Professor Oak, you'll be able to choose what you want your player character to look like. Choose the appearance that fits you, and then enter a name. Just remember that you won't be able to change these settings later unless you start a new save file!

Navigating Menus

Once your adventure begins, you'll be able to access the main menu by pressing ⊗ (or the relevant button on the controller you're playing with). The options you can select will increase as you progress through the game.

Menu Option		What You Can Do
Play with Pikachu/ Eevee		Select these icons to play with your partner or access Secret Techniques (p. 16)
Pokédex		Open up your Pokédex (p. 119) to learn about the Pokémon you've encountered
Bag		Open your Bag to use items to help your Pokémon or yourself on your journey

Menu Option		What You Can Do
Party		View your current party, move your Pokémon, or choose one to travel with you (p. 144)
Communicate		Receive Mystery Gifts (p. 158), trade Pokémon (p. 120), and battle other players (p. 140)
Save		Save your game so you don't lose your progress—there is no autosave feature in these games

Options

You can also open Options when you have the main menu open. Press ⓨ or use the equivalent input to open them. Here you can choose to adjust your gameplay in various ways, such as disabling battle effects or enabling movie skipping if you want to move more quickly through your adventure. Or you can change your battle style to Set if you want a bit of extra challenge!

What's in your Bag?

A Trainer's Bag is an essential aid in their journey! Inside it, you'll find items sorted automatically into different pockets.

Beneath these pockets, you will also find some Key Items that will come in handy throughout your adventure. These include the Town Map (which shows where in the region you are), items you can sell for cash, and more!

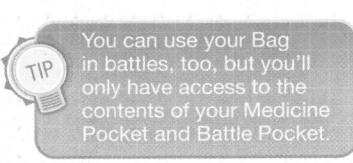

TIP: You can use your Bag in battles, too, but you'll only have access to the contents of your Medicine Pocket and Battle Pocket.

Pocket		What It Holds
Pokémon Box		If your party is full, all the rest of the Pokémon you catch will be sent here
Medicine Pocket		Items that will restore HP or heal status conditions are gathered here
TM Case		Technical Machines, or TMs, that can be used to teach moves to Pokémon (p. 131)
Power-Up Pocket		Items that can help your Pokémon evolve or grow in other ways

Pocket		What It Holds
Candy Jar		Candies you can use either to raise your Pokémon's stats through Go Power (p. 126) or to help them level up
Clothing Trunk		Outfits and accessories for you and your partner to dress up in (p. 146)
Catching Pocket		Poké Balls and Berries that can help you in your encounters with wild Pokémon (p. 116)
Battle Pocket		Items you can use in battle to temporarily boost stats and more

Version Differences

Your Partner Pokémon

The biggest difference between each game version will be the partner Pokémon that will be with you throughout your adventure. In *Pokémon: Let's Go, Pikachu!*, you'll be paired with Pikachu, a Pokémon that specializes in Electric-type moves—though this Pikachu can also learn some unique moves of other types, too. In *Pokémon: Let's Go, Eevee!*, your partner Pokémon will be the Normal-type Eevee—and this particular Eevee can learn a lot of moves of different types, based on the many ways other Eevee can evolve.

 Check out all the exclusive moves each partner can learn on pages 164 and 165!

Version-exclusive outfits

In these games, both you and your partner can dress up in special outfits, and some of them will be exclusive to one version or the other. To check out the Pikachu- or Eevee-themed outfits you'll be able to get, turn to the section beginning on page 146.

Version-Exclusive Pokémon

While the adventures that unfold in *Pokémon: Let's Go, Pikachu!* and *Pokémon: Let's Go, Eevee!* follow the same general path, some Pokémon can only be caught or received in one version of the game or the other. If you hope to obtain every last Pokémon, you'll need to trade (p. 120) with another player who has a different version!

Pokémon: Let's Go, Pikachu! exclusive Pokémon

Sandshrew · Sandslash · Oddish · Gloom · Vileplume · Mankey · Primeape · Growlithe

Arcanine · Grimer · Muk · Scyther · Alolan Sandshrew · Alolan Sandslash · Alolan Grimer · Alolan Muk

Pokémon: Let's Go, Eevee! exclusive Pokémon

Ekans · Arbok · Vulpix · Ninetales · Meowth · Persian · Bellsprout · Weepinbell

Victreebel · Koffing · Weezing · Pinsir · Alolan Vulpix · Alolan Ninetales · Alolan Meowth · Alolan Persian

GETTING STARTED

Recommended Route

This recommended route through your adventure shows you the places you'll need to go to reach the Pokémon League— as well as some locations you don't have to visit but you might want to check out! If you get stuck along the way and don't know where to go next, follow it to get back on track. Locations will be marked with ⊚ when you're returning after your first visit. Locations that are indented are optional, so check them out if you want more to do!

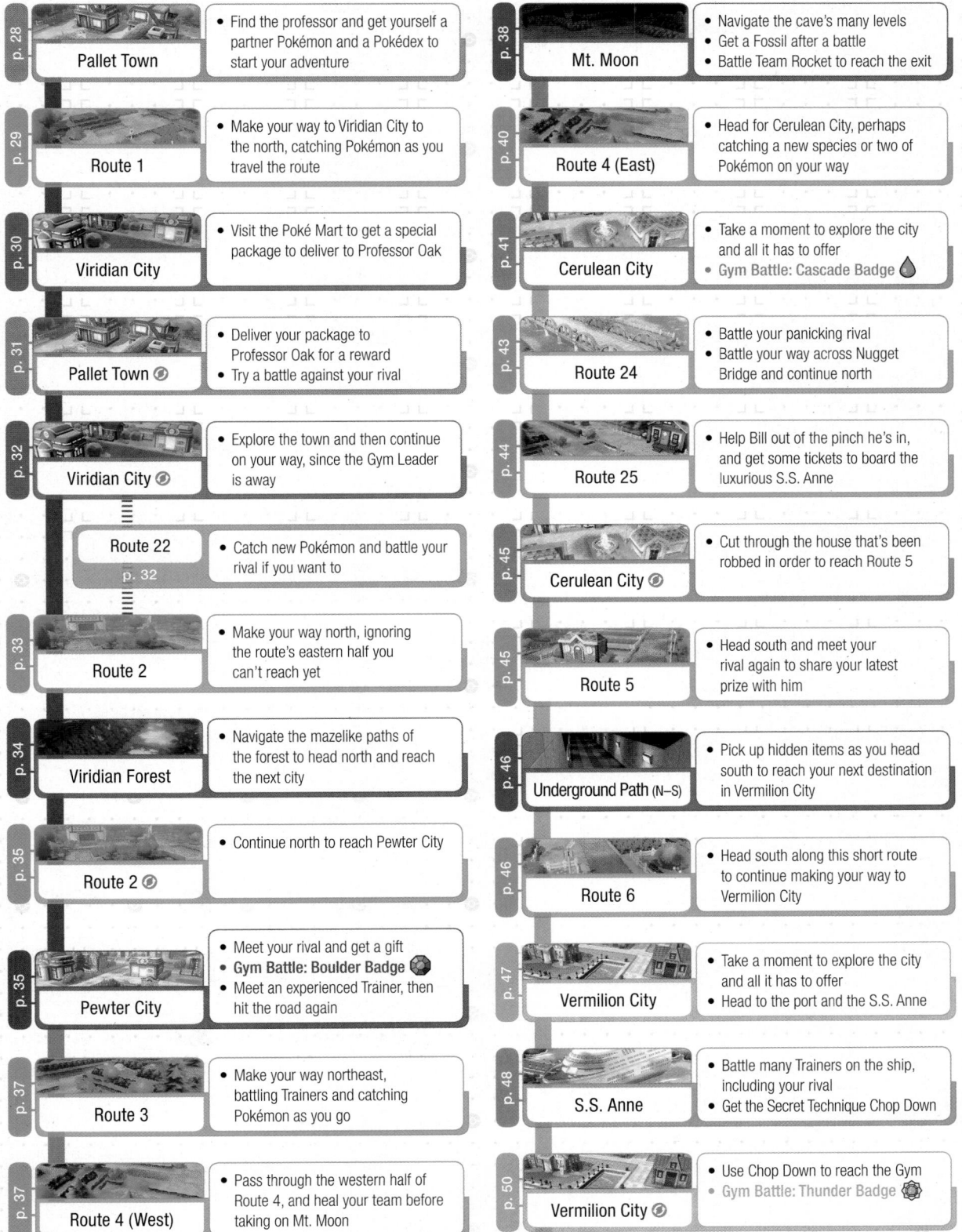

p. 28 — Pallet Town
- Find the professor and get yourself a partner Pokémon and a Pokédex to start your adventure

p. 29 — Route 1
- Make your way to Viridian City to the north, catching Pokémon as you travel the route

p. 30 — Viridian City
- Visit the Poké Mart to get a special package to deliver to Professor Oak

p. 31 — Pallet Town ⊚
- Deliver your package to Professor Oak for a reward
- Try a battle against your rival

p. 32 — Viridian City ⊚
- Explore the town and then continue on your way, since the Gym Leader is away

Route 22 — p. 32
- Catch new Pokémon and battle your rival if you want to

p. 33 — Route 2
- Make your way north, ignoring the route's eastern half you can't reach yet

p. 34 — Viridian Forest
- Navigate the mazelike paths of the forest to head north and reach the next city

p. 35 — Route 2 ⊚
- Continue north to reach Pewter City

p. 35 — Pewter City
- Meet your rival and get a gift
- **Gym Battle: Boulder Badge** 🔘
- Meet an experienced Trainer, then hit the road again

p. 37 — Route 3
- Make your way northeast, battling Trainers and catching Pokémon as you go

p. 37 — Route 4 (West)
- Pass through the western half of Route 4, and heal your team before taking on Mt. Moon

p. 38 — Mt. Moon
- Navigate the cave's many levels
- Get a Fossil after a battle
- Battle Team Rocket to reach the exit

p. 40 — Route 4 (East)
- Head for Cerulean City, perhaps catching a new species or two of Pokémon on your way

p. 41 — Cerulean City
- Take a moment to explore the city and all it has to offer
- **Gym Battle: Cascade Badge** 💧

p. 43 — Route 24
- Battle your panicking rival
- Battle your way across Nugget Bridge and continue north

p. 44 — Route 25
- Help Bill out of the pinch he's in, and get some tickets to board the luxurious S.S. Anne

p. 45 — Cerulean City ⊚
- Cut through the house that's been robbed in order to reach Route 5

p. 45 — Route 5
- Head south and meet your rival again to share your latest prize with him

p. 46 — Underground Path (N–S)
- Pick up hidden items as you head south to reach your next destination in Vermilion City

p. 46 — Route 6
- Head south along this short route to continue making your way to Vermilion City

p. 47 — Vermilion City
- Take a moment to explore the city and all it has to offer
- Head to the port and the S.S. Anne

p. 48 — S.S. Anne
- Battle many Trainers on the ship, including your rival
- Get the Secret Technique Chop Down

p. 50 — Vermilion City ⊚
- Use Chop Down to reach the Gym
- **Gym Battle: Thunder Badge** ⚙️

Route 11 — p. 52
- Unlock the Judge function if you've caught enough Pokémon

Diglett's Cave — p. 53
- Make your way through Diglett's Cave to return to Route 2's eastern side at last

Route 2 ◉ — p. 53
- Get the Secret Technique Light Up
- Take your rival's offer to zip back to Cerulean City to reach Route 9 next

Route 9 — p. 54
- Battle your way through Route 9 on your way to the next route in your journey

Route 10 — p. 55
- Battle some Team Rocket Grunts together with a new ally
- Heal your team up if they need it

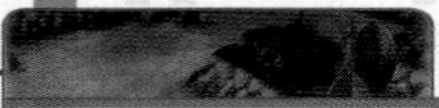

Rock Tunnel — p. 56
- Make your way through the grueling Rock Tunnel to reach the next town

Route 10 ◉ — p. 56
- Head for Lavender Town, battling some more Trainers along the way

Lavender Town — p. 57
- Check out the town, heal up your team, and then head to the Pokémon Tower

Pokémon Tower — p. 58
- Find your rival for a battle
- After your ghost hunt reaches an end, hit the road again

Lavender Town ◉ — p. 58
- Head to the west side of Lavender Town, where you'll spot Team Rocket up to some mischief

Route 8 — p. 60
- Battle your way across Route 8 as you follow after Team Rocket

Underground Path (E–W) — p. 61
- Keep an eye on your partner Pokémon for hidden items as you make use of this shortcut

Route 7 — p. 61
- Reach Celadon City at last by taking the short walk west along Route 7

Celadon City — p. 62
- Meet Brock and get some Pewter Crunchies and Tea
- Gym Battle: Rainbow Badge ✿
- Find the Team Rocket Hideout in the Rocket Game Corner

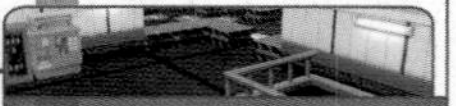

Team Rocket Hideout — p. 66
- Battle the Team Rocket Grunt on B4F and get the Lift Key
- Battle the Team Rocket Boss and get the Silph Scope

Celadon City ◉ — p. 68
- Get the Secret Technique Sky Dash, then use it to return to Lavender Town

Pokémon Tower ◉ — p. 69
- Solve the mystery of the tower
- Save Mr. Fuji from Team Rocket, and get the Poké Flute

Route 16 — p. 70
- Sky Dash back to Celadon City, then head west to Route 16
- Wake up that sleeping Snorlax to battle and catch it

Route 17 — p. 70
- Power up your team by battling Trainers and catching Pokémon

Route 18 — p. 71
- Power up your team by battling Trainers and catching Pokémon

Fuchsia City — p. 72
- Get the Secret Technique Sea Skim
- Gym Battle: Soul Badge ♡

Route 12 — p. 74
- Sky Dash back to Lavender Town, then head south to Route 12
- Wake up that sleeping Snorlax to battle and catch it

Route 13 — p. 74
- Power up your team by battling Trainers and catching Pokémon

Route 14 — p. 75
- Power up your team by battling Trainers and catching Pokémon

Route 15 — p. 76
- Power up your team by battling Trainers and catching Pokémon

Power Plant — p. 77
- Sky Dash back to Cerulean City to reach Route 10 and the Power Plant, and catch the Legendary Pokémon Zapdos

| p. 79 Saffron City | • The whole city is shut down, so head into the Silph Co. headquarters to take on Team Rocket |

| p. 81 Silph Co. | • Meet your rival and Blue and be ready for battle
• Team up with your rival against Archer
• Save the Silph Co. president from the Team Rocket Boss and get rewarded |

| p. 86 Saffron City | • Explore the city at your leisure this time
• Gym Battle: Marsh Badge
• Sky Dash back to Fuchsia City |

| p. 88 Route 19 | • Get the warden's Gold Teeth from a familiar set of troublemakers |

| p. 88 Fuchsia City | • Return the warden's Gold Teeth to get the Safari Set and the Secret Technique Strong Push |

| Route 19 p. 88 | • Head south to Route 20 |

| Route 20 p. 89 | • Use Sea Skim to head west to the Seafoam Islands |

| Seafoam Islands p. 90 | • Use Strong Push to get through the cave
• Battle and catch Articuno |

| Route 20 p. 89 | • One last push to the west to reach Cinnabar Island |

| p. 92 Cinnabar Island | • Search for the key to the Gym as you explore the small island and its facilities |

| p. 93 Pokémon Mansion | • Explore the old Pokémon Mansion, and find the Secret Key hidden within it |

| p. 95 Cinnabar Island | • Get access to the Cinnabar Pokémon Gym and its Gym Leader
• Gym Battle: Volcano Badge |

| Route 21 p. 96 | • Sea Skim north to reach Pallet Town and then Viridian City |

| p. 97 Viridian City | • Meet your rival and then head back to Pallet Town together since you can't get into the Gym |

| p. 97 Pallet Town | • Learn the secrets of Mega Evolution, and get your first Mega Stones to try out |

| p. 97 Viridian City | • Return to Viridian City, and take on the Pokémon Gym at last
• Gym Battle: Earth Badge |

| p. 99 Route 22 | • Run into your rival for one last battle before your trip to the Indigo Plateau |

| p. 100 Route 23 | • Pass through Route 23 to reach Victory Road and the grueling journey that awaits you there |

| p. 101 Victory Road | • Battle and catch the Legendary Pokémon Moltres |

| p. 100 Route 23 | • Dash north through the last bit of Route 23 to finally enter Indigo Plateau |

| p. 103 Indigo Plateau | • Battle the Elite Four
• Battle the Champion
• Enter the Pokémon League's Hall of Fame |

| p. 106 Team Rocket Hideout | • Return to the Team Rocket Hideout to battle Archer one last time |

| p. 106 Route 17 | • Battle Team Rocket one last time, and get the Blast-Off Set |

| p. 106, 110 All over Kanto | • Travel all across Kanto, and gain the titles of the 153 Master Trainers
• Have rematches with the Gym Leaders around the Kanto region |

| p. 107, 111 Indigo Plateau | • Challenge a battle legend once you've earned at least six Master Trainer titles
• Have rematches with the Elite Four |

| p. 108 Cerulean Cave | • Navigate the cave to reach and catch the Legendary Pokémon Mewtwo
• Return to battle a mysterious Trainer |

| p. 107 Celadon City | • Visit the GAME FREAK office to get your Diploma and a Shiny Charm for completing your Pokédex |

Repeat Activities

These are activities you can do over and over as you progress through your adventure. For those that can be repeated once a day, keep in mind that days are calculated by the time set on your Nintendo Switch system, with a new day starting every time it becomes 12:00 a.m.!

Buy some Pewter Crunchies — p. 35

Buy one bag of Pewter Crunchies for ₽500 from the man in the Pewter City Pokémon Center once per day.

Battle against Mina — p. 50, 107

Battle Mina daily at Vermilion Port after the S.S. Anne sets sail to receive a Bottle Cap.

Slowpoke babysitting in Pewter City — p. 35

Watch a woman's Slowpoke for her to earn a Big Pearl once per day.

Get a Nugget in Fuchsia City — p. 72

Visit the Diglett in the warden's house to receive a Nugget once per day (after obtaining the Secret Technique Strong Push).

You've gotten so strong that I just absolutely have to battle you again!

Battle Kanto's Gym Leaders — p. 110

After entering the Hall of Fame, visit Kanto's Gym Leaders for a daily rematch. They'll be much stronger this time around!

Hey, fantastic timing! I was just thinking how I'd like to battle you.

Take on the Elite Four — p. 111

Return to the Pokémon League and battle the Elite Four again to defend your Champion title as many times as you like!

TIP Once you enter the Hall of Fame and Master Trainers appear across Kanto, you can rebattle them daily after earning their title. And don't forget to go back and pick up more hidden items that may have reappeared around the region!

Walkthrough

Understanding the Walkthrough

This walkthrough will guide you through all the steps you need to complete to become a Pokémon League Champion while also pointing out extra things you can do—optional events, items to get, and more!

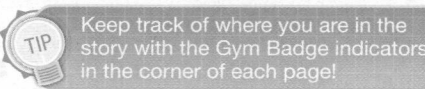

TIP Keep track of where you are in the story with the Gym Badge indicators in the corner of each page!

Maps

Every time you reach a new area, you'll be presented with a map of it. If there are items you can find in the area, those items will be listed in tables. Tables with red headers list items you'll see on the ground. In the game, these items look like Poké Balls. Tables with purple headers mark hidden items your partner can help you find (p. 143). Blue tables list items you can buy at shops.

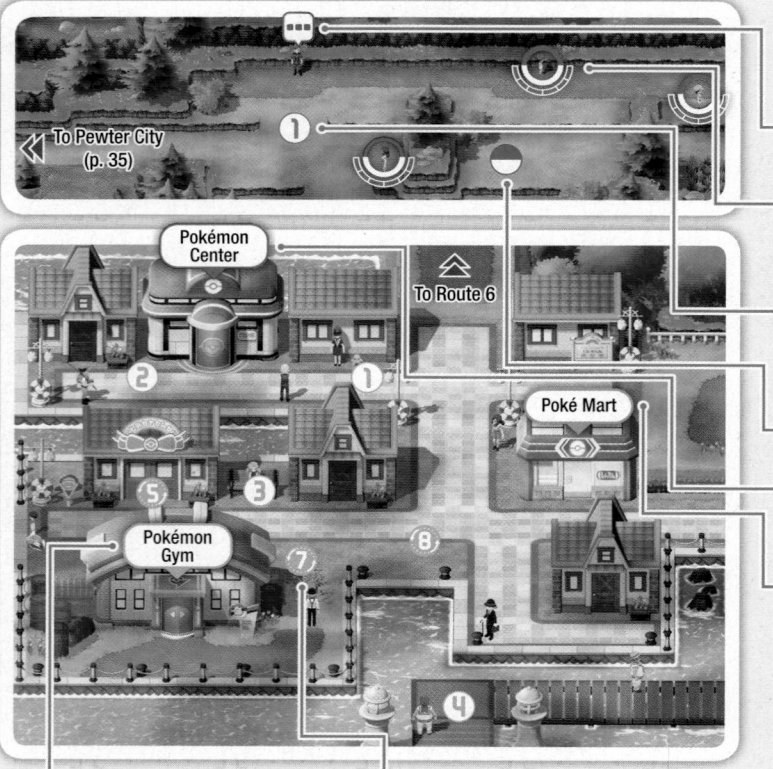

To Pewter City (p. 35)

Pokémon Center

To Route 6

Poké Mart

Pokémon Gym

Orange labels point you to important places you may want to visit.

The different colors of some revisit icons can provide a hint when you'll come back.

On maps, important features will be labeled:

These icons mark Coach Trainers you can battle. More on them on the next page!

These circles mark Trainers you can battle, and the number of sections filled in shows how many Pokémon they have.

These numbers match up to the steps you can complete in each area. Numbers like ⑤ show steps you'll complete on future revisits to an area.

These mark locations where you'll find items sitting on the ground, but remember that there may be hidden items to find, too. The fun is in finding them for yourself!

Red labels point you to places where you can heal your team.

Blue labels point you to places where you can buy items.

There are icons under the area names to show you which Secret Techniques (p. 16) you need to fully explore the area and collect every last item. Don't worry if you don't have the Secret Techniques when you first visit an area—you can always come back later!

Pokémon encounters

Below each map, you'll see the Pokémon you can encounter in that area.

Some Pokémon appear more often in one version of the game than the other. The yellow circle shows how likely the Pokémon is to appear in *Pokémon: Let's Go, Pikachu!* The brown circle shows how likely the Pokémon is to appear in *Pokémon: Let's Go, Eevee!*

In some locations, you can encounter unusual species by building up Catch Combos! They'll be listed in these boxes, so turn to page 117 if you want to know more.

These Pokémon appear in the tall grass.

Bellsprout

Pidgey

These Pokémon appear in the air.

These Pokémon appear on the surface of water.

Magikarp

Clefairy

These Pokémon appear inside caves or buildings.

⊚ frequent ○ common △ average
☆ rare ★ almost never — does not appear

Unusual Encounters Bulbasaur

Here are the names and types of the Pokémon you can encounter. (See page 399 for the complete type matchup chart.)

The colors and patterns here show where the Pokémon appears. You'll be able to encounter Pokémon on the sea or in the sky after reaching certain milestones in your journey.

Star icons indicate a species that can only be caught in this area, so try to catch one before you leave if you want to complete your Pokédex!

These six symbols you see in the yellow or brown circle show how likely you are to encounter each Pokémon. This key will appear each time there are Pokémon to encounter.

Battle boxes

This is a battle box! These boxes will help you prepare for some of the major battles during your adventure by showing you who you're about to battle and what their team lineup is.

Rival Battle!

Your Rival

Use Electric-type moves against his Pidgey or a Geodude or an Onix from Mt. Moon. He'll send out Oddish, but it'll get blown away by Flying-type moves if you've got a Pidgey or Spearow. Last comes his Eevee or Pikachu, but you know how to beat them by now!

Read the tips here if you need a bit of help winning the battle!

Pidgey Lv. 12 — WEAK AGAINST:

Oddish Lv. 12 — WEAK AGAINST:

Eevee Lv. 13 — WEAK AGAINST:

If you started with Pikachu

Pikachu Lv. 13 — WEAK AGAINST:

If you started with Eevee

Sometimes an opponent might have different Pokémon on their team based on which version of the game you're playing.

These are the Pokémon you'll be facing. Check out their levels, their types, and the types of moves they'll be weak to!

Coach battle boxes

You'll meet special Trainers called Coach Trainers that you can choose to battle if you want to claim extra rewards (p. 136).

These boxes also have some tips to help you with the battle.

Plus, you can see what Pokémon you'll have to defeat to get the reward listed at the bottom of the battle box!

Coach Battle!

Coach Trainer Oberon

If any of your Pokémon knows Double Kick or Karate Chop, you'll be in good shape to beat his Normal-type Pokémon!

TEAM:
Lv. 13

Reward: TM57 Pay Day

When running around on the field, your partner can alert you to hidden items. Pikachu's or Eevee's tail will start to wag excitedly when there's one nearby, and you'll have to find it by poking around the area and pressing Ⓐ. These hidden items are the ones listed in the purple tables on each area map—but there are other unseen items lurking around! If you have a Pokémon traveling with you (p. 144), they can also find items somewhat at random. For an idea of the kinds of items you can find, turn to page 394.

Pokémon catch boxes

These boxes highlight Pokémon you can catch in the area. They might be new species you haven't encountered before, or Pokémon that could come in handy in upcoming battles. Their types are shown with them, as well as a general idea of how difficult they tend to be to catch!

Catch!

Catch these Pokémon, and they'll come in handy for your first Gym battle!

Oddish
Catch Difficulty
Easier ◁——— Harder

Bellsprout
Catch Difficulty
Easier ◁——— Harder

WALKTHROUGH

Understanding the Walkthrough

27 ▶▶

Pallet Town

Getting
Around

1 Have a look around your room, and you won't have to go far before you get a visitor. Your rival's here to remind you that today's the day you get your own Pokémon!

TIP — Like your rival's email suggests, save your game by opening the main menu with ⊗ and selecting Save!

2 Professor Oak's not in his lab, so explore Pallet Town for a bit. When you're ready to find him, head up to the north end of town.

Map labels: Your House · To Route 1 · Your Rival's House · Oak Pokémon Research Lab · To Route 21 (p. 96)

You'll find the details of this step 3 on page 31, when you revisit Pallet Town later in your adventure!

Catch That Pokémon!

You'll barely have a chance to talk with the professor before a wild Pokémon dashes out to meet you! Follow the instructions in the game on how to ready a Poké Ball, and give it a throw to try to catch that Pokémon! There's lots more for you to learn about catching Pokémon on page 114.

3 Caught it! Or did you? Follow that bouncing Poké Ball to the lab, and claim your partner at last! You'll have the chance to give it a nickname and then check it out in your newly acquired Pokédex.

Pokémon: Pikachu or Eevee
Reward: Poké Ball ×50, Pokédex

4 The open route waits before you! Head outside and you'll get one last gift from your mom—a Town Map! Now that you'll never really be lost, let's go to Route 1.

Reward: Town Map

TIP — Find the Town Map in your Bag. The more places you visit, the more it'll tell you!

WALKTHROUGH

Route 1

Getting
Around

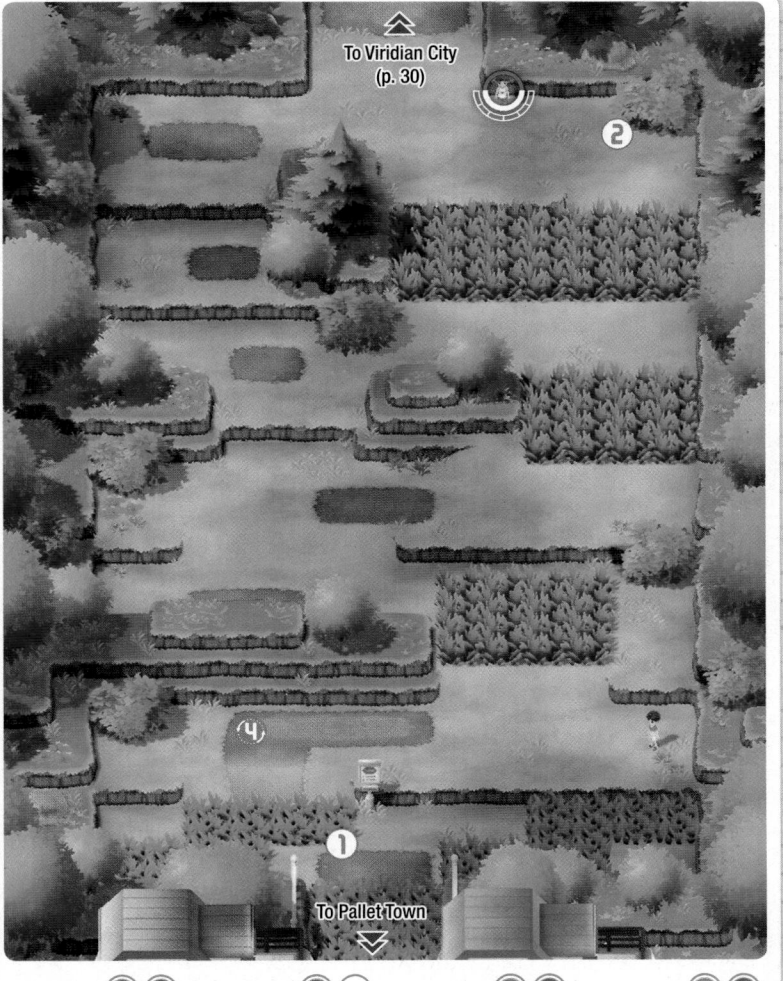

To Viridian City
(p. 30)

2

4

1

To Pallet Town

	Pidgey		Rattata		Oddish		Bellsprout

◎ frequent ○ common △ average ☆ rare ★ almost never — does not appear

TIP There's your first Trainer labeled on the map—but you won't be able to battle him on your first pass through Route 1! Look forward to testing your Pokémon against his after completing the events on page 31.

1 Now your adventure truly begins! Run through the grass along the route toward Viridian City, catching Pokémon along the way to build up your team!

2 Just before you reach the city, your partner will find a little something for you in the bushes. Pokémon traveling with you will often find items like this one (p. 143).

Reward: Razz Berry

Catch!

Catch these Pokémon, and they'll come in handy for your first Gym battle!

Oddish

Catch Difficulty

Easier ———— Harder

Bellsprout

Catch Difficulty

Easier ———— Harder

Viridian City

Getting Around

To Route 2
(p. 33)

Pokémon
Gym

④ ⑤

To Route 22
(p. 99)

Trainers'
School

Poké Mart

①

Pokémon
Center

②

⑤

To Route 1
(p. 29)

WALKTHROUGH

Poké Mart	
Before earning any Gym Badges	
Poké Ball	₽100
Potion	₽200
Antidote	₽200
Burn Heal	₽300
Ice Heal	₽100
Awakening	₽100
Paralyze Heal	₽300

?   Hidden Items   ?
Potion

 TIP In the coming pages, shop tables for Poké Marts will only show the new items that become available from earning additional Gym Badges. Find the full list of all the items that can possibly be found at Poké Marts on page 395.

① Some suspicious characters are blocking the way to Viridian Forest! So why not visit the Trainers' School to learn more about being a Trainer?

 TIP Along the narrow path that winds around the northwest corner of the town, there's a hidden item just west of a tree that blocks your way. Don't know how to find hidden items? Turn to page 143.

2 There's a clerk outside the Poké Mart, but what could he want? Talk to him and he'll give you a special request to head back to the lab in Pallet Town. Deliver the parcel to Professor Oak to get some Berries, and you'll run into your rival. It's time for your very first Trainer battle!

 Reward: Razz Berry ×20

Rival Battle!

Your Rival

Your rival's only Pokémon is the Eevee or Pikachu that he started his adventure with. If you've been catching Pokémon along Route 1, your partner Pokémon should have gained a level or two. Use same-type attack bonuses (p. 123) for a quick win!

If you started with Pikachu

Eevee
Lv. 6
WEAK AGAINST:

If you started with Eevee

Pikachu
Lv. 6
WEAK AGAINST:

 Now that you've got a taste for battle, why not battle other players? Communication features are now unlocked, so learn how to challenge others to Link Battles on page 140!

3 As you leave Pallet Town, you'll get a gift from your rival's sister. The outfit is for your partner, not you! Discover more about dressing up your partner starting on page 146. You'll also learn how to check how your partner's feeling, so try out some partner playtime from the main menu (p. 141).

 Reward: Sportswear

 Talk to your rival's sister anytime to check the love of one of your Pokémon! More about love is on page 129.

4 Let one of your Pokémon out of its Poké Ball to travel with you (p. 144) as you head back to Viridian City to continue your adventure!

Check Out Your Main Menu

Press Ⓧ and check out your main menu! Select Party to see the Pokémon in your current party, or open up your Pokédex to learn more about the Pokémon you've seen or caught. The main menu is going to be a key part of your adventure, so get a refresher on page 19 when you need it!

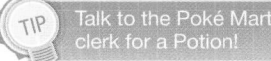 **TIP** Talk to the Poké Mart clerk for a Potion!

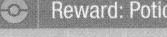 Reward: Potion

WALKTHROUGH

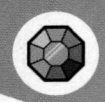

5 Back in Viridian City, you'll run into your rival and have the chance to heal up your team at the Pokémon Center. Unfortunately, the Pokémon Gym in this city seems to be closed at the moment. When you're ready, you can continue north to Route 2 now that the path is clear—or if you like, you can travel west to Route 22.

Consider a Visit to Route 22

You don't have to visit Route 22 now, but you can if you want to. There are new species of Pokémon you can catch—and an extra battle against your rival! See page 99 for the map of Route 22.

 TIP Now that you've caught a good number of Pokémon, why not try sending some to the professor to get Candies (p. 118) if you haven't already?

Rival Battle!

Your Rival

Your rival's team has grown! When he sends out Pidgey, try using Electric-type moves if you've got them. Then tackle his Eevee or Pikachu the same way as before. Pikachu's Thunder Shock can paralyze your Pokémon, so bring a Paralyze Heal just in case!

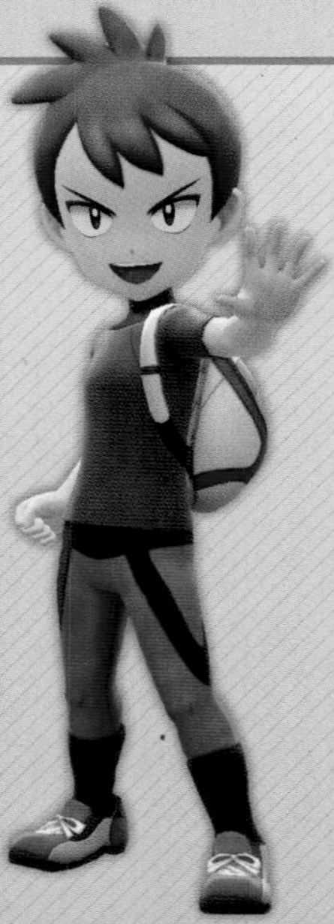

Pidgey
Lv. 3
WEAK AGAINST:

Eevee
Lv. 7
WEAK AGAINST:

If you started with Pikachu

Pikachu
Lv. 7
WEAK AGAINST:

If you started with Eevee

Catch!

Nidoran ♀ and Nidoran ♂

Catch Difficulty

Easier ———— Harder

WALKTHROUGH

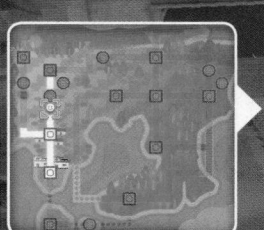

Route 2

     Getting Around

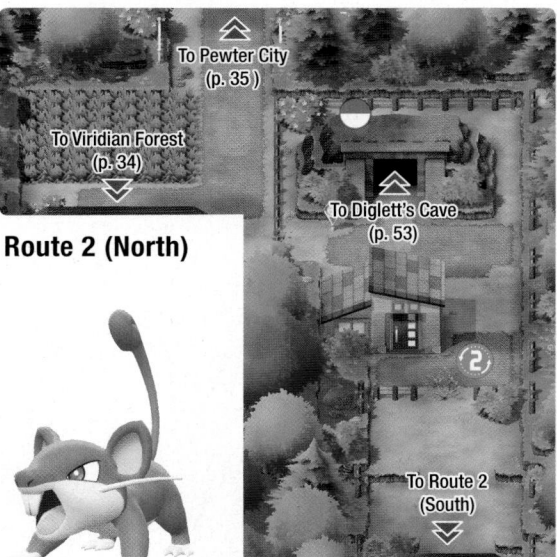

Route 2 (North)

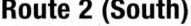

Route 2 (South)

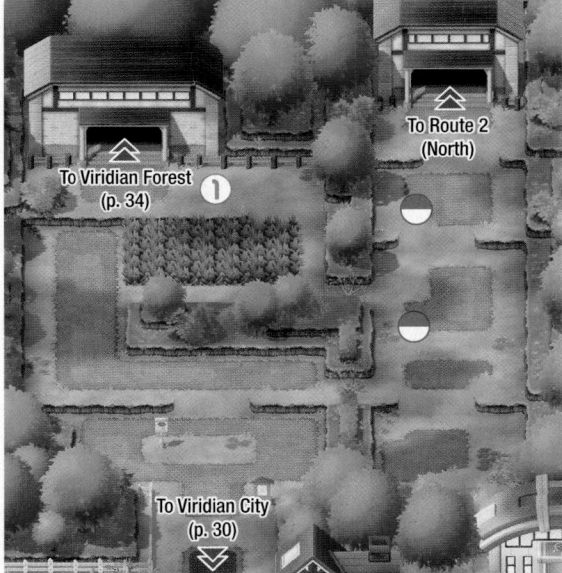

△ Caterpie	△ Weedle	○ Pidgey
○ Rattata	○ Oddish	— Bellsprout

◎ frequent ○ common △ average ☆ rare ★ almost never — does not appear

Items

North (after learning Chop Down)
☑ Great Ball ×3
South (after learning Chop Down)
☑ Leaf Stone
☑ Super Potion

① Keep following the path north toward Viridian Forest, catching some new Pokémon, such as Caterpie or Weedle, as you go along.

TIP Route 2 has a path on the right side you won't be able to reach just yet. Don't worry—you'll get there soon!

Partner Powers and Presents

Have you ever seen an icon like this appear in the corner of your screen during battle? If so, your partner may be ready to use a special power to help you out! When it's feeling up to it, your partner Pikachu or Eevee can use special exclusive moves in battle. If you see this icon out on the field, it means your partner may have a present for you! Learn more about the ways your partner Pokémon can help you on page 142.

Catch!

Caterpie

Catch Difficulty

◄ Easier   Harder ►

WALKTHROUGH

Viridian Forest

Getting Around

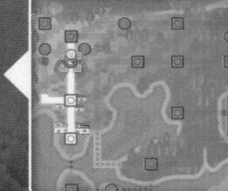

WALKTHROUGH

To Route 2 (North) (p. 33)

To Route 2 (South) (p. 33)

Unusual Encounters — Bulbasaur

Caterpie	Metapod	Butterfree
Weedle	Kakuna	Beedrill
Pidgey	Pikachu	Oddish
Bellsprout		

◎ frequent ○ common △ average ☆ rare
★ almost never — does not appear

Items

- ☑ Poké Ball ×5
- ☑ Tiny Mushroom
- ☑ Antidote
- ☑ Razz Berry ×3
- ☑ Potion
- ☑ Lure

Hidden Items

- ☑ Potion

① There are many paths to explore in this forest, but to reach Pewter City, head east first, then head north and west to find the exit to this natural maze.

 You can encounter the rare Pokémon Bulbasaur in Viridian Forest if you build up your Catch Combo. Learn more on page 117, because this is the only way to encounter Bulbasaur in the wild!

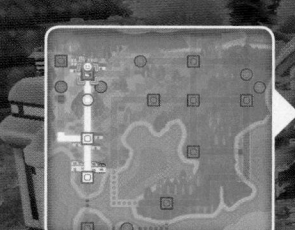

Pewter City

Getting
Around

Pewter Museum
of Science

2

Pokémon
Gym

Poké Mart

3

Pokémon
Center

To Route 3
(p. 37)

1

To Route 2 (North)
(p. 33)

Poké Mart

After earning your first Gym Badge	
☑ Great Ball	₽300
☑ Escape Rope	₽300
☑ Repel	₽400
☑ X Attack	₽550
☑ X Defense	₽500
☑ X Sp. Atk	₽350
☑ X Sp. Def	₽350
☑ X Speed	₽350
☑ X Accuracy	₽950
☑ Dire Hit	₽650
☑ Guard Spec.	₽700

For the full list of items available at Poké Marts, turn to page 395.

Items

☑ X Defense

1 Pass through Route 2's north end to reach Pewter City—and your rival! He'll give you some advice and some Potions, too. Explore the city before you rush straight to the Pokémon Gym!

◉ Reward: Potion ×5

TIP Visit the Pokémon Center here, and you can buy a bag of Pewter Crunchies once per day. Use them on a Pokémon to heal any status conditions (p. 133).

2 Help out this woman to get an item you can sell for profit. You can help her each day like this! Then pop into the museum, or sell your Big Pearl to fund some shopping at the Poké Mart.

◉ Reward: Big Pearl

WALKTHROUGH

Pewter City Pokémon Gym

Most Gyms in the Kanto region have a task you'll need to complete before you can challenge them. In the Pewter City Gym, they want to test your knowledge of type matchups, so you'll need a Water- or Grass-type Pokémon. You should have one already if you caught an Oddish or a Bellsprout back on Route 1 or 2. If not, you can go back and easily catch one.

Gym Leader Brock

Brock's Geodude and Onix are both Rock and Ground types. That means they'll take 400% damage from Grass- or Water-type moves. Using Bellsprout's Vine Whip or Oddish's Absorb should take care of his Pokémon with ease. Another wise choice would be Fighting-type moves, since they're also super effective against Rock-type Pokémon. If your partner has learned Double Kick by now, it's a solid option!

Reward: TM01 Headbutt, Boulder Badge

TM01 Headbutt

This physical move has a power of 70, plus it can cause the target to flinch. It can be learned by many different Pokémon!

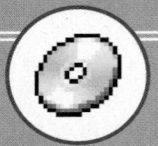

Geodude
Lv. 11
WEAK AGAINST:
4×

Onix
Lv. 12
WEAK AGAINST:
4×

3 After claiming your first Gym Badge, you'll get a gift from an experienced Trainer. Once you have it, heal up from your Gym battle at the Pokémon Center, then head east out of town to Route 3.

Reward: Great Ball ×5

TIP You can buy new items at the Poké Mart now that you've got a Gym Badge!

Smell ya later, newbie!

WALKTHROUGH

Gym Battle!

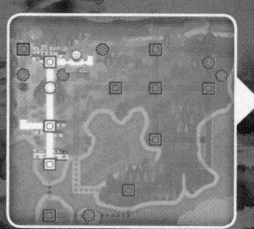

Route 3 & Route 4 (West)

   Getting Around

Items

Route 3
☑ Potion
☑ Poké Ball ×3
☑ Lure
☑ Revive
Route 4 (West)
☑ Escape Rope

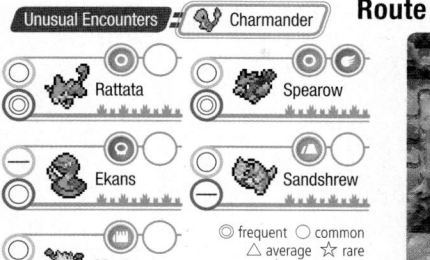

Unusual Encounters — Charmander

Rattata
Spearow
Ekans
Sandshrew
Mankey

◎ frequent ○ common
△ average ☆ rare
★ almost never
— does not appear

Route 4 (West)

Pokémon Center

To Mt. Moon (p. 38)

2

Route 3

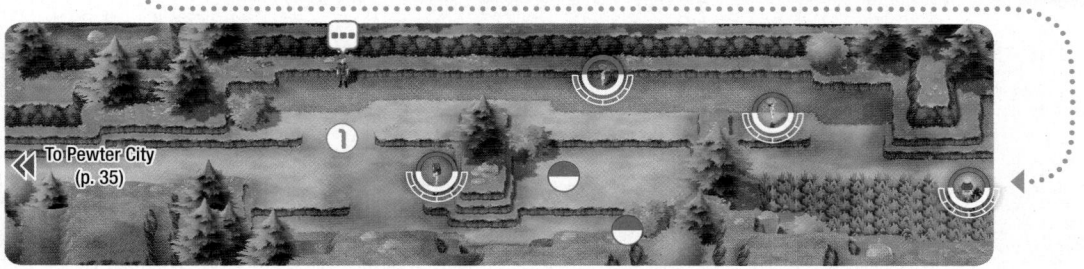

To Pewter City (p. 35)

①

① Meet your first Coach Trainer! These Trainers won't challenge you like other Trainers, but choose to battle them to earn valuable rewards. Learn more on page 136.

② Before you reach Mt. Moon, you'll pass into the west side of Route 4, where another Coach Trainer waits. Battle him, then visit the Pokémon Center before entering Mt. Moon.

> **TIP** You can buy a Magikarp from a salesman in the Pokémon Center. Magikarp isn't great in battle, but it evolves into the powerful Gyarados!

Coach Battle!

Coach Trainer Kareem

Try using a Flying-type move from Pidgey or Spearow if you've caught one!

TEAM:
Lv. 11
⊙ Reward: Revive

Coach Battle!

Coach Trainer Oberon

If any of your Pokémon knows Double Kick or Karate Chop, you'll be in good shape to beat his Normal-type Pokémon!

TEAM:
Lv. 13
⊙ Reward: TM57 Pay Day

> **TIP** Using Pay Day in battle will get you more money when you defeat Trainers!

WALKTHROUGH

Mt. Moon

Getting Around

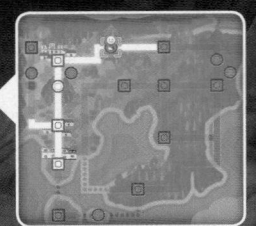

WALKTHROUGH

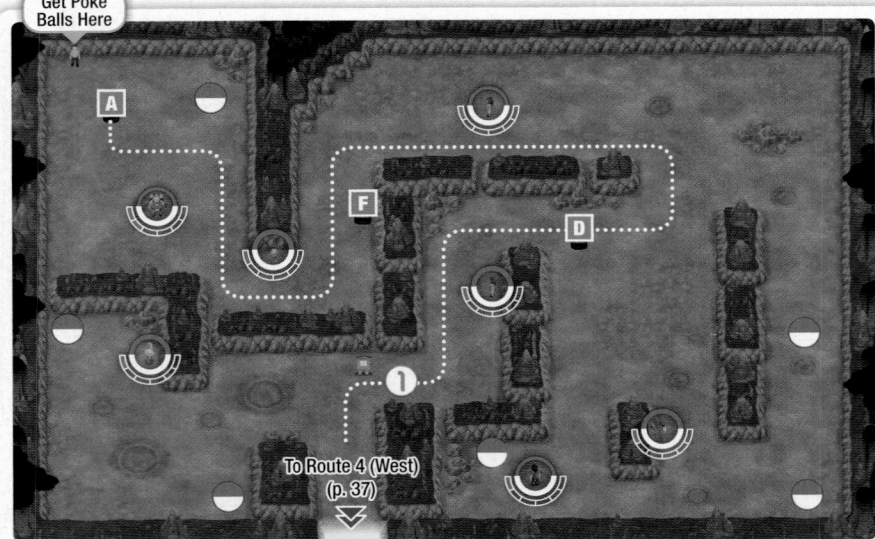

Get Poké Balls Here

To Route 4 (West) (p. 37)

1F

☆ Clefairy
☆
◎ Zubat
◎
△ Paras

◎ Geodude
◎
★ Onix
★

◎ frequent ○ common
△ average ☆ rare
★ almost never
— does not appear

B1F

Unusual Encounters ━ Chansey

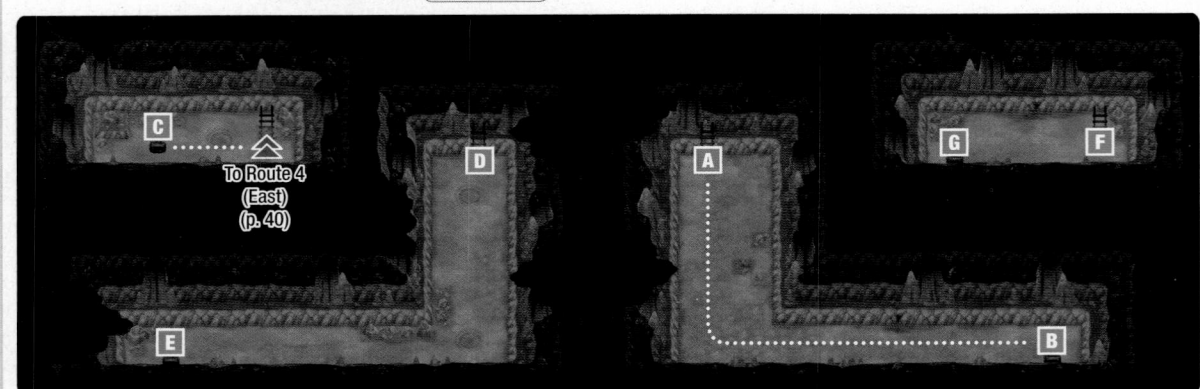

To Route 4 (East) (p. 40)

Items	
1F	
☑ Potion	
☑ Great Ball ×5	
☑ Awakening	
☑ Ether	
☑ Repel	
☑ Pearl	
B2F	
☑ Revive	
☑ Potion	
☑ Revive	
☑ Rare Candy	
☑ Nugget	

Hidden Items	
1F	
☑ Stardust	
B1F	
☑ Big Mushroom	
B2F	
☑ Moon Stone	
☑ Moon Stone	

① The path here leads east, then north, then west—just like in Viridian Forest. Follow the labels on the map in alphabetical order for the quickest route, or explore to get more items and experience!

② Travel down to B1F by heading down ladder **A** and then even deeper to B2F by heading down **B**. And what's Team Rocket doing here?

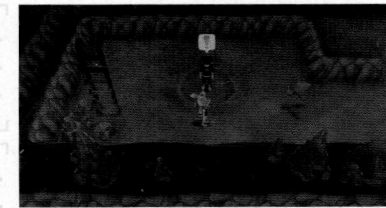

 TIP If you have fewer than 10 Poké Balls, there's a man on 1F who can give you some.

 TIP Mt. Moon is full of Rock- and Ground-type Pokémon, which will come in handy in the Vermilion City Gym, so try catching some!

	Clefairy		Clefable		Zubat		Paras		Geodude		Onix

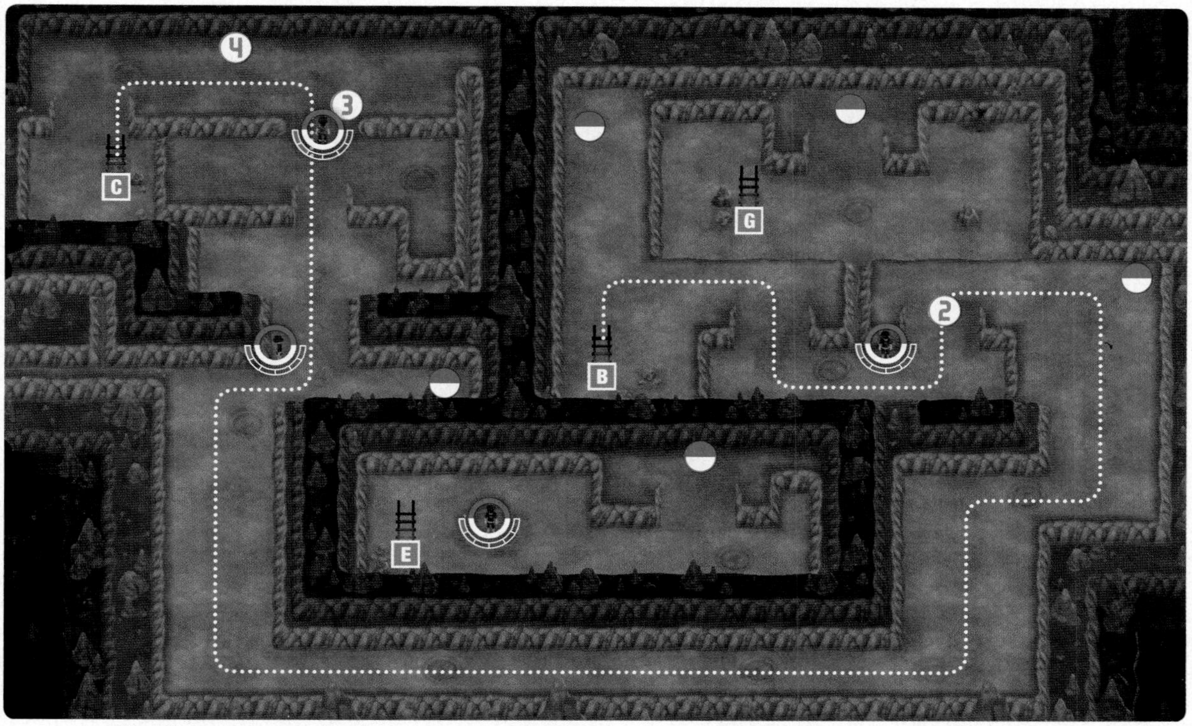

◎ frequent ○ common △ average ☆ rare ★ almost never — does not appear

---

3 When you run into Super Nerd Miguel, he won't share his Fossils willingly. Beat him in battle to get either a Helix Fossil to restore into Omanyte (p. 333) or a Dome Fossil to restore into Kabuto (p. 335). You can restore Fossils once you reach the Cinnabar Lab (p. 92)!

◉ Reward: Helix Fossil or Dome Fossil

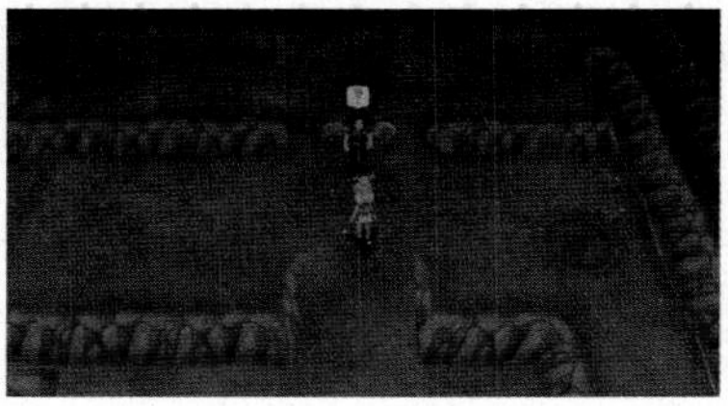

---

4 This troublesome trio won't let you go without a fight this time, so battle Jessie and James to keep moving ahead. Once you defeat them, carry on to **C** and then climb out of Mt. Moon!

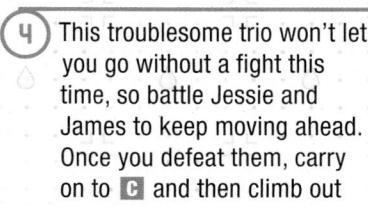

TIP Find a Moon Stone in Mt. Moon and you can evolve Clefairy with it! Hidden items can reappear, so come back later to find more!

Battle!

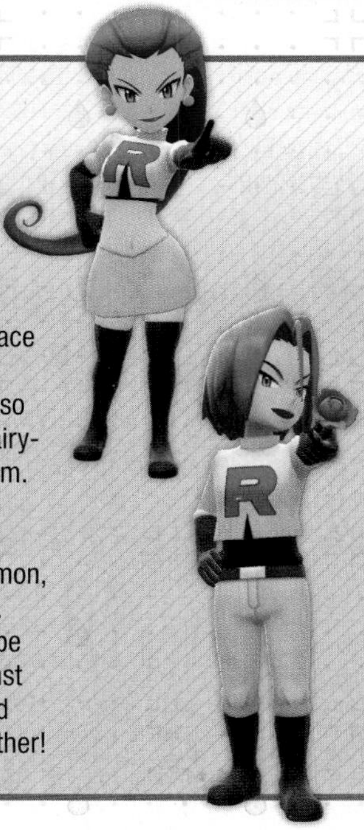

Team Rocket
Jessie and James

Both the Pokémon you'll face in your first Double Battle (p. 130) are Poison types, so don't pit your Grass- or Fairy-type Pokémon against them. Ground- and Psychic-type moves are super effective against Poison-type Pokémon, if you happen to have any. Remember that Poison-type Pokémon are strong against Fighting-type moves—and they can't be poisoned, either!

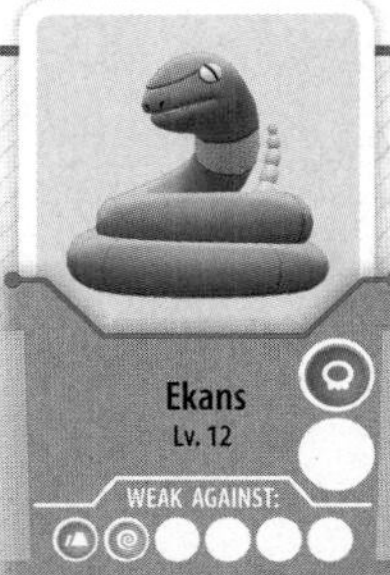

Ekans Lv. 12
WEAK AGAINST:

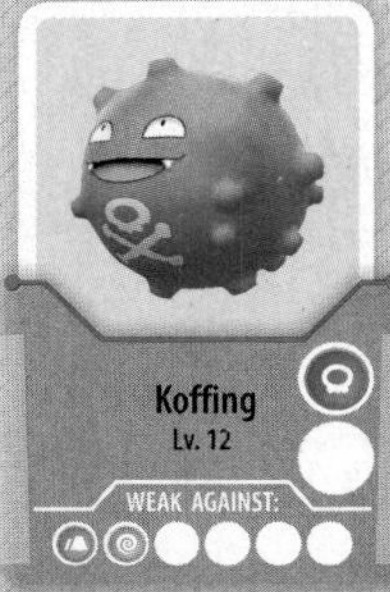

Koffing Lv. 12
WEAK AGAINST:

Route 4 (East)

Getting Around

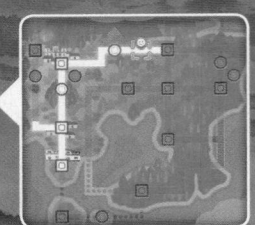

To Mt. Moon
(p. 38)

To Cerulean
Cave
(p. 108)

To Cerulean
City

①

WALKTHROUGH

Unusual Encounters — Charmander

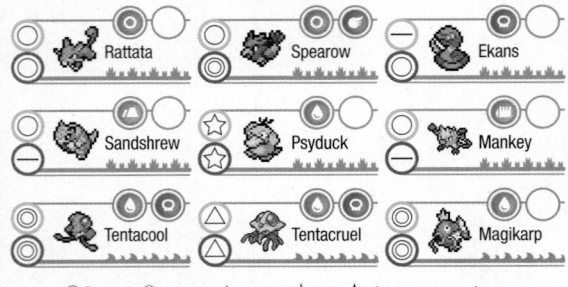

◎	Rattata	◎	Spearow	◎	Ekans
◎	Sandshrew	☆	Psyduck	—	Mankey
◎	Tentacool	△	Tentacruel	◎	Magikarp

◎ frequent ○ common △ average ☆ rare ★ almost never — does not appear

Items	
✓	Paralyze Heal
✓	Poké Ball ×5
✓	Repel
✓	Great Ball ×3
	After learning Sea Skim
✓	PP Max

? Hidden Items ?	
✓	PP Up

① It's just a short jog east to Cerulean City now. If you didn't have the chance to get a Charmander on Route 3, try to build up a Catch Combo to encounter this Fire-type Pokémon and add it to your team!

Catch!

Charmander

Catch Difficulty

Easier ◀ ▲ ▶ Harder

Cerulean City

   Getting Around

To Route 24 (p. 43)

Pokémon Center

To Cerulean Cave (p. 108)

Pokémon Gym

To Route 4 (East)

To Route 9 (p. 54)

Poké Mart

To Route 5 (p. 45)

To Route 5 (p. 45)

WALKTHROUGH

Poké Mart

After earning two Gym Badges

☐	Super Potion	₽700
☐	Lure	₽400

For the full list of items available at Poké Marts, turn to page 395.

Items

☑	Rare Candy	
☑	Burn Heal	

TIP Check out the Bike Maniac's house. If you listen to all his descriptions about his beloved bikes, he'll give you five Heart Scales!

 Reward: Heart Scale ×5

---

1 Visit this house and the woman inside will give you a Bulbasaur if you've caught at least 30 Pokémon. Bulbasaur will be a big help in the Cerulean City Gym!

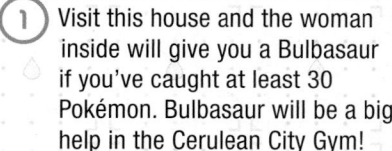

Pokémon: Bulbasaur

TIP You can visit the house on the northwest side of the city and have the man inside tell you more about each Gym Badge!

2 Talk to the Partner Move Tutor in the Pokémon Center to teach your partner Pokémon some moves only it can learn. While you're there, why not trade a Rattata you've caught for a rare Alolan Rattata (p. 191)?

Pokémon: Alolan Rattata

Cerulean City Pokémon Gym

This Gym's mission is pretty simple: you just need to show the man a Pokémon on your team that's at least Lv. 15. If you've passed this test but are still struggling against the high-level Trainers here, consider strengthening your team on Route 24 and Route 25, where you'll find lots of Trainers and wild Pokémon!

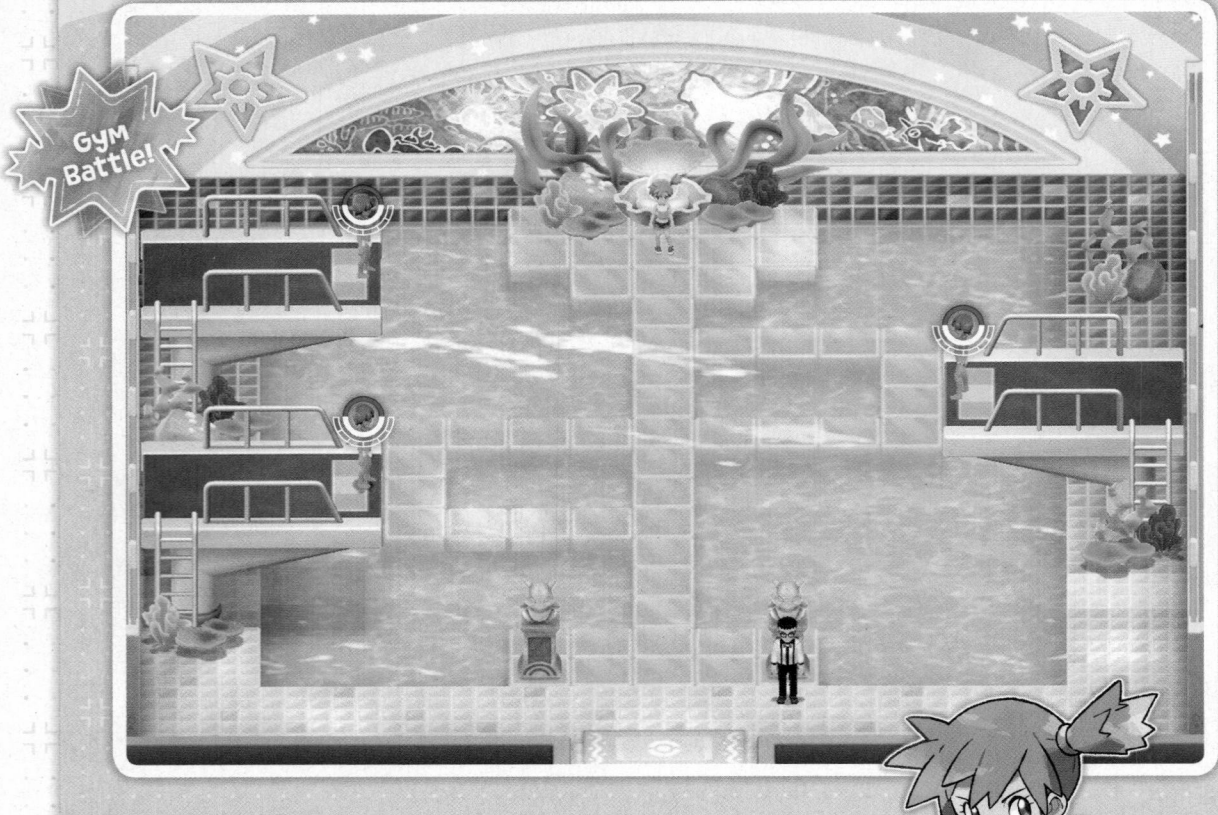

Gym Battle!

Gym Leader Misty

Misty's a master of Water-type Pokémon, so keep your Fire-, Ground-, or Rock-type Pokémon in your Pokémon Box. If you caught a Pikachu in Viridian Forest, caught a Bellsprout or an Oddish on Route 1, or picked up Bulbasaur in Cerulean City, you should be well equipped to handle Misty's Pokémon. They're weak to Grass- and Electric-type moves, so bust out that Thunder Shock or Absorb! But be careful— Bellsprout, Oddish, and Bulbasaur are all Poison types, which take double damage from Psyduck's and Starmie's Psychic-type moves! A Potion or two might come in handy here!

Psyduck
Lv. 18
WEAK AGAINST:

Starmie
Lv. 19
WEAK AGAINST:

TM29 Scald

The user shoots boiling hot water at its target. This may also leave the target with a burn. With a power of 80, this special move is great for a Water-type Pokémon!

Reward: TM29 Scald, Cascade Badge

WALKTHROUGH

Route 24

 Getting Around

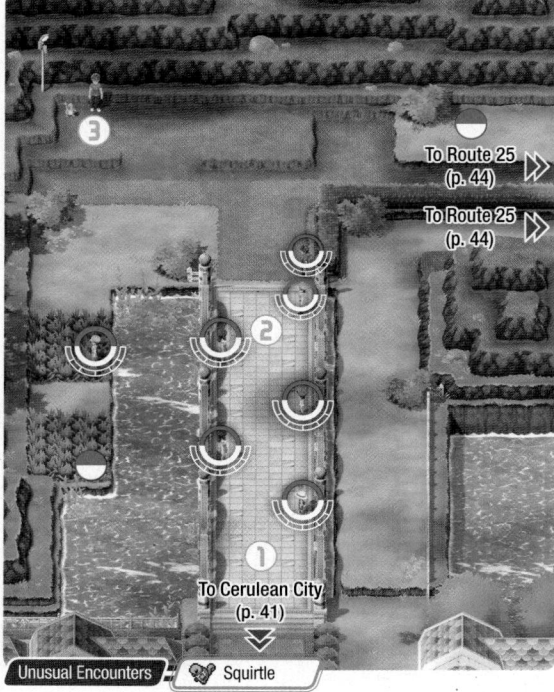

To Route 25 (p. 44) »

To Route 25 (p. 44) »

To Cerulean City (p. 41)

Unusual Encounters — Squirtle

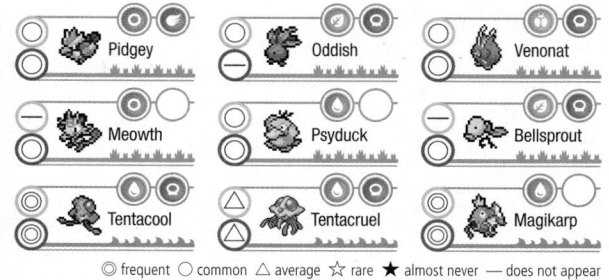

	Pidgey		Oddish		Venonat
	Meowth		Psyduck		Bellsprout
	Tentacool		Tentacruel		Magikarp

◎ frequent ○ common △ average ☆ rare ★ almost never — does not appear

① Run into your rival in front of the famous Nugget Bridge, and he'll drag you straight into battle!

Items
- ☑ Razz Berry ×3
- ☑ X Sp. Def

Hidden Items
- ☑ Pinap Berry ×3

② Heal your team at the Pokémon Center if you need to, because you'll have to battle your way across the rest of the bridge next!

⬡ Reward: Nugget

Rival Battle!

Your Rival

Use Electric-type moves against his Pidgey or a Geodude or an Onix from Mt. Moon. He'll send out Oddish, but it'll get blown away by Flying-type moves if you've got a Pidgey or Spearow. Last comes his Eevee or Pikachu, but you know how to beat them by now!

Pidgey Lv. 12 — WEAK AGAINST:

Oddish Lv. 12 — WEAK AGAINST:

Eevee Lv. 13 — WEAK AGAINST:
If you started with Pikachu

Pikachu Lv. 13 — WEAK AGAINST:
If you started with Eevee

③ This guy is looking to give his Pokémon to a worthy Trainer. This time, you'll need to have caught at least 50 Pokémon. Go catch some more in the grass south of him if you hope to get his Charmander!

⬡ Pokémon: Charmander

WALKTHROUGH

Route 25

Getting
Around

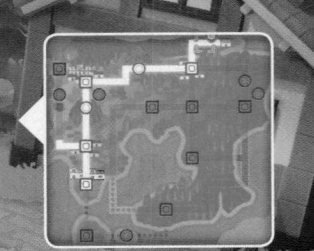

To Route 24
(p. 43)

To Route 24
(p. 43)

Bill's
House

WALKTHROUGH

| Unusual Encounters | 🐢 Squirtle |

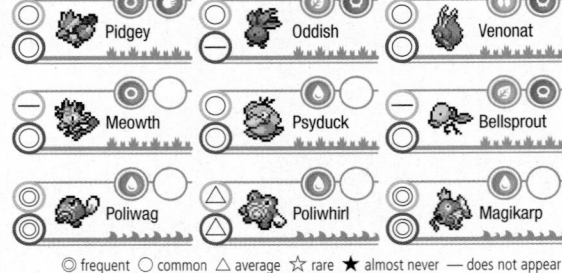

Items	
☑	Super Potion
☑	Ether
☑	Lure
	After learning Chop Down
☑	TM16 Thunder Wave

❓ Hidden Items ❓
☑ Nanab Berry ×3

	Pidgey		Oddish		Venonat
	Meowth		Psyduck		Bellsprout
	Poliwag		Poliwhirl		Magikarp

◎ frequent ○ common △ average ☆ rare ★ almost never — does not appear

① Head east to reach Bill's house, battling plenty of Trainers along the way. Then help Bill out of his pinch. He'll reward you, and you can take a peek at his PC for notes on some very rare Pokémon!

Reward: S.S. Tickets

TIP If you walk along the lower part of the path, you can get a Trainer to move out of the way when he comes to battle you. This will allow you to reach TM16 Thunder Wave! Otherwise, you'll need to come back for it when you have the Secret Technique Chop Down (p. 50).

Coach
Battle!

Coach Trainer
Amala

If you caught a Clefairy in Mt. Moon, give it a try. Otherwise, Pidgeotto or Spearow would be good choices against Amala's Machop!

TEAM:

Lv. 16

Reward: TM15 Seismic Toss

Route 5

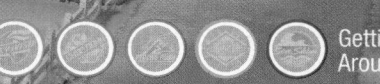

Getting
Around

To Cerulean City
(p. 41)

To Cerulean City
(p. 41)

Pokémon
Day Care

To Saffron City
(p. 79)

To Underground Path (N–S)
(p. 46)

Unusual Encounters — Chansey

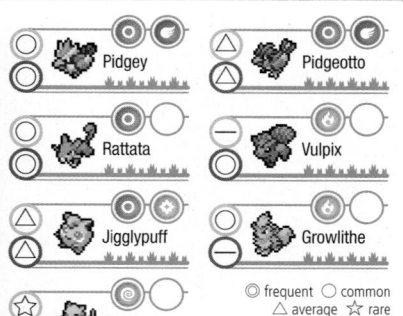

		Pidgey				Pidgeotto
Rattata						Vulpix
Jigglypuff						Growlithe
Abra						

◎ frequent ○ common
△ average ☆ rare
★ almost never
— does not appear

Items

- Ether
- Nanab Berry ×3
- Great Ball ×3

Hidden Items

- Razz Berry ×3

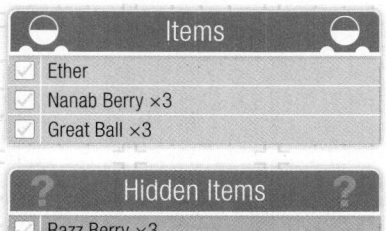

① To reach Route 5, you'll have to swing back through Cerulean City. Go into the house that had been blocked before by a police officer. Cut through it to battle a crook and claim a reward. Finally, loop around the town to the next route!

Reward: TM10 Dig

② As you travel south along Route 5, check out the Pokémon Day Care (p. 128). You can also try to catch some of the new Pokémon you'll see along the route. Then meet up with your rival, and give him one of your S.S. Tickets before you head into the Underground Path (N–S).

Reward: Revive ×3

Catch!

Get these version exclusive Fire-type Pokémon to trade with other players!

Growlithe

Catch Difficulty

Easier ————— Harder

Vulpix

Catch Difficulty

Easier ————— Harder

WALKTHROUGH

Underground Path (N–S) & Route 6

Getting Around

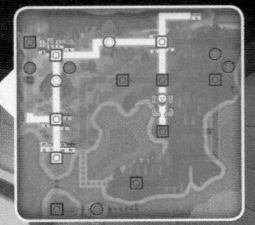

Underground Path (N–S)

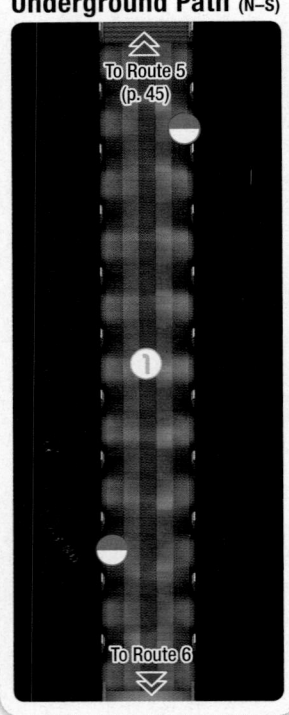

To Route 5 (p. 45)

1

To Route 6

Items

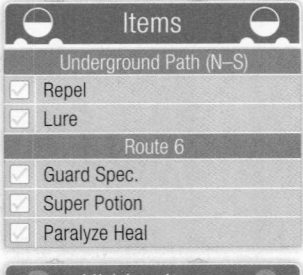

Underground Path (N–S)
- ☑ Repel
- ☑ Lure

Route 6
- ☑ Guard Spec.
- ☑ Super Potion
- ☑ Paralyze Heal

Hidden Items

Underground Path (N–S)
- ☑ Big Pearl*
- ☑ Fresh Water*
- ☑ Hyper Potion*
- ☑ Lure*
- ☑ Max Lure*
- ☑ Max Repel*
- ☑ Nugget*
- ☑ Pearl*
- ☑ Potion*
- ☑ Pretty Wing*
- ☑ Repel*
- ☑ Super Lure*
- ☑ Super Potion*
- ☑ Super Repel*

Route 6
- ☑ Rare Candy

*You have a chance to randomly find one of these items at each spot.

Route 6

To Saffron City (p. 79)

To Underground Path (N–S)

2

To Vermilion City

Unusual Encounters | **Chansey**

Pidgey	Pidgeotto	Rattata	Vulpix
Jigglypuff	Psyduck	Growlithe	Abra
Goldeen	Seaking	Magikarp	

◎ frequent ○ common
△ average ☆ rare
★ almost never
— does not appear

WALKTHROUGH

1 Make your way through the tunnel, picking up items along the way! The hidden items you find here are a bit different than the ones you've found elsewhere, as they can change each time you find them. Keep coming back to see which ones you get!

Remember to watch your partner's tail to find hidden items (p. 143)!

2 Once you leave the Underground Path, it's a short jog south along Route 6 to reach Vermilion City! Try catching an Abra along the way, as it evolves into a powerful Pokémon with high Sp. Atk.

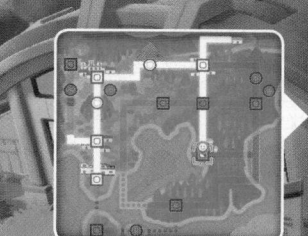

Vermilion City

   Getting Around

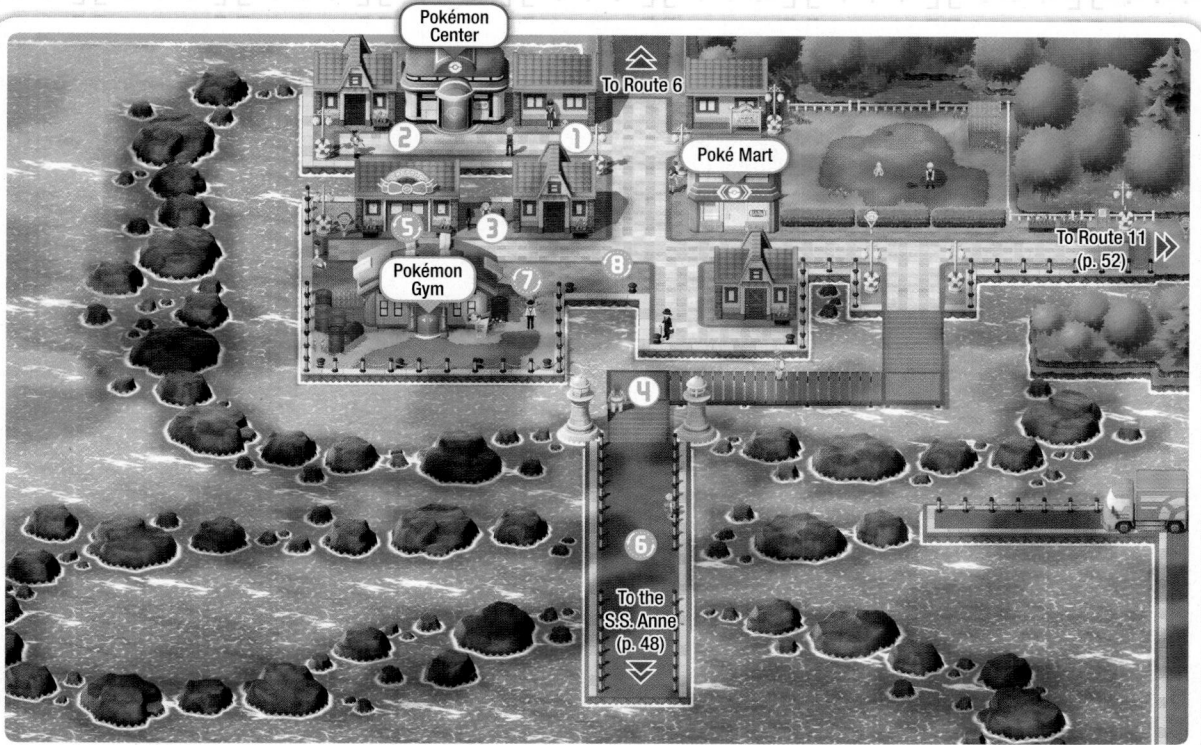

Pokémon Center

To Route 6

Poké Mart

To Route 11 (p. 52)

Pokémon Gym

To the S.S. Anne (p. 48)

WALKTHROUGH

Poké Mart

After earning three Gym Badges	
Full Heal	₽400
Revive	₽2,000
Super Repel	₽700

For the full list of items available at Poké Marts, turn to page 395.

? Hidden Items ?

☑ Full Heal
After learning Sea Skim
☑ Big Pearl
☑ Revive

1 Explore this port city for all it has to offer—which is new Pokémon for your team! Start by talking to the police officer west of the entrance from Route 6. If you've caught at least 60 Pokémon, she'll let you take the Squirtle beside her.

◉ Pokémon: Squirtle

2 Carry on to the Pokémon Center, where you can make a trade for another unusual Alolan regional variant. This time it's Geodude! When you're done there, consider popping in the house next door, where you can get some tips from other Trainers.

◉ Pokémon: Alolan Geodude

3 In *Pokémon: Let's Go, Pikachu!*, speak to the Black Belt by the Pokémon Fan Club and you can get a Persian if you've caught five Growlithe! Or get an Arcanine from a Beauty found in the same spot in *Pokémon: Let's Go, Eevee!*, if you've caught five Meowth.

◉ Pokémon: Persian or Arcanine

4 Head to Vermilion Port and get a special seafaring outfit before boarding the S.S. Anne. This is the first of several outfits you can obtain on your journey (p. 146)—just select the Clothing Trunk from your Bag whenever you feel like a fresh look!

◉ Reward: Sailor Set

S.S. Anne

Getting
Around ○ ○ ○ ○ ○

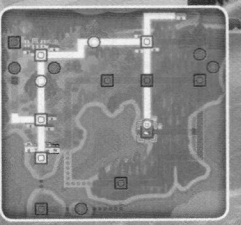

Deck

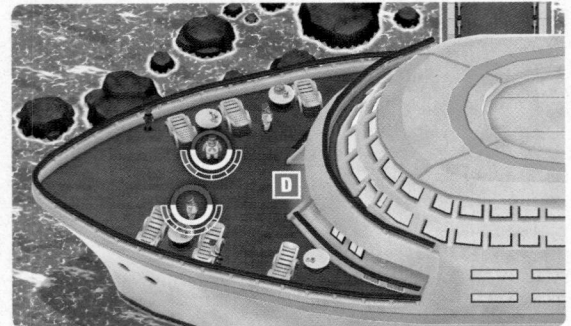

3F

Kitchen

Items	
1F	
☑	Paralyze Heal
2F	
☑	Revive
☑	Nugget
B1F	
☑	Full Heal
☑	Elixir
☑	Super Potion

Items	
Kitchen	
☑	Super Repel

? Hidden Items ?	
Kitchen	
☑	Tiny Mushroom
Deck	
☑	Pinap Berry ×3

TIP — You can heal your Pokémon whenever you need to in the room to the right of the entrance to the S.S. Anne.

① Meet some friendly faces and get a treat. Then the ship's yours to explore! Follow the markers on the maps on the next page straight to **A** and then **B** to reach step 2, but you might miss out if you do. Make sure to get all your battling done before reaching step 3—after completing it, you'll no longer be able to challenge the Trainers aboard the S.S Anne!

◉ Reward: Shalour Sable

② Whether you've run straight here or explored the kitchen, the outer deck, and the lower floors first, you'll find your rival again at the east end of 2F. It's battle time again!

Rival Battle!

Your Rival

Your rival's team is essentially the same as the last time you battled him—just a few levels higher. Use the same strategies you did before, and you'll be able to win easily as long as you've been leveling up your Pokémon properly.

Pidgeotto Lv. 20 — WEAK AGAINST:

Eevee Lv. 21 — WEAK AGAINST:

Oddish Lv. 20 — WEAK AGAINST:

Pikachu Lv. 21 — WEAK AGAINST:

If you started with Pikachu

If you started with Eevee

WALKTHROUGH

2F

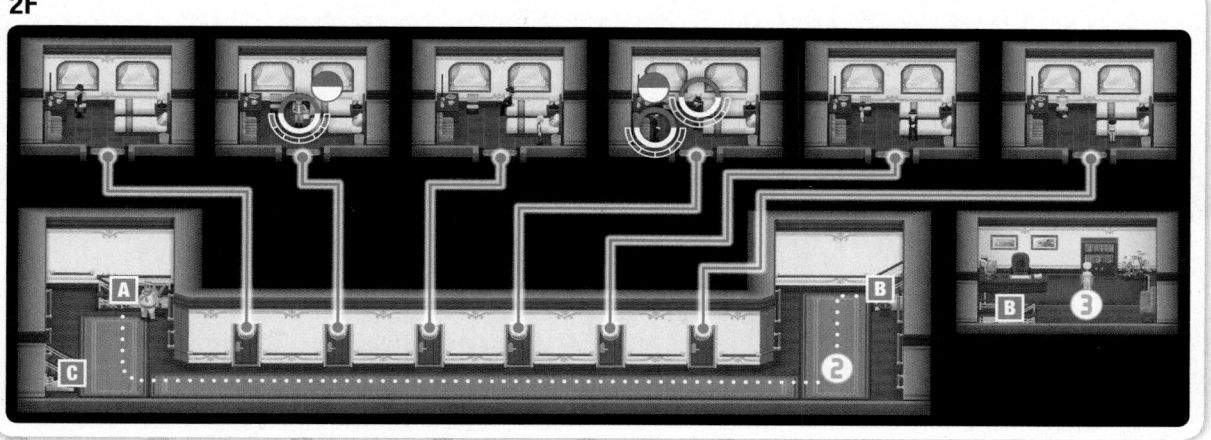

1F

Heal your party here

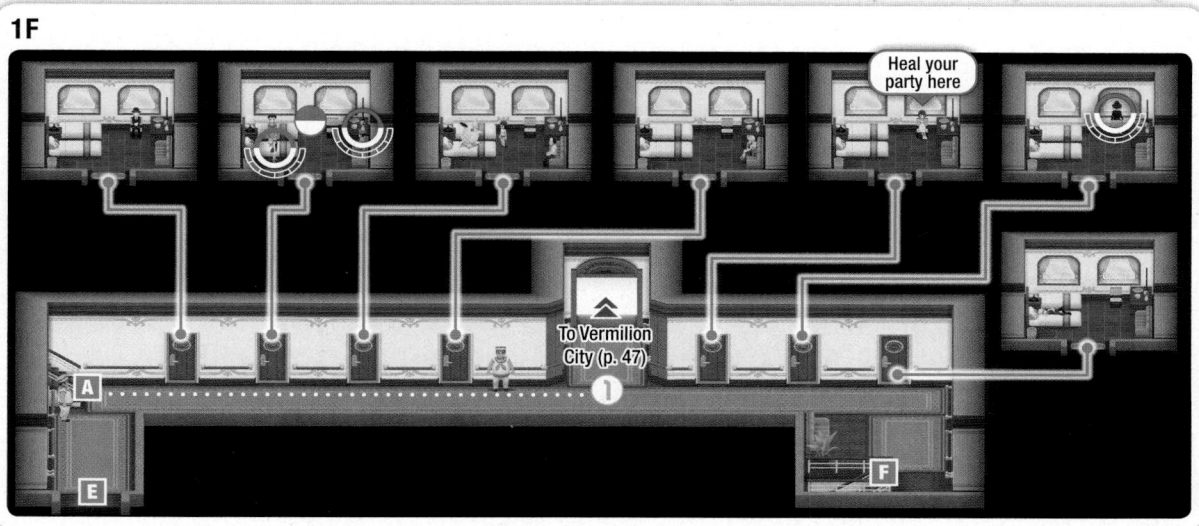

To Vermilion City (p. 47)

B1F

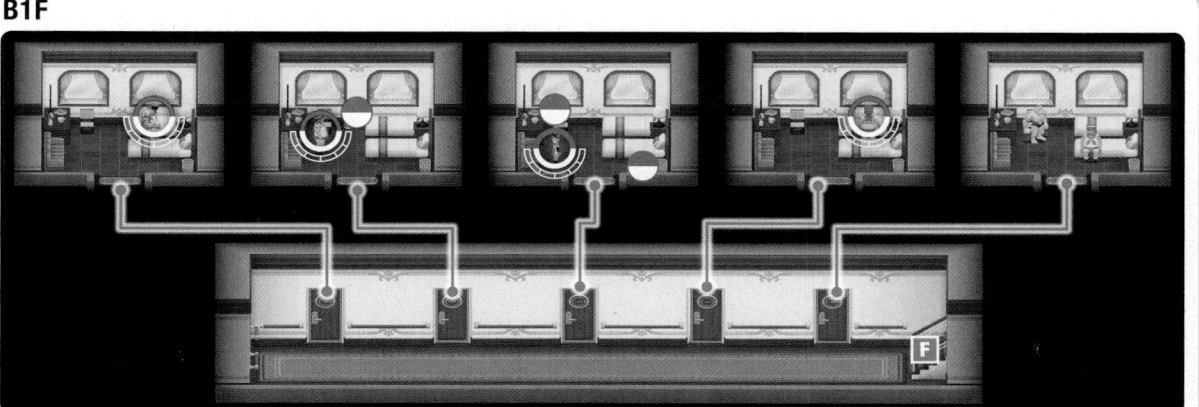

3 Help the captain out to teach your partner the Secret Technique Chop Down! You can use it in Vermilion City, but the S.S. Anne will leave as soon as you get off, so be sure you've done everything you want to do before you disembark.

Secret Technique: Chop Down

Vermilion City (Revisited)

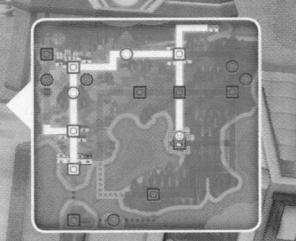

Getting Around

Turn back to page 47 if you need to refer to the map of Vermilion City again to locate any of these steps!

5 Swing into the Pokémon Fan Club and listen to the chairman's boasting to get an outfit inspired by your partner Pokémon.

Reward: Pikachu Set or Eevee Set

TIP Talk to the chairman once you've maxed out your partner Pokémon's love to get special outfits for both of you to wear! Learn how to check the love of your Pokémon on page 129.

Reward: Raichu Set or Vaporeon Set, Jolteon Set, Flareon Set, Espeon Set, Umbreon Set, Leafeon Set, Glaceon Set, Sylveon Set

6 Meet Mina, a Trainer who's traveled to Kanto from the Alola region! You can challenge her to a battle once per day. Every time you defeat her, you'll get a Bottle Cap that you can use for Hyper Training (p. 125), too.

Battle!

Pokémon Trainer Mina
Mina's a skilled Fairy-type Pokémon Trainer from the far-off Alola region! Fairy-type Pokémon are weak to Poison-type moves, so any that you have will be a great help here. Watch out, though, as her Mr. Mime also has Psychic-type moves, which are super effective against Poison-type Pokémon!

Reward: Bottle Cap

Jigglypuff Lv. 21
WEAK AGAINST:

Mr. Mime Lv. 22
WEAK AGAINST:

7 Use Chop Down on that inconvenient tree blocking the way to the Vermilion City Pokémon Gym, and you can try to claim your next Gym Badge!

TIP You've unlocked one Secret Technique now. Once your partner has learned another called Sea Skim, you'll be able to sail across the water out on the pier that led to the S.S. Anne! If you do, you'll find another pier...and something hidden beneath the truck there!

Secret Techniques

Chop Down is the first of five Secret Techniques your partner can learn during your adventure. These techniques will all help you during your quest by opening up new areas and by helping you get around more easily. Chop Down removes pesky trees that are in your way. You've probably seen one or two of them in Viridian City or Pewter City already. You can use Chop Down by walking up to a small tree and pressing Ⓐ. You can also check and use Secret Techniques when you select your partner Pokémon's face in the main menu.

WALKTHROUGH

Vermilion City Pokémon Gym

Getting past that tree was the Gym mission here, so you should be all set to take on the Gym! Ground-type Pokémon and moves will have a big advantage, if you have any. Listen to the Trainers for clues on how to disable the two barriers to reach Lt. Surge, or check the answer at the bottom of this box if you're having trouble figuring it out.

Gym Battle!

Voltorb Lv. 25	Magnemite Lv. 25	Raichu Lv. 26
WEAK AGAINST:	WEAK AGAINST:	WEAK AGAINST:

TM36 Thunderbolt

Thunderbolt is a great move for an Electric-type Pokémon to learn—or any Pokémon that can learn it! It's powerful and can cause paralysis, lowering the affected Pokémon's Speed and sometimes causing its moves to fail!

Gym Leader Lt. Surge

While Lt. Surge's Voltorb and Raichu are pure Electric-type Pokémon and weak to Ground-type moves, his Magnemite is also Steel type, meaning it's weak to Fire- and Fighting-type moves as well. Try using the Charmander you might have gotten back on Route 24 (p. 43)! If you taught any of your Pokémon Dig—using the TM you got from that Team Rocket Grunt in Cerulean City—that'll be your best move to use during this battle.

Reward: TM36 Thunderbolt, Lt. Surge's Autograph, Thunder Badge

ANSWER: First examine the trash can to the right of the blue one—then the trash can north of that one!

8 After leaving the Gym, you'll run into Misty again. She thinks you should check out Diglett's Cave, and she'll take you right there, if you want. If you turn her down, head to Route 11 whenever you're ready.

Route 11

Getting
Around

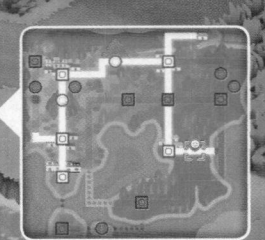

To Diglett's Cave

To Vermilion
City (p. 47)

To Route 12
(p. 74)

Unusual Encounters Chansey

Pidgey	Pidgeotto	Rattata	
	Raticate	Drowzee	Mr. Mime
	Tentacool	Tentacruel	Horsea
	Seadra	Magikarp	

◎ frequent ○ common
△ average ☆ rare
★ almost never
— does not appear

Items	
☑ Super Potion	
☑ Lure	
☑ X Defense	
☑ Super Repel	

Items	
☑ Great Ball ×5	

? Hidden Items ?	
☑ Revive	

1 You could head straight into Diglett's Cave, but if you've caught at least 30 different species of Pokémon, follow this route to the gate at the far end. On 2F, one of Professor Oak's assistants will give you the Judge function!

Have you gathered data on at least 30 species of Pokémon?

Use the Judge Function to Check Individual Strengths

Every Pokémon has different individual strengths that influence the growth of its stats—whether growth is low or high varies from stat to stat and Pokémon to Pokémon. Individual strengths can't easily be changed, but with the Judge function, they can be revealed. Learn more about individual strengths on page 125, and use this function to help you decide which of the many Pokémon you've caught you want to raise for your team!

Coach Battle!

Coach Trainer Will

Rattata is weak to Fighting-type moves, such as Double Kick. Just watch out for its Super Fang, which can cut your Pokémon's HP in half.

TEAM:

Lv. 21

Reward: Pikachu Candy ×5 or Eevee Candy ×5

WALKTHROUGH

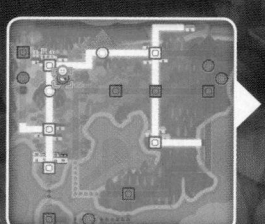

Diglett's Cave & Route 2 (Revisited)

Getting Around

A

1

B

Unusual Encounters Chansey

Diglett's Cave

△		◎	◎	Zubat
△				
◎		▲	○	Diglett
◎			☆	
☆		▲	○	Dugtrio
☆			☆	

◎ frequent ○ common
△ average ☆ rare
★ almost never
— does not appear

Top Exit

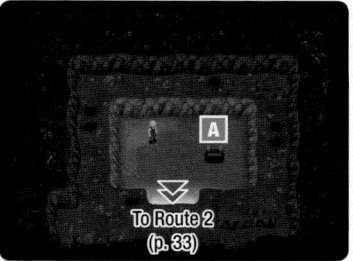

A

To Route 2
(p. 33)

Bottom Exit

B

To Vermilion
City (p. 47)

1 Head through the cave to Route 2. There's really no way to get lost in here, so simply keep heading northwest as you catch (or dodge) plenty of Diglett!

Turn back to page 33 if you need to refer to the map of Route 2 again to locate any of these steps!

Revisits with Chop Down

Now that you're back on Route 2 with Chop Down, try revisiting Viridian City and Pewter City to get some things you weren't able to before. In Viridian City, you can talk to the man sleeping by the water to get TM11 Will-O-Wisp. Use Chop Down in Pewter City to get in the back entrance of the Pewter Museum of Science and claim an Old Amber, which can be restored to a rare Pokémon later (p. 92).

◉ Reward: TM11 Will-O-Wisp, Old Amber

2 Back on Route 2 again, head south to meet Professor Oak's assistant. He'll teach your partner the Secret Technique Light Up.

Then take your rival's offer to get whisked right back to Cerulean City, where you can clear the path to Route 9 with Chop Down!

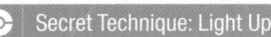

◉ Secret Technique: Light Up

WALKTHROUGH

Route 9

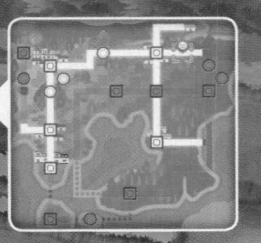

Getting Around

To Cerulean City (p. 41)

①

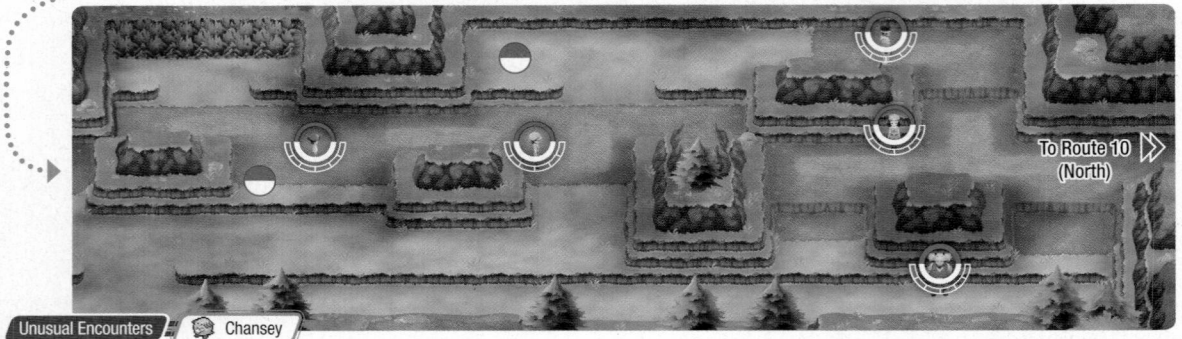

To Route 10 (North)

WALKTHROUGH

Unusual Encounters  Chansey

 Rattata

Raticate

Spearow

Fearow

 Nidoran ♀

Nidorina

Nidoran ♂

Nidorino

◎ frequent ○ common △ average ☆ rare ★ almost never — does not appear

Items

- ☑ Super Potion
- ☑ Ether
- ☑ Poké Ball ×5
- ☑ Super Potion

Hidden Items

- ☑ Pinap Berry ×5

① Battle your way through Route 9. Before you dash all the way east, consider looping up north to pick up an Ether. There are plenty of out-of-the-way corners like this on Route 9, if you look for them!

Catch!

Nidorina and Nidorino

Catch Difficulty

◀ Easier   Harder ▶

Route 10

Getting Around

To Route 9

Pokémon
Center

To Rock
Tunnel
(p. 56)

To Power
Plant (p. 77)

Unusual Encounters   Chansey

Route 10 (North)

Route 10 (South)

To Rock
Tunnel
(p. 56)

To Lavender
Town (p. 57)

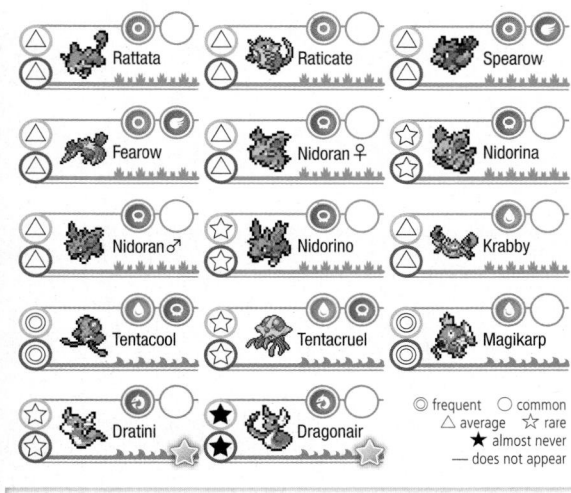

△	Rattata	△	Raticate	○	Spearow
○	Fearow	○	Nidoran ♀	☆	Nidorina
△	Nidoran ♂	☆	Nidorino	△	Krabby
△	Tentacool	☆	Tentacruel	◎	Magikarp
☆	Dratini	★	Dragonair		

◎ frequent ○ common
△ average ☆ rare
★ almost never
— does not appear

Items
North
☑ Super Potion
☑ Great Ball ×3
☑ Poké Ball ×5
After learning Sea Skim
☑ Thunder Stone
South
☑ Great Ball ×3

? Hidden Items ?
North
☑ Super Lure
South
☑ Nanab Berry ×5

② You can heal up at the Pokémon Center, but then it seems you have reached a dead end. The only way to travel down this route is to head into the depths of the Rock Tunnel!

① Carry on east and then south. Just when you see the familiar red roof of a Pokémon Center and think you're ready for a break...think again! Team Rocket is here to ruin your day. With a bit of unexpected help, fight them off!

Coach Battle!

Coach Trainer Tasha

Grass- and Electric-type moves will defeat Poliwhirl, then use Flying-, Psychic-, or Fairy-type moves to take out Primeape!

TEAM:

Lv. 25	Lv. 26				

Reward: TM13 Brick Break

WALKTHROUGH

All Floors

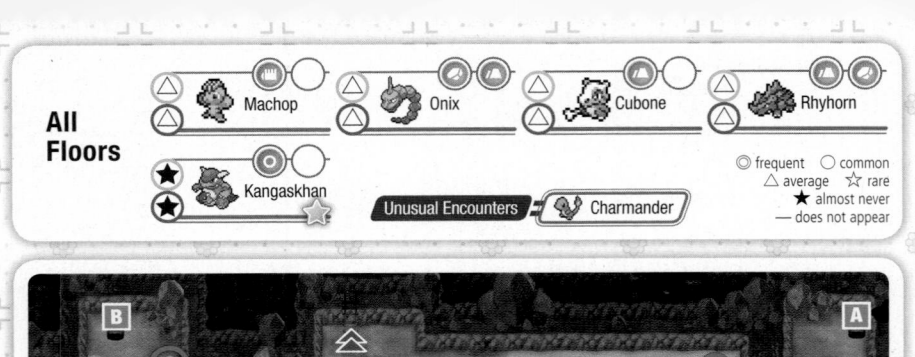

	Machop		Onix		Cubone		Rhyhorn

★	Kangaskhan
★	

⊚ frequent ○ common
△ average ☆ rare
★ almost never
— does not appear

Unusual Encounters Charmander

WALKTHROUGH

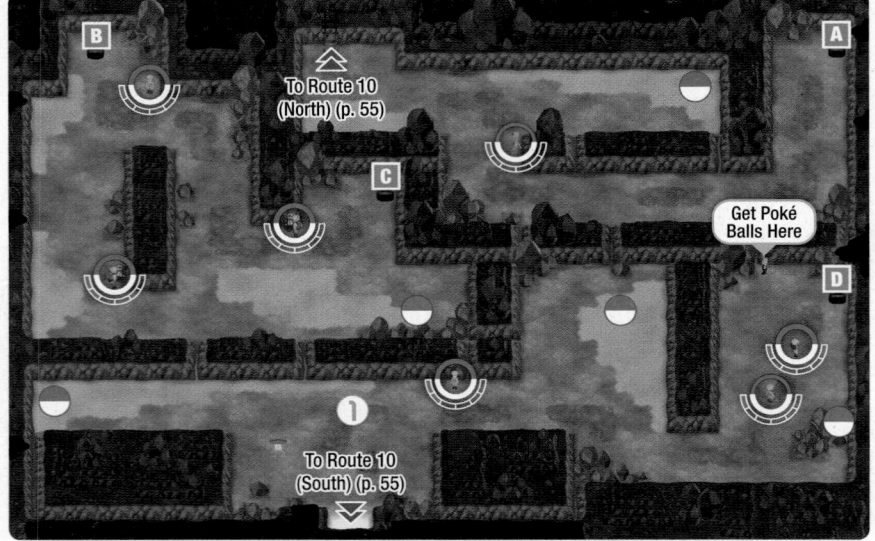

To Route 10 (North) (p. 55)

Get Poké Balls Here

To Route 10 (South) (p. 55)

1F

	Zubat		Golbat		Geodude		Graveler

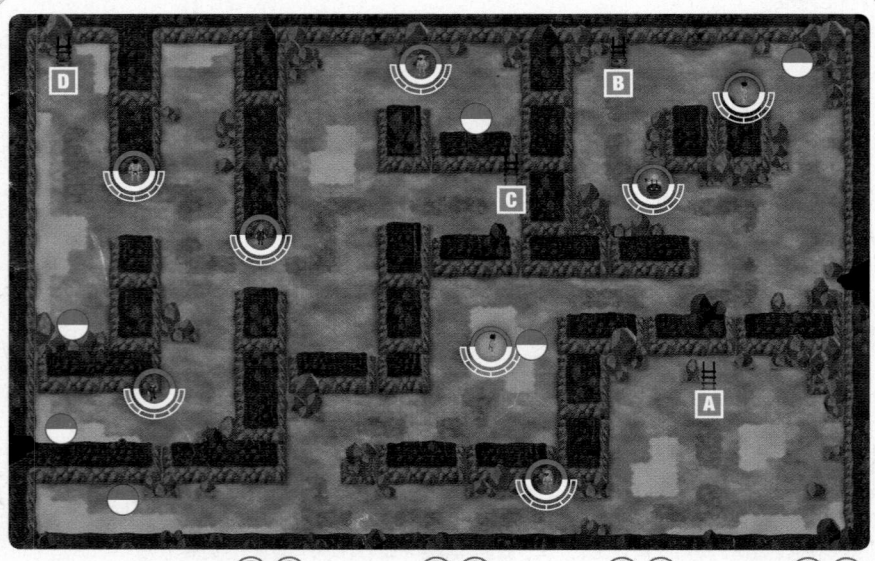

B1F

	Zubat		Golbat		Geodude		Graveler

Items

1F
- ☑ Repel
- ☑ Escape Rope
- ☑ Super Potion
- ☑ Stardust
- ☑ Pearl

B1F
- ☑ Revive
- ☑ Dire Hit
- ☑ Great Ball ×3
- ☑ Full Heal
- ☑ Stardust
- ☑ Super Potion

❓ Hidden Items ❓

1F
- ☑ Revive

B1F
- ☑ Super Potion

① Use the maps to stay on track through the twisty turns of the Rock Tunnel and find all the items lying about. When you make it through to the south end of Route 10, keep heading south to reach Lavender Town!

TIP 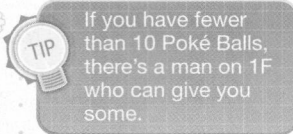 If you have fewer than 10 Poké Balls, there's a man on 1F who can give you some.

Lavender Town

Getting Around

Pokémon Center

To Route 10 (South) (p. 55)

To Pokémon Tower (p. 58)

Pokémon House

To Route 8 (p. 60)

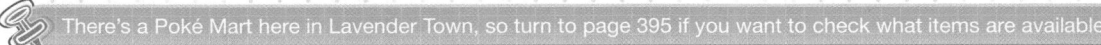

5

1

3

Poké Mart

To Route 12 (p. 74)

There's a Poké Mart here in Lavender Town, so turn to page 395 if you want to check what items are available!

1 Once you arrive in town, you'll see your rival head into a tower. Before you follow him, stop by the Pokémon Center to heal up your team and trade a Diglett for an Alolan Diglett there. Then it's off to the Pokémon Tower!

Pokémon: Alolan Diglett

WALKTHROUGH

Pokémon Tower

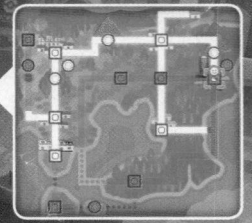

Getting Around

---

1 Talk to an old lady on 1F to get a fancy new outfit, then explore to find your rival. But be ready for a battle when you do find him up on 2F.

Reward: Formal Set

Coach Battle!

Coach Trainer Holly

Holly's Geodude is doubly weak to both Grass- and Water-type moves. If you have either, use them to make quick work of this battle!

TEAM:

Lv. 28

Reward: Pikachu Candy ×5 or Eevee Candy ×5

Rival Battle!

Your Rival

Your rival's partner Pokémon has evolved! Both Jolteon and Raichu are Electric type, so Ground-type moves, such as Dig, are your best bet when battling them. His Oddish has evolved into a Gloom, but it still has the same type weaknesses as before. You shouldn't have to change up your strategy too much from previous battles with him.

Pidgeotto Lv. 27 — WEAK AGAINST:

Jolteon Lv. 28 — WEAK AGAINST:

Gloom Lv. 27 — WEAK AGAINST:

Raichu Lv. 28 — WEAK AGAINST:

If you started with Pikachu

If you started with Eevee

2 Keep climbing the tower till you're driven back by...a ghost?! You'll get to explore the remaining floors in due time, but for now, leave the tower and head west out of town to reach Route 8.

 TIP Touch the glowing Poké Ball symbol on the floor on 5F to heal up your party.

Items	
2F	
Elixir	
X Attack	
3F	
Awakening	
Super Potion	
4F	
Escape Rope	
TM04 Teleport	
Full Heal	
5F	
Nugget	
Ice Stone	
6F	
Revive	
Ultra Ball ×3	

Items	
6F	
Hyper Potion	
Rare Candy	

Hidden Items	
2F	
Pearl	
3F	
Star Piece	
4F	
Super Potion	
5F	
Big Pearl	
6F	
PP Up	

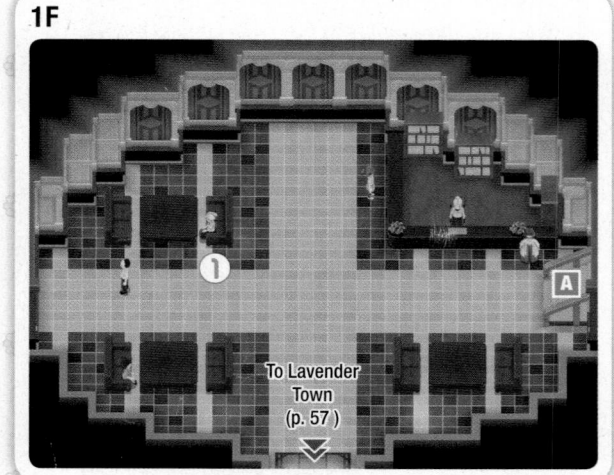

1F

To Lavender Town (p. 57)

Floors 3F through 6F

 Zubat  Golbat  Gastly  Cubone

2F

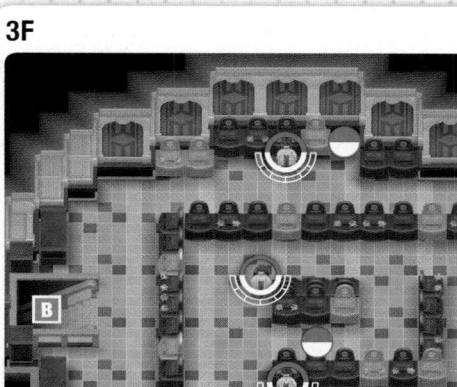

3F

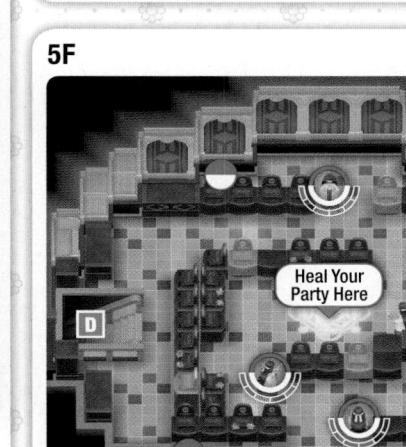 Haunter

4F

 Haunter

5F

Heal Your Party Here

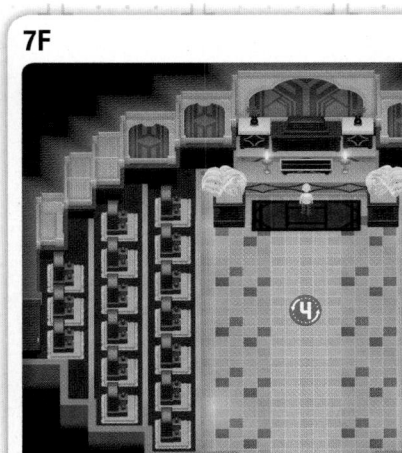 Haunter

6F

 Haunter

7F

Route 8

Getting Around

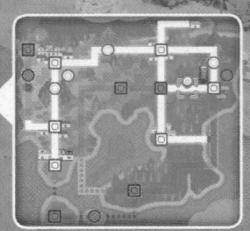

WALKTHROUGH

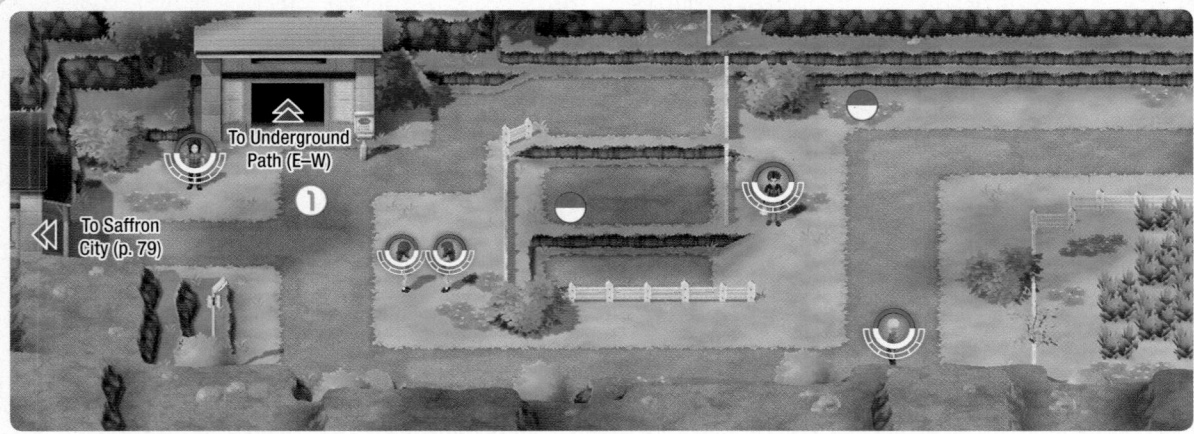

To Underground Path (E–W)

① To Saffron City (p. 79)

To Lavender Town (p. 57)

Unusual Encounters 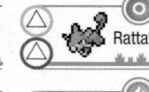 Chansey

 Pidgey
 Pidgeotto
 Rattata
 Raticate
Vulpix
Ninetales

 Jigglypuff
 Growlithe
 Arcanine
 Abra
 Kadabra

○ frequent ○ common
△ average ☆ rare
★ almost never
— does not appear

Items

- [x] Fire Stone
- [x] X Speed
- [x] Big Mushroom

Hidden Items

- [x] Silver Pinap Berry ×3

① After you witness Team Rocket up to no good again, head out along Route 8. The route leads to Saffron City, but the guard at the gate won't let you by. That leaves you with just one option: another Underground Path!

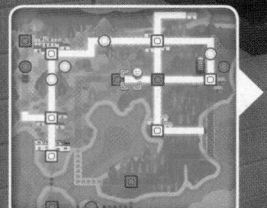

Underground Path (E–W) & Route 7

Getting Around

Underground Path (E–W)

Route 7 ◁◁ ① Route 8 ▷▷

Route 7

To Celadon City (p. 62) ②

To Saffron City (p. 79)

To Underground Path (E–W)

Unusual Encounters 🐦 Porygon

 Pidgey
 Pidgeotto
 Rattata
 Raticate

Vulpix
Ninetales
Jigglypuff
Growlithe

Arcanine
Abra
Kadabra

◎ frequent ○ common
△ average ☆ rare
★ almost never
— does not appear

Items

Underground Path (E–W)
☑ X Accuracy
☑ X Defense

Route 7
☑ Elixir

? Hidden Items ?

Underground Path (E–W)
☑ Big Pearl*
☑ Fresh Water*
☑ Hyper Potion*
☑ Lure*
☑ Max Lure*
☑ Max Repel*
☑ Nugget*
☑ Pearl*
☑ Potion*
☑ Pretty Wing*
☑ Repel*
☑ Super Lure*
☑ Super Potion*
☑ Super Repel*

Route 7
☑ Pinap Berry ×5

*You have a chance to randomly find one of these items at each spot.

WALKTHROUGH

① Once you head into the Underground Path, remember to look for hidden items. Just like the north–south Underground Path, this one also is chock-full of hidden items that can differ each time you find them.

② When you come up for air from the Underground Path, it's only a bit farther west to Celadon City. Catch some Pokémon—like the unusual Porygon—or rush right in to the big city.

Coach Battle!

Coach Trainer Alpesh

Alpesh's Farfetch'd can be zapped with an Electric-type move. Try Poison-type moves on Wigglytuff, if you have any.

TEAM:

 Lv. 29 Lv. 30

🔴 Reward: TM12 Facade

Celadon City

Getting Around

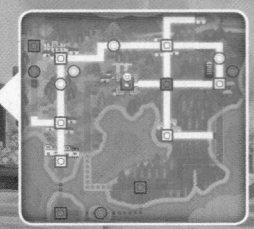

Celadon Department Store

Celadon Condominiums

Pokémon Center

Rocket Game Corner

To Route 7 (p. 61)

Pokémon Gym

To Route 16 (p. 70)

Items	
☑ Nugget	
☑ Rare Candy	
Celadon Condominiums	
☑ TM44 Play Rough	
☑ Health Candy ×3	

Hidden Items	
☑ Razz Berry ×5	
Celadon Condominiums	
☑ Fresh Water	
Rocket Game Corner	
☑ Bottle Cap*	
☑ Courage Candy*	
☑ Courage Candy L*	
☑ Courage Candy XL*	
☑ Gold Bottle Cap*	
☑ Health Candy*	
☑ Health Candy L*	
☑ Health Candy XL*	
☑ Mighty Candy*	
☑ Mighty Candy L*	
☑ Mighty Candy XL*	

Hidden Items	
Rocket Game Corner	
☑ Nanab Berry*	
☑ Pinap Berry*	
☑ PP Max*	
☑ PP Up*	
☑ Quick Candy*	
☑ Quick Candy L*	
☑ Quick Candy XL*	
☑ Razz Berry*	
☑ Smart Candy*	
☑ Smart Candy L*	
☑ Smart Candy XL*	
☑ Tough Candy*	
☑ Tough Candy L*	
☑ Tough Candy XL*	

*You have a chance to randomly find one of these items at each spot.

TIP Talk to the fortune teller—Madam Celadon—in the Pokémon Center to improve your chance of catching Pokémon with the Nature you want! Learn more about Natures on page 125 and more about Madam Celadon herself on page 388.

① There are a number of Team Rocket Grunts hanging around, but it's off to the Pokémon Center for you! The Partner Move Tutor there can teach some new moves to your partner. Plus, you can trade for another of those Alolan regional variants!

⊙ Pokémon: Alolan Sandshrew or Alolan Vulpix

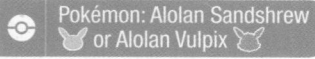

2 To the west, you'll run into Brock again. He's happy to share some treats with you. You can keep the Pewter Crunchies for your team, but that tea, on the other hand, might be put to better use...

🔴 Reward: Pewter Crunchies, Tea

Take a detour to deliver the tea you got to the guard on Route 7, opening Saffron City to you. Pop into the city once, just to make it easier to return there when you later get Sky Dash. Then it's back to Celadon City to find that poor Cubone Jessie and James tricked!

3 There's still the Celadon Department Store left to check out. Turn to the next page if you're in the mood to shop, then go check out the Rocket Game Corner. What're Jessie and James doing there? Time to search for clues!

TIP Find the back entrance to the Celadon Condominiums and walk up the stairs to find a TM!

🔵 Reward: TM44 Play Rough

4 You can talk to the Team Rocket Grunt by the poster if you're ready to solve the mystery. Turn to page 66 for more help if you do. Or take on the Celadon City Gym (p. 65) for some more Exp. Points first!

TIP Come back once your partner knows Sea Skim and talk to the man across the pond in the middle of the town to get a TM!

🔵 Reward: TM26 Poison Jab

TIP Like the Underground Paths, the Rocket Game Corner is another location where you can find hidden items that may change. They show up again from time to time, and some of them are very valuable! You might want to mark where on the map you've found hidden items, then keep coming back once in a while to check if anyone has dropped anything new!

The Celadon Department Store

This huge department store in the northwest corner of Celadon City is full of items you won't find anywhere else! There's plenty to explore here, so go through each floor as you spend your well-earned prize money.

1F
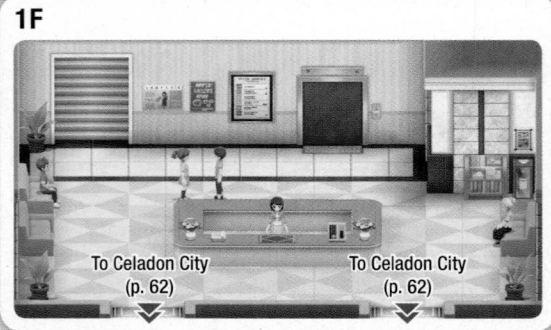
To Celadon City (p. 62)   To Celadon City (p. 62)

2F
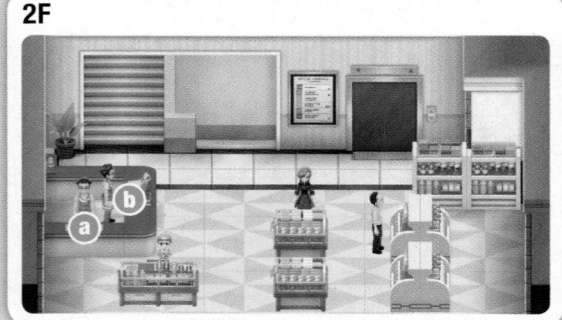

3F
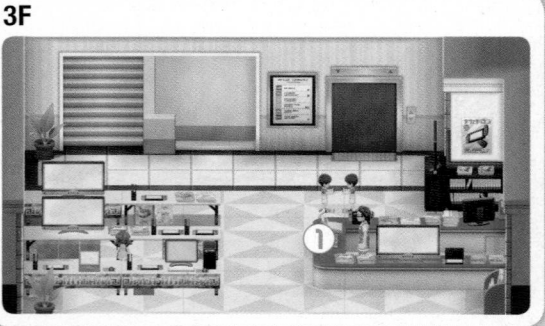

4F
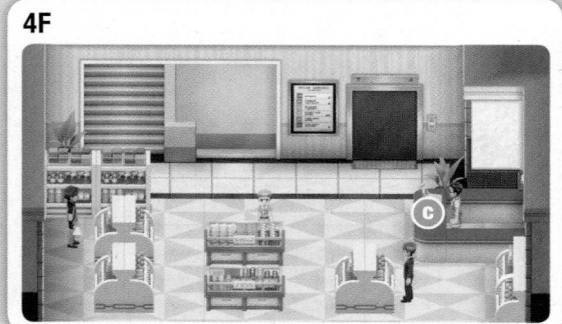

5F

Roof
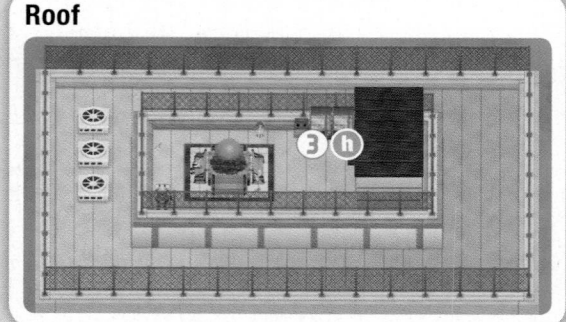

a: Poké Mart Counter   **b**: TM Counter   **c**: Evolution Stones   **d**: Hat Table   **e**: Diglett Table   **f**: Accessories Table
g: Glasses Table   **h**: Vending Machines

1 Talk to a busy man working at the shop on 3F for a TM.

Reward: TM03 Helping Hand

2 Get some rare accessories for your partner at each of the tables on 5F (p. 151).

3 Check out the vending machines on the roof to get bottles of Fresh Water, Soda Pop, or Lemonade. If you share different drinks with the little girl standing nearby, she will give you three different TMs!

TM06 Light Screen, TM07 Protect, TM09 Reflect

The Celadon Department Store is bursting with things you can buy! Check page 395 to see what may be in stock!

WALKTHROUGH

GYM BATTLE!

Celadon City Pokémon Gym

The Gym mission here is to show the girl a cute Pokémon. Beauty is in the eye of the beholder, though—so she'll love any Pokémon you show her! Trainers here use Grass-type Pokémon, lots of which are Poison type, too, so Fire-, Flying-, and Ice-type moves are your best bet in battle.

Gym Leader Erika

Unlike her Vileplume and Weepinbell, Erika's Tangela is only Grass type, so Poison-type moves are super effective against it. But Poison-type moves won't be effective against her other two Pokémon, so use other supereffective move types, such as Fire, against the rest. If you've been raising that Charmander from Route 24 or caught a Growlithe or Vulpix, moves like Ember are a great choice. And be sure to bring some Antidotes in case your Pokémon get poisoned!

Reward: TM53 Mega Drain, Rainbow Badge

Tangela Lv. 33
WEAK AGAINST:

Weepinbell Lv. 33
WEAK AGAINST:

Vileplume Lv. 34
WEAK AGAINST:

TM53 Mega Drain

While not the most powerful special move, with a power of 75, Mega Drain restores the user's HP, helping to keep your Pokémon in battle longer. Combine this with another draining move, such as Leech Seed, and your opponent is in for a tough battle!

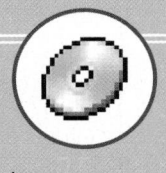

WALKTHROUGH

Team Rocket Hideout

Getting Around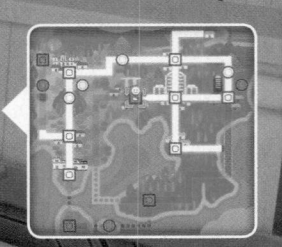

B1F

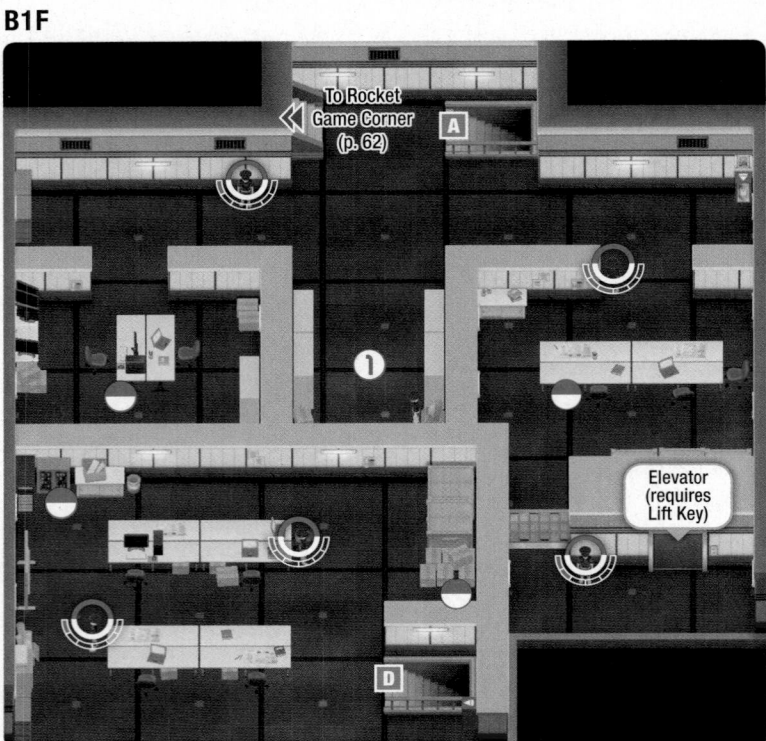

To Rocket Game Corner (p. 62)

A

1

D

Elevator (requires Lift Key)

B2F

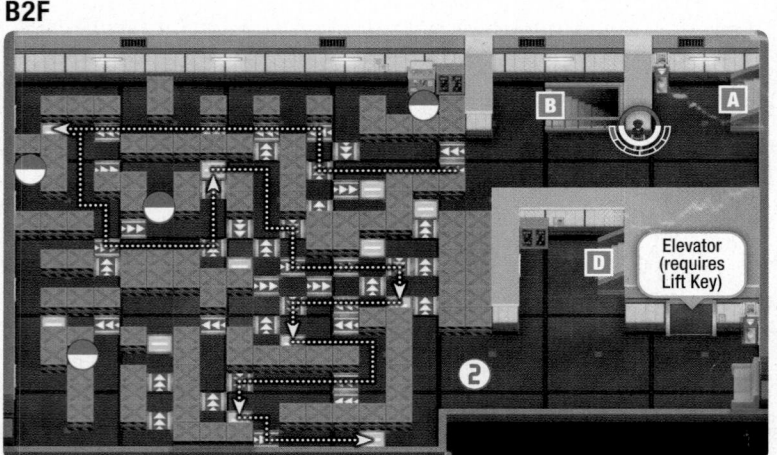

B

A

D

Elevator (requires Lift Key)

2

WALKTHROUGH

Items

B1F
☑ Ultra Ball ×5
☑ Mighty Candy ×3
☑ Great Ball ×5
☑ Hyper Potion
B2F
☑ Nugget
☑ Awakening
☑ TM05 Rest
☑ PP Up
B3F
☑ TM20 Dark Pulse
☑ Revive
☑ X Speed
☑ Rare Candy
B4F
☑ Hyper Potion
☑ PP Up
☑ Elixir

Hidden Items

B1F
☑ Full Heal
B2F
☑ X Accuracy
B3F
☑ Guard Spec.
B4F
☑ Max Revive

① Who'd have guessed that those Team Rocket baddies were hiding out underneath the Rocket Game Corner all along? You could just skip down the stairs to B2F, but first you might want to snag a couple items—plus an outfit from the mysterious Grunt at the end of the corridor that'll help you blend in as well as she does! If you're in a rush, follow the letters on the map from A to B (and so on) to hurry through this hideout.

⊙ Reward: Team Rocket Set

B3F

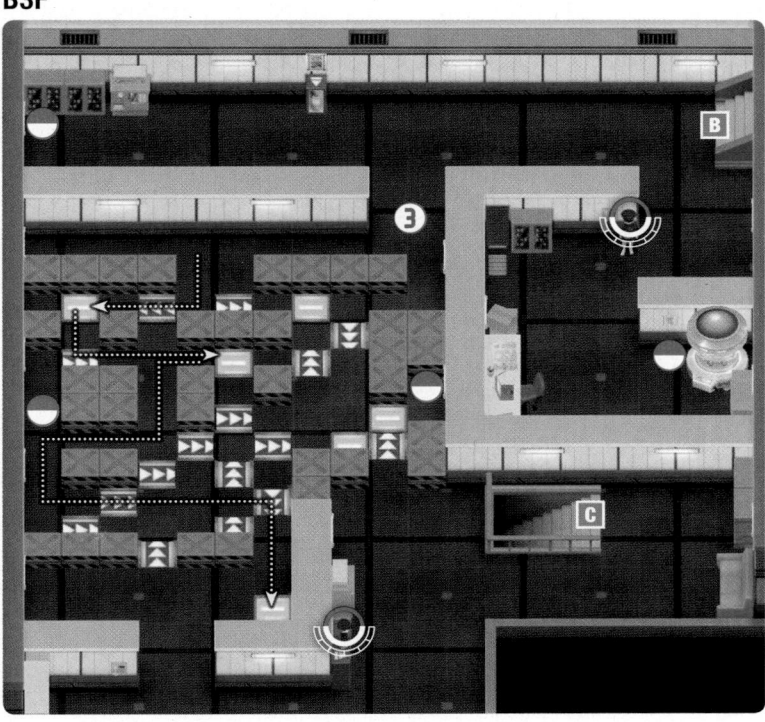

B4F

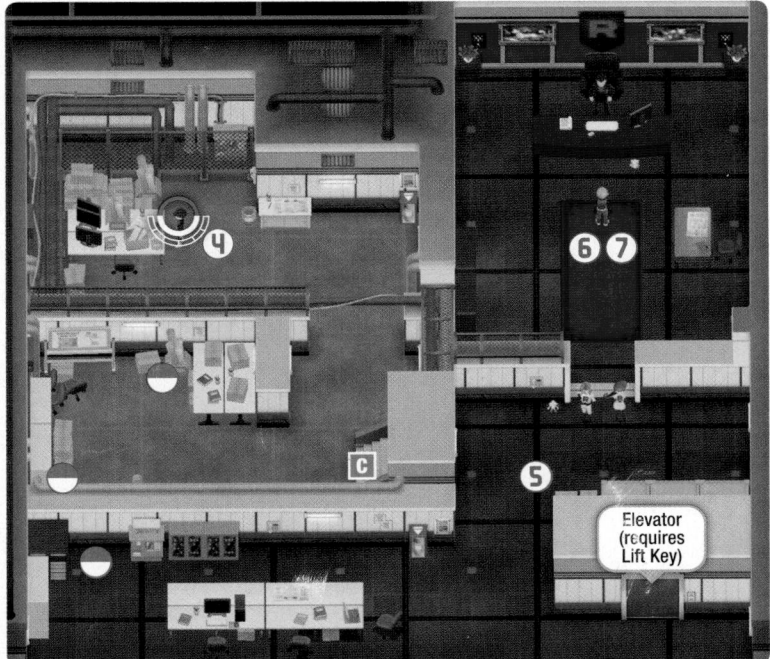

Elevator
(requires
Lift Key)

2 Again, you could go down **B** to reach B3F. But if you use the arrows on the map to find your way around to the stairs to the south, you'll be able to explore a bit of B1F that was blocked off before. You'll need to use the spin tiles.

TIP There are a lot of items to find here if you're up to the challenge! The arrows on the map only show you the easiest way to reach the stairwell, but try searching each floor for some useful items, such as TM05 Rest.

After taking the stairs **D** and picking up the items from B1F, head back down to B2F and jump on the nearest spin tile to return to the stairs and reach B3F at last...and another set of spin tiles!

3 Navigate your way through this second set of spin tiles, following the arrows on the map for the quickest way to reach the stairs to B4F. Or collect all the items along the way. You should be a pro at spin tiles by now, right?

4 On B4F, find a Grunt in the northwest corner and battle him for the Lift Key. When he throws it out of reach, try to find a way to get it. Start by examining the grating where he threw the key, and then check around the room. That air vent looks interesting...

Guide your partner along the shafts and pipes overhead, and make your way to the Lift Key—but make sure to explore as you go around if you want to eavesdrop on Team Rocket's conversations!

Reward: Lift Key

WALKTHROUGH

5 Head back to B2F and go across the spin tiles to reach the elevator on the south side of the floor. With the Lift Key, you can take it down to B4F and... Uh-oh! It's Jessie and James again!

> **TIP** You can go up to B1F, too, and unlock a passage back to the entrance if you beat a Team Rocket Grunt there. If you need to, heal up your team before taking on the coming battles.

6 Even after beating Jessie and James, you can't just walk in on  the boss. You'll have to battle Team Rocket Admin Archer first! After beating him, you'll have a chance to heal up your Pokémon if you need to before facing the big boss!

Battle!

Team Rocket Jessie and James

Their Pokémon might've gotten stronger, but they're still Poison type. Ground-type and Psychic-type moves will help you win this battle. If you caught a Diglett or an Abra near Vermilion City and have been training it, either would be a great choice here. Remember that Fairy-type Pokémon are weak to Poison-type moves, so keep your Jigglypuff or Clefairy out of this battle.

Arbok Lv. 32
WEAK AGAINST:

Weezing Lv. 32
WEAK AGAINST:

Battle!

Team Rocket Admin Archer

Like Jessie and James, Archer uses primarily Poison-type Pokémon, so the same strategy that worked on them should work here, too. Golbat is also Flying type, making it weak to Electric-, Ice-, and Rock-type moves, if you happen to have any Pokémon with moves of those types.

Weezing Lv. 33
WEAK AGAINST:

Golbat Lv. 33
WEAK AGAINST:

Battle!

Team Rocket Boss Giovanni

Unlike his flunkies, Giovanni doesn't favor Poison-type Pokémon. Instead he uses Persian, a Normal type, and Rhyhorn, a Rock- and Ground-type Pokémon. Both share a common weakness to Fighting-type moves, so a Machoke or Primeape with a move like Karate Chop would be an excellent Pokémon to use in this battle. Rhyhorn is also doubly weak to Grass- and Water-type moves, if it's still giving you trouble.

Persian Lv. 35
WEAK AGAINST:

Rhyhorn Lv. 35
WEAK AGAINST:

Reward: Silph Scope

7 After defeating the boss of Team Rocket, take your reward and be on your way! You can take the elevator right back up to B1F or explore more if you skipped over collecting any items earlier.

Step out of the Rocket Game Corner, and talk to the man with the strange balloon device just outside the entrance. You'll get the Secret Technique Sky Dash, which lets you travel to places you've visited before. Try using it to zip back to Lavender Town!

◉ Secret Technique: Sky Dash

Pokémon Tower (Revisited)

Getting Around

3 When you return to Lavender Town, you'll find your rival outside the Pokémon Tower again. Take on the tower together as you unravel the mystery of the ghosts appearing inside!

> **TIP** After clearing the Team Rocket Hideout, talk to the man standing next to the Pokémon Center and he will reward you for your victory.
>
> 🔴 Reward: Great Ball ×20

4 After you split up with your rival, continue climbing all the way up to 7F. Before you save the day, you'll have to battle some familiar faces from Team Rocket once again!

Battle!

Team Rocket Jessie and James

Deal with these persistent villains the same way as in your previous battles for a quick victory! Just use supereffective Ground- and Psychic-type moves against the Poison-type Arbok and Weezing, and Team Rocket will be blasting off again in no time.

Arbok Lv. 34
WEAK AGAINST:

Weezing Lv. 34
WEAK AGAINST:

5 You've rescued Mr. Fuji, who has been missing all this time! Return to his house and get the Poké Flute, which can awaken certain sleeping Pokémon—namely, the Snorlax you may have spotted snoozing on Route 16 and Route 12!

> 🔴 Reward: Poké Flute

Catch!

Haunter

Catch Difficulty

Easier ◄——————— Harder

> **TIP** You can now choose between two different paths toward the next stop on your adventure! Turn the page to head off down our suggested route, or skip ahead to page 74 if you can't wait to explore Routes 12, 13, 14, and 15 to the south of Lavender Town.

WALKTHROUGH

Routes 16, 17 & 18 (Optional)

Getting Around

Route 16

Snorlax

To Celadon City (p. 62)

To Route 17

Unusual Encounters 🥚 Chansey

	Pidgey		Pidgeotto		Rattata		Raticate
	Doduo		Dodrio				

◎ frequent ○ common △ average ☆ rare
★ almost never — does not appear

1 Sky Dash back to Celadon City and head west toward Route 16. Use the Poké Flute to awaken, battle, and catch the big sleeping Pokémon that's in your way!

Battle!

Snorlax

You'll have to battle Snorlax before you can get a chance at catching it. You'll want to move quick, too, as you'll only have five minutes to defeat it in battle or it'll run off! As a Normal-type Pokémon, Snorlax has only one weakness: Fighting-type moves. Try to use your best moves, and keep in mind that Snorlax is able to recover by using Rest!

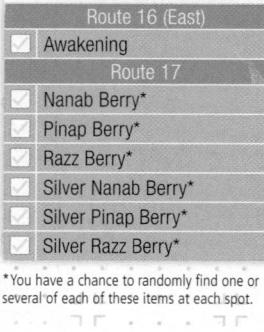

Snorlax
Lv. 34

WEAK AGAINST:

Route 17

Unusual Encounters 🥚 Chansey

To Route 16

3

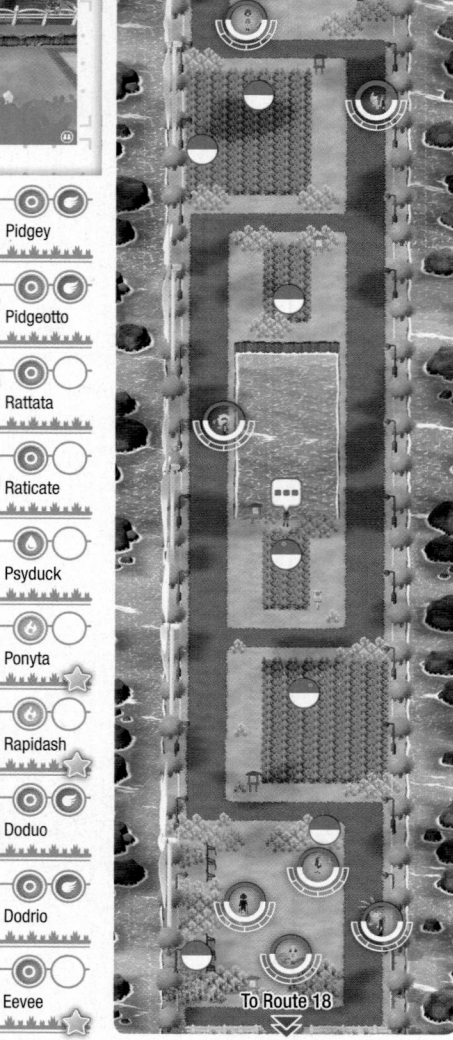

	Pidgey
	Pidgeotto
	Rattata
	Raticate
	Psyduck
	Ponyta
	Rapidash
	Doduo
	Dodrio
	Eevee

To Route 18

🔵 Items

Route 16 (East)
☑ PP Up
Route 16 (West)
☑ Super Potion
☑ Great Ball ×3
Route 17
☑ Super Potion
☑ Super Lure
☑ Great Ball ×3
☑ Elixir
☑ Rare Candy
☑ Silver Pinap Berry ×5
☑ Nugget
☑ Super Repel

❓ Hidden Items ❓

Route 16 (East)
☑ Awakening
Route 17
☑ Nanab Berry*
☑ Pinap Berry*
☑ Razz Berry*
☑ Silver Nanab Berry*
☑ Silver Pinap Berry*
☑ Silver Razz Berry*

*You have a chance to randomly find one or several of each of these items at each spot.

WALKTHROUGH

Route 18 (West)

To Route 17

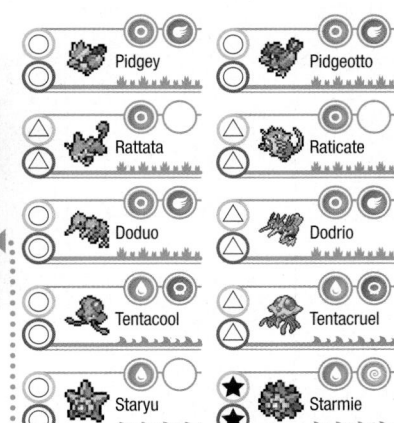

		Pidgey			Pidgeotto
		Rattata			Raticate
		Doduo			Dodrio
		Tentacool			Tentacruel
		Staryu	★		Starmie
					Magikarp

◎ frequent ○ common △ average ☆ rare
★ almost never — does not appear

Items		? Hidden Items ?
Route 18 (East)		Route 18 (West)
☑ Elixir		☑ Silver Razz Berry ×3

2 Talk to Professor Oak's assistant in the gate to get some Ultra Balls if you've caught at least 40 species of Pokémon. Then take the north path on Route 16 to find someone's secret retreat and get TM14.

> Reward: Ultra Ball ×30, TM14 Fly

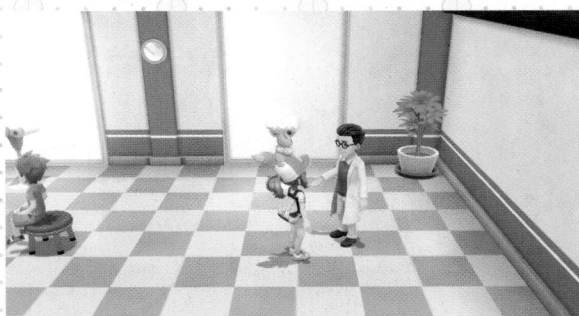

Route 18 (East)

Unusual Encounters — Chansey

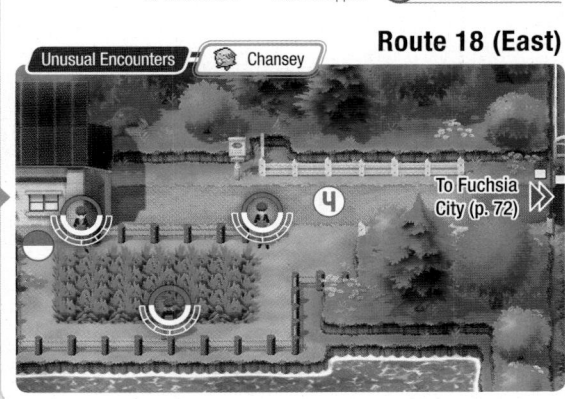

To Fuchsia City (p. 72)

> TIP Route 17 is also the only place you can catch Eevee in the wild. It can evolve into three different Pokémon—Vaporeon, Jolteon, and Flareon—so catch several if you hope to fill your Pokédex!

3 Travel south along Route 17. If you don't have any Fire-type Pokémon on your team, try catching Ponyta on this route. Fire-type Pokémon are pretty uncommon in the Kanto region, so it'll make a great ally! Don't miss the Coach Trainer here, either.

> TIP Route 17 is a great spot for harvesting Berries, so keep checking back here to see which ones you'll get!

Coach Battle!

Coach Trainer Grantley

Grantley uses a pretty varied team of Pokémon. Both Fearow and Beedrill are weak to Rock-type moves, and Fearow and Sandslash both share a weakness to Ice-type moves. Bring along Pokémon that know those types, if you happen to have them. Otherwise, try to handle each Pokémon with a different one from your team and switch out when you need to.

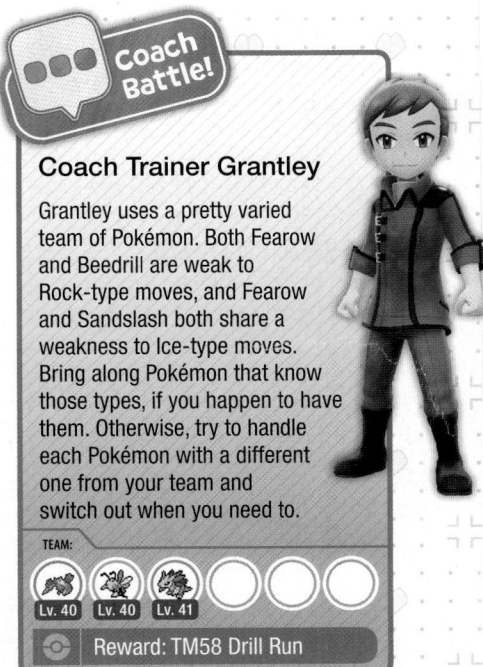

TEAM:
Lv. 40 Lv. 40 Lv. 41

> Reward: TM58 Drill Run

4 It's just a short trip to the east to reach Fuchsia City from Route 18. Try catching some Pokémon like Doduo or Dodrio here if you haven't caught them yet.

WALKTHROUGH

Fuchsia City

Getting Around

GO Park Complex

3

Poké Mart

To Route 18 (p. 70)

2

Pokémon Gym

Pokémon Center

To Route 15 (p. 74)

Warden's House

1

To Route 19 (p. 88)

Poké Mart	
After earning five Gym Badges	
☑ Max Repel	₽900

For the full list of items available at Poké Marts, turn to page 395.

Items
☑ Super Lure

TIP Did you spot that large block in the warden's house? You'll be able to push it out of the way later (p. 88) for a reward!

1 Make sure to check out the Pokémon Center before hitting the Gym. The Partner Move Tutor is here with some final moves to teach your partner, and the gentleman in the corner is also willing to trade an Alolan Marowak for a Kantonian Marowak, if you have one!

◉ Pokémon: Alolan Marowak

TIP Next to the warden's house, there's a house full of expert Trainers where you can pick up some more tips—plus a Super Lure that can be found by the back door!

2 Head to the Safari Zone in the north end of town. Talk to the man who's standing by the Lapras, and he'll teach your partner Pokémon the Secret Technique Sea Skim.

◉ Secret Technique: Sea Skim

TIP Steel-type Pokémon, such as the Mythical Pokémon Melmetal or the Magnemite and Magneton you can catch in Kanto, will be a big help in the Gym here in Fuchsia City. If you're struggling to get through it, consider taking a detour up to the Power Plant on Route 10 (p. 55) right now. You can catch both Magnemite and Magneton there.

3 Here you can finally check out the GO Park complex at the north end of the Safari Zone! The GO Park complex is where you can transfer Pokémon over from a Pokémon GO account and catch and play with them in Kanto! Learn more on page 159.

WALKTHROUGH

Fuchsia City Pokémon Gym

You'll need to have caught 50 different species of Pokémon to pass Fuchsia City's Gym mission. If you haven't hit that number yet, that's yet another reason to consider exploring the east side of the region now. You can turn the page if you want to check out Routes 12, 13, 14, and 15.

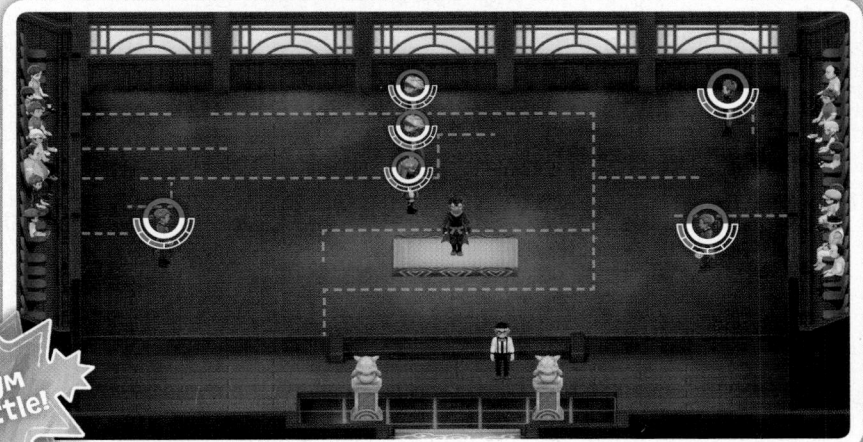

You can turn the page if you want to check out Routes 12, 13, 14, and 15.

The Trainers in this Gym use Poison-type Pokémon, which you should know how to handle thanks to fighting Team Rocket members. Ground- and Psychic-type moves are still your best choice in battle. This Gym also has invisible walls, creating a maze to Koga! Watch the smoke that appears in the Gym as it reveals the hidden walls. Or use your own secret ninja skills by taking a peek at the map right here!

Gym Battle!

Weezing
Lv. 43
WEAK AGAINST:

Muk
Lv. 43
WEAK AGAINST:

Golbat
Lv. 43
WEAK AGAINST:

Venomoth
Lv. 44
WEAK AGAINST:

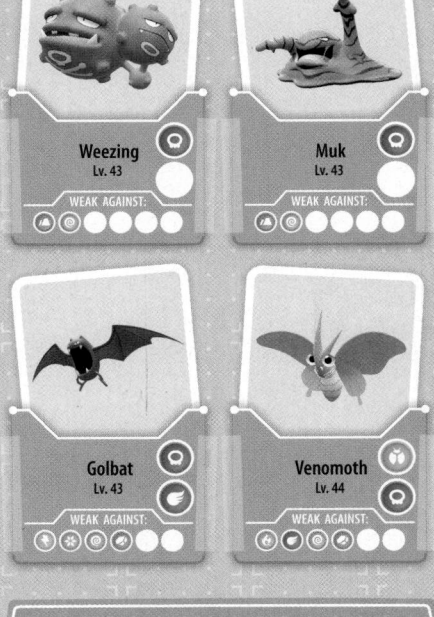

Gym Leader Koga

Koga's a famous ninja and he fights like one, too, using sneaky tactics. Very often he'll try to poison your active Pokémon and then stall to let the poison weaken your Pokémon before using a hard-hitting move to make it faint. Although Koga's Pokémon are all weak to Psychic-type moves, it might be safer to stick to a Steel-type Pokémon or even a Poison-type Pokémon yourself. Poison- and Steel-type Pokémon can't be poisoned, which shuts off a big part of Koga's strategy. Pure Grass-type Pokémon and Fairy-type Pokémon shouldn't be sent out in this battle, as Koga will have no problem taking them out. Make sure you pack some Antidotes if you aren't using a Pokémon immune to poisoning. Remember the type matchups (p. 399) and same-type attack bonuses (p. 123), and you'll make it past this master of the ninja arts!

TM27 Toxic

Toxic is a powerful move that almost every Pokémon can learn. Its increasing poison damage makes it a popular move among many expert Trainers.

⊙ Reward: TM27 Toxic, Soul Badge

WALKTHROUGH

Routes 12, 13, 14 & 15 (Optional)

Getting
Around

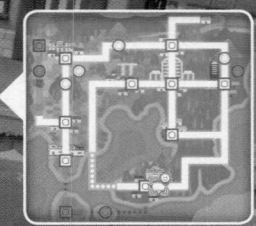

On Routes 12–15

Pidgey	Pidgeotto	Oddish
Gloom	Bellsprout	Weepinbell

◎ frequent ○ common △ average ☆ rare ★ almost never — does not appear

Items

Route 12
☑ Lure
☑ Repel
☑ Ultra Ball ×3
☑ Water Stone
☑ Awakening
☑ Max Lure
After learning Sea Skim
☑ TM24 X-Scissor

Items

Route 13
☑ PP Up
☑ Full Heal

? Hidden Items ?

Route 12
☑ Silver Pinap Berry ×5
Route 13
☑ Golden Pinap Berry
☑ Silver Nanab Berry ×5

1 You can start at either end of this long path whenever you choose to take it on. But we recommend that you fly back to Lavender Town and start from Route 12. Go upstairs in the gate that splits Route 12 to collect a TM.

◉ Reward: TM50 Roost

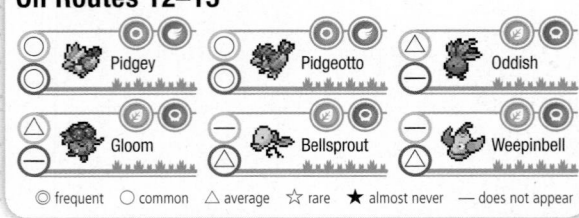

Farfetch'd	Krabby	Kingler
Tentacool	Tentacruel	Horsea	Seadra	Magikarp

Route 12

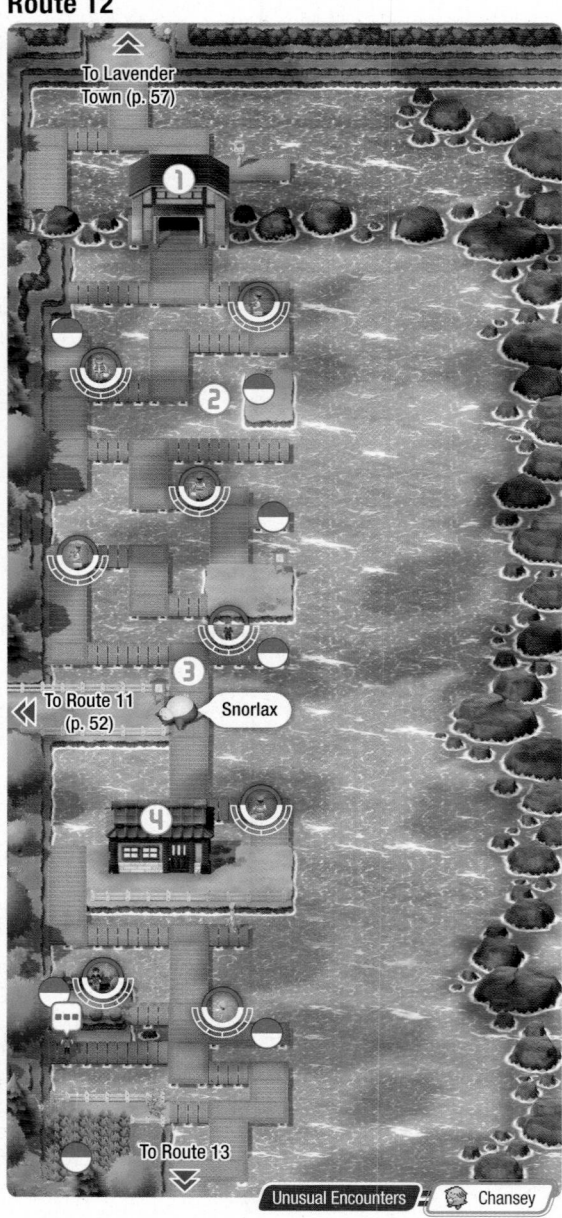

To Lavender
Town (p. 57)

1

2

3 Snorlax

To Route 11
(p. 52)

4

To Route 13

Unusual Encounters 🍳 Chansey

Route 13

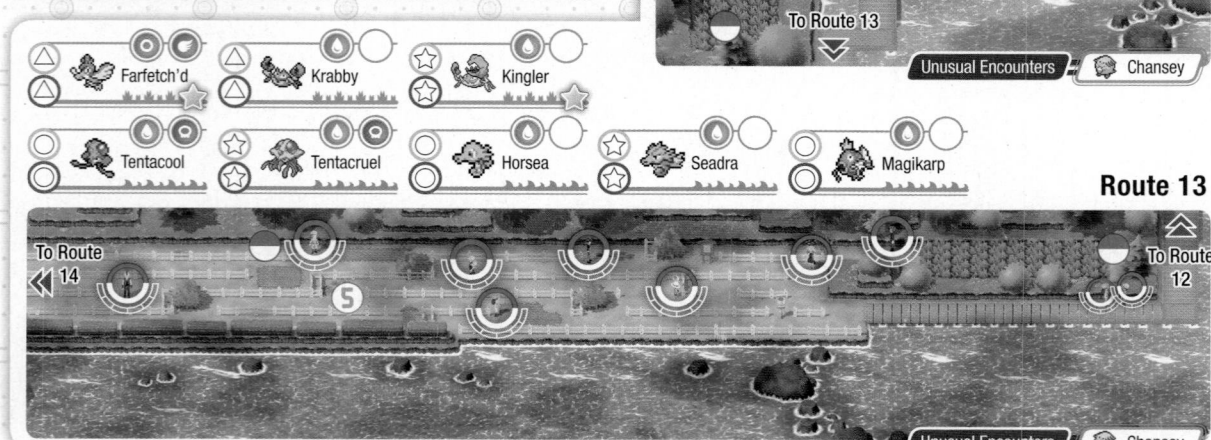

To Route
14

5

To Route
12

Unusual Encounters 🍳 Chansey

WALKTHROUGH

Route 14

To Route 13 ▶▶

◀◀ To Route 15 (p. 76)

Unusual Encounters — Chansey

△	Venonat	△	Venomoth
★	Scyther	—	Pinsir
☆ ☆	Tauros		

◎ frequent ○ common
△ average ☆ rare
★ almost never
— does not appear

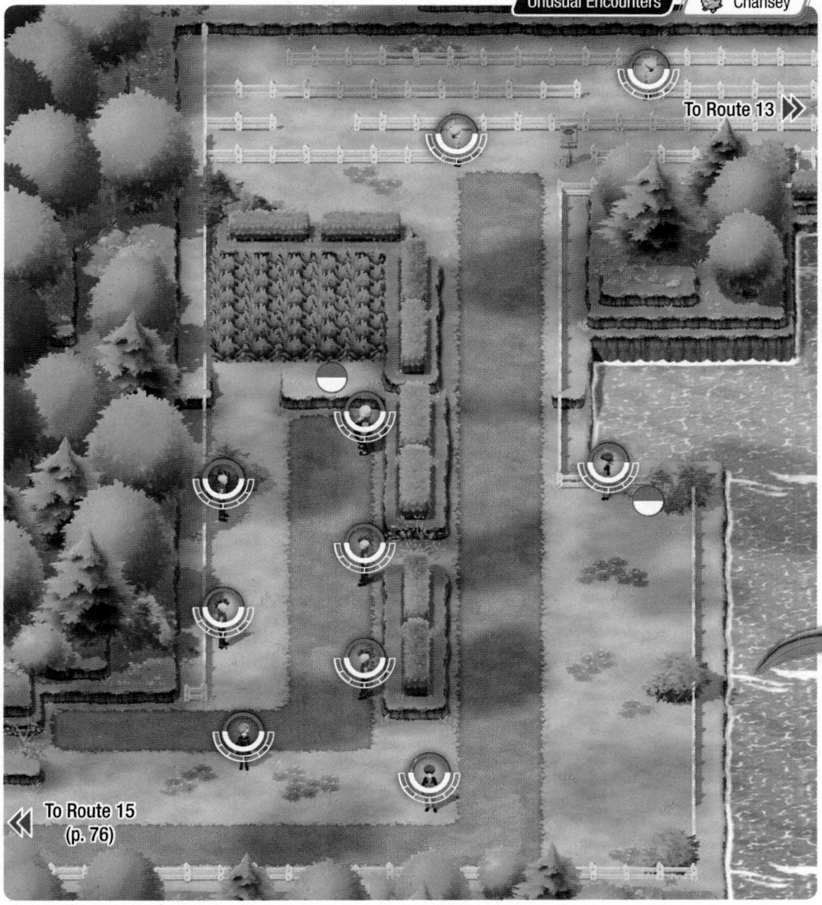

Items
- ☑ Hyper Potion
- ☑ Nugget

? Hidden Items ?
- ☑ Golden Razz Berry

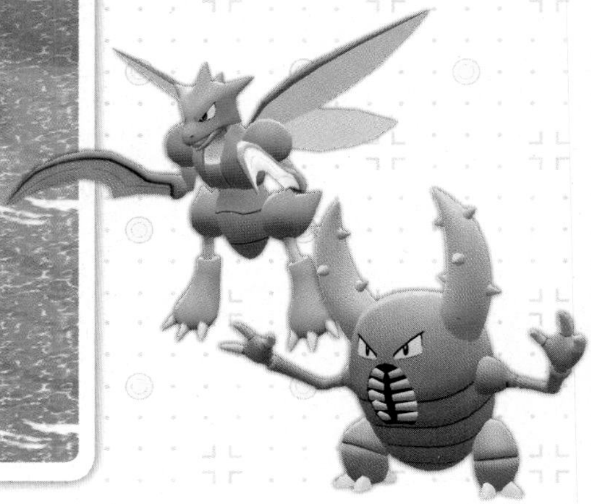

---

2 Keep heading south, taking a moment to Sea Skim out to a small island with TM24 on it. Explore the waters if you want to catch some Water-type Pokémon to add to your Pokédex.

3 Keep battling your way past Trainers until you reach Snorlax sprawled across the route! Wake up the sleeping Pokémon there with your Poké Flute to battle and catch it.

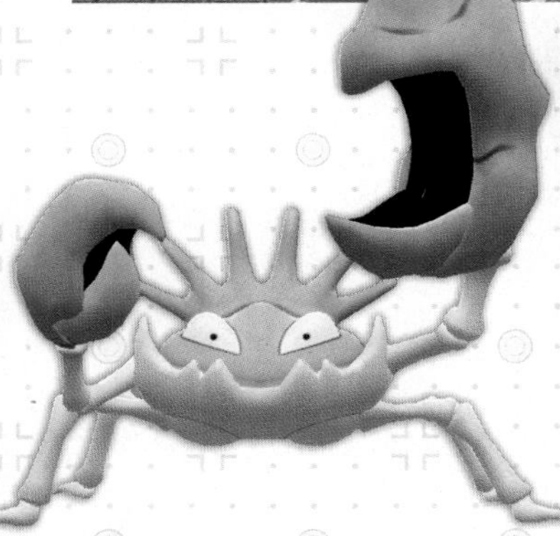

Battle!

Snorlax

This battle is slightly different from the one on Route 16—this time, Snorlax will raise its Attack at the start of battle. Strike hard with physical moves, since Snorlax's Defense is much lower than its Sp. Def., and you'll earn your chance to catch this sleepy Pokémon well before the five-minute timer runs out!

Snorlax
Lv. 34

WEAK AGAINST:

Route 15

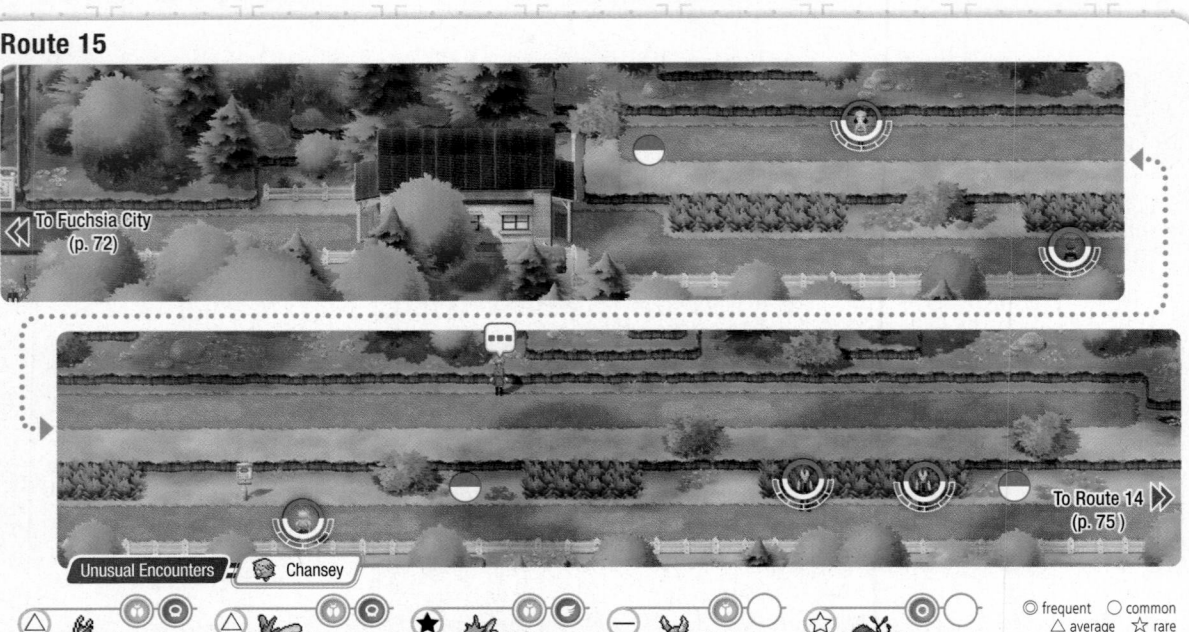

To Fuchsia City (p. 72)

To Route 14 (p. 75)

To Fuchsia City (p. 72)

To Route 14 (p. 75)

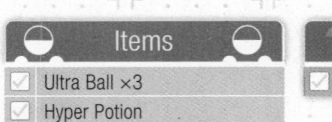

Unusual Encounters — Chansey

| | Venonat | | Venomoth | | Scyther | | Pinsir | | Tauros |

◎ frequent ○ common
△ average ☆ rare
★ almost never
— does not appear

Items			? Hidden Items ?
☑ Ultra Ball ×3			☑ Golden Nanab Berry
☑ Hyper Potion			
☑ TM47 Surf			

4 Once you're past Snorlax, carry on down Route 12 and stop in the little house. Tell the man he is Mr. Dazzling, and he'll give you another TM. Then keep heading south, where you can collect items and battle Trainers, including Coach Trainer Priya!

🔘 Reward: TM32 Dazzling Gleam

5 Travel along Routes 13, 14, and 15, battling Trainers and catching Pokémon. Make sure to pick up TM47, which contains Surf, one of the strongest Water-type moves a Pokémon can learn. Finally, challenge another Coach Trainer!

TIP If you've caught at least 50 species of Pokémon, talk to Professor Oak's assistant in the gate on Route 15 to get a smart new set of clothes for you and your partner.

🔘 Reward: Assistant Set

Coach Battle!

Coach Trainer Priya

Priya's two Pokémon are pretty different, sharing no weaknesses at all! Butterfree is most weak to Rock-type moves, being both Bug and Flying type, so a move like Rock Throw is best against it. Clefable is a Fairy-type Pokémon, so it's only weak to Poison- and Steel-type moves.

TEAM:

Lv. 38 Lv. 39

🔘 Reward: TM59 Dream Eater

Coach Battle!

Coach Trainer Midge

Midge uses two Pokémon that don't have any common weaknesses. Try to use Flying-, Psychic-, or Fairy-type moves on Machoke. Then use Water-, Ground-, or Rock-type moves on Magmar.

TEAM:

Lv. 40 Lv. 41

🔘 Reward: TM31 Fire Punch

WALKTHROUGH

Power Plant (Optional)

Getting
Around

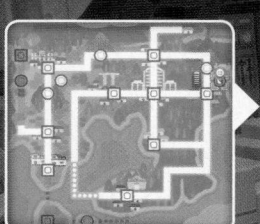

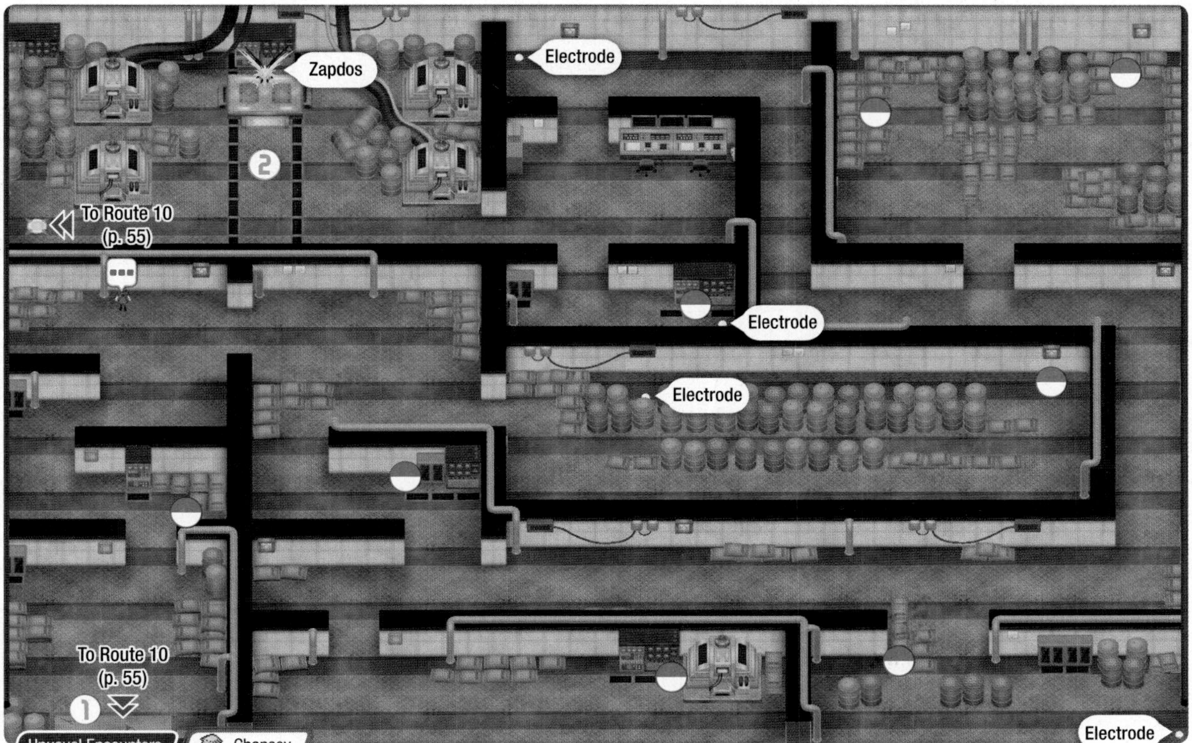

Zapdos

Electrode

2

Electrode

To Route 10
(p. 55)

Electrode

To Route 10
(p. 55)

1

Electrode

Unusual Encounters		Chansey			

	Magnemite ★		Magneton ★		Grimer		Muk		Voltorb ★		Electrode ★

	Koffing		Weezing	△	Electabuzz ★

◎ frequent ○ common △ average ☆ rare
★ almost never — does not appear

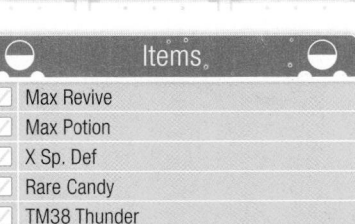

Items

- ☑ Max Revive
- ☑ Max Potion
- ☑ X Sp. Def
- ☑ Rare Candy
- ☐ TM38 Thunder
- ☑ Max Potion
- ☑ Thunder Stone
- ☑ Paralyze Heal

? Hidden Items ?

- ☑ Voltorb Candy
- ☑ Voltorb Candy
- ☑ Voltorb Candy
- ☑ Voltorb Candy
- ☑ Pretty Wing

1 Sky Dash to Cerulean City if you want to see the Power Plant—and you
should! You can catch Pokémon there that you can't catch anywhere else,
including a Legendary Pokémon! Go to Route 10 (p. 55) and then Sea Skim
over the water to enter the Power Plant.

WALKTHROUGH

2 Inside the Power Plant, you'll find plenty of items. Battle a Coach Trainer, then it's time for the main event—a chance to battle and catch the Legendary Pokémon Zapdos! Make sure you're ready for this rare chance!

TIP If you find what looks like an upside-down Poké Ball in the field, watch out! It's actually an Electrode! You'll have to battle it if you want to catch it.

Coach Battle!

Coach Trainer Mable

Mable uses all three of the ancient Pokémon you can restore from Fossils. Omastar and Kabutops are doubly weak to Grass-type moves, so make sure you use one against them. Aerodactyl is very fast but weak to Water-, Electric-, Ice-, Rock-, and Steel-type moves.

TEAM: Lv. 44, Lv. 44, Lv. 45

Reward: Rare Candy ×5

Zapdos

Zapdos
Lv. 50
WEAK AGAINST:

Just like with Snorlax, you'll only have five minutes to battle this Pokémon, and if you miss your chance, it won't appear again until after you've entered the Hall of Fame. Zapdos is a powerful Legendary Pokémon, but it does have weaknesses to Ice- and Rock-type moves. Ground-type Pokémon might be a good choice when battling, as they're immune to Zapdos's powerful Electric-type moves, but Ground-type moves don't work on Zapdos because it's also Flying type! Use moves like Rock Throw to defeat it, and then use Silver or Golden Razz Berries to help catch this rare Pokémon!

TIP Remember that Zapdos is only the first of three Legendary Pokémon you can catch before entering the Hall of Fame! You'll also be able to encounter the Ice- and Flying-type Pokémon Articuno (p. 91) and the Fire- and Flying-type Pokémon Moltres (p. 102). Try to catch all three of these incredibly powerful allies to complete your Pokédex!

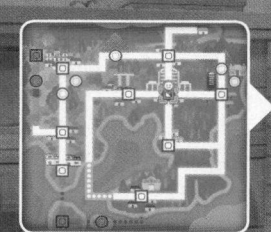

Route 10 > **Saffron City** > Silph Co.

Saffron City

Getting
Around

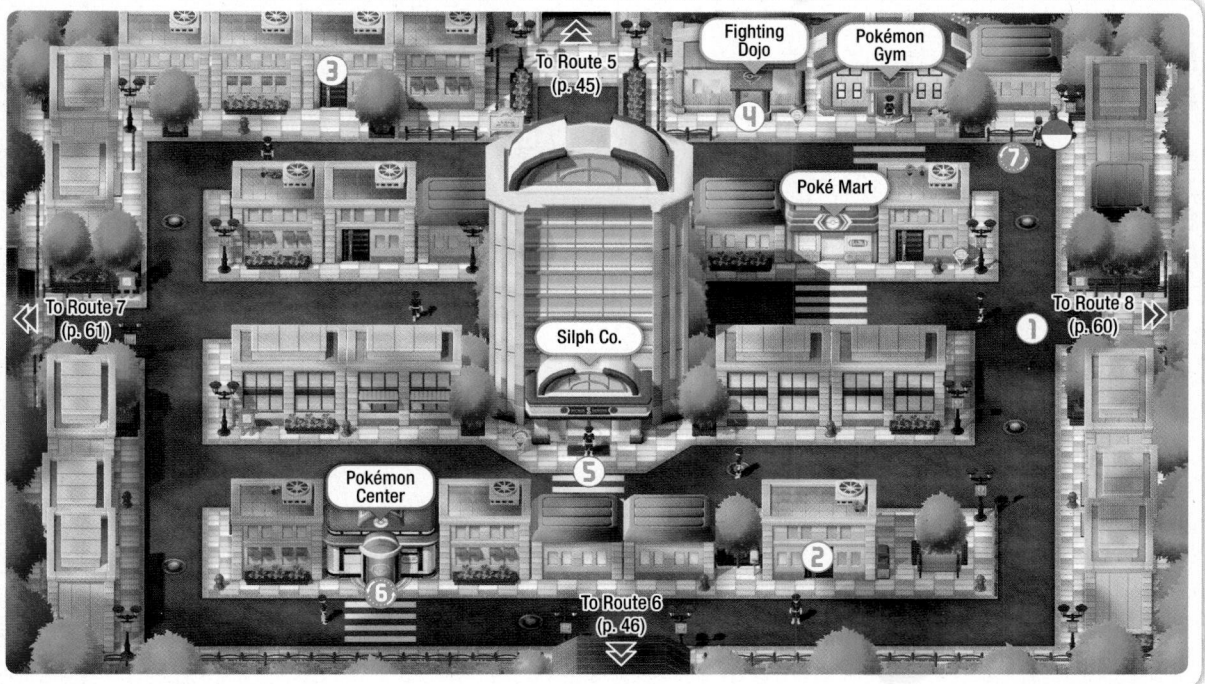

To Route 5
(p. 45)

Fighting
Dojo

Pokémon
Gym

Poké Mart

To Route 7
(p. 61)

Silph Co.

To Route 8
(p. 60)

Pokémon
Center

To Route 6
(p. 46)

Poké Mart

After earning six Gym Badges	
☐ Max Potion	₽2,500
☐ Max Lure	₽900

For the full list of items available at Poké Marts, turn to page 395.

Items

☐ X Sp. Def

Hidden Items

☐ Moon Stone

1 Sky Dash over to Saffron City. If you haven't visited it yet, Sky Dash to a nearby location, such as Lavender Town. Then pass through one of the gates outside Saffron City, giving the guard some Tea so he'll let you pass.

TIP Visit the Saffron City Pokémon Center to trade your Kantonian Raichu for an Alolan Raichu.

Pokémon: Alolan Raichu

2 Team Rocket is all over the place, and the residents of the city seem to be staying indoors. So go in to find them! In a house to the southeast, you can get a TM from a man who knows just what you came for.

Reward: TM40 Psychic

3 Swing up to the northwest corner of the city next if you want to meet the Copycat! She's upstairs in her house, and if you can show her one of her favorite Pokémon, you'll get a TM. It shouldn't take you long to guess what cute, pink Pokémon she loves most.

⊙ Reward: TM08 Substitute

4 The Gym is blocked by Team Rocket, but you can challenge the Fighting Dojo to get a rare Pokémon. There's a Coach Trainer standing on the sidelines, too!

⊙ Pokémon: Hitmonlee or Hitmonchan

The Fighting Dojo

This place used to be a Gym, but you won't get a Gym Badge here! Most of the Black Belts in this dojo use Fighting-type Pokémon, so bring Pokémon with Flying-, Psychic-, or Fairy-type moves. If you traded your Kantonian Raichu for an Alolan Raichu at the Pokémon Center in this city, you can teach it Psychic with TM40 and use it to battle here.

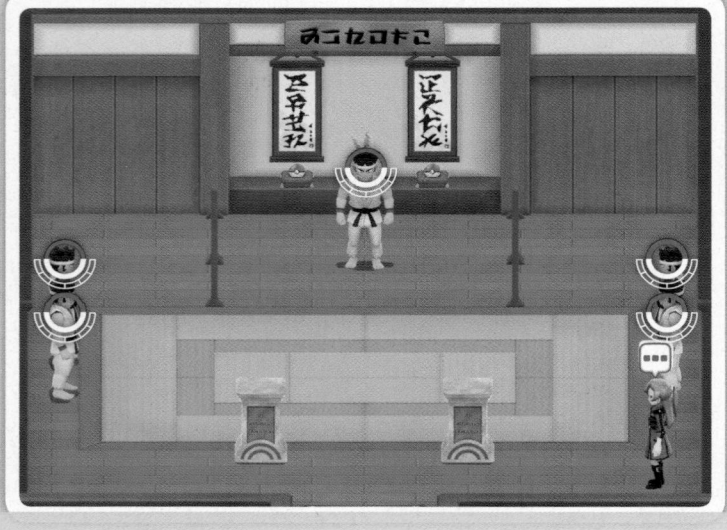

Coach Battle!

Coach Trainer Leona

Machoke is just like the other Fighting-type Pokémon you'll battle in the dojo. Electabuzz is an Electric-type Pokémon and only weak to Ground-type moves.

TEAM:
Lv. 32 Lv. 33

⊙ Reward: TM23 Thunder Punch

5 Now if you're ready, it's time to storm Silph Co.! Head to the building at the center of the city, and be ready for more battles!

WALKTHROUGH

Silph Co.

Getting Around

1F

To Saffron City
(p. 79)

To Saffron City
(p. 79)

Items

1F
☑ X Sp. Atk

TIP The maps for the upper floors of Silph Co. continue on the following pages.

1 At Silph Co., you'll meet up with Blue and your rival. Battle Blue before facing Team Rocket again.

2 You can explore every floor of Silph Co., but you probably want to make one quick trip to a specific floor. Take the elevator to 5F and defeat Archer with your rival there to get a Card Key. It'll open all the locked doors so you can explore freely.

Battle!

Pokémon Trainer Blue

Exeggutor Lv. 38
WEAK AGAINST: 4x

Charizard Lv. 40
WEAK AGAINST: 4x

The two Pokémon that Blue uses share no common weaknesses. Exeggutor is doubly weak to Bug-type moves, so use them for a quick knockout on this Pokémon. Charizard will take four times the damage from Rock-type moves, so break out that Graveler or Onix and use a move like Rock Throw. Water- and Electric-type moves are also good options when battling this Pokémon.

Battle!

Team Rocket Admin Archer and Team Rocket Grunt

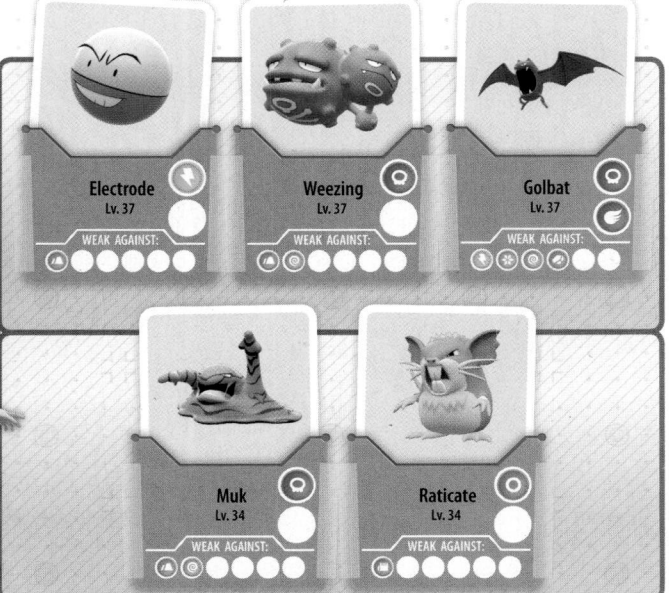

Electrode Lv. 37
WEAK AGAINST:

Weezing Lv. 37
WEAK AGAINST:

Golbat Lv. 37
WEAK AGAINST:

Muk Lv. 34
WEAK AGAINST:

Raticate Lv. 34
WEAK AGAINST:

In this battle, you'll team up with your rival against Archer and a Team Rocket Grunt. Most Pokémon you'll face in this battle are weak to Ground-type moves. Your rival even knows this and sends out a Cubone first. Be wary of Electrode—it's one of the fastest Pokémon and isn't shy about using Self-Destruct, a powerful move that will hit all other Pokémon. Use your experience from fighting other Normal- and Poison-type Pokémon to handle the rest.

WALKTHROUGH

2F

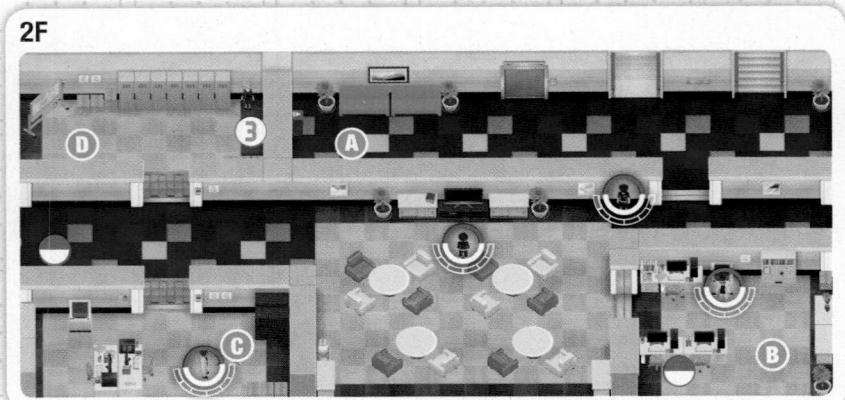

3F

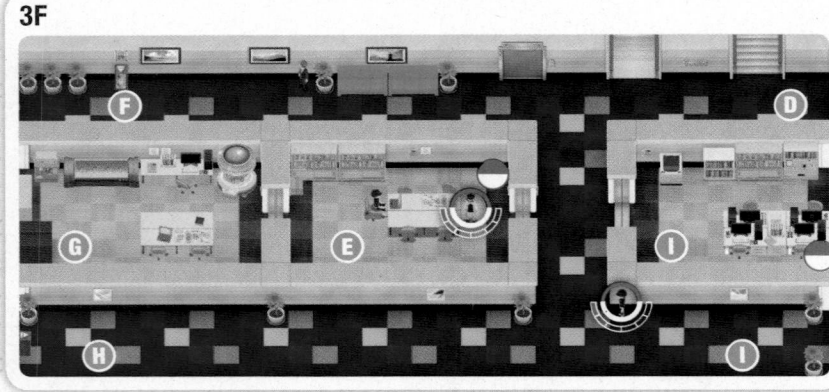

4F

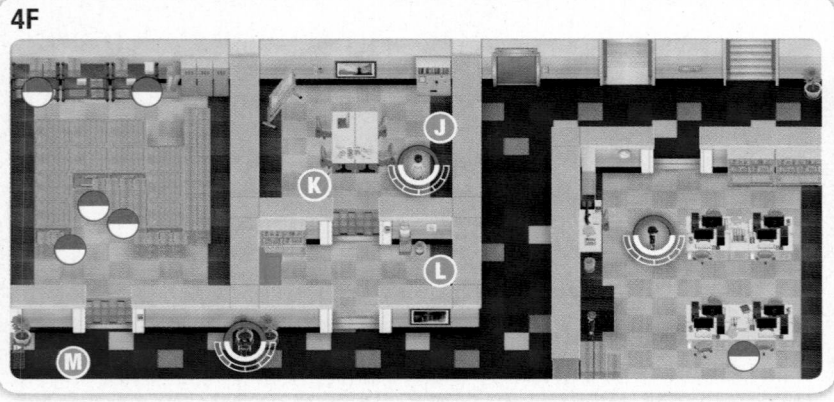

Items	
2F	
☑	X Attack
☑	Super Potion
3F	
☑	X Sp. Def
☑	Max Lure
4F	
☑	Dire Hit
☑	Full Heal
☑	Escape Rope
☑	Star Piece
☑	Great Ball ×5
☑	Revive

Hidden Items	
2F	
☑	Fresh Water
3F	
☑	Silver Razz Berry ×3
4F	
☑	Fresh Water

3 Now why don't you tackle the entire building? The uppercase markers on the map show the path through the warp panels, so feel free to use them to get some help in finding your way to the upper floors. First, try aiming to get TM42 from the woman on 2F.

Reward: TM42 Self-Destruct

5F

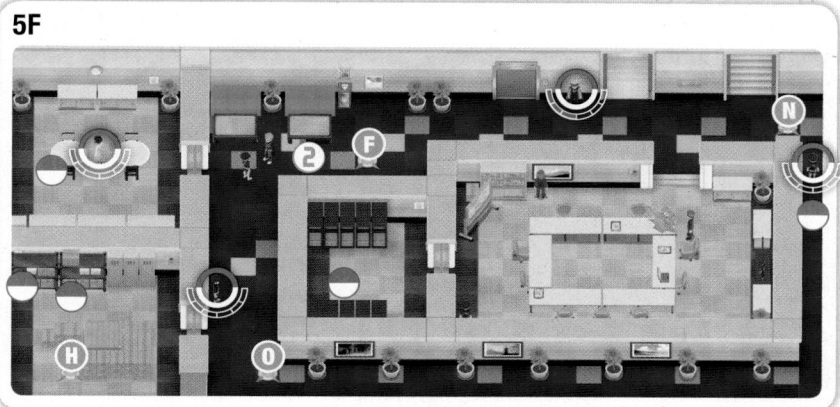

6F

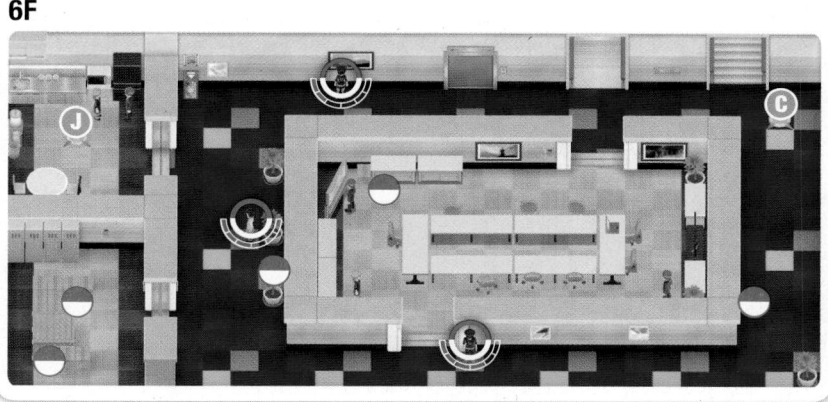

7F

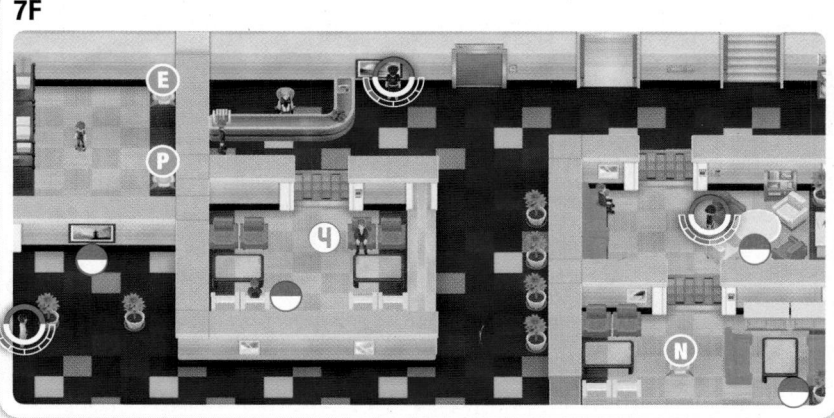

8F

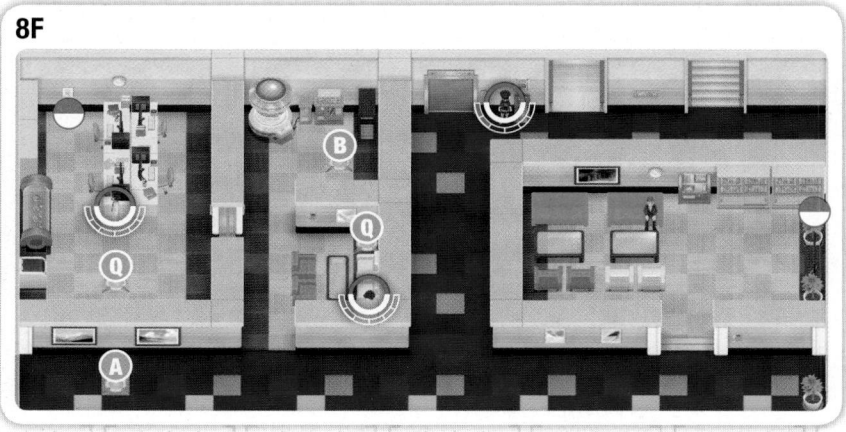

Items	
5F	
☑	Nugget
☑	Guard Spec.
☑	Max Ether
☑	TM54 Flash Cannon
☑	Poké Ball ×5
6F	
☑	X Sp. Atk
☑	Super Potion
☑	PP Up
☑	Max Repel
☑	Hyper Potion
7F	
☑	PP Up
☑	Rare Candy
☑	TM34 Dragon Pulse
☑	Smart Candy ×3
8F	
☑	X Attack
☑	Revive

? Hidden Items ?	
5F	
☑	Silver Nanab Berry ×3
6F	
☑	Fresh Water
☑	Silver Pinap Berry ×3
7F	
☑	Nanab Berry ×3
8F	
☑	Silver Razz Berry ×3

9F

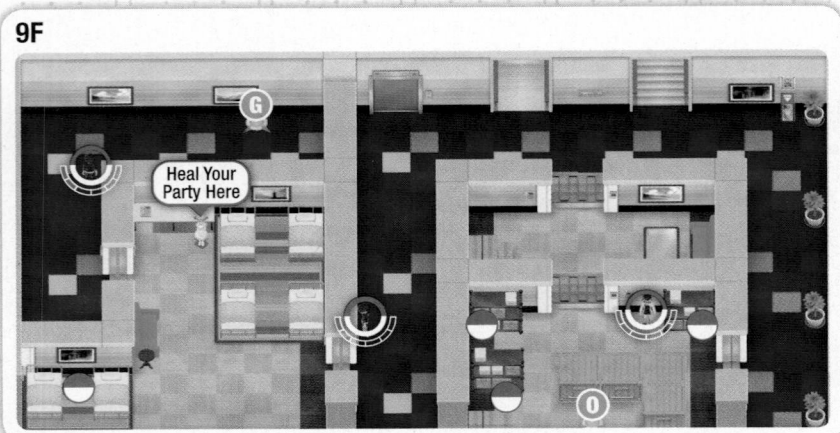

Heal Your
Party Here

Items	
9F	
☑	Ultra Ball ×3
☑	Great Ball ×3
☑	Poké Ball ×3
☑	Revive
10F	
☑	Full Heal
☑	Max Revive
☑	Rare Candy
☑	TM37 Flamethrower
11F	
☑	Max Elixir

? Hidden Items ?	
9F	
☑	Elixir
10F	
☑	X Accuracy

 TIP Stop by the rest area to heal up your Pokémon before continuing.

10F

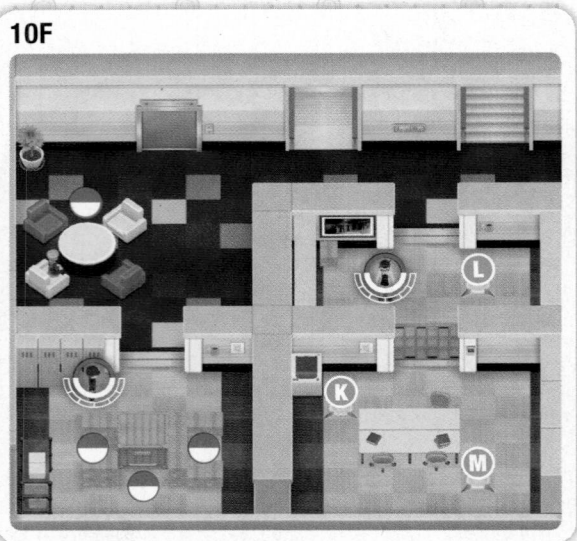

11F

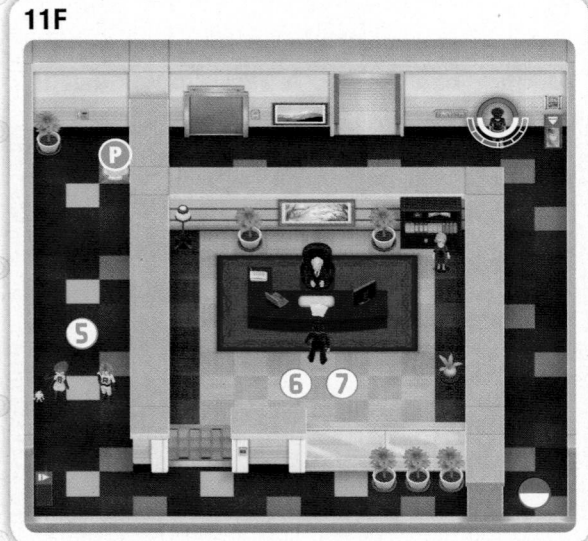

④ Continue climbing the floors, using the maps to hunt down every last item and Trainer. When you reach 7F, you'll be able to get a Lapras from a man there—which is a rare Pokémon you'll want for your team!

◉ Pokémon: Lapras

5 Keep going up through the floors till you reach 11F by stepping on the warp panel labeled **E** and then on **P**. Jessie and James are here to try to stop you again! Battle them to continue forward and reach the president.

6 It's Giovanni again! Put a stop to Silph Co.'s invasion, dashing his hopes of using the secret Poké Ball to take any Pokémon he wants for himself!

7 Get your reward from the president of Silph Co. for saving his company. It's the incredible Master Ball! This extremely rare item can catch any Pokémon without fail. Now it's time to get back to your adventure if you don't want to get left in the dust by your rival!

🔵 Reward: Master Ball

You got the Master Ball from the president!

Battle!

Team Rocket Jessie and James

These two never learn! Thankfully, you do. You should be an expert at handling their Poison-type Pokémon by now. Win this one quick with Ground- or Psychic-type moves, and confront Giovanni!

Arbok
Lv. 36
WEAK AGAINST:

Weezing
Lv. 36
WEAK AGAINST:

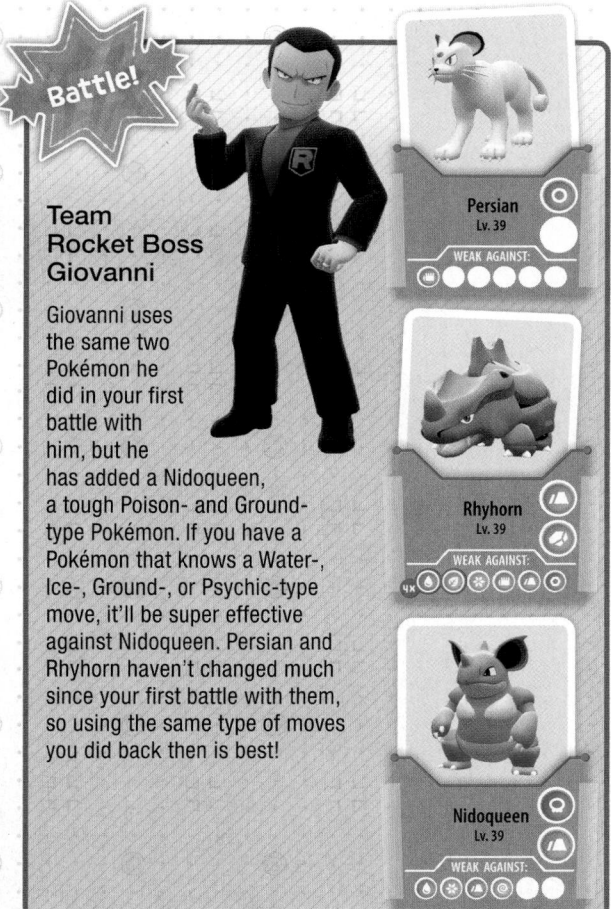

Battle!

Team Rocket Boss Giovanni

Giovanni uses the same two Pokémon he did in your first battle with him, but he has added a Nidoqueen, a tough Poison- and Ground-type Pokémon. If you have a Pokémon that knows a Water-, Ice-, Ground-, or Psychic-type move, it'll be super effective against Nidoqueen. Persian and Rhyhorn haven't changed much since your first battle with them, so using the same type of moves you did back then is best!

Persian
Lv. 39
WEAK AGAINST:

Rhyhorn
Lv. 39
WEAK AGAINST:

Nidoqueen
Lv. 39
WEAK AGAINST:

Saffron City (Revisited)

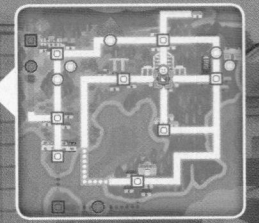

Getting
Around

6 Team Rocket's finally been foiled, so it's time to finish exploring the city before going to the Saffron City Pokémon Gym. Why don't you start by healing up your team at the Pokémon Center? Talk to the man outside with a Porygon, and he'll give it to you!

◉ Pokémon: Porygon

7 You did such a great job thwarting those villains in Silph Co., why not pick up an outfit worthy of an ally of justice by talking to the police officer on the northeastern side of Saffron City?

◉ Reward: Police Set

Turn back to page 79 if you need to refer to the map of Saffron City again to locate any of these steps!

GYM BATTLE!

Saffron City Pokémon Gym

The mission here is to show the man a Pokémon on your team that's at least Lv. 45. If you've been battling the Trainers you meet and catching lots of Pokémon, that shouldn't be too tough. If you're struggling at all, the Zapdos you can catch in the Power Plant (p. 77) can be used to clear this mission.

The Gym is full of warp panels, just like Silph Co. Follow the indications on the map to take the most direct route from A to B and so on if you want to reach Sabrina quickly.

The Trainers here use Psychic-type Pokémon. These Pokémon are weak to Bug-, Ghost-, and Dark-type moves. Dark-type Pokémon, such as Alolan Raticate, are also completely immune to Psychic-type moves, so bringing one of those along is a great choice!

Mr. Mime
Lv. 43
WEAK AGAINST:

Slowbro
Lv. 43
WEAK AGAINST:

Jynx
Lv. 43
WEAK AGAINST:

Alakazam
Lv. 44
WEAK AGAINST:

Gym Leader Sabrina

All of Sabrina's Pokémon are weak to Ghost-type moves. If you've got a Gastly or Haunter from Pokémon Tower, its Ghost-type moves will be helpful in this battle. But be careful—these two are both weak to Psychic-type moves. Bug- and Dark-type moves are also common weaknesses shared by most of Sabrina's Pokémon. You could also try using a Pokémon with high Sp. Def, such as Snorlax, since most Psychic-type moves are special moves.

> Reward: TM33 Calm Mind, Marsh Badge

TM33 Calm Mind

This status move is a great way to power up a Pokémon that focuses on special moves. Use Calm Mind to build up a Pokémon's stats, and then sweep the opponent's team with your boosted Sp. Atk!

Route 19

Getting Around

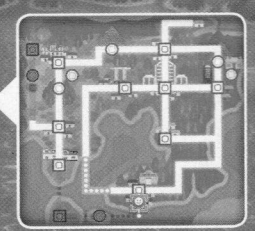

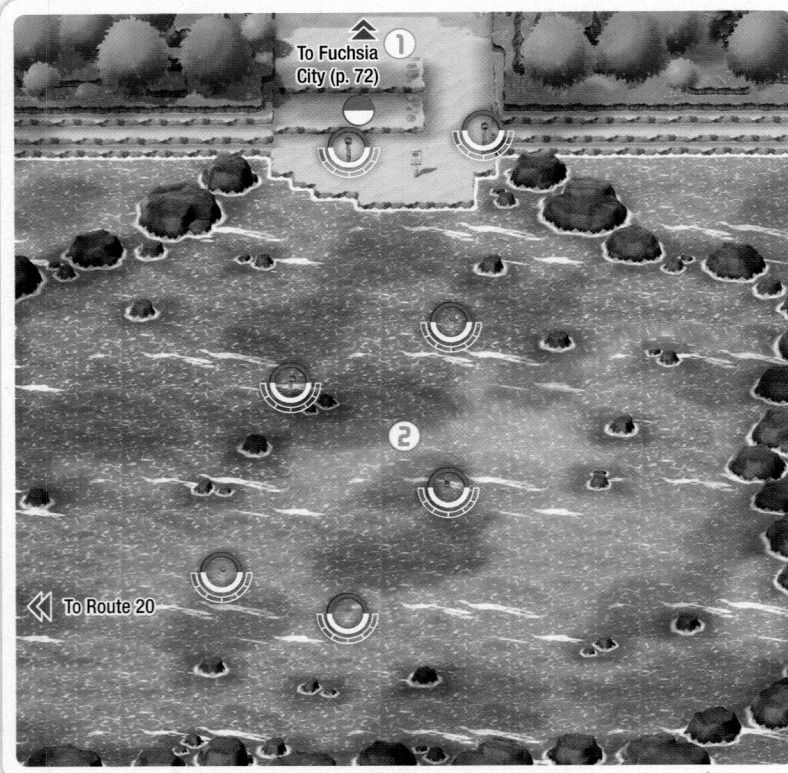

To Fuchsia City (p. 72) ①

②

To Route 20

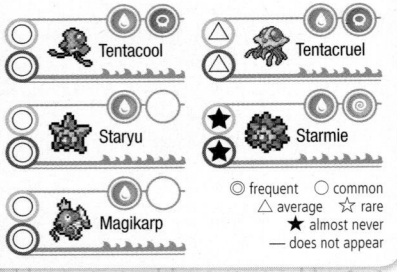

Tentacool ◎	Tentacruel △	
Staryu ◎	Starmie ★	
Magikarp ◎		

◎ frequent ○ common
△ average ☆ rare
★ almost never
— does not appear

Items

☑ Full Heal

Hidden Items

After learning Sea Skim

☑ Revive
☑ Revive

You can also ride certain Pokémon over the water, such as the Lapras you got at Silph Co.! Turn to page 144 to learn more!

---

① You've defeated Team Rocket and collected nearly all the Gym Badges, but there are still two left to go if you hope to take on the Pokémon League! To reach the next Gym, Sky Dash back to Fuchsia City and head south to Route 19. You'll run into Jessie and James, but instead of a battle, they'll give you a strange item—someone's Gold Teeth!

> 🔵 Reward: Gold Teeth

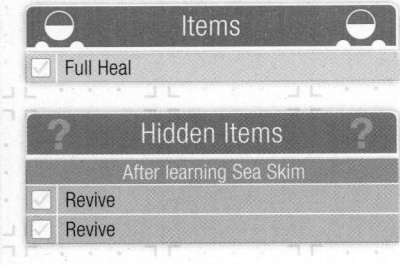

Take the teeth to the warden in the house to the east of the Fuchsia City Pokémon Center. Now that he's able to talk again, he'll teach your partner the Secret Technique Strong Push and give you both a truly wild outfit as thanks!

> 🔵 Secret Technique: Strong Push
> Reward: Safari Set

Try using Strong Push on the block in the warden's house and talking to the Diglett—it'll give you a Nugget every day (p. 24)!

> 🔵 Reward: Nugget

② Finally, you can surf out across the water to try to reach your next destination: Cinnabar Island and its Pokémon Gym! We recommend that you head south and Sea Skim through Route 19 to reach Route 20, though you could go back to Pallet Town and sail south from there. Whatever your choice, keep in mind that the Cinnabar Island Pokémon Gym focuses on Fire-type Pokémon, so try catching some Water-type Pokémon on the open seas!

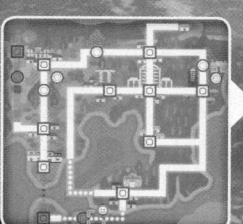

Route 20 (Optional)

Getting Around

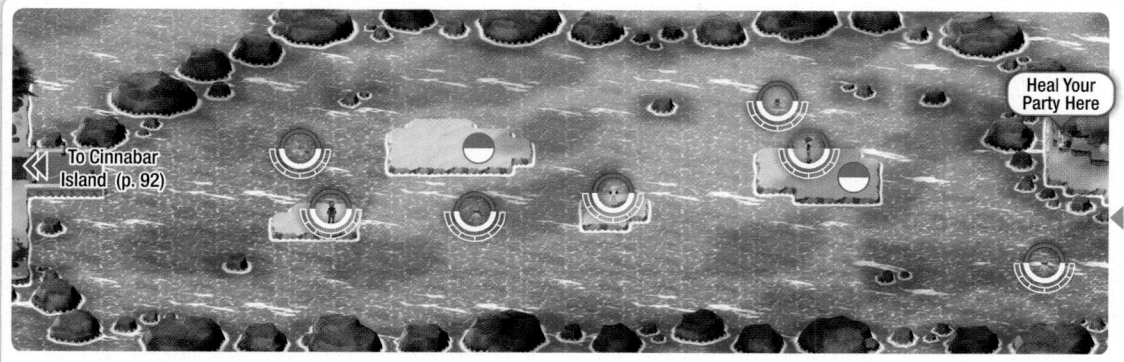

Heal Your Party Here

To Cinnabar Island (p. 92)

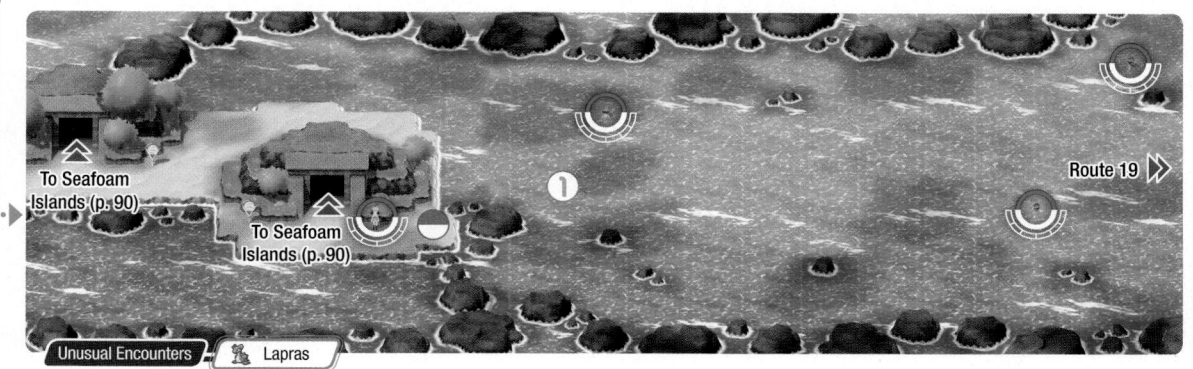

To Seafoam Islands (p. 90)

To Seafoam Islands (p. 90)

Route 19

Unusual Encounters — Lapras

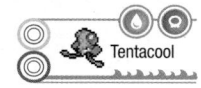 Tentacool
 Tentacruel
 Magikarp
 Gyarados

◎ frequent ○ common
△ average ☆ rare
★ almost never — does not appear

Items

- Heart Scale
- Ultra Ball ×3
- Max Repel

Hidden Items

- Revive
- Revive
- Revive
- Stardust

TIP Remember, you could also go back to Pallet Town right now and use Sea Skim to head south from there to reach Cinnabar Island, skipping Route 20 and the Seafoam Islands entirely. But you'll miss out on Exp. Points, items, and a very rare Pokémon if you do!

1. Use Sea Skim from Route 19, heading south and then west along Route 20 toward the Seafoam Islands and battling the Trainers along the way. You'll have to pass through the Seafoam Islands to continue.

Catch!

Gyarados

Catch Difficulty

Easier — Harder

Seafoam Islands (Optional)

Getting Around

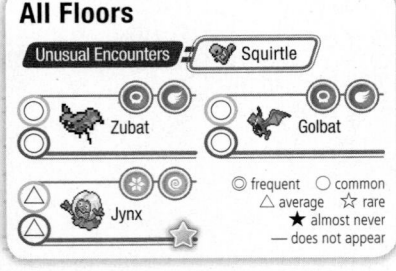

1F

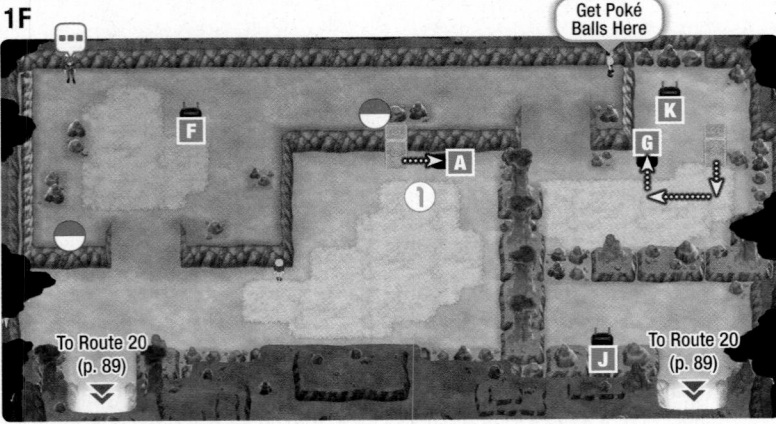

Get Poké Balls Here

To Route 20 (p. 89)

To Route 20 (p. 89)

B1F

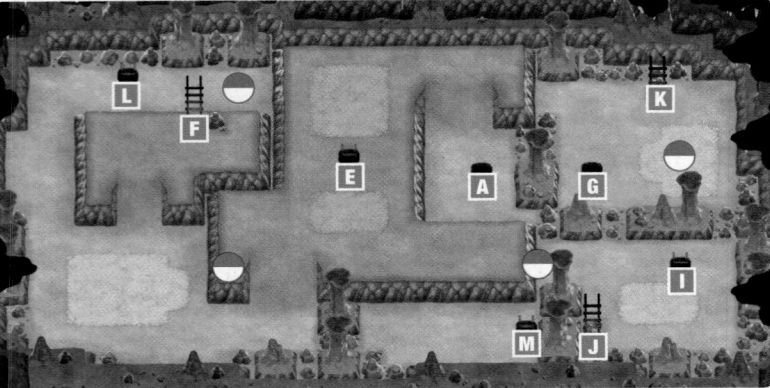

B2F

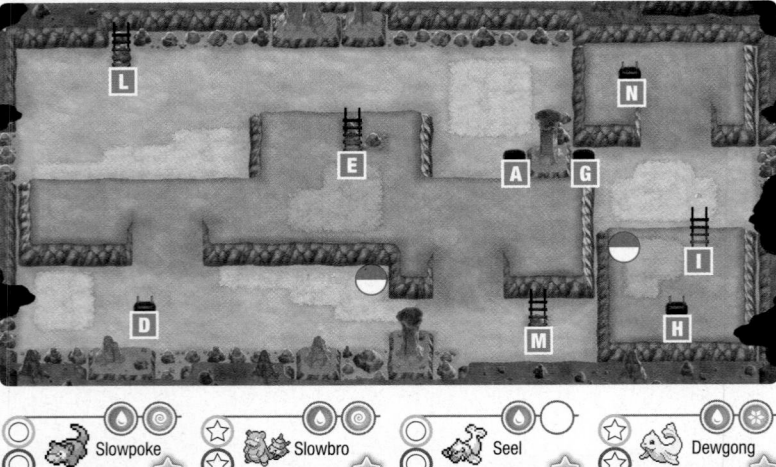

All Floors

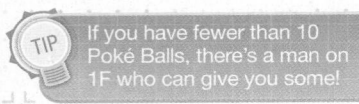

Unusual Encounters	Squirtle

Zubat — Golbat

Jynx

◎ frequent ○ common
△ average ☆ rare
★ almost never
— does not appear

TIP If you have fewer than 10 Poké Balls, there's a man on 1F who can give you some!

Items

1F	
☑	Ice Heal
☑	Escape Rope
B1F	
☑	Super Repel
☑	Max Potion
☑	Great Ball ×5
☑	Super Lure
B2F	
☑	TM55 Ice Beam
☑	Ice Stone
B3F	
☑	Super Lure
☑	X Speed
☑	Hyper Potion
☑	Ultra Ball ×3
☑	Super Repel
B4F	
☑	Big Pearl
☑	Big Pearl
☑	Big Pearl

Hidden Items

1F	
☑	Heart Scale
☑	Heart Scale
B1F	
☑	Max Revive
B2F	
☑	Heart Scale
☑	Pearl
☑	Heart Scale
☑	Heart Scale
B3F	
☑	Revive
B4F	
☑	Pretty Wing

Slowpoke — Slowbro — Seel — Dewgong

① You'll need to use Strong Push to knock the stone blocks into holes and block the water currents so you can use Sea Skim to cross. Knock the stone block by **A** down to B3F, then jump in the hole after it. Then follow the ladders in alphabetical order. Do the same for the stone near **G** on 1F, and keep following the letters.

WALKTHROUGH

 Tentacool  Tentacruel  Shellder  Cloyster  Magikarp

B3F & B4F

Coach Battle!

Coach Trainer Yas

Yas uses the three Evolutions of Eevee first discovered in the Kanto region. They don't share many common type weaknesses. Flareon and Jolteon are both weak to Ground-type moves, though.

TEAM:
Lv. 46 | Lv. 47 | Lv. 46

Reward: Rare Candy ×5

B3F

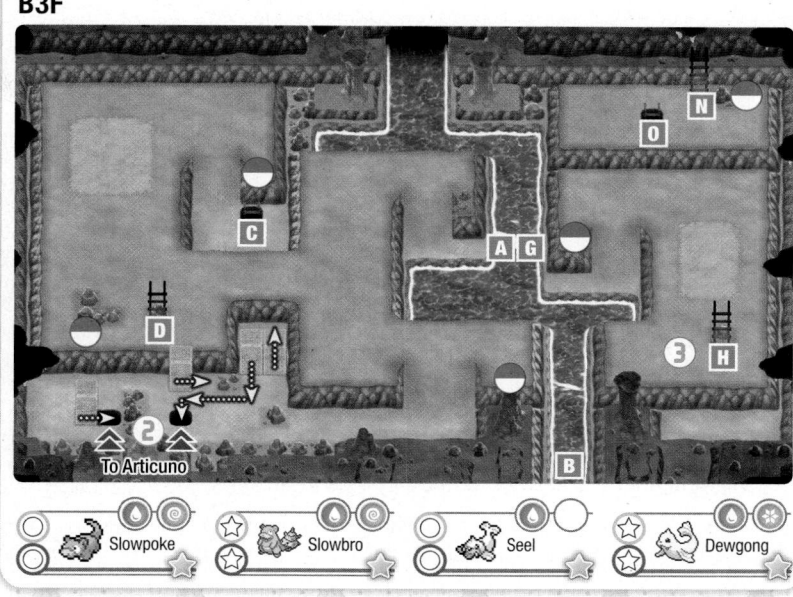

To Articuno

○ Slowpoke ☆ Slowbro ○ Seel ☆ Dewgong

2 After reaching B3F again, push the two stone blocks into the two holes to the south, moving other blocks out of the way as necessary. Then jump down either hole, save your game, and get ready to battle and catch the Legendary Pokémon Articuno!

3 Once you're ready to exit the cave, climb back to B3F via ladder **C** and use Sea Skim to reach **H**. From there, just keep climbing up to 1F!

B4F

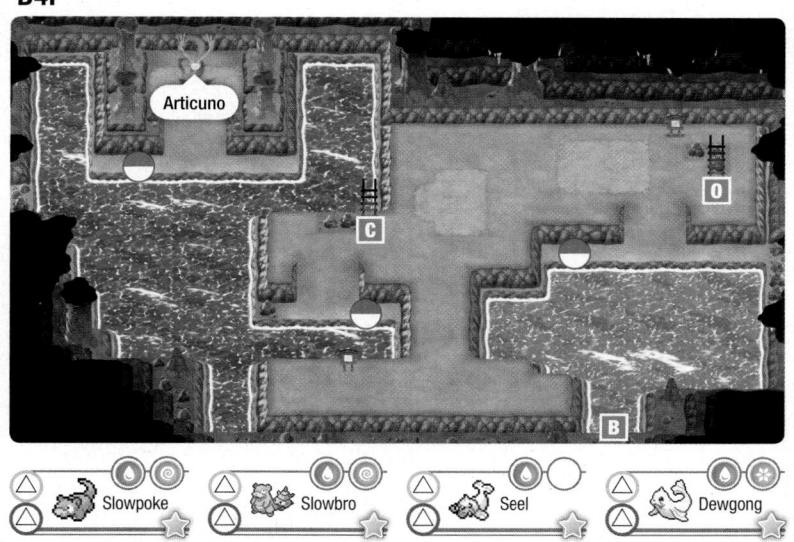

Articuno

○ Slowpoke ☆ Slowbro △ Seel △ Dewgong

Articuno

Articuno is Ice and Flying type, meaning it has a double weakness to Rock-type moves. Rock Throw or a similar move will win this battle for you pretty quickly. Otherwise, try to focus on Fire-, Electric-, or Steel-type moves, as Articuno is weak to those. Remember to keep an eye on that timer! You'll only have five minutes to defeat Articuno. If you fail, you won't be able to meet it again until you've entered the Hall of Fame. Catching this Pokémon will be just as difficult as Zapdos, so make sure to bring some Ultra Balls and try to use a Silver or Golden Razz Berry if you've got any!

Articuno
Lv. 50
WEAK AGAINST:
4x

Legendary Battle!

Cinnabar Island

Getting Around

Items

☑ Antidote

There's a Poké Mart here on the island, so turn to page 395 if you want to check what items are available.

1 Keep traveling west on Route 20, and you'll finally reach Cinnabar Island! It looks as if the Gym is locked, though, so you'll need a key. You could head straight to the Pokémon Mansion to find it, but there are a few other things you can do first on the island.

I came to visit the Cinnabar Island Gym, but the door is locked tight.

2 You can trade a Kantonian Grimer for an Alolan Grimer in *Pokémon: Let's Go, Pikachu!* and a Kantonian Meowth for an Alolan Meowth in *Pokémon: Let's Go, Eevee!* at the Cinnabar Island Pokémon Center.

⊙ Pokémon: Alolan Grimer 🐭 or Alolan Meowth ⚡

3 You can finally restore that Fossil from Mt. Moon! Head to the last room in the Cinnabar Lab, and give the scientist your Fossil. He'll restore it to the ancient Pokémon it once was. He can do the same for the Old Amber you got in Pewter City, too!

⊙ Pokémon: Aerodactyl, Kabuto, or Omanyte

Turn to page 108 to find out where you can get more Fossils that can be restored to these ancient Pokémon.

TIP Stop by another room in the Cinnabar Lab, and talk to the grumpy scientist there for a TM!

⊙ Reward: TM02 Taunt

Pokémon Mansion

Getting Around

All Floors

 Rattata

 Raticate

 Magmar

Unusual Encounters — Chansey

◎ frequent ○ common
△ average ☆ rare
★ almost never — does not appear

1F

Statue

Door

A

C

D

To Cinnabar Island

To Cinnabar Island

2F

B

Door

A   E

Door

Statue

Door

F

Grimer — ○
Muk — ☆
Koffing — ◎
Weezing — ☆
Ditto — ★

Items

1F
- [x] Max Repel
- [x] Max Lure
- [x] Silver Razz Berry ×5
- [x] Fire Stone
- [x] Max Elixir

2F
- [x] Max Ether
- [x] Ultra Ball ×3
- [x] Max Revive
- [x] PP Up
- [x] Escape Rope
- [x] Hyper Potion

3F
- [x] Full Heal
- [x] TM21 Foul Play
- [x] Rare Candy
- [x] X Accuracy

B1F
- [x] TM52 Sludge Bomb
- [x] Max Potion
- [x] Rare Candy
- [x] Max Elixir
- [x] Secret Key

Hidden Items

1F, 2F, 3F, B1F
- [x] Courage Candy*
- [x] Health Candy*
- [x] Mighty Candy*
- [x] Quick Candy*
- [x] Smart Candy*
- [x] Tough Candy*

*You have a chance to randomly find one of these items at each spot.

TIP This mansion is a Candy lover's paradise! Keep checking back here for new Candies from time to time.

WALKTHROUGH

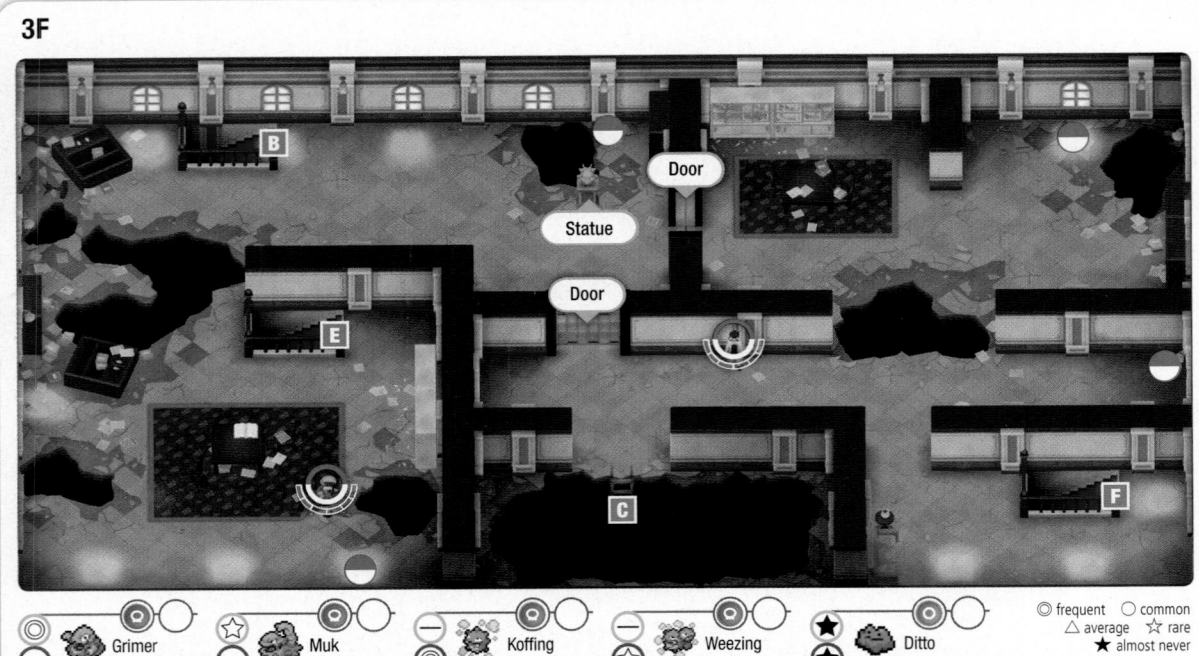

◎ frequent ○ common
△ average ☆ rare
★ almost never
— does not appear

—	Grimer	◎			★	Muk	◎	
—	Koffing	◎			—	Weezing	◎	
★	Ditto	◎		

B1F

—	Grimer	◎			△	Muk	◎	
—	Koffing	◎			△	Weezing	◎	
△	Ditto	◎		

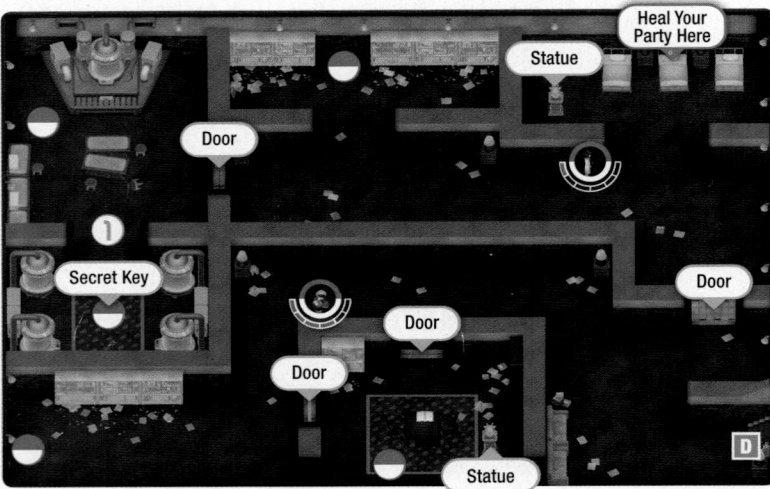

Heal Your Party Here

① This place sure is creepy! Stay tough and use the maps to guide yourself around the mansion. You'll find mysterious statues that open and close the doors on their floor. Both are marked on the maps, so you can find your way to the Secret Key and finally open the Cinnabar Island Gym. And make sure to battle the Coach Trainer to get some extra Exp. Points while you're at it!

🔄 Reward: Secret Key

Coach Battle!

Coach Trainer Rita

Rita's Pokémon are all weak to Grass-type moves, so try to bring a Pokémon that knows one.

TEAM:

| Lv. 46 | Lv. 47 | Lv. 46 | | | |

🔄 Reward: TM22 Rock Slide

Catch!

Ditto

Catch Difficulty

◄ Easier   Harder ►

WALKTHROUGH

Cinnabar Island (Revisited)

Getting Around

4 Now that you've got the Secret Key, unlock the door to the Cinnabar Island Gym. It's time to earn your seventh Badge!

GYM BATTLE!

Cinnabar Island Pokémon Gym

Gym Battle!

The Gym mission here was just to unlock the front door to the Gym, so you're all set! Trainers in this Gym use Fire-type Pokémon, so make sure you've got Pokémon with Water-, Ground-, or Rock-type moves. You'll only have to battle Trainers that have one or two Pokémon each if you get questions wrong during Blaine's quiz. You can try to answer the questions on your own, but if you're really stuck, you can check below for the answers!

Magmar
Lv. 47
WEAK AGAINST:

Rapidash
Lv. 47
WEAK AGAINST:

Ninetales
Lv. 47
WEAK AGAINST:

Arcanine
Lv. 48
WEAK AGAINST:

Gym Leader Blaine

All of Blaine's Pokémon are pure Fire type, so they're weak to Water-, Ground-, and Rock-type moves. If you caught any strong Water-type Pokémon on Routes 19 and 20 or in the Seafoam Islands, they'll be a big help in this battle. Consider using powerful Water-type TM moves, such as Surf or Scald. (If you've missed any TMs, turn to page 387.) Remember that if any of your Pokémon get burned from Blaine's toasty Fire-type moves, they'll take damage every turn and have their Attack reduced!

Reward: TM46 Fire Blast, Volcano Badge

TM46 Fire Blast

Fire Blast is an extremely powerful special move with 110 power! Be careful, though, as its accuracy is 85, meaning it will miss from time to time.

ANSWERS: 1. Magmar 2. Eight 3. Not very effective 4. False / What's that?! 5. They're all right!

WALKTHROUGH

Route 21 (Optional)

Getting Around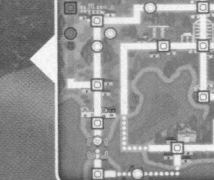

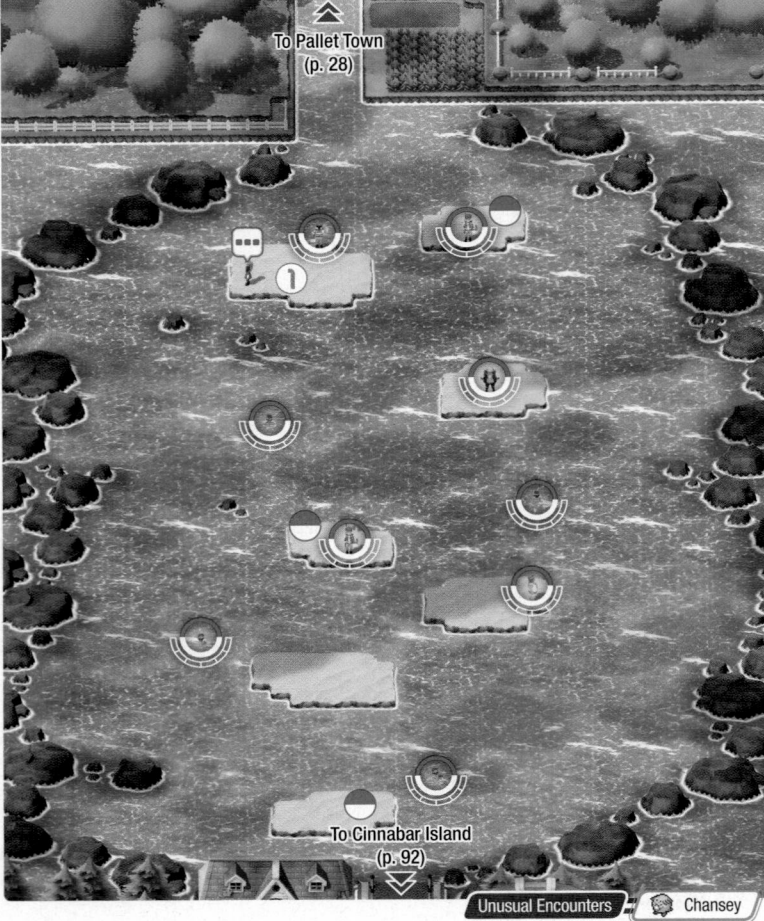

To Pallet Town
(p. 28)

To Cinnabar Island
(p. 92)

Unusual Encounters  Chansey

 Pidgey
Pidgeotto
Rattata
Raticate

Oddish
Gloom
★ Vileplume
Bellsprout

Weepinbell
★ Victreebel
Tangela
Tentacool

Tentacruel
Staryu
★ Starmie
Magikarp

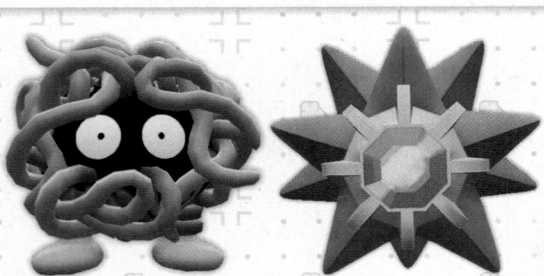

Items

- [x] PP Up
- [x] Water Stone
- [x] Hyper Potion

Hidden Items

- [x] Revive
- [x] Stardust ×3, ×5, or ×7*

*You have the chance to randomly find these items at each spot.

TIP Stardust can be sold at a high price to shops, so return here often to replenish your stock!

① Head north using Sea Skim, battle the Trainers along the route, and make your way back to Pallet Town and then Viridian City. Or you could simply use Sky Dash to be back there in a flash, if you're eager to catch up to your rival, but you'd miss the Coach Trainer on this route!

Coach Battle!

Coach Trainer Pam

Ghost-type Pokémon are a good choice in this battle. They'll be immune to Machoke and Kangaskhan's Fighting- and Normal-type moves, and Ghost-type moves are super effective against Jynx.

TEAM:
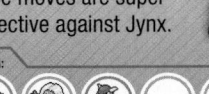 Lv. 44 | Lv. 44 | Lv. 45

 Reward: TM35 Ice Punch

WALKTHROUGH

Viridian City & Pallet Town (Revisited)

Getting Around

If you need to have another look at Viridian City's map, turn back to page 30!

4 Here you'll run into your rival again. It seems he can't get into the Gym, either, so head back to Pallet Town and ask Professor Oak for help.

Now there's a familiar face—Blue is back in town! He and Professor Oak will teach you about the incredible secrets of Mega Evolution, and you'll leave the lab with some rare Mega Stones and your very own Key Stone!

Reward: Key Stone, Venusaurite, Blastoisinite, Charizardite X, Charizardite Y

An Evolution That Surpasses All Others: Mega Evolution!

Mega Evolution is a kind of transformation certain Pokémon can undergo when they're in battle. The Pokémon's Trainer needs to have a Key Stone and that Pokémon's Mega Stone. Mega Evolution can increase the stats of a Pokémon (except for HP) and even change the Pokémon's type to give it strengths and weaknesses against different kinds of Pokémon! Note that if a Trainer has one of their Pokémon Mega Evolve in battle, they can't Mega Evolve any of their other Pokémon for the rest of that battle. To learn a little more about Mega Evolution and see the Pokémon in the Kanto region that can Mega Evolve, check out page 135.

5 Time to head back north to Viridian City. It seems the mysterious Gym Leader of the Viridian City Gym has finally returned—here's your chance to earn your eighth and final Badge, and press onward toward the Pokémon League!

WALKTHROUGH

Viridian City Pokémon Gym

Gym Battle!

Items

- [x] Revive

There's no Gym mission here, so just do your best to navigate the spinning tiles of the Gym and battle its Trainers to level up your team some more before confronting the final Gym Leader of the Kanto region! Trainers here focus mostly on Ground-type Pokémon, so be sure to use Pokémon with Water-, Grass-, or Ice-type moves. Articuno would make a great choice, as its Flying type means it's immune to Ground-type moves and it gets same-type attack bonus when using Ice Beam!

Before moving on to the next arrow, speak to the Tamer on the left. Otherwise he'll block your path.

Gym Leader Giovanni

The Gym Leader here is really Giovanni—the boss of Team Rocket! Since he uses Ground-type Pokémon, all his Pokémon share weaknesses to Water- and Ice-type moves. His powerful Rhydon is also doubly weak to Water and Grass types, so Pokémon with those types of moves are the best choice. If you'd prefer to play defensively, you can try using Flying-type Pokémon, as they're immune to Ground-type moves. Remember not to waste Electric-type moves on Ground-type Pokémon—they won't take any damage from them!

Reward: TM41 Earthquake, Earth Badge

TM41 Earthquake

The user sets off an earthquake that strikes every Pokémon around it. With a power and accuracy of 100, it's no wonder this physical move is one of the best around! Be careful in Double Battles, though—it'll hit Pokémon on your side, too!

Dugtrio Lv. 49 — WEAK AGAINST:

Nidoqueen Lv. 49 — WEAK AGAINST:

Nidoking Lv. 49 — WEAK AGAINST:

Rhydon Lv. 50 — WEAK AGAINST:

Route 22

   Getting Around

To Route 23 (South) (p. 100)

To Viridian City (p. 30)

 Rattata

 Spearow

 Nidoran♀

 Nidoran♂

 Poliwag

 Poliwhirl

 Magikarp

◎ frequent ○ common
△ average ☆ rare
★ almost never
— does not appear

Items
☑ Poké Ball ×5

? Hidden Items ?
☑ Antidote

1 After your final showdown with Giovanni, head outside to receive some surprising news from Blue about the future of the Viridian City Gym. He'll also remind you about your next destination—now that you have all eight Gym Badges, it's time to head to the Pokémon League! On the way there, you'll run into your rival on Route 22. He wants one last battle before the two of you challenge the Elite Four!

 Rival Battle!

Your Rival

Your rival's team is still made up of most of the same Pokémon from the last time the two of you battled, but he's raised his team to be ready for the Pokémon League. His Pidgeot, Vileplume, and Marowak are all weak to Ice-type moves, so maybe send in that Articuno you caught not too long ago! His Jolteon or Raichu are both Electric type, and you should know the drill battling against them by now—Ground-type moves all the way! Try out Earthquake, since you just got the TM for it from Giovanni.

Pidgeot
Lv. 50
WEAK AGAINST:

Vileplume
Lv. 50
WEAK AGAINST:

Jolteon
Lv. 51
WEAK AGAINST:

If you started with Pikachu

Marowak
Lv. 50
WEAK AGAINST:

Raichu
Lv. 51
WEAK AGAINST:

If you started with Eevee

 WALKTHROUGH

Route 23

Getting Around

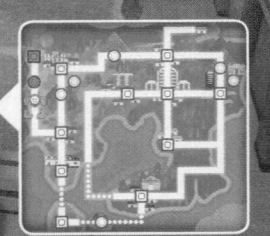

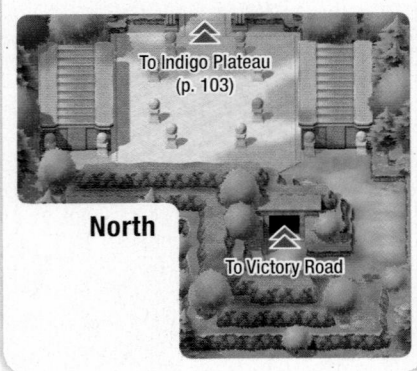

North

To Indigo Plateau (p. 103)

To Victory Road

South

To Victory Road

To Route 22 (p. 99)

Items	
☑ Golden Razz Berry ×3	
☑ Golden Nanab Berry ×3	
☑ Golden Pinap Berry ×3	

Items	
☑ Golden Razz Berry ×5	
☑ Golden Nanab Berry ×5	
☑ Golden Pinap Berry ×5	

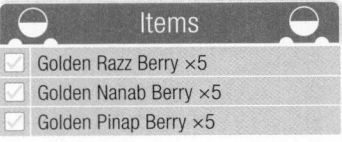

1 Make your way through the gates, showing each guard your Badges to get through. You can catch some pretty strong Pokémon here. This is also the only place you can find Exeggcute and Exeggutor!

Catch!

Exeggutor

Catch Difficulty

Easier ◄────────── Harder ►

Spearow		Fearow		Nidoran♀		Nidorina
★★ Nidoqueen		Nidoran♂		Nidorino		★★ Nidoking
Exeggcute		★★ Exeggutor		Poliwag		Poliwhirl
Magikarp						

Unusual Encounters — Chansey

◎ frequent ○ common △ average ☆ rare ★ almost never — does not appear

WALKTHROUGH

Victory Road

    Getting Around

1F

To Route 23 (South)

Unusual Encounters — Chansey

 Zubat  Golbat

 Machop  Machoke

 Geodude 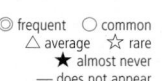 Graveler

Onix Rhyhorn

Rhydon

◎ frequent   ◯ common
△ average   ☆ rare
★ almost never
— does not appear

2F

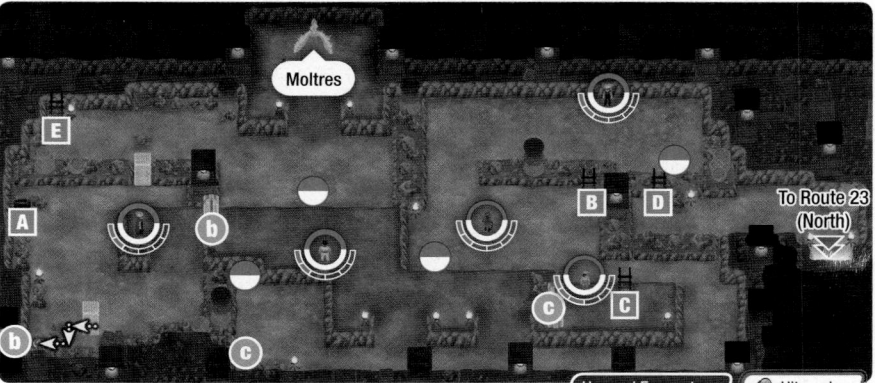

Moltres

To Route 23 (North)

Unusual Encounters — Hitmonlee

3F

Heal Your Party Here

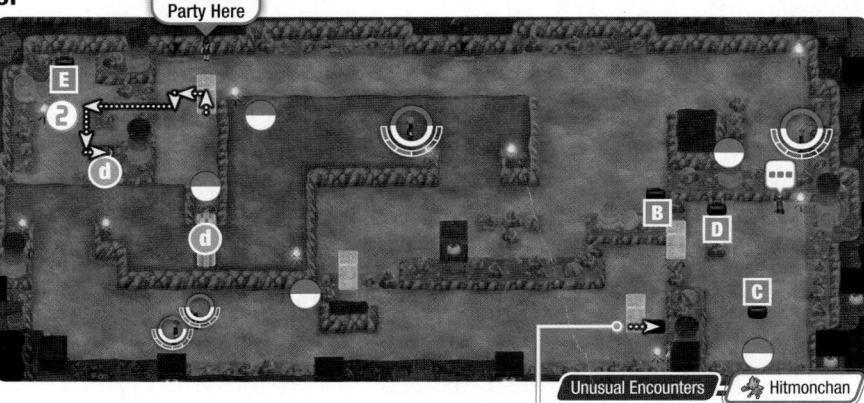

Unusual Encounters — Hitmonchan

Push this block into the hole and then keep pushing it westward to activate switch ⊙.

Items

1F
- [x] Leaf Stone
- [x] TM56 Stealth Rock
- [x] Ultra Ball ×3

2F
- [x] TM45 Solar Beam
- [x] Full Restore
- [x] TM49 Superpower
- [x] PP Max

3F
- [x] Max Revive
- [x] TM51 Blizzard
- [x] Max Potion
- [x] Golden Nanab Berry ×5
- [x] Full Restore

Hidden Items

1F, 2F, 3F
- [x] Courage Candy*
- [x] Health Candy*
- [x] Mighty Candy*
- [x] Quick Candy*
- [x] Smart Candy*
- [x] Tough Candy*

2F
- [x] Pretty Wing

3F
- [x] Fresh Water

*You have a chance to randomly find one of these items at each spot.

 TIP   If you're ever running low on Candies, remember that Victory Road is a great place for stocking up!

WALKTHROUGH

1. You'll have to find your way through the caves and battle some of Kanto's strongest Trainers to reach the Pokémon League. There are two Coach Trainers here, so make sure you battle them both! The first is on 1F to the east. The second is on 3F near **D**.

You will find some stone walls blocking your way, but fear not! The lowercase markers on the map will help you out—matching letters show you which switch will lower which wall.

TIP If you're puzzling over how to get both items at the end of the northeast path on 1F, don't worry! The blocks' positions reset when you leave the floor, so come back later to get the item you weren't able to grab the first time around.

Coach Battle!

Coach Trainer Alemana

Alemana's Ditto will transform into the Pokémon it's facing in battle. Use what you know about your Pokémon to defeat the Ditto after it's transformed!

TEAM:

Lv. 49

Reward: Pikachu Candy ×10 or Eevee Candy ×10

Coach Battle!

Coach Trainer Ryan

Ryan uses a pretty varied bunch of Pokémon. Switch out your Pokémon to handle each one at a time.

TEAM:

Lv. 48 | Lv. 48 | Lv. 48 | Lv. 49

Reward: TM39 Outrage

2. Take ladder **E** on 3F to find the fiery Moltres on 2F. Just like your other meetings with Legendary Pokémon, you'll want to battle and catch this powerful force!

TIP Find the police officer on 3F, and she'll heal up your Pokémon!

Moltres

Moltres completes the trio of winged Legendary Pokémon. You've had plenty of practice dealing with the five-minute timer, so you should be more than ready to pull off a successful battle and catch! Moltres is Fire and Flying type, so it's doubly weak to Rock-type moves. If you taught one of your Pokémon Rock Slide with the TM you got from Coach Trainer Rita, you'll defeat Moltres in no time. Break out the Razz Berries and Ultra Balls during the catch phase, and you'll nab Moltres just in time for the Pokémon League.

Moltres Lv. 50

WEAK AGAINST:

4x

Legendary Battle!

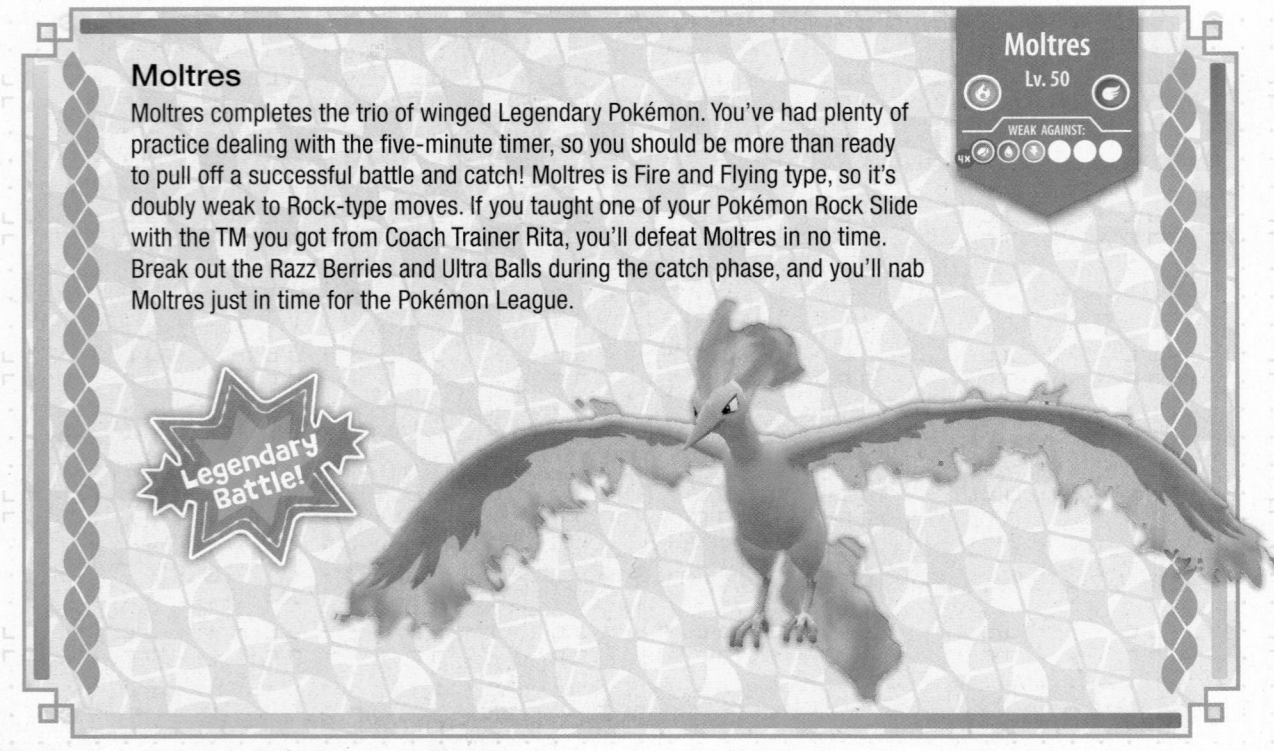

Indigo Plateau & Pokémon League

Pokémon League

Poké Mart

2 3

To Elite Four

To Indigo Plateau

Pokémon Center

Indigo Plateau

To Pokémon League

To Route 23
(North) (p. 100)

Mega Stone Seller	
After entering Hall of Fame	
Beedrillite	₽30,000
Pidgeotite	₽30,000
Alakazite	₽30,000
Slowbronite	₽30,000

Mega Stone Seller	
After entering Hall of Fame	
Gengarite	₽30,000
Kangaskhanite	₽30,000
Pinsirite	₽30,000
Gyaradosite	₽30,000
Aerodactylite	₽30,000

1 The final challenge awaits! Head north up the stairs of the Indigo Plateau and into the Pokémon League to challenge the best of the best—the Elite Four! You can also talk to the man in the corner next to the Poké Mart if you want to trade your Kantonian Exeggutor for an amazingly tall Alolan Exeggutor.

⊕ Pokémon: Alolan Exeggutor

There's a Poké Mart counter right inside the Pokémon League, with all the usual offerings listed on page 395! And once you've managed to enter the Hall of Fame, a new face will appear on the Indigo Plateau—the Mega Stone Seller! Take a look at what he's got to offer, and stock up on Mega Stones.

TIP Find Madam Memorial in the lobby and give her one of your Heart Scales, if you have any. She'll teach your Pokémon a move they have forgotten or not learned when they had the chance—or even a move they would learn by leveling up! Grab this chance before battling the Elite Four!

2 Heal up your team and consider buying some items to prepare for your battles. Once you enter the rooms of the Elite Four, you won't be able to leave until you win...or lose. This is it!

Elite Four

Each of the Elite Four specializes in a different type of Pokémon, and their weaknesses have hardly any overlaps! Use everything you've learned in your adventure so far, as well as the handy battle advice on these pages, to pick the perfect lineup from your Pokémon Box for each battle.

Elite Four Lorelei

Lorelei focuses on Ice-type Pokémon. Fire-, Fighting-, Rock-, and Steel-type moves will deal supereffective damage against Ice-type Pokémon, but remember that may change for a dual-type Pokémon, such as Lapras! Many of Lorelei's Pokémon are Water type, too. Bringing a Pokémon with Grass- or Electric-type moves will help you out. Remember to keep some Ice Heals on hand in case one of your Pokémon gets frozen!

Dewgong Lv. 51	Jynx Lv. 51	Cloyster Lv. 51	Slowbro Lv. 51	Lapras Lv. 52
WEAK AGAINST:	WEAK AGAINST:	WEAK AGAINST:	WEAK AGAINST:	WEAK AGAINST:

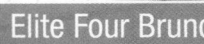

Elite Four Bruno

Bruno loves Fighting-type Pokémon, but he uses the Rock- and Ground-type Pokémon Onix, too. Most of his team can be handled with a Pokémon that knows a strong Flying-, Psychic-, or Fairy-type move, such as Psychic or Dazzling Gleam—both of which are TMs you should already have. For Onix, just make sure to have a Pokémon that knows a Water- or Grass-type move and it will take four times the damage!

Onix Lv. 52	Hitmonlee Lv. 52	Hitmonchan Lv. 52	Poliwrath Lv. 52	Machamp Lv. 53
WEAK AGAINST:	WEAK AGAINST:	WEAK AGAINST:	WEAK AGAINST:	WEAK AGAINST:

Elite Four Agatha

Agatha loves Ghost-type Pokémon, but all of her Pokémon share the Poison type. So instead of focusing on Ghost-type weaknesses, you could instead bring a Pokémon with powerful Psychic- or Ground-type moves. This is a great time to use Earthquake—which you recently got as a TM from your battle with Giovanni—to do some massive damage against this scary old lady's team!

Arbok Lv. 53	Gengar Lv. 53	Golbat Lv. 53	Weezing Lv. 53	Gengar Lv. 54
WEAK AGAINST:	WEAK AGAINST:	WEAK AGAINST:	WEAK AGAINST:	WEAK AGAINST:

Elite Four Lance

Although Lance may be a dragon master, all of his Pokémon except Dragonite share a common weakness to Electric-type moves, while all but Seadra are weak to Rock-type moves! Thunderbolt and Rock Slide would be perfect choices for this battle. Dragonite is best battled with a Fairy-type Pokémon, as Fairy types are immune to Dragon-type moves. If you don't have one, though, any Pokémon that knows an Ice-, Dragon-, or Fairy-type move will work.

Seadra
Lv. 54
WEAK AGAINST:

Aerodactyl
Lv. 54
WEAK AGAINST:

Gyarados
Lv. 54
WEAK AGAINST:

Charizard
Lv. 54
WEAK AGAINST:

Dragonite
Lv. 55
WEAK AGAINST:

---

(3) You did it! You've beaten the Elite Four, and now you're the Champion...or are you? Meet up with Professor Oak and learn about the final challenge to become a Pokémon League Champion.

Champion Battle

The last challenge before you're a Champion is your first friend and rival! Just like you've learned to do, your rival uses a very diverse team of Pokémon, with no large shared weaknesses. Both his Jolteon or Raichu and his Rapidash are weak to Ground-type moves if you want to bust out Earthquake to knock them out easily. Try sending out a Pokémon that knows a strong Electric-, Ice-, or Rock-type move first, as he'll always start the battle with his Pidgeot. It will Mega Evolve into Mega Pidgeot, too, so beat it quickly before it deals heavy damage to your team with its boosted Sp. Atk. Remember all you've learned about type matchups (p. 123). Don't be shy about using items or Mega Evolution, and you'll best your rival to go down in Kanto's history as a Pokémon League Champion!

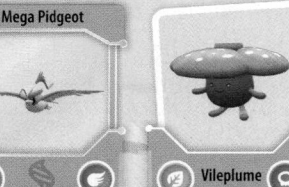

Mega Pidgeot
Lv. 56
WEAK AGAINST:

Vileplume
Lv. 56
WEAK AGAINST:

Marowak
Lv. 56
WEAK AGAINST:

Rapidash
Lv. 56
WEAK AGAINST:

Slowbro
Lv. 56
WEAK AGAINST:

If you started with Pikachu

Jolteon
Lv. 57
WEAK AGAINST:

Raichu
Lv. 57
WEAK AGAINST:

If you started with Eevee

Champion Activities

There's still more to do after becoming Champion! Buy up all the Mega Stones from the man selling them in the lobby of the Pokémon League. They aren't cheap, though, so check out page 143 for some tips on getting the cash you need.

Team Rocket may have disbanded, but Archer isn't giving up so easily! Find him in the Team Rocket Hideout in Celadon City, and battle him one last time.

Find Jessie and James on Route 17 for one last battle with them!

Battle!

Pokémon Trainer Archer

Archer's gotten tougher since your last battle with him, but you're a Pokémon League Champion now! He uses four Pokémon, but Electrode, Weezing, and Magmar share a common weakness to Ground-type moves. Bust out that Earthquake, and remind Archer why you're a champ!

Electrode Lv. 54	Magmar Lv. 54
WEAK AGAINST:	WEAK AGAINST:

Golbat Lv. 54	Weezing Lv. 54
WEAK AGAINST:	WEAK AGAINST:

Battle!

Team Rocket Jessie and James

Earthquake and Psychic are the moves you'll want to use against these two Pokémon in your last battle with Jessie and James. Earthquake will hit your other Pokémon in this Double Battle unless it's a Flying-type Pokémon, so be careful! If you're worried about being poisoned, try sending out a Poison- or Steel-type Pokémon—they're immune to this status condition.

Reward: Blast-Off Set

Arbok Lv. 52
WEAK AGAINST:

Weezing Lv. 52
WEAK AGAINST:

Master Trainers for each species of Pokémon in Kanto have appeared all across the region! Battle them or show them the Pokémon they want to see to earn their titles! Most want to battle—and only want to battle the species of Pokémon they love. Learn more about where you can find each Master Trainer starting on page 137.

TIP Master Trainers you've defeated in battle will be eager for a rematch once per day. You won't earn any Exp. Points or money from these battles, nor will your title be at stake, but it's a fun way to keep testing your beloved Pokémon so they'll remain the best of the best!

WALKTHROUGH

👑 You've met the famous Pokémon Trainer Blue during your adventure, but what about his rival? Find out how you can earn the chance to challenge the legendary battle master Red on page 137.

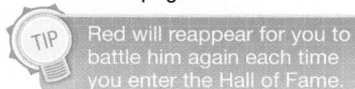

TIP: Red will reappear for you to battle him again each time you enter the Hall of Fame.

👑 Head to Celadon Condominiums and talk to the game director in the GAME FREAK Development Office when you've caught or obtained the first 150 Pokémon. You'll get a fancy diploma and a Shiny Charm that makes it easier to find Shiny Pokémon!

🔴 Reward: Diploma, Shiny Charm

Since you're at the GAME FREAK Development Office, you may as well take on the strongest Coach Trainer, who's appeared now that you've entered the Hall of Fame! Make sure your team is healed up first!

💬 Coach Battle!

Coach Trainer Morimoto

Jolteon and Flareon both share a weakness to Ground-type moves, so remember to bring a Pokémon that knows Earthquake.

TEAM: Lv. 54 · Lv. 54 · Lv. 54 · Lv. 54 · Lv. 54 · Lv. 54

🔴 Reward: PP Max ×10

👑 If you go back to Vermilion City, you can take on Mina's newly powered-up team. She'll still give you a Bottle Cap each time you defeat her.

⭐ Battle!

Pokémon Trainer Mina:

Mina's added an Alolan Ninetales to her lineup since you've entered the Hall of Fame, and her Jigglypuff has evolved! But Poison- and Steel-type moves will still win the day against this Fairy-type team.

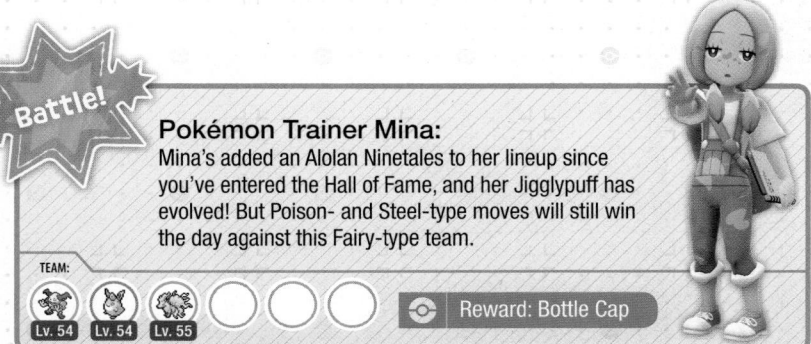

TEAM: Lv. 54 · Lv. 54 · Lv. 55

🔴 Reward: Bottle Cap

Encounter New Pokémon Midair!

If you let certain Pokémon out of their Poké Ball, you can ride on them as they fly around (p. 145). After becoming Champion, you'll find you can now encounter Pokémon midair this way! Most of these are common Pokémon, but you can encounter some particularly rare species if you find unusual encounters after building up your Catch Combos (p. 117)!

◎ frequent   ○ common   △ average   ☆ rare   ★ almost never   — does not appear

Routes 1, 2, 5, 6, 7, 8, 11, 12, 13, 14, 15, 16, 17, 18, 19, 20, 21, 24, and 25

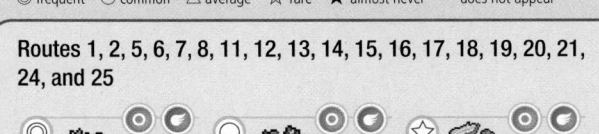

Pidgey · Pidgeotto · Pidgeot

Routes 3, 4, 9, 10, 22, and 23

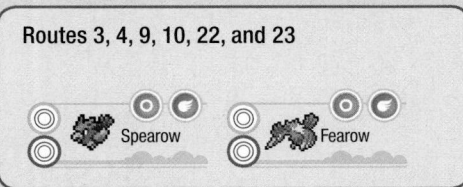

Spearow · Fearow

Once you've built up a good Catch Combo, you'll find that you start stumbling across Charizard and Dragonite pretty regularly. In stark contrast, the trio of winged Legendary Pokémon will remain elusive no matter how impressive your Catch Combo gets! Buckle down for a long search if you've got your heart set on a midair encounter with these rare Pokémon.

Unusual encounters in all of the above locations

Charizard

Dragonite

Unusual encounters in all of the above locations once you've caught Articuno, Zapdos, and Moltres in the Seafoam Islands, the Power Plant, and Victory Road

Articuno

Zapdos

Moltres

Cerulean Cave

Getting Around

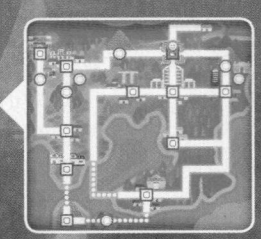

1F

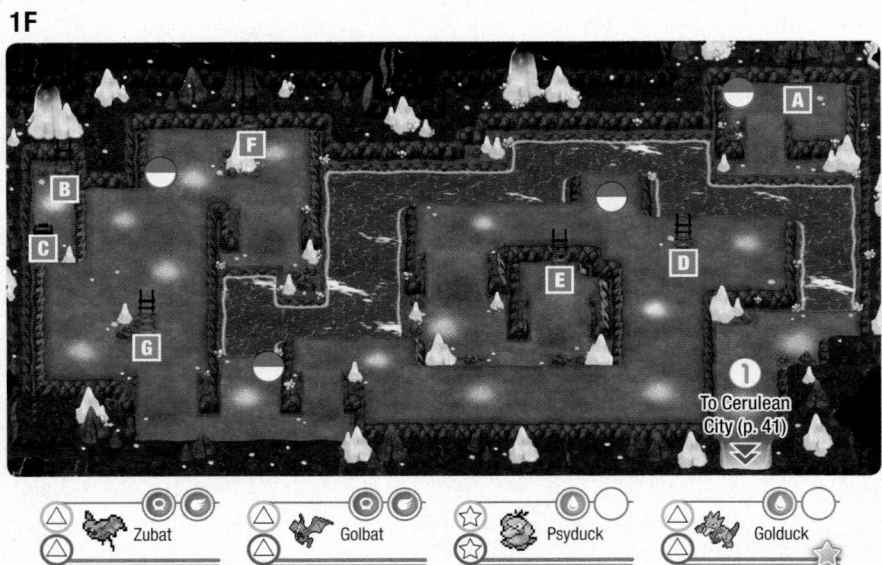

1
To Cerulean City (p. 41)

△△ Zubat	△△ Golbat	☆☆ Psyduck	△△ Golduck
△△ Geodude	△△ Graveler	☆☆ Rhydon	◎◎ Poliwag
△△ Poliwhirl	★★ Poliwrath	◎◎ Magikarp	

2F

☆☆ Zubat	◎◎ Golbat	☆☆ Geodude	Graveler
△△ Rhydon	△△ Chansey		

◎ frequent ○ common
△ average ☆ rare
★ almost never
— does not appear

All Floors

△△ Lickitung	
△△ Rhyhorn	
☆☆ Ditto	

Unusual Encounters — Snorlax

Items

1F
- ☑ PP Max
- ☑ Max Revive
- ☑ Max Repel
- ☑ Full Heal

2F
- ☑ Full Restore
- ☑ Max Revive
- ☐ Ultra Ball ×5
- ☑ Max Lure
- ☑ Rare Candy

B1F
- ☑ Escape Rope
- ☑ Full Restore
- ☑ Max Elixir

Hidden Items

1F
- ☑ Full Restore
- ☑ Rare Candy

2F
- ☑ Dome Fossil*
- ☑ Golden Nanab Berry*
- ☑ Golden Pinap Berry*
- ☑ Golden Razz Berry*
- ☑ Great Ball*
- ☑ Helix Fossil*
- ☑ Master Ball*
- ☑ Max Revive*
- ☑ Old Amber*
- ☑ Poké Ball*
- ☑ Ultra Ball*
- ☑ Ultra Ball ×10*

B1F
- ☑ Dome Fossil*
- ☑ Helix Fossil*
- ☑ Max Revive
- ☑ Old Amber*
- ☑ PP Max

*You have a chance to randomly find one of these items at each spot.

TIP Cerulean Cave is full of ultra-rare items that randomly reappear from time to time. Mark on the map where you've found hidden items, and keep coming back to try for that Fossil or Golden Berry you've been after. If you're really lucky, you might even find some more of Silph Co.'s prized Master Balls! How did they get here?

 Zubat
 Golbat
 Psyduck
 Golduck
 Geodude
 Graveler
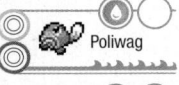 Rhydon
 Poliwag
 Poliwhirl
 Poliwrath
Magikarp

Mewtwo

1 The Coach Trainer blocking the entrance to the cave will let you in now that you're a Pokémon League Champion! A big challenge waits for you in the Cerulean Cave, so take the chance to battle the Coach Trainer for some more Exp. Points!

2 Navigate the cave and catch some of its powerful Pokémon. If you go down ladder **C** and explore B1F, you'll eventually reach the Legendary Pokémon Mewtwo. It's time to battle and catch it, so make sure you've got some Ultra Balls ready if you've already used your Master Ball!

Coach Battle!

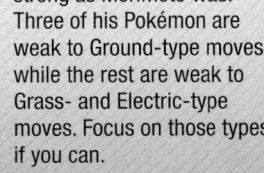

Coach Trainer Harjit

Harjit is tough but not as strong as Morimoto was. Three of his Pokémon are weak to Ground-type moves, while the rest are weak to Grass- and Electric-type moves. Focus on those types if you can.

TEAM:
 Lv. 52 Lv. 52 Lv. 52 Lv. 52 Lv. 52

🔄 Reward: TM60 Megahorn

Mewtwo

Mewtwo is a powerful Psychic-type Legendary Pokémon, but even Legendary Pokémon have weaknesses! Since its main damage-dealing move is Psychic type, try sending in a Dark-type Pokémon, such as Alolan Raticate or Alolan Persian. Their immunity to Psychic-type moves will be a big help! If you don't have either of them on your team, try focusing on Bug-, Ghost-, or Dark-type moves. Mewtwo tends to use Recover when its HP is low, so consider using an HP-sapping move, such as Toxic, so you don't end up running out of time! If you miss your chance to catch Mewtwo, you'll need to enter the Hall of Fame again for it to reappear, so make sure you're ready.

Mewtwo
Lv. 70
WEAK AGAINST:

Legendary Battle!

WALKTHROUGH

3 After you've caught Mewtwo, head outside and you'll bump into your rival! He'll mention a female Trainer who was also after this powerful Pokémon, and he'll give you some items he won't be needing anymore.

Reward: Escape Rope ×3

Following your rival's advice, return to the spot where you battled Mewtwo. This time, you'll run into Green, a skilled Trainer who also set out on an adventure with Red and Blue a while back! Battle her to get Mewtwo's Mega Stones.

TIP Itching for a rematch with Green? She will reappear near the fountain in Cerulean City whenever you enter the Hall of Fame again!

Battle!

Pokémon Trainer Green

Green might come off a bit strange at first, but she's no pushover! She's a Trainer who's just as accomplished as Red and Blue! Her Pokémon don't share many weaknesses, but Ninetales and Gengar are both weak to Ground-type moves. Green's Blastoise will Mega Evolve, so bring a Pokémon with a powerful Grass- or Electric-type move to help in your battle against it. Mega Venusaur would be a great option to handle a troublesome Mega Blastoise!

Reward: Mewtwonite X, Mewtwonite Y, Poké Ball ×5

Clefable Lv. 66 — WEAK AGAINST:
Gengar Lv. 66 — WEAK AGAINST:
Kangaskhan Lv. 66 — WEAK AGAINST:
Victreebel Lv. 66 — WEAK AGAINST:
Ninetales Lv. 66 — WEAK AGAINST:
Mega Blastoise Lv. 68 — WEAK AGAINST:

Rematches

♛ Now that you've become a Champion, it seems like everyone wants a piece of you! Visit any of the Gyms across Kanto to have a rematch with its Gym Leader once per day!

...Please allow me the privilege of facing you in battle once again!

Gym Leader Brock

All of his team, except for Aerodactyl, take four times the damage from Grass-type moves. This is a great time to use Mega Drain!

Lv. 56 Lv. 56 Lv. 56 Lv. 56 Lv. 57

Gym Leader Misty

Misty's team shares common weaknesses to Grass- and Electric-type moves. Electric is the better choice between the two, as Gyarados takes four times the damage from it. Know that Vaporeon is a Pokémon with a lot of HP. If it's giving you trouble, try sapping its strength with Leech Seed or Toxic!

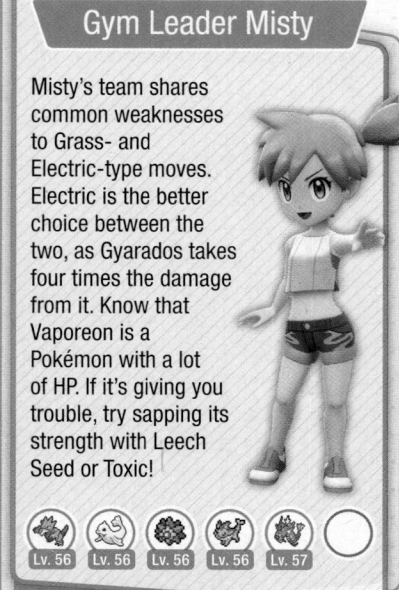

Lv. 56 Lv. 56 Lv. 56 Lv. 56 Lv. 57

Gym Leader Lt. Surge

Lt. Surge's Electric-type team may not have a lot of weaknesses, but you've got the one move that can pretty much kick them all out without any trouble—Earthquake!

Lv. 56 · Lv. 56 · Lv. 56 · Lv. 56 · Lv. 57

Gym Leader Erika

Erika's Pokémon are all weak to Fire-, Ice-, and Flying-type moves, giving you some options on what Pokémon to bring. Parasect takes four times the damage from Fire- and Flying-type moves, making those a bit of a better choice.

Lv. 56 · Lv. 56 · Lv. 56 · Lv. 56 · Lv. 57

Gym Leader Koga

Koga battles just as sneakily as he did in your first battle with him. He uses Toxic and then stalls to let the move drain your Pokémon team's HP. Remember to use Psychic- or Ground-type moves.

Lv. 56 · Lv. 56 · Lv. 56 · Lv. 56 · Lv. 57

Gym Leader Sabrina

If you've managed to get an Alolan Raticate, Alolan Persian, or Alolan Muk, their immunity to Psychic-type moves makes this battle a lot easier. Watch out for Hypnosis!

Lv. 56 · Lv. 56 · Lv. 56 · Lv. 56 · Lv. 57

Gym Leader Blaine

All of Blaine's Pokémon are pure Fire type, so it doesn't matter whether you prefer to use Water-, Ground-, or Rock-type moves to deal supereffective damage. Remember that Fire-type moves may burn your Pokémon.

Lv. 56 · Lv. 56 · Lv. 56 · Lv. 56 · Lv. 57

Gym Leader Blue

Blue's a lot stronger than the other Gym Leaders and uses a varied team with few common weaknesses, aside from Charizard, Gyarados, and Aerodactyl, which are all weak to Electric-type moves. Blue's Charizard will Mega Evolve into Mega Charizard Y, so make sure you're prepared to handle that.

Lv. 66 · Lv. 66 · Lv. 66 · Lv. 66 · Lv. 66 · Lv. 68

You can also return to the Pokémon League and have a rematch with the Elite Four! But watch out—they've gotten stronger since the first time you battled them.

Elite Four Lorelei

Grass-, Electric-, Fighting-, and Rock-type moves will be super effective against most of Lorelei's Pokémon, so bring along Pokémon with moves of these types! Alolan Sandslash and Jynx are best dealt with using strong Fire-type moves like Fire Blast or Flamethrower.

Dewgong
Lv. 61
WEAK AGAINST:

Jynx
Lv. 61
WEAK AGAINST:

Cloyster
Lv. 61
WEAK AGAINST:

Slowbro
Lv. 61
WEAK AGAINST:

Alolan Sandslash
Lv. 61
WEAK AGAINST:
4x

Lapras
Lv. 62
WEAK AGAINST:

Elite Four Bruno

Since Bruno still uses both Fighting- and Rock-type Pokémon, there isn't one type that can easily be super effective during this battle. Focus on Water- or Grass-type moves for the Rock-type Pokémon and Flying-, Psychic- and Fairy-type moves for the rest.

Onix Lv. 62

Hitmonlee Lv. 62

Hitmonchan Lv. 62

Poliwrath Lv. 62

Alolan Golem Lv. 62

Machamp Lv. 63

WEAK AGAINST:

Elite Four Agatha

Since Agatha's Pokémon are all weak to either Ground- or Psychic-type moves, use heavy damage dealers, such as Earthquake and Psychic, and you'll take down this team without too much trouble.

Arbok Lv. 63

Gengar Lv. 63

Golbat Lv. 63

Weezing Lv. 63

Alolan Marowak Lv. 63

Gengar Lv. 64

WEAK AGAINST:

Elite Four Lance

Lance's Seadra, Gyarados, and Aerodactyl will all take supereffective damage from Electric-type moves. His Dragonite and Alolan Exeggutor will take four times the damage from Ice-type moves. Lance will Mega Evolve Charizard into Mega Charizard X, turning it into a Fire- and Dragon-type Pokémon!

Seadra Lv. 64

Aerodactyl Lv. 64

Gyarados Lv. 64

Alolan Exeggutor Lv. 64

Mega Charizard X

Lv. 64

Dragonite Lv. 65

WEAK AGAINST:

Your rival's become stronger since you last saw him, too! Make sure your team is healed up with items before taking him on.

Champion Battle

Your rival's team is made up of the same Pokémon as the first time you battled him at the Pokémon League, but he's been raising his Pokémon so they've all gained 10 levels!

Mega Pidgeot

Lv. 66

Vileplume Lv. 66

Marowak Lv. 66

Rapidash Lv. 66

Slowbro Lv. 66

WEAK AGAINST:

Jolteon Lv. 67

WEAK AGAINST:

If you started with Pikachu

Raichu Lv. 67

WEAK AGAINST:

If you started with Eevee

WALKTHROUGH

Trainer
Handbook

Catching Wild Pokémon

Pokémon run wild almost everywhere in the Kanto region: popping out of the grass, swooping overhead, creeping around caves, and even splashing in the sea. You're going to want to catch plenty of them to obtain great specimens (p. 117), fill your Pokédex (p. 119), and collect Candies to help your favorite Pokémon grow (p. 126).

Tall grass

Pokémon commonly appear in the tall grass growing along many routes.

Caves and dungeons

Pokémon also like to haunt caves, abandoned buildings, and other uninhabited places.

Water surface

Once you can travel across the water (p. 72), you'll find it can be teeming with Pokémon!

Midair

After you've entered the Hall of Fame, you'll be able to encounter Pokémon flying above each route (p. 145).

 TIP You'll find that most Pokémon appear in the tall grass—but they don't always stay there! They can wander out of the grass and sometimes even follow you into towns.

Attracting rare Pokémon and decreasing encounters

Sometimes you may want to search for Pokémon that usually have only a small chance of appearing. At other times, maybe you'll want to avoid encounters entirely so you can hurry to the next town. There are items you can buy at Poké Marts or find in the field that will help you in these situations.

Items
Repel This item repels wild Pokémon so they'll disappear for a short time. Buy it at Poké Marts once you've earned one Gym Badge.
Super Repel This item repels wild Pokémon for a longer time than a normal Repel. Buy it at Poké Marts once you've earned three Gym Badges.
Max Repel This item repels wild Pokémon for longer than even a Super Repel. Buy it at Poké Marts once you've earned five Gym Badges.

Items
Lure This item increases your chances of encountering rare Pokémon for a short time. Buy it at Poké Marts once you've earned two Gym Badges.
Super Lure This item increases your chances of encountering rare Pokémon for a longer time than a normal Lure. Buy it at Poké Marts once you've earned four Gym Badges.
Max Lure This item increases your chances of encountering rare Pokémon for longer than even a Super Lure. Buy it at Poké Marts once you've earned six Gym Badges.

Becoming a Catching Pro

Once you do encounter a wild Pokémon, you've got to actually catch it! There are a number of things that'll help you be successful when it comes to catching. Let's start with the rings you see on-screen in an encounter with a wild Pokémon.

Green Ring	Yellow Ring	Orange Ring	Red Ring

Easy to catch	Normal chance to catch	Hard to catch	Very hard to catch

◄ Easier   Harder ►

The color of the ring indicates how easy it will be to catch the Pokémon. Some species are simply harder to catch than others, but there are a few things you can do to boost your chances. You can change the ring color by using a different kind of Poké Ball—or by feeding certain Berries to your target. There'll be more about those Berries on the next page.

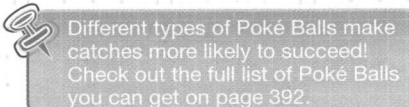

Different types of Poké Balls make catches more likely to succeed! Check out the full list of Poké Balls you can get on page 392.

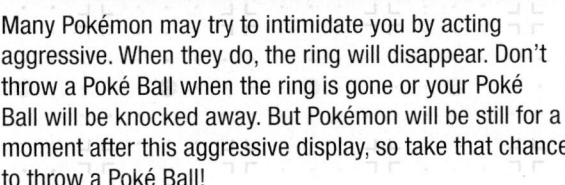

Many Pokémon may try to intimidate you by acting aggressive. When they do, the ring will disappear. Don't throw a Poké Ball when the ring is gone or your Poké Ball will be knocked away. But Pokémon will be still for a moment after this aggressive display, so take that chance to throw a Poké Ball!

Pokémon may also jump or fly around, making it harder for you to aim at them. But each species will tend to move in certain patterns, moving and then resting in turn. Watch them carefully to learn these patterns and throw your Poké Balls at the right time!

Certain rare Pokémon may also have a special aura. When this aura is activated, it will nullify the effects of any Berries you have used so far. After the aura goes away, these Berries' effects won't return but you can start using new Berries again.

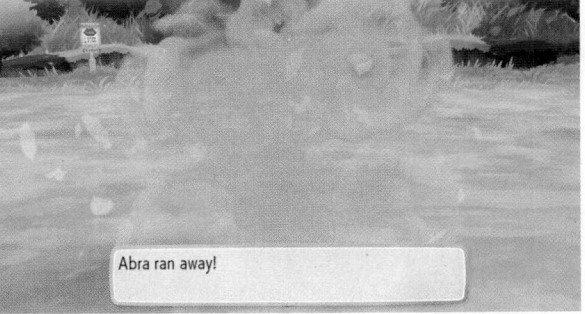

Abra ran away!

Wild Pokémon may flee if you try to catch them and fail. If they cry out without acting aggressively, they're about to flee! You'll have one last chance to get 'em before they're gone—which is especially important if you're working on a Catch Combo (p. 117)!

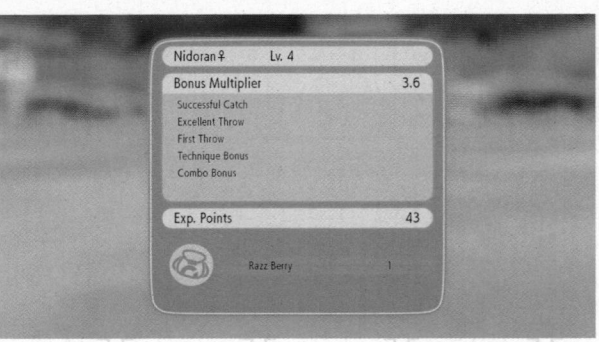

Nidoran♀	Lv. 4
Bonus Multiplier	3.6
Successful Catch	
Excellent Throw	
First Throw	
Technique Bonus	
Combo Bonus	
Exp. Points	43
Razz Berry	1

When you make a catch, you'll get more than just a new Pokémon. The Pokémon in your party will all gain Exp. Points, and you'll have a chance of getting Berries or Candies. You can maximize these rewards by earning bonuses! With bonuses, you can increase the Exp. Points your Pokémon receive by a lot—and improve your chances of getting items, too!

Bonus name	How to trigger
New Pokémon	Catch a new species of Pokémon for the first time
Successful Catch	Catch a species of Pokémon you have caught before
Nice Throw	Throw a Poké Ball through a colored ring when it's about 50–75% its max size
Great Throw	Throw a Poké Ball through a colored ring when it's about 25–50% its max size
Excellent Throw	Throw a Poké Ball through a colored ring when it's less than 25% its max size
First Throw	Catch a Pokémon with the first Poké Ball you throw
Synchronized Bonus	Catch a Pokémon by syncing with a Support Trainer (p. 18)
Technique Bonus	Catch a Pokémon by swinging a Joy-Con detached from your system or a Poké Ball Plus (p. 17)—this bonus cannot be triggered when syncing with a Support Trainer
Combo Bonus	Catch the same species multiple times in a row (p. 117)
Size Bonus	Catch a Pokémon that's unusually large or small (p. 117)

Maximize Your Chance for Success!

Some bonuses will help you catch Pokémon as well! Getting a Nice Throw, a Great Throw, or an Excellent Throw will make your catch more likely to succeed. And getting a Synchronized Bonus will boost your chance of catching a Pokémon about as much as using a Silver Razz Berry!

Berries or Candies

You may get either Berries or Candies (p. 126) after catching a Pokémon. You'll be more likely to get Berries at first, but once you've caught a good number of Pokémon, you might well earn Candies instead. You can even get rare XL or species-specific Candies if you play your cards right. Keep earning those bonuses, and use Pinap Berries to up your chances of getting items!

Use Berries wisely

There are three kinds of Berries you can use: Razz Berries, Nanab Berries, and Pinap Berries. Each comes in three varieties: normal, silver, and golden. Silver Berries will have a greater effect than normal Berries, and golden Berries will be more effective than silver ones. Collect Berries from your encounters, or find them in the field, and use them well to seize success and get rewards!

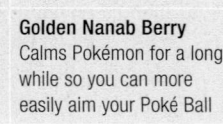 You can get Berries from the Pokémon that travels with you, too! Learn more on page 144.

Berries	Berries	Berries
Razz Berry Makes a catch a little more likely to succeed	**Nanab Berry** Calms Pokémon for a short time so you can more easily aim your Poké Ball	**Pinap Berry** Makes it a little more likely you'll get items after a catch
Silver Razz Berry Makes a catch much more likely to succeed	**Silver Nanab Berry** Calms Pokémon for a while so you can more easily aim your Poké Ball	**Silver Pinap Berry** Makes it much more likely you'll get items after a catch
Golden Razz Berry Makes a catch way more likely to succeed	**Golden Nanab Berry** Calms Pokémon for a long while so you can more easily aim your Poké Ball	**Golden Pinap Berry** Makes it way more likely you'll get items after a catch

Catch Combos

You can build up a Catch Combo by catching the same species over and over as you travel the region. This may help you get more Candies, and a combo also gives you some great bonuses! A higher Catch Combo makes you more likely to encounter extra-small or extra-large Pokémon, Pokémon with great individual strengths (p. 125), or even Shiny Pokémon!

Shiny Pokémon

Shiny Pokémon are incredibly rare Pokémon that are differently colored. They're easier to find when you build up a Catch Combo, and you can also increase your chances by using Lures or by getting a Shiny Charm after completing your Pokédex (p. 119)! You can recognize Shiny Pokémon in the field by their different coloring and the sparkles around them when they appear!

Size differences

Pokémon of the same species can come in different heights and weights, just like creatures in the real world! You won't know exactly how large or heavy a Pokémon is until you catch it, but if a Pokémon appears in the field with a red glow, it'll be far larger than normal, and if it has a blue glow, it'll be pretty tiny!

Finding large or small Pokémon can be tough if you're just waiting around, but you're far more likely to find one if you've built up a large Catch Combo. Try it out if you want to show off who caught the biggest Onix or the tiniest Tentacool!

Great stats

An average Jigglypuff caught the normal way

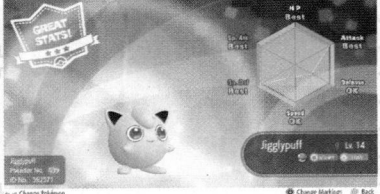

An awesome Jigglypuff caught with a high Catch Combo

Pokémon of the same species can have different stats because of their individual strengths (p. 125). Normally it's completely random what a Pokémon's individual strengths will be when you catch it. However, the longer a Catch Combo goes on, the better the chance you'll encounter a Pokémon of that species with at least one, two, three, or even four of their individual strengths maxed out!

Keep That Combo Going

The only way to build up a Catch Combo is to repeatedly catch the same species of Pokémon. Once you catch a different species, your combo will end. It will also end if the Pokémon you've encountered runs away from you or if you turn off your game. Charge up your system and settle in for a catching spree!

Unusual Encounters

The longer you continue a Catch Combo, the more likely you are to keep encountering the same species of Pokémon. But something curious will also happen: you may start to encounter Pokémon that you'd never otherwise encounter! These are the Pokémon you see listed as unusual encounters on maps, like the Bulbasaur in Viridian Forest. These unusual encounters are the only way to encounter some species, which is one more reason to give Catch Combos a try!

Your Pokémon Box

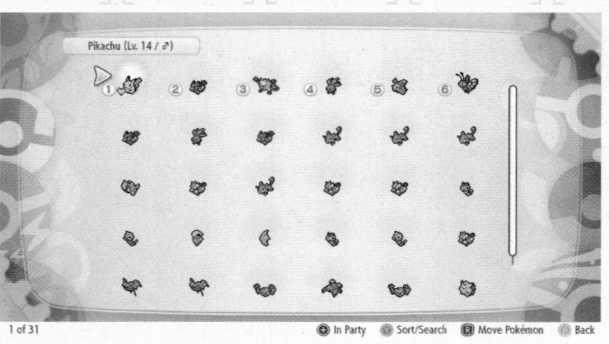

While you can only have up to six Pokémon in your party, any other Pokémon you catch will still travel with you—stored safely in your Pokémon Box. To open your Pokémon Box, just choose it from inside your Bag, or you can also press Ⓨ when you're on the Party screen. As you'll see below, it has a lot of useful functions in addition to storing your Pokémon!

Sorting and searching in your Pokémon Box

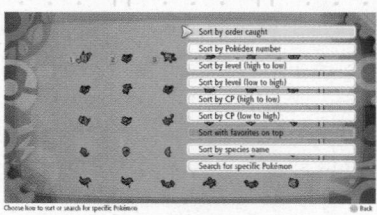
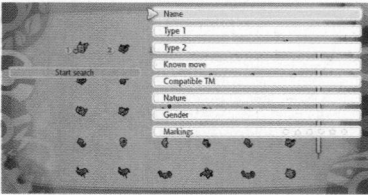

Your Pokémon Box can hold up to a thousand Pokémon, and you'll likely be catching many new friends on your journey across Kanto. The sorting and searching functions of the Pokémon Box make sure you're always able to find the right Pokémon to add to your party for an upcoming battle. Just press Ⓨ to bring up the sort/search list. You can choose all kinds of ways to sort the Pokémon in your Box, such as by catch order, by level, or alphabetically. If you want to find a specific Pokémon, you can search for it by name, types, moves it knows, or even the TMs it can learn moves from, among other search options.

 TIP Favorite a Pokémon to find it in your Pokémon Box! You can do this by choosing Change markings when you've selected a Pokémon.

Comparing Pokémon

Remember that no two Pokémon are exactly alike, even those of the same species and level! When trying to compare one Pokémon's strengths to another's, you can check the Pokémon's stat graphs, which you can learn more about on page 124. But a quick way to estimate how a Pokémon may measure up in battle is to look at its Combat Power (or CP for short). A Pokémon with higher CP will tend to do better in battle, so if you have two of the same Pokémon, you can keep the one with higher CP and send the other to Professor Oak.

Sending Pokémon to Professor Oak

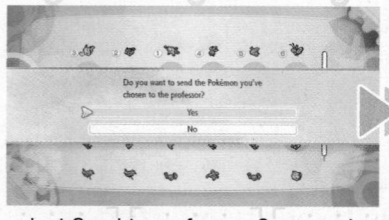
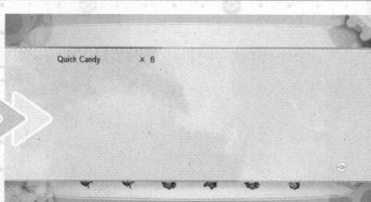

When you've got two or more of the same species of Pokémon sitting in your Box, try sending some of them to the professor for his research. He'll reward you with Candies that can power up your Pokémon in return. Choose a Pokémon from your Pokémon Box to get started, and then select Send to professor. Once you've started this process, you can keep selecting more Pokémon with Ⓐ. When you're done making selections, press Ⓨ to send them. It's that easy! Learn more about what kind of Candies you can get and what you can do with them on page 126.

 TIP You can select up to 30 Pokémon to send at one time—though you can't send Pokémon in your party or ones that you've marked as favorites!

TRAINER HANDBOOK

The Pokédex

Your Pokédex is the ultimate high-tech encyclopedia for learning all sorts of neat things about Pokémon in the Kanto region. It can be accessed easily from the main menu. While some information on a Pokémon can be viewed just by seeing that Pokémon in the wild or in a Trainer battle, you'll only be able to gather all the data on a Pokémon by catching it or trading for it. Some different forms of Pokémon also have different Pokédex data as well, so keep an eye out, and do your best to fill your Pokédex with every species and form of Pokémon to be found!

Sorting your Pokédex

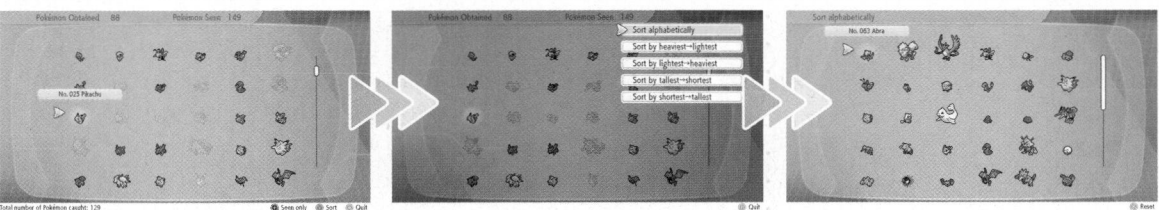

Once your Pokédex starts to fill up with the many Pokémon you discover on your adventure, it may be hard to find the one you're looking for. Or maybe you want to see which Pokémon are the biggest or heaviest. By pressing Ⓨ, you can bring up the Sort menu, allowing you to choose how Pokémon you've obtained appear: in alphabetical order, heaviest to lightest, shortest to tallest, and more. You should have no problem finding the Pokémon you're looking for!

Learn about Pokémon with your Pokédex

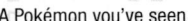

A Pokémon you've seen

A Pokémon you've caught

By choosing a Pokémon in your Pokédex, you'll be able to view its data. This includes helpful things such as the Pokémon's type. But the Pokédex also remembers fun things, such as the number of times you've caught that species of Pokémon, the lightest and heaviest you've caught of that species, and the shortest and tallest caught, too! You can also view things such as different forms, including regional variants, male and female forms, and even Shiny versions, if you've managed to obtain them. Try becoming the very best Trainer, and complete your Pokédex like no one ever has before!

Pokémon habitats

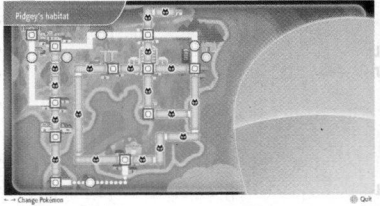
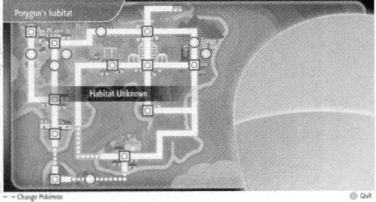

Did you see a Pokémon you liked in a Trainer battle or in the wild, only to have it escape on you? Never fear, Trainer! You can find that Pokémon in your Pokédex and choose the Check habitat option to see where in the Kanto region that Pokémon can be found! Remember, though, that even if you go to a Pokémon's habitat, it might take a while to find it. Some Pokémon are rarer than others, after all! Certain Pokémon may even have no known habitat, because that's how rare they are! You might need to use Evolution or other means to get these Pokémon. To learn more about how to obtain each Pokémon, check the Kanto Region Pokédex starting on page 161.

Complete Your Pokédex for Rewards

Completing your Pokédex will give you more than just a sense of satisfaction. If you visit the director of the GAME FREAK Development Office in the Celadon Condominiums, you can get a diploma in recognition of all your hard work. He'll also give you a Shiny Charm, which increases your chances of finding Shiny Pokémon (p. 107)!

Filling Your Pokédex

In your adventure across Kanto, you'll be able to make good progress on your Pokédex by catching every wild species you encounter. But you won't get them all that way. For example, you can only fill out certain pages in your Pokédex by evolving Pokémon to reach the next species in their Evolution chain. The entries in the Kanto Region Pokédex (p. 161) will help you fill in every last page of your Pokédex in your game, but here are some of the basics you should know as you work on completing your very own Pokédex!

Some Pokémon evolve by leveling up

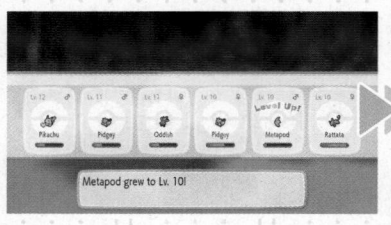

Metapod grew to Lv. 10!

Congratulations! Your Metapod evolved into Butterfree!

The most common way for a Pokémon to evolve is by leveling up. When a Pokémon that can evolve this way has reached a certain level, it will start to evolve. If you don't want it to evolve just yet, you can stop it at this time by pressing Ⓑ. But know that it will continue to try to evolve each time it levels up from that point on.

Some Pokémon evolve with items

Certain Pokémon can evolve at any level if they have special stones used on them. While you may want to evolve these Pokémon right away, they might not learn certain new moves by leveling up after they've evolved. Make sure your Pokémon have learned any moves you want before using an Evolution stone on them. Learn how to get these stones from the list of items that begins on page 382.

Evolution stones		Pokémon that evolve with them	Evolution stones		Pokémon that evolve with them
	Moon Stone	Nidorina, Nidorino, Clefairy, Jigglypuff		Thunder Stone	Pikachu, Eevee
	Fire Stone	Vulpix, Growlithe, Eevee		Leaf Stone	Gloom, Weepinbell, Exeggcute
	Water Stone	Poliwhirl, Shellder, Staryu, Eevee		Ice Stone	Alolan Sandshrew, Alolan Vulpix

 TIP Though your partner Pokémon is compatible with some Evolution stones, you won't be able to evolve it!

Some Pokémon evolve when traded

Kadabra, Machoke, Graveler, and Haunter will only evolve when they're traded to another player. Fortunately, these four Pokémon can be evolved this way at any level. Ask another player to help you evolve these Pokémon by trading the Pokémon to them and then back again, and be sure to return the favor, too!

Trading Pokémon

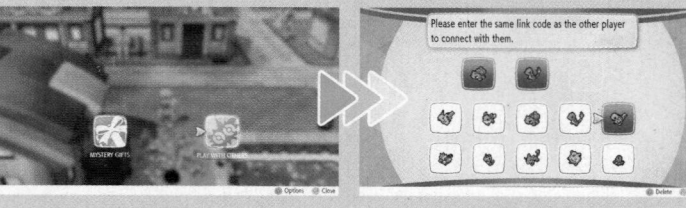

Please enter the same link code as the other player to connect with them.

Once you've delivered Oak's Parcel (p. 31), you'll be able to select the communication icon on the main menu. By choosing Communicate and then Play with Others, you'll be able to choose to connect with either someone nearby or someone far away. You and the other player will need to enter the same link code (made of three pictures of Pokémon) to begin the trade. Then each of you will have to choose one of your Pokémon to trade with the other. Trading is a great way to evolve and get certain Pokémon. Plus, Pokémon caught by another Trainer and received from a trade also gain Exp. Points faster than Pokémon you caught yourself! But be careful—traded Pokémon won't always listen to you at higher levels if you don't have enough Gym Badges!

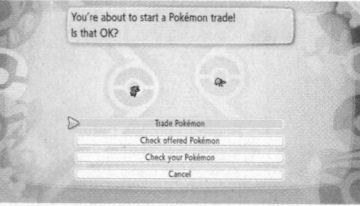

You're about to start a Pokémon trade! Is that OK?

Get exclusive Pokémon by trading

Some Pokémon may also be exclusive to one version of the game or another, as you learned back on page 20. That means you'll need to trade with players who have the other version of the game in order to fill your Pokédex with Pokémon such as Bellsprout, Oddish, and more.

TRAINER HANDBOOK

Rare Pokémon to Obtain

Still other Pokémon can only be gotten in more unusual ways. Fossils, for example, can be hard to come by, but they can be restored into Pokémon you would never encounter in the wild otherwise. Check out the Items list starting on page 389 to find out how to find these Fossils.

You can also find Alolan regional variants of some Pokémon—Pokémon originally discovered in the Kanto region that have adapted to live in the distant tropical region of Alola. You don't need to catch these forms to complete your Pokédex, but it's fun to explore their differences. They have different types and may learn different moves than their more common counterparts. Many of them can also evolve, so turn to the Kanto Region Pokédex (p. 161) to see how these regional variants may surprise you—as well as how to get each one!

Omanyte, Aerodactyl, and Kabuto

Alolan Sandshrew

Alolan Vulpix

> **TIP** There are also Pokémon that only appear in the wild as unusual encounters (p. 117), such as Hitmonlee, Hitmonchan, Lapras, and Porygon.

Legendary Pokémon

Some Pokémon are so strong and rare that they are the stuff of legends. And some of these Pokémon can only be caught once, but any of them would make a powerful ally. Try to catch all of these Legendary Pokémon to complete your Pokédex!

Articuno, Zapdos, Moltres, and Mewtwo

Mythical Pokémon

Mythical Pokémon are even harder to come by than Legendary Pokémon, so Professor Oak will still consider your Pokédex complete if you don't manage to get them. But even so, you can try to get these three Mythical Pokémon for your own satisfaction. They're also super strong, like Legendary Pokémon!

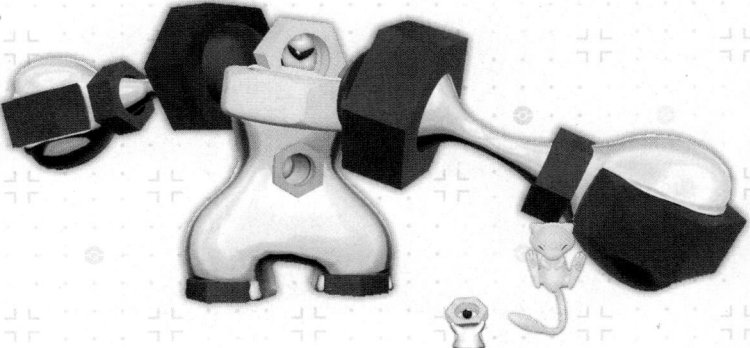

Melmetal, Meltan, and Mew

Building a Balanced Team

Every Pokémon has either one or two types that give it advantages and weaknesses against other Pokémon's attacks. Think of it like a game of rock-paper-scissors. Rock might beat scissors, but it loses to paper. The same is true in Pokémon battles. While Grass types are strong against Water-type moves, they're weak to Fire-type moves. You'll want to build a diverse team to cover all the bases!

The diagram on the right shows you how the Grass, Fire, and Water types stack up. They each deal supereffective damage against another type.

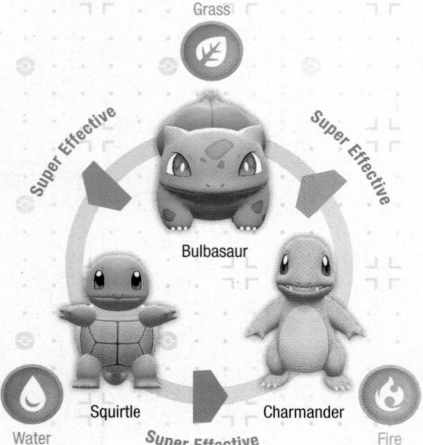

Now if we reverse the relationships, you'll see that each type is not very effective against the type that deals supereffective damage to it.

Pokémon Type Relationships

With 18 different types of Pokémon out there, remembering every type's weaknesses can be difficult at first—especially when a Pokémon has two types! Don't hesitate to use the type matchup chart on page 399 to refresh your memory whenever you need. It'll help you build teams that can dish out supereffective moves against whatever Pokémon your opponent sends out against you.

Sample Pokémon team

Let's take a look at how building a diverse team of Pokémon can aid you on your quest to be the best. There's no single perfect team, but to give you some ideas on how to make a balanced one, here's an example team you could put together pretty early in the game.

Pikachu

When putting together a team, you want to cover your weaknesses. Say you start out with Pikachu...

Bulbasaur

Pikachu is weak to Ground-type moves, so we might add Bulbasaur because Grass-type moves are super effective against Ground-type Pokémon.

Psyduck

To cover Bulbasaur's weakness to Fire-type moves, we add Psyduck. Its Water-type moves will work well on Fire-type Pokémon if they're sent out.

Pidgey

Psyduck is weak to Grass-type moves, though, so here comes Pidgey. Its Flying-type moves can easily take care of Grass-type Pokémon.

Geodude

Pidgey's weak to Ice- and Electric-type moves, though, so next we pull out a Geodude from our Pokémon Box. Its Rock- and Ground-type moves will handle Ice- and Electric-type Pokémon, respectively, with no problem!

Charmander

Lastly, we add a Charmander, because Geodude is weak to Ice- and Steel-type moves... but Charmander's Fire-type moves will fix that for us, since both Ice- and Steel-type Pokémon are weak to Fire-type moves!

TIP You may also want to have a mix of Pokémon that excel at physical moves and special moves (p. 131) so they can take on opponents with high Defense or Sp. Def!

Mastering Type Matchups

The amount of damage a move does depends on type matchups, so remember that weaknesses and resistances depend on the type of move used against your Pokémon, not the type of Pokémon dishing out the move. Think you're safe just because your Fire-type Charmander is facing the Normal-type Lickitung? Think again—because Lickitung can learn a Water-type move like Surf and wash your Charmander away! Let's look at how some moves would work in battle.

Fire-type Pokémon are weak to Water-type moves, so Charmander would take double damage from a move like Surf.

Attacks with Surf
= 200% Damage!

On the other hand, Shadow Ball, a Ghost-type move, would only deal the regular amount of damage, because Fire-type Pokémon aren't weak to or strong against Ghost-type moves.

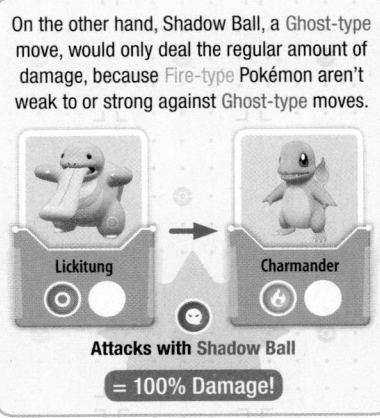

Attacks with Shadow Ball
= 100% Damage!

If Flamethrower is used on Charmander, it'll only do half damage, because Fire-type Pokémon are strong against Fire-type moves.

Attacks with Flamethrower
= 50% Damage!

What about Pokémon with two types? A Pokémon with two types has all the weaknesses and resistances of both types, meaning they can be doubly weak to some types, be doubly resistant to some types, or have the weaknesses and resistances of their two types cancel each other out so they receive the regular amount of damage.

Charizard is both Fire and Flying type. Fire types are weak to Rock-type moves, and so are Flying types, so if Charizard is hit with the Rock-type move Rock Slide, it'll take four times the usual amount of damage!

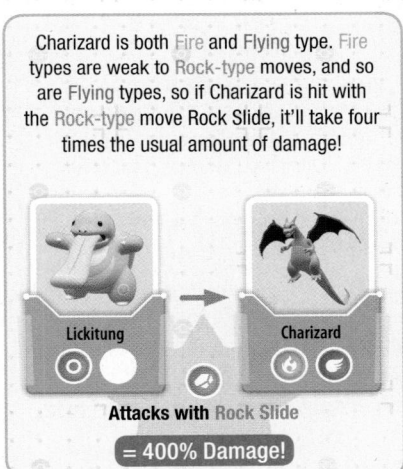

Attacks with Rock Slide
= 400% Damage!

Fire-type Pokémon are strong against Ice-type moves, but Flying-type Pokémon are weak to Ice-type moves. That means Charizard, which is Fire and Flying type, would simply take the regular amount of damage from being hit by an Ice-type move.

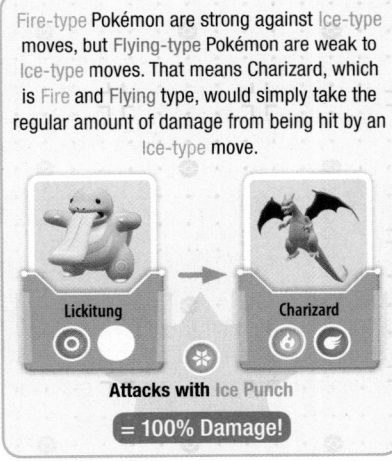

Attacks with Ice Punch
= 100% Damage!

If a Grass-type move is used on Charizard, Charizard will only receive a quarter of the usual damage, since both Fire-type Pokémon and Flying-type Pokémon resist Grass-type moves and Charizard is both of these types.

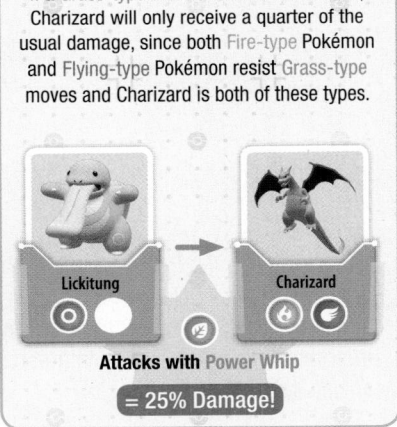

Attacks with Power Whip
= 25% Damage!

Some types of Pokémon also are completely immune to damage from certain types of moves. Ghost-type Pokémon have a well-known immunity to Normal- and Fighting-type moves, meaning that any Normal- or Fighting-type move used on a Gastly will deal no damage! To see all type matchups, including immunities like this one, check out the chart on page 399.

Same-Type Attack Bonus

In addition to weaknesses and resistances, moves also get powered up when they're used by Pokémon of the same type as the move. A Lickitung using Surf against a Rattata will deal regular damage, but a Squirtle using Surf against that Rattata will deal 1.5 times the regular amount of damage! This might make it tempting to use moves that match your Pokémon's type all the time,

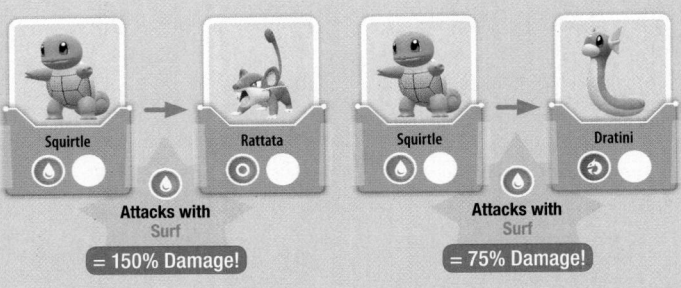

Attacks with Surf
= 150% Damage!

Attacks with Surf
= 75% Damage!

but that's not always the best choice. Remember that even Squirtle's boosted Surf will see its effectiveness cut in half against any Pokémon that's strong against Water-type moves, such as Dragon-type Pokémon. A great Trainer always picks their moves carefully!

Raising & Catching the Right Pokémon

There are over 150 species of Pokémon you can get and raise in *Pokémon: Let's Go, Pikachu!* and *Pokémon: Let's Go, Eevee!* So how do you decide which ones you want on your team? You may want to think about type matchups, as you learned about on the previous page, or the moves they can learn (p. 131). But you probably also want to consider their stats. They aren't set in stone—you can do a lot to affect the stats the Pokémon on your team end up with!

See a summary of your Pokémon

Start off by getting to know your Pokémon's summary screen. You can reach it by choosing Check summary when you've selected a Pokémon in your party or in the Pokémon Box in your Bag. You'll see information like how you met and more, but if you press Ⓐ, you can also see a good deal of useful battle information—including your Pokémon's stat graph and the moves it knows.

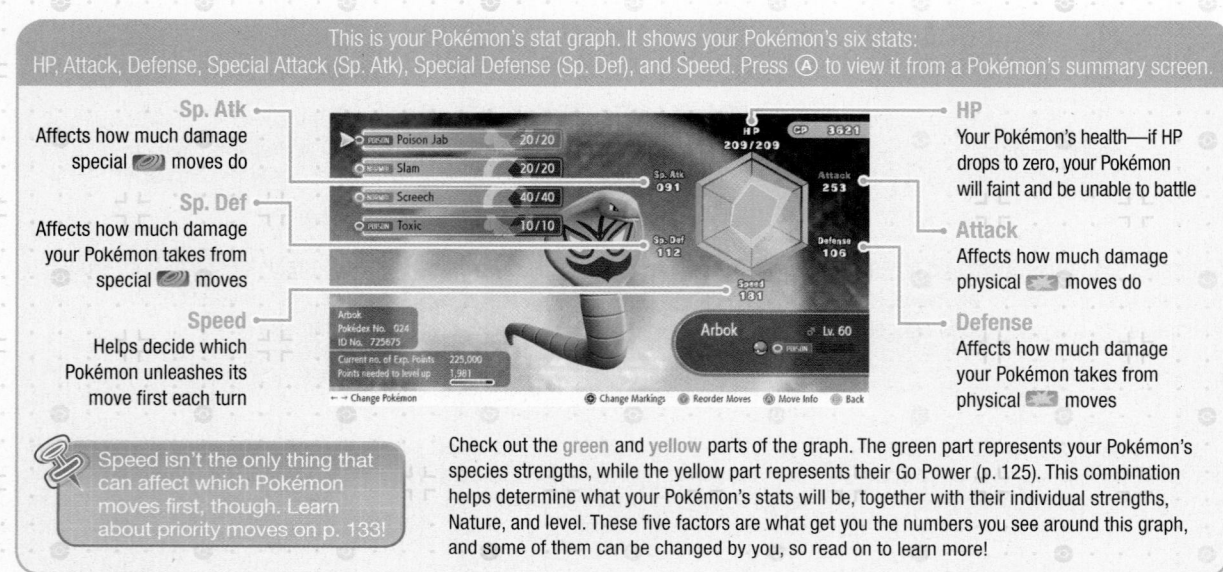

This is your Pokémon's stat graph. It shows your Pokémon's six stats: HP, Attack, Defense, Special Attack (Sp. Atk), Special Defense (Sp. Def), and Speed. Press Ⓐ to view it from a Pokémon's summary screen.

Sp. Atk
Affects how much damage special moves do

Sp. Def
Affects how much damage your Pokémon takes from special moves

Speed
Helps decide which Pokémon unleashes its move first each turn

Speed isn't the only thing that can affect which Pokémon moves first, though. Learn about priority moves on p. 133!

HP
Your Pokémon's health—if HP drops to zero, your Pokémon will faint and be unable to battle

Attack
Affects how much damage physical moves do

Defense
Affects how much damage your Pokémon takes from physical moves

Check out the green and yellow parts of the graph. The green part represents your Pokémon's species strengths, while the yellow part represents their Go Power (p. 125). This combination helps determine what your Pokémon's stats will be, together with their individual strengths, Nature, and level. These five factors are what get you the numbers you see around this graph, and some of them can be changed by you, so read on to learn more!

Species Strengths

Every species of Pokémon has its own strengths. Some are naturally speedy, while others have great defenses. You can't change these species strengths, so it's usually a good bet to start by choosing a Pokémon species that has good species strengths for the stats you're interested in. Check out the table below to get some idea of Kanto Pokémon that have great species strengths.

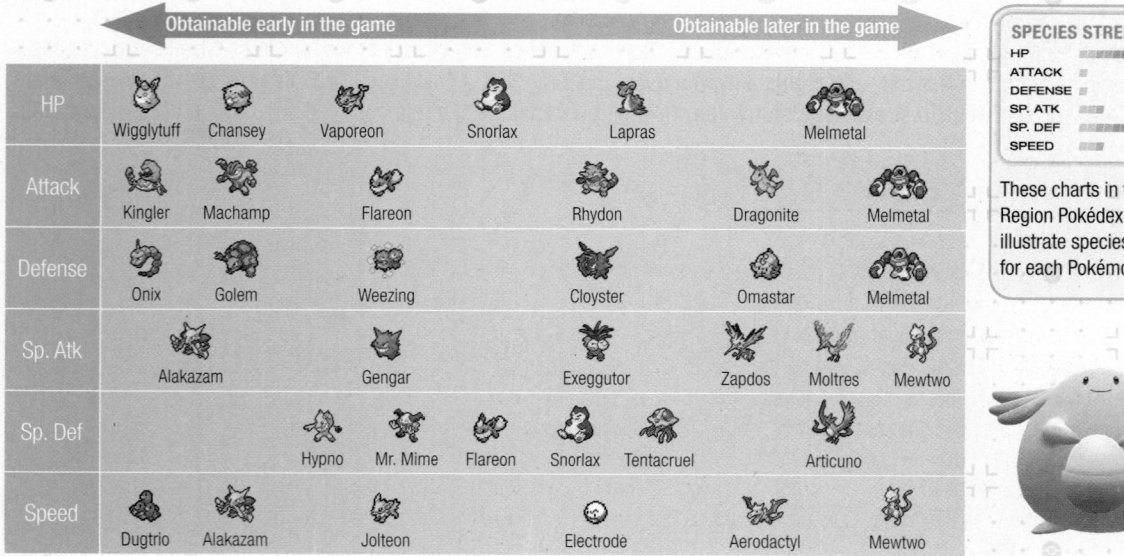

← Obtainable early in the game   Obtainable later in the game →

HP	Wigglytuff	Chansey	Vaporeon	Snorlax	Lapras		Melmetal
Attack	Kingler	Machamp	Flareon		Rhydon	Dragonite	Melmetal
Defense	Onix	Golem	Weezing		Cloyster	Omastar	Melmetal
Sp. Atk	Alakazam		Gengar		Exeggutor	Zapdos	Moltres	Mewtwo
Sp. Def		Hypno	Mr. Mime	Flareon	Snorlax	Tentacruel	Articuno	
Speed	Dugtrio	Alakazam	Jolteon		Electrode	Aerodactyl	Mewtwo

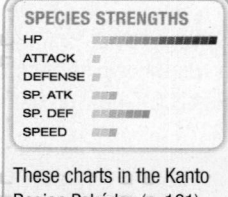

SPECIES STRENGTHS
HP
ATTACK
DEFENSE
SP. ATK
SP. DEF
SPEED

These charts in the Kanto Region Pokédex (p. 161) illustrate species strengths for each Pokémon species.

TRAINER HANDBOOK

Nature

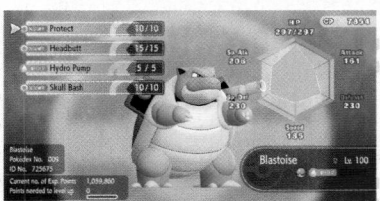

A Pokémon's Nature affects its stats as well. Most Natures help the development of one stat, so it can reach a higher max value at Lv. 100. But most Natures also hurt the development of another stat, so it will end up with a lower value. To find out which of your Pokémon's stats are affected by its Nature, check out that stat graph again.

The pink stat is getting helped by your Pokémon's Nature, while the blue stat is getting dragged down. If no stat names are colored, then your Pokémon has one of the few Natures that don't affect any stats. Natures can't be changed, so before training up a Pokémon you've caught, check if it's got the right Nature for you!

 Visit Madam Celadon for a leg up in catching Pokémon with the Nature you want! Turn to page 388 for more info.

Individual Strengths

Each Pokémon also has individual strengths. These numbers make every individual Pokémon a little different from others of its kind. Once you've got the Judge function (p. 52), press Ⓨ from your Pokémon's summary screen to check that Pokémon's individual strengths.

See the words below each stat name? If you see Best, then rest easy—your Pokémon has the best possible individual strength for that stat! And if it says Fantastic, that means that your Pokémon is just one step down from the best possible individual strength for that stat—not too shabby! Improve your chances of finding Pokémon with great individual strengths by mastering Catch Combos (p. 117), or max out the individual strengths of a Pokémon you've already caught through Hyper Training.

Hyper Training

It's possible to max out all of a Pokémon's individual strengths—but only if you raise that Pokémon to Lv. 100 and have entered the Hall of Fame. If you've done both, you can visit Mr. Hyper to have your Lv. 100 Pokémon undergo Hyper Training. You can find Mr. Hyper at the Pokémon Day Care on Route 5. Give him Bottle Caps or Gold Bottle Caps, and he'll take good care of you! You can get Bottle Caps for battling Mina once a day (p. 50). You have a small chance of finding Gold Bottle Caps in the Rocket Game Corner in Celadon City (p. 62).

Make your mark

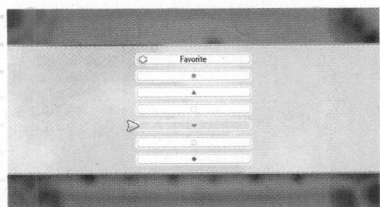

You can add markings to any of your Pokémon, helping you search for them later when you have lots of Pokémon in your Pokémon Box. Some people like to use these markings to identify Pokémon with really high or low individual strengths. You could also use these marks to be sure you don't accidentally send a great Pokémon to the professor! Press ⊕ from the Judge screen or when viewing your Pokémon's stat graph to add markings. You can also choose a Pokémon in your Pokémon Box, press Ⓐ, and select Change markings.

Go Power

With Go Power, you can raise the stats of any Pokémon you catch! If you like an adorable little Pokémon that doesn't usually pack much punch, use Go Power to give it a fighting chance in battle. You can raise each stat by as much as 200 points with Go Power, and you can max out Go Power for all six of your Pokémon's stats if you have the patience and the right Candies. There are a couple of ways to use Go Power to raise your Pokémon's stats.

 TIP Pokémon you bring from Pokémon GO will come with a little bump to their Go Power from the start!

Gains from leveling up

Pidgey grew to Lv. 11!

Each time your Pokémon levels up, it will gain an extra point for one of its stats, thanks to Go Power. Which stat is most likely to see gains after leveling up can vary from Pokémon to Pokémon and from level to level. If you want more control over which stats are increased, you'll definitely want to turn to Candies.

See the extra +1 in the HP row? You've got Go Power to thank for that extra stat point!

Gains from using Candies

You may start finding Candies after catching a large number of Pokémon. You can also get Candies from sending Pokémon to the professor for his research. With either of these methods, you can end up getting generic Candies or species-specific Candies that can be used on your Pokémon from the Candy Jar in your Bag.

Generic Candies

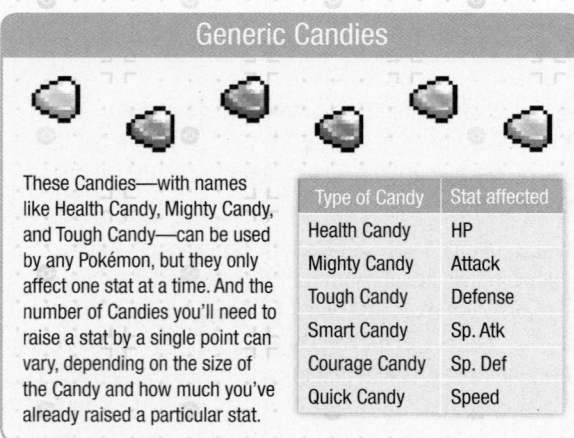

These Candies—with names like Health Candy, Mighty Candy, and Tough Candy—can be used by any Pokémon, but they only affect one stat at a time. And the number of Candies you'll need to raise a stat by a single point can vary, depending on the size of the Candy and how much you've already raised a particular stat.

Type of Candy	Stat affected
Health Candy	HP
Mighty Candy	Attack
Tough Candy	Defense
Smart Candy	Sp. Atk
Courage Candy	Sp. Def
Quick Candy	Speed

Species-specific Candies

You can also get Candies that share a name with a particular Pokémon species. If that species can evolve, any Pokémon in its Evolutionary line can use the same Candies. Check out the table on page 393 to see which species-specific Candy can be used for each species of Pokémon in the Kanto region.

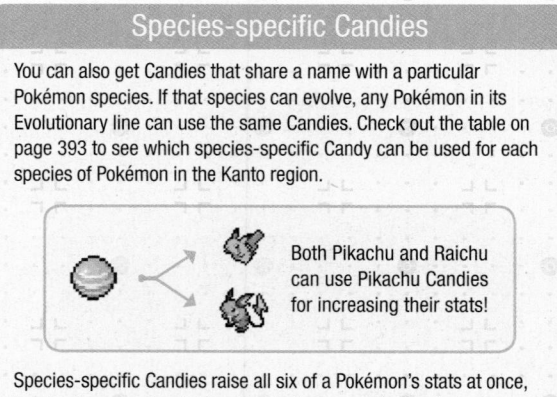

Both Pikachu and Raichu can use Pikachu Candies for increasing their stats!

Species-specific Candies raise all six of a Pokémon's stats at once, but they're much harder to come by than generic Candies!

Get Candies from catching wild Pokémon

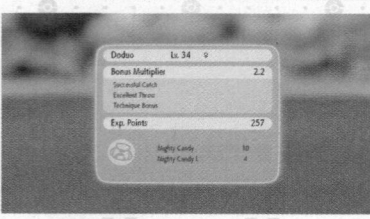

You can get Candies by catching wild Pokémon during your adventure. The types of Candy that you get from catching a particular species will be linked to the stat or stats that Pokémon species tends to excel in. The table on page 392 breaks it down for you.

Meanwhile, the size of Candy you may find after catching a Pokémon depends on how many Pokémon you've caught. Catching tons of them will boost your chances of getting rare extra-large Candies and species-specific Candies!

 TIP
The effectiveness of generic Candies goes down the more you use them on a single Pokémon, so you won't be able to max your Pokémon's stats if you don't collect L and XL Candies, too! When you look at the stat graph (p. 124), maxed-out stats will appear to spark.

Candy name	Which Pokémon can use it	Is a possible reward when you've caught
Candy	Any Pokémon	At least 30 Pokémon in total
Candy L	Pokémon Lv. 30 or above	At least 60 Pokémon in total
Candy XL	Pokémon Lv. 60 or above	At least 90 Pokémon in total
Species-specific Candy	Pokémon of the same Evolutionary line	At least 120 Pokémon in total

Maximize Your Chances of Getting More Candies

- Catch XL or XS specimens (p. 117)
- Get a Synchronized Bonus (p. 18)
- Get an Excellent Throw (p. 116)
- Catch Pokémon with your first throw
- Build up a Catch Combo (p. 117)
- Use Pinap Berries (p. 116)

 TIP
You'll also be a bit more likely to get Candies when catching a high-level or evolved Pokémon!

Get Candies by sending Pokémon to Professor Oak

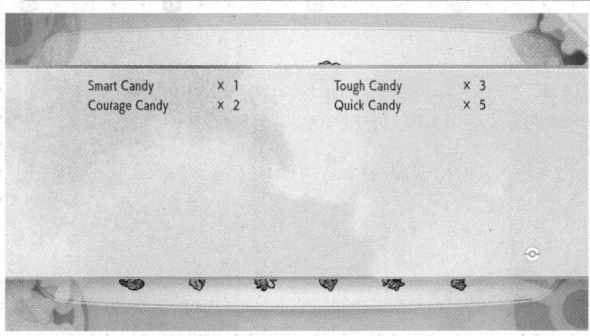

Smart Candy	x 1	Tough Candy	x 3
Courage Candy	x 2	Quick Candy	x 5

You learned back on page 118 that you can send Pokémon to Professor Oak from your Pokémon Box. This is another way you can get yourself Candies to help your other Pokémon grow stronger through Go Power!

Like the Candies you can get from catching Pokémon, the type of Candy will be linked to the stats listed for that species in the table on page 392. The size, though, will depend on how many Pokémon of that species you've ever sent to the professor.

When you send a Pokémon that has grown stronger through Go Power, you might get back some species-specific Candies, too—but only a very small number! Your hard work training that Pokémon won't go to waste, even if you decide to give it to the professor for his research.

Each time you've sent	Reward you'll receive
One Pokémon of the same species	A normal Candy
Five Pokémon of the same species	A large Candy
10 Pokémon of the same species	An extra-large Candy
50 Pokémon of the same species	A species-specific Candy

Get Those Candies

Stock up on tons of Poké Balls, and use the table to the right to pick a species that can drop the kind of Candies you want. Build up a Catch Combo (p. 117), which will make it more likely you'll keep encountering the same species, then go wild catching Pokémon! You may get Candies after successful catches, especially using the tips from the previous page.

Stat you want to raise	Species to catch	Where to catch it
HP	Nidoran♀	Route 22
Attack	Goldeen	Water's surface on Route 6
Defense	Geodude	Mt. Moon
Sp. Atk	Gastly	Upper floors of the Pokémon Tower
Sp. Def	Tentacool	Water's surface on either Route 20 or Route 24
Speed	Diglett	Diglett's Cave

If you've already unlocked the Judge function (p. 52), use it to check which Pokémon have the best individual strengths. Then send the rest to the professor for his research and claim all the Candies you get that way, too! You'll be a Go Power master in no time!

Get Candies with your Poké Ball Plus

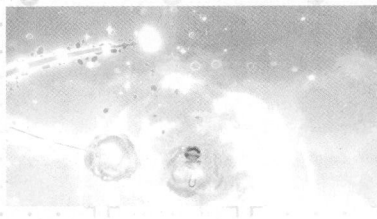

If you take a Pokémon out for a stroll in your Poké Ball Plus, you may get some species-specific Candies when it comes back to you! This is the most reliable way to get these Candies for Pokémon that you can't easily catch in the wild. Learn more on page 157 about how to maximize the rewards you can get from using the Poké Ball Plus.

Leveling Up

Your Pokémon's level is the final thing that affects your Pokémon's stats—and a lot more! Leveling up your Pokémon can also help them learn new moves (p. 131) and evolve (p. 120) or make them ready for Hyper Training (p. 125)! The main way to level up your Pokémon is by helping them earn Exp. Points through battles against other Trainers and when catching wild Pokémon.

Exp. Point bonuses

The number of Exp. Points your Pokémon gets from every battle or catch will be boosted if your Pokémon matches any of the conditions below. These bonuses also stack, so a Pokémon that came to you in a trade and now loves you a lot will have a real advantage for leveling up!

Exeggutor got a boosted 1,779 Exp. Points!

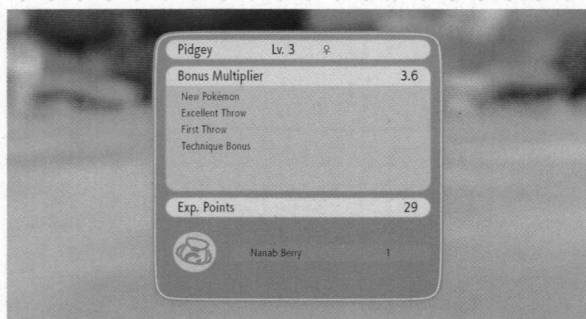

- If your Pokémon came from someone playing in a different language
- If your Pokémon was given to you in a trade (p. 120)
- If your Pokémon came from Pokémon GO (p. 159)
- If your Pokémon loves you a lot (p. 129)
- If your Pokémon was stopped from evolving so it could continue to be trained

Exp. Points earned from catches will also be boosted if you manage to achieve any of the conditions below. These also stack with each other and with the factors above. Play your cards right, and you'll have your Pokémon at Lv. 100 far quicker than usual!

- Catch an unusually small or large specimen (p. 117)
- Get a Synchronized Bonus with a Support Trainer (p. 18)
- Catch a new species of Pokémon
- Catch a Pokémon by swinging a Joy-Con detached from your system or a Poké Ball Plus (p. 17)
- Make a Nice Throw, a Great Throw, or an Excellent Throw (p. 116)
- Catch lots of the same species in a row (p. 117)
- Catch a Pokémon on the first attempt (p. 116)

Level Up in Other Ways!

There are also two other ways to help Pokémon level up! You can leave them at the Pokémon Day Care on Route 5, or you can use special items called Rare Candies. Pokémon left at the Pokémon Day Care gain Exp. Points while they are there, but the staff don't do it for free! You'll have to pay them when you pick your Pokémon up, and the longer they stayed (meaning the more they leveled up), the more you'll pay.

 Even though you pay for the privilege, leaving Pokémon at the Pokémon Day Care will also get you some other rewards. You have a chance to get Berries (p. 116) when you pick your Pokémon up—and even a Rare Candy if your Pokémon has stayed for quite a while! The longer your Pokémon stays, the better the chance you'll get multiple Berries or a rarer kind of Berry.

TRAINER HANDBOOK

Rare Candies can be found in the field sometimes. Be sure to check out any items you spot lying around on the ground, and you might get lucky! You can also sometimes get Rare Candies when you bring your Pokémon back from a stroll in the Poké Ball Plus (p. 157).

TIP Rare Candies can appear as hidden items on Route 6 or in the Cerulean Cave, which you can only visit after becoming Champion—and they even seem to reappear sometimes! Keep checking back from time to time to see if you are lucky enough to find another one! And catching Chansey in the Cerulean Cave is another great way to level up your team, since they yield lots of Exp. Points!

Feel the Love

Your Pokémon will grow to love you if you're a good Trainer, which'll give you lots of benefits in battle! Love goes up when you help your Pokémon grow stronger by having them travel with you or battle for you.

Ways to increase love

Use the handy list below to increase the love your Pokémon have for you.

- Help your Pokémon level up by earning Exp. Points or by using items on them
- Have your Pokémon travel with you by letting them out of their Poké Balls (p. 144)
- Use items on your Pokémon that boost their stats in battle (p. 134)
- Use items on your Pokémon that help them get permanently stronger (p. 134)
- Let your Pokémon take part in important battles against Gym Leaders and other tough Trainers

Love can decrease

In general, your Pokémon's love for you will not go down—but there is one surefire way to make your Pokémon feel less loving toward you. If you let your Pokémon faint in battle, its love for you will go down a little bit. It will go down even more if it was battling against a Pokémon that was way higher in level, so don't try to pit your Pokémon against opponents that completely outclass them!

Benefits of Love in Battle

Staryu toughed it out so you wouldn't feel sad!

Ponyta managed to expel the poison so you wouldn't worry!

Pokémon with higher love trust you more and will try harder in battle than other Pokémon! Depending on how high a Pokémon's love is, the effects can get better and better, so be sure to treat your Pokémon well—and try adventuring with different Pokémon on your team outside their Poké Balls to build up their love.

 To find out how much a Pokémon loves you, visit the Love Checker in Pallet Town (p. 31)!

Love Checker message	Some of the messages you might see in battle	Effects on your Pokémon in battle
"You're really starting to get friendly! I'm sure you'll be best friends in no time."	"Pikachu toughed it out so you wouldn't feel sad!"	Get a little bit more Exp. Points from battles and catching Pokémon / Very small chance of not fainting from a hit that would normally knock that Pokémon out
"It seems like Eevee likes being with you!"	"Eevee shook itself awake so you wouldn't worry!" "Eevee managed to expel the poison so you wouldn't worry!"	Get a little bit more Exp. Points from battles and catching Pokémon / Small chance of not fainting from a hit that would normally knock that Pokémon out / Medium chance of recovering from status conditions (p. 133) on its own
"I can tell Pikachu really likes you. It's saying it wants to always be with you!"	"Pikachu avoided the move in time via your shout!"	Get a little bit more Exp. Points from battles and catching Pokémon / Medium chance of not fainting from a hit that would normally knock that Pokémon out / Medium chance of recovering from status conditions on its own / Very small chance of avoiding an opponent's move entirely
"Eevee really, really, really loves you! I can tell you really trust each other!"	"Eevee landed a critical hit, wishing to be praised!"	Get a little bit more Exp. Points from battles and catching Pokémon / Good chance of not fainting from a hit that would normally knock that Pokémon out / Medium chance of recovering from status conditions on its own / Very small chance of avoiding an opponent's move entirely / Double the normal chance of landing a critical hit

Battle Formats

You'll come across all sorts of different Trainers in your journey around the Kanto region. Many of them will want to battle and test their skills against yours, and there are a few different kinds of battles they may want to have. You'll want to know about each kind of battle to be ready for anything, so let's take a look at them!

Single Battles

Single Battles are the most common kind of battle you'll find during your adventure. Single Battles are exactly what they sound like—each Trainer has a team of up to six Pokémon, and they each send out one Pokémon at a time in a turn-based battle. The Pokémon that has the higher Speed generally gets to go first each turn.

OPPONENT

VS

YOU

Double Battles

Pokémon Trainer Trace sent out Cubone!

There are a few different kinds of Double Battles, but the basics for all of them are the same—two Pokémon battling against another two Pokémon. In Double Battles during Link Battles with another player in the real world (p. 140), each Trainer uses two Pokémon in battle at the same time. During your in-game adventure, sometimes you will use two of your Pokémon but you'll be battling against two other Trainers—such as Team Rocket's Jessie and James—who each send out one of their own Pokémon to take on your two. At other times, your rival might join your side. When this happens, you'll send out one of your Pokémon to command in the battle and he'll send out one of his!

Some moves work somewhat differently in Double Battles, such as being able to hit multiple Pokémon. This makes for some exciting combinations you can't see anywhere else!

OTHER SIDE

VS

YOUR SIDE

OTHER SIDE

VS

YOUR SIDE

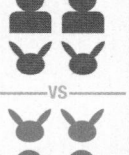

OTHER SIDE

VS

YOUR SIDE

Support Battles

When another player plays together with you as a Support Trainer (p. 18), they'll join you in battle as well! Even if they weren't on the field, they can still enter the battle by shaking their Joy-Con or Poké Ball Plus! Any battle that would normally be a Single Battle will become a Support Battle. In a Support Battle, you'll use the first Pokémon in your party while your supporter will use the second Pokémon in your party. You'll battle together against another Trainer in a two-versus-one style!

OTHER SIDE

VS

YOUR SIDE

TIP Support Trainers can't join you for Double Battles or battles against Master Trainers (p. 137), so make sure you're ready to tackle them on your own!

Mastering Moves

Pokémon can learn a lot of different moves by leveling up, evolving, and having TMs (p. 387) used on them. There are a few other ways that Pokémon can learn moves under the right conditions. Read on about all the ways Pokémon can learn moves to get the most out of your Pokémon in the many battles you'll have during your adventure in Kanto!

Leveling up

Your Pokémon may have the chance to learn a new move or moves when they level up. Check the new move's description to decide whether it's worth replacing one of your Pokémon's older moves.

> **TIP** If your Pokémon don't learn a move when they've got the chance to, either thanks to leveling up or evolving, you'll need Madam Memorial's help. Find out more about her below!

Evolving

Some Pokémon also have the chance to learn new moves when they evolve. These are often moves that the Pokémon's next Evolution can learn in the wild before being caught but which they don't otherwise learn by leveling up.

TMs

Technical Machines (TMs) can be used to teach powerful moves to many different Pokémon. You can use them as many times as you want. Select them from the TM Case in your Bag to use them on the Pokémon in your party. Turn to page 387 to find out how to get them all!

Madam Memorial

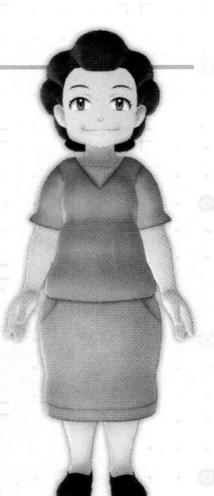

Madam Memorial is a Move Reminder—a special person who can help your Pokémon relearn moves it forgot, moves it could've learned but didn't when it had the chance, and even moves it could someday learn by leveling up! She's at the Pokémon Center on the Indigo Plateau (p. 103).

> **TIP** To use Madam Memorial's services, you'll have to pay her—but she won't accept cash! She wants Heart Scales instead, so find plenty of them as hidden items in the Seafoam Islands, as a gift from your partner (p. 142), or by playing with a Poké Ball Plus (p. 157).

Partner Move Tutor

The Partner Move Tutor can be found in Cerulean City (p. 41), Celadon City (p. 62), and Fuchsia City (p. 72), and he can help your partner Pokémon learn unique moves for free! These moves are some of the best your partner Pokémon can learn, so make good use of them. Turn to page 387 to learn more about these moves.

Know How to Use Your Moves

Each move your Pokémon learns has its own effects, but there are a handful of major categories that they all break down into. This section will introduce you to them so you can decide just what sort of move you might want to add into your strategy.

Physical and special moves

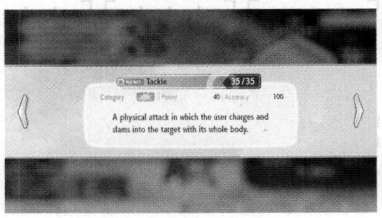

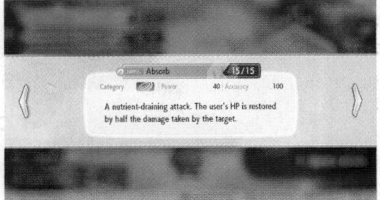

Moves that deal damage can be either physical moves or special moves. Physical moves get stronger the higher the Attack stat is for the Pokémon using the move. Special moves get stronger the higher the Sp. Atk stat is for the Pokémon using the move.

The same is true for defending, too! Physical moves will deal less damage to a Pokémon with higher Defense, and the same goes for special moves and Sp. Def.

 To check whether a move deals physical or special damage, you can turn to the Moves list beginning on page 382.

Multi-hit moves

Hit 2 times!

Most damage-dealing moves will strike once to do their damage, but some moves will hit multiple times in a row. These multi-hit moves generally have lower power, but because they hit more than once, they can make up for it!

If these moves succeed, the number of times they hit is random, but it is always at least two times. Each hit from these moves is affected by stat boosts, too, so they can do some serious damage if you boost your Pokémon's Attack. (More about that below!)

 TIP All multi-hit moves in *Pokémon: Let's Go, Pikachu!* and *Pokémon: Let's Go, Eevee!* are physical moves.

One-hit KO moves

It's a one-hit KO!

Some moves will automatically cause a Pokémon to faint, regardless of how high their HP, Defense, or Sp. Def may be! These one-hit KO moves include Fissure and Horn Drill. Their accuracy rises the lower the target's level is compared to the user's level—but at the other end, their accuracy can be as low as 30. You can recognize these moves in the moves list (p. 382) by the description "The target faints with one hit."

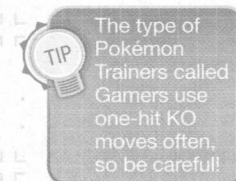 **TIP** The type of Pokémon Trainers called Gamers use one-hit KO moves often, so be careful!

Status moves

Status moves are a third kind of move different from physical and special moves. They don't deal damage, but they can affect the battle and turn the tide in your favor! These moves can be the most difficult to master, so read on to learn about some of the different things they can do.

Status moves can change stats in battle

One of the most common types of status moves are those that change the stats of a Pokémon. This works similarly to how an X Attack or X Speed would, but you don't even need an item! Even better, some of these moves can lower your opponent's Pokémon's stats!

Understanding Stat Changes

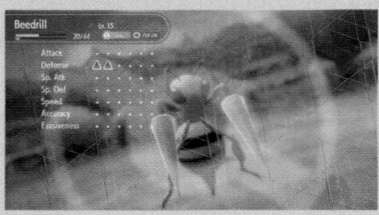

When you raise or lower a Pokémon's stats in battle with moves or items (p. 134), you'll typically change them by one or two stages at a time, up to a total of six stages maximum. In battle, you can check how many stages a Pokémon's stats have been raised or lowered if you press ⓨ and then choose the Pokémon you want to check—each red triangle represents one raised stage, while each blue triangle is a lowered stage. You should know, however, that HP cannot be raised or lowered with stat changes. And remember that stat changes only last until the end of battle or until a Pokémon is switched out! If you want to have a permanent effect on your Pokémon's stats, turn back to page 125 to read about Go Power.

Message in battle	What it means	Increase or decrease to stats
[Pokémon's stat] rose!	Stat was increased by one stage.	About 50% increase for all stats except HP. About 30% for evasiveness or accuracy.
[Pokémon's stat] rose sharply!	Stat was increased by two stages.	About 100% increase for all stats except HP. About 60% for evasiveness or accuracy.
[Pokémon's stat] fell!	Stat was decreased by one stage.	About 30% decrease for all stats except HP. About 25% for evasiveness or accuracy.
[Pokémon's stat] harshly fell!	Stat was decreased by two stages.	About 50% decrease for all stats except HP. About 40% for evasiveness or accuracy.

Status moves can make your Pokémon stronger

Ponyta's Speed rose sharply!

Moves such as Harden and Agility will boost your Pokémon's stats until the end of the battle or until the Pokémon faints or is switched out. You can use these moves multiple times to keep increasing your Pokémon's stats. Eventually, though, the Pokémon will reach a point where its stats can't be raised any higher in this way. But by the time you reach that point, you'll probably be ready to sweep through your opponent's team!

 You can also use certain items to boost your Pokémon's stats, as you'll see on page 134.

Status moves can make your opponent's Pokémon weaker

The opposing Poliwhirl's Defense harshly fell!

Moves such as Screech and Growl will lower an opposing Pokémon's stats until the end of the battle or until the Pokémon faints or is switched out. Like stat-raising moves and items, you can use these moves multiple times to keep decreasing a Pokémon's stats, but the stats will also reach a point where they can't be lowered any further.

Status Conditions Can Change the Battle

Some moves can cause status conditions. These conditions are asleep, paralyzed, burned, frozen, poisoned, and badly poisoned. Some physical and special moves have a chance of causing these in addition to the damage they deal, though the odds usually aren't high. Status moves that inflict status conditions are usually much more likely to succeed, but they deal no damage directly. Each of these status conditions has different effects, as you can see in the table below.

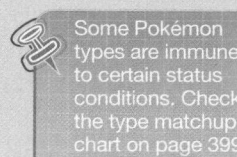

Some Pokémon types are immune to certain status conditions. Check the type matchup chart on page 399 for all the info!

There are some other conditions that can affect your Pokémon as well. Conditions like confusion don't need an item to be cured, though. You can get rid of them by switching Pokémon.

Status condition	What it does	How to cure it
ASLEEP	A Pokémon that's asleep can't use moves.	Wait until the Pokémon wakes up in battle, use a curing item, or visit a Pokémon Center.
PARALYSIS	A paralyzed Pokémon has its Speed stat lowered and randomly may not be able to use a move at all.	Use a curing item, use the move Rest, or visit a Pokémon Center.
BURNED	A burned Pokémon has its Attack stat lowered and takes damage each turn.	Use a curing item, use the move Rest, or visit a Pokémon Center.
FROZEN	A frozen Pokémon can't use moves.	Wait until the Pokémon thaws or is hit with a Fire-type move in battle, use a curing item, use the moves Flare Blitz, Scald, or Sizzly Slide, or visit a Pokémon Center.
POISONED	A poisoned Pokémon takes damage each turn.	Use a curing item, use the move Rest, or visit a Pokémon Center.
POISONED	A badly poisoned Pokémon takes increasing damage each turn.	Use a curing item, use the move Rest, or visit a Pokémon Center.

Recovery moves

There are a few moves that can restore HP to your Pokémon during battle without the need for an item. Moves such as Recover and Rest will restore a large amount of HP to your Pokémon so it can go longer in battle without fainting!

There are other kinds of moves that can restore HP to your Pokémon while doing damage to your opponent's Pokémon, too! Leech Seed and Absorb are moves like this. They won't restore as much HP as Recover or Rest, but the damage they deal might make up for it!

Priority moves

Pidgey used Quick Attack!

The Speed stat of each Pokémon normally decides which one gets to act first each turn, but priority moves go first even if your Pokémon's Speed stat is lower than an opponent's. These are moves such as Quick Attack and Sucker Punch. Using these moves when the opponent's Pokémon is close to fainting is a great way to make sure they can't strike back! Recognize these moves in the moves list (p. 382) by descriptions like "Strikes with high priority."

TIP — If two Pokémon use moves of the same priority, you'll be back to the Speed stat. Whichever Pokémon has a higher Speed stat will go first.

Understanding Items

While moves are a big part of battle, items can have an equally important role. You might overlook them, but their effects can mean the difference between a win and a loss. You'll want to use them as best you can!

In-battle items

There are a lot of different items that can be used in battle, but they can mostly be put into two groups. The first is healing and restorative items, and the second is stat-boosting and other items.

Healing and restorative items

These items may heal your Pokémon or remove status conditions, and most of them can be bought in Poké Marts—though you'll need to earn Gym Badges to be able to buy the most effective items. Check out the items list beginning on page 389 for more details on how to obtain any item you're interested in.

	Items	Effects
	Potion	Restores 20 HP to a single Pokémon.
	Super Potion	Restores 60 HP to a single Pokémon.
	Hyper Potion	Restores 120 HP to a single Pokémon.
	Max Potion	Completely restores the max HP of a single Pokémon.
	Full Restore	Fully restores the HP of a single Pokémon and heals any status conditions it has.
	Antidote	Lifts the effects of being poisoned from a single Pokémon.
	Burn Heal	Heals a single Pokémon suffering from a burn.
	Ice Heal	Thaws out a single Pokémon that has been frozen solid.
	Awakening	Rouses a single Pokémon from the clutches of sleep.
	Paralyze Heal	Frees a single Pokémon that has been paralyzed.
	Full Heal	Heals all the status conditions of a single Pokémon.

	Items	Effects
	Revive	Revives a single Pokémon that has fainted. It also restores half of the Pokémon's max HP.
	Max Revive	Revives a single Pokémon that has fainted. It also fully restores the Pokémon's max HP.
	Fresh Water	Restores 30 HP to a single Pokémon.
	Soda Pop	Restores 50 HP to a single Pokémon.
	Lemonade	Restores 70 HP to a single Pokémon.
	Ether	Restores 10 PP to a single selected move that has been learned by a Pokémon.
	Max Ether	Fully restores the PP of a single selected move that has been learned by a Pokémon.
	Elixir	Restores 10 PP to each of the moves that have been learned by a Pokémon.
	Max Elixir	Fully restores the PP of all of the moves that have been learned by a Pokémon.
	Shalour Sable	Heals all the status conditions of a single Pokémon.
	Pewter Crunchies	Heals all the status conditions of a single Pokémon.

Stat-boosting and other items

These items can be used in a battle to boost your Pokémon's stats or have other effects on how your Pokémon performs. These effects won't last if you switch out your Pokémon or the battle ends, though—if you want permanent changes, check out the next section!

	Items	Effects
	Guard Spec.	Prevents stat reduction among the user's party for five turns after it is used in battle.
	Dire Hit	Greatly raises the critical-hit ratio of a Pokémon during a battle.
	X Attack	Sharply boosts the Attack stat of a Pokémon during a battle.
	X Defense	Sharply boosts the Defense stat of a Pokémon during a battle.

	Items	Effects
	X Speed	Sharply boosts the Speed stat of a Pokémon during a battle.
	X Accuracy	Sharply boosts the accuracy of a Pokémon during a battle.
	X Sp. Atk	Sharply boosts the Sp. Atk stat of a Pokémon during a battle.
	X Sp. Def	Sharply boosts the Sp. Def stat of a Pokémon during a battle.

 Mega Stones are another type of item that can be used in battle for a temporary stat boost—but they only work for certain Pokémon! Learn more on the next page.

Outside-of-battle items

The items PP Up and PP Max can permanently improve the performance of your Pokémon in battle by increasing the PP of their moves, and Rare Candies can be used to make them level up. Use these items, if you've got any, from your Bag when you're not battling. They're hard to come by!

 You can also use Candies outside of battle to help your Pokémon get stronger! Learn more about Candies on page 126.

TRAINER HANDBOOK

Mega Evolution

When the bond between certain Pokémon and their Trainer is strong enough, a temporary transformation called Mega Evolution becomes possible during battle. Mega Evolution only lasts the duration of the battle and can only be used once per battle. Not every Pokémon can Mega Evolve either, but those that can are all covered in the table below. You can also check the Kanto Region Pokédex starting on page 161 to learn more about each.

Using Mega Evolution

Even if you have a Pokémon that can Mega Evolve, you'll need its Mega Stone to do it, along with a Key Stone. You'll get a Key Stone near the end of your journey (p. 97), but it'll be up to you to collect as many of the Mega Stones as you can. Once you have the proper Mega Stone, all you have to do is send out that Pokémon in battle! When you choose a move for your active Pokémon to use, you'll also be able to choose whether or not to Mega Evolve it for that battle. Mega Evolving isn't a move, so you can still choose a move for your Pokémon to use after it Mega Evolves, too!

> **TIP** Certain Pokémon have more than one possible Mega Evolution! You'll be able to choose which form you want as long as you have the right Mega Stones!

What does Mega Evolution do?

Mega Evolution doesn't just change how a Pokémon looks—it'll help you in battle, too! Pokémon that Mega Evolve gain higher stats. How these stats change will depend on the Pokémon's species, though HP always stays the same.

Some Pokémon also change their types. This can really shake up the battle, because it changes that Pokémon's weaknesses and which types of moves get a same-type attack bonus (p. 123). Make good use of Mega Evolution to control the battle and always stay ahead of your opponent!

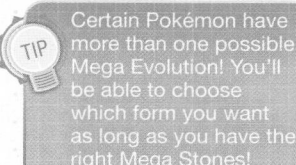

Pidgeot   Pidgeotite   Mega Pidgeot

> **TIP** If you want to know everything that changes about a Pokémon when it Mega Evolves, check out its entry in the Kanto Region Pokédex. Any stat or type that changes will be highlighted in blue.

Finding Mega Stones

If you want to collect all of the Mega Stones, the table below is your go-to guide to get them all!

Pokémon	Mega Stone needed and how to get it	Pokémon	Mega Stone needed and how to get it
Venusaur	**Venusaurite** Receive from Blue (p. 97)	Gengar	**Gengarite** Buy after entering the Hall of Fame (p. 103)
Charizard	**Charizardite X** Receive from Blue (p. 97)	Kangaskhan	**Kangaskhanite** Buy after entering the Hall of Fame (p. 103)
Charizard	**Charizardite Y** Receive from Blue (p. 97)	Pinsir	**Pinsirite** Buy after entering the Hall of Fame (p. 103)
Blastoise	**Blastoisinite** Receive from Blue (p. 97)	Gyarados	**Gyaradosite** Buy after entering the Hall of Fame (p. 103)
Beedrill	**Beedrillite** Buy after entering the Hall of Fame (p. 103)	Aerodactyl	**Aerodactylite** Buy after entering the Hall of Fame (p. 103)
Pidgeot	**Pidgeotite** Buy after entering the Hall of Fame (p. 103)	Mewtwo	**Mewtwonite X** Receive from Green after defeating her (p. 110)
Alakazam	**Alakazite** Buy after entering the Hall of Fame (p. 103)	Mewtwo	**Mewtwonite Y** Receive from Green after defeating her (p. 110)
Slowbro	**Slowbronite** Buy after entering the Hall of Fame (p. 103)		

Coach Trainers

While there are all sorts of Trainers across the Kanto region who you can battle to earn prize money and help your Pokémon grow, there's one special kind of Trainer that is particularly worth challenging if you aspire to become a Pokémon League Champion! These are called Coach Trainers, and they're here to support you on your adventure.

What Are Coach Trainers?

Every Trainer needs a little help on their journey, and learning from other Trainers is a great way to learn more about battling! Coach Trainers are all about that. They're Trainers who will challenge you a little more, often using rarer and stronger Pokémon than most other Trainers in the area around them.

Thanks to the ⋯ above each Coach Trainer's head, you'll be able to spot one from a distance. Coach Trainers may give you a challenge in battle, but the rewards will be worth it! Coach Trainers give you useful items that any Trainer would be happy to have—things like Revives to restore some of your fainted Pokémon or even TMs to teach your Pokémon moves they can't learn anywhere else! Check the chart below to know where you can find each Coach Trainer in Kanto!

\ Where to find Coach Trainers

All of the Coach Trainers in Kanto are listed below. You'll also find them marked on the maps where they appear throughout the walkthrough—plus you'll find special battle boxes for them that give you an idea of what Pokémon they have and what reward they'll give!

Where they are	Recommended Pokémon level	Reward
Route 3 (p. 37)	Level 11	Revive
Route 4 (West) (p. 37)	Level 13	TM57 Pay Day
Route 25 (p. 44)	Level 16	TM15 Seismic Toss
Route 11 (p. 52)	Level 21	Pikachu Candy ×5 (*Pokémon: Let's Go, Pikachu!*) Eevee Candy ×5 (*Pokémon: Let's Go, Eevee!*)
Route 10 (p. 55)	Level 26	TM13 Brick Break
Pokémon Tower (p. 58)	Level 28	Pikachu Candy ×5 (*Pokémon: Let's Go, Pikachu!*) Eevee Candy ×5 (*Pokémon: Let's Go, Eevee!*)
Route 7 (p. 61)	Level 30	TM12 Facade
Fighting Dojo (p. 80)	Level 33	TM23 Thunder Punch
Route 12 (p. 76)	Level 39	TM59 Dream Eater
Route 17 (p. 71)	Level 41	TM58 Drill Run
Route 15 (p. 76)	Level 41	TM31 Fire Punch
Route 21 (p. 96)	Level 45	TM35 Ice Punch
Power Plant (p. 78)	Level 45	Rare Candy ×5
Seafoam Islands (p. 91)	Level 47	Rare Candy ×5
Pokémon Mansion (p. 94)	Level 47	TM22 Rock Slide
Victory Road (p. 102)	Level 49	Pikachu Candy ×10 (*Pokémon: Let's Go, Pikachu!*) Eevee Candy ×10 (*Pokémon: Let's Go, Eevee!*)
Victory Road (p. 102)	Level 49	TM39 Outrage
Cerulean City (p. 109)	Level 52	TM60 Megahorn
Celadon City (p. 107)	Level 54	PP Max ×10

TIP
Coach Trainers look like Ace Trainers wearing green!

Master Trainers

There are also some Trainers who love a certain species of Pokémon so much that they devote themselves completely to training that Pokémon. These Trainers are known as Master Trainers and can be found all over the Kanto region after you've entered the Hall of Fame. They wear red, and they have nothing but their favorite Pokémon on their mind, so you'll know exactly what Pokémon they're using!

Hiker   Master Hiker

Most of these Master Trainers want to battle another Trainer who uses the species of Pokémon they love, but don't expect these battles to be easy. These Trainers use Pokémon between Lv. 65 and Lv. 80, with high stats thanks to Go Power—plus you can't use items in these battles! If you're ready to take one of them on, put the Pokémon they love at the head of your party and be prepared. It'll be the only Pokémon you can use in the battle!

For the few Master Trainers who don't want to fight, impress them instead with your training skills. Show them a specimen with a particular high CP to satisfy the Master Trainers who specialize in the species listed to the right.

Species	CP Requirement
Ditto, Meltan	4,000 or more
Articuno, Zapdos, Moltres	7,500 or more
Mew, Melmetal	8,000 or more
Mewtwo	9,000 or more

Titles

Yo, Porygon Master!
A fitting title for you, indeed.

When you beat a Master Trainer, you'll gain a new title showing your true mastery of that species of Pokémon. You can choose which title you'd like to set as active by visiting GAME FREAK's Development Office in Celadon City (p. 62). Your active title will be viewable when you connect with other players for Link Battles (p. 140), so pick your favorite title to show off!

TIP
Obtain the Grand Master title by obtaining the Master Trainer titles for the first 150 Pokémon in the Kanto region!

The Battle Master

Once you've managed to obtain at least six titles, a special challenge will become available! Head over to the Indigo Plateau to find the Pokémon Trainer Red, Blue's longtime rival and friend, waiting for you. Talk to him to battle, but be warned! Red is no pushover. He has a team of six powerful Pokémon, so bring your strongest team to face him.

TIP
Winning against Red will grant you the one-of-a-kind Battle Master title, a true way to show you've become one of the best!

Battle!

Battle Master Red

Red is a Trainer well known for his skill in battle. Using Pokémon with a wide variety of types, he's sure to push your battle know-how to the absolute limit! While his team doesn't all share one common weakness, have some Fighting-, Ground-, Flying-, Psychic-, and Rock-type moves on hand. Each will be super effective on a couple of his Pokémon!

Red's Pokémon are all Lv. 85 and they're quite strong, thanks to Go Power! Don't expect an easy fight, even if your Pokémon are higher level than Red's. His Venusaur will also Mega Evolve into Mega Venusaur, raising its stats significantly! You'll probably want to bring a Pokémon that can Mega Evolve, too, so you can match his!

TRAINER HANDBOOK

Indigo Plateau

Indigo Plateau
- ☑ Battle Master Red (Lv. 85)

Route 23 (North)
- ☑ Venusaur Master (Lv. 75)
- ☑ Charizard Master (Lv. 75)

Victory Road
- ☑ Golbat Master (Lv. 75)
- ☑ Graveler Master (Lv. 70)
- ☐ Moltres Master

Route 23 (South)
- ☐ Nidoqueen Master (Lv. 75)
- ☐ Nidoking Master (Lv. 80)
- ☐ Dratini Master (Lv. 65)

Pewter City
- ☑ Spearow Master (Lv. 70)
- ☑ Jigglypuff Master (Lv. 70)
- ☑ Gloom Master (Lv. 70)
- ☑ Kabutops Master (Lv. 75)

Pewter Museum of Science
- ☑ Golem Master (Lv. 75)
- ☑ Aerodactyl Master (Lv. 75)

Route 3
- ☐ Nidoran♀ Master (Lv. 65)

Mt. Moon
- ☐ Clefable Master (Lv. 80)
- ☐ Paras Master (Lv. 70)
- ☐ Omanyte Master (Lv. 70)
- ☐ Kabuto Master (Lv. 70)

Route 4 (West)
- ☐ Nidoran♂ Master (Lv. 70)
- ☐ Magikarp Master (Lv. 65)

Viridian Forest
- ☑ Butterfree Master (Lv. 75)
- ☑ Weedle Master (Lv. 65)
- ☑ Pikachu Master (Lv. 75)

Route 2
- ☑ Pidgey Master (Lv. 65)
- ☑ Parasect Master (Lv. 75)

Route 16
- ☑ Pidgeotto Master (Lv. 70)
- ☑ Lickitung Master (Lv. 70)
- ☑ Snorlax Master (Lv. 75)

Celadon City
- ☑ Arcanine Master (Lv. 75)
- ☑ Victreebel Master (Lv. 75)
- ☑ Grimer Master (Lv. 70)
- ☑ Gyarados Master (Lv. 75)

Team Rocket Hideout
- ☑ Arbok Master (Lv. 75)
- ☑ Persian Master (Lv. 75)
- ☑ Weezing Master (Lv. 75)
- ☑ Rhydon Master (Lv. 75)

Celadon Condominiums
- ☑ Charmander Master (Lv. 65)
- ☑ Mr. Mime Master (Lv. 70)

Rocket Game Corner
- ☑ Porygon Master (Lv. 70)

Celadon Department Store
- ☑ Vaporeon Master (Lv. 75)
- ☑ Jolteon Master (Lv. 75)
- ☑ Flareon Master (Lv. 75)

Viridian City
- ☑ Oddish Master (Lv. 65)
- ☑ Meowth Master (Lv. 70)
- ☑ Abra Master (Lv. 70)
- ☑ Bellsprout Master (Lv. 65)
- ☑ Drowzee Master (Lv. 70)

Route 17 (Pokémon Road)
- ☑ Electrode Master (Lv. 75)
- ☑ Koffing Master (Lv. 70)
- ☑ Rhyhorn Master (Lv. 70)
- ☑ Eevee Master (Lv. 75)

Route 18
- ☑ Caterpie Master (Lv. 65)
- ☑ Fearow Master (Lv. 80)
- ☑ Pinsir Master (Lv. 75)

Route 21
- ☐ Psyduck Master (Lv. 70)
- ☐ Slowpoke Master (Lv. 70)
- ☐ Slowbro Master (Lv. 75)

Cinnabar Island
- ☑ Exeggutor Master (Lv. 75)

Pokémon Mansion
- ☑ Muk Master (Lv. 75)
- ☑ Magmar Master (Lv. 75)
- ☑ Ditto Master
- ☑ Mewtwo Master
- ☑ Mew Master
- ☑ Meltan Master
- ☑ Melmetal Master

Cinnabar Laboratory
- ☑ Omastar Master (Lv. 75)

Route 20 (West)
- ☐ Wartortle Master (Lv. 70)
- ☐ Tentacruel Master (Lv. 80)
- ☐ Cloyster Master (Lv. 75)

Seafoam Islands
- ☐ Seel Master (Lv. 70)
- ☐ Dewgong Master (Lv. 75)
- ☐ Articuno Master
- ☐ Dragonair Master (Lv. 70)

Route 20 (East)
- ☐ Blastoise Master (Lv. 80)
- ☐ Tentacool Master (Lv. 75)

Map labels: Indigo Plateau, Route 23, Victory Road, Pewter City, Route 3, Mt. Moon, Route 4, Celadon City, Route 16, Viridian City, Route 2, Route 22, Route 1, Route 17, Pallet Town, Route 21, Route 18, Route 19, Route 20, Seafoam Islands, Cinnabar Island

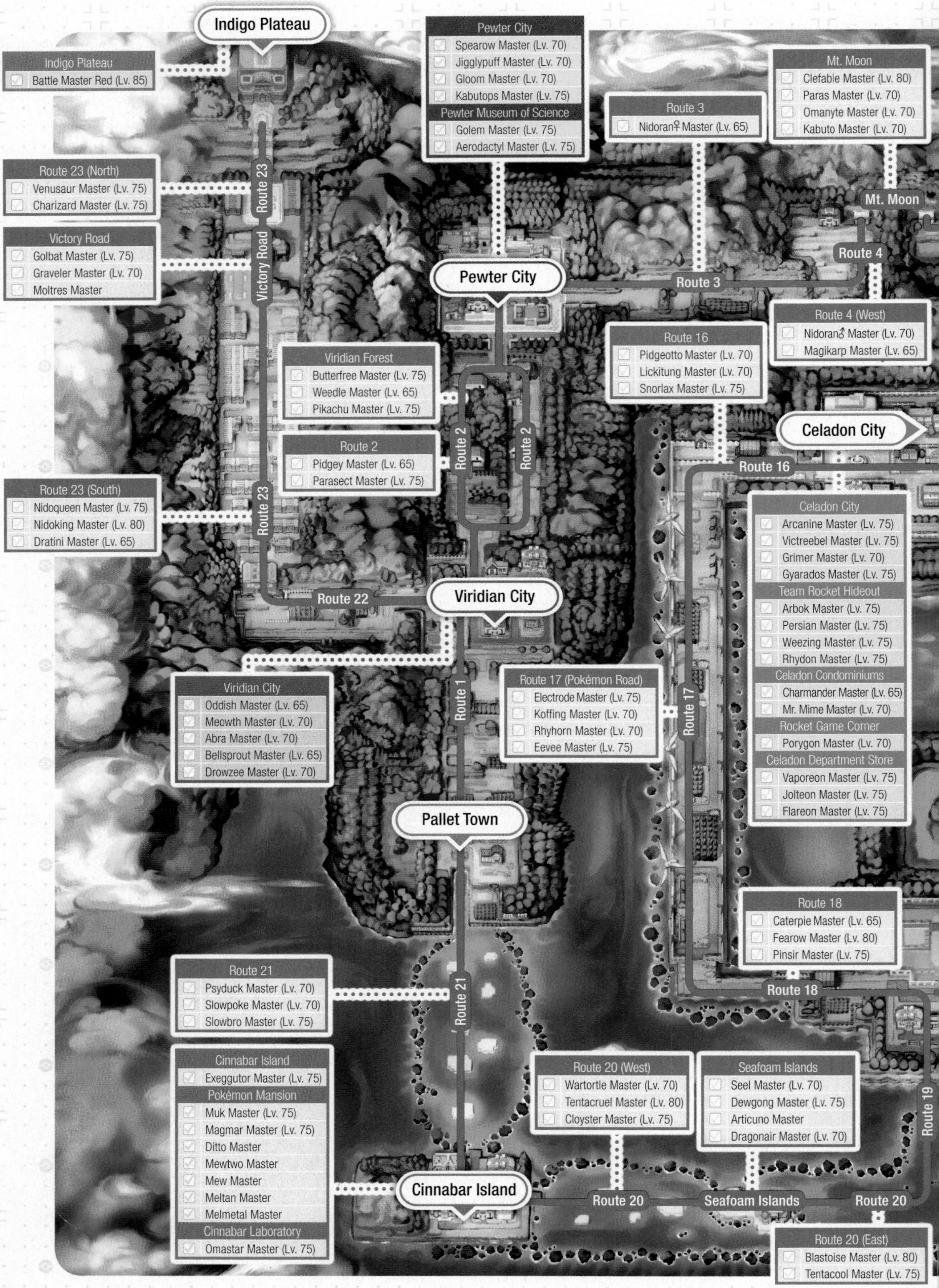

With 153 Master Trainers in Kanto, there's a lot of work to get your Pokémon ready. Be sure to consult the section on page 128 for ways to raise your Pokémon faster! Once you're ready to face a Master Trainer, use the map here to find whichever Master Trainer you want to take on! If you can battle the Trainer listed, the level of his or her Pokémon will be shown in parentheses.

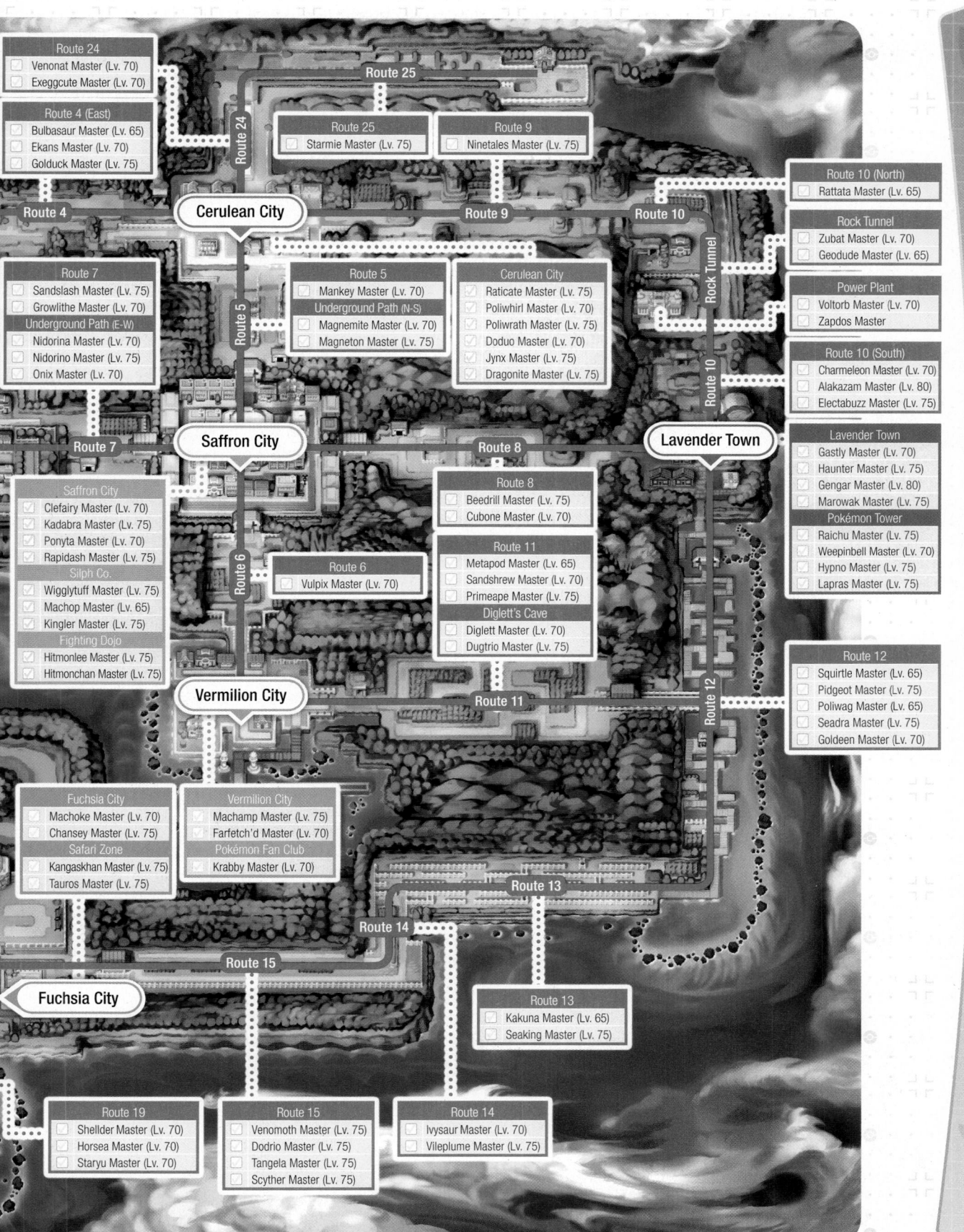

Route 24
- ☐ Venonat Master (Lv. 70)
- ☐ Exeggcute Master (Lv. 70)

Route 4 (East)
- ☐ Bulbasaur Master (Lv. 65)
- ☐ Ekans Master (Lv. 70)
- ☐ Golduck Master (Lv. 75)

Route 4

Route 7
- ☐ Sandslash Master (Lv. 75)
- ☐ Growlithe Master (Lv. 70)

Underground Path (E-W)
- ☐ Nidorina Master (Lv. 70)
- ☐ Nidorino Master (Lv. 75)
- ☐ Onix Master (Lv. 70)

Route 7

Saffron City
- ☑ Clefairy Master (Lv. 70)
- ☑ Kadabra Master (Lv. 75)
- ☑ Ponyta Master (Lv. 70)
- ☑ Rapidash Master (Lv. 75)

Silph Co.
- ☑ Wigglytuff Master (Lv. 75)
- ☑ Machop Master (Lv. 65)
- ☑ Kingler Master (Lv. 75)

Fighting Dojo
- ☑ Hitmonlee Master (Lv. 75)
- ☑ Hitmonchan Master (Lv. 75)

Vermilion City

Fuchsia City
- ☑ Machoke Master (Lv. 70)
- ☐ Chansey Master (Lv. 75)

Safari Zone
- ☐ Kangaskhan Master (Lv. 75)
- ☐ Tauros Master (Lv. 75)

Vermilion City
- ☑ Machamp Master (Lv. 75)
- ☑ Farfetch'd Master (Lv. 70)

Pokémon Fan Club
- ☐ Krabby Master (Lv. 70)

Fuchsia City

Route 15

Route 14

Route 19
- ☐ Shellder Master (Lv. 70)
- ☐ Horsea Master (Lv. 70)
- ☐ Staryu Master (Lv. 70)

Route 15
- ☐ Venomoth Master (Lv. 75)
- ☐ Dodrio Master (Lv. 75)
- ☐ Tangela Master (Lv. 75)
- ☐ Scyther Master (Lv. 75)

Route 14
- ☐ Ivysaur Master (Lv. 70)
- ☐ Vileplume Master (Lv. 75)

Route 25

Cerulean City

Route 25
- ☐ Starmie Master (Lv. 75)

Route 9
- ☐ Ninetales Master (Lv. 75)

Route 9

Route 5
- ☐ Mankey Master (Lv. 70)

Underground Path (N-S)
- ☐ Magnemite Master (Lv. 70)
- ☐ Magneton Master (Lv. 75)

Cerulean City
- ☐ Raticate Master (Lv. 75)
- ☐ Poliwhirl Master (Lv. 70)
- ☐ Poliwrath Master (Lv. 75)
- ☐ Doduo Master (Lv. 70)
- ☑ Jynx Master (Lv. 75)
- ☐ Dragonite Master (Lv. 75)

Saffron City

Route 8
- ☐ Beedrill Master (Lv. 75)
- ☐ Cubone Master (Lv. 70)

Route 8

Route 11
- ☐ Metapod Master (Lv. 65)
- ☐ Sandshrew Master (Lv. 70)
- ☐ Primeape Master (Lv. 75)

Diglett's Cave
- ☐ Diglett Master (Lv. 70)
- ☐ Dugtrio Master (Lv. 75)

Route 6
- ☐ Vulpix Master (Lv. 70)

Route 11

Route 13

Route 13
- ☐ Kakuna Master (Lv. 65)
- ☐ Seaking Master (Lv. 75)

Route 10

Route 10 (North)
- ☐ Rattata Master (Lv. 65)

Rock Tunnel
- ☐ Zubat Master (Lv. 70)
- ☐ Geodude Master (Lv. 65)

Power Plant
- ☐ Voltorb Master (Lv. 70)
- ☐ Zapdos Master

Route 10 (South)
- ☐ Charmeleon Master (Lv. 70)
- ☐ Alakazam Master (Lv. 80)
- ☐ Electabuzz Master (Lv. 75)

Lavender Town
- ☐ Gastly Master (Lv. 70)
- ☐ Haunter Master (Lv. 75)
- ☐ Gengar Master (Lv. 80)
- ☐ Marowak Master (Lv. 75)

Pokémon Tower
- ☐ Raichu Master (Lv. 75)
- ☐ Weepinbell Master (Lv. 70)
- ☐ Hypno Master (Lv. 75)
- ☐ Lapras Master (Lv. 75)

Lavender Town

Route 12
- ☐ Squirtle Master (Lv. 65)
- ☐ Pidgeot Master (Lv. 75)
- ☐ Poliwag Master (Lv. 65)
- ☐ Seadra Master (Lv. 75)
- ☐ Goldeen Master (Lv. 70)

Link Battles

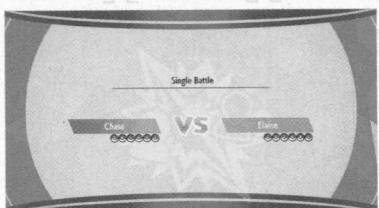

In the world of Pokémon, when two Trainers meet, they will battle. With Link Battles, the same can be true of two Trainers in the real world, too! Link Battles let you battle someone else with their own *Pokémon: Let's Go, Pikachu!* or *Pokémon: Let's Go, Eevee!* game. Just as you may face different battle formats with the Trainers you meet in your adventures in Kanto, there are a few different battle options the two of you can choose from for Link Battles.

Setting Up a Link Battle

Link Battles are started by selecting the Communicate option in the main menu. Then select Play with Others. From here you'll have the option to connect with someone nearby or someone who is far away, and this changes things a bit, so read on about how each one works.

 TIP To battle or trade with players online, you must have an active Nintendo Switch Online membership.

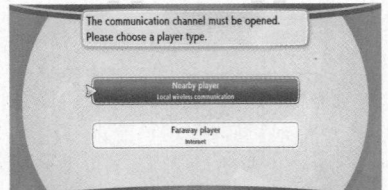

Nearby players

To connect with a nearby player, you'll likely need to be in the same room as that player. If the two of you move any farther apart, the connection may not be strong enough, so make sure the two of you are close to each other!

Faraway players

Connecting with a faraway player requires an internet connection for both players. As long as both players have an internet connection, it doesn't matter how far away they are!

Link codes

To connect with another player, you'll have to select a link code made up of three Pokémon chosen from Pikachu, Eevee, Bulbasaur, Charmander, Squirtle, Pidgey, Caterpie, Rattata, Jigglypuff, and Diglett.

You and the player you want to connect to must select the same code in order to connect with each other, so make sure you both know the code you want to use!

Choosing the rules

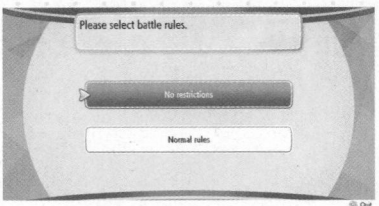

Once you and the other player have successfully connected, you'll be able to choose whether you want a Single Battle or a Double Battle. (Turn back to page 130 if you need to review battle formats!) Then you'll have a different kind of rules choice you won't see in the usual battles in the Kanto region. You'll be able to choose to battle with no restrictions or with normal rules.

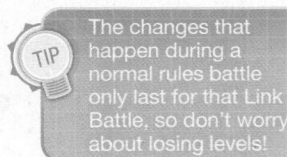 **TIP** The changes that happen during a normal rules battle only last for that Link Battle, so don't worry about losing levels!

No restrictions

No restrictions is exactly what it sounds like. Each of you will use your team of Pokémon with no limits on their stats or level. This means that if you've been playing for a long time and your opponent only just started their adventure, the battle may be pretty unfair and end without being much fun. So use the no restrictions rules when you've both been playing for the same amount of time and want to go all out!

Normal rules

Normal rules are for when you want to have a fair battle between players who haven't been playing for the same amount of time. Normal rules will set the level of any Pokémon used to Lv. 50, regardless of whether they were actually above or below Lv. 50 in the player's own game. Any stat gains from Go Power (p. 125) will be removed, and the Pokémon's love (p. 129) will be set to be equal. This way, you and another player can battle together even if one of you has only just started your adventure in the Kanto region!

Playtime with Your Partner

Your partner does much more than just join you on your adventure and in battle. They share a bond with you like no other Pokémon, and it only grows stronger the longer you two are together! Treating your partner Pikachu or partner Eevee well earns you different rewards, so read on to learn all about how to take care of your partner Pokémon!

Play with Your Partner Pokémon

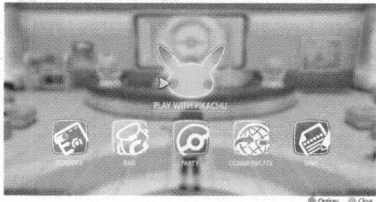

Once your partner starts to ride on either your shoulder (*Pokémon: Let's Go, Pikachu!*) or your head (*Pokémon: Let's Go, Eevee!*) and you leave Pallet Town, you'll be able to play with your partner Pokémon anytime by selecting the Pikachu or Eevee icon from the main menu or simply by shaking your controller.

You'll be able to see how your partner's feeling on this screen. If you want to do even more than that, choose Partner Play! Depending on the play mode you've chosen (p. 17), you can pet your partner either with your controller or by using your finger on the touch screen of your Nintendo Switch!

Change your partner's hairstyle

When you pet your partner via the Nintendo Switch touch screen, try using multiple fingers and petting its head. Doing this correctly should change your partner Pokémon's hairstyle! Which new stylin' hairdo you get depends on how many fingers you use. Check page 155 for each style and how to get it!

Feed your partner some Berries

Berries can be used for more than just helping catch Pokémon! You can also feed them to your partner Pokémon. Just like wild Pokémon, your partner Pikachu or Eevee loves Berries, and it will grow closer to you if you're generous with them. It likes silver Berries and golden Berries even more than regular ones, so share them when you've got some to spare.

Your partner's spirit and mood

Your partner's spirit and mood will influence how it acts with you. The higher the spirit your Pokémon has, the more energetic it will be. And the better its mood is, the more friendly it will be. Check the handy chart on the right to see how both spirit and mood change your partner's attitude!

There are many things that can increase your Pokémon's spirit and mood. Sending your partner Pokémon out in battle can increase its spirit, and using healing items on it can increase its mood. Giving your partner Berries will increase both! Remember, though, that both spirit and mood can decrease as you play, so take good care of your partner!

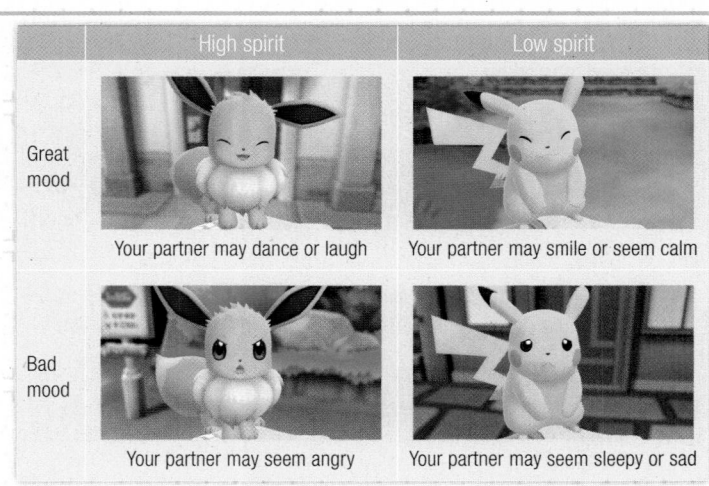

	High spirit	Low spirit
Great mood	Your partner may dance or laugh	Your partner may smile or seem calm
Bad mood	Your partner may seem angry	Your partner may seem sleepy or sad

Your Partner Can Help in Battle

Your partner also has special partner powers! If you ever see a dancing icon of your partner Pikachu or partner Eevee in battle, be sure to shake your Joy-Con or Poké Ball Plus, and your partner Pokémon will use its special power to help you in battle. What exactly it does depends on whether your partner Pokémon is the one battling or not.

TIP

This icon won't appear in handheld mode, though. Detach a Joy-Con or play with a Poké Ball Plus to see it!

If your partner Pokémon is the one battling, it'll use a signature move that can only be triggered in this way. Your partner Pikachu will use Pika Papow, while your partner Eevee uses Veevee Volley. The power of these moves depends on your partner's love (p. 129). But if your partner Pokémon isn't the one battling, it'll use its partner powers to boost all stats of your Pokémon in battle instead (p. 132)! However, keep in mind that this will count as your action for the turn and that your battling Pokémon will have to wait until next turn to use one of its moves.

When your partner is in battle, it will use its signature move on the opponent's Pokémon!

When your partner isn't in battle, it'll help out your battling Pokémon by boosting its stats!

Your partner won't always help out, though. It'll need some motivation from its best friend—and that's you! Feeding your partner Pokémon Berries—especially silver and golden Berries—is a great way to increase the chance of having your partner help in battle. Playing with your partner Pokémon will help, too! If your partner Pokémon ever wants you to play a short game by touching its hands or paws, do it! Your partner will be feeling powered up in no time!

Your Partner May Give You Gifts

Apart from helping you in battle, your partner Pikachu or partner Eevee may also want to give you a present while you're out adventuring in the field. Shake your Joy-Con or Poké Ball Plus when you see the dancing partner Pokémon icon in the field—or select your partner icon on the main menu when you see the icon bouncing up and down—and your partner may give you something! There are a number of items it can give you—and some of them can't be found anywhere else! They can generally be sold at Poké Marts for some extra cash.

 Instead of selling Heart Scales, hold on to them and use them for Madam Memorial (p. 131)!

Item	Value
Stretchy Spring	₽10
Chalky Stone	₽30
Heart Scale	₽50
Marble	₽150
Tiny Mushroom	₽250
Lone Earring	₽300

Item	Value
Beach Glass	₽400
Gold Leaf	₽500
Silver Leaf	₽500
Pretty Wing	₽500
Polished Mud Ball	₽600
Tropical Shell	₽1,000

Item	Value
Stardust	₽1,500
Leaf Letter *Pokémon: Let's Go, Pikachu!*	A treasured item that can't be sold!
Leaf Letter *Pokémon: Let's Go, Eevee!*	A treasured item that can't be sold!
Small Bouquet	A treasured item that can't be sold!

Making Money in the Kanto Region

Getting gifts from your partner is one way to make more money, whether you need to buy useful items for battle or just want to deck out your partner with the greatest accessories (p. 150). But there are still other ways to make that money.

Sell valuable items
While you can sell most items at a Poké Mart, they generally won't be worth too much cash. However, a few items are meant only to be sold for money. Check in your Bag for their descriptions, which will often say something about being able to sell the item to a shop for a good price. The Underground Paths (p. 46 and 61) are full of hidden items that reappear, including those that can be sold for a high price!

Get dough daily
Once per day, you can babysit a woman's Slowpoke outside the Pewter Museum of Science (p. 35) or visit a burrowing Diglett in Fuchsia City (p. 88) to get some items that can be sold for a good amount of money.

Boost battle rewards
Using the move Pay Day increases the amount of money you'll receive at the end of a battle. Meowth is a Pokémon that learns the move by leveling up. Also, early in the game, you can get the TM for Pay Day from a Coach Trainer in order to teach it to other Pokémon (p. 37).

Item	Value
Tiny Mushroom	₽250
Big Mushroom	₽2,500
Pearl	₽1,000
Big Pearl	₽4,000
Stardust	₽1,500
Star Piece	₽6,000
Nugget	₽5,000

Your Partner Helps You Find Hidden Items

When out exploring in the Kanto region, keep an eye on your partner Pokémon's tail. If it starts to wag, you know that an item is nearby! While this will happen for items you can see on the ground, it can also be a clue that you're near a hidden item that you can't see.

While walking along...

watch for your partner's tail to start wagging...

Then check the ground nearby for a hidden item!

When you're far from the hidden item, your partner's tail will wag from side to side slowly. When you get closer, the wagging will become quicker. When this happens, try moving around a bit while pressing Ⓐ and you should be able to find the hidden item! Your partner Pikachu or partner Eevee's tail will only wag if you're facing toward the item, so if you see it wagging, keep moving in that direction.

TIP Many hidden items can be found again after waiting a day or after walking around for a while, so be sure to revisit towns and routes and always watch your partner Pokémon's tail!

Pokémon That Travel with You

While your partner Pokémon will always be with you, it's not the only Pokémon you can have travel with you on your adventure. You can choose to let any other Pokémon in your party out of its Poké Ball to travel together with you! Just select the Pokémon from the Party menu and press ⊕. This is possible with any species of Pokémon, no matter how big or small. Read below to see how traveling with Pokémon can help you.

Pokémon that travel with you have a lot on their mind

While a Pokémon is outside of its Poké Ball, you can talk to it with Ⓐ. There are many different ways it may react, depending on its spirit, mood, status, location, and even species. Try talking to all sorts of different Pokémon you're traveling with as you visit the many sights of Kanto!

Porygon is making a strange humming sound. Could it be reacting to the game?

Having a Pokémon travel with you increases its love

Ponyta toughed it out so you wouldn't feel sad!

Traveling with a Pokémon outside of its Poké Ball is also a great way to increase its love! The Pokémon's love will slowly increase as long as you're walking and it's traveling with you. A Pokémon with high love will gain all sorts of helpful effects in battle—find out more on page 129.

Travel together with a Pokémon, and its love will grow!

A Pokémon traveling with you can find items you'd miss

A Pokémon you're traveling with may suddenly stop and head over to a bush or other spot during your adventure. When this happens, it might have found an item to give to you! You can only find items like this if you have a Pokémon out of its Poké Ball and traveling with you. Find out more about these items on page 394.

Get Around by Riding Pokémon

While most Pokémon outside of their Poké Ball will simply travel with you as you walk, certain Pokémon will let you ride on them! Overall, there are three types of Pokémon you can ride on—those you ride on the ground, on the water, or in the air. Many of them can help you get around faster than you would on your own, so they make for great Pokémon to travel with!

Pokémon that travel on the ground
You'll be able to ride these Pokémon as soon as you get them.

| Persian | Arcanine | Machamp | Rapidash | Dodrio | Haunter | Onix | Rhyhorn |

| Rhydon | Kangaskhan | Starmie | Tauros | Snorlax |

Pokémon that swim across the water
Even if you have one of these Pokémon, you'll need Sea Skim before you can ride it across the water.

Gyarados   Lapras

TRAINER HANDBOOK

Pokémon that fly in the air

You can ride these Pokémon as soon as you get them, but you'll be flying low to the ground. The only places you'll be able to fly high up at first will be Route 16, Route 17, and Route 18 (p. 70). Once you enter the Hall of Fame, you'll be able to fly high in the sky no matter where you are!

Charizard

Aerodactyl

Dragonite

Find Pokémon in the Sky

When flying on a Pokémon after you've entered the Hall of Fame, you'll see other Pokémon flying up in the air, too! You can catch them just like the ones you'd find on the ground.

Pidgey	**Pidgeotto**	**Pidgeot**	**Spearow**	**Fearow**

Get Catch Combos in the Sky for Rare Pokémon

Building up a Catch Combo can give you a chance to find some especially rare Pokémon in the air, just like on the ground. You can even find Articuno, Zapdos, and Moltres, provided that you've caught them all before, but such an encounter is *exceedingly* rare! Just remember that these unusual encounters will only be possible after becoming Champion (p. 107). Learn more about building Catch Combos on page 117.

Extremely Rare!

Charizard	**Dragonite**	**Articuno**	**Zapdos**	**Moltres**

Dress for Success

As you're going through your adventure, you might want to dress the part! There are a number of special outfits you can get to dress up in—and matching outfits for your partner to wear, too. What's more, you can mix and match the different parts of these outfits to create your own unique look! You can check out all of them on the following three pages, though note that there are a couple you can only get in *Pokémon: Let's Go, Pikachu!*—as well as a number you can only get in *Pokémon: Let's Go, Eevee!*

How to get outfits

Beneath each outfit, you can find information on how you can get it and references to pages where you can learn more. Many outfits become yours just through normal gameplay, but you'll have to put in a little effort to get them all!

How to change outfits

You can change outfits via your Bag. Open up the main menu whenever you're not in an event or a battle, and select Bag. In your Bag, choose your Clothing Trunk, and there you'll find the two options that'll let you choose an outfit for your partner or yourself.

Choosing an outfit for your partner

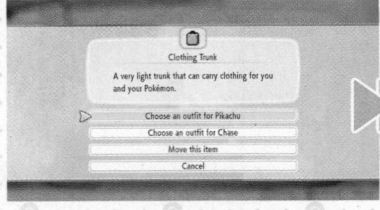  

Choosing an outfit for yourself

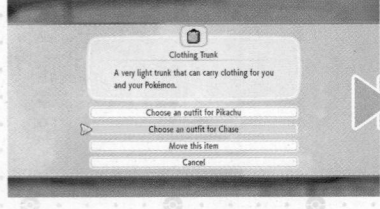  

Outfits

Sportswear

You'll be wearing this outfit by default, and you can get a matching set for your partner when you start your adventure together in Pallet Town (p. 31)!

Sailor Set

Get this set for you and your partner when you first board the S.S. Anne (p. 47)!

Formal Set

Get this set for you and your partner when you visit the Pokémon Tower (p. 58)!

Team Rocket Set

Get this set for you and your partner when you infiltrate the Team Rocket Hideout (p. 66)!

Assistant Set

Get this set for you and your partner on Route 15 if you've caught enough Pokémon (p. 76)!

Police Set

Get this set for you and your partner in Saffron City after you've helped run some criminals out of town (p. 86)!

Safari Set

Get this set for you and your partner in Fuchsia City when you help the warden out of a gummy situation (p. 88)!

Blast-Off Set

Get this set for you and your partner if you defeat Jessie and James after you've entered the Hall of Fame (p. 106)!

Pikachu Set

Get this set for yourself at the Pokémon Fan Club in Vermilion City (p. 50)!

Raichu Set

Get this set for you and your partner at the Pokémon Fan Club in Vermilion City (p. 50)!

Eevee Set

Get this set for yourself at the Pokémon Fan Club in Vermilion City (p. 50)!

Vaporeon Set

Get this set for you and your partner at the Pokémon Fan Club in Vermilion City (p. 50)!

Jolteon Set

Get this set for you and your partner at the Pokémon Fan Club in Vermilion City (p. 50)!

Flareon Set

Get this set for you and your partner at the Pokémon Fan Club in Vermilion City (p. 50)!

Espeon Set

Get this set for you and your partner at the Pokémon Fan Club in Vermilion City (p. 50)!

Umbreon Set

Get this set for you and your partner at the Pokémon Fan Club in Vermilion City (p. 50)!

Leafeon Set

Get this set for you and your partner at the Pokémon Fan Club in Vermilion City (p. 50)!

Glaceon Set

Get this set for you and your partner at the Pokémon Fan Club in Vermilion City (p. 50)!

Sylveon Set

Get this set for you and your partner at the Pokémon Fan Club in Vermilion City (p. 50)!

Pretty Up Your Partner

There are more fashion items you can get for your partner, if you think it needs a bit more style. These can be bought at the Celadon Department Store in Celadon City (p. 62). You'll find hats, glasses, and a whole array of bows, bandannas, and flower accessories in different colors.

Putting On Accessories

While there may be only one way to normally wear glasses and hats, the other accessories you get for your partner can be put on its ear, chest, back, or tail. You can put on multiple accessories at a time, sticking them on any of these parts as you please.

 **TIP** If you hope to get all of these accessories, they'll cost you. Turn back to page 143 for more on how to make money in your game if you're having a hard time getting enough together!

Hats

Buy it at the hat table for ₽10,000.

Buy it at the hat table for ₽20,000.

Buy it at the hat table for ₽20,000.

Buy it at the hat table for ₽999,999.

Diglett Cap

Buy it at the Diglett table for ₽50.

Accessories

Little Red Bow

Buy it at the accessory table for ₽1,000.

Little Green Bow

Buy it at the accessory table for ₽1,000.

Little Blue Bow

Buy it at the accessory table for ₽1,000.

Little Black Bow

Buy it at the accessory table for ₽1,000.

Little Plaid Bow

Buy it at the accessory table for ₽1,000.

Little Formal Bow

Buy it at the accessory table for ₽1,000.

Little Polka-Dot Bow

Buy it at the accessory table for ₽1,000.

Little Bow

Buy it at the accessory table for ₽1,000.

Fancy Red Bow

Buy it at the accessory table for ₽2,000.

Fancy Green Bow

Buy it at the accessory table for ₽2,000.

Fancy Blue Bow

Buy it at the accessory table for ₽2,000.

Fancy Black Bow

Buy it at the accessory table for ₽2,000.

Fancy Plaid Bow

Buy it at the accessory table for ₽2,000.

Fancy Polka-Dot Bow

Buy it at the accessory table for ₽2,000.

Fancy Cute Bow

Buy it at the accessory table for ₽2,000.

Fancy Frilly Bow

Buy it at the accessory table for ₽2,000.

Sailor Bandanna

Buy it at the accessory table for ₽3,000.

Safari Bandanna

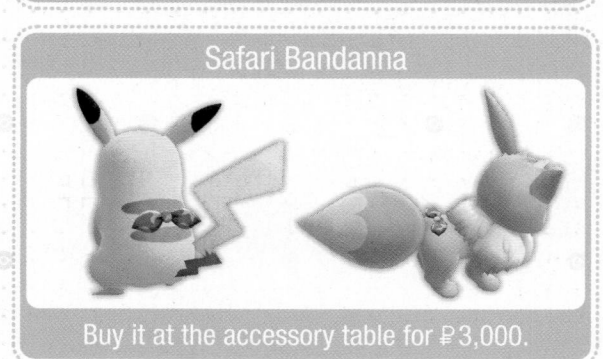

Buy it at the accessory table for ₽3,000.

Polka-Dot Bandanna

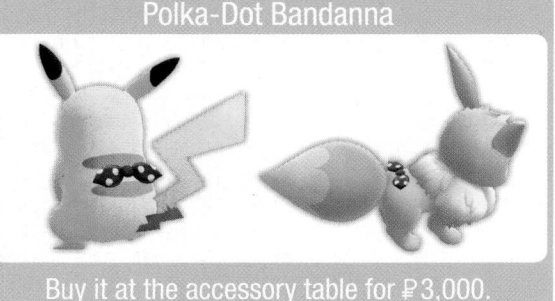

Buy it at the accessory table for ₽3,000.

Ruby Bandanna

Buy it at the accessory table for ₽3,000.

Sapphire Bandanna

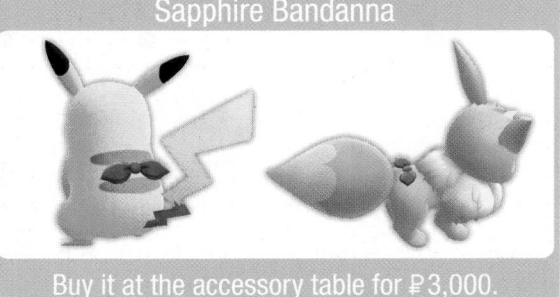

Buy it at the accessory table for ₽3,000.

Emerald Bandanna

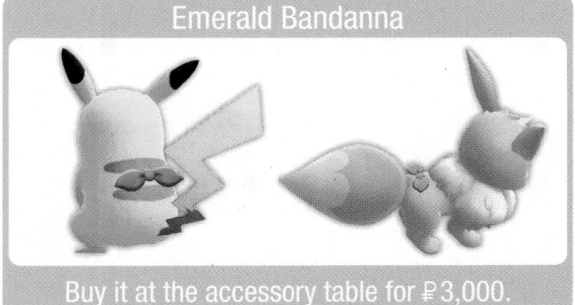

Buy it at the accessory table for ₽3,000.

Black Bandanna

Buy it at the accessory table for ₽3,000.

White Bandanna

Buy it at the accessory table for ₽3,000.

Red Flowers

Buy them at the accessory table for ₽5,000.

Pink Flowers

Buy them at the accessory table for ₽5,000.

Blue Flowers

Buy them at the accessory table for ₽5,000.

White Flowers

Buy them at the accessory table for ₽5,000.

Orange Flowers

Buy them at the accessory table for ₽5,000.

Purple Flowers

Buy them at the accessory table for ₽5,000.

Pale Blue Flowers

Buy them at the accessory table for ₽5,000.

Green Flowers

Buy them at the accessory table for ₽5,000.

Glasses

Black Framed Glasses

Buy them at the glasses table for ₽8,000.

Red Framed Glasses

Buy them at the glasses table for ₽8,000.

Green Framed Glasses

Buy them at the glasses table for ₽8,000.

Brown Framed Glasses

Buy them at the glasses table for ₽12,000.

Thick Glasses

Buy them at the glasses table for ₽5,000.

Blue Sky Sunglasses

Buy them at the glasses table for ₽10,000.

Dawn Sunglasses

Buy them at the glasses table for ₽10,000.

Dusk Sunglasses

Buy them at the glasses table for ₽10,000.

Midnight Sunglasses

Buy them at the glasses table for ₽10,000.

Special Hairstyles

When it comes to style, there's no need to stop at clothes and accessories! You can also style your partner's hair in a number of surprising ways. Perhaps you've managed to do so by accident when playing with your Pokémon. If not, read on to find out exactly how to achieve these various looks!

Changing hairstyles

You can change your partner's hair when playing with them. Select the Pikachu or Eevee icon on the main menu—or shake your Joy-Con or Poké Ball Plus—whenever you're not in the middle of a battle or event. Once your partner appears on your arm, give it a little poke or select the Partner Play option on the right side of the screen.

When you're playing with your partner, try giving it a little rub using at least two fingers. If you start brushing back and forth, you may see its head start to jiggle a bit. After a few moments of rubbing side to side across its forehead, with your fingers not leaving the touch screen, your partner will be transformed with a new hairdo!

Give it a try for a while and you can trigger a number of different hairstyles. But how can you see them all? Try using a different number of fingers! The more fingers you use, the more styles you may trigger. Some of them are pretty tricky to get, but luckily these styles don't grow out—they'll stay how you left them unless you muss up your partner's hair again yourself!

Two to four fingers

Use two to four fingers to trigger four different hairstyles for Pikachu or Eevee. You can also return their hair to normal this way, going through all these possible hairstyles.

Five to seven fingers

Use anywhere from five to seven fingers, and you may trigger three more special hairstyles for Pikachu or Eevee.

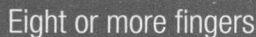

Eight or more fingers

Try ruffling your partner's hair with eight or more fingers, and you may be able to trigger one amazing hairstyle! This one might be tough to accomplish, so try starting with a few fingers and then adding more as you go.

The Poké Ball Plus

The Poké Ball Plus is a Poké Ball–shaped controller that can be used to play *Pokémon: Let's Go, Pikachu!* and *Pokémon: Let's Go, Eevee!* You can also have one of your Pokémon hop into your Poké Ball Plus to accompany you for a stroll in the real world.

Top Button

Control Stick

TIP Don't worry—your Pokémon won't disappear from your game if you take it for a stroll! You can continue to use it in-game while you're on your adventure. And if you ever lose your Poké Ball Plus, you can still summon your Pokémon back to your game. They'll just lose any of the rewards they would've normally earned from their stroll.

Take Your Pokémon for a Stroll

The more you walk and play with your Pokémon while it's out for a stroll, the more rewards you'll get in *Pokémon: Let's Go, Pikachu!* or *Pokémon: Let's Go, Eevee!* But if you're playing with a new Poké Ball Plus, you'll first have to claim your Mew to be able to take a Pokémon for a stroll. Turn to the next page to learn how, if you need to!

Depositing Pokémon

Before you can head out in the real world with a Pokémon, you'll need to deposit one in your Poké Ball Plus. To do this, open the main menu and choose Save. Then select "Take your Pokémon for a stroll." You'll have to connect the Poké Ball Plus you want to use if you haven't already. You can connect the Poké Ball Plus the same way you'd connect it to use it as a controller (p. 17) by pressing the Top Button or the Control Stick and waiting for your game to recognize it.

Next, choose whether you want to take your partner Pokémon for a stroll or another Pokémon from your Pokémon Box. If you choose the Pokémon Box, you'll be able to choose any of your Pokémon to take for a stroll with you. Just wait a few moments for your Pokémon to hop over into your Poké Ball Plus, and that's it! Now you can bring your Pokémon with you wherever you go!

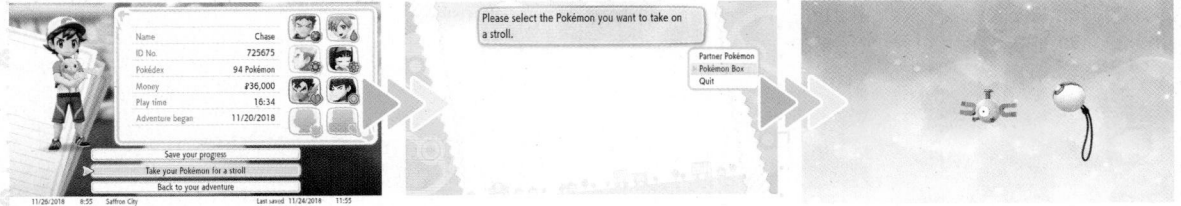

Withdrawing Pokémon

When you'd like to bring your Pokémon back from your Poké Ball Plus, go back to the Save menu and select "Take your Pokémon for a stroll." Connect your Poké Ball Plus to your Nintendo Switch once again. When you're asked whether you want your Pokémon to come back from its stroll or not, choose Yes to welcome it back and claim your rewards!

Two ways to play

While out for a stroll with your Pokémon, you have two different ways of playing with your Poké Ball Plus—standard mode and play mode. Standard mode is the default and can be used simply by walking around with your device. In this mode, the Poké Ball Plus will track your steps and also work like a Pokémon GO Plus if connected to your Pokémon GO app.

Play mode can be turned on by holding down the Control Stick. When you do, you should see a light from your Poké Ball Plus that's the same color as a primary color of the Pokémon you took with you for a stroll. In this mode you can shake, gently toss, or roll your Poké Ball Plus to play with your Pokémon. If you see a rainbow flash of lights, you did something it really liked!

To go back to standard mode, quickly click down the Control Stick. You should see the light on the Poké Ball Plus turn off. This means it's back to standard mode.

Getting Rewards

Taking a Pokémon out for a stroll with you isn't just fun—it can get your Pokémon Exp. Points and even helpful items in *Pokémon: Let's Go, Pikachu!* or *Pokémon: Let's Go, Eevee!* What you get depends on what you do during your stroll with the Poké Ball Plus.

When a Pokémon returns from its stroll, you'll see a list of the different things you did together while it was in your Poké Ball Plus. The more you do in each of these categories, the more points you get. Check the table on the right for all the different things you can do to earn points for rewards and Exp. Points.

You'll get better rewards as the points you earn add up over time. Check below to see the rewards you can get from going on strolls with your Pokémon!

Results you may see after a stroll	How to earn these results
Walked together	Walk with your Poké Ball Plus
Played / Enjoyed playing / Enjoyed playing very much	Play with your Pokémon in play mode or answer your Pokémon's cry in standard mode
Called out to you	Get your Pokémon to cry out to you in standard mode
Replied to a callout	Answer your Pokémon's cry in standard mode
Worked hard in Pokémon GO	Find Pokémon in Pokémon GO, try to catch Pokémon in Pokémon GO, and visit PokéStops in Pokémon GO
Helped Pokémon GO	Catch Pokémon in Pokémon GO, spin PokéStops in Pokémon GO, and get items from PokéStops in Pokémon GO

Reward	Points needed
Random Berries	50
Heart Scales	500
Random generic Candies	1,000
Random generic L Candies	2,000

Reward	Points needed
Random generic XL Candies	3,000
Species-specific Candies (any Pokémon you've gone for a stroll with)	10,000
Rare Candy ×1 / Rare Candy ×2 / Rare Candy ×3	10,000 / 20,000 / 30,000

Get Mew from Your Poké Ball Plus

When you first get your Poké Ball Plus, it will have the Mythical Pokémon Mew waiting in it! Until you receive it in your copy of *Pokémon: Let's Go, Pikachu!* or *Pokémon: Let's Go, Eevee!*, you won't be able to use your Poké Ball Plus, so get this extremely rare Pokémon right away.

To get Mew, connect your Poké Ball Plus to your Nintendo Switch as a controller (p. 17) by pressing either the Top Button or the Control Stick, then open the main menu. Choose Communicate and then Mystery Gifts. If your Poké Ball Plus is connected, you should see an option appear here to receive a gift from your Poké Ball Plus. Choose this option and follow the instructions on the screen to receive Mew in your game and get full access to all the fun features of your Poké Ball Plus!

TIP: You'll need to be connected to the internet to receive Mew as a Mystery Gift!

Mystery Gifts

Using your Poké Ball Plus isn't the only way to get Mystery Gifts. Choose Communicate from the main menu and then Mystery Gifts. You'll see you also have the option to get Mystery Gifts via the internet or with a code or password. You can also check the Mystery Gifts you've received on this screen.

Get via internet

This option will connect you to the internet to see if there are any Mystery Gifts available for you to receive. You will need a Nintendo Account and an internet connection for this. Special Mystery Gifts are sometimes available from The Pokémon Company International, so keep an eye on the official website at www.pokemon.com for announcements!

Get with code/password

You'll need a special code or password to receive a Mystery Gift this way. These codes and passwords are sometimes given out for certain events, which may be announced on www.pokemon.com, and you'll also need to connect to the internet (which requires setting up a Nintendo Account) to get these gifts. Enter the code or password to receive your special Mystery Gift!

Check Mystery Gifts

Choose this option if you want to see the Mystery Gifts you've collected in your game.

Get Going with Pokémon GO

Do you or does someone you know play Pokémon GO? Great! Pokémon can be sent from Pokémon GO over to *Pokémon: Let's Go, Pikachu!* or *Pokémon: Let's Go, Eevee!* Not only that, but you can also then play with those Pokémon in the GO Park complex in Fuchsia City (p. 72).

 TIP Bringing Pokémon from Pokémon GO is the only way to get the Mythical Pokémon Meltan and Melmetal (p. 350)!

Connecting to Pokémon GO

Before you can send Pokémon from Pokémon GO to your game, you'll need to connect your Nintendo Switch to a smartphone with the Pokémon GO app installed on it.

Open the main menu in *Pokémon: Let's Go, Pikachu!* or *Pokémon: Let's Go, Eevee!* with Ⓧ. Then press Ⓨ to open the Options menu and choose Open Pokémon GO Settings. Follow the instructions on-screen, and your Nintendo Switch will begin to search for a Pokémon GO account to connect with.

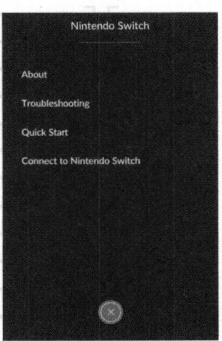

Screenshot image subject to change.

While your Nintendo Switch is searching for a Pokémon GO account, open up Pokémon GO on the smartphone you want to use. Tap the Poké Ball icon on the bottom of the screen, and then tap the Settings icon in the upper right. Near the bottom of this menu is an option to connect your game to a Nintendo Switch. Choose to connect to a Nintendo Switch, and you should see a message on your console asking if you want to pair your two games. Agree to pair them and you'll be all set! Remember, you'll need to have Bluetooth enabled on the smartphone you want to use.

Send Pokémon from Pokémon GO

Now that you've paired your game with a Pokémon GO account, you'll be able to receive Pokémon from Pokémon GO. Head to the GO Park complex and talk to the receptionist there. Choose the Bring Pokémon option, and then select which GO Park you'd like to send Pokémon to.

 TIP Each GO Park can hold up to 50 Pokémon, and you have 20 GO Parks to use.

Once you choose which GO Park to use, communication will start with your linked Pokémon GO account. Your Nintendo Switch will search for the Pokémon GO account you paired with your game. After choosing which Pokémon you want to bring over from Pokémon GO to *Pokémon: Let's Go, Pikachu!* or *Pokémon: Let's Go, Eevee!*, the two devices will be able to connect.

 **TIP** Pokémon sent to a GO Park can't be sent back to Pokémon GO!

Visit Your GO Parks

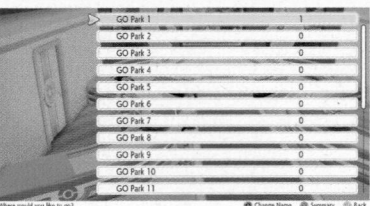

To see the Pokémon that have come over from Pokémon GO, talk to the receptionist and choose to enter a GO Park, then select which GO Park you want to enter. You'll be able to see how many Pokémon are in each one before choosing. You can check what Pokémon are in a GO Park by pressing Ⓨ, and you can change the park's name with ⊕. Customize and sort your parks however you like!

Exploring your GO Parks

Once you've entered one of your GO Parks, have a look around! You should be able to find all the Pokémon that you've sent to that park from Pokémon GO. You can watch them explore and even play with each other!

If you'd like to have a Pokémon move to another GO Park, walk up to that Pokémon and press Ⓐ. Choose the Move option and then the GO Park you'd like to send it to. You can adjust the zoom of the camera in a GO Park with Ⓨ and save the game or leave that GO Park with Ⓧ.

Catching Pokémon in GO Parks

Even after a Pokémon has come over to your GO Park from a Pokémon GO account, you can't immediately use it on your team. It'll stay in your GO Park until you catch it! Walk up to a Pokémon you want to catch and press Ⓐ, then choose the Catch option. You'll be able to catch the Pokémon like you would any other wild Pokémon! Don't forget to stock up on Poké Balls!

 TIP Even if you don't catch it the first time, the Pokémon will stay in the GO Park and you can try again.

Once a Pokémon is caught and brought out of a GO Park, its stats and moves will be different from what they were in Pokémon GO. Something about the mysterious way Pokémon travel to GO Parks causes these changes. Perhaps you could become a Pokémon Professor and research these secrets yourself!

 TIP Shiny Pokémon you've sent over from Pokémon GO will still be Shiny after you catch them in a GO Park!

Pokémon Chase

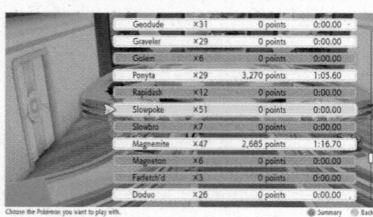

By talking to the GO Park complex receptionist, you can also play the Pokémon Chase minigame! You'll need at least 25 Pokémon of the same species in the GO Park complex, but it doesn't matter if they're in the same GO Parks or not.

To play the minigame, just choose the option to enter the Play Yard and then select the species of Pokémon you'd like to play with.

When the game starts, you'll have three minutes to gather up all 25 of the Pokémon and bring them to the north end of the Play Yard. Watch out, though, as Pokémon will pop up from the ground and startle your gathered group, making them scatter! The faster you complete the minigame and the larger the group of Pokémon you bring to the goal at a time, the better your score will be!

Just like in a GO Park, you can adjust the camera with Ⓨ and bring up the menu with Ⓧ.

 TIP Each time you complete the minigame, you'll get a random generic Candy!

Kanto Region
Pokédex

Kanto Region Pokédex

This is a list of all of the Pokémon in the Kanto Region Pokédex, ordered by Pokédex number. There is also an alphabetical list of all the Pokémon species back on page 9. Remember: Pokémon with numbers greater than 150 don't have to be obtained for your Pokédex to be considered complete (p. 119)!

001 Bulbasaur 166	039 Jigglypuff 217	077 Ponyta 263	115 Kangaskhan 307
002 Ivysaur...................167	040 Wigglytuff...............218	078 Rapidash.................264	116 Horsea 309
003 Venusaur 168	041 Zubat 219	079 Slowpoke.................265	117 Seadra 310
004 Charmander...........170	042 Golbat....................220	080 Slowbro 266	118 Goldeen 311
005 Charmeleon 171	043 Oddish....................221	081 Magnemite...............268	119 Seaking 312
006 Charizard 172	044 Gloom.....................222	082 Magneton.................269	120 Staryu 313
007 Squirtle...................175	045 Vileplume.................223	083 Farfetch'd 270	121 Starmie 314
008 Wartortle 176	046 Paras 224	084 Doduo.....................271	122 Mr. Mime 315
009 Blastoise.................177	047 Parasect 225	085 Dodrio.....................272	123 Scyther 316
010 Caterpie 179	048 Venonat 226	086 Seel 273	124 Jynx 317
011 Metapod 180	049 Venomoth 227	087 Dewgong 274	125 Electabuzz 318
012 Butterfree 181	050 Diglett.....................228	088 Grimer 275	126 Magmar 319
013 Weedle...................182	051 Dugtrio....................230	089 Muk 277	127 Pinsir 320
014 Kakuna 183	052 Meowth 232	090 Shellder 279	128 Tauros 322
015 Beedrill 184	053 Persian 234	091 Cloyster 280	129 Magikarp 323
016 Pidgey.....................186	054 Psyduck...................236	092 Gastly 281	130 Gyarados 324
017 Pidgeotto 187	055 Golduck 237	093 Haunter 282	131 Lapras 326
018 Pidgeot 188	056 Mankey 238	094 Gengar....................283	132 Ditto 327
019 Rattata....................190	057 Primeape 239	095 Onix 285	133 Eevee......................328
020 Raticate 192	058 Growlithe 240	096 Drowzee 286	134 Vaporeon 329
021 Spearow 194	059 Arcanine 241	097 Hypno 287	135 Jolteon.....................330
022 Fearow 195	060 Poliwag 242	098 Krabby 288	136 Flareon 331
023 Ekans 196	061 Poliwhirl..................243	099 Kingler 289	137 Porygon 332
024 Arbok.......................197	062 Poliwrath 244	100 Voltorb 290	138 Omanyte 333
025 Pikachu....................198	063 Abra 245	101 Electrode 291	139 Omastar 334
026 Raichu.....................199	064 Kadabra 246	102 Exeggcute 292	140 Kabuto 335
027 Sandshrew 201	065 Alakazam 247	103 Exeggutor 293	141 Kabutops..................336
028 Sandslash 203	066 Machop 249	104 Cubone 295	142 Aerodactyl 337
029 Nidoran♀ 205	067 Machoke 250	105 Marowak 296	143 Snorlax.....................339
030 Nidorina 206	068 Machamp 251	106 Hitmonlee 298	144 Articuno 340
031 Nidoqueen 207	069 Bellsprout 252	107 Hitmonchan 299	145 Zapdos.....................341
032 Nidoran♂ 208	070 Weepinbell 253	108 Lickitung...................300	146 Moltres 342
033 Nidorino 209	071 Victreebel 254	109 Koffing 301	147 Dratini 343
034 Nidoking 210	072 Tentacool 255	110 Weezing 302	148 Dragonair 344
035 Clefairy 211	073 Tentacruel 256	111 Rhyhorn 303	149 Dragonite..................345
036 Clefable 212	074 Geodude 257	112 Rhydon.....................304	150 Mewtwo....................346
037 Vulpix......................213	075 Graveler 259	113 Chansey 305	151 Mew.........................349
038 Ninetales 215	076 Golem 261	114 Tangela 306	152 Meltan 350
			153 Melmetal..............350

Mega-Evolved Pokémon

Mega Venusaur 169	Mega Beedrill.................185	Mega Gengar 284	Mega Aerodactyl............338
Mega Charizard X 173	Mega Pidgeot................189	Mega Kangaskhan 308	Mega Mewtwo X 347
Mega Charizard Y 174	Mega Alakazam 248	Mega Pinsir...................321	Mega Mewtwo Y............348
Mega Blastoise 178	Mega Slowbro................267	Mega Gyarados..............325	

Alolan Regional Variants

Alolan Rattata................191	Alolan Vulpix 214	Alolan Persian...............235	Alolan Muk....................278
Alolan Raticate...............193	Alolan Ninetales............216	Alolan Geodude.............258	Alolan Exeggutor...........294
Alolan Raichu................200	Alolan Diglett 229	Alolan Graveler 260	Alolan Marowak 297
Alolan Sandshrew 202	Alolan Dugtrio 231	Alolan Golem 262	
Alolan Sandslash 204	Alolan Meowth..............233	Alolan Grimer 276	

Understanding Pokédex Entries

On the next 187 pages, you will see entries about each of the Pokémon species you can obtain in these games, as well as some of the different forms they can appear in. The guide below breaks down what information you'll find in standard entries.

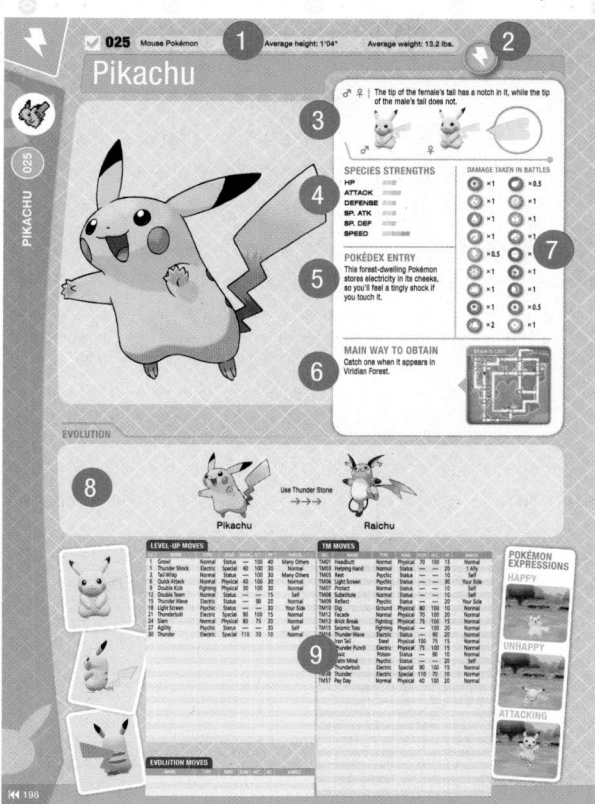

4. Species strengths

You'll find the strengths that are typical of this species here. If you haven't already, learn about species strengths on page 124.

5. Pokédex entry

Some interesting facts about each Pokémon can be found here in its Pokédex entry.

6. Main way to obtain

Here you will find recommendations on the best ways to get this Pokémon yourself, whether through catching one in the wild, Evolution, trading, or other methods.

7. Damage taken in battles

This handy chart shows you exactly how moves of each type will affect this species, dealing anywhere from 0.25 to 4 times the basic damage.

8. Evolution

If the Pokémon can evolve in these games, you can see its Evolutionary chain here.

> **TIP**
> A number of Pokemon may have further Evolutions or different ways to evolve in other Pokemon games which aren't featured in *Pokémon: Let's Go, Pikachu!* or *Pokémon: Let's Go, Eevee!* Check out www.pokemon.com to learn more about the ever-growing number of discovered Pokémon!

1. Basic info

At the top of each page, you'll find basic info, such as the Pokémon species' name, its Pokédex number, its category, and its average height and weight.

2. Types

These icons here represent the type or types this Pokémon has. If you need a refresher on the type symbols, turn to the type matchup chart on page 399.

3. Gender descriptions

If the males and females of the species look different, you'll find a description and images here!

> **TIP**
> The special entries for Mega-Evolved Pokémon will have a bit less info, but you'll notice some of it appears outlined in blue. Anything that will have changed by a Pokémon undergoing Mega Evolution—such as its height, types, or species strengths—will be marked in blue!

9. Move tables

Nestled among images showing species in different ways are tables of all the moves that species can learn, broken down by category. If you need help understanding the meaning of the different columns in these tables, refer to page 382, where you can learn about move ranges, power, accuracy, and more!

Partner Pikachu ☑ **025** Mouse Pokémon

Average height: 1'04" | Average weight: 13.2 lbs.

GET IT WHEN YOU PLAY

♂ ♀ | The tip of the female's tail has a notch in it, while the tip of the male's tail does not.

 ♂  ♀

SPECIES STRENGTHS

HP	▪▪▪
ATTACK	▪▪▪▪
DEFENSE	▪▪▪
SP. ATK	▪▪▪▪
SP. DEF	▪▪▪
SPEED	▪▪▪▪▪▪

DAMAGE TAKEN IN BATTLES

⊙	×1	⊙	×0.5
🔥	×1	◎	×1
💧	×1	⊙	×1
🍃	×1	⊙	×1
⚡	×0.5	⊙	×1
❄	×1	⊙	×1
👊	×1	◗	×1
☁	×1	⊙	×0.5
⛰	×2	✦	×1

HOW TO OBTAIN

This special Pikachu will be your partner if you are playing *Pokémon: Let's Go, Pikachu!* If you are looking for information about the Pikachu you can catch in the wild, turn to page 198.

LOOKS & MOVES

LEVEL-UP MOVES

LV.	NAME	TYPE	KIND	POW.	ACC.	PP	RANGE
1	Growl	Normal	Status	—	100	40	Many Others
1	Thunder Shock	Electric	Special	40	100	30	Normal
3	Tail Whip	Normal	Status	—	100	30	Many Others
6	Quick Attack	Normal	Physical	40	100	30	Normal
9	Double Kick	Fighting	Physical	30	100	30	Normal
12	Double Team	Normal	Status	—	—	15	Self
15	Thunder Wave	Electric	Status	—	90	20	Normal
18	Light Screen	Psychic	Status	—	—	30	Your Side
21	Thunderbolt	Electric	Special	90	100	15	Normal
24	Slam	Normal	Physical	80	75	20	Normal
27	Agility	Psychic	Status	—	—	30	Self
30	Thunder	Electric	Special	110	70	10	Normal

TM MOVES

NO.	NAME	TYPE	KIND	POW.	ACC.	PP	RANGE
TM01	Headbutt	Normal	Physical	70	100	15	Normal
TM03	Helping Hand	Normal	Status	—	—	20	1 Ally
TM05	Rest	Psychic	Status	—	—	10	Self
TM06	Light Screen	Psychic	Status	—	—	30	Your Side
TM07	Protect	Normal	Status	—	—	10	Self
TM08	Substitute	Normal	Status	—	—	10	Self
TM09	Reflect	Psychic	Status	—	—	20	Your Side
TM10	Dig	Ground	Physical	80	100	10	Normal
TM12	Facade	Normal	Physical	70	100	20	Normal
TM13	Brick Break	Fighting	Physical	75	100	15	Normal
TM15	Seismic Toss	Fighting	Physical	—	100	10	Normal
TM16	Thunder Wave	Electric	Status	—	90	20	Normal
TM19	Iron Tail	Steel	Physical	100	75	15	Normal
TM23	Thunder Punch	Electric	Physical	75	100	15	Normal
TM27	Toxic	Poison	Status	—	90	10	Normal
TM33	Calm Mind	Psychic	Status	—	—	20	Self
TM36	Thunderbolt	Electric	Special	90	100	15	Normal
TM38	Thunder	Electric	Special	110	70	10	Normal
TM57	Pay Day	Normal	Physical	40	100	20	Normal

MOVES TAUGHT BY PEOPLE

NAME	TYPE	KIND	POW.	ACC.	PP	RANGE	CAN BE LEARNED
Zippy Zap	Electric	Physical	50	100	15	Normal	After reaching Cerulean City
Floaty Fall	Flying	Physical	90	95	15	Normal	After reaching Celadon City
Splishy Splash	Water	Special	90	100	15	Many Others	After reaching Fuchsia City

Your partner also has access to special partner powers (p. 142), which can manifest in the special move Pika Papow! This Electric-type move never misses an opponent in the field, and its power is based on how much your partner loves you (p. 129). It can become the most powerful move your partner knows, if your friendship grows!

☑ **133** Evolution Pokémon

Partner Eevee

Average height: 1'00" | Average weight: 14.3 lbs.

GET IT WHEN YOU PLAY

♂ ♀ | The white tip of the female's tail has larger, rounder scallops than the male's tail.

SPECIES STRENGTHS

HP	▪▪▪
ATTACK	▪▪▪
DEFENSE	▪▪▪▪
SP. ATK	▪▪▪
SP. DEF	▪▪▪▪
SPEED	▪▪▪▪

DAMAGE TAKEN IN BATTLES

◎	×1	🍃	×1
🔥	×1	🌀	×1
💧	×1	🦋	×1
⚡	×1	🪨	×1
🌿	×1	👁	×0
❄	×1	🔥	×1
🥊	×2	🌙	×1
☠	×1	◉	×1
⛰	×1	✦	×1

HOW TO OBTAIN

This special Eevee will be your partner if you are playing *Pokémon: Let's Go, Eevee!* If you are looking for information about the Eevee you can catch in the wild, turn to page 328.

LOOKS & MOVES

LEVEL-UP MOVES

LV.	NAME	TYPE	KIND	POW.	ACC.	PP	RANGE
1	Growl	Normal	Status	—	100	40	Many Others
1	Tackle	Normal	Physical	40	100	35	Normal
3	Tail Whip	Normal	Status	—	100	30	Many Others
6	Quick Attack	Normal	Physical	40	100	30	Normal
10	Double Kick	Fighting	Physical	30	100	30	Normal
14	Sand Attack	Ground	Status	—	100	15	Normal
17	Bite	Dark	Physical	60	100	25	Normal
21	Swift	Normal	Special	60	—	20	Many Others
24	Take Down	Normal	Physical	90	85	20	Normal
28	Double-Edge	Normal	Physical	120	100	15	Normal
31	Helping Hand	Normal	Status	—	—	20	1 Ally

TM MOVES

NO.	NAME	TYPE	KIND	POW.	ACC.	PP	RANGE
TM01	Headbutt	Normal	Physical	70	100	15	Normal
TM03	Helping Hand	Normal	Status	—	—	20	1 Ally
TM05	Rest	Psychic	Status	—	—	10	Self
TM07	Protect	Normal	Status	—	—	10	Self
TM08	Substitute	Normal	Status	—	—	10	Self
TM09	Reflect	Psychic	Status	—	—	20	Your Side
TM10	Dig	Ground	Physical	80	100	10	Normal
TM12	Facade	Normal	Physical	70	100	20	Normal
TM19	Iron Tail	Steel	Physical	100	75	15	Normal
TM27	Toxic	Poison	Status	—	90	10	Normal
TM43	Shadow Ball	Ghost	Special	80	100	15	Normal
TM57	Pay Day	Normal	Physical	40	100	20	Normal

MOVES TAUGHT BY PEOPLE

NAME	TYPE	KIND	POW.	ACC.	PP	RANGE	CAN BE LEARNED
Bouncy Bubble	Water	Special	90	100	15	Normal	After reaching Cerulean City
Buzzy Buzz	Electric	Special	90	100	15	Normal	After reaching Cerulean City
Sizzly Slide	Fire	Physical	90	100	15	Normal	After reaching Cerulean City
Glitzy Glow	Psychic	Special	90	100	15	Normal	After reaching Celadon City
Baddy Bad	Dark	Special	90	100	15	Normal	After reaching Celadon City
Sappy Seed	Grass	Physical	90	100	15	Normal	After reaching Fuchsia City
Freezy Frost	Ice	Special	90	100	15	Normal	After reaching Fuchsia City
Sparkly Swirl	Fairy	Special	90	100	15	Normal	After reaching Fuchsia City

Your partner also has access to special partner powers (p. 142), which can manifest in the physical move Veevee Volley! This Normal-type move never misses an opponent in the field, and its power is based on how much your partner loves you (p. 129). It can become the most powerful move your partner knows, if your friendship grows!

Bulbasaur

BULBASAUR   001

♂ ♀ | Same form for male/female

SPECIES STRENGTHS

HP	▪▪▪
ATTACK	▪▪▪
DEFENSE	▪▪▪
SP. ATK	▪▪▪▪
SP. DEF	▪▪▪▪
SPEED	▪▪▪

DAMAGE TAKEN IN BATTLES

◉ ×1		🍃 ×2	
🔥 ×2		◎ ×2	
💧 ×0.5		⚡ ×1	
🍂 ×0.25		👊 ×1	
✋ ×0.5		◓ ×1	
❄ ×2		✦ ×1	
🪨 ×0.5		☾ ×1	
◐ ×1		◉ ×1	
◿ ×1		✧ ×0.5	

POKÉDEX ENTRY

It can go for days without eating a single morsel. In the bulb on its back, it stores energy.

MAIN WAY TO OBTAIN

Receive one from a lady in Cerulean City (p. 41). Or catch one when it appears as an unusual encounter during a Catch Combo (p. 117) in Viridian Forest.

Where to catch
Unusual Encounter

EVOLUTION

Bulbasaur

Lv. 16 →→→

Ivysaur

Lv. 32 →→→

Venusaur

LEVEL-UP MOVES

LV.	NAME	TYPE	KIND	POW.	ACC.	PP	RANGE
1	Growl	Normal	Status	—	100	40	Many Others
1	Tackle	Normal	Physical	40	100	35	Normal
5	Vine Whip	Grass	Physical	45	100	25	Normal
9	Leech Seed	Grass	Status	—	90	10	Normal
14	Poison Powder	Poison	Status	—	75	35	Normal
14	Sleep Powder	Grass	Status	—	75	15	Normal
18	Take Down	Normal	Physical	90	85	20	Normal
23	Razor Leaf	Grass	Physical	55	95	25	Many Others
27	Growth	Normal	Status	—	—	20	Self
32	Double-Edge	Normal	Physical	120	100	15	Normal

TM MOVES

NO.	NAME	TYPE	KIND	POW.	ACC.	PP	RANGE
TM01	Headbutt	Normal	Physical	70	100	15	Normal
TM05	Rest	Psychic	Status	—	—	10	Self
TM06	Light Screen	Psychic	Status	—	—	30	Your Side
TM07	Protect	Normal	Status	—	—	10	Self
TM08	Substitute	Normal	Status	—	—	10	Self
TM09	Reflect	Psychic	Status	—	—	20	Your Side
TM12	Facade	Normal	Physical	70	100	20	Normal
TM27	Toxic	Poison	Status	—	90	10	Normal
TM39	Outrage	Dragon	Physical	120	100	10	1 Random
TM45	Solar Beam	Grass	Special	200	100	10	Normal
TM52	Sludge Bomb	Poison	Special	90	100	10	Normal
TM53	Mega Drain	Grass	Special	75	100	10	Normal

POKÉMON EXPRESSIONS

HAPPY

UNHAPPY

ATTACKING

EVOLUTION MOVES

NAME	TYPE	KIND	POW.	ACC.	PP	RANGE

Ivysaur

♂ ♀ | Same form for male/female

SPECIES STRENGTHS

HP	▪▪▪
ATTACK	▪▪▪
DEFENSE	▪▪▪
SP. ATK	▪▪▪▪
SP. DEF	▪▪▪▪
SPEED	▪▪▪

DAMAGE TAKEN IN BATTLES

×1		×2	
×2		×2	
×0.5		×1	
×0.25		×1	
×0.5		×1	
×2		×1	
×0.5		×1	
×1		×1	
×1		×0.5	

POKÉDEX ENTRY

The bud on its back grows by drawing energy. It gives off an aroma when it is ready to bloom.

MAIN WAY TO OBTAIN

Obtain a Bulbasaur, then level it up to Lv. 16 or higher to evolve it into Ivysaur.

Where to catch

Habitat Unknown

EVOLUTION

Bulbasaur

Lv. 16 →→→

Ivysaur

Lv. 32 →→→

Venusaur

POKÉMON EXPRESSIONS

HAPPY

UNHAPPY

ATTACKING

LEVEL-UP MOVES

LV.	NAME	TYPE	KIND	POW.	ACC.	PP	RANGE
1	Growl	Normal	Status	—	100	40	Many Others
1	Leech Seed	Grass	Status	—	90	10	Normal
1	Tackle	Normal	Physical	40	100	35	Normal
1	Vine Whip	Grass	Physical	45	100	25	Normal
5	Vine Whip	Grass	Physical	45	100	25	Normal
9	Leech Seed	Grass	Status	—	90	10	Normal
14	Poison Powder	Poison	Status	—	75	35	Normal
14	Sleep Powder	Grass	Status	—	75	15	Normal
22	Take Down	Normal	Physical	90	85	20	Normal
31	Razor Leaf	Grass	Physical	55	95	25	Many Others
39	Growth	Normal	Status	—	—	20	Self
48	Double-Edge	Normal	Physical	120	100	15	Normal
56	Solar Beam	Grass	Special	200	100	10	Normal

TM MOVES

NO.	NAME	TYPE	KIND	POW.	ACC.	PP	RANGE
TM01	Headbutt	Normal	Physical	70	100	15	Normal
TM05	Rest	Psychic	Status	—	—	10	Self
TM06	Light Screen	Psychic	Status	—	—	30	Your Side
TM07	Protect	Normal	Status	—	—	10	Self
TM08	Substitute	Normal	Status	—	—	10	Self
TM09	Reflect	Psychic	Status	—	—	20	Your Side
TM12	Facade	Normal	Physical	70	100	20	Normal
TM27	Toxic	Poison	Status	—	90	10	Normal
TM39	Outrage	Dragon	Physical	120	100	10	1 Random
TM45	Solar Beam	Grass	Special	200	100	10	Normal
TM52	Sludge Bomb	Poison	Special	90	100	10	Normal
TM53	Mega Drain	Grass	Special	75	100	10	Normal

EVOLUTION MOVES

NAME	TYPE	KIND	POW.	ACC.	PP	RANGE

VENUSAUR 003

003 Seed Pokémon — Average height: 6'07" — Average weight: 220.5 lbs.

Venusaur

♂ ♀ | The female has a pistil in its bloom, but the male has none.

♂   ♀

SPECIES STRENGTHS

HP	▰▰▰▱▱
ATTACK	▰▰▰▱▱
DEFENSE	▰▰▰▱▱
SP. ATK	▰▰▰▰▱
SP. DEF	▰▰▰▰▱
SPEED	▰▰▰▱▱

DAMAGE TAKEN IN BATTLES

◎	×1		×2
	×2		×2
	×0.5		×1
	×0.25		×1
	×0.5		×1
	×2		×1
	×0.5		×1
	×1		×1
	×1		×0.5

POKÉDEX ENTRY

The flower on its back catches the sun's rays. The sunlight is then absorbed and used for energy.

MAIN WAY TO OBTAIN

Obtain an Ivysaur, then level it up to Lv. 32 or higher to evolve it into Venusaur.

Where to catch

Habitat Unknown

EVOLUTION

Bulbasaur

Lv. 16 →→→

Ivysaur

Lv. 32 →→→

Venusaur

LEVEL-UP MOVES

LV.	NAME	TYPE	KIND	POW.	ACC.	PP	RANGE
1	Amnesia	Psychic	Status	—	—	20	Self
1	Growl	Normal	Status	—	100	40	Many Others
1	Leech Seed	Grass	Status	—	90	10	Normal
1	Petal Dance	Grass	Special	120	100	10	1 Random
1	Power Whip	Grass	Physical	120	85	10	Normal
1	Tackle	Normal	Physical	40	100	35	Normal
1	Vine Whip	Grass	Physical	45	100	25	Normal
1	Vine Whip	Grass	Physical	45	100	25	Normal
9	Leech Seed	Grass	Status	—	90	10	Normal
14	Poison Powder	Poison	Status	—	75	35	Normal
14	Sleep Powder	Grass	Status	—	75	15	Normal
22	Take Down	Normal	Physical	90	85	20	Normal
31	Razor Leaf	Grass	Physical	55	95	25	Many Others
44	Growth	Normal	Status	—	—	20	Self
58	Double-Edge	Normal	Physical	120	100	15	Normal
71	Solar Beam	Grass	Special	200	100	10	Normal

TM MOVES

NO.	NAME	TYPE	KIND	POW.	ACC.	PP	RANGE
TM01	Headbutt	Normal	Physical	70	100	15	Normal
TM05	Rest	Psychic	Status	—	—	10	Self
TM06	Light Screen	Psychic	Status	—	—	30	Your Side
TM07	Protect	Normal	Status	—	—	10	Self
TM08	Substitute	Normal	Status	—	—	10	Self
TM09	Reflect	Psychic	Status	—	—	20	Your Side
TM12	Facade	Normal	Physical	70	100	20	Normal
TM27	Toxic	Poison	Status	—	90	10	Normal
TM39	Outrage	Dragon	Physical	120	100	10	1 Random
TM41	Earthquake	Ground	Physical	100	100	10	All Others
TM45	Solar Beam	Grass	Special	200	100	10	Normal
TM48	Hyper Beam	Normal	Special	150	90	5	Normal
TM52	Sludge Bomb	Poison	Special	90	100	10	Normal
TM53	Mega Drain	Grass	Special	75	100	10	Normal

EVOLUTION MOVES

NAME	TYPE	KIND	POW.	ACC.	PP	RANGE
Petal Dance	Grass	Special	120	100	10	1 Random

POKÉMON EXPRESSIONS

HAPPY

UNHAPPY

ATTACKING

Mega Venusaur

MEGA EVOLUTION

Venusaur

Get a Venusaurite from Blue (p. 96), then Mega Evolve Venusaur during battle.

→→→

Mega Venusaur

SPECIES STRENGTHS

HP	▪▪▪▫▫
ATTACK	▪▪▪▫▫
DEFENSE	▪▪▪▪▪▪▫
SP. ATK	▪▪▪▪▪▫
SP. DEF	▪▪▪▪▪▫
SPEED	▪▪▪▫▫

REQUIRED MEGA STONE: VENUSAURITE

Receive it from Blue when you return to Pallet Town near the end of your adventure (p. 97).

DAMAGE TAKEN IN BATTLES

⊙	×1	⟁	×2
🔥	×2	◎	×2
💧	×0.5	⊛	×1
🍃	×0.25	⚔	×1
⚡	×0.5	☉	×1
❄	×2	👊	×1
▦	×0.5	☾	×1
☯	×1	⊙	×1
◭	×1	✶	×0.5

✓ **004** Lizard Pokémon　Average height: 2'00"　Average weight: 18.7 lbs.

Charmander

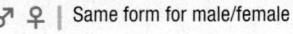

♂ ♀ | Same form for male/female

SPECIES STRENGTHS

HP	▮▮▮
ATTACK	▮▮▮▮
DEFENSE	▮▮▮
SP. ATK	▮▮▮▮
SP. DEF	▮▮▮
SPEED	▮▮▮▮

DAMAGE TAKEN IN BATTLES

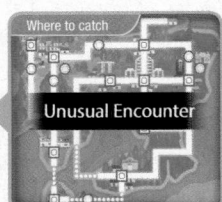

⊙	×1		×1
	×0.5		×1
	×2		×0.5
	×0.5		×2
	×1		×1
	×0.5		×1
	×1		×1
	×1		×0.5
	×2		×0.5

POKÉDEX ENTRY

The flame at the tip of its tail makes a sound as it burns. You can only hear it in quiet places.

MAIN WAY TO OBTAIN

Receive one from a man north of Nugget Bridge on Route 24 (p. 43). Or catch one when it appears as an unusual encounter during a Catch Combo (p. 117) on Route 3 or Route 4 (East) or in the Rock Tunnel.

Where to catch

Unusual Encounter

EVOLUTION

Lv. 16
→→→

Lv. 36
→→→

Charmander　　　**Charmeleon**　　　**Charizard**

LEVEL-UP MOVES

LV.	NAME	TYPE	KIND	POW.	ACC.	PP	RANGE
1	Scratch	Normal	Physical	40	100	35	Normal
4	Growl	Normal	Status	—	100	40	Many Others
9	Smokescreen	Normal	Status	—	100	20	Normal
13	Ember	Fire	Special	40	100	25	Normal
18	Fury Swipes	Normal	Physical	18	80	15	Normal
22	Dragon Rage	Dragon	Special	—	100	10	Normal
27	Fire Spin	Fire	Special	35	85	15	Normal
31	Slash	Normal	Physical	70	100	20	Normal
36	Flamethrower	Fire	Special	90	100	15	Normal

TM MOVES

NO.	NAME	TYPE	KIND	POW.	ACC.	PP	RANGE
TM01	Headbutt	Normal	Physical	70	100	15	Normal
TM05	Rest	Psychic	Status	—	—	10	Self
TM07	Protect	Normal	Status	—	—	10	Self
TM08	Substitute	Normal	Status	—	—	10	Self
TM09	Reflect	Psychic	Status	—	—	20	Your Side
TM10	Dig	Ground	Physical	80	100	10	Normal
TM11	Will-O-Wisp	Fire	Status	—	85	15	Normal
TM12	Facade	Normal	Physical	70	100	20	Normal
TM13	Brick Break	Fighting	Physical	75	100	15	Normal
TM15	Seismic Toss	Fighting	Physical	—	100	20	Normal
TM19	Iron Tail	Steel	Physical	100	75	15	Normal
TM22	Rock Slide	Rock	Physical	75	90	10	Many Others
TM23	Thunder Punch	Electric	Physical	75	100	15	Normal
TM27	Toxic	Poison	Status	—	90	10	Normal
TM31	Fire Punch	Fire	Physical	75	100	15	Normal
TM34	Dragon Pulse	Dragon	Special	85	100	10	Normal
TM37	Flamethrower	Fire	Special	90	100	15	Normal
TM39	Outrage	Dragon	Physical	120	100	10	1 Random
TM46	Fire Blast	Fire	Special	110	85	5	Normal

EVOLUTION MOVES

NAME	TYPE	KIND	POW.	ACC.	PP	RANGE

POKÉMON EXPRESSIONS

HAPPY

UNHAPPY

ATTACKING

Charmeleon

♂ ♀ | Same form for male/female

SPECIES STRENGTHS

HP
ATTACK
DEFENSE
SP. ATK
SP. DEF
SPEED

DAMAGE TAKEN IN BATTLES

◎ ×1		🍃 ×1	
🔥 ×0.5		🌀 ×1	
💧 ×2		🔮 ×0.5	
⚡ ×0.5		🌿 ×2	
❄ ×1		⚫ ×1	
❄ ×0.5		👊 ×1	
🗻 ×1		🌙 ×1	
👻 ×1		⭕ ×0.5	
🔩 ×2		✦ ×0.5	

POKÉDEX ENTRY

Tough fights could excite this Pokémon. When excited, it may breathe out bluish-white flames.

MAIN WAY TO OBTAIN

Obtain a Charmander, then level it up to Lv. 16 or higher to evolve it into Charmeleon.

Where to catch

Habitat Unknown

EVOLUTION

Charmander

Lv. 16 →→→

Charmeleon

Lv. 36 →→→

Charizard

POKÉMON EXPRESSIONS

HAPPY

UNHAPPY

ATTACKING

LEVEL-UP MOVES

LV.	NAME	TYPE	KIND	POW.	ACC.	PP	RANGE
1	Ember	Fire	Special	40	100	25	Normal
1	Growl	Normal	Status	—	100	40	Many Others
1	Scratch	Normal	Physical	40	100	35	Normal
1	Smokescreen	Normal	Status	—	100	20	Normal
4	Growl	Normal	Status	—	100	40	Many Others
9	Smokescreen	Normal	Status	—	100	20	Normal
13	Ember	Fire	Special	40	100	25	Normal
20	Fury Swipes	Normal	Physical	18	80	15	Normal
26	Dragon Rage	Dragon	Special	—	100	10	Normal
33	Fire Spin	Fire	Special	35	85	15	Normal
39	Slash	Normal	Physical	70	100	20	Normal
46	Flamethrower	Fire	Special	90	100	15	Normal

TM MOVES

NO.	NAME	TYPE	KIND	POW.	ACC.	PP	RANGE
TM01	Headbutt	Normal	Physical	70	100	15	Normal
TM05	Rest	Psychic	Status	—	—	10	Self
TM07	Protect	Normal	Status	—	—	10	Self
TM08	Substitute	Normal	Status	—	—	10	Self
TM09	Reflect	Psychic	Status	—	—	20	Your Side
TM10	Dig	Ground	Physical	80	100	10	Normal
TM11	Will-O-Wisp	Fire	Status	—	85	15	Normal
TM12	Facade	Normal	Physical	70	100	20	Normal
TM13	Brick Break	Fighting	Physical	75	100	15	Normal
TM15	Seismic Toss	Fighting	Physical	—	100	20	Normal
TM19	Iron Tail	Steel	Physical	100	75	15	Normal
TM22	Rock Slide	Rock	Physical	75	90	10	Many Others
TM23	Thunder Punch	Electric	Physical	75	100	15	Normal
TM27	Toxic	Poison	Status	—	90	10	Normal
TM31	Fire Punch	Fire	Physical	75	100	15	Normal
TM34	Dragon Pulse	Dragon	Special	85	100	10	Normal
TM37	Flamethrower	Fire	Special	90	100	15	Normal
TM39	Outrage	Dragon	Physical	120	100	10	1 Random
TM46	Fire Blast	Fire	Special	110	85	5	Normal

EVOLUTION MOVES

NAME	TYPE	KIND	POW.	ACC.	PP	RANGE

Charizard

♂ ♀ | Same form for male/female

SPECIES STRENGTHS

HP	▨▨▨▨
ATTACK	▨▨▨▨
DEFENSE	▨▨▨▨
SP. ATK	▨▨▨▨▨
SP. DEF	▨▨▨▨
SPEED	▨▨▨▨▨

DAMAGE TAKEN IN BATTLES

⬤	×1	〰	×1
🔥	×0.5	◎	×1
💧	×2	🌸	×0.25
🍃	×0.25	✦	×4
⚡	×2	🌀	×1
❄	×1	🪨	×1
▨	×0.5	◐	×1
◌	×1	◉	×0.5
△	×0	✸	×0.5

POKÉDEX ENTRY

When this Pokémon expels a blast of superhot fire, the red flame at the tip of its tail burns more intensely.

MAIN WAY TO OBTAIN

Obtain a Charmeleon, then level it up to Lv. 36 or higher to evolve it into Charizard. Or catch one when it appears in the sky as an unusual encounter during a Catch Combo after becoming Champion (p. 107).

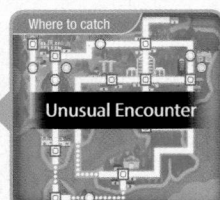

Where to catch

Unusual Encounter

EVOLUTION

Charmander	Lv. 16 →→→	Charmeleon	Lv. 36 →→→	Charizard

LEVEL-UP MOVES

LV.	NAME	TYPE	KIND	POW.	ACC.	PP	RANGE
1	Counter	Fighting	Physical	—	100	20	Varies
1	Crunch	Dark	Physical	80	100	15	Normal
1	Ember	Fire	Special	40	100	25	Normal
1	Growl	Normal	Status	—	100	40	Many Others
1	Heat Wave	Fire	Special	95	90	10	Many Others
1	Scratch	Normal	Physical	40	100	35	Normal
1	Smokescreen	Normal	Status	—	100	20	Normal
1	Wing Attack	Flying	Physical	60	100	35	Normal
4	Growl	Normal	Status	—	100	40	Many Others
9	Smokescreen	Normal	Status	—	100	20	Normal
13	Ember	Fire	Special	40	100	25	Normal
20	Fury Swipes	Normal	Physical	18	80	15	Normal
26	Dragon Rage	Dragon	Special	—	100	10	Normal
33	Fire Spin	Fire	Special	35	85	15	Normal
43	Slash	Normal	Physical	70	100	20	Normal
54	Flamethrower	Fire	Special	90	100	15	Normal
62	Air Slash	Flying	Special	75	95	15	Normal
75	Flare Blitz	Fire	Physical	120	100	15	Normal

TM MOVES

NO.	NAME	TYPE	KIND	POW.	ACC.	PP	RANGE
TM01	Headbutt	Normal	Physical	70	100	15	Normal
TM05	Rest	Psychic	Status	—	—	10	Self
TM07	Protect	Normal	Status	—	—	10	Self
TM08	Substitute	Normal	Status	—	—	10	Self
TM09	Reflect	Psychic	Status	—	—	20	Your Side
TM10	Dig	Ground	Physical	80	100	10	Normal
TM11	Will-O-Wisp	Fire	Status	—	85	15	Normal
TM12	Facade	Normal	Physical	70	100	20	Normal
TM13	Brick Break	Fighting	Physical	75	100	15	Normal
TM14	Fly	Flying	Physical	90	95	15	Normal
TM15	Seismic Toss	Fighting	Physical	—	100	20	Normal
TM17	Dragon Tail	Dragon	Physical	60	90	10	Normal
TM19	Iron Tail	Steel	Physical	100	75	15	Normal
TM22	Rock Slide	Rock	Physical	75	90	10	Many Others
TM23	Thunder Punch	Electric	Physical	75	100	15	Normal
TM27	Toxic	Poison	Status	—	90	10	Normal
TM31	Fire Punch	Fire	Physical	75	100	15	Normal
TM34	Dragon Pulse	Dragon	Special	85	100	10	Normal
TM37	Flamethrower	Fire	Special	90	100	15	Normal
TM39	Outrage	Dragon	Physical	120	100	10	1 Random
TM41	Earthquake	Ground	Physical	100	100	10	All Others
TM45	Solar Beam	Grass	Special	200	100	10	Normal
TM46	Fire Blast	Fire	Special	110	85	5	Normal
TM48	Hyper Beam	Normal	Special	150	90	5	Normal
TM50	Roost	Flying	Status	—	—	10	Self

EVOLUTION MOVES

NAME	TYPE	KIND	POW.	ACC.	PP	RANGE
Wing Attack	Flying	Physical	60	100	35	Normal

Mega Charizard X

MEGA EVOLUTION

Charizard

→ → →

Get a Charizardite X from Blue, then Mega Evolve Charizard during battle by selecting the X icon.

Mega Charizard X

SPECIES STRENGTHS

HP	▩▩▩▩
ATTACK	▩▩▩▩▩▩
DEFENSE	▩▩▩▩▩
SP. ATK	▩▩▩▩▩▩
SP. DEF	▩▩▩▩
SPEED	▩▩▩▩▩

DAMAGE TAKEN IN BATTLES

⊙	×1	◗	×1
🔥	×0.25	◉	×1
💧	×1	⊙	×0.5
🍃	×0.25	🍂	×2
⚡	×0.5	👁	×1
❄	×1	✦	×2
👊	×1	☾	×1
☣	×1	⊙	×0.5
⛰	×2	✦	×1

 REQUIRED MEGA STONE: CHARIZARDITE X

Receive it from Blue when you return to Pallet Town near the end of your adventure (p. 97).

✓ **006** Flame Pokémon   Average height: 5'07"   Average weight: 221.6 lbs.

Mega Charizard Y

MEGA EVOLUTION

Charizard

Get a Charizardite Y from Blue, then Mega Evolve Charizard during battle by selecting the Y icon.

Mega Charizard Y

SPECIES STRENGTHS

HP	▰▰▰▰▱
ATTACK	▰▰▰▰▰▰
DEFENSE	▰▰▰▱▱
SP. ATK	▰▰▰▰▰▰▰▰
SP. DEF	▰▰▰▰▰
SPEED	▰▰▰▰▰

DAMAGE TAKEN IN BATTLES

⊙	×1	🍃	×1
🔥	×0.5	◎	×1
💧	×2	☯	×0.25
⚡	×0.25	🍂	×4
⚡	×2	◉	×1
❄	×1	☬	×1
🏰	×0.5	☾	×1
◐	×1	⊚	×0.5
⛰	×0	✦	×0.5

⊙ REQUIRED MEGA STONE: CHARIZARDITE Y

Receive it from Blue when you return to Pallet Town near the end of your adventure (p. 97).

Squirtle

♂ ♀ | Same form for male/female

SPECIES STRENGTHS

HP
ATTACK
DEFENSE
SP. ATK
SP. DEF
SPEED

DAMAGE TAKEN IN BATTLES

◎	×1		×1
	×0.5		×1
	×0.5		×1
	×2		×1
	×2		×1
	×0.5		×1
	×1		×1
	×1		×0.5
	×1		×1

POKÉDEX ENTRY

Shoots water at prey while in the water. Withdraws into its shell when in danger.

MAIN WAY TO OBTAIN

Receive one from a police officer in Vermilion City (p. 47). Or catch one when it appears as an unusual encounter during a Catch Combo (p. 117) on Route 24 or Route 25 or in the Seafoam Islands.

Where to catch
Unusual Encounter

EVOLUTION

 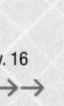  

Squirtle → Lv. 16 → Wartortle → Lv. 36 → Blastoise

POKÉMON EXPRESSIONS

HAPPY

UNHAPPY

ATTACKING

LEVEL-UP MOVES

LV.	NAME	TYPE	KIND	POW.	ACC.	PP	RANGE
1	Tackle	Normal	Physical	40	100	35	Normal
5	Tail Whip	Normal	Status	—	100	30	Many Others
9	Bubble	Water	Special	40	100	30	Many Others
14	Withdraw	Water	Status	—	—	40	Self
18	Water Gun	Water	Special	40	100	25	Normal
23	Bite	Dark	Physical	60	100	25	Normal
27	Bubble Beam	Water	Special	65	100	20	Normal
32	Protect	Normal	Status	—	—	10	Self
36	Headbutt	Normal	Physical	70	100	15	Normal
41	Hydro Pump	Water	Special	110	80	5	Normal
45	Skull Bash	Normal	Physical	130	100	10	Normal

TM MOVES

NO.	NAME	TYPE	KIND	POW.	ACC.	PP	RANGE
TM01	Headbutt	Normal	Physical	70	100	15	Normal
TM05	Rest	Psychic	Status	—	—	10	Self
TM07	Protect	Normal	Status	—	—	10	Self
TM08	Substitute	Normal	Status	—	—	10	Self
TM09	Reflect	Psychic	Status	—	—	20	Your Side
TM10	Dig	Ground	Physical	80	100	10	Normal
TM12	Facade	Normal	Physical	70	100	20	Normal
TM13	Brick Break	Fighting	Physical	75	100	15	Normal
TM15	Seismic Toss	Fighting	Physical	—	100	20	Normal
TM19	Iron Tail	Steel	Physical	100	75	15	Normal
TM22	Rock Slide	Rock	Physical	75	90	10	Many Others
TM25	Waterfall	Water	Physical	80	100	15	Normal
TM27	Toxic	Poison	Status	—	90	10	Normal
TM29	Scald	Water	Special	80	100	15	Normal
TM34	Dragon Pulse	Dragon	Special	85	100	10	Normal
TM35	Ice Punch	Ice	Physical	75	100	15	Normal
TM39	Outrage	Dragon	Physical	120	100	10	1 Random
TM47	Surf	Water	Special	90	100	15	All Others
TM51	Blizzard	Ice	Special	110	70	5	Many Others
TM55	Ice Beam	Ice	Special	90	100	10	Normal

EVOLUTION MOVES

NAME	TYPE	KIND	POW.	ACC.	PP	RANGE

Wartortle

WARTORTLE 008

♂ ♀ | Same form for male/female

SPECIES STRENGTHS

HP	▪▪▪▫
ATTACK	▪▪▪▫
DEFENSE	▪▪▪▪▫
SP. ATK	▪▪▪▫
SP. DEF	▪▪▪▪▫
SPEED	▪▪▪▫

DAMAGE TAKEN IN BATTLES

◎	×1		×1
	×0.5		×1
	×0.5		×1
	×2		×1
	×2		×1
	×0.5		×1
	×1		×1
	×1		×0.5
	×1		×1

POKÉDEX ENTRY

When tapped on its head, this Pokémon will pull it in, but its tail will still stick out a little bit.

MAIN WAY TO OBTAIN

Obtain a Squirtle, then level it up to Lv. 16 or higher to evolve it into Wartortle.

Where to catch

Habitat Unknown

EVOLUTION

 Squirtle → Lv. 16 → → →  Wartortle → Lv. 36 → → →  Blastoise

LEVEL-UP MOVES

LV.	NAME	TYPE	KIND	POW.	ACC.	PP	RANGE
1	Bubble	Water	Special	40	100	30	Many Others
1	Tackle	Normal	Physical	40	100	35	Normal
1	Tail Whip	Normal	Status	—	100	30	Many Others
1	Withdraw	Water	Status	—	—	40	Self
5	Tail Whip	Normal	Status	—	100	30	Many Others
9	Bubble	Water	Special	40	100	30	Many Others
14	Withdraw	Water	Status	—	—	40	Self
20	Water Gun	Water	Special	40	100	25	Normal
27	Bite	Dark	Physical	60	100	25	Normal
33	Bubble Beam	Water	Special	65	100	20	Normal
40	Protect	Normal	Status	—	—	10	Self
46	Headbutt	Normal	Physical	70	100	15	Normal
53	Hydro Pump	Water	Special	110	80	5	Normal
59	Skull Bash	Normal	Physical	130	100	10	Normal

TM MOVES

NO.	NAME	TYPE	KIND	POW.	ACC.	PP	RANGE
TM01	Headbutt	Normal	Physical	70	100	15	Normal
TM05	Rest	Psychic	Status	—	—	10	Self
TM07	Protect	Normal	Status	—	—	10	Self
TM08	Substitute	Normal	Status	—	—	10	Self
TM09	Reflect	Psychic	Status	—	—	20	Your Side
TM10	Dig	Ground	Physical	80	100	10	Normal
TM12	Facade	Normal	Physical	70	100	20	Normal
TM13	Brick Break	Fighting	Physical	75	100	15	Normal
TM15	Seismic Toss	Fighting	Physical	—	100	20	Normal
TM19	Iron Tail	Steel	Physical	100	75	15	Normal
TM22	Rock Slide	Rock	Physical	75	90	10	Many Others
TM25	Waterfall	Water	Physical	80	100	15	Normal
TM27	Toxic	Poison	Status	—	90	10	Normal
TM29	Scald	Water	Special	80	100	15	Normal
TM34	Dragon Pulse	Dragon	Special	85	100	10	Normal
TM35	Ice Punch	Ice	Physical	75	100	15	Normal
TM39	Outrage	Dragon	Physical	120	100	10	1 Random
TM47	Surf	Water	Special	90	100	15	All Others
TM51	Blizzard	Ice	Special	110	70	5	Many Others
TM55	Ice Beam	Ice	Special	90	100	10	Normal

POKÉMON EXPRESSIONS

HAPPY

UNHAPPY

ATTACKING

EVOLUTION MOVES

NAME	TYPE	KIND	POW.	ACC.	PP	RANGE

Blastoise

♂ ♀ | Same form for male/female

SPECIES STRENGTHS

HP	
ATTACK	
DEFENSE	
SP. ATK	
SP. DEF	
SPEED	

DAMAGE TAKEN IN BATTLES

◎	×1	🍃	×1
🔥	×0.5	⚪	×1
💧	×0.5	🌀	×1
🍃	×2	🔮	×1
❄	×2	👁	×1
✴	×0.5	🔴	×1
👊	×1	🌙	×1
☠	×1	⚙	×0.5
⛰	×1	✦	×1

POKÉDEX ENTRY

Once it takes aim at its enemy, it blasts out water with even more force than a fire hose.

MAIN WAY TO OBTAIN

Obtain a Wartortle, then level it up to Lv. 36 or higher to evolve it into Blastoise.

Where to catch

Habitat Unknown

EVOLUTION

	Lv. 16		Lv. 36	
Squirtle	→→→	**Wartortle**	→→→	**Blastoise**

POKÉMON EXPRESSIONS

HAPPY

UNHAPPY

ATTACKING

LEVEL-UP MOVES

LV.	NAME	TYPE	KIND	POW.	ACC.	PP	RANGE
1	Aqua Jet	Water	Physical	40	100	20	Normal
1	Bubble	Water	Special	40	100	30	Many Others
1	Fake Out	Normal	Physical	40	100	10	Normal
1	Flash Cannon	Steel	Special	80	100	10	Normal
1	Tackle	Normal	Physical	40	100	35	Normal
1	Tail Whip	Normal	Status	—	100	30	Many Others
1	Withdraw	Water	Status	—	—	40	Self
5	Tail Whip	Normal	Status	—	100	30	Many Others
9	Bubble	Water	Special	40	100	30	Many Others
14	Withdraw	Water	Status	—	—	40	Self
20	Water Gun	Water	Special	40	100	25	Normal
27	Bite	Dark	Physical	60	100	25	Normal
33	Bubble Beam	Water	Special	65	100	20	Normal
44	Protect	Normal	Status	—	—	10	Self
54	Headbutt	Normal	Physical	70	100	15	Normal
65	Hydro Pump	Water	Special	110	80	5	Normal
75	Skull Bash	Normal	Physical	130	100	10	Normal

TM MOVES

NO.	NAME	TYPE	KIND	POW.	ACC.	PP	RANGE
TM01	Headbutt	Normal	Physical	70	100	15	Normal
TM05	Rest	Psychic	Status	—	—	10	Self
TM07	Protect	Normal	Status	—	—	10	Self
TM08	Substitute	Normal	Status	—	—	10	Self
TM09	Reflect	Psychic	Status	—	—	20	Your Side
TM10	Dig	Ground	Physical	80	100	10	Normal
TM12	Facade	Normal	Physical	70	100	20	Normal
TM13	Brick Break	Fighting	Physical	75	100	15	Normal
TM15	Seismic Toss	Fighting	Physical	—	100	20	Normal
TM17	Dragon Tail	Dragon	Physical	60	90	10	Normal
TM19	Iron Tail	Steel	Physical	100	75	15	Normal
TM20	Dark Pulse	Dark	Special	80	100	15	Normal
TM22	Rock Slide	Rock	Physical	75	90	10	Many Others
TM25	Waterfall	Water	Physical	80	100	15	Normal
TM27	Toxic	Poison	Status	—	90	10	Normal
TM29	Scald	Water	Special	80	100	15	Normal
TM34	Dragon Pulse	Dragon	Special	85	100	10	Normal
TM35	Ice Punch	Ice	Physical	75	100	15	Normal
TM39	Outrage	Dragon	Physical	120	100	10	1 Random
TM41	Earthquake	Ground	Physical	100	100	10	All Others
TM47	Surf	Water	Special	90	100	15	All Others
TM48	Hyper Beam	Normal	Special	150	90	5	Normal
TM51	Blizzard	Ice	Special	110	70	5	Many Others
TM54	Flash Cannon	Steel	Special	80	100	10	Normal
TM55	Ice Beam	Ice	Special	90	100	10	Normal

EVOLUTION MOVES

NAME	TYPE	KIND	POW.	ACC.	PP	RANGE

Mega Blastoise

MEGA BLASTOISE

MEGA EVOLUTION

Blastoise

Get a Blastoisinite from Blue, then Mega Evolve Blastoise during battle.

→→→

Mega Blastoise

SPECIES STRENGTHS

HP	▪▪▪▪▪
ATTACK	▪▪▪▪▪▪▪
DEFENSE	▪▪▪▪▪▪▪▪
SP. ATK	▪▪▪▪▪▪▪▪
SP. DEF	▪▪▪▪▪▪▪
SPEED	▪▪▪▪▪

DAMAGE TAKEN IN BATTLES

⬤	×1	◈	×1
🔥	×0.5	◉	×1
💧	×0.5	◍	×1
⚡	×2	◐	×1
🍂	×2	◑	×1
❄	×0.5	◒	×1
▦	×1	◓	×1
◎	×1	◔	×0.5
◭	×1	✦	×1

REQUIRED MEGA STONE: BLASTOISINITE

Receive it from Blue when you return to Pallet Town near the end of your adventure (p. 97).

Caterpie

♂ ♀ | Same form for male/female

SPECIES STRENGTHS

HP
ATTACK
DEFENSE
SP. ATK
SP. DEF
SPEED

DAMAGE TAKEN IN BATTLES

×1		×2	
×2		×1	
×1		×1	
×0.5		×2	
×1		×1	
×1		×1	
×0.5		×1	
×1		×1	
×0.5		×1	

POKÉDEX ENTRY

If you touch the feeler on top of its head, it will release a horrible stink to protect itself.

MAIN WAY TO OBTAIN

Catch one when it appears on Route 2 or more commonly in Viridian Forest.

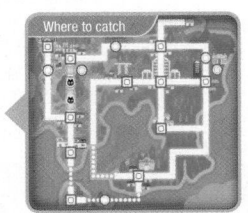
Where to catch

EVOLUTION

 Caterpie → Lv. 7 → Metapod → Lv. 10 → Butterfree

POKÉMON EXPRESSIONS

HAPPY

UNHAPPY

ATTACKING

LEVEL-UP MOVES

LV.	NAME	TYPE	KIND	POW.	ACC.	PP	RANGE
1	String Shot	Bug	Status	—	95	40	Many Others
1	Tackle	Normal	Physical	40	100	35	Normal

TM MOVES

NO.	NAME	TYPE	KIND	POW.	ACC.	PP	RANGE

EVOLUTION MOVES

NAME	TYPE	KIND	POW.	ACC.	PP	RANGE

✓ **011** Cocoon Pokémon   Average height: 2'04"   Average weight: 21.8 lbs.

Metapod

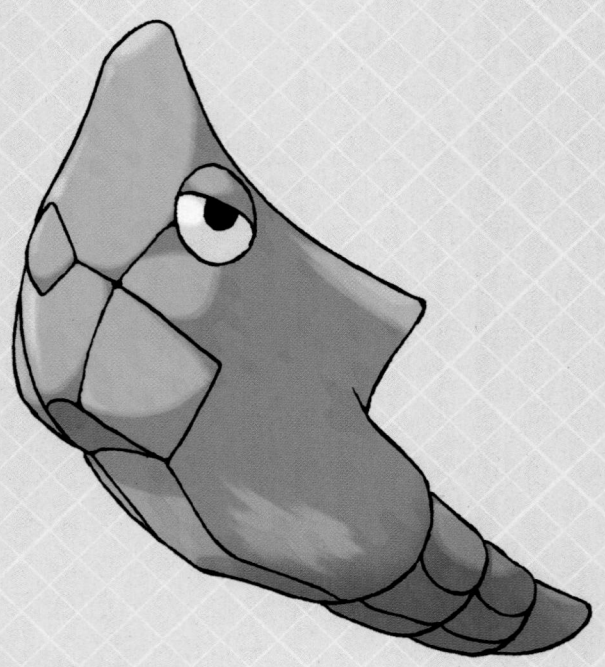

♂ ♀ | Same form for male/female

SPECIES STRENGTHS

HP	▰▰
ATTACK	▰
DEFENSE	▰▰▰▰
SP. ATK	▰
SP. DEF	▰
SPEED	▰

DAMAGE TAKEN IN BATTLES

◉	×1	🜁	×2
🔥	×2	◎	×1
💧	×1	🌀	×1
🌿	×0.5	✦	×2
⚡	×1	◈	×1
❄	×1	☯	×1
🥊	×0.5	☾	×1
☣	×1	●	×1
⛰	×0.5	✺	×1

POKÉDEX ENTRY

Hardens its shell to protect itself. However, a large impact may cause it to pop out of its shell.

MAIN WAY TO OBTAIN

Catch one when it appears in Viridian Forest. Or obtain a Caterpie, then level it up to Lv. 7 or higher to evolve it into Metapod.

Where to catch

EVOLUTION

 Caterpie → Lv. 7 →  Metapod → Lv. 10 →  Butterfree

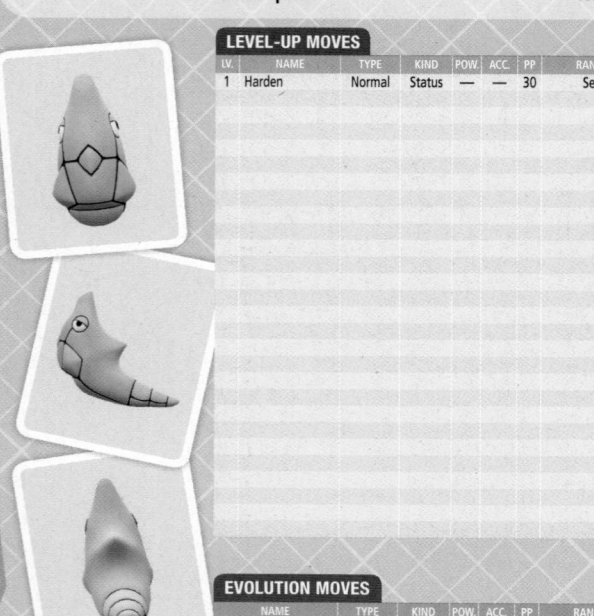

LEVEL-UP MOVES

LV.	NAME	TYPE	KIND	POW.	ACC.	PP	RANGE
1	Harden	Normal	Status	—	—	30	Self

TM MOVES

NO.	NAME	TYPE	KIND	POW.	ACC.	PP	RANGE

EVOLUTION MOVES

NAME	TYPE	KIND	POW.	ACC.	PP	RANGE
Harden	Normal	Status	—	—	30	Self

POKÉMON EXPRESSIONS

HAPPY

UNHAPPY

ATTACKING

Butterfree

♂ ♀ | The female has a black section on its lower wings where the male does not.

♂   ♀

SPECIES STRENGTHS

HP	▰▰▰
ATTACK	▰▰▰
DEFENSE	▰▰▰
SP. ATK	▰▰▰▰▰
SP. DEF	▰▰▰▰
SPEED	▰▰▰▰

DAMAGE TAKEN IN BATTLES

⊙ ×1		🔥 ×2
💧 ×2		⚙ ×1
💧 ×1		🌿 ×0.5
⚡ ×0.25		⚔ ×4
❄ ×2		🌑 ×1
❄ ×2		🔴 ×1
✊ ×0.25		🌙 ×1
⊙ ×1		⊙ ×1
◼ ×0		◈ ×1

POKÉDEX ENTRY

Its wings, covered with poisonous powder, repel water. This allows it to fly in the rain.

MAIN WAY TO OBTAIN

Catch one when it appears in Viridian Forest in *Pokémon: Let's Go, Pikachu!* Or obtain a Metapod, then level it up to Lv. 10 or higher to evolve it into Butterfree.

Where to catch

EVOLUTION

Caterpie   Lv. 7 →→→   **Metapod**   Lv. 10 →→→   **Butterfree**

POKÉMON EXPRESSIONS

HAPPY

UNHAPPY

ATTACKING

LEVEL-UP MOVES

LV.	NAME	TYPE	KIND	POW.	ACC.	PP	RANGE
1	Confusion	Psychic	Special	50	100	25	Normal
1	Gust	Flying	Special	40	100	35	Normal
13	Poison Powder	Poison	Status	—	75	35	Normal
13	Sleep Powder	Grass	Status	—	75	15	Normal
13	Stun Spore	Grass	Status	—	75	30	Normal
16	Psybeam	Psychic	Special	65	100	20	Normal
19	Supersonic	Normal	Status	—	55	20	Normal
22	Quiver Dance	Bug	Status	—	—	20	Self
25	Whirlwind	Normal	Status	—	—	20	Normal
28	Air Slash	Flying	Special	75	95	15	Normal
31	Bug Buzz	Bug	Special	90	100	10	Normal

TM MOVES

NO.	NAME	TYPE	KIND	POW.	ACC.	PP	RANGE
TM01	Headbutt	Normal	Physical	70	100	15	Normal
TM04	Teleport	Psychic	Status	—	—	20	Self
TM05	Rest	Psychic	Status	—	—	10	Self
TM07	Protect	Normal	Status	—	—	10	Self
TM08	Substitute	Normal	Status	—	—	10	Self
TM09	Reflect	Psychic	Status	—	—	20	Your Side
TM12	Facade	Normal	Physical	70	100	20	Normal
TM18	U-turn	Bug	Physical	70	100	20	Normal
TM27	Toxic	Poison	Status	—	90	10	Normal
TM40	Psychic	Psychic	Special	90	100	10	Normal
TM43	Shadow Ball	Ghost	Special	80	100	15	Normal
TM45	Solar Beam	Grass	Special	200	100	10	Normal
TM48	Hyper Beam	Normal	Special	150	90	5	Normal
TM50	Roost	Flying	Status	—	—	10	Self
TM53	Mega Drain	Grass	Special	75	100	10	Normal
TM59	Dream Eater	Psychic	Special	100	100	15	Normal

EVOLUTION MOVES

NAME	TYPE	KIND	POW.	ACC.	PP	RANGE
Gust	Flying	Special	40	100	35	Normal

Hairy Bug Pokémon   Average height: 1'00"   Average weight: 7.1 lbs.

Weedle

♂ ♀ | Same form for male/female

SPECIES STRENGTHS

HP
ATTACK
DEFENSE
SP. ATK
SP. DEF
SPEED

DAMAGE TAKEN IN BATTLES

×1		×2	
×2		×2	
×1		×0.5	
×0.25		×2	
×1		×1	
×1		×1	
×0.25		×1	
×0.5		×1	
×1		×0.5	

POKÉDEX ENTRY

Beware of the sharp stinger on its head. It hides in grass and bushes where it eats leaves.

MAIN WAY TO OBTAIN

Catch one when it appears on Route 2 or more commonly in Viridian Forest.

Where to catch

EVOLUTION

Weedle   Lv. 7 →→→   **Kakuna**   Lv. 10 →→→   **Beedrill**

LEVEL-UP MOVES

LV.	NAME	TYPE	KIND	POW.	ACC.	PP	RANGE
1	Poison Sting	Poison	Physical	15	100	35	Normal
1	String Shot	Bug	Status	—	95	40	Many Others

TM MOVES

NO.	NAME	TYPE	KIND	POW.	ACC.	PP	RANGE

EVOLUTION MOVES

NAME	TYPE	KIND	POW.	ACC.	PP	RANGE

POKÉMON EXPRESSIONS

HAPPY

UNHAPPY

ATTACKING

Average height: 2'00"   Average weight: 22.0 lbs.   Cocoon Pokémon **014**

Kakuna

♂ ♀ | Same form for male/female

SPECIES STRENGTHS

HP
ATTACK
DEFENSE
SP. ATK
SP. DEF
SPEED

DAMAGE TAKEN IN BATTLES

×1		×2	
×2		×2	
×1		×0.5	
×0.25		×2	
×1		×1	
×1		×1	
×0.25		×1	
×0.5		×1	
×1		×0.5	

POKÉDEX ENTRY

Able to move only slightly. When endangered, it may stick out its stinger and poison its enemy.

MAIN WAY TO OBTAIN

Catch one when it appears in Viridian Forest. Or obtain a Weedle, then level it up to Lv. 7 or higher to evolve it into Kakuna.

EVOLUTION

Weedle → Lv. 7 → **Kakuna** → Lv. 10 → **Beedrill**

POKÉMON EXPRESSIONS

HAPPY

UNHAPPY

ATTACKING

LEVEL-UP MOVES

LV.	NAME	TYPE	KIND	POW.	ACC.	PP	RANGE
1	Harden	Normal	Status	—	—	30	Self

TM MOVES

NO.	NAME	TYPE	KIND	POW.	ACC.	PP	RANGE

EVOLUTION MOVES

NAME	TYPE	KIND	POW.	ACC.	PP	RANGE
Harden	Normal	Status	—	—	30	Self

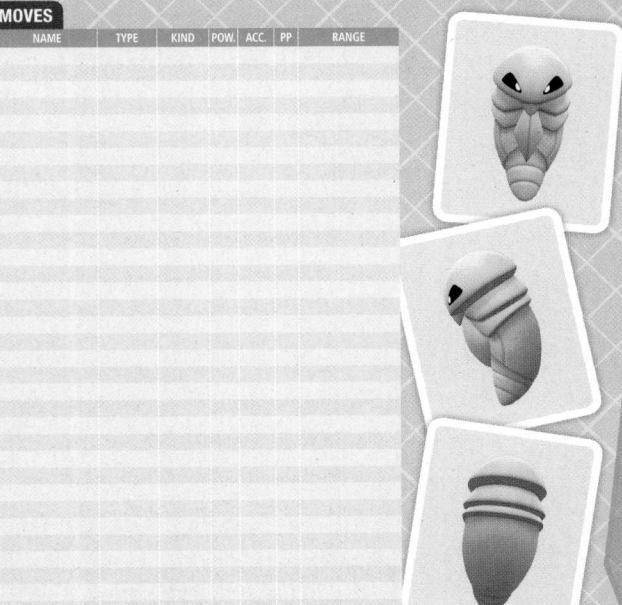

BEEDRILL 015

☑ **015** Poison Bee Pokémon Average height: 3'03" Average weight: 65.0 lbs.

Beedrill

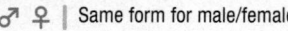
♂ ♀ | Same form for male/female

SPECIES STRENGTHS

HP	▰▰▰
ATTACK	▰▰▰▰▰
DEFENSE	▰▰▰
SP. ATK	▰▰▰
SP. DEF	▰▰▰▰▰
SPEED	▰▰▰▰

DAMAGE TAKEN IN BATTLES

◎ ×1		×2
×2		×2
×1		×0.5
×0.25		×2
×1		×1
×1		×1
×0.25		×1
×0.5		×1
×1		×0.5

POKÉDEX ENTRY

It has three poisonous stingers on its forelegs and its tail. They are used to jab its enemy repeatedly.

MAIN WAY TO OBTAIN

Catch one when it appears in Viridian Forest in *Pokémon: Let's Go, Eevee!* Or obtain a Kakuna, then level it up to Lv. 10 or higher to evolve it into Beedrill.

Where to catch

EVOLUTION

Weedle

Lv. 7 →→→

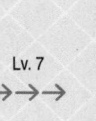

Kakuna

Lv. 10 →→→

Beedrill

LEVEL-UP MOVES

LV.	NAME	TYPE	KIND	POW.	ACC.	PP	RANGE
1	Peck	Flying	Physical	35	100	35	Normal
1	Twineedle	Bug	Physical	25	100	20	Normal
13	Rage	Normal	Physical	20	100	20	Normal
16	Fury Attack	Normal	Physical	15	85	20	Normal
19	Focus Energy	Normal	Status	—	—	30	Self
22	Poison Jab	Poison	Physical	80	100	20	Normal
25	Agility	Psychic	Status	—	—	30	Self
28	Pin Missile	Bug	Physical	25	95	20	Normal
31	Outrage	Dragon	Physical	120	100	10	1 Random

TM MOVES

NO.	NAME	TYPE	KIND	POW.	ACC.	PP	RANGE
TM01	Headbutt	Normal	Physical	70	100	15	Normal
TM05	Rest	Psychic	Status	—	—	10	Self
TM07	Protect	Normal	Status	—	—	10	Self
TM08	Substitute	Normal	Status	—	—	10	Self
TM09	Reflect	Psychic	Status	—	—	20	Your Side
TM12	Facade	Normal	Physical	70	100	20	Normal
TM13	Brick Break	Fighting	Physical	75	100	15	Normal
TM18	U-turn	Bug	Physical	70	100	20	Normal
TM24	X-Scissor	Bug	Physical	80	100	15	Normal
TM26	Poison Jab	Poison	Physical	80	100	20	Normal
TM27	Toxic	Poison	Status	—	90	10	Normal
TM39	Outrage	Dragon	Physical	120	100	10	1 Random
TM45	Solar Beam	Grass	Special	200	100	10	Normal
TM48	Hyper Beam	Normal	Special	150	90	5	Normal
TM50	Roost	Flying	Status	—	—	10	Self
TM52	Sludge Bomb	Poison	Special	90	100	10	Normal
TM53	Mega Drain	Grass	Special	75	100	10	Normal
TM58	Drill Run	Ground	Physical	80	95	10	Normal

POKÉMON EXPRESSIONS

HAPPY

UNHAPPY

ATTACKING

EVOLUTION MOVES

NAME	TYPE	KIND	POW.	ACC.	PP	RANGE
Twineedle	Bug	Physical	25	100	20	Normal

Mega Beedrill

MEGA EVOLUTION

Beedrill

Buy a Beedrillite, then
Mega Evolve Beedrill
during battle.

→→→

Mega Beedrill

SPECIES STRENGTHS

HP	
ATTACK	
DEFENSE	
SP. ATK	
SP. DEF	
SPEED	

DAMAGE TAKEN IN BATTLES

⬤	×1	🪽	×2
🔥	×2	🌀	×2
💧	×1	☯	×0.5
🌿	×0.25	🔮	×2
⚡	×1	🐛	×1
❄	×1	👊	×1
🪨	×0.25	🌙	×1
⬤	×0.5	⬤	×1
🔻	×1	✦	×0.5

**REQUIRED MEGA STONE:
BEEDRILLITE**

Buy it from a seller who appears at
the Pokémon League once you have
become Champion (p. 103).

016 Tiny Bird Pokémon | Average height: 1'00" | Average weight: 4.0 lbs.

Pidgey

PIDGEY 016

♂ ♀ | Same form for male/female

SPECIES STRENGTHS

HP
ATTACK
DEFENSE
SP. ATK
SP. DEF
SPEED

DAMAGE TAKEN IN BATTLES

⊙ ×1		⬤ ×1	
×1		×1	
×1		×0.5	
×0.5		×2	
×2		×0	
×2		×1	
×1		×1	
×1		×1	
×0		×1	

POKÉDEX ENTRY

Very docile. If attacked, it will often kick up sand to protect itself rather than fight back.

MAIN WAY TO OBTAIN

Catch one when it appears on Route 1, Route 2, or elsewhere.

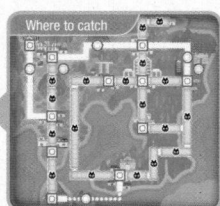

Where to catch

EVOLUTION

Pidgey

Lv. 18 →→→

Pidgeotto

Lv. 36 →→→

Pidgeot

LEVEL-UP MOVES

LV.	NAME	TYPE	KIND	POW.	ACC.	PP	RANGE
1	Tackle	Normal	Physical	40	100	35	Normal
3	Sand Attack	Ground	Status	—	100	15	Normal
5	Gust	Flying	Special	40	100	35	Normal
9	Mirror Move	Flying	Status	—	—	20	Normal
11	Quick Attack	Normal	Physical	40	100	30	Normal
15	Wing Attack	Flying	Physical	60	100	35	Normal
17	Roost	Flying	Status	—	—	10	Self
21	Whirlwind	Normal	Status	—	—	20	Normal
23	Agility	Psychic	Status	—	—	30	Self
27	Air Slash	Flying	Special	75	95	15	Normal
29	Razor Wind	Normal	Special	80	100	10	Many Others

TM MOVES

NO.	NAME	TYPE	KIND	POW.	ACC.	PP	RANGE
TM01	Headbutt	Normal	Physical	70	100	15	Normal
TM05	Rest	Psychic	Status	—	—	10	Self
TM07	Protect	Normal	Status	—	—	10	Self
TM08	Substitute	Normal	Status	—	—	10	Self
TM09	Reflect	Psychic	Status	—	—	20	Your Side
TM12	Facade	Normal	Physical	70	100	20	Normal
TM14	Fly	Flying	Physical	90	95	15	Normal
TM18	U-turn	Bug	Physical	70	100	20	Normal
TM27	Toxic	Poison	Status	—	90	10	Normal
TM50	Roost	Flying	Status	—	—	10	Self

POKÉMON EXPRESSIONS

HAPPY

UNHAPPY

ATTACKING

EVOLUTION MOVES

NAME	TYPE	KIND	POW.	ACC.	PP	RANGE

Pidgeotto

♂ ♀ | Same form for male/female

SPECIES STRENGTHS

HP	▦▦▦
ATTACK	▦▦▦
DEFENSE	▦▦▦
SP. ATK	▦▦
SP. DEF	▦▦
SPEED	▦▦▦▦

DAMAGE TAKEN IN BATTLES

◉	×1	〰	×1
🔥	×1	🌀	×1
💧	×1	☯	×0.5
🍃	×0.5	✦	×2
⚡	×2	⚫	×0
❄	×2	☾	×1
👊	×1	◒	×1
☠	×1	◎	×1
⛰	×0	◈	×1

POKÉDEX ENTRY

This Pokémon is full of vitality. It constantly flies around its large territory in search of prey.

MAIN WAY TO OBTAIN

Catch one when it appears on Route 5, Route 6, or elsewhere. Or obtain a Pidgey, then level it up to Lv. 18 or higher to evolve it into Pidgeotto.

Where to catch

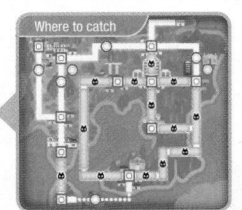

EVOLUTION

Pidgey

Lv. 18
→→→

Pidgeotto

Lv. 36
→→→

Pidgeot

POKÉMON EXPRESSIONS

HAPPY

UNHAPPY

ATTACKING

LEVEL-UP MOVES

LV.	NAME	TYPE	KIND	POW.	ACC.	PP	RANGE
1	Gust	Flying	Special	40	100	35	Normal
1	Quick Attack	Normal	Physical	40	100	30	Normal
1	Sand Attack	Ground	Status	—	100	15	Normal
1	Tackle	Normal	Physical	40	100	35	Normal
3	Sand Attack	Ground	Status	—	100	15	Normal
5	Gust	Flying	Special	40	100	35	Normal
9	Quick Attack	Normal	Physical	40	100	30	Normal
11	Mirror Move	Flying	Status	—	—	20	Normal
15	Wing Attack	Flying	Physical	60	100	35	Normal
17	Roost	Flying	Status	—	—	10	Self
25	Whirlwind	Normal	Status	—	—	20	Normal
31	Agility	Psychic	Status	—	—	30	Self
39	Air Slash	Flying	Special	75	95	15	Normal
45	Razor Wind	Normal	Special	80	100	10	Many Others

TM MOVES

NO.	NAME	TYPE	KIND	POW.	ACC.	PP	RANGE
TM01	Headbutt	Normal	Physical	70	100	15	Normal
TM05	Rest	Psychic	Status	—	—	10	Self
TM07	Protect	Normal	Status	—	—	10	Self
TM08	Substitute	Normal	Status	—	—	10	Self
TM09	Reflect	Psychic	Status	—	—	20	Your Side
TM12	Facade	Normal	Physical	70	100	20	Normal
TM14	Fly	Flying	Physical	90	95	15	Normal
TM18	U-turn	Bug	Physical	70	100	20	Normal
TM27	Toxic	Poison	Status	—	90	10	Normal
TM50	Roost	Flying	Status	—	—	10	Self

EVOLUTION MOVES

NAME	TYPE	KIND	POW.	ACC.	PP	RANGE

✓ 018 Bird Pokémon Average height: 4'11" Average weight: 87.1 lbs.

Pidgeot

♂ ♀ | Same form for male/female

SPECIES STRENGTHS

HP	▪▪▪
ATTACK	▪▪▪▪
DEFENSE	▪▪▪▪
SP. ATK	▪▪▪
SP. DEF	▪▪▪▪
SPEED	▪▪▪▪▪

DAMAGE TAKEN IN BATTLES

×1		×1	
×1		×1	
×1		×0.5	
×0.5		×2	
×2		×0	
×2		×1	
×1		×1	
×1		×1	
×0		×1	

POKÉDEX ENTRY

This Pokémon flies at Mach 2 speed, seeking prey. Its large talons are feared as wicked weapons.

MAIN WAY TO OBTAIN

Obtain a Pidgeotto, then level it up to Lv. 36 or higher to evolve it into Pidgeot. Or catch one when it appears in the sky after becoming Champion (p. 107).

Where to catch

Habitat Unknown

EVOLUTION

Pidgey

Lv. 18 →→→

Pidgeotto

Lv. 36 →→→

Pidgeot

LEVEL-UP MOVES

LV.	NAME	TYPE	KIND	POW.	ACC.	PP	RANGE
1	Gust	Flying	Special	40	100	35	Normal
1	Heat Wave	Fire	Special	95	90	10	Many Others
1	Quick Attack	Normal	Physical	40	100	30	Normal
1	Sand Attack	Ground	Status	—	100	15	Normal
1	Sky Attack	Flying	Physical	200	90	5	Normal
1	Tackle	Normal	Physical	40	100	35	Normal
3	Sand Attack	Ground	Status	—	100	15	Normal
5	Gust	Flying	Special	40	100	35	Normal
9	Quick Attack	Normal	Physical	40	100	30	Normal
11	Mirror Move	Flying	Status	—	—	20	Normal
15	Wing Attack	Flying	Physical	60	100	35	Normal
17	Roost	Flying	Status	—	—	10	Self
25	Whirlwind	Normal	Status	—	—	20	Normal
31	Agility	Psychic	Status	—	—	30	Self
43	Air Slash	Flying	Special	75	95	15	Normal
53	Razor Wind	Normal	Special	80	100	10	Many Others

TM MOVES

NO.	NAME	TYPE	KIND	POW.	ACC.	PP	RANGE
TM01	Headbutt	Normal	Physical	70	100	15	Normal
TM05	Rest	Psychic	Status	—	—	10	Self
TM07	Protect	Normal	Status	—	—	10	Self
TM08	Substitute	Normal	Status	—	—	10	Self
TM09	Reflect	Psychic	Status	—	—	20	Your Side
TM12	Facade	Normal	Physical	70	100	20	Normal
TM14	Fly	Flying	Physical	90	95	15	Normal
TM18	U-turn	Bug	Physical	70	100	20	Normal
TM27	Toxic	Poison	Status	—	90	10	Normal
TM48	Hyper Beam	Normal	Special	150	90	5	Normal
TM50	Roost	Flying	Status	—	—	10	Self

POKÉMON EXPRESSIONS

HAPPY

UNHAPPY

ATTACKING

EVOLUTION MOVES

NAME	TYPE	KIND	POW.	ACC.	PP	RANGE

Mega Pidgeot

MEGA EVOLUTION

Pidgeot

Buy a Pidgeotite, then Mega Evolve Pidgeot during battle.

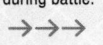

Mega Pidgeot

SPECIES STRENGTHS

HP	
ATTACK	
DEFENSE	
SP. ATK	
SP. DEF	
SPEED	

DAMAGE TAKEN IN BATTLES

○	×1	🌿	×1
🔥	×1	◎	×1
💧	×1	🍃	×0.5
⚡	×0.5	🔮	×2
❄	×2	👁	×0
❄	×2	✊	×1
〰	×1	☽	×1
💢	×1	⊙	×1
⛰	×0	✿	×1

 **REQUIRED MEGA STONE: PIDGEOTITE**

Buy it from a seller who appears at the Pokémon League once you have become Champion (p. 103).

Mouse Pokémon   Average height: 1'00"   Average weight: 7.7 lbs.

Rattata

♂ ♀ | The female has shorter whiskers than the male.

 ♂    ♀

SPECIES STRENGTHS

HP	▣▣
ATTACK	▣▣▣▣
DEFENSE	▣▣▣
SP. ATK	▣▣
SP. DEF	▣▣▣
SPEED	▣▣▣▣▣

DAMAGE TAKEN IN BATTLES

◉ ×1		×1
×1		×1
×1		×1
×1		×0
×1		×1
×2		×1
×1		×1
×1		×1

POKÉDEX ENTRY

Will chew on anything with its fangs. If you see one, you can be certain that 40 more live in the area.

MAIN WAY TO OBTAIN

Catch one when it appears on Route 1, Route 2, or elsewhere.

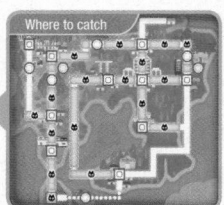

Where to catch

EVOLUTION

Rattata → → → Lv. 20 → Raticate

Rattata   Raticate

LEVEL-UP MOVES

Lv.	NAME	TYPE	KIND	POW.	ACC.	PP	RANGE
1	Tackle	Normal	Physical	40	100	35	Normal
3	Tail Whip	Normal	Status	—	100	30	Many Others
6	Quick Attack	Normal	Physical	40	100	30	Normal
9	Focus Energy	Normal	Status	—	—	30	Self
12	Bite	Dark	Physical	60	100	25	Normal
15	Super Fang	Normal	Physical	—	90	10	Normal
18	Crunch	Dark	Physical	80	100	15	Normal
21	Hyper Fang	Normal	Physical	80	90	15	Normal
24	Sucker Punch	Dark	Physical	70	100	5	Normal
27	Double-Edge	Normal	Physical	120	100	15	Normal

TM MOVES

NO.	NAME	TYPE	KIND	POW.	ACC.	PP	RANGE
TM01	Headbutt	Normal	Physical	70	100	15	Normal
TM02	Taunt	Dark	Status	—	100	20	Normal
TM05	Rest	Psychic	Status	—	—	10	Self
TM07	Protect	Normal	Status	—	—	10	Self
TM08	Substitute	Normal	Status	—	—	10	Self
TM10	Dig	Ground	Physical	80	100	10	Normal
TM12	Facade	Normal	Physical	70	100	20	Normal
TM16	Thunder Wave	Electric	Status	—	90	20	Normal
TM18	U-turn	Bug	Physical	70	100	20	Normal
TM19	Iron Tail	Steel	Physical	100	75	15	Normal
TM27	Toxic	Poison	Status	—	90	10	Normal
TM36	Thunderbolt	Electric	Special	90	100	15	Normal
TM38	Thunder	Electric	Special	110	70	10	Normal
TM43	Shadow Ball	Ghost	Special	80	100	15	Normal
TM51	Blizzard	Ice	Special	110	70	5	Many Others
TM55	Ice Beam	Ice	Special	90	100	10	Normal

EVOLUTION MOVES

NAME	TYPE	KIND	POW.	ACC.	PP	RANGE

POKÉMON EXPRESSIONS

HAPPY

UNHAPPY

ATTACKING

Rattata

♂ ♀ | Same form for male/female

ALOLA FORM

SPECIES STRENGTHS

HP
ATTACK
DEFENSE
SP. ATK
SP. DEF
SPEED

DAMAGE TAKEN IN BATTLES

⊙ ×1		🌀 ×1
🔥 ×1		◎ ×0
💧 ×1		🍃 ×2
⚡ ×1		🗡 ×1
🌿 ×1		👁 ×0
❄ ×1		🔮 ×1
👊 ×4		🌙 ×0.5
☠ ×1		⊙ ×1
⛰ ×1		✦ ×2

POKÉDEX ENTRY

Its whiskers provide it with a keen sense of smell, enabling it to pick up the scent of hidden food and locate it instantly.

MAIN WAY TO OBTAIN

Trade a Rattata for one in the Pokémon Center in Cerulean City (p. 41).

Where to catch

Habitat Unknown

EVOLUTION

Lv. 20
→→→

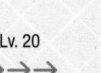

Alolan Rattata   Alolan Raticate

POKÉMON EXPRESSIONS

HAPPY

UNHAPPY

ATTACKING

LEVEL-UP MOVES

LV.	NAME	TYPE	KIND	POW.	ACC.	PP	RANGE
1	Tackle	Normal	Physical	40	100	35	Normal
3	Tail Whip	Normal	Status	—	100	30	Many Others
6	Quick Attack	Normal	Physical	40	100	30	Normal
9	Focus Energy	Normal	Status	—	—	30	Self
12	Bite	Dark	Physical	60	100	25	Normal
15	Super Fang	Normal	Physical	—	90	10	Normal
18	Crunch	Dark	Physical	80	100	15	Normal
21	Hyper Fang	Normal	Physical	80	90	15	Normal
24	Sucker Punch	Dark	Physical	70	100	5	Normal
27	Double-Edge	Normal	Physical	120	100	15	Normal

TM MOVES

NO.	NAME	TYPE	KIND	POW.	ACC.	PP	RANGE
TM01	Headbutt	Normal	Physical	70	100	15	Normal
TM02	Taunt	Dark	Status	—	100	20	Normal
TM05	Rest	Psychic	Status	—	—	10	Self
TM07	Protect	Normal	Status	—	—	10	Self
TM08	Substitute	Normal	Status	—	—	10	Self
TM10	Dig	Ground	Physical	80	100	10	Normal
TM12	Facade	Normal	Physical	70	100	20	Normal
TM18	U-turn	Bug	Physical	70	100	20	Normal
TM19	Iron Tail	Steel	Physical	100	75	15	Normal
TM20	Dark Pulse	Dark	Special	80	100	15	Normal
TM27	Toxic	Poison	Status	—	90	10	Normal
TM43	Shadow Ball	Ghost	Special	80	100	15	Normal
TM51	Blizzard	Ice	Special	110	70	5	Many Others
TM52	Sludge Bomb	Poison	Special	90	100	10	Normal
TM55	Ice Beam	Ice	Special	90	100	10	Normal

EVOLUTION MOVES

NAME	TYPE	KIND	POW.	ACC.	PP	RANGE

Raticate

♂ ♀ | The female has shorter whiskers than the male.

SPECIES STRENGTHS

HP	▰▰▰
ATTACK	▰▰▰▰
DEFENSE	▰▰▰
SP. ATK	▰▰
SP. DEF	▰▰▰
SPEED	▰▰▰▰

DAMAGE TAKEN IN BATTLES

×1		×1	
×1		×1	
×1		×1	
×1		×1	
×1		×0	
×1		×1	
×2		×1	
×1		×1	
×1		×1	

POKÉDEX ENTRY

Its hind feet are webbed. They act as flippers, so it can swim in rivers and hunt for prey.

MAIN WAY TO OBTAIN

Catch one when it appears in the Pokémon Mansion, on Route 21, or elsewhere. Or obtain a Rattata, then level it up to Lv. 20 or higher to evolve it into Raticate.

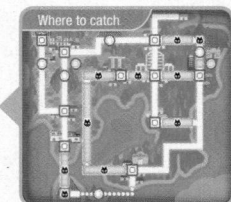
Where to catch

EVOLUTION

Rattata

Lv. 20
→ → →

Raticate

LEVEL-UP MOVES

LV.	NAME	TYPE	KIND	POW.	ACC.	PP	RANGE
1	Counter	Fighting	Physical	—	100	20	Varies
1	Focus Energy	Normal	Status	—	—	30	Self
1	Fury Swipes	Normal	Physical	18	80	15	Normal
1	Quick Attack	Normal	Physical	40	100	30	Normal
1	Swords Dance	Normal	Status	—	—	20	Self
1	Tackle	Normal	Physical	40	100	35	Normal
1	Tail Whip	Normal	Status	—	100	30	Many Others
3	Tail Whip	Normal	Status	—	100	30	Many Others
6	Quick Attack	Normal	Physical	40	100	30	Normal
9	Focus Energy	Normal	Status	—	—	30	Self
12	Bite	Dark	Physical	60	100	25	Normal
15	Super Fang	Normal	Physical	—	90	10	Normal
18	Crunch	Dark	Physical	80	100	15	Normal
26	Hyper Fang	Normal	Physical	80	90	15	Normal
34	Sucker Punch	Dark	Physical	70	100	5	Normal
42	Double-Edge	Normal	Physical	120	100	15	Normal

TM MOVES

NO.	NAME	TYPE	KIND	POW.	ACC.	PP	RANGE
TM01	Headbutt	Normal	Physical	70	100	15	Normal
TM02	Taunt	Dark	Status	—	100	20	Normal
TM05	Rest	Psychic	Status	—	—	10	Self
TM07	Protect	Normal	Status	—	—	10	Self
TM08	Substitute	Normal	Status	—	—	10	Self
TM10	Dig	Ground	Physical	80	100	10	Normal
TM12	Facade	Normal	Physical	70	100	20	Normal
TM16	Thunder Wave	Electric	Status	—	90	20	Normal
TM18	U-turn	Bug	Physical	70	100	20	Normal
TM19	Iron Tail	Steel	Physical	100	75	15	Normal
TM27	Toxic	Poison	Status	—	90	10	Normal
TM36	Thunderbolt	Electric	Special	90	100	15	Normal
TM38	Thunder	Electric	Special	110	70	10	Normal
TM43	Shadow Ball	Ghost	Special	80	100	15	Normal
TM48	Hyper Beam	Normal	Special	150	90	5	Normal
TM51	Blizzard	Ice	Special	110	70	5	Many Others
TM55	Ice Beam	Ice	Special	90	100	10	Normal

EVOLUTION MOVES

NAME	TYPE	KIND	POW.	ACC.	PP	RANGE

POKÉMON EXPRESSIONS

HAPPY

UNHAPPY

ATTACKING

Raticate

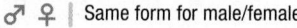

♂ ♀ | Same form for male/female

ALOLA FORM

SPECIES STRENGTHS

HP	▧▧▧▧▧
ATTACK	▧▧▧▧▧
DEFENSE	▧▧▧▧▧
SP. ATK	▧▧▧
SP. DEF	▧▧▧▧
SPEED	▧▧▧▧▧

DAMAGE TAKEN IN BATTLES

⊙	×1	🍃	×1
🔥	×1	🌀	×0
💧	×1	☄	×2
🌿	×1	🪨	×1
⚡	×1	👁	×0
❄	×1	🐉	×1
👊	×4	🌙	×0.5
☠	×1	⚙	×1
🏔	×1	✦	×2

POKÉDEX ENTRY

It makes its Rattata underlings gather food for it, dining solely on the most nutritious and delicious fare.

MAIN WAY TO OBTAIN

Obtain an Alolan Rattata, then level it up to Lv. 20 or higher to evolve it into Alolan Raticate.

Where to catch

Habitat Unknown

EVOLUTION

 →→→ Lv. 20 →→→

Alolan Rattata   Alolan Raticate

POKÉMON EXPRESSIONS

HAPPY

UNHAPPY

ATTACKING

LEVEL-UP MOVES

LV.	NAME	TYPE	KIND	POW.	ACC.	PP	RANGE
1	Counter	Fighting	Physical	—	100	20	Varies
1	Focus Energy	Normal	Status	—	—	30	Self
1	Fury Swipes	Normal	Physical	18	80	15	Normal
1	Quick Attack	Normal	Physical	40	100	30	Normal
1	Swords Dance	Normal	Status	—	—	20	Self
1	Tackle	Normal	Physical	40	100	35	Normal
1	Tail Whip	Normal	Status	—	100	30	Many Others
3	Tail Whip	Normal	Status	—	100	30	Many Others
6	Quick Attack	Normal	Physical	40	100	30	Normal
9	Focus Energy	Normal	Status	—	—	30	Self
12	Bite	Dark	Physical	60	100	25	Normal
15	Super Fang	Normal	Physical	—	90	10	Normal
18	Crunch	Dark	Physical	80	100	15	Normal
26	Hyper Fang	Normal	Physical	80	90	15	Normal
34	Sucker Punch	Dark	Physical	70	100	5	Normal
42	Double-Edge	Normal	Physical	120	100	15	Normal

TM MOVES

NO.	NAME	TYPE	KIND	POW.	ACC.	PP	RANGE
TM01	Headbutt	Normal	Physical	70	100	15	Normal
TM02	Taunt	Dark	Status	—	100	20	Normal
TM05	Rest	Psychic	Status	—	—	10	Self
TM07	Protect	Normal	Status	—	—	10	Self
TM08	Substitute	Normal	Status	—	—	10	Self
TM10	Dig	Ground	Physical	80	100	10	Normal
TM12	Facade	Normal	Physical	70	100	20	Normal
TM18	U-turn	Bug	Physical	70	100	20	Normal
TM19	Iron Tail	Steel	Physical	100	75	15	Normal
TM20	Dark Pulse	Dark	Special	80	100	15	Normal
TM27	Toxic	Poison	Status	—	90	10	Normal
TM30	Bulk Up	Fighting	Status	—	—	20	Self
TM43	Shadow Ball	Ghost	Special	80	100	15	Normal
TM48	Hyper Beam	Normal	Special	150	90	5	Normal
TM51	Blizzard	Ice	Special	110	70	5	Many Others
TM52	Sludge Bomb	Poison	Special	90	100	10	Normal
TM55	Ice Beam	Ice	Special	90	100	10	Normal

EVOLUTION MOVES

NAME	TYPE	KIND	POW.	ACC.	PP	RANGE

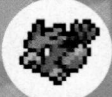

021 Tiny Bird Pokémon | Average height: 1'00" | Average weight: 4.4 lbs.

021

SPEAROW

Spearow

♂ ♀ | Same form for male/female

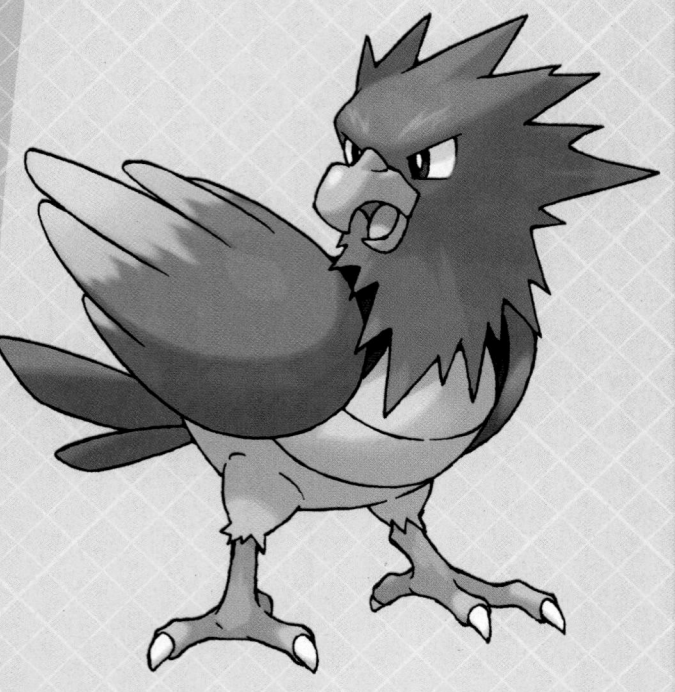

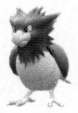

SPECIES STRENGTHS

HP

ATTACK

DEFENSE

SP. ATK

SP. DEF

SPEED

POKÉDEX ENTRY

Inept at flying high. However, it can fly around very fast to protect its territory.

DAMAGE TAKEN IN BATTLES

×1	×1
×1	×1
×1	×0.5
×0.5	×2
×2	×0
×2	×1
×1	×1
×1	×1
×0	×1

MAIN WAY TO OBTAIN

Catch one when it appears on Route 3, Route 4 (East), or elsewhere.

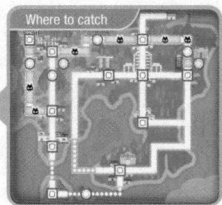

EVOLUTION

Spearow

Lv. 20

Fearow

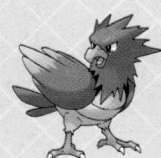

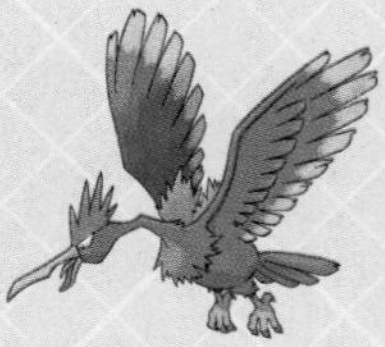

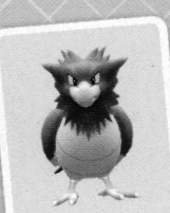

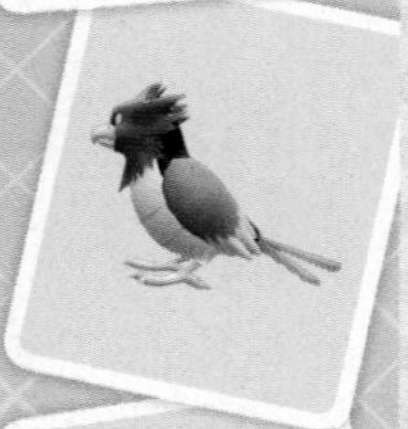

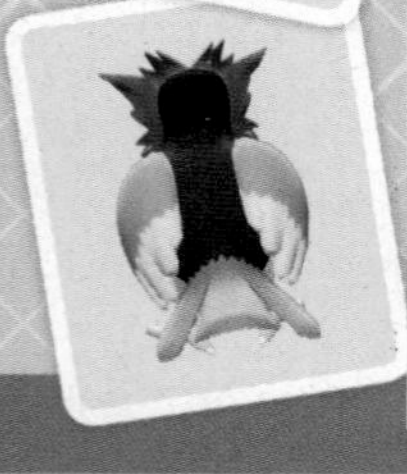

LEVEL-UP MOVES

LV.	NAME	TYPE	KIND	POW.	ACC.	PP	RANGE
1	Peck	Flying	Physical	35	100	35	Normal
3	Growl	Normal	Status	—	100	40	Many Others
8	Leer	Normal	Status	—	100	30	Many Others
11	Focus Energy	Normal	Status	—	—	30	Self
16	Fury Attack	Normal	Physical	15	85	20	Normal
19	Mirror Move	Flying	Status	—	—	20	Normal
24	Roost	Flying	Status	—	—	10	Self
27	Agility	Psychic	Status	—	—	30	Self
32	Drill Peck	Flying	Physical	80	100	20	Normal

EVOLUTION MOVES

NAME	TYPE	KIND	POW.	ACC.	PP	RANGE

TM MOVES

NO.	NAME	TYPE	KIND	POW.	ACC.	PP	RANGE
TM01	Headbutt	Normal	Physical	70	100	15	Normal
TM05	Rest	Psychic	Status	—	—	10	Self
TM07	Protect	Normal	Status	—	—	10	Self
TM08	Substitute	Normal	Status	—	—	10	Self
TM12	Facade	Normal	Physical	70	100	20	Normal
TM14	Fly	Flying	Physical	90	95	15	Normal
TM18	U-turn	Bug	Physical	70	100	20	Normal
TM27	Toxic	Poison	Status	—	90	10	Normal
TM28	Tri Attack	Normal	Special	80	100	10	Normal
TM50	Roost	Flying	Status	—	—	10	Self
TM58	Drill Run	Ground	Physical	80	95	10	Normal

POKÉMON EXPRESSIONS

HAPPY

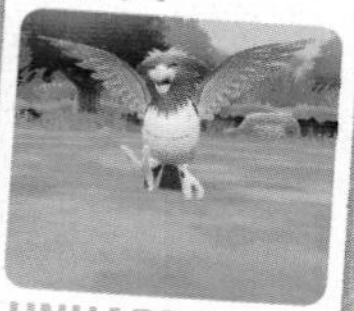

UNHAPPY

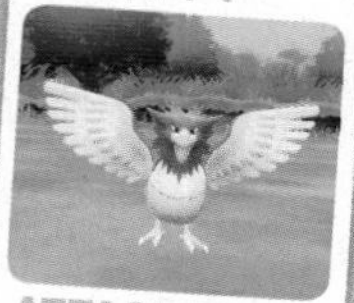

ATTACKING

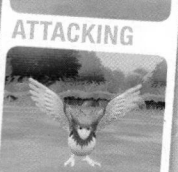

Fearow

♂ ♀ | Same form for male/female

SPECIES STRENGTHS

HP	▬▬▬
ATTACK	▬▬▬▬▬
DEFENSE	▬▬▬
SP. ATK	▬▬▬
SP. DEF	▬▬▬
SPEED	▬▬▬▬▬

DAMAGE TAKEN IN BATTLES

×1		×1	
×1		×1	
×1		×0.5	
×0.5		×2	
×2		×0	
×2		×1	
×1		×1	
×1		×1	
×0		×1	

POKÉDEX ENTRY

A Pokémon that dates back many years. If it senses danger, it flies high and away, instantly.

MAIN WAY TO OBTAIN

Catch one when it appears on Route 9, Route 10 (North), or elsewhere. Or obtain a Spearow, then level it up to Lv. 20 or higher to evolve it into Fearow.

Where to catch

EVOLUTION

Spearow

Lv. 20
→→→

Fearow

POKÉMON EXPRESSIONS

HAPPY

UNHAPPY

ATTACKING

LEVEL-UP MOVES

LV.	NAME	TYPE	KIND	POW.	ACC.	PP	RANGE
1	Drill Run	Ground	Physical	80	95	10	Normal
1	Focus Energy	Normal	Status	—	—	30	Self
1	Growl	Normal	Status	—	100	40	Many Others
1	Leer	Normal	Status	—	100	30	Many Others
1	Peck	Flying	Physical	35	100	35	Normal
1	Quick Attack	Normal	Physical	40	100	30	Normal
1	Sky Attack	Flying	Physical	200	90	5	Normal
3	Growl	Normal	Status	—	100	40	Many Others
8	Leer	Normal	Status	—	100	30	Many Others
11	Focus Energy	Normal	Status	—	—	30	Self
16	Fury Attack	Normal	Physical	15	85	20	Normal
19	Mirror Move	Flying	Status	—	—	20	Normal
29	Roost	Flying	Status	—	—	10	Self
37	Agility	Psychic	Status	—	—	30	Self
47	Drill Peck	Flying	Physical	80	100	20	Normal

TM MOVES

NO.	NAME	TYPE	KIND	POW.	ACC.	PP	RANGE
TM01	Headbutt	Normal	Physical	70	100	15	Normal
TM05	Rest	Psychic	Status	—	—	10	Self
TM07	Protect	Normal	Status	—	—	10	Self
TM08	Substitute	Normal	Status	—	—	10	Self
TM12	Facade	Normal	Physical	70	100	20	Normal
TM14	Fly	Flying	Physical	90	95	15	Normal
TM18	U-turn	Bug	Physical	70	100	20	Normal
TM27	Toxic	Poison	Status	—	90	10	Normal
TM28	Tri Attack	Normal	Special	80	100	10	Normal
TM48	Hyper Beam	Normal	Special	150	90	5	Normal
TM50	Roost	Flying	Status	—	—	10	Self
TM58	Drill Run	Ground	Physical	80	95	10	Normal

EVOLUTION MOVES

NAME	TYPE	KIND	POW.	ACC.	PP	RANGE

023 ☑ Snake Pokémon   Average height: 6'07"   Average weight: 15.2 lbs.

Ekans

EKANS 023

♂ ♀ | Same form for male/female

SPECIES STRENGTHS

HP	▪▪▪
ATTACK	▪▪▪▪
DEFENSE	▪▪▪
SP. ATK	▪▪▪
SP. DEF	▪▪▪▪
SPEED	▪▪▪▪

DAMAGE TAKEN IN BATTLES

◎ ×1		🍃 ×1	
🔥 ×1		◉ ×2	
💧 ×1		🌿 ×0.5	
⚡ ×0.5		🦋 ×1	
⚡ ×1		👁 ×1	
❄ ×1		✊ ×1	
🥊 ×0.5		☾ ×1	
💬 ×0.5		⬡ ×1	
⛰ ×2		✦ ×0.5	

POKÉDEX ENTRY

The older it gets, the longer it grows. At night, it wraps its long body around tree branches to rest.

MAIN WAY TO OBTAIN

Obtain one in a trade if you are playing *Pokémon: Let's Go, Pikachu!*, as it does not appear in that game. Catch one when it appears on Route 3 or Route 4 (East) in *Pokémon: Let's Go, Eevee!*

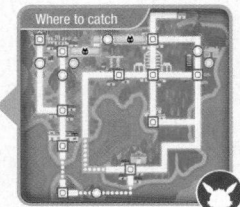

Where to catch

EVOLUTION

Ekans → → → Arbok

Lv. 22

LEVEL-UP MOVES

LV.	NAME	TYPE	KIND	POW.	ACC.	PP	RANGE
1	Poison Sting	Poison	Physical	15	100	35	Normal
1	Wrap	Normal	Physical	15	90	20	Normal
4	Leer	Normal	Status	—	100	30	Many Others
8	Acid	Poison	Special	40	100	30	Many Others
12	Bite	Dark	Physical	60	100	25	Normal
16	Haze	Ice	Status	—	—	30	Both Sides
20	Glare	Normal	Status	—	100	30	Normal
24	Poison Jab	Poison	Physical	80	100	20	Normal
28	Slam	Normal	Physical	80	75	20	Normal
32	Screech	Normal	Status	—	85	40	Normal
36	Toxic	Poison	Status	—	90	10	Normal

TM MOVES

NO.	NAME	TYPE	KIND	POW.	ACC.	PP	RANGE
TM01	Headbutt	Normal	Physical	70	100	15	Normal
TM05	Rest	Psychic	Status	—	—	10	Self
TM07	Protect	Normal	Status	—	—	10	Self
TM08	Substitute	Normal	Status	—	—	10	Self
TM10	Dig	Ground	Physical	80	100	10	Normal
TM12	Facade	Normal	Physical	70	100	20	Normal
TM19	Iron Tail	Steel	Physical	100	75	15	Normal
TM20	Dark Pulse	Dark	Special	80	100	15	Normal
TM22	Rock Slide	Rock	Physical	75	90	10	Many Others
TM26	Poison Jab	Poison	Physical	80	100	20	Normal
TM27	Toxic	Poison	Status	—	90	10	Normal
TM41	Earthquake	Ground	Physical	100	100	10	All Others
TM52	Sludge Bomb	Poison	Special	90	100	10	Normal
TM53	Mega Drain	Grass	Special	75	100	10	Normal

POKÉMON EXPRESSIONS

HAPPY

UNHAPPY

ATTACKING

EVOLUTION MOVES

NAME	TYPE	KIND	POW.	ACC.	PP	RANGE

Arbok

♂ ♀ | Same form for male/female

SPECIES STRENGTHS

HP	▪▪▪▫▫
ATTACK	▪▪▪▪▫
DEFENSE	▪▪▪▫▫
SP. ATK	▪▪▫▫▫
SP. DEF	▪▪▪▫▫
SPEED	▪▪▪▫▫

DAMAGE TAKEN IN BATTLES

⊙ ×1		🍃 ×1	
🔥 ×1		◎ ×2	
💧 ×1		🌱 ×0.5	
⚡ ×0.5		◇ ×1	
❄ ×1		🧠 ×1	
❄ ×1		🌀 ×1	
👊 ×0.5		☾ ×1	
☁ ×0.5		⚪ ×1	
◿ ×2		✦ ×0.5	

POKÉDEX ENTRY

The frightening patterns on its belly have been studied. Six variations have been confirmed.

MAIN WAY TO OBTAIN

Obtain an Ekans, then level it up to Lv. 22 or higher to evolve it into Arbok.

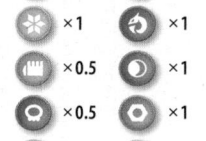

Where to catch

Habitat Unknown

EVOLUTION

Ekans

Lv. 22
→→→

Arbok

POKÉMON EXPRESSIONS

HAPPY

UNHAPPY

ATTACKING

LEVEL-UP MOVES

LV.	NAME	TYPE	KIND	POW.	ACC.	PP	RANGE
1	Acid	Poison	Special	40	100	30	Many Others
1	Crunch	Dark	Physical	80	100	15	Normal
1	Leer	Normal	Status	—	100	30	Many Others
1	Poison Sting	Poison	Physical	15	100	35	Normal
1	Sucker Punch	Dark	Physical	70	100	5	Normal
1	Wrap	Normal	Physical	15	90	20	Normal
4	Leer	Normal	Status	—	100	30	Many Others
9	Acid	Poison	Special	40	100	30	Many Others
12	Bite	Dark	Physical	60	100	25	Normal
16	Haze	Ice	Status	—	—	30	Both Sides
20	Glare	Normal	Status	—	100	30	Normal
28	Poison Jab	Poison	Physical	80	100	20	Normal
36	Slam	Normal	Physical	80	75	20	Normal
44	Screech	Normal	Status	—	85	40	Normal
52	Toxic	Poison	Status	—	90	10	Normal

TM MOVES

NO.	NAME	TYPE	KIND	POW.	ACC.	PP	RANGE
TM01	Headbutt	Normal	Physical	70	100	15	Normal
TM05	Rest	Psychic	Status	—	—	10	Self
TM07	Protect	Normal	Status	—	—	10	Self
TM08	Substitute	Normal	Status	—	—	10	Self
TM10	Dig	Ground	Physical	80	100	10	Normal
TM12	Facade	Normal	Physical	70	100	20	Normal
TM17	Dragon Tail	Dragon	Physical	60	90	10	Normal
TM19	Iron Tail	Steel	Physical	100	75	15	Normal
TM20	Dark Pulse	Dark	Special	80	100	15	Normal
TM22	Rock Slide	Rock	Physical	75	90	10	Many Others
TM26	Poison Jab	Poison	Physical	80	100	20	Normal
TM27	Toxic	Poison	Status	—	90	10	Normal
TM41	Earthquake	Ground	Physical	100	100	10	All Others
TM48	Hyper Beam	Normal	Special	150	90	5	Normal
TM52	Sludge Bomb	Poison	Special	90	100	10	Normal
TM53	Mega Drain	Grass	Special	75	100	10	Normal

EVOLUTION MOVES

NAME	TYPE	KIND	POW.	ACC.	PP	RANGE
Crunch	Dark	Physical	80	100	15	Normal

Pikachu

♂ ♀ | The tip of the female's tail has a notch in it, while the tip of the male's tail does not.

♂ ♀

SPECIES STRENGTHS

HP	▮▮▮
ATTACK	▮▮▮▮
DEFENSE	▮▮▮
SP. ATK	▮▮▮
SP. DEF	▮▮▮
SPEED	▮▮▮▮▮▮

DAMAGE TAKEN IN BATTLES

◉	×1	◐	×0.5
🔥	×1	◎	×1
💧	×1	🌀	×1
🍃	×1	👁	×1
⚡	×0.5	🌙	×1
❄	×1	🔆	×1
👊	×1	◑	×1
☠	×1	◉	×0.5
🔺	×2	✦	×1

POKÉDEX ENTRY

This forest-dwelling Pokémon stores electricity in its cheeks, so you'll feel a tingly shock if you touch it.

MAIN WAY TO OBTAIN

Catch one when it appears in Viridian Forest.

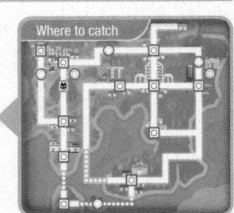

Where to catch

EVOLUTION

Use Thunder Stone
→ → →

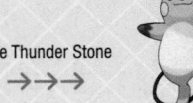

Pikachu   Raichu

LEVEL-UP MOVES

LV.	NAME	TYPE	KIND	POW.	ACC.	PP	RANGE
1	Growl	Normal	Status	—	100	40	Many Others
1	Thunder Shock	Electric	Special	40	100	30	Normal
3	Tail Whip	Normal	Status	—	100	30	Many Others
6	Quick Attack	Normal	Physical	40	100	30	Normal
9	Double Kick	Fighting	Physical	30	100	30	Normal
12	Double Team	Normal	Status	—	—	15	Self
15	Thunder Wave	Electric	Status	—	90	20	Normal
18	Light Screen	Psychic	Status	—	—	30	Your Side
21	Thunderbolt	Electric	Special	90	100	15	Normal
24	Slam	Normal	Physical	80	75	20	Normal
27	Agility	Psychic	Status	—	—	30	Self
30	Thunder	Electric	Special	110	70	10	Normal

TM MOVES

NO.	NAME	TYPE	KIND	POW.	ACC.	PP	RANGE
TM01	Headbutt	Normal	Physical	70	100	15	Normal
TM03	Helping Hand	Normal	Status	—	—	20	1 Ally
TM05	Rest	Psychic	Status	—	—	10	Self
TM06	Light Screen	Psychic	Status	—	—	30	Your Side
TM07	Protect	Normal	Status	—	—	10	Self
TM08	Substitute	Normal	Status	—	—	10	Self
TM09	Reflect	Psychic	Status	—	—	20	Your Side
TM10	Dig	Ground	Physical	80	100	10	Normal
TM12	Facade	Normal	Physical	70	100	20	Normal
TM13	Brick Break	Fighting	Physical	75	100	15	Normal
TM15	Seismic Toss	Fighting	Physical	—	100	20	Normal
TM16	Thunder Wave	Electric	Status	—	90	20	Normal
TM19	Iron Tail	Steel	Physical	100	75	15	Normal
TM23	Thunder Punch	Electric	Physical	75	100	15	Normal
TM27	Toxic	Poison	Status	—	90	10	Normal
TM33	Calm Mind	Psychic	Status	—	—	20	Self
TM36	Thunderbolt	Electric	Special	90	100	15	Normal
TM38	Thunder	Electric	Special	110	70	10	Normal
TM57	Pay Day	Normal	Physical	40	100	20	Normal

EVOLUTION MOVES

NAME	TYPE	KIND	POW.	ACC.	PP	RANGE

POKÉMON EXPRESSIONS

HAPPY

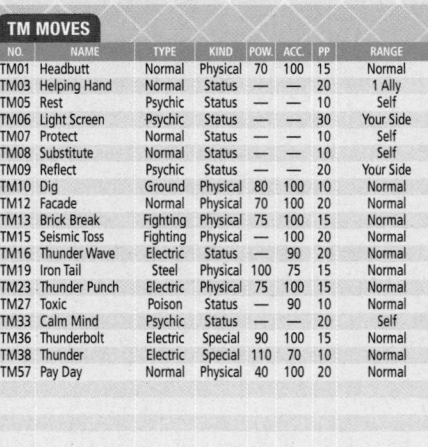

UNHAPPY

ATTACKING

Raichu

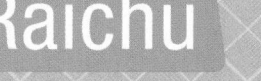

♂ ♀ | The tip of the female's tail is flat, while the tip of the male's tail is pointed.

 ♂  ♀

SPECIES STRENGTHS

HP
ATTACK
DEFENSE
SP. ATK
SP. DEF
SPEED

DAMAGE TAKEN IN BATTLES

⊙	×1	🍃	×0.5
🔥	×1	🌀	×1
💧	×1	☀	×1
🍃	×1	🌙	×1
⚡	×0.5	👊	×1
❄	×1	🔮	×1
🐛	×1	⚪	×1
💬	×1	⊙	×0.5
⛰	×2	✦	×1

POKÉDEX ENTRY

When electricity builds up inside its body, it becomes feisty. It also glows in the dark.

MAIN WAY TO OBTAIN

Obtain a Pikachu, then use a Thunder Stone on it to evolve it into Raichu. Note that your partner Pikachu will not evolve into Raichu if you are playing *Pokémon: Let's Go, Pikachu!*

Where to catch
Habitat Unknown

EVOLUTION

Use Thunder Stone
→ → →

Pikachu Raichu

POKÉMON EXPRESSIONS

HAPPY

UNHAPPY

ATTACKING

LEVEL-UP MOVES

LV.	NAME	TYPE	KIND	POW.	ACC.	PP	RANGE
1	Encore	Normal	Status	—	100	5	Normal
1	Fake Out	Normal	Physical	40	100	10	Normal
1	Growl	Normal	Status	—	100	40	Many Others
1	Quick Attack	Normal	Physical	40	100	30	Normal
1	Tail Whip	Normal	Status	—	100	30	Many Others
1	Thunder Punch	Electric	Physical	75	100	15	Normal
1	Thunder Shock	Electric	Special	40	100	30	Normal

TM MOVES

NO.	NAME	TYPE	KIND	POW.	ACC.	PP	RANGE
TM01	Headbutt	Normal	Physical	70	100	15	Normal
TM03	Helping Hand	Normal	Status	—	—	20	1 Ally
TM05	Rest	Psychic	Status	—	—	10	Self
TM06	Light Screen	Psychic	Status	—	—	30	Your Side
TM07	Protect	Normal	Status	—	—	10	Self
TM08	Substitute	Normal	Status	—	—	10	Self
TM09	Reflect	Psychic	Status	—	—	20	Your Side
TM10	Dig	Ground	Physical	80	100	10	Normal
TM12	Facade	Normal	Physical	70	100	20	Normal
TM13	Brick Break	Fighting	Physical	75	100	15	Normal
TM15	Seismic Toss	Fighting	Physical	—	100	20	Normal
TM16	Thunder Wave	Electric	Status	—	90	20	Normal
TM19	Iron Tail	Steel	Physical	100	75	15	Normal
TM23	Thunder Punch	Electric	Physical	75	100	15	Normal
TM27	Toxic	Poison	Status	—	90	10	Normal
TM33	Calm Mind	Psychic	Status	—	—	20	Self
TM36	Thunderbolt	Electric	Special	90	100	15	Normal
TM38	Thunder	Electric	Special	110	70	10	Normal
TM48	Hyper Beam	Normal	Special	150	90	5	Normal
TM57	Pay Day	Normal	Physical	40	100	20	Normal

EVOLUTION MOVES

NAME	TYPE	KIND	POW.	ACC.	PP	RANGE
Thunder Punch	Electric	Physical	75	100	15	Normal

Raichu

RAICHU
ALOLA FORM

026

ALOLA FORM

 ♂ ♀ | Same form for male/female

SPECIES STRENGTHS

HP	▦▦▦
ATTACK	▦▦▦▦
DEFENSE	▦▦
SP. ATK	▦▦▦▦▦
SP. DEF	▦▦▦▦
SPEED	▦▦▦▦▦

DAMAGE TAKEN IN BATTLES

⬤	×1	🪶	×0.5
🔥	×1	🌀	×0.5
💧	×1	🪨	×2
🍃	×1	👻	×1
⚡	×0.5	🐉	×2
❄️	×1	🌑	×1
👊	×0.5	🌙	×2
☠️	×1	⚙️	×0.5
⛰️	×2	✨	×1

POKÉDEX ENTRY

It loves pancakes prepared with a secret Alolan recipe. Some wonder whether that recipe holds the key to this Pokémon's evolution.

MAIN WAY TO OBTAIN

Trade a Raichu for one in the Pokémon Center in Saffron City (p. 79).

Where to catch

Habitat Unknown

EVOLUTION

(DOES NOT EVOLVE)

LEVEL-UP MOVES

LV.	NAME	TYPE	KIND	POW.	ACC.	PP	RANGE
1	Double Team	Normal	Status	—	—	15	Self
1	Encore	Normal	Status	—	100	5	Normal
1	Fake Out	Normal	Physical	40	100	10	Normal
1	Growl	Normal	Status	—	100	40	Many Others
1	Psychic	Psychic	Special	90	100	10	Normal
1	Tail Whip	Normal	Status	—	100	30	Many Others
1	Thunder Shock	Electric	Special	40	100	30	Normal

TM MOVES

NO.	NAME	TYPE	KIND	POW.	ACC.	PP	RANGE
TM01	Headbutt	Normal	Physical	70	100	15	Normal
TM03	Helping Hand	Normal	Status	—	—	20	1 Ally
TM04	Teleport	Psychic	Status	—	—	20	Self
TM05	Rest	Psychic	Status	—	—	10	Self
TM06	Light Screen	Psychic	Status	—	—	30	Your Side
TM07	Protect	Normal	Status	—	—	10	Self
TM08	Substitute	Normal	Status	—	—	10	Self
TM09	Reflect	Psychic	Status	—	—	20	Your Side
TM10	Dig	Ground	Physical	80	100	10	Normal
TM12	Facade	Normal	Physical	70	100	20	Normal
TM13	Brick Break	Fighting	Physical	75	100	15	Normal
TM15	Seismic Toss	Fighting	Physical	—	100	20	Normal
TM16	Thunder Wave	Electric	Status	—	90	20	Normal
TM19	Iron Tail	Steel	Physical	100	75	15	Normal
TM23	Thunder Punch	Electric	Physical	75	100	15	Normal
TM27	Toxic	Poison	Status	—	90	10	Normal
TM33	Calm Mind	Psychic	Status	—	—	20	Self
TM36	Thunderbolt	Electric	Special	90	100	15	Normal
TM38	Thunder	Electric	Special	110	70	10	Normal
TM40	Psychic	Psychic	Special	90	100	10	Normal
TM48	Hyper Beam	Normal	Special	150	90	5	Normal
TM57	Pay Day	Normal	Physical	40	100	20	Normal

EVOLUTION MOVES

NAME	TYPE	KIND	POW.	ACC.	PP	RANGE
Psychic	Psychic	Special	90	100	10	Normal

POKÉMON EXPRESSIONS

HAPPY

UNHAPPY

ATTACKING

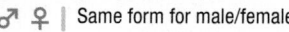

Sandshrew

♂ ♀ | Same form for male/female

SPECIES STRENGTHS

HP	▬▬▬
ATTACK	▬▬▬▬▬
DEFENSE	▬▬▬▬▬
SP. ATK	▬▬
SP. DEF	▬▬
SPEED	▬▬▬

DAMAGE TAKEN IN BATTLES

⊙ ×1		🪶 ×1	
🔥 ×1		🌀 ×1	
💧 ×2		🌿 ×1	
⚡ ×2		🔮 ×0.5	
🥊 ×0		● ×1	
❄ ×2		🌑 ×1	
🗿 ×1		☾ ×1	
🐍 ×0.5		◉ ×1	
⛰ ×1		✦ ×1	

POKÉDEX ENTRY

Its body is dry. When it gets cold at night, its hide is said to become coated with a fine dew.

MAIN WAY TO OBTAIN

Catch one when it appears on Route 3 or Route 4 (East) in *Pokémon: Let's Go, Pikachu!* Obtain one in a trade if you are playing *Pokémon: Let's Go, Eevee!*, as it does not appear in that game.

Where to catch

EVOLUTION

Sandshrew

Lv. 22
⟶⟶⟶

Sandslash

POKÉMON EXPRESSIONS

HAPPY

UNHAPPY

ATTACKING

LEVEL-UP MOVES

LV.	NAME	TYPE	KIND	POW.	ACC.	PP	RANGE
1	Defense Curl	Normal	Status	—	—	40	Self
1	Scratch	Normal	Physical	40	100	35	Normal
4	Poison Sting	Poison	Physical	15	100	35	Normal
8	Sand Attack	Ground	Status	—	100	15	Normal
12	Swift	Normal	Special	60	—	20	Many Others
16	Fury Swipes	Normal	Physical	18	80	15	Normal
20	Dig	Ground	Physical	80	100	10	Normal
24	Protect	Normal	Status	—	—	10	Self
28	Swords Dance	Normal	Status	—	—	20	Self
32	Slash	Normal	Physical	70	100	20	Normal
36	Earthquake	Ground	Physical	100	100	10	All Others

TM MOVES

NO.	NAME	TYPE	KIND	POW.	ACC.	PP	RANGE
TM01	Headbutt	Normal	Physical	70	100	15	Normal
TM05	Rest	Psychic	Status	—	—	10	Self
TM07	Protect	Normal	Status	—	—	10	Self
TM08	Substitute	Normal	Status	—	—	10	Self
TM10	Dig	Ground	Physical	80	100	10	Normal
TM12	Facade	Normal	Physical	70	100	20	Normal
TM13	Brick Break	Fighting	Physical	75	100	15	Normal
TM15	Seismic Toss	Fighting	Physical	—	100	20	Normal
TM19	Iron Tail	Steel	Physical	100	75	15	Normal
TM22	Rock Slide	Rock	Physical	75	90	10	Many Others
TM24	X-Scissor	Bug	Physical	80	100	15	Normal
TM26	Poison Jab	Poison	Physical	80	100	20	Normal
TM27	Toxic	Poison	Status	—	90	10	Normal
TM41	Earthquake	Ground	Physical	100	100	10	All Others
TM56	Stealth Rock	Rock	Status	—	—	20	Other Side

EVOLUTION MOVES

NAME	TYPE	KIND	POW.	ACC.	PP	RANGE

027 Mouse Pokémon Average height: 2'04" Average weight: 88.2 lbs.

Sandshrew

ALOLA FORM

♂ ♀ | Same form for male/female

SPECIES STRENGTHS

HP	▰▰▰
ATTACK	▰▰▰▰
DEFENSE	▰▰▰▰▰▰
SP. ATK	▰
SP. DEF	▰▰▰
SPEED	▰▰▰

DAMAGE TAKEN IN BATTLES

×0.5		×0.5	
×4		×0.5	
×1		×0.5	
×0.5		×1	
×1		×1	
×0.25		×0.5	
×4		×1	
×0		×1	
×2		×0.5	

POKÉDEX ENTRY

Its ice-covered body lets it slide across the ground with bullet-like speed, sending its enemies flying when it hits them.

MAIN WAY TO OBTAIN

Trade a Sandshrew for one in the Pokémon Center in Celadon City (p. 62) in *Pokémon: Let's Go, Pikachu!* Obtain one in a trade if you are playing *Pokémon: Let's Go, Eevee!*, as it does not appear in that game.

Where to catch

Habitat Unknown

EVOLUTION

Use Ice Stone
→ → →

Alolan Sandshrew   **Alolan Sandslash**

LEVEL-UP MOVES

LV.	NAME	TYPE	KIND	POW.	ACC.	PP	RANGE
1	Defense Curl	Normal	Status	—	—	40	Self
1	Scratch	Normal	Physical	40	100	35	Normal
4	Bide	Normal	Physical	—	—	10	Self
8	Ice Shard	Ice	Physical	40	100	30	Normal
12	Swift	Normal	Special	60	—	20	Many Others
16	Mirror Coat	Psychic	Special	—	100	20	Varies
20	Fury Swipes	Normal	Physical	18	80	15	Normal
24	Ice Punch	Ice	Physical	75	100	15	Normal
28	Swords Dance	Normal	Status	—	—	20	Self
32	Slash	Normal	Physical	70	100	20	Normal
36	Blizzard	Ice	Special	110	70	5	Many Others

TM MOVES

NO.	NAME	TYPE	KIND	POW.	ACC.	PP	RANGE
TM01	Headbutt	Normal	Physical	70	100	15	Normal
TM05	Rest	Psychic	Status	—	—	10	Self
TM07	Protect	Normal	Status	—	—	10	Self
TM08	Substitute	Normal	Status	—	—	10	Self
TM10	Dig	Ground	Physical	80	100	10	Normal
TM12	Facade	Normal	Physical	70	100	20	Normal
TM13	Brick Break	Fighting	Physical	75	100	15	Normal
TM15	Seismic Toss	Fighting	Physical	—	100	20	Normal
TM19	Iron Tail	Steel	Physical	100	75	15	Normal
TM22	Rock Slide	Rock	Physical	75	90	10	Many Others
TM24	X-Scissor	Bug	Physical	80	100	15	Normal
TM26	Poison Jab	Poison	Physical	80	100	20	Normal
TM27	Toxic	Poison	Status	—	90	10	Normal
TM35	Ice Punch	Ice	Physical	75	100	15	Normal
TM41	Earthquake	Ground	Physical	100	100	10	All Others
TM51	Blizzard	Ice	Special	110	70	5	Many Others
TM55	Ice Beam	Ice	Special	90	100	10	Normal
TM56	Stealth Rock	Rock	Status	—	—	20	Other Side

POKÉMON EXPRESSIONS

HAPPY

UNHAPPY

ATTACKING

EVOLUTION MOVES

NAME	TYPE	KIND	POW.	ACC.	PP	RANGE

Sandslash

♂ ♀ | Same form for male/female

SPECIES STRENGTHS

HP	▮▮▮▮
ATTACK	▮▮▮▮▮
DEFENSE	▮▮▮▮▮▮
SP. ATK	▮▮▮
SP. DEF	▮▮▮▮
SPEED	▮▮▮▮

DAMAGE TAKEN IN BATTLES

◉	×1	🖐	×1
🔥	×1	◎	×1
💧	×2	🍃	×1
⚡	×2	✦	×0.5
🍂	×0	●	×1
❄	×2	✊	×1
▥	×1	☾	×1
◐	×0.5	◉	×1
◭	×1	◈	×1

POKÉDEX ENTRY

It is skilled at slashing enemies with its claws. If broken, they start to grow back in a day.

MAIN WAY TO OBTAIN

Obtain a Sandshrew, then level it up to Lv. 22 or higher to evolve it into Sandslash.

Where to catch

Habitat Unknown

EVOLUTION

Sandshrew

Lv. 22
→→→

Sandslash

POKÉMON EXPRESSIONS

HAPPY

UNHAPPY

ATTACKING

LEVEL-UP MOVES

LV.	NAME	TYPE	KIND	POW.	ACC.	PP	RANGE
1	Counter	Fighting	Physical	—	100	20	Varies
1	Defense Curl	Normal	Status	—	—	40	Self
1	Poison Sting	Poison	Physical	15	100	35	Normal
1	Sand Attack	Ground	Status	—	100	15	Normal
1	Scratch	Normal	Physical	40	100	35	Normal
4	Poison Sting	Poison	Physical	15	100	35	Normal
8	Sand Attack	Ground	Status	—	100	15	Normal
12	Swift	Normal	Special	60	—	20	Many Others
16	Fury Swipes	Normal	Physical	18	80	15	Normal
20	Dig	Ground	Physical	80	100	10	Normal
28	Protect	Normal	Status	—	—	10	Self
36	Swords Dance	Normal	Status	—	—	20	Self
44	Slash	Normal	Physical	70	100	20	Normal
52	Earthquake	Ground	Physical	100	100	10	All Others

TM MOVES

NO.	NAME	TYPE	KIND	POW.	ACC.	PP	RANGE
TM01	Headbutt	Normal	Physical	70	100	15	Normal
TM05	Rest	Psychic	Status	—	—	10	Self
TM07	Protect	Normal	Status	—	—	10	Self
TM08	Substitute	Normal	Status	—	—	10	Self
TM10	Dig	Ground	Physical	80	100	10	Normal
TM12	Facade	Normal	Physical	70	100	20	Normal
TM13	Brick Break	Fighting	Physical	75	100	15	Normal
TM15	Seismic Toss	Fighting	Physical	—	100	20	Normal
TM19	Iron Tail	Steel	Physical	100	75	15	Normal
TM22	Rock Slide	Rock	Physical	75	90	10	Many Others
TM24	X-Scissor	Bug	Physical	80	100	15	Normal
TM26	Poison Jab	Poison	Physical	80	100	20	Normal
TM27	Toxic	Poison	Status	—	90	10	Normal
TM41	Earthquake	Ground	Physical	100	100	10	All Others
TM48	Hyper Beam	Normal	Special	150	90	5	Normal
TM56	Stealth Rock	Rock	Status	—	—	20	Other Side
TM58	Drill Run	Ground	Physical	80	95	10	Normal

EVOLUTION MOVES

NAME	TYPE	KIND	POW.	ACC.	PP	RANGE

028 Mouse Pokémon   Average height: 3'11"   Average weight: 121.3 lbs.

Sandslash

SANDSLASH
ALOLA FORM

028

ALOLA FORM

♂ ♀ | Same form for male/female

SPECIES STRENGTHS

HP	▚▚▚▚▚
ATTACK	▚▚▚▚▚
DEFENSE	▚▚▚▚▚▚▚
SP. ATK	▚▚
SP. DEF	▚▚▚
SPEED	▚▚▚

DAMAGE TAKEN IN BATTLES

◎	×0.5	🌀	×0.5
🔥	×4	🌐	×0.5
💧	×1	🐛	×0.5
🍃	×0.5	◐	×1
⚡	×1	👊	×1
❄	×0.25	🌙	×0.5
🪨	×4	◉	×1
👻	×0	◎	×1
🔩	×2	✦	×0.5

POKÉDEX ENTRY

This is Sandslash's form after adaptation to a frigid environment. The cold air emitted by its body sharpens its icy spikes.

MAIN WAY TO OBTAIN

Obtain an Alolan Sandshrew, then use an Ice Stone on it to evolve it into Alolan Sandslash.

Where to catch

Habitat Unknown

EVOLUTION

Alolan Sandshrew

Use Ice Stone
→ → →

Alolan Sandslash

LEVEL-UP MOVES

LV.	NAME	TYPE	KIND	POW.	ACC.	PP	RANGE
1	Bide	Normal	Physical	—	—	10	Self
1	Counter	Fighting	Physical	—	100	20	Varies
1	Defense Curl	Normal	Status	—	—	40	Self
1	Ice Shard	Ice	Physical	40	100	30	Normal
1	Scratch	Normal	Physical	40	100	35	Normal

TM MOVES

NO.	NAME	TYPE	KIND	POW.	ACC.	PP	RANGE
TM01	Headbutt	Normal	Physical	70	100	15	Normal
TM05	Rest	Psychic	Status	—	—	10	Self
TM07	Protect	Normal	Status	—	—	10	Self
TM08	Substitute	Normal	Status	—	—	10	Self
TM10	Dig	Ground	Physical	80	100	10	Normal
TM12	Facade	Normal	Physical	70	100	20	Normal
TM13	Brick Break	Fighting	Physical	75	100	15	Normal
TM15	Seismic Toss	Fighting	Physical	—	100	20	Normal
TM19	Iron Tail	Steel	Physical	100	75	15	Normal
TM22	Rock Slide	Rock	Physical	75	90	10	Many Others
TM24	X-Scissor	Bug	Physical	80	100	15	Normal
TM26	Poison Jab	Poison	Physical	80	100	20	Normal
TM27	Toxic	Poison	Status	—	90	10	Normal
TM35	Ice Punch	Ice	Physical	75	100	15	Normal
TM41	Earthquake	Ground	Physical	100	100	10	All Others
TM48	Hyper Beam	Normal	Special	150	90	5	Normal
TM51	Blizzard	Ice	Special	110	70	5	Many Others
TM55	Ice Beam	Ice	Special	90	100	10	Normal
TM56	Stealth Rock	Rock	Status	—	—	20	Other Side
TM58	Drill Run	Ground	Physical	80	95	10	Normal

EVOLUTION MOVES

NAME	TYPE	KIND	POW.	ACC.	PP	RANGE

POKÉMON EXPRESSIONS

HAPPY

UNHAPPY

ATTACKING

Nidoran ♀

♀ | Female only

SPECIES STRENGTHS

HP ▪▪▪
ATTACK ▪▪▪
DEFENSE ▪▪▪▪
SP. ATK ▪▪▪
SP. DEF ▪▪▪
SPEED ▪▪▪

DAMAGE TAKEN IN BATTLES

○ ×1		✊ ×1	
🔥 ×1		◎ ×2	
💧 ×1		🍃 ×0.5	
⚡ ×0.5		🌸 ×1	
🍃 ×1		👁 ×1	
❄ ×1		🌀 ×1	
👊 ×0.5		🌙 ×1	
☠ ×0.5		⚪ ×1	
⛰ ×2		✦ ×0.5	

POKÉDEX ENTRY

A mild-mannered Pokémon that does not like to fight. Beware— its small horn secretes venom.

MAIN WAY TO OBTAIN

Catch one when it appears on Route 22, Route 9, or elsewhere.

Where to catch

EVOLUTION

Nidoran ♀

→→→ Lv. 16

Nidorina

→→→ Use Moon Stone

Nidoqueen

POKÉMON EXPRESSIONS

HAPPY

UNHAPPY

ATTACKING

LEVEL-UP MOVES

LV.	NAME	TYPE	KIND	POW.	ACC.	PP	RANGE
1	Growl	Normal	Status	—	100	40	Many Others
1	Scratch	Normal	Physical	40	100	35	Normal
3	Tail Whip	Normal	Status	—	100	30	Many Others
6	Poison Sting	Poison	Physical	15	100	35	Normal
9	Double Kick	Fighting	Physical	30	100	30	Normal
12	Bite	Dark	Physical	60	100	25	Normal
15	Helping Hand	Normal	Status	—	—	20	1 Ally
18	Toxic	Poison	Status	—	90	10	Normal
21	Fury Swipes	Normal	Physical	18	80	15	Normal
24	Crunch	Dark	Physical	80	100	15	Normal
27	Super Fang	Normal	Physical	—	90	10	Normal

TM MOVES

NO.	NAME	TYPE	KIND	POW.	ACC.	PP	RANGE
TM01	Headbutt	Normal	Physical	70	100	15	Normal
TM03	Helping Hand	Normal	Status	—	—	20	1 Ally
TM05	Rest	Psychic	Status	—	—	10	Self
TM07	Protect	Normal	Status	—	—	10	Self
TM08	Substitute	Normal	Status	—	—	10	Self
TM09	Reflect	Psychic	Status	—	—	20	Your Side
TM10	Dig	Ground	Physical	80	100	10	Normal
TM12	Facade	Normal	Physical	70	100	20	Normal
TM19	Iron Tail	Steel	Physical	100	75	15	Normal
TM26	Poison Jab	Poison	Physical	80	100	20	Normal
TM27	Toxic	Poison	Status	—	90	10	Normal
TM36	Thunderbolt	Electric	Special	90	100	15	Normal
TM38	Thunder	Electric	Special	110	70	10	Normal
TM51	Blizzard	Ice	Special	110	70	5	Many Others
TM52	Sludge Bomb	Poison	Special	90	100	10	Normal
TM55	Ice Beam	Ice	Special	90	100	10	Normal

EVOLUTION MOVES

NAME	TYPE	KIND	POW.	ACC.	PP	RANGE

Poison Pin Pokémon   Average height: 2'07"   Average weight: 44.1 lbs.

Nidorina

030
NIDORINA

♀ | Female only

SPECIES STRENGTHS

HP	▬▬▬▬▬
ATTACK	▬▬▬▬
DEFENSE	▬▬▬▬
SP. ATK	▬▬▬
SP. DEF	▬▬▬
SPEED	▬▬▬

DAMAGE TAKEN IN BATTLES

⬤	×1	🌫	×1
🔥	×1	◎	×2
💧	×1	🌀	×0.5
🍃	×0.5	🦋	×1
⚡	×1	🪨	×1
❄	×1	👊	×1
🥊	×0.5	🌙	×1
👁	×0.5	⬤	×1
🔔	×2	✦	×0.5

POKÉDEX ENTRY

When resting deep in its burrow, its barbs always retract. This is proof that it is relaxed.

MAIN WAY TO OBTAIN

Catch one when it appears on Route 9 or Route 10 (North), or more commonly on Route 23 (South). Or obtain a Nidoran ♀, then level it up to Lv. 16 or higher to evolve it into Nidorina.

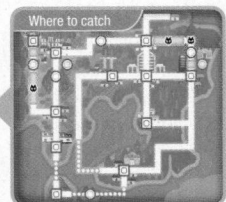

Where to catch

EVOLUTION

Nidoran ♀

Lv. 16
→→→

Nidorina

Use Moon Stone
→→→

Nidoqueen

LEVEL-UP MOVES

LV.	NAME	TYPE	KIND	POW.	ACC.	PP	RANGE
1	Growl	Normal	Status	—	100	40	Many Others
1	Poison Sting	Poison	Physical	15	100	35	Normal
1	Scratch	Normal	Physical	40	100	35	Normal
1	Tail Whip	Normal	Status	—	100	30	Many Others
3	Tail Whip	Normal	Status	—	100	30	Many Others
6	Poison Sting	Poison	Physical	15	100	35	Normal
9	Double Kick	Fighting	Physical	30	100	30	Normal
12	Bite	Dark	Physical	60	100	25	Normal
15	Helping Hand	Normal	Status	—	—	20	1 Ally
23	Toxic	Poison	Status	—	90	10	Normal
31	Fury Swipes	Normal	Physical	18	80	15	Normal
39	Crunch	Dark	Physical	80	100	15	Normal
47	Super Fang	Normal	Physical	—	90	10	Normal

TM MOVES

NO.	NAME	TYPE	KIND	POW.	ACC.	PP	RANGE
TM01	Headbutt	Normal	Physical	70	100	15	Normal
TM03	Helping Hand	Normal	Status	—	—	20	1 Ally
TM05	Rest	Psychic	Status	—	—	10	Self
TM07	Protect	Normal	Status	—	—	10	Self
TM08	Substitute	Normal	Status	—	—	10	Self
TM09	Reflect	Psychic	Status	—	—	20	Your Side
TM10	Dig	Ground	Physical	80	100	10	Normal
TM12	Facade	Normal	Physical	70	100	20	Normal
TM19	Iron Tail	Steel	Physical	100	75	15	Normal
TM26	Poison Jab	Poison	Physical	80	100	20	Normal
TM27	Toxic	Poison	Status	—	90	10	Normal
TM36	Thunderbolt	Electric	Special	90	100	15	Normal
TM38	Thunder	Electric	Special	110	70	10	Normal
TM51	Blizzard	Ice	Special	110	70	5	Many Others
TM52	Sludge Bomb	Poison	Special	90	100	10	Normal
TM55	Ice Beam	Ice	Special	90	100	10	Normal

EVOLUTION MOVES

NAME	TYPE	KIND	POW.	ACC.	PP	RANGE

POKÉMON EXPRESSIONS

HAPPY

UNHAPPY

ATTACKING

Nidoqueen

♀ | Female only

SPECIES STRENGTHS

HP	▰▰▰▰▱
ATTACK	▰▰▰▱▱
DEFENSE	▰▰▰▰▱
SP. ATK	▰▰▱▱▱
SP. DEF	▰▰▱▱▱
SPEED	▰▰▱▱▱

DAMAGE TAKEN IN BATTLES

⬤	×1	🪶	×1
🔥	×1	◎	×2
💧	×2	🌿	×0.5
🍃	×1	✦	×0.5
⚡	×0	◑	×1
❄	×2	↻	×1
🥊	×0.5	🌙	×1
💧	×0.25	◉	×1
🔺	×2	✧	×0.5

POKÉDEX ENTRY

Tough scales cover the sturdy body of this Pokémon. It appears that the scales grow in cycles.

MAIN WAY TO OBTAIN

Catch one when it appears on Route 23 (South). Or obtain a Nidorina, then use a Moon Stone on it to evolve it into Nidoqueen.

Where to catch

EVOLUTION

Nidoran ♀

Lv. 16
→→→

Nidorina

Use Moon Stone
→→→

Nidoqueen

POKÉMON EXPRESSIONS

HAPPY

UNHAPPY

ATTACKING

LEVEL-UP MOVES

LV.	NAME	TYPE	KIND	POW.	ACC.	PP	RANGE
1	Body Slam	Normal	Physical	85	100	15	Normal
1	Counter	Fighting	Physical	—	100	20	Varies
1	Growl	Normal	Status	—	100	40	Many Others
1	Poison Sting	Poison	Physical	15	100	35	Normal
1	Scratch	Normal	Physical	40	100	35	Normal
1	Supersonic	Normal	Status	—	55	20	Normal
1	Tail Whip	Normal	Status	—	100	30	Many Others
55	Superpower	Fighting	Physical	120	100	5	Normal

EVOLUTION MOVES

NAME	TYPE	KIND	POW.	ACC.	PP	RANGE
Body Slam	Normal	Physical	85	100	15	Normal

TM MOVES

NO.	NAME	TYPE	KIND	POW.	ACC.	PP	RANGE
TM01	Headbutt	Normal	Physical	70	100	15	Normal
TM02	Taunt	Dark	Status	—	100	20	Normal
TM03	Helping Hand	Normal	Status	—	—	20	1 Ally
TM05	Rest	Psychic	Status	—	—	10	Self
TM07	Protect	Normal	Status	—	—	10	Self
TM08	Substitute	Normal	Status	—	—	10	Self
TM09	Reflect	Psychic	Status	—	—	20	Your Side
TM10	Dig	Ground	Physical	80	100	10	Normal
TM12	Facade	Normal	Physical	70	100	20	Normal
TM13	Brick Break	Fighting	Physical	75	100	15	Normal
TM15	Seismic Toss	Fighting	Physical	—	100	20	Normal
TM17	Dragon Tail	Dragon	Physical	60	90	10	Normal
TM19	Iron Tail	Steel	Physical	100	75	15	Normal
TM22	Rock Slide	Rock	Physical	75	90	10	Many Others
TM23	Thunder Punch	Electric	Physical	75	100	15	Normal
TM26	Poison Jab	Poison	Physical	80	100	20	Normal
TM27	Toxic	Poison	Status	—	90	10	Normal
TM31	Fire Punch	Fire	Physical	75	100	15	Normal
TM34	Dragon Pulse	Dragon	Special	85	100	10	Normal
TM35	Ice Punch	Ice	Physical	75	100	15	Normal
TM36	Thunderbolt	Electric	Special	90	100	15	Normal
TM37	Flamethrower	Fire	Special	90	100	15	Normal
TM38	Thunder	Electric	Special	110	70	10	Normal
TM39	Outrage	Dragon	Physical	120	100	10	1 Random
TM41	Earthquake	Ground	Physical	100	100	10	All Others
TM43	Shadow Ball	Ghost	Special	80	100	15	Normal
TM46	Fire Blast	Fire	Special	110	85	5	Normal
TM47	Surf	Water	Special	90	100	15	All Others
TM48	Hyper Beam	Normal	Special	150	90	5	Normal
TM49	Superpower	Fighting	Physical	120	100	5	Normal
TM51	Blizzard	Ice	Special	110	70	5	Many Others
TM52	Sludge Bomb	Poison	Special	90	100	10	Normal
TM55	Ice Beam	Ice	Special	90	100	10	Normal
TM56	Stealth Rock	Rock	Status	—	—	20	Other Side
TM57	Pay Day	Normal	Physical	40	100	20	Normal
TM58	Drill Run	Ground	Physical	80	95	10	Normal

Nidoran♂

032

NIDORAN♂

♂ | Male only

SPECIES STRENGTHS

HP	▦▦
ATTACK	▦▦▦
DEFENSE	▦▦▦
SP. ATK	▦▦
SP. DEF	▦▦
SPEED	▦▦▦

DAMAGE TAKEN IN BATTLES

⊙	×1	🍃	×1
🔥	×1	🌀	×2
💧	×1	🪨	×0.5
🌿	×0.5	👊	×1
⚡	×1	👁	×1
❄	×1	↪	×1
🏛	×0.5	🌙	×1
🔮	×0.5	⊚	×1
🪨	×2	✦	×0.5

POKÉDEX ENTRY

Its large ears are always kept upright. If it senses danger, it will attack with a poisonous sting.

MAIN WAY TO OBTAIN

Catch one when it appears on Route 22, Route 9, or elsewhere.

Where to catch

EVOLUTION

Nidoran♂   Lv. 16 →→→   Nidorino   Use Moon Stone →→→   Nidoking

LEVEL-UP MOVES

LV.	NAME	TYPE	KIND	POW.	ACC.	PP	RANGE
1	Leer	Normal	Status	—	100	30	Many Others
1	Peck	Flying	Physical	35	100	35	Normal
3	Focus Energy	Normal	Status	—	—	30	Self
6	Poison Sting	Poison	Physical	15	100	35	Normal
9	Double Kick	Fighting	Physical	30	100	30	Normal
12	Horn Attack	Normal	Physical	65	100	25	Normal
15	Helping Hand	Normal	Status	—	—	20	1 Ally
18	Toxic	Poison	Status	—	90	10	Normal
21	Fury Attack	Normal	Physical	15	85	20	Normal
24	Poison Jab	Poison	Physical	80	100	20	Normal
27	Horn Drill	Normal	Physical	—	30	5	Normal

TM MOVES

NO.	NAME	TYPE	KIND	POW.	ACC.	PP	RANGE
TM01	Headbutt	Normal	Physical	70	100	15	Normal
TM03	Helping Hand	Normal	Status	—	—	20	1 Ally
TM05	Rest	Psychic	Status	—	—	10	Self
TM07	Protect	Normal	Status	—	—	10	Self
TM08	Substitute	Normal	Status	—	—	10	Self
TM09	Reflect	Psychic	Status	—	—	20	Your Side
TM10	Dig	Ground	Physical	80	100	10	Normal
TM12	Facade	Normal	Physical	70	100	20	Normal
TM19	Iron Tail	Steel	Physical	100	75	15	Normal
TM26	Poison Jab	Poison	Physical	80	100	20	Normal
TM27	Toxic	Poison	Status	—	90	10	Normal
TM36	Thunderbolt	Electric	Special	90	100	15	Normal
TM38	Thunder	Electric	Special	110	70	10	Normal
TM51	Blizzard	Ice	Special	110	70	5	Many Others
TM52	Sludge Bomb	Poison	Special	90	100	10	Normal
TM55	Ice Beam	Ice	Special	90	100	10	Normal
TM58	Drill Run	Ground	Physical	80	95	10	Normal

EVOLUTION MOVES

NAME	TYPE	KIND	POW.	ACC.	PP	RANGE

POKÉMON EXPRESSIONS

HAPPY

UNHAPPY

ATTACKING

Nidorino

♂ | Male only

SPECIES STRENGTHS

HP ▬▬▬
ATTACK ▬▬▬▬
DEFENSE ▬▬▬
SP. ATK ▬▬▬
SP. DEF ▬▬▬
SPEED ▬▬▬▬

DAMAGE TAKEN IN BATTLES

⊙ ×1		✊ ×1	
🔥 ×1		🌀 ×2	
💧 ×1		🐛 ×0.5	
⚡ ×0.5		🌙 ×1	
🍃 ×1		👁 ×1	
❄ ×1		🐉 ×1	
👊 ×0.5		◑ ×1	
☠ ×0.5		⬡ ×1	
⛰ ×2		✦ ×0.5	

POKÉDEX ENTRY

Its horn contains venom. If it stabs an enemy with the horn, the impact makes the poison leak out.

MAIN WAY TO OBTAIN

Catch one when it appears on Route 9 or Route 10 (North), or more commonly on Route 23 (South). Or obtain a Nidoran ♂, then level it up to Lv. 16 or higher to evolve it into Nidorino.

Where to catch

EVOLUTION

Nidoran ♂

Lv. 16
→→→

Nidorino

Use Moon Stone
→→→

Nidoking

POKÉMON EXPRESSIONS

HAPPY

UNHAPPY

ATTACKING

LEVEL-UP MOVES

LV.	NAME	TYPE	KIND	POW.	ACC.	PP	RANGE
1	Focus Energy	Normal	Status	—	—	30	Self
1	Leer	Normal	Status	—	100	30	Many Others
1	Peck	Flying	Physical	35	100	35	Normal
1	Poison Sting	Poison	Physical	15	100	35	Normal
3	Focus Energy	Normal	Status	—	—	30	Self
6	Poison Sting	Poison	Physical	15	100	35	Normal
9	Double Kick	Fighting	Physical	30	100	30	Normal
12	Horn Attack	Normal	Physical	65	100	25	Normal
15	Helping Hand	Normal	Status	—	—	20	1 Ally
23	Toxic	Poison	Status	—	90	10	Normal
31	Fury Attack	Normal	Physical	15	85	20	Normal
39	Poison Jab	Poison	Physical	80	100	20	Normal
47	Horn Drill	Normal	Physical	—	30	5	Normal

TM MOVES

NO.	NAME	TYPE	KIND	POW.	ACC.	PP	RANGE
TM01	Headbutt	Normal	Physical	70	100	15	Normal
TM03	Helping Hand	Normal	Status	—	—	20	1 Ally
TM05	Rest	Psychic	Status	—	—	10	Self
TM07	Protect	Normal	Status	—	—	10	Self
TM08	Substitute	Normal	Status	—	—	10	Self
TM09	Reflect	Psychic	Status	—	—	20	Your Side
TM10	Dig	Ground	Physical	80	100	10	Normal
TM12	Facade	Normal	Physical	70	100	20	Normal
TM19	Iron Tail	Steel	Physical	100	75	15	Normal
TM26	Poison Jab	Poison	Physical	80	100	20	Normal
TM27	Toxic	Poison	Status	—	90	10	Normal
TM36	Thunderbolt	Electric	Special	90	100	15	Normal
TM38	Thunder	Electric	Special	110	70	10	Normal
TM51	Blizzard	Ice	Special	110	70	5	Many Others
TM52	Sludge Bomb	Poison	Special	90	100	10	Normal
TM55	Ice Beam	Ice	Special	90	100	10	Normal
TM58	Drill Run	Ground	Physical	80	95	10	Normal

EVOLUTION MOVES

NAME	TYPE	KIND	POW.	ACC.	PP	RANGE

Nidoking

♂ | Male only

SPECIES STRENGTHS

HP	▮▮▮▯▯▯
ATTACK	▮▮▮▮▯▯
DEFENSE	▮▮▮▮▯▯
SP. ATK	▮▮▮▯▯▯
SP. DEF	▮▮▮▯▯▯
SPEED	▮▮▮▮▯▯

DAMAGE TAKEN IN BATTLES

◎	×1	✋	×1
🔥	×1	🌀	×2
💧	×2	🦋	×0.5
🍃	×1	🪨	×0.5
⚡	×0	👻	×1
❄	×2	☄	×1
👊	×0.5	🌙	×1
☠	×0.25	⚙	×1
⛰	×2	✨	×0.5

POKÉDEX ENTRY

Its steel-like hide adds to its powerful tackle. Its horns are so hard, they can pierce a diamond.

MAIN WAY TO OBTAIN

Catch one when it appears on Route 23 (South). Or obtain a Nidorino, then use a Moon Stone on it to evolve it into Nidoking.

Where to catch

EVOLUTION

Nidoran ♂

Lv. 16
⇒⇒⇒

Nidorino

Use Moon Stone
⇒⇒⇒

Nidoking

LEVEL-UP MOVES

LV.	NAME	TYPE	KIND	POW.	ACC.	PP	RANGE
1	Counter	Fighting	Physical	—	100	20	Varies
1	Focus Energy	Normal	Status	—	—	30	Self
1	Leer	Normal	Status	—	100	30	Many Others
1	Peck	Flying	Physical	35	100	35	Normal
1	Poison Sting	Poison	Physical	15	100	35	Normal
1	Supersonic	Normal	Status	—	55	20	Normal
1	Thrash	Normal	Physical	120	100	10	1 Random
55	Megahorn	Bug	Physical	120	85	10	Normal

EVOLUTION MOVES

NAME	TYPE	KIND	POW.	ACC.	PP	RANGE
Thrash	Normal	Physical	120	100	10	1 Random

TM MOVES

NO.	NAME	TYPE	KIND	POW.	ACC.	PP	RANGE
TM01	Headbutt	Normal	Physical	70	100	15	Normal
TM02	Taunt	Dark	Status	—	100	20	Normal
TM03	Helping Hand	Normal	Status	—	—	20	1 Ally
TM05	Rest	Psychic	Status	—	—	10	Self
TM07	Protect	Normal	Status	—	—	10	Self
TM08	Substitute	Normal	Status	—	—	10	Self
TM09	Reflect	Psychic	Status	—	—	20	Your Side
TM10	Dig	Ground	Physical	80	100	10	Normal
TM12	Facade	Normal	Physical	70	100	20	Normal
TM13	Brick Break	Fighting	Physical	75	100	15	Normal
TM15	Seismic Toss	Fighting	Physical	—	100	20	Normal
TM17	Dragon Tail	Dragon	Physical	60	90	10	Normal
TM19	Iron Tail	Steel	Physical	100	75	15	Normal
TM22	Rock Slide	Rock	Physical	75	90	10	Many Others
TM23	Thunder Punch	Electric	Physical	75	100	15	Normal
TM26	Poison Jab	Poison	Physical	80	100	20	Normal
TM27	Toxic	Poison	Status	—	90	10	Normal
TM31	Fire Punch	Fire	Physical	75	100	15	Normal
TM34	Dragon Pulse	Dragon	Special	85	100	10	Normal
TM35	Ice Punch	Ice	Physical	75	100	15	Normal
TM36	Thunderbolt	Electric	Special	90	100	15	Normal
TM37	Flamethrower	Fire	Special	90	100	15	Normal
TM38	Thunder	Electric	Special	110	70	10	Normal
TM39	Outrage	Dragon	Physical	120	100	10	Normal
TM41	Earthquake	Ground	Physical	100	100	10	All Others
TM43	Shadow Ball	Ghost	Special	80	100	15	Normal
TM46	Fire Blast	Fire	Special	110	85	5	Normal
TM47	Surf	Water	Special	90	100	15	All Others
TM48	Hyper Beam	Normal	Special	150	90	5	Normal
TM49	Superpower	Fighting	Physical	120	100	5	Normal
TM51	Blizzard	Ice	Special	110	70	5	Many Others
TM52	Sludge Bomb	Poison	Special	90	100	10	Normal
TM55	Ice Beam	Ice	Special	90	100	10	Normal
TM56	Stealth Rock	Rock	Status	—	—	20	Other Side
TM57	Pay Day	Normal	Physical	40	100	20	Normal
TM58	Drill Run	Ground	Physical	80	95	10	Normal
TM60	Megahorn	Bug	Physical	120	85	10	Normal

POKÉMON EXPRESSIONS

HAPPY

UNHAPPY

ATTACKING

Clefairy

♂ ♀ | Same form for male/female

SPECIES STRENGTHS

HP	▨▨▨▨
ATTACK	▨▨▨
DEFENSE	▨▨▨
SP. ATK	▨▨▨▨
SP. DEF	▨▨▨▨
SPEED	▨▨▨

DAMAGE TAKEN IN BATTLES

◎	×1	〰	×1
🔥	×1	◉	×1
💧	×1	🔮	×0.5
🍃	×1	◈	×1
⚡	×1	👁	×1
❄	×1	🌀	×0
👊	×0.5	🌙	×0.5
☣	×2	⦿	×2
⛰	×1	✦	×1

POKÉDEX ENTRY

Adored for their cute looks and playfulness. They are thought to be rare, as they do not appear often.

MAIN WAY TO OBTAIN

Catch one when it appears in Mt. Moon, especially on B2F.

Where to catch
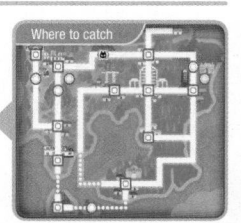

EVOLUTION

Clefairy

Use Moon Stone
→ → →

Clefable

POKÉMON EXPRESSIONS

HAPPY

UNHAPPY

ATTACKING

LEVEL-UP MOVES

LV.	NAME	TYPE	KIND	POW.	ACC.	PP	RANGE
1	Growl	Normal	Status	—	100	40	Many Others
1	Pound	Normal	Physical	40	100	35	Normal
4	Defense Curl	Normal	Status	—	—	40	Self
6	Sing	Normal	Status	—	55	15	Normal
10	Minimize	Normal	Status	—	—	10	Self
12	Double Slap	Normal	Physical	15	85	10	Normal
16	Amnesia	Psychic	Status	—	—	20	Self
18	Metronome	Normal	Status	—	—	10	Self
22	Encore	Normal	Status	—	100	5	Normal
24	Body Slam	Normal	Physical	85	100	15	Normal
28	Moonblast	Fairy	Special	95	100	15	Normal

TM MOVES

NO.	NAME	TYPE	KIND	POW.	ACC.	PP	RANGE
TM01	Headbutt	Normal	Physical	70	100	15	Normal
TM03	Helping Hand	Normal	Status	—	—	20	1 Ally
TM04	Teleport	Psychic	Status	—	—	20	Self
TM05	Rest	Psychic	Status	—	—	10	Self
TM06	Light Screen	Psychic	Status	—	—	30	Your Side
TM07	Protect	Normal	Status	—	—	10	Self
TM08	Substitute	Normal	Status	—	—	10	Self
TM09	Reflect	Psychic	Status	—	—	20	Your Side
TM10	Dig	Ground	Physical	80	100	10	Normal
TM12	Facade	Normal	Physical	70	100	20	Normal
TM13	Brick Break	Fighting	Physical	75	100	15	Normal
TM15	Seismic Toss	Fighting	Physical	—	100	20	Normal
TM16	Thunder Wave	Electric	Status	—	90	20	Normal
TM19	Iron Tail	Steel	Physical	100	75	15	Normal
TM23	Thunder Punch	Electric	Physical	75	100	15	Normal
TM27	Toxic	Poison	Status	—	90	10	Normal
TM28	Tri Attack	Normal	Special	80	100	10	Normal
TM31	Fire Punch	Fire	Physical	75	100	15	Normal
TM32	Dazzling Gleam	Fairy	Special	80	100	10	Many Others
TM33	Calm Mind	Psychic	Status	—	—	20	Self
TM35	Ice Punch	Ice	Physical	75	100	15	Normal
TM36	Thunderbolt	Electric	Special	90	100	15	Normal
TM37	Flamethrower	Fire	Special	90	100	15	Normal
TM38	Thunder	Electric	Special	110	70	10	Normal
TM40	Psychic	Psychic	Special	90	100	10	Normal
TM43	Shadow Ball	Ghost	Special	80	100	15	Normal
TM44	Play Rough	Fairy	Physical	90	90	10	Normal
TM45	Solar Beam	Grass	Special	200	100	10	Normal
TM46	Fire Blast	Fire	Special	110	85	5	Normal
TM51	Blizzard	Ice	Special	110	70	5	Many Others
TM55	Ice Beam	Ice	Special	90	100	10	Normal
TM56	Stealth Rock	Rock	Status	—	—	20	Other Side
TM59	Dream Eater	Psychic	Special	100	100	15	Normal

EVOLUTION MOVES

NAME	TYPE	KIND	POW.	ACC.	PP	RANGE

Clefable

CLEFABLE 036

♂ ♀ | Same form for male/female

SPECIES STRENGTHS

HP	▰▰▰▱▱▱
ATTACK	▰▰▰▰▱▱
DEFENSE	▰▰▰▱▱▱
SP. ATK	▰▰▰▰▱▱
SP. DEF	▰▰▰▰▰▱
SPEED	▰▰▰▱▱▱

DAMAGE TAKEN IN BATTLES

◎	×1	🌀	×1
🔥	×1	◉	×1
💧	×1	🌙	×0.5
🍃	×1	⚔	×1
⚡	×1	○	×1
❄	×1	◐	×0
👊	×0.5	🌑	×0.5
☠	×2	⚙	×2
⛰	×1	✦	×1

POKÉDEX ENTRY

They appear to be very protective of their own world. It is a kind of fairy, rarely seen by people.

MAIN WAY TO OBTAIN

Catch one when it appears in Mt. Moon (B2F). Or obtain a Clefairy, then use a Moon Stone on it to evolve it into Clefable.

Where to catch

EVOLUTION

Use Moon Stone
→ → →

Clefairy **Clefable**

LEVEL-UP MOVES

LV.	NAME	TYPE	KIND	POW.	ACC.	PP	RANGE
1	Defense Curl	Normal	Status	—	—	40	Self
1	Growl	Normal	Status	—	100	40	Many Others
1	Metronome	Normal	Status	—	—	10	Self
1	Pound	Normal	Physical	40	100	35	Normal
1	Sing	Normal	Status	—	55	15	Normal

EVOLUTION MOVES

NAME	TYPE	KIND	POW.	ACC.	PP	RANGE
Metronome	Normal	Status	—	—	10	Self

TM MOVES

NO.	NAME	TYPE	KIND	POW.	ACC.	PP	RANGE
TM01	Headbutt	Normal	Physical	70	100	15	Normal
TM03	Helping Hand	Normal	Status	—	—	20	1 Ally
TM04	Teleport	Psychic	Status	—	—	20	Self
TM05	Rest	Psychic	Status	—	—	10	Self
TM06	Light Screen	Psychic	Status	—	—	30	Your Side
TM07	Protect	Normal	Status	—	—	10	Self
TM08	Substitute	Normal	Status	—	—	10	Self
TM09	Reflect	Psychic	Status	—	—	20	Your Side
TM10	Dig	Ground	Physical	80	100	10	Normal
TM12	Facade	Normal	Physical	70	100	20	Normal
TM13	Brick Break	Fighting	Physical	75	100	15	Normal
TM15	Seismic Toss	Fighting	Physical	—	100	20	Normal
TM16	Thunder Wave	Electric	Status	—	90	20	Normal
TM19	Iron Tail	Steel	Physical	100	75	15	Normal
TM23	Thunder Punch	Electric	Physical	75	100	15	Normal
TM27	Toxic	Poison	Status	—	90	10	Normal
TM28	Tri Attack	Normal	Special	80	100	10	Normal
TM31	Fire Punch	Fire	Physical	75	100	15	Normal
TM32	Dazzling Gleam	Fairy	Special	80	100	10	Many Others
TM33	Calm Mind	Psychic	Status	—	—	20	Self
TM35	Ice Punch	Ice	Physical	75	100	15	Normal
TM36	Thunderbolt	Electric	Special	90	100	15	Normal
TM37	Flamethrower	Fire	Special	90	100	15	Normal
TM38	Thunder	Electric	Special	110	70	10	Normal
TM40	Psychic	Psychic	Special	90	100	10	Normal
TM43	Shadow Ball	Ghost	Special	80	100	15	Normal
TM44	Play Rough	Fairy	Physical	90	90	10	Normal
TM45	Solar Beam	Grass	Special	200	100	10	Normal
TM46	Fire Blast	Fire	Special	110	85	5	Normal
TM48	Hyper Beam	Normal	Special	150	90	5	Normal
TM51	Blizzard	Ice	Special	110	70	5	Many Others
TM55	Ice Beam	Ice	Special	90	100	10	Normal
TM56	Stealth Rock	Rock	Status	—	—	20	Other Side
TM59	Dream Eater	Psychic	Special	100	100	15	Normal

POKÉMON EXPRESSIONS

HAPPY

UNHAPPY

ATTACKING

Vulpix

♂ ♀ | Same form for male/female

SPECIES STRENGTHS

HP
ATTACK
DEFENSE
SP. ATK
SP. DEF
SPEED

DAMAGE TAKEN IN BATTLES

⚫ ×1		🕊 ×1	
🔥 ×0.5		⊚ ×1	
💧 ×2		🍃 ×0.5	
⚡ ×0.5		✦ ×2	
⚡ ×1		👁 ×1	
❄ ×0.5		🥊 ×1	
〰 ×1		◐ ×1	
🌀 ×1		⊙ ×0.5	
⛰ ×2		✺ ×0.5	

POKÉDEX ENTRY

Both its fur and its tails are
beautiful. As it grows, the tails
split and form more tails.

MAIN WAY TO OBTAIN

Obtain one in a trade if you are
playing *Pokémon: Let's Go, Pikachu!*,
as it does not appear in that game.
Catch one when it appears on
Route 5, Route 6, or elsewhere in
Pokémon: Let's Go, Eevee!

Where to catch

EVOLUTION

Use Fire Stone
→ → →

Vulpix   Ninetales

POKÉMON EXPRESSIONS

HAPPY

UNHAPPY

ATTACKING

LEVEL-UP MOVES

LV.	NAME	TYPE	KIND	POW.	ACC.	PP	RANGE
1	Tackle	Normal	Physical	40	100	35	Normal
3	Tail Whip	Normal	Status	—	100	30	Many Others
7	Ember	Fire	Special	40	100	25	Normal
10	Quick Attack	Normal	Physical	40	100	30	Normal
14	Confuse Ray	Ghost	Status	—	100	10	Normal
17	Will-O-Wisp	Fire	Status	—	85	15	Normal
21	Fire Spin	Fire	Special	35	85	15	Normal
24	Flamethrower	Fire	Special	90	100	15	Normal
28	Roar	Normal	Status	—	—	20	Normal
31	Fire Blast	Fire	Special	110	85	5	Normal

TM MOVES

NO.	NAME	TYPE	KIND	POW.	ACC.	PP	RANGE
TM01	Headbutt	Normal	Physical	70	100	15	Normal
TM05	Rest	Psychic	Status	—	—	10	Self
TM07	Protect	Normal	Status	—	—	10	Self
TM08	Substitute	Normal	Status	—	—	10	Self
TM09	Reflect	Psychic	Status	—	—	20	Your Side
TM10	Dig	Ground	Physical	80	100	10	Normal
TM11	Will-O-Wisp	Fire	Status	—	85	15	Normal
TM12	Facade	Normal	Physical	70	100	20	Normal
TM19	Iron Tail	Steel	Physical	100	75	15	Normal
TM20	Dark Pulse	Dark	Special	80	100	15	Normal
TM21	Foul Play	Dark	Physical	95	100	15	Normal
TM27	Toxic	Poison	Status	—	90	10	Normal
TM37	Flamethrower	Fire	Special	90	100	15	Normal
TM46	Fire Blast	Fire	Special	110	85	5	Normal

EVOLUTION MOVES

NAME	TYPE	KIND	POW.	ACC.	PP	RANGE

Vulpix

ALOLA FORM

VULPIX
ALOLA FORM
037

♂ ♀ | Same form for male/female

SPECIES STRENGTHS

HP	▬▬
ATTACK	▬▬
DEFENSE	▬▬
SP. ATK	▬▬
SP. DEF	▬▬▬
SPEED	▬▬▬

DAMAGE TAKEN IN BATTLES

⬤	×1	🪶	×1
🔥	×2	🌀	×1
💧	×1	🌱	×1
🍃	×1	👁	×2
⚡	×1	🐛	×1
❄	×0.5	🪨	×1
👊	×2	🌙	×1
☠	×1	⚙	×2
⛰	×1	✦	×1

POKÉDEX ENTRY

It looks like snow come to life, and the breath it exhales is −58 degrees Fahrenheit. Another name for it is Keokeo.

MAIN WAY TO OBTAIN

Obtain one in a trade if you are playing *Pokémon: Let's Go, Pikachu!*, as it does not appear in that game. Trade a Vulpix for one in the Pokémon Center in Celadon City (p. 62) in *Pokémon: Let's Go, Eevee!*

Where to catch

Habitat Unknown

EVOLUTION

Use Ice Stone
→ → →

Alolan Vulpix   **Alolan Ninetales**

LEVEL-UP MOVES

LV.	NAME	TYPE	KIND	POW.	ACC.	PP	RANGE
1	Tackle	Normal	Physical	40	100	35	Normal
3	Tail Whip	Normal	Status	—	100	30	Many Others
7	Mist	Ice	Status	—	—	30	Your Side
10	Ice Shard	Ice	Physical	40	100	30	Normal
14	Confuse Ray	Ghost	Status	—	100	10	Normal
17	Aurora Beam	Ice	Special	65	100	20	Normal
21	Dazzling Gleam	Fairy	Special	80	100	10	Many Others
24	Ice Beam	Ice	Special	90	100	10	Normal
28	Roar	Normal	Status	—	—	20	Normal
31	Blizzard	Ice	Special	110	70	5	Many Others

TM MOVES

NO.	NAME	TYPE	KIND	POW.	ACC.	PP	RANGE
TM01	Headbutt	Normal	Physical	70	100	15	Normal
TM05	Rest	Psychic	Status	—	—	10	Self
TM07	Protect	Normal	Status	—	—	10	Self
TM08	Substitute	Normal	Status	—	—	10	Self
TM09	Reflect	Psychic	Status	—	—	20	Your Side
TM10	Dig	Ground	Physical	80	100	10	Normal
TM12	Facade	Normal	Physical	70	100	20	Normal
TM19	Iron Tail	Steel	Physical	100	75	15	Normal
TM20	Dark Pulse	Dark	Special	80	100	15	Normal
TM21	Foul Play	Dark	Physical	95	100	15	Normal
TM27	Toxic	Poison	Status	—	90	10	Normal
TM32	Dazzling Gleam	Fairy	Special	80	100	10	Many Others
TM51	Blizzard	Ice	Special	110	70	5	Many Others
TM55	Ice Beam	Ice	Special	90	100	10	Normal

POKÉMON EXPRESSIONS

HAPPY

UNHAPPY

ATTACKING

EVOLUTION MOVES

NAME	TYPE	KIND	POW.	ACC.	PP	RANGE

Ninetales

♂ ♀ | Same form for male/female

SPECIES STRENGTHS

HP	▪▪▪□□
ATTACK	▪▪▪□□
DEFENSE	▪▪▪□□
SP. ATK	▪▪▪□□
SP. DEF	▪▪▪□□
SPEED	▪▪▪▪□

DAMAGE TAKEN IN BATTLES

⊙ ×1		🪶 ×1	
🔥 ×0.5		🌀 ×1	
💧 ×2		🐛 ×0.5	
🍃 ×0.5		🪨 ×2	
⚡ ×1		👻 ×1	
❄ ×0.5		🐉 ×1	
👊 ×1		🌑 ×1	
☠ ×1		⚙ ×0.5	
⛰ ×2		✦ ×0.5	

POKÉDEX ENTRY

According to an enduring legend, nine noble saints were united and reincarnated as this Pokémon.

MAIN WAY TO OBTAIN

Catch one when it appears on Route 7 or Route 8 in *Pokémon: Let's Go, Eevee!* Or obtain a Vulpix, then use a Fire Stone on it to evolve it into Ninetales.

Where to catch

EVOLUTION

Use Fire Stone
→ → →

Vulpix

Ninetales

POKÉMON EXPRESSIONS

HAPPY

UNHAPPY

ATTACKING

LEVEL-UP MOVES

LV.	NAME	TYPE	KIND	POW.	ACC.	PP	RANGE
1	Ember	Fire	Special	40	100	25	Normal
1	Hypnosis	Psychic	Status	—	60	20	Normal
1	Nasty Plot	Dark	Status	—	—	20	Self
1	Quick Attack	Normal	Physical	40	100	30	Normal
1	Tackle	Normal	Physical	40	100	35	Normal
1	Tail Whip	Normal	Status	—	100	30	Many Others

TM MOVES

NO.	NAME	TYPE	KIND	POW.	ACC.	PP	RANGE
TM01	Headbutt	Normal	Physical	70	100	15	Normal
TM05	Rest	Psychic	Status	—	—	10	Self
TM07	Protect	Normal	Status	—	—	10	Self
TM08	Substitute	Normal	Status	—	—	10	Self
TM09	Reflect	Psychic	Status	—	—	20	Your Side
TM10	Dig	Ground	Physical	80	100	10	Normal
TM11	Will-O-Wisp	Fire	Status	—	85	15	Normal
TM12	Facade	Normal	Physical	70	100	20	Normal
TM19	Iron Tail	Steel	Physical	100	75	15	Normal
TM20	Dark Pulse	Dark	Special	80	100	15	Normal
TM21	Foul Play	Dark	Physical	95	100	15	Normal
TM27	Toxic	Poison	Status	—	90	10	Normal
TM33	Calm Mind	Psychic	Status	—	—	20	Self
TM37	Flamethrower	Fire	Special	90	100	15	Normal
TM45	Solar Beam	Grass	Special	200	100	10	Normal
TM46	Fire Blast	Fire	Special	110	85	5	Normal
TM48	Hyper Beam	Normal	Special	150	90	5	Normal
TM59	Dream Eater	Psychic	Special	100	100	15	Normal

EVOLUTION MOVES

NAME	TYPE	KIND	POW.	ACC.	PP	RANGE

Ninetales

ALOLA FORM

♂ ♀ | Same form for male/female

SPECIES STRENGTHS

HP	▪▪▪▫▫▫
ATTACK	▪▪▪▫▫▫
DEFENSE	▪▪▪▪▫▫
SP. ATK	▪▪▪▪▫▫
SP. DEF	▪▪▪▪▫▫
SPEED	▪▪▪▪▪▫

DAMAGE TAKEN IN BATTLES

◎	×1	◿	×1
🔥	×2	💧	×1
💧	×1	🦋	×0.5
🍃	×1	⚔	×2
⚡	×1	💠	×1
❄	×0.5	👊	×0
▦	×1	☾	×0.5
◉	×2	⦿	×4
△	×1	✦	×1

POKÉDEX ENTRY

It lives on mountains perpetually covered in snow and is revered as a deity incarnate. It appears draped in a blizzard.

MAIN WAY TO OBTAIN

Obtain an Alolan Vulpix, then use an Ice Stone on it to evolve it into Alolan Ninetales.

Where to catch

Habitat Unknown

EVOLUTION

Alolan Vulpix

Use Ice Stone
→ → →

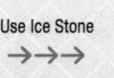

Alolan Ninetales

LEVEL-UP MOVES

LV.	NAME	TYPE	KIND	POW.	ACC.	PP	RANGE
1	Hypnosis	Psychic	Status	—	60	20	Normal
1	Ice Shard	Ice	Physical	40	100	30	Normal
1	Mist	Ice	Status	—	—	30	Your Side
1	Nasty Plot	Dark	Status	—	—	20	Self
1	Tackle	Normal	Physical	40	100	35	Normal
1	Tail Whip	Normal	Status	—	100	30	Many Others

TM MOVES

NO.	NAME	TYPE	KIND	POW.	ACC.	PP	RANGE
TM01	Headbutt	Normal	Physical	70	100	15	Normal
TM05	Rest	Psychic	Status	—	—	10	Self
TM07	Protect	Normal	Status	—	—	10	Self
TM08	Substitute	Normal	Status	—	—	10	Self
TM09	Reflect	Psychic	Status	—	—	20	Your Side
TM10	Dig	Ground	Physical	80	100	10	Normal
TM12	Facade	Normal	Physical	70	100	20	Normal
TM19	Iron Tail	Steel	Physical	100	75	15	Normal
TM20	Dark Pulse	Dark	Special	80	100	15	Normal
TM21	Foul Play	Dark	Physical	95	100	15	Normal
TM27	Toxic	Poison	Status	—	90	10	Normal
TM32	Dazzling Gleam	Fairy	Special	80	100	10	Many Others
TM33	Calm Mind	Psychic	Status	—	—	20	Self
TM48	Hyper Beam	Normal	Special	150	90	5	Normal
TM51	Blizzard	Ice	Special	110	70	5	Many Others
TM55	Ice Beam	Ice	Special	90	100	10	Normal
TM59	Dream Eater	Psychic	Special	100	100	15	Normal

EVOLUTION MOVES

NAME	TYPE	KIND	POW.	ACC.	PP	RANGE

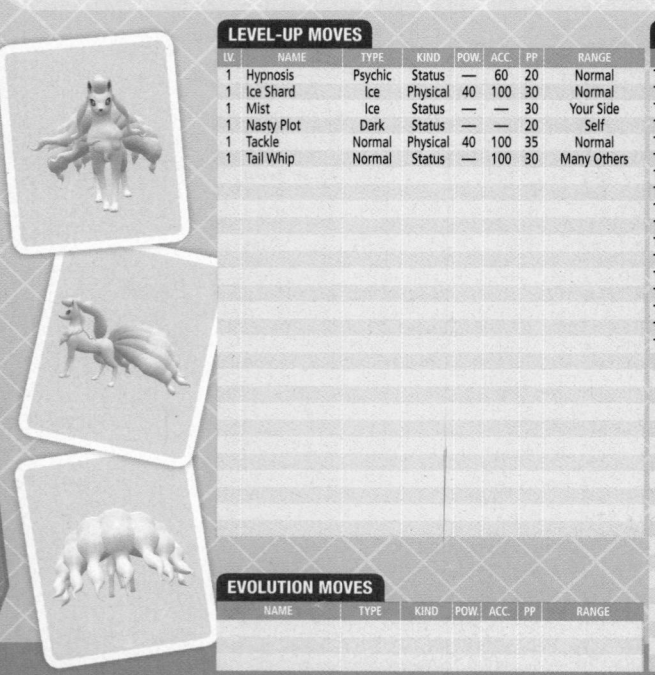

POKÉMON EXPRESSIONS

HAPPY

UNHAPPY

ATTACKING

Jigglypuff

♂ ♀ | Same form for male/female

SPECIES STRENGTHS

HP	▮▮▮▮▮
ATTACK	▮▮
DEFENSE	▮
SP. ATK	▮▮
SP. DEF	▮
SPEED	▮

DAMAGE TAKEN IN BATTLES

⦿ ×1	🌀 ×1		
🔥 ×1	🌀 ×1		
💧 ×1	☀ ×0.5		
🍃 ×1	🍂 ×1		
⚡ ×1	⚪ ×0		
❄ ×1	🌙 ×0		
👊 ×1	🌙 ×0.5		
☠ ×2	⦿ ×2		
⛰ ×1	✦ ×1		

POKÉDEX ENTRY

Uses its cute round eyes to enrapture its foe. It then sings a pleasing melody that lulls the foe to sleep.

MAIN WAY TO OBTAIN

Catch one when it appears on Route 5, Route 6, or elsewhere.

Where to catch

EVOLUTION

 **Jigglypuff**

Use Moon Stone
→ → →

 **Wigglytuff**

POKÉMON EXPRESSIONS

HAPPY

UNHAPPY

ATTACKING

LEVEL-UP MOVES

LV.	NAME	TYPE	KIND	POW.	ACC.	PP	RANGE
1	Sing	Normal	Status	—	55	15	Normal
4	Pound	Normal	Physical	40	100	35	Normal
6	Defense Curl	Normal	Status	—	—	40	Self
10	Bide	Normal	Physical	—	—	10	Self
12	Double Slap	Normal	Physical	15	85	10	Normal
16	Disable	Normal	Status	—	100	20	Normal
18	Rest	Psychic	Status	—	—	10	Self
22	Body Slam	Normal	Physical	85	100	15	Normal
24	Mimic	Normal	Status	—	—	10	Normal
28	Double-Edge	Normal	Physical	120	100	15	Normal

TM MOVES

NO.	NAME	TYPE	KIND	POW.	ACC.	PP	RANGE
TM01	Headbutt	Normal	Physical	70	100	15	Normal
TM03	Helping Hand	Normal	Status	—	—	20	1 Ally
TM04	Teleport	Psychic	Status	—	—	20	Self
TM05	Rest	Psychic	Status	—	—	10	Self
TM06	Light Screen	Psychic	Status	—	—	30	Your Side
TM07	Protect	Normal	Status	—	—	10	Self
TM08	Substitute	Normal	Status	—	—	10	Self
TM09	Reflect	Psychic	Status	—	—	20	Your Side
TM10	Dig	Ground	Physical	80	100	10	Normal
TM12	Facade	Normal	Physical	70	100	20	Normal
TM13	Brick Break	Fighting	Physical	75	100	15	Normal
TM15	Seismic Toss	Fighting	Physical	—	100	20	Normal
TM16	Thunder Wave	Electric	Status	—	90	20	Normal
TM23	Thunder Punch	Electric	Physical	75	100	15	Normal
TM27	Toxic	Poison	Status	—	90	10	Normal
TM28	Tri Attack	Normal	Special	80	100	10	Normal
TM31	Fire Punch	Fire	Physical	75	100	15	Normal
TM32	Dazzling Gleam	Fairy	Special	80	100	10	Many Others
TM35	Ice Punch	Ice	Physical	75	100	15	Normal
TM36	Thunderbolt	Electric	Special	90	100	15	Normal
TM37	Flamethrower	Fire	Special	90	100	15	Normal
TM38	Thunder	Electric	Special	110	70	10	Normal
TM40	Psychic	Psychic	Special	90	100	10	Normal
TM43	Shadow Ball	Ghost	Special	80	100	15	Normal
TM44	Play Rough	Fairy	Physical	90	90	10	Normal
TM45	Solar Beam	Grass	Special	200	100	10	Normal
TM46	Fire Blast	Fire	Special	110	85	5	Normal
TM51	Blizzard	Ice	Special	110	70	5	Many Others
TM55	Ice Beam	Ice	Special	90	100	10	Normal
TM56	Stealth Rock	Rock	Status	—	—	20	Other Side
TM59	Dream Eater	Psychic	Special	100	100	15	Normal

EVOLUTION MOVES

NAME	TYPE	KIND	POW.	ACC.	PP	RANGE

Wigglytuff

♂ ♀ | Same form for male/female

SPECIES STRENGTHS

HP	
ATTACK	
DEFENSE	
SP. ATK	
SP. DEF	
SPEED	

DAMAGE TAKEN IN BATTLES

	×1		×1
	×1		×1
	×1		×0.5
	×1		×1
	×1		×0
	×1		×0
	×1		×0.5
	×2		×2
	×1		×1

POKÉDEX ENTRY

Its body is very elastic. By inhaling deeply, it can continue to inflate itself without limit.

MAIN WAY TO OBTAIN

Obtain a Jigglypuff, then use a Moon Stone on it to evolve it into Wigglytuff.

Where to catch

Habitat Unknown

EVOLUTION

Jigglypuff

Use Moon Stone →→→

Wigglytuff

LEVEL-UP MOVES

LV.	NAME	TYPE	KIND	POW.	ACC.	PP	RANGE
1	Bide	Normal	Physical	—	—	10	Self
1	Minimize	Normal	Status	—	—	10	Self
1	Pound	Normal	Physical	40	100	35	Normal
1	Sing	Normal	Status	—	55	15	Normal

EVOLUTION MOVES

NAME	TYPE	KIND	POW.	ACC.	PP	RANGE

TM MOVES

NO.	NAME	TYPE	KIND	POW.	ACC.	PP	RANGE
TM01	Headbutt	Normal	Physical	70	100	15	Normal
TM03	Helping Hand	Normal	Status	—	—	20	1 Ally
TM04	Teleport	Psychic	Status	—	—	20	Self
TM05	Rest	Psychic	Status	—	—	10	Self
TM06	Light Screen	Psychic	Status	—	—	30	Your Side
TM07	Protect	Normal	Status	—	—	10	Self
TM08	Substitute	Normal	Status	—	—	10	Self
TM09	Reflect	Psychic	Status	—	—	20	Your Side
TM10	Dig	Ground	Physical	80	100	10	Normal
TM12	Facade	Normal	Physical	70	100	20	Normal
TM13	Brick Break	Fighting	Physical	75	100	15	Normal
TM15	Seismic Toss	Fighting	Physical	—	100	20	Normal
TM16	Thunder Wave	Electric	Status	—	90	20	Normal
TM23	Thunder Punch	Electric	Physical	75	100	15	Normal
TM27	Toxic	Poison	Status	—	90	10	Normal
TM28	Tri Attack	Normal	Special	80	100	10	Normal
TM31	Fire Punch	Fire	Physical	75	100	15	Normal
TM32	Dazzling Gleam	Fairy	Special	80	100	10	Many Others
TM35	Ice Punch	Ice	Physical	75	100	15	Normal
TM36	Thunderbolt	Electric	Special	90	100	15	Normal
TM37	Flamethrower	Fire	Special	90	100	15	Normal
TM38	Thunder	Electric	Special	110	70	10	Normal
TM40	Psychic	Psychic	Special	90	100	10	Normal
TM43	Shadow Ball	Ghost	Special	80	100	15	Normal
TM44	Play Rough	Fairy	Physical	90	90	10	Normal
TM45	Solar Beam	Grass	Special	200	100	10	Normal
TM46	Fire Blast	Fire	Special	110	85	5	Normal
TM48	Hyper Beam	Normal	Special	150	90	5	Normal
TM51	Blizzard	Ice	Special	110	70	5	Many Others
TM55	Ice Beam	Ice	Special	90	100	10	Normal
TM56	Stealth Rock	Rock	Status	—	—	20	Other Side
TM59	Dream Eater	Psychic	Special	100	100	15	Normal

POKÉMON EXPRESSIONS

HAPPY

UNHAPPY

ATTACKING

Zubat

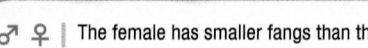

♂ ♀ | The female has smaller fangs than the male.

♂   ♀

SPECIES STRENGTHS

HP
ATTACK
DEFENSE
SP. ATK
SP. DEF
SPEED

DAMAGE TAKEN IN BATTLES

⚪ ×1		🕊 ×1	
🔥 ×1		🌀 ×2	
💧 ×1		⚫ ×0.25	
⚡ ×0.25		💠 ×2	
🍃 ×2		👁 ×1	
❄ ×2		🌑 ×1	
👊 ×0.25		◐ ×1	
☠ ×0.5		⊙ ×1	
🔺 ×0		✴ ×0.5	

POKÉDEX ENTRY

Emits ultrasonic cries while it flies. They act as a sonar used to check for objects in its way.

MAIN WAY TO OBTAIN

Catch one when it appears in Mt. Moon, in the Rock Tunnel, or elsewhere.

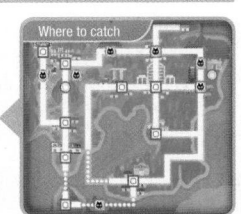

Where to catch

EVOLUTION

Zubat

Lv. 22
→ → →

Golbat

POKÉMON EXPRESSIONS

HAPPY

UNHAPPY

ATTACKING

LEVEL-UP MOVES

LV.	NAME	TYPE	KIND	POW.	ACC.	PP	RANGE
1	Absorb	Grass	Special	40	100	15	Normal
1	Supersonic	Normal	Status	—	55	20	Normal
4	Wing Attack	Flying	Physical	60	100	35	Normal
9	Bite	Dark	Physical	60	100	25	Normal
12	Swift	Normal	Special	60	—	20	Many Others
17	Confuse Ray	Ghost	Status	—	100	10	Normal
20	Haze	Ice	Status	—	—	30	Both Sides
25	Leech Life	Bug	Physical	80	100	10	Normal
28	Toxic	Poison	Status	—	90	10	Normal
33	Air Slash	Flying	Special	75	95	15	Normal

TM MOVES

NO.	NAME	TYPE	KIND	POW.	ACC.	PP	RANGE
TM01	Headbutt	Normal	Physical	70	100	15	Normal
TM02	Taunt	Dark	Status	—	100	20	Normal
TM05	Rest	Psychic	Status	—	—	10	Self
TM07	Protect	Normal	Status	—	—	10	Self
TM08	Substitute	Normal	Status	—	—	10	Self
TM12	Facade	Normal	Physical	70	100	20	Normal
TM14	Fly	Flying	Physical	90	95	15	Normal
TM18	U-turn	Bug	Physical	70	100	20	Normal
TM27	Toxic	Poison	Status	—	90	10	Normal
TM43	Shadow Ball	Ghost	Special	80	100	15	Normal
TM50	Roost	Flying	Status	—	—	10	Self
TM52	Sludge Bomb	Poison	Special	90	100	10	Normal
TM53	Mega Drain	Grass	Special	75	100	10	Normal

EVOLUTION MOVES

NAME	TYPE	KIND	POW.	ACC.	PP	RANGE

GOLBAT 042

☑ **042** Bat Pokémon   Average height: 5'03"   Average weight: 121.3 lbs.

Golbat

♂ ♀ | The female has smaller fangs than the male.

SPECIES STRENGTHS

HP
ATTACK
DEFENSE
SP. ATK
SP. DEF
SPEED

DAMAGE TAKEN IN BATTLES

×1		×1	
×1		×2	
×1		×0.25	
×0.25		×2	
×2		×1	
×2		×1	
×0.25		×1	
×0.5		×1	
×0		×0.5	

POKÉDEX ENTRY

It attacks in a stealthy manner, without warning. Its sharp fangs are used to bite and to suck blood.

MAIN WAY TO OBTAIN

Catch one when it appears in the Rock Tunnel, in the Seafoam Islands, or elsewhere. Or obtain a Zubat, then level it up to Lv. 22 or higher to evolve it into Golbat.

Where to catch

EVOLUTION

Zubat

Lv. 22
→→→

Golbat

LEVEL-UP MOVES

LV.	NAME	TYPE	KIND	POW.	ACC.	PP	RANGE
1	Absorb	Grass	Special	40	100	15	Normal
1	Bite	Dark	Physical	60	100	25	Normal
1	Crunch	Dark	Physical	80	100	15	Normal
1	Quick Attack	Normal	Physical	40	100	30	Normal
1	Supersonic	Normal	Status	—	55	20	Normal
1	Whirlwind	Normal	Status	—	—	20	Normal
1	Wing Attack	Flying	Physical	60	100	35	Normal
4	Wing Attack	Flying	Physical	60	100	35	Normal
8	Bite	Dark	Physical	60	100	25	Normal
12	Swift	Normal	Special	60	—	20	Many Others
17	Confuse Ray	Ghost	Status	—	100	10	Normal
20	Haze	Ice	Status	—	—	30	Both Sides
31	Leech Life	Bug	Physical	80	100	10	Normal
40	Toxic	Poison	Status	—	90	10	Normal
51	Air Slash	Flying	Special	75	95	15	Normal

TM MOVES

NO.	NAME	TYPE	KIND	POW.	ACC.	PP	RANGE
TM01	Headbutt	Normal	Physical	70	100	15	Normal
TM02	Taunt	Dark	Status	—	100	20	Normal
TM05	Rest	Psychic	Status	—	—	10	Self
TM07	Protect	Normal	Status	—	—	10	Self
TM08	Substitute	Normal	Status	—	—	10	Self
TM12	Facade	Normal	Physical	70	100	20	Normal
TM14	Fly	Flying	Physical	90	95	15	Normal
TM18	U-turn	Bug	Physical	70	100	20	Normal
TM27	Toxic	Poison	Status	—	90	10	Normal
TM43	Shadow Ball	Ghost	Special	80	100	15	Normal
TM48	Hyper Beam	Normal	Special	150	90	5	Normal
TM50	Roost	Flying	Status	—	—	10	Self
TM52	Sludge Bomb	Poison	Special	90	100	10	Normal
TM53	Mega Drain	Grass	Special	75	100	10	Normal

EVOLUTION MOVES

NAME	TYPE	KIND	POW.	ACC.	PP	RANGE
Crunch	Dark	Physical	80	100	15	Normal

POKÉMON EXPRESSIONS

HAPPY

UNHAPPY

ATTACKING

Oddish

♂ ♀ | Same form for male/female

SPECIES STRENGTHS

HP
ATTACK
DEFENSE
SP. ATK
SP. DEF
SPEED

DAMAGE TAKEN IN BATTLES

×1		×2	
×2		×2	
×0.5		×1	
×0.25		×1	
×0.5		×1	
×2		×1	
×0.5		×1	
×1		×1	
×1		×0.5	

POKÉDEX ENTRY

It may be mistaken for a clump of weeds. If you try to yank it out of the ground, it shrieks horribly.

MAIN WAY TO OBTAIN

Catch one when it appears on Route 1, Route 2, or elsewhere in *Pokémon: Let's Go, Pikachu!* Obtain one in a trade if you are playing *Pokémon: Let's Go, Eevee!*, as it does not appear in that game.

Where to catch

EVOLUTION

 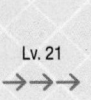  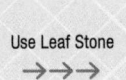 

Oddish　　Lv. 21 →→→　　**Gloom**　　Use Leaf Stone →→→　　**Vileplume**

POKÉMON EXPRESSIONS

HAPPY

UNHAPPY

ATTACKING

LEVEL-UP MOVES

LV.	NAME	TYPE	KIND	POW.	ACC.	PP	RANGE
1	Absorb	Grass	Special	40	100	15	Normal
4	Growth	Normal	Status	—	—	20	Self
8	Acid	Poison	Special	40	100	30	Many Others
12	Poison Powder	Poison	Status	—	75	35	Normal
13	Stun Spore	Grass	Status	—	75	30	Normal
14	Sleep Powder	Grass	Status	—	75	15	Normal
18	Razor Leaf	Grass	Physical	55	95	25	Many Others
22	Mega Drain	Grass	Special	75	100	10	Normal
26	Toxic	Poison	Status	—	90	10	Normal
30	Moonblast	Fairy	Special	95	100	15	Normal

TM MOVES

NO.	NAME	TYPE	KIND	POW.	ACC.	PP	RANGE
TM01	Headbutt	Normal	Physical	70	100	15	Normal
TM05	Rest	Psychic	Status	—	—	10	Self
TM07	Protect	Normal	Status	—	—	10	Self
TM08	Substitute	Normal	Status	—	—	10	Self
TM09	Reflect	Psychic	Status	—	—	20	Your Side
TM12	Facade	Normal	Physical	70	100	20	Normal
TM27	Toxic	Poison	Status	—	90	10	Normal
TM32	Dazzling Gleam	Fairy	Special	80	100	10	Many Others
TM45	Solar Beam	Grass	Special	200	100	10	Normal
TM52	Sludge Bomb	Poison	Special	90	100	10	Normal
TM53	Mega Drain	Grass	Special	75	100	10	Normal

EVOLUTION MOVES

NAME	TYPE	KIND	POW.	ACC.	PP	RANGE

Gloom

♂ ♀ | The female has one large spot per petal, while the male has multiple small spots.

SPECIES STRENGTHS

HP	▧▧▧
ATTACK	▧▧▧
DEFENSE	▧▧▧▧
SP. ATK	▧▧▧
SP. DEF	▧▧▧▧
SPEED	▧▧

DAMAGE TAKEN IN BATTLES

⊙	×1	🕊	×2
🔥	×2	🌀	×2
💧	×0.5	👊	×1
🍃	×0.25	🔷	×1
⚡	×0.5	👻	×1
❄	×2	☯	×1
✊	×0.5	🌙	×1
💧	×1	⊙	×1
⛰	×1	☀	×0.5

POKÉDEX ENTRY

Smells incredibly foul! However, around one out of a thousand people enjoy sniffing its nose-bending stink.

MAIN WAY TO OBTAIN

Catch one when it appears on Route 12, Route 13, or elsewhere in *Pokémon: Let's Go, Pikachu!* Or obtain an Oddish, then level it up to Lv. 21 or higher to evolve it into Gloom.

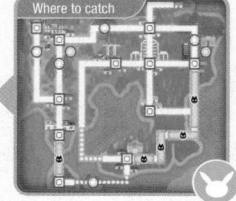
Where to catch

EVOLUTION

 **Oddish** → Lv. 21 →→→  **Gloom** → Use Leaf Stone →→→  **Vileplume**

LEVEL-UP MOVES

LV.	NAME	TYPE	KIND	POW.	ACC.	PP	RANGE
1	Absorb	Grass	Special	40	100	15	Normal
1	Acid	Poison	Special	40	100	30	Many Others
1	Growth	Normal	Status	—	—	20	Self
1	Poison Powder	Poison	Status	—	75	35	Normal
4	Growth	Normal	Status	—	—	20	Self
8	Acid	Poison	Special	40	100	30	Many Others
12	Poison Powder	Poison	Status	—	75	35	Normal
13	Stun Spore	Grass	Status	—	75	30	Normal
14	Sleep Powder	Grass	Status	—	75	15	Normal
18	Razor Leaf	Grass	Physical	55	95	25	Many Others
27	Mega Drain	Grass	Special	75	100	10	Normal
36	Toxic	Poison	Status	—	90	10	Normal
45	Moonblast	Fairy	Special	95	100	15	Normal

TM MOVES

NO.	NAME	TYPE	KIND	POW.	ACC.	PP	RANGE
TM01	Headbutt	Normal	Physical	70	100	15	Normal
TM05	Rest	Psychic	Status	—	—	10	Self
TM07	Protect	Normal	Status	—	—	10	Self
TM08	Substitute	Normal	Status	—	—	10	Self
TM09	Reflect	Psychic	Status	—	—	20	Your Side
TM12	Facade	Normal	Physical	70	100	20	Normal
TM27	Toxic	Poison	Status	—	90	10	Normal
TM32	Dazzling Gleam	Fairy	Special	80	100	10	Many Others
TM45	Solar Beam	Grass	Special	200	100	10	Normal
TM52	Sludge Bomb	Poison	Special	90	100	10	Normal
TM53	Mega Drain	Grass	Special	75	100	10	Normal

EVOLUTION MOVES

NAME	TYPE	KIND	POW.	ACC.	PP	RANGE

POKÉMON EXPRESSIONS

HAPPY

UNHAPPY

ATTACKING

Vileplume

♂ ♀ | The female has large spots on its petals, while the male has small spots on its petals.

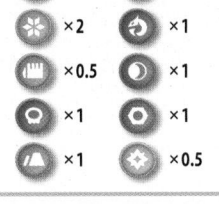
♂

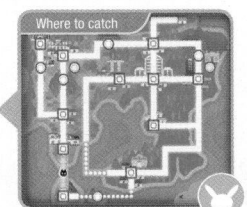
♀

SPECIES STRENGTHS

HP
ATTACK
DEFENSE
SP. ATK
SP. DEF
SPEED

DAMAGE TAKEN IN BATTLES

⊙ ×1		🪶 ×2
🔥 ×2		⊚ ×2
💧 ×0.5		🍃 ×1
⚡ ×0.25		👁 ×1
⚔ ×0.5		◑ ×1
❄ ×2		🐦 ×1
👊 ×0.5		☾ ×1
☠ ×1		⊙ ×1
🗻 ×1		✦ ×0.5

POKÉDEX ENTRY

Flaps its broad flower petals to scatter its poisonous pollen. The flapping sound is very loud.

MAIN WAY TO OBTAIN

Catch one when it appears on Route 21 in *Pokémon: Let's Go, Pikachu!* Or obtain a Gloom, then use a Leaf Stone on it to evolve it into Vileplume.

Where to catch

EVOLUTION

Oddish

Lv. 21
→→→

Gloom

Use Leaf Stone
→→→

Vileplume

POKÉMON EXPRESSIONS

HAPPY

UNHAPPY

ATTACKING

LEVEL-UP MOVES

LV.	NAME	TYPE	KIND	POW.	ACC.	PP	RANGE
1	Absorb	Grass	Special	40	100	15	Normal
1	Acid	Poison	Special	40	100	30	Many Others
1	Growth	Normal	Status	—	—	20	Self
1	Poison Powder	Poison	Status	—	75	35	Normal
1	Solar Beam	Grass	Special	200	100	10	Normal
54	Petal Dance	Grass	Special	120	100	10	1 Random

TM MOVES

NO.	NAME	TYPE	KIND	POW.	ACC.	PP	RANGE
TM01	Headbutt	Normal	Physical	70	100	15	Normal
TM05	Rest	Psychic	Status	—	—	10	Self
TM07	Protect	Normal	Status	—	—	10	Self
TM08	Substitute	Normal	Status	—	—	10	Self
TM09	Reflect	Psychic	Status	—	—	20	Your Side
TM12	Facade	Normal	Physical	70	100	20	Normal
TM27	Toxic	Poison	Status	—	90	10	Normal
TM32	Dazzling Gleam	Fairy	Special	80	100	10	Many Others
TM45	Solar Beam	Grass	Special	200	100	10	Normal
TM48	Hyper Beam	Normal	Special	150	90	5	Normal
TM52	Sludge Bomb	Poison	Special	90	100	10	Normal
TM53	Mega Drain	Grass	Special	75	100	10	Normal

EVOLUTION MOVES

NAME	TYPE	KIND	POW.	ACC.	PP	RANGE

Average height: 1'00" Average weight: 11.9 lbs.

PARAS 046

Paras

♂ ♀ | Same form for male/female

SPECIES STRENGTHS

HP	▰▰▰
ATTACK	▰▰▰▰▰
DEFENSE	▰▰▰▰
SP. ATK	▰▰▰
SP. DEF	▰▰▰▰
SPEED	▰▰

DAMAGE TAKEN IN BATTLES

◉	×1	🪶	×4
🔥	×4	🌀	×1
💧	×0.5		×2
⚡	×0.25		×2
	×0.5		×1
❄	×2		×1
	×0.5	☾	×1
	×2		×1
	×0.25	✦	×1

POKÉDEX ENTRY

Burrows under the ground to gnaw on tree roots. The mushrooms on its back absorb most of the nutrition.

MAIN WAY TO OBTAIN

Catch one when it appears in Mt. Moon.

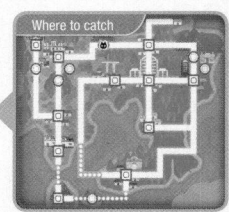

Where to catch

EVOLUTION

Paras

Lv. 24 →→→

Parasect

LEVEL-UP MOVES

LV.	NAME	TYPE	KIND	POW.	ACC.	PP	RANGE
1	Scratch	Normal	Physical	40	100	35	Normal
2	Sleep Powder	Grass	Status	—	75	15	Normal
4	Stun Spore	Grass	Status	—	75	30	Normal
6	Poison Powder	Poison	Status	—	75	35	Normal
9	Absorb	Grass	Special	40	100	15	Normal
12	Growth	Normal	Status	—	—	20	Self
15	Fury Swipes	Normal	Physical	18	80	15	Normal
19	Slash	Normal	Physical	70	100	20	Normal
23	Leech Life	Bug	Physical	80	100	10	Normal
27	Spore	Grass	Status	—	100	15	Normal
31	X-Scissor	Bug	Physical	80	100	15	Normal

TM MOVES

NO.	NAME	TYPE	KIND	POW.	ACC.	PP	RANGE
TM01	Headbutt	Normal	Physical	70	100	15	Normal
TM05	Rest	Psychic	Status	—	—	10	Self
TM06	Light Screen	Psychic	Status	—	—	30	Your Side
TM07	Protect	Normal	Status	—	—	10	Self
TM08	Substitute	Normal	Status	—	—	10	Self
TM09	Reflect	Psychic	Status	—	—	20	Your Side
TM10	Dig	Ground	Physical	80	100	10	Normal
TM12	Facade	Normal	Physical	70	100	20	Normal
TM13	Brick Break	Fighting	Physical	75	100	15	Normal
TM24	X-Scissor	Bug	Physical	80	100	15	Normal
TM27	Toxic	Poison	Status	—	90	10	Normal
TM45	Solar Beam	Grass	Special	200	100	10	Normal
TM52	Sludge Bomb	Poison	Special	90	100	10	Normal
TM53	Mega Drain	Grass	Special	75	100	10	Normal

EVOLUTION MOVES

NAME	TYPE	KIND	POW.	ACC.	PP	RANGE

POKÉMON EXPRESSIONS

HAPPY

UNHAPPY

ATTACKING

Parasect

♂ ♀ | Same form for male/female

SPECIES STRENGTHS

HP	
ATTACK	
DEFENSE	
SP. ATK	
SP. DEF	
SPEED	

DAMAGE TAKEN IN BATTLES

×1		×4	
×4		×1	
×0.5		×2	
×0.25		×2	
×0.5		×1	
×2		×1	
×0.5		×1	
×2		×1	
×0.25		×1	

POKÉDEX ENTRY

The bug host is drained of energy by the mushroom on its back. The mushroom appears to do all the thinking.

MAIN WAY TO OBTAIN

Obtain a Paras, then level it up to Lv. 24 or higher to evolve it into Parasect.

Where to catch

Habitat Unknown

EVOLUTION

Lv. 24
→→→

Paras → Parasect

POKÉMON EXPRESSIONS

HAPPY

UNHAPPY

ATTACKING

LEVEL-UP MOVES

LV.	NAME	TYPE	KIND	POW.	ACC.	PP	RANGE
1	Leech Seed	Grass	Status	—	90	10	Normal
1	Poison Powder	Poison	Status	—	75	35	Normal
1	Scratch	Normal	Physical	40	100	35	Normal
1	Screech	Normal	Status	—	85	40	Normal
1	Sleep Powder	Grass	Status	—	75	15	Normal
1	Stun Spore	Grass	Status	—	75	30	Normal
2	Sleep Powder	Grass	Status	—	75	15	Normal
4	Stun Spore	Grass	Status	—	75	30	Normal
6	Poison Powder	Poison	Status	—	75	35	Normal
9	Absorb	Grass	Special	40	100	15	Normal
12	Growth	Normal	Status	—	—	20	Self
15	Fury Swipes	Normal	Physical	18	80	15	Normal
19	Slash	Normal	Physical	70	100	20	Normal
23	Leech Life	Bug	Physical	80	100	10	Normal
33	Spore	Grass	Status	—	100	15	Normal
43	X-Scissor	Bug	Physical	80	100	15	Normal

TM MOVES

NO.	NAME	TYPE	KIND	POW.	ACC.	PP	RANGE
TM01	Headbutt	Normal	Physical	70	100	15	Normal
TM05	Rest	Psychic	Status	—	—	10	Self
TM06	Light Screen	Psychic	Status	—	—	30	Your Side
TM07	Protect	Normal	Status	—	—	10	Self
TM08	Substitute	Normal	Status	—	—	10	Self
TM09	Reflect	Psychic	Status	—	—	20	Your Side
TM10	Dig	Ground	Physical	80	100	10	Normal
TM12	Facade	Normal	Physical	70	100	20	Normal
TM13	Brick Break	Fighting	Physical	75	100	15	Normal
TM24	X-Scissor	Bug	Physical	80	100	15	Normal
TM27	Toxic	Poison	Status	—	90	10	Normal
TM45	Solar Beam	Grass	Special	200	100	10	Normal
TM48	Hyper Beam	Normal	Special	150	90	5	Normal
TM52	Sludge Bomb	Poison	Special	90	100	10	Normal
TM53	Mega Drain	Grass	Special	75	100	10	Normal

EVOLUTION MOVES

NAME	TYPE	KIND	POW.	ACC.	PP	RANGE

Venonat

♂ ♀ | Same form for male/female

SPECIES STRENGTHS

HP	
ATTACK	
DEFENSE	
SP. ATK	
SP. DEF	
SPEED	

DAMAGE TAKEN IN BATTLES

×1		×2	
×2		×2	
×1		×0.5	
×0.25		×2	
×1		×1	
×1		×1	
×0.25		×1	
×0.5		×1	
×1		×0.5	

POKÉDEX ENTRY

Its large eyes act as radar. In a bright place, you can see that they are clusters of many tiny eyes.

MAIN WAY TO OBTAIN

Catch one when it appears on Route 24, Route 25, or elsewhere.

Where to catch

EVOLUTION

Lv. 31
→→→

Venonat   **Venomoth**

LEVEL-UP MOVES

LV.	NAME	TYPE	KIND	POW.	ACC.	PP	RANGE
1	Tackle	Normal	Physical	40	100	35	Normal
4	Disable	Normal	Status	—	100	20	Normal
8	Supersonic	Normal	Status	—	55	20	Normal
12	Confusion	Psychic	Special	50	100	25	Normal
14	Poison Powder	Poison	Status	—	75	35	Normal
16	Stun Spore	Grass	Status	—	75	30	Normal
20	Psybeam	Psychic	Special	65	100	20	Normal
24	Sleep Powder	Grass	Status	—	75	15	Normal
28	Leech Life	Bug	Physical	80	100	10	Normal
32	Psychic	Psychic	Special	90	100	10	Normal

TM MOVES

NO.	NAME	TYPE	KIND	POW.	ACC.	PP	RANGE
TM01	Headbutt	Normal	Physical	70	100	15	Normal
TM05	Rest	Psychic	Status	—	—	10	Self
TM07	Protect	Normal	Status	—	—	10	Self
TM08	Substitute	Normal	Status	—	—	10	Self
TM09	Reflect	Psychic	Status	—	—	20	Your Side
TM12	Facade	Normal	Physical	70	100	20	Normal
TM27	Toxic	Poison	Status	—	90	10	Normal
TM40	Psychic	Psychic	Special	90	100	10	Normal
TM45	Solar Beam	Grass	Special	200	100	10	Normal
TM52	Sludge Bomb	Poison	Special	90	100	10	Normal
TM53	Mega Drain	Grass	Special	75	100	10	Normal

POKÉMON EXPRESSIONS

HAPPY

UNHAPPY

ATTACKING

EVOLUTION MOVES

NAME	TYPE	KIND	POW.	ACC.	PP	RANGE

Venomoth

♂ ♀ | Same form for male/female

SPECIES STRENGTHS

HP	▦▦▦
ATTACK	▦▦
DEFENSE	▦▦
SP. ATK	▦▦▦▦
SP. DEF	▦▦▦
SPEED	▦▦▦▦

DAMAGE TAKEN IN BATTLES

◉	×1	🍃	×2
🔥	×2	◎	×2
💧	×1		×0.5
	×0.25		×2
	×1		×1
❄	×1		×1
	×0.25	☾	×1
	×0.5	◉	×1
	×1	✦	×0.5

POKÉDEX ENTRY

The powdery scales on its wings are hard to remove from skin. They also contain poison that leaks out on contact.

MAIN WAY TO OBTAIN

Catch one when it appears on Route 14 or Route 15. Or obtain a Venonat, then level it up to Lv. 31 or higher to evolve it into Venomoth.

Where to catch
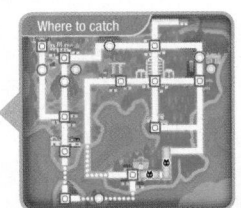

EVOLUTION

Venonat

Lv. 31
→ → →

Venomoth

POKÉMON EXPRESSIONS

HAPPY

UNHAPPY

ATTACKING

LEVEL-UP MOVES

LV.	NAME	TYPE	KIND	POW.	ACC.	PP	RANGE
1	Agility	Psychic	Status	—	—	30	Self
1	Confusion	Psychic	Special	50	100	25	Normal
1	Disable	Normal	Status	—	100	20	Normal
1	Gust	Flying	Special	40	100	35	Normal
1	Screech	Normal	Status	—	85	40	Normal
1	Supersonic	Normal	Status	—	55	20	Normal
1	Tackle	Normal	Physical	40	100	35	Normal
4	Disable	Normal	Status	—	100	20	Normal
8	Supersonic	Normal	Status	—	55	20	Normal
12	Confusion	Psychic	Special	50	100	25	Normal
14	Poison Powder	Poison	Status	—	75	35	Normal
16	Stun Spore	Grass	Status	—	75	30	Normal
20	Psybeam	Psychic	Special	65	100	20	Normal
24	Sleep Powder	Grass	Status	—	75	15	Normal
28	Leech Life	Bug	Physical	80	100	10	Normal
37	Psychic	Psychic	Special	90	100	10	Normal
46	Bug Buzz	Bug	Special	90	100	10	Normal
55	Quiver Dance	Bug	Status	—	—	20	Self

TM MOVES

NO.	NAME	TYPE	KIND	POW.	ACC.	PP	RANGE
TM01	Headbutt	Normal	Physical	70	100	15	Normal
TM04	Teleport	Psychic	Status	—	—	20	Self
TM05	Rest	Psychic	Status	—	—	10	Self
TM07	Protect	Normal	Status	—	—	10	Self
TM08	Substitute	Normal	Status	—	—	10	Self
TM09	Reflect	Psychic	Status	—	—	20	Your Side
TM12	Facade	Normal	Physical	70	100	20	Normal
TM18	U-turn	Bug	Physical	70	100	20	Normal
TM27	Toxic	Poison	Status	—	90	10	Normal
TM40	Psychic	Psychic	Special	90	100	10	Normal
TM45	Solar Beam	Grass	Special	200	100	10	Normal
TM48	Hyper Beam	Normal	Special	150	90	5	Normal
TM50	Roost	Flying	Status	—	—	10	Self
TM52	Sludge Bomb	Poison	Special	90	100	10	Normal
TM53	Mega Drain	Grass	Special	75	100	10	Normal
TM59	Dream Eater	Psychic	Special	100	100	15	Normal

EVOLUTION MOVES

NAME	TYPE	KIND	POW.	ACC.	PP	RANGE
Gust	Flying	Special	40	100	35	Normal

Diglett

DIGLETT / 050

♂ ♀ | Same form for male/female

SPECIES STRENGTHS

HP
ATTACK
DEFENSE
SP. ATK
SP. DEF
SPEED

DAMAGE TAKEN IN BATTLES

×1		×1	
×1		×1	
×2		×1	
×2		×0.5	
×0		×1	
×2		×1	
×1		×1	
×0.5		×1	
×1		×1	

POKÉDEX ENTRY

It prefers dark places. It spends most of its time underground, though it may pop up in caves.

MAIN WAY TO OBTAIN

Catch one when it appears in Diglett's Cave.

Where to catch

EVOLUTION

Lv. 26
→ → →

Diglett   Dugtrio

LEVEL-UP MOVES

LV.	NAME	TYPE	KIND	POW.	ACC.	PP	RANGE
1	Scratch	Normal	Physical	40	100	35	Normal
4	Sand Attack	Ground	Status	—	100	15	Normal
8	Growl	Normal	Status	—	100	40	Many Others
12	Agility	Psychic	Status	—	—	30	Self
15	Fury Swipes	Normal	Physical	18	80	15	Normal
18	Dig	Ground	Physical	80	100	10	Normal
21	Slash	Normal	Physical	70	100	20	Normal
25	Sucker Punch	Dark	Physical	70	100	5	Normal
29	Earthquake	Ground	Physical	100	100	10	All Others
33	Fissure	Ground	Physical	—	30	5	Normal

TM MOVES

NO.	NAME	TYPE	KIND	POW.	ACC.	PP	RANGE
TM01	Headbutt	Normal	Physical	70	100	15	Normal
TM05	Rest	Psychic	Status	—	—	10	Self
TM07	Protect	Normal	Status	—	—	10	Self
TM08	Substitute	Normal	Status	—	—	10	Self
TM10	Dig	Ground	Physical	80	100	10	Normal
TM12	Facade	Normal	Physical	70	100	20	Normal
TM22	Rock Slide	Rock	Physical	75	90	10	Many Others
TM27	Toxic	Poison	Status	—	90	10	Normal
TM41	Earthquake	Ground	Physical	100	100	10	All Others
TM52	Sludge Bomb	Poison	Special	90	100	10	Normal
TM56	Stealth Rock	Rock	Status	—	—	20	Other Side

POKÉMON EXPRESSIONS

HAPPY

UNHAPPY

ATTACKING

EVOLUTION MOVES

NAME	TYPE	KIND	POW.	ACC.	PP	RANGE

Diglett

♂ ♀ | Same form for male/female

ALOLA FORM

SPECIES STRENGTHS

HP	▪
ATTACK	▪▪▪
DEFENSE	▪▪
SP. ATK	▪▪▪
SP. DEF	▪▪▪
SPEED	▪▪▪▪▪▪

DAMAGE TAKEN IN BATTLES

⬡	×0.5	💨	×0.5
🔥	×2	🌀	×0.5
💧	×2	🍃	×0.5
⚡	×1	🗡	×0.25
🍂	×0	👁	×1
❄	×1	🔮	×0.5
👊	×2	🌙	×1
☠	×0	⬤	×0.5
⛰	×2	✦	×0.5

POKÉDEX ENTRY

After living in soil with high iron content for some time, three steel whiskers sprouted from the top of its head.

MAIN WAY TO OBTAIN

Trade a Diglett for one in the Pokémon Center in Lavender Town (p. 57).

Where to catch

Habitat Unknown

EVOLUTION

Alolan Diglett

Lv. 26
→ → →

Alolan Dugtrio

POKÉMON EXPRESSIONS

HAPPY

UNHAPPY

ATTACKING

LEVEL-UP MOVES

LV.	NAME	TYPE	KIND	POW.	ACC.	PP	RANGE
1	Scratch	Normal	Physical	40	100	35	Normal
4	Sand Attack	Ground	Status	—	100	15	Normal
8	Growl	Normal	Status	—	100	40	Many Others
12	Agility	Psychic	Status	—	—	30	Self
15	Fury Swipes	Normal	Physical	18	80	15	Normal
18	Dig	Ground	Physical	80	100	10	Normal
21	Slash	Normal	Physical	70	100	20	Normal
25	Sucker Punch	Dark	Physical	70	100	5	Normal
29	Earthquake	Ground	Physical	100	100	10	All Others
33	Fissure	Ground	Physical	—	30	5	Normal

TM MOVES

NO.	NAME	TYPE	KIND	POW.	ACC.	PP	RANGE
TM01	Headbutt	Normal	Physical	70	100	15	Normal
TM05	Rest	Psychic	Status	—	—	10	Self
TM07	Protect	Normal	Status	—	—	10	Self
TM08	Substitute	Normal	Status	—	—	10	Self
TM10	Dig	Ground	Physical	80	100	10	Normal
TM12	Facade	Normal	Physical	70	100	20	Normal
TM22	Rock Slide	Rock	Physical	75	90	10	Many Others
TM27	Toxic	Poison	Status	—	90	10	Normal
TM41	Earthquake	Ground	Physical	100	100	10	All Others
TM52	Sludge Bomb	Poison	Special	90	100	10	Normal
TM54	Flash Cannon	Steel	Special	80	100	10	Normal
TM56	Stealth Rock	Rock	Status	—	—	20	Other Side

EVOLUTION MOVES

NAME	TYPE	KIND	POW	ACC.	PP	RANGE

Dugtrio

♂ ♀ | Same form for male/female

SPECIES STRENGTHS

- HP
- ATTACK
- DEFENSE
- SP. ATK
- SP. DEF
- SPEED

DAMAGE TAKEN IN BATTLES

×1		×1	
×1		×1	
×2		×1	
×2		×0.5	
×0		×1	
×2		×1	
×1		×1	
×0.5		×1	
×1		×1	

POKÉDEX ENTRY

A team of triplets that can burrow to a depth of 60 miles. It's reported that this triggers an earthquake.

MAIN WAY TO OBTAIN

Catch one when it appears in Diglett's Cave. Or obtain a Diglett, then level it up to Lv. 26 or higher to evolve it into Dugtrio.

Where to catch

EVOLUTION

Diglett

Lv. 26
→→→

Dugtrio

LEVEL-UP MOVES

LV.	NAME	TYPE	KIND	POW.	ACC.	PP	RANGE
1	Agility	Psychic	Status	—	—	30	Self
1	Growl	Normal	Status	—	100	40	Many Others
1	Sand Attack	Ground	Status	—	100	15	Normal
1	Scratch	Normal	Physical	40	100	35	Normal
1	Screech	Normal	Status	—	85	40	Normal
1	Tri Attack	Normal	Special	80	100	10	Normal
4	Sand Attack	Ground	Status	—	100	15	Normal
8	Growl	Normal	Status	—	100	40	Many Others
12	Agility	Psychic	Status	—	—	30	Self
15	Fury Swipes	Normal	Physical	18	80	15	Normal
18	Dig	Ground	Physical	80	100	10	Normal
21	Slash	Normal	Physical	70	100	20	Normal
25	Sucker Punch	Dark	Physical	70	100	5	Normal
35	Earthquake	Ground	Physical	100	100	10	All Others
45	Fissure	Ground	Physical	—	30	5	Normal

TM MOVES

NO.	NAME	TYPE	KIND	POW.	ACC.	PP	RANGE
TM01	Headbutt	Normal	Physical	70	100	15	Normal
TM05	Rest	Psychic	Status	—	—	10	Self
TM07	Protect	Normal	Status	—	—	10	Self
TM08	Substitute	Normal	Status	—	—	10	Self
TM10	Dig	Ground	Physical	80	100	10	Normal
TM12	Facade	Normal	Physical	70	100	20	Normal
TM22	Rock Slide	Rock	Physical	75	90	10	Many Others
TM27	Toxic	Poison	Status	—	90	10	Normal
TM28	Tri Attack	Normal	Special	80	100	10	Normal
TM41	Earthquake	Ground	Physical	100	100	10	All Others
TM48	Hyper Beam	Normal	Special	150	90	5	Normal
TM52	Sludge Bomb	Poison	Special	90	100	10	Normal
TM56	Stealth Rock	Rock	Status	—	—	20	Other Side

EVOLUTION MOVES

NAME	TYPE	KIND	POW.	ACC.	PP	RANGE
Tri Attack	Normal	Special	80	100	10	Normal

POKÉMON EXPRESSIONS

HAPPY

UNHAPPY

ATTACKING

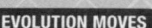

Dugtrio

♂ ♀ | Same form for male/female

ALOLA FORM

SPECIES STRENGTHS

HP	▨▨
ATTACK	▨▨▨▨▨
DEFENSE	▨▨▨
SP. ATK	▨▨
SP. DEF	▨▨▨▨
SPEED	▨▨▨▨

DAMAGE TAKEN IN BATTLES

⬡ ×0.5	🍃 ×0.5
🔥 ×2	◎ ×0.5
💧 ×2	🧿 ×0.5
🍃 ×1	⚔ ×0.25
⚡ ×0	👁 ×1
❄ ×1	🜂 ×0.5
👊 ×2	☾ ×1
☠ ×0	⬡ ×0.5
🗻 ×2	✦ ×0.5

POKÉDEX ENTRY

They're referred to as triplets, but they're not identical—the metallic elements in their bodies differ slightly. The proof shows in their whiskers!

MAIN WAY TO OBTAIN

Obtain an Alolan Diglett, then level it up to Lv. 26 or higher to evolve it into Alolan Dugtrio.

Where to catch
Habitat Unknown

EVOLUTION

Alolan Diglett

Lv. 26
→→→

Alolan Dugtrio

POKÉMON EXPRESSIONS

HAPPY

UNHAPPY

ATTACKING

LEVEL-UP MOVES

LV.	NAME	TYPE	KIND	POW.	ACC.	PP	RANGE
1	Agility	Psychic	Status	—	—	30	Self
1	Growl	Normal	Status	—	100	40	Many Others
1	Sand Attack	Ground	Status	—	100	15	Normal
1	Scratch	Normal	Physical	40	100	35	Normal
1	Screech	Normal	Status	—	85	40	Normal
1	Tri Attack	Normal	Special	80	100	10	Normal
4	Sand Attack	Ground	Status	—	100	15	Normal
8	Growl	Normal	Status	—	100	40	Many Others
12	Agility	Psychic	Status	—	—	30	Self
15	Fury Swipes	Normal	Physical	18	80	15	Normal
18	Dig	Ground	Physical	80	100	10	Normal
21	Slash	Normal	Physical	70	100	20	Normal
25	Sucker Punch	Dark	Physical	70	100	5	Normal
35	Earthquake	Ground	Physical	100	100	10	All Others
45	Fissure	Ground	Physical	—	30	5	Normal

TM MOVES

NO.	NAME	TYPE	KIND	POW.	ACC.	PP	RANGE
TM01	Headbutt	Normal	Physical	70	100	15	Normal
TM05	Rest	Psychic	Status	—	—	10	Self
TM07	Protect	Normal	Status	—	—	10	Self
TM08	Substitute	Normal	Status	—	—	10	Self
TM10	Dig	Ground	Physical	80	100	10	Normal
TM12	Facade	Normal	Physical	70	100	20	Normal
TM22	Rock Slide	Rock	Physical	75	90	10	Many Others
TM27	Toxic	Poison	Status	—	90	10	Normal
TM28	Tri Attack	Normal	Special	80	100	10	Normal
TM41	Earthquake	Ground	Physical	100	100	10	All Others
TM48	Hyper Beam	Normal	Special	150	90	5	Normal
TM52	Sludge Bomb	Poison	Special	90	100	10	Normal
TM54	Flash Cannon	Steel	Special	80	100	10	Normal
TM56	Stealth Rock	Rock	Status	—	—	20	Other Side

EVOLUTION MOVES

NAME	TYPE	KIND	POW.	ACC.	PP	RANGE
Tri Attack	Normal	Special	80	100	10	Normal

Meowth

♂ ♀ | Same form for male/female

SPECIES STRENGTHS

HP	▰▰▰
ATTACK	▰▰▰
DEFENSE	▰▰▰
SP. ATK	▰▰▰
SP. DEF	▰▰▰
SPEED	▰▰▰▰▰▰

DAMAGE TAKEN IN BATTLES

◎	×1	🔥	×1
🔥	×1	🌀	×1
💧	×1	🐛	×1
🍃	×1	🪨	×1
👊	×1	👻	×0
❄	×1	↻	×1
🏰	×2	🌙	×1
☯	×1	⚙	×1
🔥	×1	✦	×1

POKÉDEX ENTRY

Appears to be more active at night. It loves round and shiny things. It can't stop itself from picking them up.

MAIN WAY TO OBTAIN

Obtain one in a trade if you are playing *Pokémon: Let's Go, Pikachu!*, as it does not appear in that game. Catch one when it appears on Route 24 or Route 25 in *Pokémon: Let's Go, Eevee!*

Where to catch

EVOLUTION

Meowth → Lv. 28 →→→→ Persian

LEVEL-UP MOVES

LV.	NAME	TYPE	KIND	POW.	ACC.	PP	RANGE
1	Bite	Dark	Physical	60	100	25	Normal
1	Fake Out	Normal	Physical	40	100	10	Normal
1	Growl	Normal	Status	—	100	40	Many Others
1	Scratch	Normal	Physical	40	100	35	Normal
3	Bite	Dark	Physical	60	100	25	Normal
6	Fake Out	Normal	Physical	40	100	10	Normal
9	Taunt	Dark	Status	—	100	20	Normal
12	Pay Day	Normal	Physical	40	100	20	Normal
15	Feint	Normal	Physical	30	100	10	Normal
19	Fury Swipes	Normal	Physical	18	80	15	Normal
23	Screech	Normal	Status	—	85	40	Normal
27	Slash	Normal	Physical	70	100	20	Normal
31	Nasty Plot	Dark	Status	—	—	20	Self
35	Play Rough	Fairy	Physical	90	90	10	Normal

TM MOVES

NO.	NAME	TYPE	KIND	POW.	ACC.	PP	RANGE
TM01	Headbutt	Normal	Physical	70	100	15	Normal
TM02	Taunt	Dark	Status	—	100	20	Normal
TM05	Rest	Psychic	Status	—	—	10	Self
TM07	Protect	Normal	Status	—	—	10	Self
TM08	Substitute	Normal	Status	—	—	10	Self
TM10	Dig	Ground	Physical	80	100	10	Normal
TM12	Facade	Normal	Physical	70	100	20	Normal
TM18	U-turn	Bug	Physical	70	100	20	Normal
TM19	Iron Tail	Steel	Physical	100	75	15	Normal
TM20	Dark Pulse	Dark	Special	80	100	15	Normal
TM21	Foul Play	Dark	Physical	95	100	15	Normal
TM27	Toxic	Poison	Status	—	90	10	Normal
TM36	Thunderbolt	Electric	Special	90	100	15	Normal
TM38	Thunder	Electric	Special	110	70	10	Normal
TM43	Shadow Ball	Ghost	Special	80	100	15	Normal
TM44	Play Rough	Fairy	Physical	90	90	10	Normal
TM57	Pay Day	Normal	Physical	40	100	20	Normal

EVOLUTION MOVES

NAME	TYPE	KIND	POW.	ACC.	PP	RANGE

POKÉMON EXPRESSIONS

HAPPY

UNHAPPY

ATTACKING

Meowth

♂ ♀ | Same form for male/female

ALOLA FORM

MEOWTH
ALOLA FORM
052

SPECIES STRENGTHS

HP	■■■
ATTACK	■■■
DEFENSE	■■■
SP. ATK	■■■
SP. DEF	■■■
SPEED	■■■■■

DAMAGE TAKEN IN BATTLES

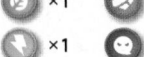

●×1		◐×1	
●×1		◉×0	
●×1		◉×2	
●×1		◉×1	
●×1		◉×0.5	
●×1		◉×1	
●×2		◉×0.5	
●×1		◉×1	
●×1		◉×2	

POKÉDEX ENTRY

Highly intelligent and prideful, it's famously difficult to handle—but that's also a reason for its popularity.

MAIN WAY TO OBTAIN

Obtain one in a trade if you are playing *Pokémon: Let's Go, Pikachu!*, as it does not appear in that game. Trade a Meowth for one in the Pokémon Center on Cinnabar Island (p. 92) in *Pokémon: Let's Go, Eevee!*

Where to catch
Habitat Unknown

EVOLUTION

Lv. 28
→→→

Alolan Meowth   **Alolan Persian**

POKÉMON EXPRESSIONS

HAPPY

UNHAPPY

ATTACKING

LEVEL-UP MOVES

LV.	NAME	TYPE	KIND	POW.	ACC.	PP	RANGE
1	Bite	Dark	Physical	60	100	25	Normal
1	Fake Out	Normal	Physical	40	100	10	Normal
1	Growl	Normal	Status	—	100	40	Many Others
1	Scratch	Normal	Physical	40	100	35	Normal
3	Bite	Dark	Physical	60	100	25	Normal
6	Fake Out	Normal	Physical	40	100	10	Normal
9	Taunt	Dark	Status	—	100	20	Normal
12	Pay Day	Normal	Physical	40	100	20	Normal
15	Feint	Normal	Physical	30	100	10	Normal
19	Fury Swipes	Normal	Physical	18	80	15	Normal
23	Screech	Normal	Status	—	85	40	Normal
27	Slash	Normal	Physical	70	100	20	Normal
31	Nasty Plot	Dark	Status	—	—	20	Self
35	Play Rough	Fairy	Physical	90	90	10	Normal

TM MOVES

NO.	NAME	TYPE	KIND	POW.	ACC.	PP	RANGE
TM01	Headbutt	Normal	Physical	70	100	15	Normal
TM02	Taunt	Dark	Status	—	100	20	Normal
TM05	Rest	Psychic	Status	—	—	10	Self
TM07	Protect	Normal	Status	—	—	10	Self
TM08	Substitute	Normal	Status	—	—	10	Self
TM12	Facade	Normal	Physical	70	100	20	Normal
TM18	U-turn	Bug	Physical	70	100	20	Normal
TM19	Iron Tail	Steel	Physical	100	75	15	Normal
TM20	Dark Pulse	Dark	Special	80	100	15	Normal
TM21	Foul Play	Dark	Physical	95	100	15	Normal
TM27	Toxic	Poison	Status	—	90	10	Normal
TM36	Thunderbolt	Electric	Special	90	100	15	Normal
TM38	Thunder	Electric	Special	110	70	10	Normal
TM43	Shadow Ball	Ghost	Special	80	100	15	Normal
TM44	Play Rough	Fairy	Physical	90	90	10	Normal
TM57	Pay Day	Normal	Physical	40	100	20	Normal
TM59	Dream Eater	Psychic	Special	100	100	15	Normal

EVOLUTION MOVES

NAME	TYPE	KIND	POW.	ACC.	PP	RANGE

053 Classy Cat Pokémon   Average height: 3'03"   Average weight: 70.5 lbs.

Persian

♂ ♀ | Same form for male/female

SPECIES STRENGTHS

HP	▦▦▦
ATTACK	▦▦▦
DEFENSE	▦▦▦
SP. ATK	▦▦▦
SP. DEF	▦▦▦
SPEED	▦▦▦▦▦

DAMAGE TAKEN IN BATTLES

◎ ×1		🖐 ×1
🔥 ×1		🌀 ×1
💧 ×1		🌸 ×1
🍃 ×1		🌿 ×1
⚡ ×1		⚪ ×0
❄ ×1		🗡 ×1
👊 ×2		🌙 ×1
☠ ×1		◉ ×1
🔔 ×1		✦ ×1

POKÉDEX ENTRY

The gem in its forehead glows on its own! It walks with all the grace and elegance of a proud queen.

MAIN WAY TO OBTAIN

Obtain a Meowth, then level it up to Lv. 28 or higher to evolve it into Persian. Or get one from a Black Belt in Vermilion City (p. 47) in *Pokémon: Let's Go, Pikachu!*

Where to catch

Habitat Unknown

EVOLUTION

Meowth — Lv. 28 →→→ **Persian**

LEVEL-UP MOVES

LV.	NAME	TYPE	KIND	POW.	ACC.	PP	RANGE
1	Amnesia	Psychic	Status	—	—	20	Self
1	Bite	Dark	Physical	60	100	25	Normal
1	Fake Out	Normal	Physical	40	100	10	Normal
1	Growl	Normal	Status	—	100	40	Many Others
1	Hypnosis	Psychic	Status	—	60	20	Normal
1	Scratch	Normal	Physical	40	100	35	Normal
1	Swift	Normal	Special	60	—	20	Many Others
3	Bite	Dark	Physical	60	100	25	Normal
6	Fake Out	Normal	Physical	40	100	10	Normal
9	Taunt	Dark	Status	—	100	20	Normal
12	Pay Day	Normal	Physical	40	100	20	Normal
15	Feint	Normal	Physical	30	100	10	Normal
19	Fury Swipes	Normal	Physical	18	80	15	Normal
23	Screech	Normal	Status	—	85	40	Normal
27	Slash	Normal	Physical	70	100	20	Normal
37	Nasty Plot	Dark	Status	—	—	20	Self
47	Play Rough	Fairy	Physical	90	90	10	Normal

TM MOVES

NO.	NAME	TYPE	KIND	POW.	ACC.	PP	RANGE
TM01	Headbutt	Normal	Physical	70	100	15	Normal
TM02	Taunt	Dark	Status	—	100	20	Normal
TM05	Rest	Psychic	Status	—	—	10	Self
TM07	Protect	Normal	Status	—	—	10	Self
TM08	Substitute	Normal	Status	—	—	10	Self
TM10	Dig	Ground	Physical	80	100	10	Normal
TM12	Facade	Normal	Physical	70	100	20	Normal
TM18	U-turn	Bug	Physical	70	100	20	Normal
TM19	Iron Tail	Steel	Physical	100	75	15	Normal
TM20	Dark Pulse	Dark	Special	80	100	15	Normal
TM21	Foul Play	Dark	Physical	95	100	15	Normal
TM27	Toxic	Poison	Status	—	90	10	Normal
TM36	Thunderbolt	Electric	Special	90	100	15	Normal
TM38	Thunder	Electric	Special	110	70	10	Normal
TM43	Shadow Ball	Ghost	Special	80	100	15	Normal
TM44	Play Rough	Fairy	Physical	90	90	10	Normal
TM48	Hyper Beam	Normal	Special	150	90	5	Normal
TM57	Pay Day	Normal	Physical	40	100	20	Normal
TM59	Dream Eater	Psychic	Special	100	100	15	Normal

EVOLUTION MOVES

NAME	TYPE	KIND	POW.	ACC.	PP	RANGE
Swift	Normal	Special	60	—	20	Many Others

Persian

ALOLA FORM

♂ ♀ | Same form for male/female

SPECIES STRENGTHS

HP	
ATTACK	
DEFENSE	
SP. ATK	
SP. DEF	
SPEED	

DAMAGE TAKEN IN BATTLES

◉	×1	🍃	×1
🔥	×1	◎	×0
💧	×1	🧷	×2
⚡	×1	🗡	×1
✦	×1	●	×0.5
❄	×1	👊	×1
🏛	×2	🌙	×0.5
◉	×1	◉	×1
🪨	×1	✧	×2

POKÉDEX ENTRY

It has the classiest coat. The rippling of its fur in the heat of battle has a beauty all its own.

MAIN WAY TO OBTAIN

Obtain an Alolan Meowth, then level it up to Lv. 28 or higher to evolve it into Alolan Persian.

Where to catch

Habitat Unknown

EVOLUTION

Lv. 28
→→→

Alolan Meowth   **Alolan Persian**

POKÉMON EXPRESSIONS

HAPPY

UNHAPPY

ATTACKING

LEVEL-UP MOVES

LV.	NAME	TYPE	KIND	POW.	ACC.	PP	RANGE
1	Amnesia	Psychic	Status	—	—	20	Self
1	Bite	Dark	Physical	60	100	25	Normal
1	Fake Out	Normal	Physical	40	100	10	Normal
1	Growl	Normal	Status	—	100	40	Many Others
1	Hypnosis	Psychic	Status	—	60	20	Normal
1	Scratch	Normal	Physical	40	100	35	Normal
1	Swift	Normal	Special	60	—	20	Many Others
3	Bite	Dark	Physical	60	100	25	Normal
6	Fake Out	Normal	Physical	40	100	10	Normal
9	Taunt	Dark	Status	—	100	20	Normal
12	Pay Day	Normal	Physical	40	100	20	Normal
16	Feint	Normal	Physical	30	100	10	Normal
19	Fury Swipes	Normal	Physical	18	80	15	Normal
23	Screech	Normal	Status	—	85	40	Normal
27	Slash	Normal	Physical	70	100	20	Normal
37	Nasty Plot	Dark	Status	—	—	20	Self
47	Play Rough	Fairy	Physical	90	90	10	Normal

TM MOVES

NO.	NAME	TYPE	KIND	POW.	ACC.	PP	RANGE
TM01	Headbutt	Normal	Physical	70	100	15	Normal
TM02	Taunt	Dark	Status	—	100	20	Normal
TM05	Rest	Psychic	Status	—	—	10	Self
TM07	Protect	Normal	Status	—	—	10	Self
TM08	Substitute	Normal	Status	—	—	10	Self
TM12	Facade	Normal	Physical	70	100	20	Normal
TM18	U-turn	Bug	Physical	70	100	20	Normal
TM19	Iron Tail	Steel	Physical	100	75	15	Normal
TM20	Dark Pulse	Dark	Special	80	100	15	Normal
TM21	Foul Play	Dark	Physical	95	100	15	Normal
TM27	Toxic	Poison	Status	—	90	10	Normal
TM36	Thunderbolt	Electric	Special	90	100	15	Normal
TM38	Thunder	Electric	Special	110	70	10	Normal
TM43	Shadow Ball	Ghost	Special	80	100	15	Normal
TM44	Play Rough	Fairy	Physical	90	90	10	Normal
TM48	Hyper Beam	Normal	Special	150	90	5	Normal
TM57	Pay Day	Normal	Physical	40	100	20	Normal
TM59	Dream Eater	Psychic	Special	100	100	15	Normal

EVOLUTION MOVES

NAME	TYPE	KIND	POW.	ACC.	PP	RANGE
Swift	Normal	Special	60	—	20	Many Others

Psyduck

♂ ♀ | Same form for male/female

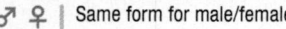

SPECIES STRENGTHS

HP	▰▰▰
ATTACK	▰▰▰
DEFENSE	▰▰
SP. ATK	▰▰▰
SP. DEF	▰▰
SPEED	▰▰▰

DAMAGE TAKEN IN BATTLES

⬤ ×1		🪶 ×1	
🔥 ×0.5		⚪ ×1	
💧 ×0.5		🍃 ×1	
🌿 ×2		👊 ×1	
⚡ ×2		👻 ×1	
❄ ×0.5		🐉 ×1	
✊ ×1		🌑 ×1	
☠ ×1		⚙ ×0.5	
⛰ ×1		✨ ×1	

POKÉDEX ENTRY

Always tormented by headaches. It uses psychic powers, but whether it intends to do so is not known.

MAIN WAY TO OBTAIN

Catch one when it appears on Route 24, Route 25, or elsewhere.

Where to catch

EVOLUTION

Psyduck → Lv. 33 →→→ Golduck

LEVEL-UP MOVES

LV.	NAME	TYPE	KIND	POW.	ACC.	PP	RANGE
1	Scratch	Normal	Physical	40	100	35	Normal
5	Tail Whip	Normal	Status	—	100	30	Many Others
9	Water Gun	Water	Special	40	100	25	Normal
14	Confusion	Psychic	Special	50	100	25	Normal
18	Fury Swipes	Normal	Physical	18	80	15	Normal
23	Disable	Normal	Status	—	100	20	Normal
27	Psybeam	Psychic	Special	65	100	20	Normal
32	Screech	Normal	Status	—	85	40	Normal
36	Surf	Water	Special	90	100	15	All Others
41	Amnesia	Psychic	Status	—	—	20	Self
45	Hydro Pump	Water	Special	110	80	5	Normal

TM MOVES

NO.	NAME	TYPE	KIND	POW.	ACC.	PP	RANGE
TM01	Headbutt	Normal	Physical	70	100	15	Normal
TM05	Rest	Psychic	Status	—	—	10	Self
TM06	Light Screen	Psychic	Status	—	—	30	Your Side
TM07	Protect	Normal	Status	—	—	10	Self
TM08	Substitute	Normal	Status	—	—	10	Self
TM10	Dig	Ground	Physical	80	100	10	Normal
TM12	Facade	Normal	Physical	70	100	20	Normal
TM13	Brick Break	Fighting	Physical	75	100	15	Normal
TM15	Seismic Toss	Fighting	Physical	—	100	20	Normal
TM19	Iron Tail	Steel	Physical	100	75	15	Normal
TM25	Waterfall	Water	Physical	80	100	15	Normal
TM27	Toxic	Poison	Status	—	90	10	Normal
TM29	Scald	Water	Special	80	100	15	Normal
TM33	Calm Mind	Psychic	Status	—	—	20	Self
TM35	Ice Punch	Ice	Physical	75	100	15	Normal
TM40	Psychic	Psychic	Special	90	100	10	Normal
TM47	Surf	Water	Special	90	100	15	All Others
TM51	Blizzard	Ice	Special	110	70	5	Many Others
TM55	Ice Beam	Ice	Special	90	100	10	Normal
TM57	Pay Day	Normal	Physical	40	100	20	Normal

EVOLUTION MOVES

NAME	TYPE	KIND	POW.	ACC.	PP	RANGE

POKÉMON EXPRESSIONS

HAPPY

UNHAPPY

ATTACKING

Golduck

♂ ♀ | Same form for male/female

SPECIES STRENGTHS

HP	
ATTACK	
DEFENSE	
SP. ATK	
SP. DEF	
SPEED	

DAMAGE TAKEN IN BATTLES

◉ ×1		◉ ×1	
◉ ×0.5		◉ ×1	
◉ ×0.5		◉ ×1	
◉ ×2		◉ ×1	
◉ ×2		◉ ×1	
◉ ×0.5		◉ ×1	
◉ ×1		◉ ×1	
◉ ×1		◉ ×0.5	
◉ ×1		◉ ×1	

POKÉDEX ENTRY

Its long, slim limbs end in broad flippers. They are used for swimming gracefully in lakes.

MAIN WAY TO OBTAIN

Catch one when it appears in the Cerulean Cave (1F or B1F). Or obtain a Psyduck, then level it up to Lv. 33 or higher to evolve it into Golduck.

Where to catch

EVOLUTION

Psyduck

Lv. 33
→→→

Golduck

POKÉMON EXPRESSIONS

HAPPY

UNHAPPY

ATTACKING

LEVEL-UP MOVES

LV.	NAME	TYPE	KIND	POW.	ACC.	PP	RANGE
1	Confusion	Psychic	Special	50	100	25	Normal
1	Encore	Normal	Status	—	100	5	Normal
1	Scratch	Normal	Physical	40	100	35	Normal
1	Tail Whip	Normal	Status	—	100	30	Many Others
1	Water Gun	Water	Special	40	100	25	Normal
1	Yawn	Normal	Status	—	—	10	Normal
5	Tail Whip	Normal	Status	—	100	30	Many Others
9	Water Gun	Water	Special	40	100	25	Normal
14	Confusion	Psychic	Special	50	100	25	Normal
18	Fury Swipes	Normal	Physical	18	80	15	Normal
23	Disable	Normal	Status	—	100	20	Normal
27	Psybeam	Psychic	Special	65	100	20	Normal
32	Screech	Normal	Status	—	85	40	Normal
42	Surf	Water	Special	90	100	15	All Others
53	Amnesia	Psychic	Status	—	—	20	Self
63	Hydro Pump	Water	Special	110	80	5	Normal

TM MOVES

NO.	NAME	TYPE	KIND	POW.	ACC.	PP	RANGE
TM01	Headbutt	Normal	Physical	70	100	15	Normal
TM05	Rest	Psychic	Status	—	—	10	Self
TM06	Light Screen	Psychic	Status	—	—	30	Your Side
TM07	Protect	Normal	Status	—	—	10	Self
TM08	Substitute	Normal	Status	—	—	10	Self
TM10	Dig	Ground	Physical	80	100	10	Normal
TM12	Facade	Normal	Physical	70	100	20	Normal
TM13	Brick Break	Fighting	Physical	75	100	15	Normal
TM15	Seismic Toss	Fighting	Physical	—	100	20	Normal
TM19	Iron Tail	Steel	Physical	100	75	15	Normal
TM25	Waterfall	Water	Physical	80	100	15	Normal
TM27	Toxic	Poison	Status	—	90	10	Normal
TM29	Scald	Water	Special	80	100	15	Normal
TM33	Calm Mind	Psychic	Status	—	—	20	Self
TM35	Ice Punch	Ice	Physical	75	100	15	Normal
TM40	Psychic	Psychic	Special	90	100	10	Normal
TM47	Surf	Water	Special	90	100	15	All Others
TM48	Hyper Beam	Normal	Special	150	90	5	Normal
TM51	Blizzard	Ice	Special	110	70	5	Many Others
TM55	Ice Beam	Ice	Special	90	100	10	Normal
TM57	Pay Day	Normal	Physical	40	100	20	Normal

EVOLUTION MOVES

NAME	TYPE	KIND	POW.	ACC.	PP	RANGE

056 Pig Monkey Pokémon · Average height: 1'08" · Average weight: 61.7 lbs.

Mankey

♂ ♀ | Same form for male/female

SPECIES STRENGTHS

HP	▰▰▰
ATTACK	▰▰▰▰
DEFENSE	▰▰▰
SP. ATK	▰▰▰
SP. DEF	▰▰▰
SPEED	▰▰▰▰

DAMAGE TAKEN IN BATTLES

⊙	×1	✊	×2
🔥	×1	◎	×2
💧	×1	🍃	×0.5
🌿	×1	◈	×0.5
⚡	×1	👁	×1
❄	×1	🌀	×1
🐛	×1	☾	×0.5
⊙	×1	⊙	×1
🪨	×1	✦	×2

POKÉDEX ENTRY

An agile Pokémon that lives in trees. It angers easily and will not hesitate to attack anything.

MAIN WAY TO OBTAIN

Catch one when it appears on Route 3 or Route 4 (East) in *Pokémon: Let's Go, Pikachu!* Obtain one in a trade if you are playing *Pokémon: Let's Go, Eevee!*, as it does not appear in that game.

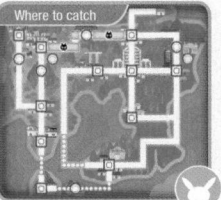

Where to catch

EVOLUTION

Lv. 28
→→→

Mankey

Primeape

POKÉMON EXPRESSIONS

HAPPY

UNHAPPY

ATTACKING

LEVEL-UP MOVES

LV.	NAME	TYPE	KIND	POW.	ACC.	PP	RANGE
1	Leer	Normal	Status	—	100	30	Many Others
1	Scratch	Normal	Physical	40	100	35	Normal
5	Focus Energy	Normal	Status	—	—	30	Self
8	Taunt	Dark	Status	—	100	20	Normal
13	Karate Chop	Fighting	Physical	50	100	25	Normal
16	Fury Swipes	Normal	Physical	18	80	15	Normal
21	Low Kick	Fighting	Physical	—	100	20	Normal
24	Seismic Toss	Fighting	Physical	—	100	20	Normal
29	U-turn	Bug	Physical	70	100	20	Normal
32	Screech	Normal	Status	—	85	40	Normal
37	Thrash	Normal	Physical	120	100	10	1 Random
40	Outrage	Dragon	Physical	120	100	10	1 Random

TM MOVES

NO.	NAME	TYPE	KIND	POW.	ACC.	PP	RANGE
TM01	Headbutt	Normal	Physical	70	100	15	Normal
TM02	Taunt	Dark	Status	—	100	20	Normal
TM03	Helping Hand	Normal	Status	—	—	20	1 Ally
TM05	Rest	Psychic	Status	—	—	10	Self
TM07	Protect	Normal	Status	—	—	10	Self
TM08	Substitute	Normal	Status	—	—	10	Self
TM10	Dig	Ground	Physical	80	100	10	Normal
TM12	Facade	Normal	Physical	70	100	20	Normal
TM13	Brick Break	Fighting	Physical	75	100	15	Normal
TM15	Seismic Toss	Fighting	Physical	—	100	20	Normal
TM18	U-turn	Bug	Physical	70	100	20	Normal
TM19	Iron Tail	Steel	Physical	100	75	15	Normal
TM22	Rock Slide	Rock	Physical	75	90	10	Many Others
TM23	Thunder Punch	Electric	Physical	75	100	15	Normal
TM26	Poison Jab	Poison	Physical	80	100	20	Normal
TM27	Toxic	Poison	Status	—	90	10	Normal
TM30	Bulk Up	Fighting	Status	—	—	20	Self
TM31	Fire Punch	Fire	Physical	75	100	15	Normal
TM35	Ice Punch	Ice	Physical	75	100	15	Normal
TM36	Thunderbolt	Electric	Special	90	100	15	Normal
TM38	Thunder	Electric	Special	110	70	10	Normal
TM39	Outrage	Dragon	Physical	120	100	10	1 Random
TM41	Earthquake	Ground	Physical	100	100	10	All Others
TM57	Pay Day	Normal	Physical	40	100	20	Normal

EVOLUTION MOVES

NAME	TYPE	KIND	POW.	ACC.	PP	RANGE

Primeape

♂ ♀ | Same form for male/female

SPECIES STRENGTHS

HP
ATTACK
DEFENSE
SP. ATK
SP. DEF
SPEED

DAMAGE TAKEN IN BATTLES

⊙ ×1		🜁 ×2
🔥 ×1		🌀 ×2
💧 ×1		🦋 ×0.5
🍃 ×1		👁 ×0.5
⚡ ×1		😈 ×1
❄ ×1		🐉 ×1
👊 ×1		🌙 ×0.5
☠ ×1		⭕ ×1
⛰ ×1		✦ ×2

POKÉDEX ENTRY

It stops being angry only when nobody else is around. To view this moment is very difficult.

MAIN WAY TO OBTAIN

Obtain a Mankey, then level it up to Lv. 28 or higher to evolve it into Primeape.

Where to catch
Habitat Unknown

EVOLUTION

Mankey

Lv. 28
→→→

Primeape

POKÉMON EXPRESSIONS

HAPPY

UNHAPPY

ATTACKING

LEVEL-UP MOVES

LV.	NAME	TYPE	KIND	POW.	ACC.	PP	RANGE
1	Counter	Fighting	Physical	—	100	20	Varies
1	Encore	Normal	Status	—	100	5	Normal
1	Focus Energy	Normal	Status	—	—	30	Self
1	Leer	Normal	Status	—	100	30	Many Others
1	Rage	Normal	Physical	20	100	20	Normal
1	Scratch	Normal	Physical	40	100	35	Normal
1	Taunt	Dark	Status	—	100	20	Normal
5	Focus Energy	Normal	Status	—	—	30	Self
8	Taunt	Dark	Status	—	100	20	Normal
13	Karate Chop	Fighting	Physical	50	100	25	Normal
16	Fury Swipes	Normal	Physical	18	80	15	Normal
21	Low Kick	Fighting	Physical	—	100	20	Normal
24	Seismic Toss	Fighting	Physical	—	100	20	Normal
33	U-turn	Bug	Physical	70	100	20	Normal
40	Screech	Normal	Status	—	85	40	Normal
49	Thrash	Normal	Physical	120	100	10	1 Random
56	Outrage	Dragon	Physical	120	100	10	1 Random

TM MOVES

NO.	NAME	TYPE	KIND	POW.	ACC.	PP	RANGE
TM01	Headbutt	Normal	Physical	70	100	15	Normal
TM02	Taunt	Dark	Status	—	100	20	Normal
TM03	Helping Hand	Normal	Status	—	—	20	1 Ally
TM05	Rest	Psychic	Status	—	—	10	Self
TM07	Protect	Normal	Status	—	—	10	Self
TM08	Substitute	Normal	Status	—	—	10	Self
TM10	Dig	Ground	Physical	80	100	10	Normal
TM12	Facade	Normal	Physical	70	100	20	Normal
TM13	Brick Break	Fighting	Physical	75	100	15	Normal
TM15	Seismic Toss	Fighting	Physical	—	100	20	Normal
TM18	U-turn	Bug	Physical	70	100	20	Normal
TM19	Iron Tail	Steel	Physical	100	75	15	Normal
TM22	Rock Slide	Rock	Physical	75	90	10	Many Others
TM23	Thunder Punch	Electric	Physical	75	100	15	Normal
TM26	Poison Jab	Poison	Physical	80	100	20	Normal
TM27	Toxic	Poison	Status	—	90	10	Normal
TM30	Bulk Up	Fighting	Status	—	—	20	Self
TM31	Fire Punch	Fire	Physical	75	100	15	Normal
TM35	Ice Punch	Ice	Physical	75	100	15	Normal
TM36	Thunderbolt	Electric	Special	90	100	15	Normal
TM38	Thunder	Electric	Special	110	70	10	Normal
TM39	Outrage	Dragon	Physical	120	100	10	1 Random
TM41	Earthquake	Ground	Physical	100	100	10	All Others
TM48	Hyper Beam	Normal	Special	150	90	5	Normal
TM57	Pay Day	Normal	Physical	40	100	20	Normal

EVOLUTION MOVES

NAME	TYPE	KIND	POW.	ACC.	PP	RANGE
Rage	Normal	Physical	20	100	20	Normal

Growlithe

♂ ♀ | Same form for male/female

SPECIES STRENGTHS

HP	▮▮▮
ATTACK	▮▮▮▮
DEFENSE	▮▮▮
SP. ATK	▮▮▮▮
SP. DEF	▮▮▮
SPEED	▮▮▮

DAMAGE TAKEN IN BATTLES

◉ ×1		×1
×0.5		×1
×2		×0.5
×0.5		×2
×1		×1
×0.5		×1
×1		×1
×1		×0.5
×2		×0.5

POKÉDEX ENTRY

A Pokémon with a friendly nature. However, it will bark fiercely at anything invading its territory.

MAIN WAY TO OBTAIN

Catch one when it appears on Route 5, Route 6, or elsewhere in *Pokémon: Let's Go, Pikachu!* Obtain one in a trade if you are playing *Pokémon: Let's Go, Eevee!*, as it does not appear in that game.

Where to catch

EVOLUTION

Use Fire Stone
→→→

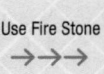

Growlithe   **Arcanine**

LEVEL-UP MOVES

LV.	NAME	TYPE	KIND	POW.	ACC.	PP	RANGE
1	Bite	Dark	Physical	60	100	25	Normal
1	Roar	Normal	Status	—	—	20	Normal
3	Ember	Fire	Special	40	100	25	Normal
7	Leer	Normal	Status	—	100	30	Many Others
10	Helping Hand	Normal	Status	—	—	20	1 Ally
14	Take Down	Normal	Physical	90	85	20	Normal
17	Flamethrower	Fire	Special	90	100	15	Normal
21	Agility	Psychic	Status	—	—	30	Self
24	Heat Wave	Fire	Special	95	90	10	Many Others
28	Crunch	Dark	Physical	80	100	15	Normal
31	Outrage	Dragon	Physical	120	100	10	1 Random
35	Play Rough	Fairy	Physical	90	90	10	Normal
38	Flare Blitz	Fire	Physical	120	100	15	Normal

TM MOVES

NO.	NAME	TYPE	KIND	POW.	ACC.	PP	RANGE
TM01	Headbutt	Normal	Physical	70	100	15	Normal
TM03	Helping Hand	Normal	Status	—	—	20	1 Ally
TM05	Rest	Psychic	Status	—	—	10	Self
TM07	Protect	Normal	Status	—	—	10	Self
TM08	Substitute	Normal	Status	—	—	10	Self
TM09	Reflect	Psychic	Status	—	—	20	Your Side
TM10	Dig	Ground	Physical	80	100	10	Normal
TM11	Will-O-Wisp	Fire	Status	—	85	15	Normal
TM12	Facade	Normal	Physical	70	100	20	Normal
TM19	Iron Tail	Steel	Physical	100	75	15	Normal
TM27	Toxic	Poison	Status	—	90	10	Normal
TM37	Flamethrower	Fire	Special	90	100	15	Normal
TM39	Outrage	Dragon	Physical	120	100	10	1 Random
TM44	Play Rough	Fairy	Physical	90	90	10	Normal
TM46	Fire Blast	Fire	Special	110	85	5	Normal

EVOLUTION MOVES

NAME	TYPE	KIND	POW.	ACC.	PP	RANGE

POKÉMON EXPRESSIONS

HAPPY

UNHAPPY

ATTACKING

Arcanine

♂ ♀ | Same form for male/female

SPECIES STRENGTHS

HP	▪▪▪▪▫▫
ATTACK	▪▪▪▪▪▫
DEFENSE	▪▪▪▫▫
SP. ATK	▪▪▪▪▫
SP. DEF	▪▪▪▫▫
SPEED	▪▪▪▪▪▫

DAMAGE TAKEN IN BATTLES

⊙	×1	🍃	×1
🔥	×0.5	◎	×1
💧	×2	⬡	×0.5
🌿	×0.5	🌀	×2
⚡	×1	👁	×1
❄	×0.5	✊	×1
⛰	×1	☾	×1
⊙	×1	⊙	×0.5
◢	×2	✦	×0.5

POKÉDEX ENTRY

A legendary Pokémon in the East. Many people are charmed by the grace and beauty of its running.

MAIN WAY TO OBTAIN

Catch one when it appears on Route 7 or Route 8 in *Pokémon: Let's Go, Pikachu!* Get one from a Beauty in Vermilion City (p. 47) in *Pokémon: Let's Go, Eevee!* Or obtain a Growlithe, then use a Fire Stone on it to evolve it into Arcanine.

Where to catch

EVOLUTION

Growlithe

Use Fire Stone
→→→

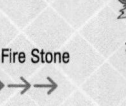

Arcanine

LEVEL-UP MOVES

LV.	NAME	TYPE	KIND	POW.	ACC.	PP	RANGE
1	Bite	Dark	Physical	60	100	25	Normal
1	Double-Edge	Normal	Physical	120	100	15	Normal
1	Ember	Fire	Special	40	100	25	Normal
1	Leer	Normal	Status	—	100	30	Many Others
1	Roar	Normal	Status	—	—	20	Normal

TM MOVES

NO.	NAME	TYPE	KIND	POW.	ACC.	PP	RANGE
TM01	Headbutt	Normal	Physical	70	100	15	Normal
TM03	Helping Hand	Normal	Status	—	—	20	1 Ally
TM04	Teleport	Psychic	Status	—	—	20	Self
TM05	Rest	Psychic	Status	—	—	10	Self
TM07	Protect	Normal	Status	—	—	10	Self
TM08	Substitute	Normal	Status	—	—	10	Self
TM09	Reflect	Psychic	Status	—	—	20	Your Side
TM10	Dig	Ground	Physical	80	100	10	Normal
TM11	Will-O-Wisp	Fire	Status	—	85	15	Normal
TM12	Facade	Normal	Physical	70	100	20	Normal
TM19	Iron Tail	Steel	Physical	100	75	15	Normal
TM27	Toxic	Poison	Status	—	90	10	Normal
TM34	Dragon Pulse	Dragon	Special	85	100	10	Normal
TM37	Flamethrower	Fire	Special	90	100	15	Normal
TM39	Outrage	Dragon	Physical	120	100	10	1 Random
TM44	Play Rough	Fairy	Physical	90	90	10	Normal
TM45	Solar Beam	Grass	Special	200	100	10	Normal
TM46	Fire Blast	Fire	Special	110	85	5	Normal
TM48	Hyper Beam	Normal	Special	150	90	5	Normal
TM49	Superpower	Fighting	Physical	120	100	5	Normal

EVOLUTION MOVES

NAME	TYPE	KIND	POW.	ACC.	PP	RANGE

☑ **060** Tadpole Pokémon   Average height: 2'00"   Average weight: 27.3 lbs.

Poliwag

♂ ♀ | Same form for male/female

SPECIES STRENGTHS

- HP
- ATTACK
- DEFENSE
- SP. ATK
- SP. DEF
- SPEED

DAMAGE TAKEN IN BATTLES

×1		×1	
×0.5		×1	
×0.5		×1	
×2		×1	
×2		×1	
×0.5		×1	
×1		×1	
×1		×0.5	
×1		×1	

POKÉDEX ENTRY

The direction of the spiral on the belly differs by area. It is more adept at swimming than walking.

MAIN WAY TO OBTAIN

Catch one when it appears on the water's surface on Route 22, Route 23 (South), or elsewhere.

Where to catch

EVOLUTION

Poliwag → Lv. 25 →→→ **Poliwhirl** → Use Water Stone →→→ **Poliwrath**

LEVEL-UP MOVES

LV.	NAME	TYPE	KIND	POW.	ACC.	PP	RANGE
1	Bubble	Water	Special	40	100	30	Many Others
4	Pound	Normal	Physical	40	100	35	Normal
8	Hypnosis	Psychic	Status	—	60	20	Normal
12	Water Gun	Water	Special	40	100	25	Normal
16	Double Slap	Normal	Physical	15	85	10	Normal
21	Bubble Beam	Water	Special	65	100	20	Normal
26	Low Kick	Fighting	Physical	—	100	20	Normal
31	Body Slam	Normal	Physical	85	100	15	Normal
36	Hydro Pump	Water	Special	110	80	5	Normal

TM MOVES

NO.	NAME	TYPE	KIND	POW.	ACC.	PP	RANGE
TM01	Headbutt	Normal	Physical	70	100	15	Normal
TM03	Helping Hand	Normal	Status	—	—	20	1 Ally
TM05	Rest	Psychic	Status	—	—	10	Self
TM07	Protect	Normal	Status	—	—	10	Self
TM08	Substitute	Normal	Status	—	—	10	Self
TM10	Dig	Ground	Physical	80	100	10	Normal
TM12	Facade	Normal	Physical	70	100	20	Normal
TM25	Waterfall	Water	Physical	80	100	15	Normal
TM27	Toxic	Poison	Status	—	90	10	Normal
TM29	Scald	Water	Special	80	100	15	Normal
TM40	Psychic	Psychic	Special	90	100	10	Normal
TM47	Surf	Water	Special	90	100	15	All Others
TM51	Blizzard	Ice	Special	110	70	5	Many Others
TM55	Ice Beam	Ice	Special	90	100	10	Normal

EVOLUTION MOVES

NAME	TYPE	KIND	POW.	ACC.	PP	RANGE

POKÉMON EXPRESSIONS

HAPPY

UNHAPPY

ATTACKING

Poliwhirl

♂ ♀ | Same form for male/female

SPECIES STRENGTHS

HP	▰▰▱
ATTACK	▰▰▱
DEFENSE	▰▰▰
SP. ATK	▰▰▱
SP. DEF	▰▰▱
SPEED	▰▰▰▰

DAMAGE TAKEN IN BATTLES

◎ ×1		⚡ ×1	
🔥 ×0.5		⚪ ×1	
💧 ×0.5		🍃 ×1	
🌿 ×2		👁 ×1	
⚡ ×2		🌀 ×1	
❄ ×0.5		✊ ×1	
👊 ×1		🌙 ×1	
☠ ×1		⭕ ×0.5	
🪨 ×1		✨ ×1	

POKÉDEX ENTRY

Under attack, it uses its belly spiral to put the foe to sleep. It then makes its escape.

MAIN WAY TO OBTAIN

Catch one when it appears on the water's surface on Route 22, Route 23 (South), or elsewhere. Or obtain a Poliwag, then level it up to Lv. 25 or higher to evolve it into Poliwhirl.

Where to catch

EVOLUTION

Poliwag	Lv. 25 →→→	Poliwhirl	Use Water Stone →→→	Poliwrath

POKÉMON EXPRESSIONS

HAPPY

UNHAPPY

ATTACKING

LEVEL-UP MOVES

LV.	NAME	TYPE	KIND	POW.	ACC.	PP	RANGE
1	Bubble	Water	Special	40	100	30	Many Others
1	Hypnosis	Psychic	Status	—	60	20	Normal
1	Pound	Normal	Physical	40	100	35	Normal
1	Water Gun	Water	Special	40	100	25	Normal
4	Pound	Normal	Physical	40	100	35	Normal
8	Hypnosis	Psychic	Status	—	60	20	Normal
12	Water Gun	Water	Special	40	100	25	Normal
16	Double Slap	Normal	Physical	15	85	10	Normal
21	Bubble Beam	Water	Special	65	100	20	Normal
30	Low Kick	Fighting	Physical	—	100	20	Normal
39	Body Slam	Normal	Physical	85	100	15	Normal
48	Hydro Pump	Water	Special	110	80	5	Normal

TM MOVES

NO.	NAME	TYPE	KIND	POW.	ACC.	PP	RANGE
TM01	Headbutt	Normal	Physical	70	100	15	Normal
TM03	Helping Hand	Normal	Status	—	—	20	1 Ally
TM05	Rest	Psychic	Status	—	—	10	Self
TM07	Protect	Normal	Status	—	—	10	Self
TM08	Substitute	Normal	Status	—	—	10	Self
TM10	Dig	Ground	Physical	80	100	10	Normal
TM12	Facade	Normal	Physical	70	100	20	Normal
TM13	Brick Break	Fighting	Physical	75	100	15	Normal
TM15	Seismic Toss	Fighting	Physical	—	100	20	Normal
TM25	Waterfall	Water	Physical	80	100	15	Normal
TM27	Toxic	Poison	Status	—	90	10	Normal
TM29	Scald	Water	Special	80	100	15	Normal
TM35	Ice Punch	Ice	Physical	75	100	15	Normal
TM40	Psychic	Psychic	Special	90	100	10	Normal
TM41	Earthquake	Ground	Physical	100	100	10	All Others
TM47	Surf	Water	Special	90	100	15	All Others
TM51	Blizzard	Ice	Special	110	70	5	Many Others
TM55	Ice Beam	Ice	Special	90	100	10	Normal

EVOLUTION MOVES

NAME	TYPE	KIND	POW.	ACC.	PP	RANGE

062 Tadpole Pokémon | Average height: 4'03" | Average weight: 119.0 lbs.

Poliwrath

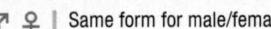 ♂ ♀ | Same form for male/female

SPECIES STRENGTHS

HP	▰▰▰▱▱
ATTACK	▰▰▰▰▱
DEFENSE	▰▰▰▰▱
SP. ATK	▰▰▱▱▱
SP. DEF	▰▰▰▱▱
SPEED	▰▰▱▱▱

DAMAGE TAKEN IN BATTLES

×1		×2	
×0.5		×2	
×0.5		×0.5	
×2		×0.5	
×2		×1	
×0.5		×1	
×1		×0.5	
×1		×0.5	
×1		×2	

POKÉDEX ENTRY

Swims powerfully using all the muscles in its body. It can even overtake world-class swimmers.

MAIN WAY TO OBTAIN

Catch one when it appears on the water's surface in the Cerulean Cave (1F or B1F). Or obtain a Poliwhirl, then use a Water Stone on it to evolve it into Poliwrath.

Where to catch

EVOLUTION

Poliwag

Lv. 25
→→→

Poliwhirl

Use Water Stone
→→→

Poliwrath

LEVEL-UP MOVES

LV.	NAME	TYPE	KIND	POW.	ACC.	PP	RANGE
1	Bubble	Water	Special	40	100	30	Many Others
1	Bulk Up	Fighting	Status	—	—	20	Self
1	Haze	Ice	Status	—	—	30	Both Sides
1	Hypnosis	Psychic	Status	—	60	20	Normal
1	Mist	Ice	Status	—	—	30	Your Side
1	Pound	Normal	Physical	40	100	35	Normal
1	Submission	Fighting	Physical	80	80	20	Normal
1	Water Gun	Water	Special	40	100	25	Normal
57	Superpower	Fighting	Physical	120	100	5	Normal

TM MOVES

NO.	NAME	TYPE	KIND	POW.	ACC.	PP	RANGE
TM01	Headbutt	Normal	Physical	70	100	15	Normal
TM03	Helping Hand	Normal	Status	—	—	20	1 Ally
TM05	Rest	Psychic	Status	—	—	10	Self
TM07	Protect	Normal	Status	—	—	10	Self
TM08	Substitute	Normal	Status	—	—	10	Self
TM10	Dig	Ground	Physical	80	100	10	Normal
TM12	Facade	Normal	Physical	70	100	20	Normal
TM13	Brick Break	Fighting	Physical	75	100	15	Normal
TM15	Seismic Toss	Fighting	Physical	—	100	20	Normal
TM22	Rock Slide	Rock	Physical	75	90	10	Many Others
TM25	Waterfall	Water	Physical	80	100	15	Normal
TM26	Poison Jab	Poison	Physical	80	100	20	Normal
TM27	Toxic	Poison	Status	—	90	10	Normal
TM29	Scald	Water	Special	80	100	15	Normal
TM30	Bulk Up	Fighting	Status	—	—	20	Self
TM35	Ice Punch	Ice	Physical	75	100	15	Normal
TM40	Psychic	Psychic	Special	90	100	10	Normal
TM41	Earthquake	Ground	Physical	100	100	10	All Others
TM47	Surf	Water	Special	90	100	15	All Others
TM48	Hyper Beam	Normal	Special	150	90	5	Normal
TM49	Superpower	Fighting	Physical	120	100	5	Normal
TM51	Blizzard	Ice	Special	110	70	5	Many Others
TM55	Ice Beam	Ice	Special	90	100	10	Normal

EVOLUTION MOVES

NAME	TYPE	KIND	POW.	ACC.	PP	RANGE
Submission	Fighting	Physical	80	80	20	Normal

POKÉMON EXPRESSIONS

HAPPY

UNHAPPY

ATTACKING

Abra

♂ ♀ | Same form for male/female

SPECIES STRENGTHS

HP	▪▪
ATTACK	▪▪
DEFENSE	▪
SP. ATK	▪▪▪▪▪▪▪
SP. DEF	▪▪▪▪
SPEED	▪▪▪▪▪▪

DAMAGE TAKEN IN BATTLES

◉	×1	🍃	×1
🔥	×1	◎	×0.5
💧	×1	🍂	×2
⚡	×1	🌀	×1
💪	×1	👁	×2
❄	×1	↻	×1
🏔	×0.5	🌙	×2
🟣	×1	◉	×1
🔺	×1	✦	×1

POKÉDEX ENTRY

Sleeps 18 hours a day. If it senses danger, it will teleport itself to safety even as it sleeps.

MAIN WAY TO OBTAIN

Catch one when it appears on Route 5, Route 6, or elsewhere.

Where to catch

EVOLUTION

Abra

Lv. 16

Kadabra

Trade Kadabra

Alakazam

POKÉMON EXPRESSIONS

HAPPY

UNHAPPY

ATTACKING

LEVEL-UP MOVES

LV.	NAME	TYPE	KIND	POW.	ACC.	PP	RANGE
1	Teleport	Psychic	Status	—	—	20	Self

TM MOVES

NO.	NAME	TYPE	KIND	POW.	ACC.	PP	RANGE
TM01	Headbutt	Normal	Physical	70	100	15	Normal
TM02	Taunt	Dark	Status	—	100	20	Normal
TM04	Teleport	Psychic	Status	—	—	20	Self
TM05	Rest	Psychic	Status	—	—	10	Self
TM06	Light Screen	Psychic	Status	—	—	30	Your Side
TM07	Protect	Normal	Status	—	—	10	Self
TM08	Substitute	Normal	Status	—	—	10	Self
TM09	Reflect	Psychic	Status	—	—	20	Your Side
TM12	Facade	Normal	Physical	70	100	20	Normal
TM15	Seismic Toss	Fighting	Physical	—	100	20	Normal
TM16	Thunder Wave	Electric	Status	—	90	20	Normal
TM19	Iron Tail	Steel	Physical	100	75	15	Normal
TM21	Foul Play	Dark	Physical	95	100	15	Normal
TM23	Thunder Punch	Electric	Physical	75	100	15	Normal
TM27	Toxic	Poison	Status	—	90	10	Normal
TM28	Tri Attack	Normal	Special	80	100	10	Normal
TM31	Fire Punch	Fire	Physical	75	100	15	Normal
TM32	Dazzling Gleam	Fairy	Special	80	100	10	Many Others
TM33	Calm Mind	Psychic	Status	—	—	20	Self
TM35	Ice Punch	Ice	Physical	75	100	15	Normal
TM40	Psychic	Psychic	Special	90	100	10	Normal
TM43	Shadow Ball	Ghost	Special	80	100	15	Normal
TM59	Dream Eater	Psychic	Special	100	100	15	Normal

EVOLUTION MOVES

NAME	TYPE	KIND	POW.	ACC.	PP	RANGE

Kadabra

KADABRA 064

♂ ♀ | The female has shorter whiskers than the male.

♂   ♀

SPECIES STRENGTHS

HP	▮▮▮
ATTACK	▮▮▮
DEFENSE	▮▮
SP. ATK	▮▮▮▮▮▮▮
SP. DEF	▮▮▮▮
SPEED	▮▮▮▮▮▮

DAMAGE TAKEN IN BATTLES

◉ ×1		✦ ×1
🔥 ×1		🌀 ×0.5
💧 ×1		⚙ ×2
🍃 ×1		✴ ×1
⚡ ×1		🌙 ×2
❄ ×1		↻ ×1
👊 ×0.5		☾ ×2
☠ ×1		◎ ×1
⛰ ×1		✧ ×1

POKÉDEX ENTRY

Many odd things happen if this Pokémon is close by. For example, it makes clocks run backward.

MAIN WAY TO OBTAIN

Catch one when it appears on Route 7 or Route 8. Or obtain an Abra, then level it up to Lv. 16 or higher to evolve it into Kadabra.

Where to catch

EVOLUTION

Abra → Lv. 16 → **Kadabra** → Trade Kadabra → **Alakazam**

LEVEL-UP MOVES

LV.	NAME	TYPE	KIND	POW.	ACC.	PP	RANGE
1	Confusion	Psychic	Special	50	100	25	Normal
1	Disable	Normal	Status	—	100	20	Normal
1	Flash	Normal	Status	—	100	20	Normal
1	Kinesis	Psychic	Status	—	80	15	Normal
1	Psybeam	Psychic	Special	65	100	20	Normal
1	Teleport	Psychic	Status	—	—	20	Self
6	Disable	Normal	Status	—	100	20	Normal
13	Flash	Normal	Status	—	100	20	Normal
19	Night Shade	Ghost	Special	—	100	15	Normal
26	Substitute	Normal	Status	—	—	10	Self
32	Reflect	Psychic	Status	—	—	20	Your Side
39	Recover	Normal	Status	—	—	10	Self
45	Psychic	Psychic	Special	90	100	10	Normal

TM MOVES

NO.	NAME	TYPE	KIND	POW.	ACC.	PP	RANGE
TM01	Headbutt	Normal	Physical	70	100	15	Normal
TM02	Taunt	Dark	Status	—	100	20	Normal
TM04	Teleport	Psychic	Status	—	—	20	Self
TM05	Rest	Psychic	Status	—	—	10	Self
TM06	Light Screen	Psychic	Status	—	—	30	Your Side
TM07	Protect	Normal	Status	—	—	10	Self
TM08	Substitute	Normal	Status	—	—	10	Self
TM09	Reflect	Psychic	Status	—	—	20	Your Side
TM10	Dig	Ground	Physical	80	100	10	Normal
TM12	Facade	Normal	Physical	70	100	20	Normal
TM15	Seismic Toss	Fighting	Physical	—	100	20	Normal
TM16	Thunder Wave	Electric	Status	—	90	20	Normal
TM19	Iron Tail	Steel	Physical	100	75	15	Normal
TM21	Foul Play	Dark	Physical	95	100	15	Normal
TM23	Thunder Punch	Electric	Physical	75	100	15	Normal
TM27	Toxic	Poison	Status	—	90	10	Normal
TM28	Tri Attack	Normal	Special	80	100	10	Normal
TM31	Fire Punch	Fire	Physical	75	100	15	Normal
TM32	Dazzling Gleam	Fairy	Special	80	100	10	Many Others
TM33	Calm Mind	Psychic	Status	—	—	20	Self
TM35	Ice Punch	Ice	Physical	75	100	15	Normal
TM40	Psychic	Psychic	Special	90	100	10	Normal
TM43	Shadow Ball	Ghost	Special	80	100	15	Normal
TM59	Dream Eater	Psychic	Special	100	100	15	Normal

POKÉMON EXPRESSIONS

HAPPY

UNHAPPY

ATTACKING

EVOLUTION MOVES

NAME	TYPE	KIND	POW.	ACC.	PP	RANGE
Kinesis	Psychic	Status	—	80	15	Normal
Psybeam	Psychic	Special	65	100	20	Normal

Alakazam

♂ ♀ | The female has shorter whiskers than the male.

♂ ♀

SPECIES STRENGTHS

HP	▰▰▰
ATTACK	▰▰▰
DEFENSE	▰▰▰
SP. ATK	▰▰▰▰▰▰▰
SP. DEF	▰▰▰▰▰▰
SPEED	▰▰▰▰▰▰▰

DAMAGE TAKEN IN BATTLES

◎	×1	🖐	×1
🔥	×1	🌀	×0.5
💧	×1	🍃	×2
⚡	×1	🍂	×1
❄	×1	☯	×2
✴	×1	🌙	×1
👊	×0.5	🌑	×2
☠	×1	⚙	×1
🔻	×1	✦	×1

POKÉDEX ENTRY

A Pokémon that can memorize anything. It never forgets what it learns—that's why this Pokémon is smart.

MAIN WAY TO OBTAIN

Receive a Kadabra in a trade, and it will immediately evolve into Alakazam.

Where to catch

Habitat Unknown

EVOLUTION

Abra

Lv. 16
→→→

Kadabra

Trade Kadabra
→→→

Alakazam

POKÉMON EXPRESSIONS

HAPPY

UNHAPPY

ATTACKING

LEVEL-UP MOVES

LV.	NAME	TYPE	KIND	POW.	ACC.	PP	RANGE
1	Barrier	Psychic	Status	—	—	20	Self
1	Calm Mind	Psychic	Status	—	—	20	Self
1	Confusion	Psychic	Special	50	100	25	Normal
1	Disable	Normal	Status	—	100	20	Normal
1	Encore	Normal	Status	—	100	5	Normal
1	Flash	Normal	Status	—	100	20	Normal
1	Kinesis	Psychic	Status	—	80	15	Normal
1	Psybeam	Psychic	Special	65	100	20	Normal
1	Teleport	Psychic	Status	—	—	20	Self
6	Disable	Normal	Status	—	100	20	Normal
13	Flash	Normal	Status	—	100	20	Normal
19	Night Shade	Ghost	Special	—	100	15	Normal
26	Substitute	Normal	Status	—	—	10	Self
32	Reflect	Psychic	Status	—	—	20	Your Side
39	Recover	Normal	Status	—	—	10	Self
45	Psychic	Psychic	Special	90	100	10	Normal

TM MOVES

NO.	NAME	TYPE	KIND	POW.	ACC.	PP	RANGE
TM01	Headbutt	Normal	Physical	70	100	15	Normal
TM02	Taunt	Dark	Status	—	100	20	Normal
TM04	Teleport	Psychic	Status	—	—	20	Self
TM05	Rest	Psychic	Status	—	—	10	Self
TM06	Light Screen	Psychic	Status	—	—	30	Your Side
TM07	Protect	Normal	Status	—	—	10	Self
TM08	Substitute	Normal	Status	—	—	10	Self
TM09	Reflect	Psychic	Status	—	—	20	Your Side
TM10	Dig	Ground	Physical	80	100	10	Normal
TM12	Facade	Normal	Physical	70	100	20	Normal
TM15	Seismic Toss	Fighting	Physical	—	100	20	Normal
TM16	Thunder Wave	Electric	Status	—	90	20	Normal
TM19	Iron Tail	Steel	Physical	100	75	15	Normal
TM21	Foul Play	Dark	Physical	95	100	15	Normal
TM23	Thunder Punch	Electric	Physical	75	100	15	Normal
TM27	Toxic	Poison	Status	—	90	10	Normal
TM28	Tri Attack	Normal	Special	80	100	10	Normal
TM31	Fire Punch	Fire	Physical	75	100	15	Normal
TM32	Dazzling Gleam	Fairy	Special	80	100	10	Many Others
TM33	Calm Mind	Psychic	Status	—	—	20	Self
TM35	Ice Punch	Ice	Physical	75	100	15	Normal
TM40	Psychic	Psychic	Special	90	100	10	Normal
TM43	Shadow Ball	Ghost	Special	80	100	15	Normal
TM48	Hyper Beam	Normal	Special	150	90	5	Normal
TM59	Dream Eater	Psychic	Special	100	100	15	Normal

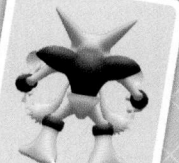

EVOLUTION MOVES

NAME	TYPE	KIND	POW.	ACC.	PP	RANGE
Calm Mind	Psychic	Status	—	—	20	Self

Mega Alakazam

MEGA EVOLUTION

Alakazam

→→→

Buy an Alakazite, then Mega Evolve Alakazam during battle.

Mega Alakazam

SPECIES STRENGTHS

HP	▰▰▰▱▱
ATTACK	▰▰▱▱▱
DEFENSE	▰▰▰▱▱
SP. ATK	▰▰▰▰▰▰▰▰▰▰
SP. DEF	▰▰▰▰▰▱
SPEED	▰▰▰▰▰▰▰▰

DAMAGE TAKEN IN BATTLES

◎	×1	◜	×1
♨	×1	◉	×0.5
◍	×1	◐	×2
✿	×1	◑	×1
⚡	×1	◔	×2
❄	×1	◓	×1
▥	×0.5	◗	×2
◒	×1	◉	×1
◭	×1	✸	×1

⬤ **REQUIRED MEGA STONE: ALAKAZITE**

Buy it from a seller who appears at the Pokémon League once you have become Champion (p. 103).

Machop

♂ ♀ | Same form for male/female

SPECIES STRENGTHS

HP	▪▪▪▫▫
ATTACK	▪▪▪▪▫
DEFENSE	▪▪▫▫▫
SP. ATK	▪▪▫▫▫
SP. DEF	▪▪▫▫▫
SPEED	▪▪▫▫▫

DAMAGE TAKEN IN BATTLES

⊙ ×1		🕊 ×2	
🔥 ×1		🌀 ×2	
💧 ×1		🌿 ×0.5	
⚡ ×1		🍃 ×0.5	
⚡ ×1		👁 ×1	
❄ ×1		🌙 ×1	
👊 ×1		🌑 ×0.5	
☠ ×1		◎ ×1	
⛰ ×1		✦ ×2	

POKÉDEX ENTRY

Very powerful in spite of its small size. Its mastery of many types of martial arts makes it very tough.

MAIN WAY TO OBTAIN

Catch one when it appears in the Rock Tunnel or on Victory Road.

Where to catch

EVOLUTION

Machop	→ Lv. 28 →	Machoke	→ Trade Machoke →	Machamp

 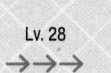

POKÉMON EXPRESSIONS

HAPPY

UNHAPPY

ATTACKING

LEVEL-UP MOVES

LV.	NAME	TYPE	KIND	POW.	ACC.	PP	RANGE
1	Leer	Normal	Status	—	100	30	Many Others
1	Low Kick	Fighting	Physical	—	100	20	Normal
4	Focus Energy	Normal	Status	—	—	30	Self
8	Bide	Normal	Physical	—	—	10	Self
12	Seismic Toss	Fighting	Physical	—	100	20	Normal
16	Karate Chop	Fighting	Physical	50	100	25	Normal
21	Brick Break	Fighting	Physical	75	100	15	Normal
26	Submission	Fighting	Physical	80	80	20	Normal
31	Bulk Up	Fighting	Status	—	—	20	Self
36	Superpower	Fighting	Physical	120	100	5	Normal

TM MOVES

NO.	NAME	TYPE	KIND	POW.	ACC.	PP	RANGE
TM01	Headbutt	Normal	Physical	70	100	15	Normal
TM03	Helping Hand	Normal	Status	—	—	20	1 Ally
TM05	Rest	Psychic	Status	—	—	10	Self
TM06	Light Screen	Psychic	Status	—	—	30	Your Side
TM07	Protect	Normal	Status	—	—	10	Self
TM08	Substitute	Normal	Status	—	—	10	Self
TM10	Dig	Ground	Physical	80	100	10	Normal
TM12	Facade	Normal	Physical	70	100	20	Normal
TM13	Brick Break	Fighting	Physical	75	100	15	Normal
TM15	Seismic Toss	Fighting	Physical	—	100	20	Normal
TM22	Rock Slide	Rock	Physical	75	90	10	Many Others
TM23	Thunder Punch	Electric	Physical	75	100	15	Normal
TM26	Poison Jab	Poison	Physical	80	100	20	Normal
TM27	Toxic	Poison	Status	—	90	10	Normal
TM30	Bulk Up	Fighting	Status	—	—	20	Self
TM31	Fire Punch	Fire	Physical	75	100	15	Normal
TM35	Ice Punch	Ice	Physical	75	100	15	Normal
TM37	Flamethrower	Fire	Special	90	100	15	Normal
TM41	Earthquake	Ground	Physical	100	100	10	All Others
TM46	Fire Blast	Fire	Special	110	85	5	Normal
TM49	Superpower	Fighting	Physical	120	100	5	Normal

EVOLUTION MOVES

NAME	TYPE	KIND	POW.	ACC.	PP	RANGE

Machoke

MACHOKE 067

♂ ♀ | Same form for male/female

SPECIES STRENGTHS

HP	▰▰▰▱▱
ATTACK	▰▰▰▰▱
DEFENSE	▰▰▰▱▱
SP. ATK	▰▰▱▱▱
SP. DEF	▰▰▱▱▱
SPEED	▰▰▱▱▱

DAMAGE TAKEN IN BATTLES

⊙	×1		×2
	×1		×2
	×1		×0.5
	×1		×0.5
	×1		×1
❄	×1		×1
	×1		×0.5
	×1		×1
	×1		×2

POKÉDEX ENTRY

The belt around its waist holds back its energy. Without it, this Pokémon would be unstoppable.

MAIN WAY TO OBTAIN

Catch one when it appears on Victory Road. Or obtain a Machop, then level it up to Lv. 28 or higher to evolve it into Machoke.

Where to catch

EVOLUTION

Machop

Lv. 28
→→→

Machoke

Trade Machoke
→→→

Machamp

LEVEL-UP MOVES

LV.	NAME	TYPE	KIND	POW.	ACC.	PP	RANGE
1	Bide	Normal	Physical	—	—	10	Self
1	Focus Energy	Normal	Status	—	—	30	Self
1	Leer	Normal	Status	—	100	30	Many Others
1	Low Kick	Fighting	Physical	—	100	20	Normal
4	Focus Energy	Normal	Status	—	—	30	Self
8	Bide	Normal	Physical	—	—	10	Self
12	Seismic Toss	Fighting	Physical	—	100	20	Normal
16	Karate Chop	Fighting	Physical	50	100	25	Normal
21	Brick Break	Fighting	Physical	75	100	15	Normal
26	Submission	Fighting	Physical	80	80	20	Normal
37	Bulk Up	Fighting	Status	—	—	20	Self
48	Superpower	Fighting	Physical	120	100	5	Normal

TM MOVES

NO.	NAME	TYPE	KIND	POW.	ACC.	PP	RANGE
TM01	Headbutt	Normal	Physical	70	100	15	Normal
TM03	Helping Hand	Normal	Status	—	—	20	1 Ally
TM05	Rest	Psychic	Status	—	—	10	Self
TM06	Light Screen	Psychic	Status	—	—	30	Your Side
TM07	Protect	Normal	Status	—	—	10	Self
TM08	Substitute	Normal	Status	—	—	10	Self
TM10	Dig	Ground	Physical	80	100	10	Normal
TM12	Facade	Normal	Physical	70	100	20	Normal
TM13	Brick Break	Fighting	Physical	75	100	15	Normal
TM15	Seismic Toss	Fighting	Physical	—	100	20	Normal
TM22	Rock Slide	Rock	Physical	75	90	10	Many Others
TM23	Thunder Punch	Electric	Physical	75	100	15	Normal
TM26	Poison Jab	Poison	Physical	80	100	20	Normal
TM27	Toxic	Poison	Status	—	90	10	Normal
TM30	Bulk Up	Fighting	Status	—	—	20	Self
TM31	Fire Punch	Fire	Physical	75	100	15	Normal
TM35	Ice Punch	Ice	Physical	75	100	15	Normal
TM37	Flamethrower	Fire	Special	90	100	15	Normal
TM41	Earthquake	Ground	Physical	100	100	10	All Others
TM46	Fire Blast	Fire	Special	110	85	5	Normal
TM49	Superpower	Fighting	Physical	120	100	5	Normal

POKÉMON EXPRESSIONS

HAPPY

UNHAPPY

ATTACKING

EVOLUTION MOVES

NAME	TYPE	KIND	POW.	ACC.	PP	RANGE

Machamp

♂ ♀ | Same form for male/female

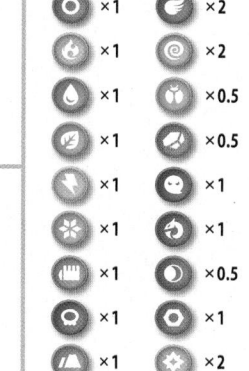

SPECIES STRENGTHS

HP ▪▪▪▪▪
ATTACK ▪▪▪▪▪▪▪
DEFENSE ▪▪▪▪
SP. ATK ▪▪▪
SP. DEF ▪▪▪
SPEED ▪▪▪

DAMAGE TAKEN IN BATTLES

◎ ×1		🖐 ×2	
🔥 ×1		@ ×2	
💧 ×1		🌿 ×0.5	
⚡ ×1		🗡 ×0.5	
⚡ ×1		👁 ×1	
❄ ×1		↻ ×1	
👊 ×1		🌙 ×0.5	
☣ ×1		◉ ×1	
⛰ ×1		✦ ×2	

POKÉDEX ENTRY

One arm alone can move mountains. Using all four arms, this Pokémon fires off awesome punches.

MAIN WAY TO OBTAIN

Receive a Machoke in a trade and it will immediately evolve into Machamp.

Where to catch
Habitat Unknown

EVOLUTION

 **Machop** → Lv. 28 →  **Machoke** → Trade Machoke →  **Machamp**

LEVEL-UP MOVES

LV.	NAME	TYPE	KIND	POW.	ACC.	PP	RANGE
1	Bide	Normal	Physical	—	—	10	Self
1	Counter	Fighting	Physical	—	100	20	Varies
1	Encore	Normal	Status	—	100	5	Normal
1	Focus Energy	Normal	Status	—	—	30	Self
1	Leer	Normal	Status	—	100	30	Many Others
1	Low Kick	Fighting	Physical	—	100	20	Normal
1	Strength	Normal	Physical	80	100	15	Normal
4	Focus Energy	Normal	Status	—	—	30	Self
8	Bide	Normal	Physical	—	—	10	Self
12	Seismic Toss	Fighting	Physical	—	100	20	Normal
16	Karate Chop	Fighting	Physical	50	100	25	Normal
21	Brick Break	Fighting	Physical	75	100	15	Normal
26	Submission	Fighting	Physical	80	80	20	Normal
37	Bulk Up	Fighting	Status	—	—	20	Self
48	Superpower	Fighting	Physical	120	100	5	Normal

TM MOVES

NO.	NAME	TYPE	KIND	POW.	ACC.	PP	RANGE
TM01	Headbutt	Normal	Physical	70	100	15	Normal
TM03	Helping Hand	Normal	Status	—	—	20	1 Ally
TM05	Rest	Psychic	Status	—	—	10	Self
TM06	Light Screen	Psychic	Status	—	—	30	Your Side
TM07	Protect	Normal	Status	—	—	10	Self
TM08	Substitute	Normal	Status	—	—	10	Self
TM10	Dig	Ground	Physical	80	100	10	Normal
TM12	Facade	Normal	Physical	70	100	20	Normal
TM13	Brick Break	Fighting	Physical	75	100	15	Normal
TM15	Seismic Toss	Fighting	Physical	—	100	20	Normal
TM22	Rock Slide	Rock	Physical	75	90	10	Many Others
TM23	Thunder Punch	Electric	Physical	75	100	15	Normal
TM26	Poison Jab	Poison	Physical	80	100	20	Normal
TM27	Toxic	Poison	Status	—	90	10	Normal
TM30	Bulk Up	Fighting	Status	—	—	20	Self
TM31	Fire Punch	Fire	Physical	75	100	15	Normal
TM35	Ice Punch	Ice	Physical	75	100	15	Normal
TM37	Flamethrower	Fire	Special	90	100	15	Normal
TM41	Earthquake	Ground	Physical	100	100	10	All Others
TM46	Fire Blast	Fire	Special	110	85	5	Normal
TM48	Hyper Beam	Normal	Special	150	90	5	Normal
TM49	Superpower	Fighting	Physical	120	100	5	Normal

EVOLUTION MOVES

NAME	TYPE	KIND	POW.	ACC.	PP	RANGE
Strength	Normal	Physical	80	100	15	Normal

Bellsprout

♂ ♀ | Same form for male/female

SPECIES STRENGTHS

HP	▭▭
ATTACK	▭▭▭▭
DEFENSE	▭▭▭
SP. ATK	▭▭▭▭
SP. DEF	▭▭
SPEED	▭▭▭

DAMAGE TAKEN IN BATTLES

◎	×1	🍃	×2
✊	×2	⚪	×2
💧	×0.5	🐛	×1
🌿	×0.25	👻	×1
⚡	×0.5	☯	×1
❄	×2	🔥	×1
👊	×0.5	🌑	×1
☠	×1	⚙	×1
⛰	×1	✦	×0.5

POKÉDEX ENTRY

Prefers hot and humid places. It ensnares tiny bugs with its vines and devours them.

MAIN WAY TO OBTAIN

Obtain one in a trade if you are playing *Pokémon: Let's Go, Pikachu!*, as it does not appear in that game. Catch one when it appears on Route 1, Route 2, or elsewhere in *Pokémon: Let's Go, Eevee!*

Where to catch

EVOLUTION

Bellsprout

Lv. 21 →→→

Weepinbell

Use Leaf Stone →→→

Victreebel

LEVEL-UP MOVES

LV.	NAME	TYPE	KIND	POW.	ACC.	PP	RANGE
1	Vine Whip	Grass	Physical	45	100	25	Normal
4	Growth	Normal	Status	—	—	20	Self
8	Wrap	Normal	Physical	15	90	20	Normal
12	Acid	Poison	Special	40	100	30	Many Others
16	Sleep Powder	Grass	Status	—	75	15	Normal
17	Poison Powder	Poison	Status	—	75	35	Normal
18	Stun Spore	Grass	Status	—	75	30	Normal
22	Razor Leaf	Grass	Physical	55	95	25	Many Others
26	Poison Jab	Poison	Physical	80	100	20	Normal
30	Slam	Normal	Physical	80	75	20	Normal

TM MOVES

NO.	NAME	TYPE	KIND	POW.	ACC.	PP	RANGE
TM01	Headbutt	Normal	Physical	70	100	15	Normal
TM05	Rest	Psychic	Status	—	—	10	Self
TM07	Protect	Normal	Status	—	—	10	Self
TM08	Substitute	Normal	Status	—	—	10	Self
TM09	Reflect	Psychic	Status	—	—	20	Your Side
TM12	Facade	Normal	Physical	70	100	20	Normal
TM26	Poison Jab	Poison	Physical	80	100	20	Normal
TM27	Toxic	Poison	Status	—	90	10	Normal
TM45	Solar Beam	Grass	Special	200	100	10	Normal
TM52	Sludge Bomb	Poison	Special	90	100	10	Normal
TM53	Mega Drain	Grass	Special	75	100	10	Normal

EVOLUTION MOVES

NAME	TYPE	KIND	POW.	ACC.	PP	RANGE

POKÉMON EXPRESSIONS

HAPPY

UNHAPPY

ATTACKING

Weepinbell

♂ ♀ | Same form for male/female

SPECIES STRENGTHS

HP	▰▰▰
ATTACK	▰▰▰▰
DEFENSE	▰▰
SP. ATK	▰▰▰
SP. DEF	▰▰
SPEED	▰▰

DAMAGE TAKEN IN BATTLES

◉	×1	🖐	×2
🔥	×2	🌀	×2
💧	×0.5	🧠	×1
⚡	×0.25	⚔	×1
🍃	×0.5	🪨	×1
❄	×2	👻	×1
👊	×0.5	◐	×1
☠	×1	⚙	×1
⛰	×1	✦	×0.5

POKÉDEX ENTRY

When hungry, it swallows anything that moves. Its hapless prey is dissolved by strong acids.

MAIN WAY TO OBTAIN

Catch one when it appears on Route 12, Route 13, or elsewhere in *Pokémon: Let's Go, Eevee!* Or obtain a Bellsprout, then level it up to Lv. 21 or higher to evolve it into Weepinbell.

Where to catch

EVOLUTION

Bellsprout

Lv. 21
→→→

Weepinbell

Use Leaf Stone
→→→

Victreebel

POKÉMON EXPRESSIONS

HAPPY

UNHAPPY

ATTACKING

LEVEL-UP MOVES

LV.	NAME	TYPE	KIND	POW.	ACC.	PP	RANGE
1	Acid	Poison	Special	40	100	30	Many Others
1	Growth	Normal	Status	—	—	20	Self
1	Vine Whip	Grass	Physical	45	100	25	Normal
1	Wrap	Normal	Physical	15	90	20	Normal
4	Growth	Normal	Status	—	—	20	Self
8	Wrap	Normal	Physical	15	90	20	Normal
12	Acid	Poison	Special	40	100	30	Many Others
16	Sleep Powder	Grass	Status	—	75	15	Normal
17	Poison Powder	Poison	Status	—	75	35	Normal
18	Stun Spore	Grass	Status	—	75	30	Normal
27	Razor Leaf	Grass	Physical	55	95	25	Many Others
36	Poison Jab	Poison	Physical	80	100	20	Normal
45	Slam	Normal	Physical	80	75	20	Normal

TM MOVES

NO.	NAME	TYPE	KIND	POW.	ACC.	PP	RANGE
TM01	Headbutt	Normal	Physical	70	100	15	Normal
TM05	Rest	Psychic	Status	—	—	10	Self
TM07	Protect	Normal	Status	—	—	10	Self
TM08	Substitute	Normal	Status	—	—	10	Self
TM09	Reflect	Psychic	Status	—	—	20	Your Side
TM12	Facade	Normal	Physical	70	100	20	Normal
TM26	Poison Jab	Poison	Physical	80	100	20	Normal
TM27	Toxic	Poison	Status	—	90	10	Normal
TM45	Solar Beam	Grass	Special	200	100	10	Normal
TM52	Sludge Bomb	Poison	Special	90	100	10	Normal
TM53	Mega Drain	Grass	Special	75	100	10	Normal

EVOLUTION MOVES

NAME	TYPE	KIND	POW.	ACC.	PP	RANGE

Victreebel

VICTREEBEL 071

♂ ♀ | Same form for male/female

SPECIES STRENGTHS

HP
ATTACK
DEFENSE
SP. ATK
SP. DEF
SPEED

DAMAGE TAKEN IN BATTLES

◉	×1		×2
	×2		×2
	×0.5		×1
	×0.25		×1
	×0.5		×1
	×2		×1
	×0.5		×1
	×1		×1
	×1		×0.5

POKÉDEX ENTRY

Lures prey with the sweet aroma of honey. Swallowed whole, the prey is dissolved in a day, bones and all.

MAIN WAY TO OBTAIN

Catch one when it appears on Route 21 in *Pokémon: Let's Go, Eevee!* Or obtain a Weepinbell, then use a Leaf Stone on it to evolve it into Victreebel.

Where to catch

EVOLUTION

Bellsprout

Lv. 21
→→→

Weepinbell

Use Leaf Stone
→→→

Victreebel

LEVEL-UP MOVES

LV.	NAME	TYPE	KIND	POW.	ACC.	PP	RANGE
1	Acid	Poison	Special	40	100	30	Many Others
1	Clear Smog	Poison	Special	50	—	15	Normal
1	Growth	Normal	Status	—	—	20	Self
1	Leech Life	Bug	Physical	80	100	10	Normal
1	Power Whip	Grass	Physical	120	85	10	Normal
1	Sucker Punch	Dark	Physical	70	100	5	Normal
1	Swords Dance	Normal	Status	—	—	20	Self
1	Vine Whip	Grass	Physical	45	100	25	Normal
1	Wrap	Normal	Physical	15	90	20	Normal
54	Power Whip	Grass	Physical	120	85	10	Normal

TM MOVES

NO.	NAME	TYPE	KIND	POW.	ACC.	PP	RANGE
TM01	Headbutt	Normal	Physical	70	100	15	Normal
TM05	Rest	Psychic	Status	—	—	10	Self
TM07	Protect	Normal	Status	—	—	10	Self
TM08	Substitute	Normal	Status	—	—	10	Self
TM09	Reflect	Psychic	Status	—	—	20	Your Side
TM12	Facade	Normal	Physical	70	100	20	Normal
TM26	Poison Jab	Poison	Physical	80	100	20	Normal
TM27	Toxic	Poison	Status	—	90	10	Normal
TM45	Solar Beam	Grass	Special	200	100	10	Normal
TM48	Hyper Beam	Normal	Special	150	90	5	Normal
TM52	Sludge Bomb	Poison	Special	90	100	10	Normal
TM53	Mega Drain	Grass	Special	75	100	10	Normal

EVOLUTION MOVES

NAME	TYPE	KIND	POW.	ACC.	PP	RANGE

POKÉMON EXPRESSIONS

HAPPY

UNHAPPY

ATTACKING

Tentacool

♂ ♀ | Same form for male/female

SPECIES STRENGTHS

HP	▪▪
ATTACK	▪▪
DEFENSE	▪▪
SP. ATK	▪▪
SP. DEF	▪▪▪▪
SPEED	▪▪▪

DAMAGE TAKEN IN BATTLES

⊙	×1	🔥	×1
🥊	×0.5	🌀	×2
💧	×0.5	🍃	×0.5
⚡	×1	❄	×1
⛏	×2	👁	×1
❄	×0.5	🌙	×1
🐛	×0.5	☾	×1
👻	×0.5	⭕	×0.5
🗿	×2	✦	×0.5

POKÉDEX ENTRY

It can sometimes be found all dry and shriveled up on a beach. Toss it back into the sea to revive it.

MAIN WAY TO OBTAIN

Catch one when it appears on the water's surface on Route 4 (East), Route 24, or elsewhere.

Where to catch

EVOLUTION

Tentacool

Lv. 30
→→→→

Tentacruel

POKÉMON EXPRESSIONS

HAPPY

UNHAPPY

ATTACKING

LEVEL-UP MOVES

LV.	NAME	TYPE	KIND	POW.	ACC.	PP	RANGE
1	Poison Sting	Poison	Physical	15	100	35	Normal
4	Constrict	Normal	Physical	10	100	35	Normal
9	Supersonic	Normal	Status	—	55	20	Normal
13	Acid	Poison	Special	40	100	30	Many Others
18	Bubble Beam	Water	Special	65	100	20	Normal
22	Wrap	Normal	Physical	15	90	20	Normal
27	Surf	Water	Special	90	100	15	All Others
31	Barrier	Psychic	Status	—	—	20	Self
36	Poison Jab	Poison	Physical	80	100	20	Normal
40	Screech	Normal	Status	—	85	40	Normal
45	Hydro Pump	Water	Special	110	80	5	Normal

TM MOVES

NO.	NAME	TYPE	KIND	POW.	ACC.	PP	RANGE
TM01	Headbutt	Normal	Physical	70	100	15	Normal
TM05	Rest	Psychic	Status	—	—	10	Self
TM07	Protect	Normal	Status	—	—	10	Self
TM08	Substitute	Normal	Status	—	—	10	Self
TM09	Reflect	Psychic	Status	—	—	20	Your Side
TM12	Facade	Normal	Physical	70	100	20	Normal
TM25	Waterfall	Water	Physical	80	100	15	Normal
TM26	Poison Jab	Poison	Physical	80	100	20	Normal
TM27	Toxic	Poison	Status	—	90	10	Normal
TM29	Scald	Water	Special	80	100	15	Normal
TM32	Dazzling Gleam	Fairy	Special	80	100	10	Many Others
TM47	Surf	Water	Special	90	100	15	All Others
TM51	Blizzard	Ice	Special	110	70	5	Many Others
TM52	Sludge Bomb	Poison	Special	90	100	10	Normal
TM53	Mega Drain	Grass	Special	75	100	10	Normal
TM55	Ice Beam	Ice	Special	90	100	10	Normal

EVOLUTION MOVES

NAME	TYPE	KIND	POW.	ACC.	PP	RANGE

Tentacruel

♂ ♀ | Same form for male/female

SPECIES STRENGTHS

HP	▰▰▰▰▱
ATTACK	▰▰▰▰▱
DEFENSE	▰▰▰▱
SP. ATK	▰▰▰▰▱
SP. DEF	▰▰▰▰▰▰▰
SPEED	▰▰▰▰▰

DAMAGE TAKEN IN BATTLES

⊙	×1	⟐	×1
🔥	×0.5	⬡	×2
💧	×0.5	🐛	×0.5
⚡	×1	👻	×1
🍃	×2	◉	×1
❄	×0.5	⟁	×1
👊	×0.5	◐	×1
☠	×0.5	⬤	×0.5
⛰	×2	✴	×0.5

POKÉDEX ENTRY

Its 80 tentacles can stretch and contract freely. They wrap around prey and weaken it with poison.

MAIN WAY TO OBTAIN

Catch one when it appears on the water's surface on Route 18 (West), Route 19, or elsewhere. Or obtain a Tentacool, then level it up to Lv. 30 or higher to evolve it into Tentacruel.

Where to catch

EVOLUTION

Tentacool

 Lv. 30 →→→

Tentacruel

LEVEL-UP MOVES

LV.	NAME	TYPE	KIND	POW.	ACC.	PP	RANGE
1	Acid	Poison	Special	40	100	30	Many Others
1	Constrict	Normal	Physical	10	100	35	Normal
1	Haze	Ice	Status	—	—	30	Both Sides
1	Mirror Coat	Psychic	Special	—	100	20	Varies
1	Poison Sting	Poison	Physical	15	100	35	Normal
1	Supersonic	Normal	Status	—	55	20	Normal
4	Constrict	Normal	Physical	10	100	35	Normal
9	Supersonic	Normal	Status	—	55	20	Normal
13	Acid	Poison	Special	40	100	30	Many Others
18	Bubble Beam	Water	Special	65	100	20	Normal
22	Wrap	Normal	Physical	15	90	20	Normal
27	Surf	Water	Special	90	100	15	All Others
36	Barrier	Psychic	Status	—	—	20	Self
46	Poison Jab	Poison	Physical	80	100	20	Normal
55	Screech	Normal	Status	—	85	40	Normal
65	Hydro Pump	Water	Special	110	80	5	Normal

TM MOVES

NO.	NAME	TYPE	KIND	POW.	ACC.	PP	RANGE
TM01	Headbutt	Normal	Physical	70	100	15	Normal
TM05	Rest	Psychic	Status	—	—	10	Self
TM07	Protect	Normal	Status	—	—	10	Self
TM08	Substitute	Normal	Status	—	—	10	Self
TM09	Reflect	Psychic	Status	—	—	20	Your Side
TM12	Facade	Normal	Physical	70	100	20	Normal
TM25	Waterfall	Water	Physical	80	100	15	Normal
TM26	Poison Jab	Poison	Physical	80	100	20	Normal
TM27	Toxic	Poison	Status	—	90	10	Normal
TM29	Scald	Water	Special	80	100	15	Normal
TM32	Dazzling Gleam	Fairy	Special	80	100	10	Many Others
TM47	Surf	Water	Special	90	100	15	All Others
TM48	Hyper Beam	Normal	Special	150	90	5	Normal
TM51	Blizzard	Ice	Special	110	70	5	Many Others
TM52	Sludge Bomb	Poison	Special	90	100	10	Normal
TM53	Mega Drain	Grass	Special	75	100	10	Normal
TM55	Ice Beam	Ice	Special	90	100	10	Normal

EVOLUTION MOVES

NAME	TYPE	KIND	POW.	ACC.	PP	RANGE

POKÉMON EXPRESSIONS

HAPPY

UNHAPPY

ATTACKING

Geodude

♂ ♀ | Same form for male/female

SPECIES STRENGTHS

HP ▪▪▪
ATTACK ▪▪▪▪▪
DEFENSE ▪▪▪▪▪▪
SP. ATK ▪▪
SP. DEF ▪▪
SPEED ▪▪

DAMAGE TAKEN IN BATTLES

×0.5		×0.5	
×0.5		×1	
×4		×1	
×4		×0.5	
×0		×1	
×2		×1	
×2		×1	
×0.25		×2	
×2		×1	

POKÉDEX ENTRY

Commonly found near mountain trails and the like. If you step on one by accident, it gets angry.

MAIN WAY TO OBTAIN

Catch one when it appears in Mt. Moon, in the Rock Tunnel, or elsewhere.

Where to catch

EVOLUTION

| Geodude | Lv. 25 →→→ | Graveler | Trade Graveler →→→ | Golem |

POKÉMON EXPRESSIONS

HAPPY

UNHAPPY

ATTACKING

LEVEL-UP MOVES

LV.	NAME	TYPE	KIND	POW.	ACC.	PP	RANGE
1	Defense Curl	Normal	Status	—	—	40	Self
1	Tackle	Normal	Physical	40	100	35	Normal
3	Sand Attack	Ground	Status	—	100	15	Normal
6	Bide	Normal	Physical	—	—	10	Self
9	Rock Throw	Rock	Physical	50	90	15	Normal
12	Stealth Rock	Rock	Status	—	—	20	Other Side
15	Take Down	Normal	Physical	90	85	20	Normal
19	Self-Destruct	Normal	Physical	200	100	5	All Others
23	Rock Slide	Rock	Physical	75	90	10	Many Others
27	Earthquake	Ground	Physical	100	100	10	All Others
31	Double-Edge	Normal	Physical	120	100	15	Normal
35	Explosion	Normal	Physical	250	100	5	All Others

TM MOVES

NO.	NAME	TYPE	KIND	POW.	ACC.	PP	RANGE
TM01	Headbutt	Normal	Physical	70	100	15	Normal
TM05	Rest	Psychic	Status	—	—	10	Self
TM07	Protect	Normal	Status	—	—	10	Self
TM08	Substitute	Normal	Status	—	—	10	Self
TM10	Dig	Ground	Physical	80	100	10	Normal
TM12	Facade	Normal	Physical	70	100	20	Normal
TM13	Brick Break	Fighting	Physical	75	100	15	Normal
TM15	Seismic Toss	Fighting	Physical	—	100	20	Normal
TM22	Rock Slide	Rock	Physical	75	90	10	Many Others
TM23	Thunder Punch	Electric	Physical	75	100	15	Normal
TM27	Toxic	Poison	Status	—	90	10	Normal
TM31	Fire Punch	Fire	Physical	75	100	15	Normal
TM37	Flamethrower	Fire	Special	90	100	15	Normal
TM41	Earthquake	Ground	Physical	100	100	10	All Others
TM42	Self-Destruct	Normal	Physical	200	100	5	All Others
TM46	Fire Blast	Fire	Special	110	85	5	Normal
TM49	Superpower	Fighting	Physical	120	100	5	Normal
TM56	Stealth Rock	Rock	Status	—	—	20	Other Side

EVOLUTION MOVES

NAME	TYPE	KIND	POW.	ACC.	PP	RANGE

 074 Rock Pokémon | Average height: 1'04" | Average weight: 44.8 lbs.

Geodude

GEODUDE
ALOLA FORM
074

ALOLA FORM

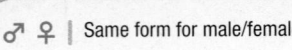 ♂ ♀ | Same form for male/female

SPECIES STRENGTHS

HP	▓▓▓
ATTACK	▓▓▓▓▓
DEFENSE	▓▓▓▓▓▓
SP. ATK	▓▓
SP. DEF	▓▓▓
SPEED	▓▓

DAMAGE TAKEN IN BATTLES

◉	×0.5	🍃	×0.25
🔥	×0.5	💧	×1
💧	×2	🌿	×1
🍃	×2	❄	×1
⚡	×0.5	👊	×1
❄	×1	🔥	×1
🥊	×2	🌙	×1
⚫	×0.5	⬤	×1
🔺	×4	✦	×1

POKÉDEX ENTRY

Its stone head is imbued with electricity and magnetism. If you carelessly step on one, you'll be in for a painful shock.

MAIN WAY TO OBTAIN

Trade a Geodude for one in the Pokémon Center in Vermilion City (p. 47).

Where to catch

Habitat Unknown

EVOLUTION

Alolan Geodude

Lv. 25
→ → →

Alolan Graveler

Trade Alolan Graveler
→ → →

Alolan Golem

LEVEL-UP MOVES

LV.	NAME	TYPE	KIND	POW.	ACC.	PP	RANGE
1	Defense Curl	Normal	Status	—	—	40	Self
1	Tackle	Normal	Physical	40	100	35	Normal
3	Thunder Shock	Electric	Special	40	100	30	Normal
6	Bide	Normal	Physical	—	—	10	Self
9	Rock Throw	Rock	Physical	50	90	15	Normal
12	Stealth Rock	Rock	Status	—	—	20	Other Side
15	Take Down	Normal	Physical	90	85	20	Normal
19	Self-Destruct	Normal	Physical	200	100	5	All Others
23	Rock Slide	Rock	Physical	75	90	10	Many Others
27	Thunder Punch	Electric	Physical	75	100	15	Normal
31	Double-Edge	Normal	Physical	120	100	15	Normal
35	Explosion	Normal	Physical	250	100	5	All Others

TM MOVES

NO.	NAME	TYPE	KIND	POW.	ACC.	PP	RANGE
TM01	Headbutt	Normal	Physical	70	100	15	Normal
TM05	Rest	Psychic	Status	—	—	10	Self
TM07	Protect	Normal	Status	—	—	10	Self
TM08	Substitute	Normal	Status	—	—	10	Self
TM10	Dig	Ground	Physical	80	100	10	Normal
TM12	Facade	Normal	Physical	70	100	20	Normal
TM13	Brick Break	Fighting	Physical	75	100	15	Normal
TM15	Seismic Toss	Fighting	Physical	—	100	20	Normal
TM16	Thunder Wave	Electric	Status	—	90	20	Normal
TM22	Rock Slide	Rock	Physical	75	90	10	Many Others
TM23	Thunder Punch	Electric	Physical	75	100	15	Normal
TM27	Toxic	Poison	Status	—	90	10	Normal
TM31	Fire Punch	Fire	Physical	75	100	15	Normal
TM36	Thunderbolt	Electric	Special	90	100	15	Normal
TM37	Flamethrower	Fire	Special	90	100	15	Normal
TM38	Thunder	Electric	Special	110	70	10	Normal
TM41	Earthquake	Ground	Physical	100	100	10	All Others
TM42	Self-Destruct	Normal	Physical	200	100	5	All Others
TM46	Fire Blast	Fire	Special	110	85	5	Normal
TM49	Superpower	Fighting	Physical	120	100	5	Normal
TM56	Stealth Rock	Rock	Status	—	—	20	Other Side

EVOLUTION MOVES

NAME	TYPE	KIND	POW.	ACC.	PP	RANGE

POKÉMON EXPRESSIONS

HAPPY

UNHAPPY

ATTACKING

Graveler

♂ ♀ | Same form for male/female

SPECIES STRENGTHS

HP	▰▰▰
ATTACK	▰▰▰▰▰
DEFENSE	▰▰▰▰▰▰
SP. ATK	▰▰
SP. DEF	▰▰▰
SPEED	▰▰▰

DAMAGE TAKEN IN BATTLES

⬡	×0.5	🔥	×0.5
🔥	×0.5	◎	×1
💧	×4	🍃	×1
🌿	×4	◈	×0.5
⚡	×0	◐	×1
❄	×2	◓	×1
👊	×2	◑	×1
☣	×0.25	◉	×2
⛰	×2	✦	×1

POKÉDEX ENTRY

Often seen rolling down mountain trails. Obstacles are just things to roll straight over, not avoid.

MAIN WAY TO OBTAIN

Catch one when it appears in the Rock Tunnel, on Victory Road, or elsewhere. Or obtain a Geodude, then level it up to Lv. 25 or higher to evolve it into Graveler.

Where to catch

EVOLUTION

Geodude	Lv. 25 →→→ **Graveler**	Trade Graveler →→→ **Golem**

POKÉMON EXPRESSIONS

HAPPY

UNHAPPY

ATTACKING

LEVEL-UP MOVES

LV.	NAME	TYPE	KIND	POW.	ACC.	PP	RANGE
1	Bide	Normal	Physical	—	—	10	Self
1	Defense Curl	Normal	Status	—	—	40	Self
1	Sand Attack	Ground	Status	—	100	15	Normal
1	Tackle	Normal	Physical	40	100	35	Normal
3	Sand Attack	Ground	Status	—	100	15	Normal
6	Bide	Normal	Physical	—	—	10	Self
9	Rock Throw	Rock	Physical	50	90	15	Normal
12	Stealth Rock	Rock	Status	—	—	20	Other Side
15	Take Down	Normal	Physical	90	85	20	Normal
19	Self-Destruct	Normal	Physical	200	100	5	All Others
23	Rock Slide	Rock	Physical	75	90	10	Many Others
31	Earthquake	Ground	Physical	100	100	10	All Others
39	Double-Edge	Normal	Physical	120	100	15	Normal
47	Explosion	Normal	Physical	250	100	5	All Others

TM MOVES

NO.	NAME	TYPE	KIND	POW.	ACC.	PP	RANGE
TM01	Headbutt	Normal	Physical	70	100	15	Normal
TM05	Rest	Psychic	Status	—	—	10	Self
TM07	Protect	Normal	Status	—	—	10	Self
TM08	Substitute	Normal	Status	—	—	10	Self
TM10	Dig	Ground	Physical	80	100	10	Normal
TM12	Facade	Normal	Physical	70	100	20	Normal
TM13	Brick Break	Fighting	Physical	75	100	15	Normal
TM15	Seismic Toss	Fighting	Physical	—	100	20	Normal
TM22	Rock Slide	Rock	Physical	75	90	10	Many Others
TM23	Thunder Punch	Electric	Physical	75	100	15	Normal
TM27	Toxic	Poison	Status	—	90	10	Normal
TM31	Fire Punch	Fire	Physical	75	100	15	Normal
TM37	Flamethrower	Fire	Special	90	100	15	Normal
TM41	Earthquake	Ground	Physical	100	100	10	All Others
TM42	Self-Destruct	Normal	Physical	200	100	5	All Others
TM46	Fire Blast	Fire	Special	110	85	5	Normal
TM49	Superpower	Fighting	Physical	120	100	5	Normal
TM56	Stealth Rock	Rock	Status	—	—	20	Other Side

EVOLUTION MOVES

NAME	TYPE	KIND	POW.	ACC.	PP	RANGE

Graveler

GRAVELER
ALOLA FORM

075

ALOLA FORM

♂ ♀ | Same form for male/female

SPECIES STRENGTHS

HP	
ATTACK	
DEFENSE	
SP. ATK	
SP. DEF	
SPEED	

DAMAGE TAKEN IN BATTLES

⊙	×0.5		×0.25
	×0.5		×1
	×2		×1
	×2		×1
	×0.5		×1
	×1		×1
	×2		×1
	×0.5		×1
	×4		×1

POKÉDEX ENTRY

When it comes rolling down a mountain path, anything in its way gets zapped by electricity and sent flying.

MAIN WAY TO OBTAIN

Obtain an Alolan Geodude, then level it up to Lv. 25 or higher to evolve it into Alolan Graveler.

Where to catch

Habitat Unknown

EVOLUTION

Alolan Geodude

Lv. 25
→→→

Alolan Graveler

Trade Alolan Graveler
→→→

Alolan Golem

LEVEL-UP MOVES

LV.	NAME	TYPE	KIND	POW.	ACC.	PP	RANGE
1	Bide	Normal	Physical	—	—	10	Self
1	Defense Curl	Normal	Status	—	—	40	Self
1	Tackle	Normal	Physical	40	100	35	Normal
1	Thunder Shock	Electric	Special	40	100	30	Normal
3	Thunder Shock	Electric	Special	40	100	30	Normal
6	Bide	Normal	Physical	—	—	10	Self
9	Rock Throw	Rock	Physical	50	90	15	Normal
12	Stealth Rock	Rock	Status	—	—	20	Other Side
15	Take Down	Normal	Physical	90	85	20	Normal
19	Self-Destruct	Normal	Physical	200	100	5	All Others
23	Rock Slide	Rock	Physical	75	90	10	Many Others
31	Thunder Punch	Electric	Physical	75	100	15	Normal
39	Double-Edge	Normal	Physical	120	100	15	Normal
47	Explosion	Normal	Physical	250	100	5	All Others

TM MOVES

NO.	NAME	TYPE	KIND	POW.	ACC.	PP	RANGE
TM01	Headbutt	Normal	Physical	70	100	15	Normal
TM05	Rest	Psychic	Status	—	—	10	Self
TM07	Protect	Normal	Status	—	—	10	Self
TM08	Substitute	Normal	Status	—	—	10	Self
TM10	Dig	Ground	Physical	80	100	10	Normal
TM12	Facade	Normal	Physical	70	100	20	Normal
TM13	Brick Break	Fighting	Physical	75	100	15	Normal
TM15	Seismic Toss	Fighting	Physical	—	100	20	Normal
TM16	Thunder Wave	Electric	Status	—	90	20	Normal
TM22	Rock Slide	Rock	Physical	75	90	10	Many Others
TM23	Thunder Punch	Electric	Physical	75	100	15	Normal
TM27	Toxic	Poison	Status	—	90	10	Normal
TM31	Fire Punch	Fire	Physical	75	100	15	Normal
TM36	Thunderbolt	Electric	Special	90	100	15	Normal
TM37	Flamethrower	Fire	Special	90	100	15	Normal
TM38	Thunder	Electric	Special	110	70	10	Normal
TM41	Earthquake	Ground	Physical	100	100	10	All Others
TM42	Self-Destruct	Normal	Physical	200	100	5	All Others
TM46	Fire Blast	Fire	Special	110	85	5	Normal
TM49	Superpower	Fighting	Physical	120	100	5	Normal
TM56	Stealth Rock	Rock	Status	—	—	20	Other Side

EVOLUTION MOVES

NAME	TYPE	KIND	POW.	ACC.	PP	RANGE

POKÉMON EXPRESSIONS

HAPPY

UNHAPPY

ATTACKING

Golem

♂ ♀ | Same form for male/female

SPECIES STRENGTHS

HP	▰▰▰
ATTACK	▰▰▰▰▰▰
DEFENSE	▰▰▰▰▰▰
SP. ATK	▰▰▰
SP. DEF	▰▰▰
SPEED	▰▰▰

DAMAGE TAKEN IN BATTLES

⬡	×0.5	🪶	×0.5
🔥	×0.5	🌀	×1
💧	×4	🍃	×1
⚡	×4	🔮	×0.5
🌿	×0	◉	×1
❄	×2	🌑	×1
🥊	×2	🌙	×1
☠	×0.25	⚙	×2
🗻	×2	✦	×1

POKÉDEX ENTRY

Once it sheds its skin, its body turns tender and whitish. Its hide hardens when it's exposed to air.

MAIN WAY TO OBTAIN

Receive a Graveler in a trade and it will immediately evolve into Golem.

Where to catch
Habitat Unknown

EVOLUTION

   Lv. 25 → → →      Trade Graveler → → →   

Geodude   **Graveler**   **Golem**

POKÉMON EXPRESSIONS

HAPPY

UNHAPPY

ATTACKING

LEVEL-UP MOVES

LV.	NAME	TYPE	KIND	POW.	ACC.	PP	RANGE
1	Bide	Normal	Physical	—	—	10	Self
1	Defense Curl	Normal	Status	—	—	40	Self
1	Mega Punch	Normal	Physical	80	85	20	Normal
1	Sand Attack	Ground	Status	—	100	15	Normal
1	Tackle	Normal	Physical	40	100	35	Normal
3	Sand Attack	Ground	Status	—	100	15	Normal
6	Bide	Normal	Physical	—	—	10	Self
9	Rock Throw	Rock	Physical	50	90	15	Normal
12	Stealth Rock	Rock	Status	—	—	20	Other Side
15	Take Down	Normal	Physical	90	85	20	Normal
19	Self-Destruct	Normal	Physical	200	100	5	All Others
23	Rock Slide	Rock	Physical	75	90	10	Many Others
31	Earthquake	Ground	Physical	100	100	10	All Others
39	Double-Edge	Normal	Physical	120	100	15	Normal
47	Explosion	Normal	Physical	250	100	5	All Others

TM MOVES

NO.	NAME	TYPE	KIND	POW.	ACC.	PP	RANGE
TM01	Headbutt	Normal	Physical	70	100	15	Normal
TM05	Rest	Psychic	Status	—	—	10	Self
TM07	Protect	Normal	Status	—	—	10	Self
TM08	Substitute	Normal	Status	—	—	10	Self
TM10	Dig	Ground	Physical	80	100	10	Normal
TM12	Facade	Normal	Physical	70	100	20	Normal
TM13	Brick Break	Fighting	Physical	75	100	15	Normal
TM15	Seismic Toss	Fighting	Physical	—	100	20	Normal
TM22	Rock Slide	Rock	Physical	75	90	10	Many Others
TM23	Thunder Punch	Electric	Physical	75	100	15	Normal
TM27	Toxic	Poison	Status	—	90	10	Normal
TM31	Fire Punch	Fire	Physical	75	100	15	Normal
TM37	Flamethrower	Fire	Special	90	100	15	Normal
TM41	Earthquake	Ground	Physical	100	100	10	All Others
TM42	Self-Destruct	Normal	Physical	200	100	5	All Others
TM46	Fire Blast	Fire	Special	110	85	5	Normal
TM48	Hyper Beam	Normal	Special	150	90	5	Normal
TM49	Superpower	Fighting	Physical	120	100	5	Normal
TM56	Stealth Rock	Rock	Status	—	—	20	Other Side

EVOLUTION MOVES

NAME	TYPE	KIND	POW.	ACC.	PP	RANGE

Golem

ALOLA FORM

♂ ♀ | Same form for male/female

SPECIES STRENGTHS

HP	▨▨▨▨▨
ATTACK	▨▨▨▨▨▨▨
DEFENSE	▨▨▨▨▨▨▨
SP. ATK	▨▨▨
SP. DEF	▨▨▨
SPEED	▨▨

DAMAGE TAKEN IN BATTLES

◉	×0.5		×0.25
	×0.5		×1
	×2		×1
	×2		×1
	×0.5		×1
❄	×1		×1
	×2		×1
	×0.5	◉	×1
	×4	✦	×1

POKÉDEX ENTRY

It uses magnetism to accelerate and fire off rocks tinged with electricity. Even if it doesn't score a direct hit, the jolt of electricity will do the job.

MAIN WAY TO OBTAIN

Receive an Alolan Graveler in a trade and it will immediately evolve into Alolan Golem.

Where to catch

Habitat Unknown

EVOLUTION

Alolan Geodude

Lv. 25
→→→

Alolan Graveler

Trade Alolan Graveler
→→→

Alolan Golem

LEVEL-UP MOVES

LV.	NAME	TYPE	KIND	POW.	ACC.	PP	RANGE
1	Bide	Normal	Physical	—	—	10	Self
1	Defense Curl	Normal	Status	—	—	40	Self
1	Mega Punch	Normal	Physical	80	85	20	Normal
1	Tackle	Normal	Physical	40	100	35	Normal
1	Thunder Shock	Electric	Special	40	100	30	Normal
3	Thunder Shock	Electric	Special	40	100	30	Normal
6	Bide	Normal	Physical	—	—	10	Self
9	Rock Throw	Rock	Physical	50	90	15	Normal
12	Stealth Rock	Rock	Status	—	—	20	Other Side
15	Take Down	Normal	Physical	90	85	20	Normal
19	Self-Destruct	Normal	Physical	200	100	5	All Others
23	Rock Slide	Rock	Physical	75	90	10	Many Others
31	Thunder Punch	Electric	Physical	75	100	15	Normal
39	Double-Edge	Normal	Physical	120	100	15	Normal
47	Explosion	Normal	Physical	250	100	5	All Others

TM MOVES

NO.	NAME	TYPE	KIND	POW.	ACC.	PP	RANGE
TM01	Headbutt	Normal	Physical	70	100	15	Normal
TM05	Rest	Psychic	Status	—	—	10	Self
TM07	Protect	Normal	Status	—	—	10	Self
TM08	Substitute	Normal	Status	—	—	10	Self
TM10	Dig	Ground	Physical	80	100	10	Normal
TM12	Facade	Normal	Physical	70	100	20	Normal
TM13	Brick Break	Fighting	Physical	75	100	15	Normal
TM15	Seismic Toss	Fighting	Physical	—	100	20	Normal
TM16	Thunder Wave	Electric	Status	—	90	20	Normal
TM22	Rock Slide	Rock	Physical	75	90	10	Many Others
TM23	Thunder Punch	Electric	Physical	75	100	15	Normal
TM27	Toxic	Poison	Status	—	90	10	Normal
TM31	Fire Punch	Fire	Physical	75	100	15	Normal
TM36	Thunderbolt	Electric	Special	90	100	15	Normal
TM37	Flamethrower	Fire	Special	90	100	15	Normal
TM38	Thunder	Electric	Special	110	70	10	Normal
TM41	Earthquake	Ground	Physical	100	100	10	All Others
TM42	Self-Destruct	Normal	Physical	200	100	5	All Others
TM46	Fire Blast	Fire	Special	110	85	5	Normal
TM48	Hyper Beam	Normal	Special	150	90	5	Normal
TM49	Superpower	Fighting	Physical	120	100	5	Normal
TM56	Stealth Rock	Rock	Status	—	—	20	Other Side

POKÉMON EXPRESSIONS

HAPPY

UNHAPPY

ATTACKING

EVOLUTION MOVES

NAME	TYPE	KIND	POW.	ACC.	PP	RANGE

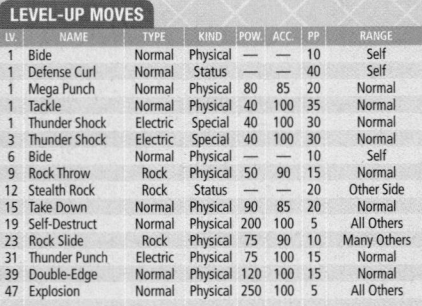

Ponyta

♂ ♀ | Same form for male/female

SPECIES STRENGTHS

HP	▪▪▪
ATTACK	▪▪▪▪▪
DEFENSE	▪▪▪
SP. ATK	▪▪▪▪
SP. DEF	▪▪▪▪
SPEED	▪▪▪▪▪▪

DAMAGE TAKEN IN BATTLES

◉ ×1		🍃 ×1	
🔥 ×0.5		🌀 ×1	
💧 ×2		🕊 ×0.5	
🍃 ×0.5		◐ ×2	
⚡ ×1		⊙ ×1	
❄ ×0.5		🥊 ×1	
🔲 ×1		🌙 ×1	
◉ ×1		◉ ×0.5	
⛰ ×2		✦ ×0.5	

POKÉDEX ENTRY

Capable of jumping incredibly
high. Its hooves and sturdy
legs absorb the impact of a
hard landing.

MAIN WAY TO OBTAIN

Catch one when it appears
on Route 17.

Where to catch

EVOLUTION

Ponyta

Lv. 40
→→→

Rapidash

POKÉMON EXPRESSIONS

HAPPY

UNHAPPY

ATTACKING

LEVEL-UP MOVES

LV.	NAME	TYPE	KIND	POW.	ACC.	PP	RANGE
1	Growl	Normal	Status	—	100	40	Many Others
1	Tackle	Normal	Physical	40	100	35	Normal
1	Tail Whip	Normal	Status	—	100	30	Many Others
5	Ember	Fire	Special	40	100	25	Normal
10	Quick Attack	Normal	Physical	40	100	30	Normal
15	Double Kick	Fighting	Physical	30	100	30	Normal
20	Stomp	Normal	Physical	65	100	20	Normal
26	Fire Spin	Fire	Special	35	85	15	Normal
32	Agility	Psychic	Status	—	—	30	Self
38	Fire Blast	Fire	Special	110	85	5	Normal
44	Take Down	Normal	Physical	90	85	20	Normal
51	Flare Blitz	Fire	Physical	120	100	15	Normal

TM MOVES

NO.	NAME	TYPE	KIND	POW.	ACC.	PP	RANGE
TM01	Headbutt	Normal	Physical	70	100	15	Normal
TM05	Rest	Psychic	Status	—	—	10	Self
TM07	Protect	Normal	Status	—	—	10	Self
TM08	Substitute	Normal	Status	—	—	10	Self
TM09	Reflect	Psychic	Status	—	—	20	Your Side
TM11	Will-O-Wisp	Fire	Status	—	85	15	Normal
TM12	Facade	Normal	Physical	70	100	20	Normal
TM19	Iron Tail	Steel	Physical	100	75	15	Normal
TM27	Toxic	Poison	Status	—	90	10	Normal
TM37	Flamethrower	Fire	Special	90	100	15	Normal
TM45	Solar Beam	Grass	Special	200	100	10	Normal
TM46	Fire Blast	Fire	Special	110	85	5	Normal

EVOLUTION MOVES

NAME	TYPE	KIND	POW.	ACC.	PP	RANGE

078 Fire Horse Pokémon Average height: 5'07" Average weight: 209.4 lbs.

Rapidash

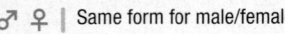
♂ ♀ | Same form for male/female

SPECIES STRENGTHS

HP	
ATTACK	
DEFENSE	
SP. ATK	
SP. DEF	
SPEED	

DAMAGE TAKEN IN BATTLES

×1		×1	
×0.5		×1	
×2		×0.5	
×0.5		×2	
×1		×1	
×0.5		×1	
×1		×1	
×1		×0.5	
×2		×0.5	

POKÉDEX ENTRY

Just loves to run. If it sees something faster than itself, it will give chase at top speed.

MAIN WAY TO OBTAIN

Catch one when it appears on Route 17. Or obtain a Ponyta, then level it up to Lv. 40 or higher to evolve it into Rapidash.

Where to catch

EVOLUTION

Ponyta

Lv. 40
→→→

Rapidash

LEVEL-UP MOVES

LV.	NAME	TYPE	KIND	POW.	ACC.	PP	RANGE
1	Ember	Fire	Special	40	100	25	Normal
1	Fury Attack	Normal	Physical	15	85	20	Normal
1	Growl	Normal	Status	—	100	40	Many Others
1	Horn Drill	Normal	Physical	—	30	5	Normal
1	Hypnosis	Psychic	Status	—	60	20	Normal
1	Megahorn	Bug	Physical	120	85	10	Normal
1	Poison Jab	Poison	Physical	80	100	20	Normal
1	Tackle	Normal	Physical	40	100	35	Normal
1	Tail Whip	Normal	Status	—	100	30	Many Others
5	Ember	Fire	Special	40	100	25	Normal
10	Quick Attack	Normal	Physical	40	100	30	Normal
15	Double Kick	Fighting	Physical	30	100	30	Normal
20	Stomp	Normal	Physical	65	100	20	Normal
26	Fire Spin	Fire	Special	35	85	15	Normal
32	Agility	Psychic	Status	—	—	30	Self
38	Fire Blast	Fire	Special	110	85	5	Normal
51	Take Down	Normal	Physical	90	85	20	Normal
65	Flare Blitz	Fire	Physical	120	100	15	Normal

TM MOVES

NO.	NAME	TYPE	KIND	POW.	ACC.	PP	RANGE
TM01	Headbutt	Normal	Physical	70	100	15	Normal
TM05	Rest	Psychic	Status	—	—	10	Self
TM07	Protect	Normal	Status	—	—	10	Self
TM08	Substitute	Normal	Status	—	—	10	Self
TM09	Reflect	Psychic	Status	—	—	20	Your Side
TM11	Will-O-Wisp	Fire	Status	—	85	15	Normal
TM12	Facade	Normal	Physical	70	100	20	Normal
TM19	Iron Tail	Steel	Physical	100	75	15	Normal
TM26	Poison Jab	Poison	Physical	80	100	20	Normal
TM27	Toxic	Poison	Status	—	90	10	Normal
TM37	Flamethrower	Fire	Special	90	100	15	Normal
TM45	Solar Beam	Grass	Special	200	100	10	Normal
TM46	Fire Blast	Fire	Special	110	85	5	Normal
TM48	Hyper Beam	Normal	Special	150	90	5	Normal
TM58	Drill Run	Ground	Physical	80	95	10	Normal
TM60	Megahorn	Bug	Physical	120	85	10	Normal

EVOLUTION MOVES

NAME	TYPE	KIND	POW.	ACC.	PP	RANGE
Fury Attack	Normal	Physical	15	85	20	Normal

Slowpoke

♂ ♀ | Same form for male/female

SPECIES STRENGTHS

HP ▰▰▰▰▰
ATTACK ▰▰▰
DEFENSE ▰▰▰
SP. ATK ▰▰
SP. DEF ▰▰
SPEED ▰

POKÉDEX ENTRY

Incredibly slow and sluggish. It is quite content to loll about without worrying about the time.

DAMAGE TAKEN IN BATTLES

×1		×1	
×0.5		×0.5	
×0.5		×2	
×2		×1	
×2		×2	
×0.5		×1	
×0.5		×2	
×1		×0.5	
×1		×1	

MAIN WAY TO OBTAIN

Catch one when it appears in the Seafoam Islands.

Where to catch

EVOLUTION

 → → →
Slowpoke   Lv. 37   Slowbro

POKÉMON EXPRESSIONS

HAPPY

UNHAPPY

ATTACKING

LEVEL-UP MOVES

LV.	NAME	TYPE	KIND	POW.	ACC.	PP	RANGE
1	Tackle	Normal	Physical	40	100	35	Normal
1	Yawn	Normal	Status	—	—	10	Normal
6	Growl	Normal	Status	—	100	40	Many Others
12	Water Gun	Water	Special	40	100	25	Normal
18	Confusion	Psychic	Special	50	100	25	Normal
24	Disable	Normal	Status	—	100	20	Normal
30	Rest	Psychic	Status	—	—	10	Self
36	Surf	Water	Special	90	100	15	All Others
42	Psychic	Psychic	Special	90	100	10	Normal
48	Amnesia	Psychic	Status	—	—	20	Self

TM MOVES

NO.	NAME	TYPE	KIND	POW.	ACC.	PP	RANGE
TM01	Headbutt	Normal	Physical	70	100	15	Normal
TM04	Teleport	Psychic	Status	—	—	20	Self
TM05	Rest	Psychic	Status	—	—	10	Self
TM06	Light Screen	Psychic	Status	—	—	30	Your Side
TM07	Protect	Normal	Status	—	—	10	Self
TM08	Substitute	Normal	Status	—	—	10	Self
TM09	Reflect	Psychic	Status	—	—	20	Your Side
TM10	Dig	Ground	Physical	80	100	10	Normal
TM12	Facade	Normal	Physical	70	100	20	Normal
TM16	Thunder Wave	Electric	Status	—	90	20	Normal
TM19	Iron Tail	Steel	Physical	100	75	15	Normal
TM27	Toxic	Poison	Status	—	90	10	Normal
TM28	Tri Attack	Normal	Special	80	100	10	Normal
TM29	Scald	Water	Special	80	100	15	Normal
TM33	Calm Mind	Psychic	Status	—	—	20	Self
TM37	Flamethrower	Fire	Special	90	100	10	Normal
TM40	Psychic	Psychic	Special	90	100	10	Normal
TM41	Earthquake	Ground	Physical	100	100	10	All Others
TM43	Shadow Ball	Ghost	Special	80	100	15	Normal
TM46	Fire Blast	Fire	Special	110	85	5	Normal
TM47	Surf	Water	Special	90	100	15	All Others
TM51	Blizzard	Ice	Special	110	70	5	Many Others
TM55	Ice Beam	Ice	Special	90	100	10	Normal
TM57	Pay Day	Normal	Physical	40	100	20	Normal
TM59	Dream Eater	Psychic	Special	100	100	15	Normal

EVOLUTION MOVES

NAME	TYPE	KIND	POW.	ACC.	PP	RANGE

Hermit Crab Pokémon | Average height: 5'03" | Average weight: 173.1 lbs.

Slowbro

♂ ♀ | Same form for male/female

SPECIES STRENGTHS

HP	▰▰▰▰▱
ATTACK	▰▰▰▱▱
DEFENSE	▰▰▰▰▰▰
SP. ATK	▰▰▰▰▱
SP. DEF	▰▰▰▰▱
SPEED	▰▱

DAMAGE TAKEN IN BATTLES

⊙	×1	🌀	×1
🔥	×0.5		×0.5
💧	×0.5	🍃	×2
⚡	×2		×1
⚡	×2		×2
❄	×0.5		×1
👊	×0.5	◐	×2
☁	×1	◉	×0.5
⛰	×1	✦	×1

POKÉDEX ENTRY

Lives lazily by the sea. If the Shellder on its tail comes off, it becomes a Slowpoke again.

MAIN WAY TO OBTAIN

Catch one when it appears in the Seafoam Islands, especially on B4F. Or obtain a Slowpoke, then level it up to Lv. 37 or higher to evolve it into Slowbro.

Where to catch

EVOLUTION

Slowpoke

Lv. 37
→→→

Slowbro

LEVEL-UP MOVES

LV.	NAME	TYPE	KIND	POW.	ACC.	PP	RANGE
1	Growl	Normal	Status	—	100	40	Many Others
1	Stomp	Normal	Physical	65	100	20	Normal
1	Tackle	Normal	Physical	40	100	35	Normal
1	Water Gun	Water	Special	40	100	25	Normal
1	Withdraw	Water	Status	—	—	40	Self
1	Yawn	Normal	Status	—	—	10	Normal
6	Growl	Normal	Status	—	100	40	Many Others
12	Water Gun	Water	Special	40	100	25	Normal
18	Confusion	Psychic	Special	50	100	25	Normal
24	Disable	Normal	Status	—	100	20	Normal
30	Rest	Psychic	Status	—	—	10	Self
36	Surf	Water	Special	90	100	15	All Others
49	Psychic	Psychic	Special	90	100	10	Normal
62	Amnesia	Psychic	Status	—	—	20	Self

EVOLUTION MOVES

NAME	TYPE	KIND	POW.	ACC.	PP	RANGE
Withdraw	Water	Status	—	—	40	Self

TM MOVES

NO.	NAME	TYPE	KIND	POW.	ACC.	PP	RANGE
TM01	Headbutt	Normal	Physical	70	100	15	Normal
TM04	Teleport	Psychic	Status	—	—	20	Self
TM05	Rest	Psychic	Status	—	—	10	Self
TM06	Light Screen	Psychic	Status	—	—	30	Your Side
TM07	Protect	Normal	Status	—	—	10	Self
TM08	Substitute	Normal	Status	—	—	10	Self
TM09	Reflect	Psychic	Status	—	—	20	Your Side
TM10	Dig	Ground	Physical	80	100	10	Normal
TM12	Facade	Normal	Physical	70	100	20	Normal
TM13	Brick Break	Fighting	Physical	75	100	15	Normal
TM15	Seismic Toss	Fighting	Physical	—	100	20	Normal
TM16	Thunder Wave	Electric	Status	—	90	20	Normal
TM19	Iron Tail	Steel	Physical	100	75	15	Normal
TM21	Foul Play	Dark	Physical	95	100	15	Normal
TM27	Toxic	Poison	Status	—	90	10	Normal
TM28	Tri Attack	Normal	Special	80	100	10	Normal
TM29	Scald	Water	Special	80	100	15	Normal
TM33	Calm Mind	Psychic	Status	—	—	20	Self
TM35	Ice Punch	Ice	Physical	75	100	15	Normal
TM37	Flamethrower	Fire	Special	90	100	15	Normal
TM40	Psychic	Psychic	Special	90	100	10	Normal
TM41	Earthquake	Ground	Physical	100	100	10	All Others
TM43	Shadow Ball	Ghost	Special	80	100	15	Normal
TM46	Fire Blast	Fire	Special	110	85	5	Normal
TM47	Surf	Water	Special	90	100	15	All Others
TM48	Hyper Beam	Normal	Special	150	90	5	Normal
TM51	Blizzard	Ice	Special	110	70	5	Many Others
TM55	Ice Beam	Ice	Special	90	100	10	Normal
TM57	Pay Day	Normal	Physical	40	100	20	Normal
TM59	Dream Eater	Psychic	Special	100	100	15	Normal

POKÉMON EXPRESSIONS

HAPPY

UNHAPPY

ATTACKING

Mega Slowbro

MEGA EVOLUTION

Slowbro

→→→

Buy a Slowbronite, then
Mega Evolve Slowbro
during battle.

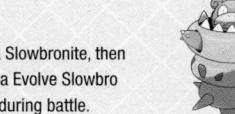

Mega Slowbro

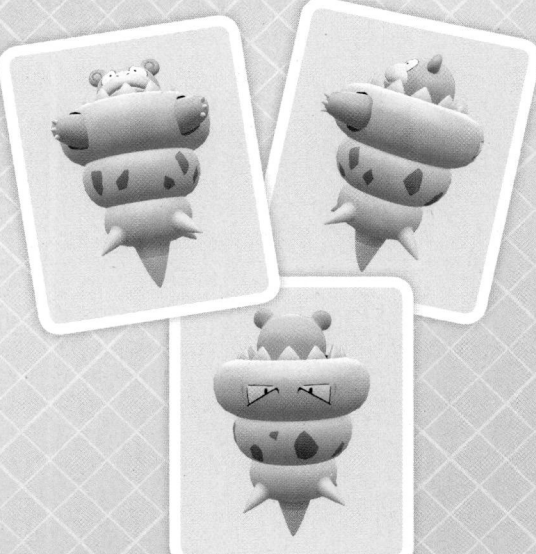

SPECIES STRENGTHS

HP	▰▰▰▰▱
ATTACK	▰▰▰▰▱
DEFENSE	▰▰▰▰▰▰▰▰▰▱
SP. ATK	▰▰▰▰▰▰▱
SP. DEF	▰▰▰▰▱
SPEED	▰▱

DAMAGE TAKEN IN BATTLES

⬡	×1	🪶	×1
🔥	×0.5	🌀	×0.5
💧	×0.5	🐛	×2
🌿	×2	✦	×1
⚡	×2	👻	×2
❄	×0.5	🐉	×1
👊	×0.5	◐	×2
☠	×1	⭕	×0.5
⛰	×1	✹	×1

⬤ **REQUIRED MEGA STONE:
SLOWBRONITE**

Buy it from a seller who appears at
the Pokémon League once you have
become Champion (p. 103).

Magnemite

MAGNEMITE ⟨081⟩

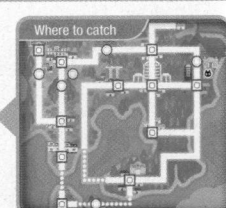

— | Gender unknown

SPECIES STRENGTHS

HP	■■
ATTACK	■■■
DEFENSE	■■■■
SP. ATK	■■■■■
SP. DEF	■■■
SPEED	■■

DAMAGE TAKEN IN BATTLES

×0.5		×0.25	
×2		×0.5	
×1		×0.5	
×0.5		×0.5	
×0.5		×1	
×0.5		×0.5	
×2		×1	
×0		×0.25	
×4		×0.5	

POKÉDEX ENTRY

It is hatched with the ability to defy gravity. It floats while emitting powerful electromagnetic waves.

MAIN WAY TO OBTAIN

Catch one when it appears in the Power Plant.

Where to catch

EVOLUTION

Lv. 30
→ → →

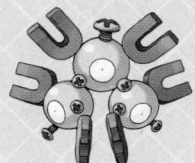

Magnemite   Magneton

LEVEL-UP MOVES

LV.	NAME	TYPE	KIND	POW.	ACC.	PP	RANGE
1	Supersonic	Normal	Status	—	55	20	Normal
1	Tackle	Normal	Physical	40	100	35	Normal
5	Thunder Shock	Electric	Special	40	100	30	Normal
10	Thunder Wave	Electric	Status	—	90	20	Normal
15	Sonic Boom	Normal	Special	—	90	20	Normal
20	Light Screen	Psychic	Status	—	—	30	Your Side
26	Thunderbolt	Electric	Special	90	100	15	Normal
32	Screech	Normal	Status	—	85	40	Normal
38	Flash Cannon	Steel	Special	80	100	10	Normal
44	Thunder	Electric	Special	110	70	10	Normal

TM MOVES

NO.	NAME	TYPE	KIND	POW.	ACC.	PP	RANGE
TM01	Headbutt	Normal	Physical	70	100	15	Normal
TM04	Teleport	Psychic	Status	—	—	20	Self
TM05	Rest	Psychic	Status	—	—	10	Self
TM06	Light Screen	Psychic	Status	—	—	30	Your Side
TM07	Protect	Normal	Status	—	—	10	Self
TM08	Substitute	Normal	Status	—	—	10	Self
TM09	Reflect	Psychic	Status	—	—	20	Your Side
TM12	Facade	Normal	Physical	70	100	20	Normal
TM16	Thunder Wave	Electric	Status	—	90	20	Normal
TM27	Toxic	Poison	Status	—	90	10	Normal
TM36	Thunderbolt	Electric	Special	90	100	15	Normal
TM38	Thunder	Electric	Special	110	70	10	Normal
TM54	Flash Cannon	Steel	Special	80	100	10	Normal

EVOLUTION MOVES

NAME	TYPE	KIND	POW.	ACC.	PP	RANGE

POKÉMON EXPRESSIONS

HAPPY

UNHAPPY

ATTACKING

Magneton

— | Gender unknown

SPECIES STRENGTHS

HP ▮▮
ATTACK ▮▮▮
DEFENSE ▮▮▮▮▮▮
SP. ATK ▮▮▮▮▮▮▮▮
SP. DEF ▮▮▮▮
SPEED ▮▮▮▮

DAMAGE TAKEN IN BATTLES

◉ ×0.5		🍃 ×0.25
🔥 ×2		◎ ×0.5
💧 ×1		🌼 ×0.5
⚡ ×0.5		🗡 ×0.5
❄ ×0.5		☯ ×1
❄ ×0.5		🌙 ×0.5
🥊 ×2		🌑 ×1
☁ ×0		⬤ ×0.25
🪨 ×4		✦ ×0.5

POKÉDEX ENTRY

Generates strange radio signals. It raises the temperature by 3.6 degrees Fahrenheit within 3,300 feet.

MAIN WAY TO OBTAIN

Catch one when it appears in the Power Plant. Or obtain a Magnemite, then level it up to Lv. 30 or higher to evolve it into Magneton.

Where to catch

EVOLUTION

Magnemite — Lv. 30 →→→ **Magneton**

POKÉMON EXPRESSIONS

HAPPY

UNHAPPY

ATTACKING

LEVEL-UP MOVES

LV.	NAME	TYPE	KIND	POW.	ACC.	PP	RANGE
1	Supersonic	Normal	Status	—	55	20	Normal
1	Tackle	Normal	Physical	40	100	35	Normal
1	Thunder Shock	Electric	Special	40	100	30	Normal
1	Thunder Wave	Electric	Status	—	90	20	Normal
1	Tri Attack	Normal	Special	80	100	10	Normal
5	Thunder Shock	Electric	Special	40	100	30	Normal
10	Thunder Wave	Electric	Status	—	90	20	Normal
15	Sonic Boom	Normal	Special	—	90	20	Normal
20	Light Screen	Psychic	Status	—	—	30	Your Side
26	Thunderbolt	Electric	Special	90	100	15	Normal
36	Screech	Normal	Status	—	85	40	Normal
46	Flash Cannon	Steel	Special	80	100	10	Normal
56	Thunder	Electric	Special	110	70	10	Normal

TM MOVES

NO.	NAME	TYPE	KIND	POW.	ACC.	PP	RANGE
TM01	Headbutt	Normal	Physical	70	100	15	Normal
TM04	Teleport	Psychic	Status	—	—	20	Self
TM05	Rest	Psychic	Status	—	—	10	Self
TM06	Light Screen	Psychic	Status	—	—	30	Your Side
TM07	Protect	Normal	Status	—	—	10	Self
TM08	Substitute	Normal	Status	—	—	10	Self
TM09	Reflect	Psychic	Status	—	—	20	Your Side
TM12	Facade	Normal	Physical	70	100	20	Normal
TM16	Thunder Wave	Electric	Status	—	90	20	Normal
TM27	Toxic	Poison	Status	—	90	10	Normal
TM28	Tri Attack	Normal	Special	80	100	10	Normal
TM36	Thunderbolt	Electric	Special	90	100	15	Normal
TM38	Thunder	Electric	Special	110	70	10	Normal
TM48	Hyper Beam	Normal	Special	150	90	5	Normal
TM54	Flash Cannon	Steel	Special	80	100	10	Normal

EVOLUTION MOVES

NAME	TYPE	KIND	POW.	ACC.	PP	RANGE
Tri Attack	Normal	Special	80	100	10	Normal

Farfetch'd

FARFETCH'D 083

♂ ♀ | Same form for male/female

SPECIES STRENGTHS

HP	
ATTACK	
DEFENSE	
SP. ATK	
SP. DEF	
SPEED	

DAMAGE TAKEN IN BATTLES

⬤	×1	💧	×1
🔥	×1	◎	×1
💧	×1	✴	×0.5
🍃	×0.5	🌀	×2
✊	×2	👁	×0
❄	×2	⬤	×1
🔩	×1	☾	×1
⬤	×1	⬤	×1
🔔	×0	✦	×1

POKÉDEX ENTRY

They live where reedy plants grow. Farfetch'd are rarely seen, so it's thought their numbers are decreasing.

MAIN WAY TO OBTAIN

Catch one when it appears on Route 12 or Route 13.

Where to catch

EVOLUTION

(DOES NOT EVOLVE)

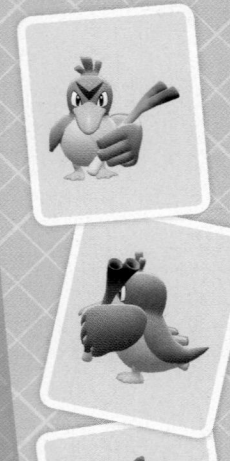

LEVEL-UP MOVES

LV.	NAME	TYPE	KIND	POW.	ACC.	PP	RANGE
1	Feint	Normal	Physical	30	100	10	Normal
1	Leer	Normal	Status	—	100	30	Many Others
1	Mirror Move	Flying	Status	—	—	20	Normal
1	Peck	Flying	Physical	35	100	35	Normal
1	Poison Jab	Poison	Physical	80	100	20	Normal
1	Quick Attack	Normal	Physical	40	100	30	Normal
1	Sand Attack	Ground	Status	—	100	15	Normal
4	Focus Energy	Normal	Status	—	—	30	Self
9	Cut	Normal	Physical	50	95	30	Normal
13	Razor Leaf	Grass	Physical	55	95	25	Many Others
18	Fury Attack	Normal	Physical	15	85	20	Normal
22	Agility	Psychic	Status	—	—	30	Self
27	Slash	Normal	Physical	70	100	20	Normal
31	Air Slash	Flying	Special	75	95	15	Normal
36	Swords Dance	Normal	Status	—	—	20	Self
40	Sky Attack	Flying	Physical	200	90	5	Normal

TM MOVES

NO.	NAME	TYPE	KIND	POW.	ACC.	PP	RANGE
TM01	Headbutt	Normal	Physical	70	100	15	Normal
TM03	Helping Hand	Normal	Status	—	—	20	1 Ally
TM05	Rest	Psychic	Status	—	—	10	Self
TM07	Protect	Normal	Status	—	—	10	Self
TM08	Substitute	Normal	Status	—	—	10	Self
TM09	Reflect	Psychic	Status	—	—	20	Your Side
TM12	Facade	Normal	Physical	70	100	20	Normal
TM14	Fly	Flying	Physical	90	95	15	Normal
TM18	U-turn	Bug	Physical	70	100	20	Normal
TM19	Iron Tail	Steel	Physical	100	75	15	Normal
TM26	Poison Jab	Poison	Physical	80	100	20	Normal
TM27	Toxic	Poison	Status	—	90	10	Normal
TM50	Roost	Flying	Status	—	—	10	Self

EVOLUTION MOVES

NAME	TYPE	KIND	POW.	ACC.	PP	RANGE

POKÉMON EXPRESSIONS

HAPPY

UNHAPPY

ATTACKING

Doduo

♂ ♀ | The female has beige necks, while the male has black necks.

 ♂    ♀

SPECIES STRENGTHS

HP	
ATTACK	
DEFENSE	
SP. ATK	
SP. DEF	
SPEED	

DAMAGE TAKEN IN BATTLES

◎	×1	🌀	×1
🔥	×1	◉	×1
💧	×1	🍃	×0.5
⚡	×0.5	✨	×2
🌿	×2	👁	×0
❄	×2	🐉	×1
👊	×1	🌙	×1
☠	×1	⬡	×1
⛰	×0	✦	×1

POKÉDEX ENTRY

Its short wings make flying difficult. Instead, this Pokémon runs at high speed on developed legs.

MAIN WAY TO OBTAIN

Catch one when it appears on Route 16, Route 17, or Route 18 (East).

Where to catch

EVOLUTION

   Lv. 31
→→→

Doduo   **Dodrio**

POKÉMON EXPRESSIONS

HAPPY

UNHAPPY

ATTACKING

LEVEL-UP MOVES

LV.	NAME	TYPE	KIND	POW.	ACC.	PP	RANGE
1	Growl	Normal	Status	—	100	40	Many Others
1	Peck	Flying	Physical	35	100	35	Normal
5	Quick Attack	Normal	Physical	40	100	30	Normal
10	Rage	Normal	Physical	20	100	20	Normal
16	Fury Attack	Normal	Physical	15	85	20	Normal
22	Agility	Psychic	Status	—	—	30	Self
27	Drill Peck	Flying	Physical	80	100	20	Normal
32	Swords Dance	Normal	Status	—	—	20	Self
38	Jump Kick	Fighting	Physical	100	95	10	Normal
44	Thrash	Normal	Physical	120	100	10	1 Random

TM MOVES

NO.	NAME	TYPE	KIND	POW.	ACC.	PP	RANGE
TM01	Headbutt	Normal	Physical	70	100	15	Normal
TM05	Rest	Psychic	Status	—	—	10	Self
TM07	Protect	Normal	Status	—	—	10	Self
TM08	Substitute	Normal	Status	—	—	10	Self
TM09	Reflect	Psychic	Status	—	—	20	Your Side
TM12	Facade	Normal	Physical	70	100	20	Normal
TM14	Fly	Flying	Physical	90	95	15	Normal
TM27	Toxic	Poison	Status	—	90	10	Normal
TM50	Roost	Flying	Status	—	—	10	Self

EVOLUTION MOVES

NAME	TYPE	KIND	POW.	ACC.	PP	RANGE

Triple Bird Pokémon   Average height: 5'11"   Average weight: 187.8 lbs.

Dodrio

♂ ♀ | The female has beige necks, while the male has black necks.

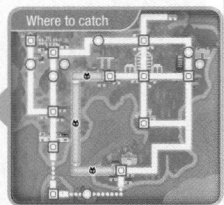

♂ ♀

SPECIES STRENGTHS

HP	▪▪▪
ATTACK	▪▪▪▪▪▪
DEFENSE	▪▪▪▪
SP. ATK	▪▪▪
SP. DEF	▪▪▪
SPEED	▪▪▪▪▪▪

DAMAGE TAKEN IN BATTLES

×1		×1	
×1		×1	
×1		×0.5	
×0.5		×2	
×2		×0	
×2		×1	
×1		×1	
×1		×1	
×0		×1	

POKÉDEX ENTRY

One of Doduo's two heads splits to form a unique species. It runs close to 40 mph in prairies.

MAIN WAY TO OBTAIN

Catch one when it appears on Route 16 or Route 17, or more commonly on Route 18 (East). Or obtain a Doduo, then level it up to Lv. 31 or higher to evolve it into Dodrio.

Where to catch

EVOLUTION

Lv. 31
→ → →

Doduo   **Dodrio**

LEVEL-UP MOVES

LV.	NAME	TYPE	KIND	POW.	ACC.	PP	RANGE
1	Growl	Normal	Status	—	100	40	Many Others
1	Mirror Move	Flying	Status	—	—	20	Normal
1	Peck	Flying	Physical	35	100	35	Normal
1	Quick Attack	Normal	Physical	40	100	30	Normal
1	Rage	Normal	Physical	20	100	20	Normal
1	Supersonic	Normal	Status	—	55	20	Normal
1	Tri Attack	Normal	Special	80	100	10	Normal
5	Quick Attack	Normal	Physical	40	100	30	Normal
10	Rage	Normal	Physical	20	100	20	Normal
16	Fury Attack	Normal	Physical	15	85	20	Normal
22	Agility	Psychic	Status	—	—	30	Self
27	Drill Peck	Flying	Physical	80	100	20	Normal
37	Swords Dance	Normal	Status	—	—	20	Self
48	Jump Kick	Fighting	Physical	100	95	10	Normal
59	Thrash	Normal	Physical	120	100	10	1 Random

TM MOVES

NO.	NAME	TYPE	KIND	POW.	ACC.	PP	RANGE
TM01	Headbutt	Normal	Physical	70	100	15	Normal
TM02	Taunt	Dark	Status	—	100	20	Normal
TM05	Rest	Psychic	Status	—	—	10	Self
TM07	Protect	Normal	Status	—	—	10	Self
TM08	Substitute	Normal	Status	—	—	10	Self
TM09	Reflect	Psychic	Status	—	—	20	Your Side
TM12	Facade	Normal	Physical	70	100	20	Normal
TM14	Fly	Flying	Physical	90	95	15	Normal
TM27	Toxic	Poison	Status	—	90	10	Normal
TM28	Tri Attack	Normal	Special	80	100	10	Normal
TM48	Hyper Beam	Normal	Special	150	90	5	Normal
TM50	Roost	Flying	Status	—	—	10	Self

EVOLUTION MOVES

NAME	TYPE	KIND	POW.	ACC.	PP	RANGE
Tri Attack	Normal	Special	80	100	10	Normal

Seel

♂ ♀ | Same form for male/female

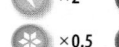

SPECIES STRENGTHS

HP	▨▨
ATTACK	▨▨
DEFENSE	▨▨▨
SP. ATK	▨▨
SP. DEF	▨▨▨
SPEED	▨▨

DAMAGE TAKEN IN BATTLES

◉	×1	🕊	×1
🔥	×0.5	🌀	×1
💧	×0.5	🍃	×1
⚡	×2	🌿	×1
🌱	×2	🌑	×1
❄	×0.5	✊	×1
👊	×1	🌙	×1
☠	×1	⚙	×0.5
⛰	×1	✦	×1

POKÉDEX ENTRY

Loves freezing-cold conditions. Relishes swimming in a frigid climate of around 14 degrees Fahrenheit.

MAIN WAY TO OBTAIN

Catch one when it appears in the Seafoam Islands.

Where to catch

EVOLUTION

Seel

Lv. 34
→→→

Dewgong

POKÉMON EXPRESSIONS

HAPPY

UNHAPPY

ATTACKING

LEVEL-UP MOVES

LV.	NAME	TYPE	KIND	POW.	ACC.	PP	RANGE
1	Headbutt	Normal	Physical	70	100	15	Normal
4	Growl	Normal	Status	—	100	40	Many Others
8	Encore	Normal	Status	—	100	5	Normal
12	Aqua Jet	Water	Physical	40	100	20	Normal
16	Ice Shard	Ice	Physical	40	100	30	Normal
20	Rest	Psychic	Status	—	—	10	Self
26	Aurora Beam	Ice	Special	65	100	20	Normal
32	Waterfall	Water	Physical	80	100	15	Normal
38	Take Down	Normal	Physical	90	85	20	Normal
44	Ice Beam	Ice	Special	90	100	10	Normal
50	Double-Edge	Normal	Physical	120	100	15	Normal

TM MOVES

NO.	NAME	TYPE	KIND	POW.	ACC.	PP	RANGE
TM01	Headbutt	Normal	Physical	70	100	15	Normal
TM03	Helping Hand	Normal	Status	—	—	20	1 Ally
TM05	Rest	Psychic	Status	—	—	10	Self
TM07	Protect	Normal	Status	—	—	10	Self
TM08	Substitute	Normal	Status	—	—	10	Self
TM12	Facade	Normal	Physical	70	100	20	Normal
TM19	Iron Tail	Steel	Physical	100	75	15	Normal
TM25	Waterfall	Water	Physical	80	100	15	Normal
TM27	Toxic	Poison	Status	—	90	10	Normal
TM47	Surf	Water	Special	90	100	15	All Others
TM51	Blizzard	Ice	Special	110	70	5	Many Others
TM55	Ice Beam	Ice	Special	90	100	10	Normal
TM57	Pay Day	Normal	Physical	40	100	20	Normal
TM58	Drill Run	Ground	Physical	80	95	10	Normal
TM60	Megahorn	Bug	Physical	120	85	10	Normal

EVOLUTION MOVES

NAME	TYPE	KIND	POW.	ACC.	PP	RANGE

Sea Lion Pokémon   Average height: 5'07"   Average weight: 264.6 lbs.

Dewgong

♂ ♀ | Same form for male/female

SPECIES STRENGTHS

HP	▰▰▰▰▰▱
ATTACK	▰▰▰▰▱
DEFENSE	▰▰▰▰▱
SP. ATK	▰▰▰▰▱
SP. DEF	▰▰▰▰▰▱
SPEED	▰▰▰▰▱

DAMAGE TAKEN IN BATTLES

◎ ×1		🕊 ×1	
🔥 ×1		⊙ ×1	
💧 ×0.5		🍃 ×1	
🍃 ×2		⚔ ×2	
⚡ ×2		🌑 ×1	
❄ ×0.25		👊 ×1	
🪨 ×2		◐ ×1	
💬 ×1		◉ ×1	
🔔 ×1		✦ ×1	

POKÉDEX ENTRY

Its entire body is a snowy white. Unharmed by even intense cold, it swims powerfully in icy waters.

MAIN WAY TO OBTAIN

Catch one when it appears in the Seafoam Islands, especially on B4F. Or obtain a Seel, then level it up to Lv. 34 or higher to evolve it into Dewgong.

Where to catch

EVOLUTION

Seel   Lv. 34 →→→   **Dewgong**

LEVEL-UP MOVES

LV.	NAME	TYPE	KIND	POW.	ACC.	PP	RANGE
1	Aqua Jet	Water	Physical	40	100	20	Normal
1	Encore	Normal	Status	—	100	5	Normal
1	Fake Out	Normal	Physical	40	100	10	Normal
1	Growl	Normal	Status	—	100	40	Many Others
1	Headbutt	Normal	Physical	70	100	15	Normal
1	Horn Drill	Normal	Physical	—	30	5	Normal
4	Growl	Normal	Status	—	100	40	Many Others
8	Encore	Normal	Status	—	100	5	Normal
12	Aqua Jet	Water	Physical	40	100	20	Normal
15	Ice Shard	Ice	Physical	40	100	30	Normal
20	Rest	Psychic	Status	—	—	10	Self
26	Aurora Beam	Ice	Special	65	100	20	Normal
32	Waterfall	Water	Physical	80	100	15	Normal
42	Take Down	Normal	Physical	90	85	20	Normal
52	Ice Beam	Ice	Special	90	100	10	Normal
62	Double-Edge	Normal	Physical	120	100	15	Normal

TM MOVES

NO.	NAME	TYPE	KIND	POW.	ACC.	PP	RANGE
TM01	Headbutt	Normal	Physical	70	100	15	Normal
TM03	Helping Hand	Normal	Status	—	—	20	1 Ally
TM05	Rest	Psychic	Status	—	—	10	Self
TM07	Protect	Normal	Status	—	—	10	Self
TM08	Substitute	Normal	Status	—	—	10	Self
TM12	Facade	Normal	Physical	70	100	20	Normal
TM19	Iron Tail	Steel	Physical	100	75	15	Normal
TM25	Waterfall	Water	Physical	80	100	15	Normal
TM27	Toxic	Poison	Status	—	90	10	Normal
TM47	Surf	Water	Special	90	100	15	All Others
TM48	Hyper Beam	Normal	Special	150	90	5	Normal
TM51	Blizzard	Ice	Special	110	70	5	Many Others
TM55	Ice Beam	Ice	Special	90	100	10	Normal
TM57	Pay Day	Normal	Physical	40	100	20	Normal
TM58	Drill Run	Ground	Physical	80	95	10	Normal
TM60	Megahorn	Bug	Physical	120	85	10	Normal

EVOLUTION MOVES

NAME	TYPE	KIND	POW.	ACC.	PP	RANGE

POKÉMON EXPRESSIONS

HAPPY

UNHAPPY

ATTACKING

Grimer

♂ ♀ | Same form for male/female

SPECIES STRENGTHS

HP	▩▩▩▩
ATTACK	▩▩▩▩
DEFENSE	▩▩▩
SP. ATK	▩▩▩
SP. DEF	▩▩▩
SPEED	▩▩

DAMAGE TAKEN IN BATTLES

◎	×1	🍃	×1
🔥	×1	◉	×2
💧	×1	🍄	×0.5
⚡	×0.5	🗡	×1
⚡	×1	◐	×1
❄	×1	↻	×1
👊	×0.5	🌙	×1
☠	×0.5	◎	×1
⛰	×2	✦	×0.5

POKÉDEX ENTRY

Made of congealed sludge. It smells too putrid to touch. Even weeds won't grow in its path.

MAIN WAY TO OBTAIN

Catch one when it appears in the Power Plant or the Pokémon Mansion in *Pokémon: Let's Go, Pikachu!* Obtain one in a trade if you are playing *Pokémon: Let's Go, Eevee!*, as it does not appear in that game.

Where to catch

EVOLUTION

Lv. 38
→→→

Grimer **Muk**

POKÉMON EXPRESSIONS

HAPPY

UNHAPPY

ATTACKING

LEVEL-UP MOVES

LV.	NAME	TYPE	KIND	POW.	ACC.	PP	RANGE
1	Poison Gas	Poison	Status	—	90	40	Many Others
1	Pound	Normal	Physical	40	100	35	Normal
6	Harden	Normal	Status	—	—	30	Self
12	Minimize	Normal	Status	—	—	10	Self
18	Disable	Normal	Status	—	100	20	Normal
24	Sludge	Poison	Special	65	100	20	Normal
30	Screech	Normal	Status	—	85	40	Normal
36	Toxic	Poison	Status	—	90	10	Normal
42	Acid Armor	Poison	Status	—	—	20	Self
48	Sludge Bomb	Poison	Special	90	100	10	Normal

TM MOVES

NO.	NAME	TYPE	KIND	POW.	ACC.	PP	RANGE
TM01	Headbutt	Normal	Physical	70	100	15	Normal
TM02	Taunt	Dark	Status	—	100	20	Normal
TM03	Helping Hand	Normal	Status	—	—	20	1 Ally
TM05	Rest	Psychic	Status	—	—	10	Self
TM07	Protect	Normal	Status	—	—	10	Self
TM08	Substitute	Normal	Status	—	—	10	Self
TM10	Dig	Ground	Physical	80	100	10	Normal
TM12	Facade	Normal	Physical	70	100	20	Normal
TM22	Rock Slide	Rock	Physical	75	90	10	Many Others
TM23	Thunder Punch	Electric	Physical	75	100	15	Normal
TM26	Poison Jab	Poison	Physical	80	100	20	Normal
TM27	Toxic	Poison	Status	—	90	10	Normal
TM31	Fire Punch	Fire	Physical	75	100	15	Normal
TM35	Ice Punch	Ice	Physical	75	100	15	Normal
TM36	Thunderbolt	Electric	Special	90	100	15	Normal
TM37	Flamethrower	Fire	Special	90	100	15	Normal
TM38	Thunder	Electric	Special	110	70	10	Normal
TM42	Self-Destruct	Normal	Physical	200	100	5	All Others
TM43	Shadow Ball	Ghost	Special	80	100	15	Normal
TM46	Fire Blast	Fire	Special	110	85	5	Normal
TM52	Sludge Bomb	Poison	Special	90	100	10	Normal
TM53	Mega Drain	Grass	Special	75	100	10	Normal

EVOLUTION MOVES

NAME	TYPE	KIND	POW.	ACC.	PP	RANGE

Grimer

GRIMER
ALOLA FORM
088

ALOLA FORM

♂ ♀ | Same form for male/female

SPECIES STRENGTHS

HP	▬▬▬▬
ATTACK	▬▬▬▬
DEFENSE	▬▬
SP. ATK	▬▬
SP. DEF	▬▬
SPEED	▬

DAMAGE TAKEN IN BATTLES

⊙	×1	🪶	×1
🔥	×1	◎	×0
💧	×1	🌿	×1
⚡	×0.5	🧊	×1
👊	×1	☠	×0.5
❄	×1	🪨	×1
🧠	×1	◐	×0.5
👁	×0.5	⬡	×1
🌊	×2	✦	×1

POKÉDEX ENTRY

It has a passion for trash above all else, speedily digesting it and creating brilliant crystals of sparkling poison.

MAIN WAY TO OBTAIN

Trade a Grimer for one in the Pokémon Center on Cinnabar Island (p. 92) in *Pokémon: Let's Go, Pikachu!* Obtain one in a trade if you are playing *Pokémon: Let's Go, Eevee!*, as it does not appear in that game.

Where to catch
Habitat Unknown

EVOLUTION

Alolan Grimer — Lv. 38 →→→ — **Alolan Muk**

LEVEL-UP MOVES

LV.	NAME	TYPE	KIND	POW.	ACC.	PP	RANGE
1	Poison Gas	Poison	Status	—	90	40	Many Others
1	Pound	Normal	Physical	40	100	35	Normal
6	Harden	Normal	Status	—	—	30	Self
12	Minimize	Normal	Status	—	—	10	Self
18	Disable	Normal	Status	—	100	20	Normal
24	Bite	Dark	Physical	60	100	25	Normal
30	Screech	Normal	Status	—	85	40	Normal
36	Crunch	Dark	Physical	80	100	15	Normal
42	Acid Armor	Poison	Status	—	—	20	Self
48	Sludge Bomb	Poison	Special	90	100	10	Normal

TM MOVES

NO.	NAME	TYPE	KIND	POW.	ACC.	PP	RANGE
TM01	Headbutt	Normal	Physical	70	100	15	Normal
TM02	Taunt	Dark	Status	—	100	20	Normal
TM03	Helping Hand	Normal	Status	—	—	20	1 Ally
TM05	Rest	Psychic	Status	—	—	10	Self
TM07	Protect	Normal	Status	—	—	10	Self
TM08	Substitute	Normal	Status	—	—	10	Self
TM10	Dig	Ground	Physical	80	100	10	Normal
TM12	Facade	Normal	Physical	70	100	20	Normal
TM22	Rock Slide	Rock	Physical	75	90	10	Many Others
TM23	Thunder Punch	Electric	Physical	75	100	15	Normal
TM26	Poison Jab	Poison	Physical	80	100	20	Normal
TM27	Toxic	Poison	Status	—	90	10	Normal
TM31	Fire Punch	Fire	Physical	75	100	15	Normal
TM35	Ice Punch	Ice	Physical	75	100	15	Normal
TM37	Flamethrower	Fire	Special	90	100	15	Normal
TM42	Self-Destruct	Normal	Physical	200	100	5	All Others
TM43	Shadow Ball	Ghost	Special	80	100	15	Normal
TM46	Fire Blast	Fire	Special	110	85	5	Normal
TM52	Sludge Bomb	Poison	Special	90	100	10	Normal
TM53	Mega Drain	Grass	Special	75	100	10	Normal

EVOLUTION MOVES

NAME	TYPE	KIND	POW.	ACC.	PP	RANGE

POKÉMON EXPRESSIONS

HAPPY

UNHAPPY

ATTACKING

Muk

♂ ♀ | Same form for male/female

SPECIES STRENGTHS

HP	▪▪▪▪▪▪▫
ATTACK	▪▪▪▪▪▫
DEFENSE	▪▪▪▫▫
SP. ATK	▪▪▪▫
SP. DEF	▪▪▪▪▪▫
SPEED	▪▪▪

DAMAGE TAKEN IN BATTLES

◉ ×1		🍃 ×1	
🔥 ×1		◎ ×2	
💧 ×1		🌿 ×0.5	
⚡ ×0.5		👁 ×1	
🗡 ×1		👻 ×1	
❄ ×1		🐉 ×1	
👊 ×0.5		🌙 ×1	
💠 ×0.5		◉ ×1	
🪨 ×2		✦ ×0.5	

POKÉDEX ENTRY

Smells so awful, it can cause fainting. Through degeneration of its nose, it lost its sense of smell.

MAIN WAY TO OBTAIN

Catch one when it appears in the Power Plant or the Pokémon Mansion, especially on B1F, in *Pokémon: Let's Go, Pikachu!* Or obtain a Grimer, then level it up to Lv. 38 or higher to evolve it into Muk.

Where to catch

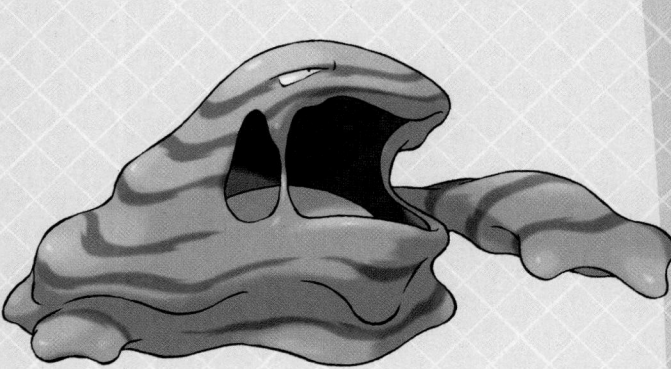

EVOLUTION

Grimer

Lv. 38
→→→

Muk

POKÉMON EXPRESSIONS

HAPPY

UNHAPPY

ATTACKING

LEVEL-UP MOVES

LV.	NAME	TYPE	KIND	POW.	ACC.	PP	RANGE
1	Harden	Normal	Status	—	—	30	Self
1	Haze	Ice	Status	—	—	30	Both Sides
1	Minimize	Normal	Status	—	—	10	Self
1	Moonblast	Fairy	Special	95	100	15	Normal
1	Poison Gas	Poison	Status	—	90	40	Many Others
1	Pound	Normal	Physical	40	100	35	Normal
6	Harden	Normal	Status	—	—	30	Self
12	Minimize	Normal	Status	—	—	10	Self
18	Disable	Normal	Status	—	100	20	Normal
24	Sludge	Poison	Special	65	100	20	Normal
30	Screech	Normal	Status	—	85	40	Normal
36	Toxic	Poison	Status	—	90	10	Normal
48	Acid Armor	Poison	Status	—	—	20	Self
60	Sludge Bomb	Poison	Special	90	100	10	Normal

TM MOVES

NO.	NAME	TYPE	KIND	POW.	ACC.	PP	RANGE
TM01	Headbutt	Normal	Physical	70	100	15	Normal
TM02	Taunt	Dark	Status	—	100	20	Normal
TM03	Helping Hand	Normal	Status	—	—	20	1 Ally
TM05	Rest	Psychic	Status	—	—	10	Self
TM07	Protect	Normal	Status	—	—	10	Self
TM08	Substitute	Normal	Status	—	—	10	Self
TM10	Dig	Ground	Physical	80	100	10	Normal
TM12	Facade	Normal	Physical	70	100	20	Normal
TM13	Brick Break	Fighting	Physical	75	100	15	Normal
TM20	Dark Pulse	Dark	Special	80	100	15	Normal
TM22	Rock Slide	Rock	Physical	75	90	10	Many Others
TM23	Thunder Punch	Electric	Physical	75	100	15	Normal
TM26	Poison Jab	Poison	Physical	80	100	20	Normal
TM27	Toxic	Poison	Status	—	90	10	Normal
TM31	Fire Punch	Fire	Physical	75	100	15	Normal
TM35	Ice Punch	Ice	Physical	75	100	15	Normal
TM36	Thunderbolt	Electric	Special	90	100	15	Normal
TM37	Flamethrower	Fire	Special	90	100	15	Normal
TM38	Thunder	Electric	Special	110	70	10	Normal
TM42	Self-Destruct	Normal	Physical	200	100	5	All Others
TM43	Shadow Ball	Ghost	Special	80	100	15	Normal
TM46	Fire Blast	Fire	Special	110	85	5	Normal
TM48	Hyper Beam	Normal	Special	150	90	5	Normal
TM52	Sludge Bomb	Poison	Special	90	100	10	Normal
TM53	Mega Drain	Grass	Special	75	100	10	Normal

EVOLUTION MOVES

NAME	TYPE	KIND	POW.	ACC.	PP	RANGE

089

MUK
ALOLA FORM

Muk

ALOLA FORM

♂ ♀ | Same form for male/female

SPECIES STRENGTHS

HP	▰▰▰▰▰▰▱
ATTACK	▰▰▰▰▰▰▱
DEFENSE	▰▰▰▱▱
SP. ATK	▰▰▰▱
SP. DEF	▰▰▰▰▰▰▱
SPEED	▰▰▱

DAMAGE TAKEN IN BATTLES

⊙	×1	🪶	×1
🔥	×1	⭕	×0
💧	×1	⚙	×1
🌿	×0.5	🔆	×1
⚡	×1	👁	×0.5
❄	×1	↻	×1
👊	×1	🌙	×0.5
☠	×0.5	◉	×1
⛰	×2	✦	×1

POKÉDEX ENTRY

Muk's coloration becomes increasingly vivid the more it feasts on its favorite dish—trash.

MAIN WAY TO OBTAIN

Obtain an Alolan Grimer, then level it up to Lv. 38 or higher to evolve it into Alolan Muk.

Where to catch

Habitat Unknown

EVOLUTION

Lv. 38
→→→

Alolan Grimer   **Alolan Muk**

LEVEL-UP MOVES

LV.	NAME	TYPE	KIND	POW.	ACC.	PP	RANGE
1	Harden	Normal	Status	—	—	30	Self
1	Haze	Ice	Status	—	—	30	Both Sides
1	Minimize	Normal	Status	—	—	10	Self
1	Moonblast	Fairy	Special	95	100	15	Normal
1	Poison Gas	Poison	Status	—	90	40	Many Others
1	Pound	Normal	Physical	40	100	35	Normal
6	Harden	Normal	Status	—	—	30	Self
12	Minimize	Normal	Status	—	—	10	Self
18	Disable	Normal	Status	—	100	20	Normal
24	Bite	Dark	Physical	60	100	25	Normal
30	Screech	Normal	Status	—	85	40	Normal
36	Crunch	Dark	Physical	80	100	15	Normal
48	Acid Armor	Poison	Status	—	—	20	Self
60	Sludge Bomb	Poison	Special	90	100	10	Normal

TM MOVES

NO.	NAME	TYPE	KIND	POW.	ACC.	PP	RANGE
TM01	Headbutt	Normal	Physical	70	100	15	Normal
TM02	Taunt	Dark	Status	—	100	20	Normal
TM03	Helping Hand	Normal	Status	—	—	20	1 Ally
TM05	Rest	Psychic	Status	—	—	10	Self
TM07	Protect	Normal	Status	—	—	10	Self
TM08	Substitute	Normal	Status	—	—	10	Self
TM10	Dig	Ground	Physical	80	100	10	Normal
TM12	Facade	Normal	Physical	70	100	20	Normal
TM13	Brick Break	Fighting	Physical	75	100	15	Normal
TM20	Dark Pulse	Dark	Special	80	100	15	Normal
TM21	Foul Play	Dark	Physical	95	100	15	Normal
TM22	Rock Slide	Rock	Physical	75	90	10	Many Others
TM23	Thunder Punch	Electric	Physical	75	100	15	Normal
TM26	Poison Jab	Poison	Physical	80	100	20	Normal
TM27	Toxic	Poison	Status	—	90	10	Normal
TM31	Fire Punch	Fire	Physical	75	100	15	Normal
TM35	Ice Punch	Ice	Physical	75	100	15	Normal
TM37	Flamethrower	Fire	Special	90	100	15	Normal
TM42	Self-Destruct	Normal	Physical	200	100	5	All Others
TM43	Shadow Ball	Ghost	Special	80	100	15	Normal
TM46	Fire Blast	Fire	Special	110	85	5	Normal
TM48	Hyper Beam	Normal	Special	150	90	5	Normal
TM52	Sludge Bomb	Poison	Special	90	100	10	Normal
TM53	Mega Drain	Grass	Special	75	100	10	Normal

EVOLUTION MOVES

NAME	TYPE	KIND	POW.	ACC.	PP	RANGE

POKÉMON EXPRESSIONS

HAPPY

UNHAPPY

ATTACKING

Shellder

♂ ♀ | Same form for male/female

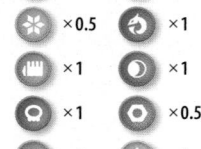

SPECIES STRENGTHS

HP	▰▰
ATTACK	▰▰▰
DEFENSE	▰▰▰▰▰▰
SP. ATK	▰▰▰
SP. DEF	▰▰
SPEED	▰▰▰

DAMAGE TAKEN IN BATTLES

⊙	×1	🌊	×1
🔥	×0.5	@	×1
💧	×0.5	⚙	×1
🍃	×2	⚔	×1
⚡	×2	◐	×1
❄	×0.5	↺	×1
👊	×1	☾	×1
☁	×1	◉	×0.5
🔺	×1	✦	×1

POKÉDEX ENTRY

The shell can withstand any attack. However, when it is open, the tender body is exposed.

MAIN WAY TO OBTAIN

Catch one when it appears in the Seafoam Islands (B3F or B4F).

Where to catch

EVOLUTION

Use Water Stone
→ → →

Shellder   Cloyster

POKÉMON EXPRESSIONS

HAPPY

UNHAPPY

ATTACKING

LEVEL-UP MOVES

LV.	NAME	TYPE	KIND	POW.	ACC.	PP	RANGE
1	Tackle	Normal	Physical	40	100	35	Normal
1	Water Gun	Water	Special	40	100	25	Normal
4	Withdraw	Water	Status	—	—	40	Self
9	Leer	Normal	Status	—	100	30	Many Others
13	Ice Shard	Ice	Physical	40	100	30	Normal
18	Supersonic	Normal	Status	—	55	20	Normal
22	Clamp	Water	Physical	35	85	15	Normal
27	Aurora Beam	Ice	Special	65	100	20	Normal
31	Protect	Normal	Status	—	—	10	Self
36	Ice Beam	Ice	Special	90	100	10	Normal
40	Shell Smash	Normal	Status	—	—	15	Self
45	Hydro Pump	Water	Special	110	80	5	Normal

TM MOVES

NO.	NAME	TYPE	KIND	POW.	ACC.	PP	RANGE
TM01	Headbutt	Normal	Physical	70	100	15	Normal
TM04	Teleport	Psychic	Status	—	—	20	Self
TM05	Rest	Psychic	Status	—	—	10	Self
TM07	Protect	Normal	Status	—	—	10	Self
TM08	Substitute	Normal	Status	—	—	10	Self
TM09	Reflect	Psychic	Status	—	—	20	Your Side
TM12	Facade	Normal	Physical	70	100	20	Normal
TM27	Toxic	Poison	Status	—	90	10	Normal
TM28	Tri Attack	Normal	Special	80	100	10	Normal
TM42	Self-Destruct	Normal	Physical	200	100	5	All Others
TM47	Surf	Water	Special	90	100	15	All Others
TM51	Blizzard	Ice	Special	110	70	5	Many Others
TM55	Ice Beam	Ice	Special	90	100	10	Normal

EVOLUTION MOVES

NAME	TYPE	KIND	POW.	ACC.	PP	RANGE

091 Bivalve Pokémon · Average height: 4'11" · Average weight: 292.1 lbs.

Cloyster

♂ ♀ | Same form for male/female

SPECIES STRENGTHS

HP	▮▮▮
ATTACK	▮▮▮▮▮
DEFENSE	▮▮▮▮▮▮▮▮▮▮
SP. ATK	▮▮▮▮▮
SP. DEF	▮▮▮
SPEED	▮▮▮▮▮

DAMAGE TAKEN IN BATTLES

×1		×1	
×1		×1	
×0.5		×1	
×2		×2	
×2		×1	
×0.25		×1	
×2		×1	
×1		×1	
×1		×1	

POKÉDEX ENTRY

For protection, it uses its harder-than-diamond shell. It also shoots spikes from the shell.

MAIN WAY TO OBTAIN

Catch one when it appears in the Seafoam Islands (B3F or B4F). Or obtain a Shellder, then use a Water Stone on it to evolve it into Cloyster.

Where to catch

EVOLUTION

Use Water Stone
→→→

Shellder → Cloyster

LEVEL-UP MOVES

LV.	NAME	TYPE	KIND	POW.	ACC.	PP	RANGE
1	Barrier	Psychic	Status	—	—	20	Self
1	Leer	Normal	Status	—	100	30	Many Others
1	Spike Cannon	Normal	Physical	20	100	15	Normal
1	Tackle	Normal	Physical	40	100	35	Normal
1	Twineedle	Bug	Physical	25	100	20	Normal
1	Water Gun	Water	Special	40	100	25	Normal
1	Withdraw	Water	Status	—	—	40	Self

TM MOVES

NO.	NAME	TYPE	KIND	POW.	ACC.	PP	RANGE
TM01	Headbutt	Normal	Physical	70	100	15	Normal
TM04	Teleport	Psychic	Status	—	—	20	Self
TM05	Rest	Psychic	Status	—	—	10	Self
TM07	Protect	Normal	Status	—	—	10	Self
TM08	Substitute	Normal	Status	—	—	10	Self
TM09	Reflect	Psychic	Status	—	—	20	Your Side
TM12	Facade	Normal	Physical	70	100	20	Normal
TM26	Poison Jab	Poison	Physical	80	100	20	Normal
TM27	Toxic	Poison	Status	—	90	10	Normal
TM28	Tri Attack	Normal	Special	80	100	10	Normal
TM42	Self-Destruct	Normal	Physical	200	100	5	All Others
TM47	Surf	Water	Special	90	100	15	All Others
TM48	Hyper Beam	Normal	Special	150	90	5	Normal
TM51	Blizzard	Ice	Special	110	70	5	Many Others
TM55	Ice Beam	Ice	Special	90	100	10	Normal

POKÉMON EXPRESSIONS

HAPPY

UNHAPPY

ATTACKING

EVOLUTION MOVES

NAME	TYPE	KIND	POW.	ACC.	PP	RANGE
Spike Cannon	Normal	Physical	20	100	15	Normal

Gastly

♂ ♀ | Same form for male/female

SPECIES STRENGTHS

HP	▮▮
ATTACK	▮▮▮
DEFENSE	▮▮
SP. ATK	▮▮▮▮▮▮
SP. DEF	▮▮▮
SPEED	▮▮▮▮▮

DAMAGE TAKEN IN BATTLES

◎	×0	✦	×1
🔥	×1	◉	×2
💧	×1	◉	×0.25
🌿	×0.5	◈	×1
⚡	×1	◉	×2
❄	×1	↻	×1
👊	×0	◑	×2
◉	×0.25	◎	×1
◣	×2	✷	×0.5

POKÉDEX ENTRY

Said to appear in decrepit, deserted buildings. It has no real shape, as it appears to be made of a gas.

MAIN WAY TO OBTAIN

Catch one when it appears in the Pokémon Tower (3F through 6F) once you have the Silph Scope.

Where to catch

EVOLUTION

Gastly

Lv. 25
→→→

Haunter

Trade Haunter
→→→

Gengar

POKÉMON EXPRESSIONS

HAPPY

UNHAPPY

ATTACKING

LEVEL-UP MOVES

LV.	NAME	TYPE	KIND	POW.	ACC.	PP	RANGE
1	Hypnosis	Psychic	Status	—	60	20	Normal
1	Lick	Ghost	Physical	30	100	30	Normal
1	Smog	Poison	Special	30	70	20	Normal
5	Confuse Ray	Ghost	Status	—	100	10	Normal
7	Poison Gas	Poison	Status	—	90	40	Many Others
12	Night Shade	Ghost	Special	—	100	15	Normal
14	Will-O-Wisp	Fire	Status	—	85	15	Normal
19	Sucker Punch	Dark	Physical	70	100	5	Normal
21	Toxic	Poison	Status	—	90	10	Normal
26	Shadow Ball	Ghost	Special	80	100	15	Normal
28	Dark Pulse	Dark	Special	80	100	15	Normal
33	Dream Eater	Psychic	Special	100	100	15	Normal

TM MOVES

NO.	NAME	TYPE	KIND	POW.	ACC.	PP	RANGE
TM01	Headbutt	Normal	Physical	70	100	15	Normal
TM02	Taunt	Dark	Status	—	100	20	Normal
TM05	Rest	Psychic	Status	—	—	10	Self
TM07	Protect	Normal	Status	—	—	10	Self
TM08	Substitute	Normal	Status	—	—	10	Self
TM11	Will-O-Wisp	Fire	Status	—	85	15	Normal
TM12	Facade	Normal	Physical	70	100	20	Normal
TM20	Dark Pulse	Dark	Special	80	100	15	Normal
TM21	Foul Play	Dark	Physical	95	100	15	Normal
TM23	Thunder Punch	Electric	Physical	75	100	15	Normal
TM27	Toxic	Poison	Status	—	90	10	Normal
TM31	Fire Punch	Fire	Physical	75	100	15	Normal
TM32	Dazzling Gleam	Fairy	Special	80	100	10	Many Others
TM35	Ice Punch	Ice	Physical	75	100	15	Normal
TM36	Thunderbolt	Electric	Special	90	100	15	Normal
TM38	Thunder	Electric	Special	110	70	10	Normal
TM40	Psychic	Psychic	Special	90	100	10	Normal
TM42	Self-Destruct	Normal	Physical	200	100	5	All Others
TM43	Shadow Ball	Ghost	Special	80	100	15	Normal
TM52	Sludge Bomb	Poison	Special	90	100	10	Normal
TM53	Mega Drain	Grass	Special	75	100	10	Normal
TM59	Dream Eater	Psychic	Special	100	100	15	Normal

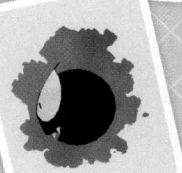

EVOLUTION MOVES

NAME	TYPE	KIND	POW.	ACC.	PP	RANGE

✓ **093** Gas Pokémon | Average height: 5'03" | Average weight: 0.2 lbs.

Haunter

♂ ♀ | Same form for male/female

SPECIES STRENGTHS

HP	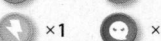
ATTACK	
DEFENSE	
SP. ATK	
SP. DEF	
SPEED	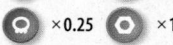

DAMAGE TAKEN IN BATTLES

◉	×0	🍃	×1
🔥	×1	🌀	×2
💧	×1	🪨	×0.25
🌿	×0.5	💠	×1
⚡	×1	👊	×2
❄	×1	🦅	×1
🐛	×0	🌙	×2
◐	×0.25	⚙	×1
🔺	×2	✦	×0.5

POKÉDEX ENTRY

By licking, it saps the victim's life. It causes shaking that won't stop until the victim's demise.

MAIN WAY TO OBTAIN

Catch one when it appears in the Pokémon Tower (3F through 6F, but most commonly on 6F) once you have the Silph Scope. Or obtain a Gastly, then level it up to Lv. 25 or higher to evolve it into Haunter.

Where to catch

EVOLUTION

Gastly — Lv. 25 →→→ **Haunter** — Trade Haunter →→→ **Gengar**

LEVEL-UP MOVES

LV.	NAME	TYPE	KIND	POW.	ACC.	PP	RANGE
1	Confuse Ray	Ghost	Status	—	100	10	Normal
1	Hypnosis	Psychic	Status	—	60	20	Normal
1	Lick	Ghost	Physical	30	100	30	Normal
1	Smog	Poison	Special	30	70	20	Normal
5	Confuse Ray	Ghost	Status	—	100	10	Normal
7	Poison Gas	Poison	Status	—	90	40	Many Others
12	Night Shade	Ghost	Special	—	100	15	Normal
14	Will-O-Wisp	Fire	Status	—	85	15	Normal
19	Sucker Punch	Dark	Physical	70	100	5	Normal
21	Toxic	Poison	Status	—	90	10	Normal
30	Shadow Ball	Ghost	Special	80	100	15	Normal
36	Dark Pulse	Dark	Special	80	100	15	Normal
45	Dream Eater	Psychic	Special	100	100	15	Normal

TM MOVES

NO.	NAME	TYPE	KIND	POW.	ACC.	PP	RANGE
TM01	Headbutt	Normal	Physical	70	100	15	Normal
TM02	Taunt	Dark	Status	—	100	20	Normal
TM05	Rest	Psychic	Status	—	—	10	Self
TM07	Protect	Normal	Status	—	—	10	Self
TM08	Substitute	Normal	Status	—	—	10	Self
TM11	Will-O-Wisp	Fire	Status	—	85	15	Normal
TM12	Facade	Normal	Physical	70	100	20	Normal
TM20	Dark Pulse	Dark	Special	80	100	15	Normal
TM21	Foul Play	Dark	Physical	95	100	15	Normal
TM23	Thunder Punch	Electric	Physical	75	100	15	Normal
TM26	Poison Jab	Poison	Physical	80	100	20	Normal
TM27	Toxic	Poison	Status	—	90	10	Normal
TM31	Fire Punch	Fire	Physical	75	100	15	Normal
TM32	Dazzling Gleam	Fairy	Special	80	100	10	Many Others
TM35	Ice Punch	Ice	Physical	75	100	15	Normal
TM36	Thunderbolt	Electric	Special	90	100	15	Normal
TM38	Thunder	Electric	Special	110	70	10	Normal
TM40	Psychic	Psychic	Special	90	100	10	Normal
TM42	Self-Destruct	Normal	Physical	200	100	5	All Others
TM43	Shadow Ball	Ghost	Special	80	100	15	Normal
TM52	Sludge Bomb	Poison	Special	90	100	10	Normal
TM53	Mega Drain	Grass	Special	75	100	10	Normal
TM59	Dream Eater	Psychic	Special	100	100	15	Normal

EVOLUTION MOVES

NAME	TYPE	KIND	POW.	ACC.	PP	RANGE

Gengar

♂ ♀ | Same form for male/female

SPECIES STRENGTHS

HP	▪▪▪
ATTACK	▪▪▪
DEFENSE	▪▪▪
SP. ATK	▪▪▪▪▪▪
SP. DEF	▪▪▪▪
SPEED	▪▪▪▪▪▪

DAMAGE TAKEN IN BATTLES

⊙	×0	🍃	×1
🔥	×1	◎	×2
💧	×1	⊕	×0.25
🌱	×0.5	🗡	×1
⚡	×1	👁	×2
❄	×1	🌀	×1
👊	×0	🌙	×2
☠	×0.25	⊙	×1
⛰	×2	✦	×0.5

POKÉDEX ENTRY

A Gengar is close by if you feel a sudden chill. It may be trying to lay a curse on you.

MAIN WAY TO OBTAIN

Receive a Haunter in a trade and it will immediately evolve into Gengar.

Where to catch

Habitat Unknown

EVOLUTION

Gastly	Lv. 25 → → → **Haunter**	Trade Haunter → → → **Gengar**

POKÉMON EXPRESSIONS

HAPPY

UNHAPPY

ATTACKING

LEVEL-UP MOVES

LV.	NAME	TYPE	KIND	POW.	ACC.	PP	RANGE
1	Confuse Ray	Ghost	Status	—	100	10	Normal
1	Disable	Normal	Status	—	100	20	Normal
1	Haze	Ice	Status	—	—	30	Both Sides
1	Hypnosis	Psychic	Status	—	60	20	Normal
1	Lick	Ghost	Physical	30	100	30	Normal
1	Smog	Poison	Special	30	70	20	Normal
5	Confuse Ray	Ghost	Status	—	100	10	Normal
7	Poison Gas	Poison	Status	—	90	40	Many Others
12	Night Shade	Ghost	Special	—	100	15	Normal
14	Will-O-Wisp	Fire	Status	—	85	15	Normal
19	Sucker Punch	Dark	Physical	70	100	5	Normal
21	Toxic	Poison	Status	—	90	10	Normal
30	Shadow Ball	Ghost	Special	80	100	15	Normal
36	Dark Pulse	Dark	Special	80	100	15	Normal
45	Dream Eater	Psychic	Special	100	100	15	Normal

TM MOVES

NO.	NAME	TYPE	KIND	POW.	ACC.	PP	RANGE
TM01	Headbutt	Normal	Physical	70	100	15	Normal
TM02	Taunt	Dark	Status	—	100	20	Normal
TM05	Rest	Psychic	Status	—	—	10	Self
TM07	Protect	Normal	Status	—	—	10	Self
TM08	Substitute	Normal	Status	—	—	10	Self
TM11	Will-O-Wisp	Fire	Status	—	85	15	Normal
TM12	Facade	Normal	Physical	70	100	20	Normal
TM13	Brick Break	Fighting	Physical	75	100	15	Normal
TM15	Seismic Toss	Fighting	Physical	—	100	20	Normal
TM20	Dark Pulse	Dark	Special	80	100	15	Normal
TM21	Foul Play	Dark	Physical	95	100	15	Normal
TM23	Thunder Punch	Electric	Physical	75	100	15	Normal
TM26	Poison Jab	Poison	Physical	80	100	20	Normal
TM27	Toxic	Poison	Status	—	90	10	Normal
TM31	Fire Punch	Fire	Physical	75	100	15	Normal
TM32	Dazzling Gleam	Fairy	Special	80	100	15	Many Others
TM35	Ice Punch	Ice	Physical	75	100	15	Normal
TM36	Thunderbolt	Electric	Special	90	100	15	Normal
TM38	Thunder	Electric	Special	110	70	10	Normal
TM40	Psychic	Psychic	Special	90	100	10	Normal
TM42	Self-Destruct	Normal	Physical	200	100	5	All Others
TM43	Shadow Ball	Ghost	Special	80	100	15	Normal
TM48	Hyper Beam	Normal	Special	150	90	5	Normal
TM52	Sludge Bomb	Poison	Special	90	100	10	Normal
TM53	Mega Drain	Grass	Special	75	100	10	Normal
TM59	Dream Eater	Psychic	Special	100	100	15	Normal

EVOLUTION MOVES

NAME	TYPE	KIND	POW.	ACC.	PP	RANGE

094 Shadow Pokémon · Average height: 4'07" · Average weight: 89.3 lbs.

Mega Gengar

MEGA EVOLUTION

Gengar

Buy a Gengarite, then Mega Evolve Gengar during battle.

Mega Gengar

SPECIES STRENGTHS

HP	
ATTACK	
DEFENSE	
SP. ATK	
SP. DEF	
SPEED	

DAMAGE TAKEN IN BATTLES

⊙	×0	🌀	×1
🔥	×1	🌪	×2
💧	×1	⚪	×0.25
🍃	×0.5	🗡	×1
⚡	×1	🔵	×2
❄	×1	🔆	×1
👊	×0	🌙	×2
☠	×0.25	⊙	×1
⛰	×2	✦	×0.5

REQUIRED MEGA STONE: GENGARITE

Buy it from a seller who appears at the Pokémon League once you have become Champion (p. 103).

Onix

♂ ♀ | Same form for male/female

SPECIES STRENGTHS

HP	▪▪▪
ATTACK	▪▪▪
DEFENSE	▪▪▪▪▪▪▪▪
SP. ATK	▪▪
SP. DEF	▪▪▪
SPEED	▪▪▪▪

DAMAGE TAKEN IN BATTLES

◎	×0.5	🍃	×0.5
🔥	×0.5	◉	×1
💧	×4	🌟	×1
🌿	×4	🦋	×0.5
⚡	×0	👊	×1
❄	×2	🌀	×1
👊	×2	🌙	×1
◯	×0.25	◉	×2
🔺	×2	✦	×1

POKÉDEX ENTRY

Burrows at high speed in search of food. The tunnels it leaves are used as homes by Diglett.

MAIN WAY TO OBTAIN

Catch one when it appears in Mt. Moon, or more commonly in the Rock Tunnel or on Victory Road.

Where to catch

EVOLUTION

(DOES NOT EVOLVE)

LEVEL-UP MOVES

LV.	NAME	TYPE	KIND	POW.	ACC.	PP	RANGE
1	Bind	Normal	Physical	15	85	20	Normal
1	Harden	Normal	Status	—	—	30	Self
1	Rock Throw	Rock	Physical	50	90	15	Normal
1	Tackle	Normal	Physical	40	100	35	Normal
5	Stealth Rock	Rock	Status	—	—	20	Other Side
10	Rage	Normal	Physical	20	100	20	Normal
15	Screech	Normal	Status	—	85	40	Normal
20	Dig	Ground	Physical	80	100	10	Normal
25	Slam	Normal	Physical	80	75	20	Normal
30	Rock Slide	Rock	Physical	75	90	10	Many Others
35	Earthquake	Ground	Physical	100	100	10	All Others
40	Iron Tail	Steel	Physical	100	75	15	Normal
45	Double-Edge	Normal	Physical	120	100	15	Normal

TM MOVES

NO.	NAME	TYPE	KIND	POW.	ACC.	PP	RANGE
TM01	Headbutt	Normal	Physical	70	100	15	Normal
TM02	Taunt	Dark	Status	—	100	20	Normal
TM05	Rest	Psychic	Status	—	—	10	Self
TM07	Protect	Normal	Status	—	—	10	Self
TM08	Substitute	Normal	Status	—	—	10	Self
TM10	Dig	Ground	Physical	80	100	10	Normal
TM12	Facade	Normal	Physical	70	100	20	Normal
TM17	Dragon Tail	Dragon	Physical	60	90	10	Normal
TM19	Iron Tail	Steel	Physical	100	75	15	Normal
TM22	Rock Slide	Rock	Physical	75	90	10	Many Others
TM27	Toxic	Poison	Status	—	90	10	Normal
TM34	Dragon Pulse	Dragon	Special	85	100	10	Normal
TM41	Earthquake	Ground	Physical	100	100	10	All Others
TM42	Self-Destruct	Normal	Physical	200	100	5	All Others
TM54	Flash Cannon	Steel	Special	80	100	10	Normal
TM56	Stealth Rock	Rock	Status	—	—	20	Other Side

EVOLUTION MOVES

NAME	TYPE	KIND	POW.	ACC.	PP	RANGE

Drowzee

DROWZEE 096

♂ ♀ | Same form for male/female

SPECIES STRENGTHS

HP	▰▰▰
ATTACK	▰▰▰
DEFENSE	▰▰▰
SP. ATK	▰▰▰
SP. DEF	▰▰▰▰▰
SPEED	▰▰▰

DAMAGE TAKEN IN BATTLES

◉ ×1		🪶 ×1
🔥 ×1		💧 ×0.5
💧 ×1		⚡ ×2
🍃 ×1		⚔ ×1
🌀 ×1		☠ ×2
❄ ×1		🪨 ×1
🥊 ×0.5		🌙 ×2
👁 ×1		⬤ ×1
🔺 ×1		✦ ×1

POKÉDEX ENTRY

If you sleep by it all the time, it will sometimes show you dreams it had eaten in the past.

MAIN WAY TO OBTAIN

Catch one when it appears on Route 11.

Where to catch

EVOLUTION

Lv. 26
→→→

Drowzee   Hypno

LEVEL-UP MOVES

LV.	NAME	TYPE	KIND	POW.	ACC.	PP	RANGE
1	Hypnosis	Psychic	Status	—	60	20	Normal
1	Pound	Normal	Physical	40	100	35	Normal
4	Disable	Normal	Status	—	100	20	Normal
9	Confusion	Psychic	Special	50	100	25	Normal
13	Poison Gas	Poison	Status	—	90	40	Many Others
18	Meditate	Psychic	Status	—	—	40	Self
22	Psybeam	Psychic	Special	65	100	20	Normal
27	Headbutt	Normal	Physical	70	100	15	Normal
31	Psychic	Psychic	Special	90	100	10	Normal
36	Nasty Plot	Dark	Status	—	—	20	Self
40	Dream Eater	Psychic	Special	100	100	15	Normal

TM MOVES

NO.	NAME	TYPE	KIND	POW.	ACC.	PP	RANGE
TM01	Headbutt	Normal	Physical	70	100	15	Normal
TM02	Taunt	Dark	Status	—	100	20	Normal
TM04	Teleport	Psychic	Status	—	—	20	Self
TM05	Rest	Psychic	Status	—	—	10	Self
TM06	Light Screen	Psychic	Status	—	—	30	Your Side
TM07	Protect	Normal	Status	—	—	10	Self
TM08	Substitute	Normal	Status	—	—	10	Self
TM09	Reflect	Psychic	Status	—	—	20	Your Side
TM12	Facade	Normal	Physical	70	100	20	Normal
TM13	Brick Break	Fighting	Physical	75	100	15	Normal
TM15	Seismic Toss	Fighting	Physical	—	100	20	Normal
TM16	Thunder Wave	Electric	Status	—	90	20	Normal
TM21	Foul Play	Dark	Physical	95	100	15	Normal
TM23	Thunder Punch	Electric	Physical	75	100	15	Normal
TM27	Toxic	Poison	Status	—	90	10	Normal
TM28	Tri Attack	Normal	Special	80	100	10	Normal
TM31	Fire Punch	Fire	Physical	75	100	15	Normal
TM32	Dazzling Gleam	Fairy	Special	80	100	10	Many Others
TM33	Calm Mind	Psychic	Status	—	—	20	Self
TM35	Ice Punch	Ice	Physical	75	100	15	Normal
TM40	Psychic	Psychic	Special	90	100	10	Normal
TM43	Shadow Ball	Ghost	Special	80	100	15	Normal
TM59	Dream Eater	Psychic	Special	100	100	15	Normal

EVOLUTION MOVES

NAME	TYPE	KIND	POW.	ACC.	PP	RANGE

POKÉMON EXPRESSIONS

HAPPY

UNHAPPY

ATTACKING

Hypno

♂ ♀ | The fur around the female's neck is longer than the fur around the male's neck.

 ♂  ♀

SPECIES STRENGTHS

HP	▰▰▰▱▱
ATTACK	▰▰▰▱▱
DEFENSE	▰▰▰▱▱
SP. ATK	▰▰▰▱▱
SP. DEF	▰▰▰▰▰▰
SPEED	▰▰▱▱▱

DAMAGE TAKEN IN BATTLES

⬡	×1	🪽	×1
🔥	×1	⚪	×0.5
💧	×1	🖐	×2
🍃	×1	🗡	×1
⚡	×1	●	×2
❄	×1	🌀	×1
💨	×0.5	🌑	×2
⬢	×1	⚙	×1
🪨	×1	✦	×1

POKÉDEX ENTRY

Avoid eye contact if you come across one. It will try to put you to sleep by using its pendulum.

MAIN WAY TO OBTAIN

Obtain a Drowzee, then level it up to Lv. 26 or higher to evolve it into Hypno.

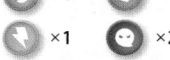

Where to catch

Habitat Unknown

EVOLUTION

Drowzee   Lv. 26 →→→   **Hypno**

POKÉMON EXPRESSIONS

HAPPY

UNHAPPY

ATTACKING

LEVEL-UP MOVES

LV.	NAME	TYPE	KIND	POW.	ACC.	PP	RANGE
1	Barrier	Psychic	Status	—	—	20	Self
1	Confusion	Psychic	Special	50	100	25	Normal
1	Disable	Normal	Status	—	100	20	Normal
1	Hypnosis	Psychic	Status	—	60	20	Normal
1	Pound	Normal	Physical	40	100	35	Normal
4	Disable	Normal	Status	—	100	20	Normal
9	Confusion	Psychic	Special	50	100	25	Normal
13	Poison Gas	Poison	Status	—	90	40	Many Others
18	Meditate	Psychic	Status	—	—	40	Self
22	Psybeam	Psychic	Special	65	100	20	Normal
27	Headbutt	Normal	Physical	70	100	15	Normal
36	Psychic	Psychic	Special	90	100	10	Normal
46	Nasty Plot	Dark	Status	—	—	20	Self
55	Dream Eater	Psychic	Special	100	100	15	Normal

TM MOVES

NO.	NAME	TYPE	KIND	POW.	ACC.	PP	RANGE
TM01	Headbutt	Normal	Physical	70	100	15	Normal
TM02	Taunt	Dark	Status	—	100	20	Normal
TM04	Teleport	Psychic	Status	—	—	20	Self
TM05	Rest	Psychic	Status	—	—	10	Self
TM06	Light Screen	Psychic	Status	—	—	30	Your Side
TM07	Protect	Normal	Status	—	—	10	Self
TM08	Substitute	Normal	Status	—	—	10	Self
TM09	Reflect	Psychic	Status	—	—	20	Your Side
TM12	Facade	Normal	Physical	70	100	20	Normal
TM13	Brick Break	Fighting	Physical	75	100	15	Normal
TM15	Seismic Toss	Fighting	Physical	—	100	20	Normal
TM16	Thunder Wave	Electric	Status	—	90	20	Normal
TM21	Foul Play	Dark	Physical	95	100	15	Normal
TM23	Thunder Punch	Electric	Physical	75	100	15	Normal
TM27	Toxic	Poison	Status	—	90	10	Normal
TM28	Tri Attack	Normal	Special	80	100	10	Normal
TM31	Fire Punch	Fire	Physical	75	100	15	Normal
TM32	Dazzling Gleam	Fairy	Special	80	100	10	Many Others
TM33	Calm Mind	Psychic	Status	—	—	20	Self
TM35	Ice Punch	Ice	Physical	75	100	15	Normal
TM40	Psychic	Psychic	Special	90	100	10	Normal
TM43	Shadow Ball	Ghost	Special	80	100	15	Normal
TM48	Hyper Beam	Normal	Special	150	90	5	Normal
TM59	Dream Eater	Psychic	Special	100	100	15	Normal

EVOLUTION MOVES

NAME	TYPE	KIND	POW.	ACC.	PP	RANGE

098 River Crab Pokémon Average height: 1'04" Average weight: 14.3 lbs.

Krabby

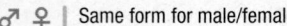

♂ ♀ | Same form for male/female

SPECIES STRENGTHS

HP	▇▇
ATTACK	▇▇▇▇▇▇
DEFENSE	▇▇▇▇▇
SP. ATK	▇▇
SP. DEF	▇▇
SPEED	▇▇▇

DAMAGE TAKEN IN BATTLES

◎	×1		×1
	×0.5		×1
	×0.5		×1
	×2		×1
	×2		×1
	×0.5		×1
	×1		×1
	×1		×0.5
	×1		×1

POKÉDEX ENTRY

Its pincers are superb weapons. They sometimes break off during battle, but they grow back fast.

MAIN WAY TO OBTAIN

Catch one when it appears on Route 10 (North), Route 12, or Route 13.

Where to catch

EVOLUTION

Lv. 28
→ → →

Krabby   **Kingler**

LEVEL-UP MOVES

LV.	NAME	TYPE	KIND	POW.	ACC.	PP	RANGE
1	Bubble	Water	Special	40	100	30	Many Others
5	Vice Grip	Normal	Physical	55	100	30	Normal
9	Leer	Normal	Status	—	100	30	Many Others
14	Harden	Normal	Status	—	—	30	Self
18	Bubble Beam	Water	Special	65	100	20	Normal
23	Stomp	Normal	Physical	65	100	20	Normal
27	Protect	Normal	Status	—	—	10	Self
32	Slam	Normal	Physical	80	75	20	Normal
36	Crabhammer	Water	Physical	100	90	10	Normal
41	Guillotine	Normal	Physical	—	30	5	Normal

TM MOVES

NO.	NAME	TYPE	KIND	POW.	ACC.	PP	RANGE
TM01	Headbutt	Normal	Physical	70	100	15	Normal
TM05	Rest	Psychic	Status	—	—	10	Self
TM07	Protect	Normal	Status	—	—	10	Self
TM08	Substitute	Normal	Status	—	—	10	Self
TM10	Dig	Ground	Physical	80	100	10	Normal
TM12	Facade	Normal	Physical	70	100	20	Normal
TM13	Brick Break	Fighting	Physical	75	100	15	Normal
TM22	Rock Slide	Rock	Physical	75	90	10	Many Others
TM24	X-Scissor	Bug	Physical	80	100	15	Normal
TM27	Toxic	Poison	Status	—	90	10	Normal
TM29	Scald	Water	Special	80	100	15	Normal
TM47	Surf	Water	Special	90	100	15	All Others
TM49	Superpower	Fighting	Physical	120	100	5	Normal
TM51	Blizzard	Ice	Special	110	70	5	Many Others
TM55	Ice Beam	Ice	Special	90	100	10	Normal

POKÉMON EXPRESSIONS

HAPPY

UNHAPPY

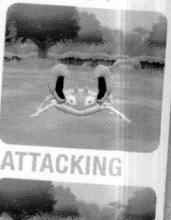

ATTACKING

EVOLUTION MOVES

NAME	TYPE	KIND	POW.	ACC.	PP	RANGE

Kingler

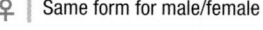

♂ ♀ | Same form for male/female

SPECIES STRENGTHS

HP	▮▮▮
ATTACK	▮▮▮▮▮▮▮
DEFENSE	▮▮▮▮▮▮▮
SP. ATK	▮▮▮
SP. DEF	▮▮▮
SPEED	▮▮▮▮▮

DAMAGE TAKEN IN BATTLES

◉ ×1		🍃 ×1
🔥 ×0.5		⊚ ×1
💧 ×0.5		🌱 ×1
⚡ ×2		◈ ×1
⚡ ×2		◑ ×1
❄ ×0.5		🌀 ×1
👊 ×1		☾ ×1
☁ ×1		◉ ×0.5
◢ ×1		⚙ ×1

POKÉDEX ENTRY

One claw grew massively
and is as hard as steel. It has
10,000-horsepower strength.
However, it is too heavy.

MAIN WAY TO OBTAIN

Catch one when it appears on
Route 12 or Route 13. Or obtain a
Krabby, then level it up to Lv. 28 or
higher to evolve it into Kingler.

Where to catch

EVOLUTION

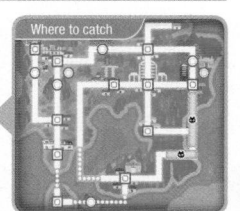

Lv. 28
→→→

Krabby	**Kingler**

POKÉMON EXPRESSIONS

HAPPY

UNHAPPY

ATTACKING

LEVEL-UP MOVES

LV.	NAME	TYPE	KIND	POW.	ACC.	PP	RANGE
1	Agility	Psychic	Status	—	—	30	Self
1	Amnesia	Psychic	Status	—	—	20	Self
1	Bubble	Water	Special	40	100	30	Many Others
1	Harden	Normal	Status	—	—	30	Self
1	Leer	Normal	Status	—	100	30	Many Others
1	Vice Grip	Normal	Physical	55	100	30	Normal
5	Vice Grip	Normal	Physical	55	100	30	Normal
9	Leer	Normal	Status	—	100	30	Many Others
14	Harden	Normal	Status	—	—	30	Self
18	Bubble Beam	Water	Special	65	100	20	Normal
23	Stomp	Normal	Physical	65	100	20	Normal
27	Protect	Normal	Status	—	—	10	Self
37	Slam	Normal	Physical	80	75	20	Normal
41	Crabhammer	Water	Physical	100	90	10	Normal
56	Guillotine	Normal	Physical	—	30	5	Normal

TM MOVES

NO.	NAME	TYPE	KIND	POW.	ACC.	PP	RANGE
TM01	Headbutt	Normal	Physical	70	100	15	Normal
TM05	Rest	Psychic	Status	—	—	10	Self
TM07	Protect	Normal	Status	—	—	10	Self
TM08	Substitute	Normal	Status	—	—	10	Self
TM10	Dig	Ground	Physical	80	100	10	Normal
TM12	Facade	Normal	Physical	70	100	20	Normal
TM13	Brick Break	Fighting	Physical	75	100	15	Normal
TM22	Rock Slide	Rock	Physical	75	90	10	Many Others
TM24	X-Scissor	Bug	Physical	80	100	15	Normal
TM27	Toxic	Poison	Status	—	90	10	Normal
TM29	Scald	Water	Special	80	100	15	Normal
TM47	Surf	Water	Special	90	100	15	All Others
TM48	Hyper Beam	Normal	Special	150	90	5	Normal
TM49	Superpower	Fighting	Physical	120	100	5	Normal
TM51	Blizzard	Ice	Special	110	70	5	Many Others
TM55	Ice Beam	Ice	Special	90	100	10	Normal

EVOLUTION MOVES

NAME	TYPE	KIND	POW.	ACC.	PP	RANGE

Voltorb

VOLTORB 100

— | Gender unknown

SPECIES STRENGTHS

HP	▪▪▪
ATTACK	▪▪
DEFENSE	▪▪▪
SP. ATK	▪▪▪▪
SP. DEF	▪▪▪▪
SPEED	▪▪▪▪▪▪

DAMAGE TAKEN IN BATTLES

×1		×0.5	
×1		×1	
×1		×1	
×1		×1	
×0.5		×1	
×1		×1	
×1		×1	
×1		×0.5	
×2		×1	

POKÉDEX ENTRY

It is said to camouflage itself as a Poké Ball. It will self-destruct with very little stimulus.

MAIN WAY TO OBTAIN

Catch one when it appears in the Power Plant.

Where to catch

EVOLUTION

Lv. 30
→→→

Voltorb   Electrode

LEVEL-UP MOVES

LV.	NAME	TYPE	KIND	POW.	ACC.	PP	RANGE
1	Tackle	Normal	Physical	40	100	35	Normal
3	Light Screen	Psychic	Status	—	—	30	Your Side
6	Sonic Boom	Normal	Special	—	90	20	Normal
9	Thunder Shock	Electric	Special	40	100	30	Normal
14	Swift	Normal	Special	60	—	20	Many Others
19	Self-Destruct	Normal	Physical	200	100	5	All Others
24	Screech	Normal	Status	—	85	40	Normal
31	Thunderbolt	Electric	Special	90	100	15	Normal
38	Mirror Coat	Psychic	Special	—	100	20	Varies
45	Explosion	Normal	Physical	250	100	5	All Others

TM MOVES

NO.	NAME	TYPE	KIND	POW.	ACC.	PP	RANGE
TM01	Headbutt	Normal	Physical	70	100	15	Normal
TM02	Taunt	Dark	Status	—	100	20	Normal
TM04	Teleport	Psychic	Status	—	—	20	Self
TM05	Rest	Psychic	Status	—	—	10	Self
TM06	Light Screen	Psychic	Status	—	—	30	Your Side
TM07	Protect	Normal	Status	—	—	10	Self
TM08	Substitute	Normal	Status	—	—	10	Self
TM09	Reflect	Psychic	Status	—	—	20	Your Side
TM12	Facade	Normal	Physical	70	100	20	Normal
TM16	Thunder Wave	Electric	Status	—	90	20	Normal
TM21	Foul Play	Dark	Physical	95	100	15	Normal
TM27	Toxic	Poison	Status	—	90	10	Normal
TM36	Thunderbolt	Electric	Special	90	100	15	Normal
TM38	Thunder	Electric	Special	110	70	10	Normal
TM42	Self-Destruct	Normal	Physical	200	100	5	All Others

EVOLUTION MOVES

NAME	TYPE	KIND	POW.	ACC.	PP	RANGE

POKÉMON EXPRESSIONS

HAPPY

UNHAPPY

ATTACKING

Electrode

— | Gender unknown

SPECIES STRENGTHS

HP
ATTACK
DEFENSE
SP. ATK
SP. DEF
SPEED

DAMAGE TAKEN IN BATTLES

◎	×1	🍃	×0.5
🔥	×1	◎	×1
💧	×1	🍄	×1
⚡	×1	🗡	×1
⚡	×0.5	👊	×1
❄	×1	🌀	×1
🧱	×1	☾	×1
◎	×1	◎	×0.5
🔺	×2	✦	×1

POKÉDEX ENTRY

Stores electrical energy inside its body. Even the slightest shock could trigger a huge explosion.

MAIN WAY TO OBTAIN

Catch one when it appears in the Power Plant. Or obtain a Voltorb, then level it up to Lv. 30 or higher to evolve it into Electrode.

Where to catch

EVOLUTION

Lv. 30
→→→

Voltorb   **Electrode**

POKÉMON EXPRESSIONS

HAPPY

UNHAPPY

ATTACKING

LEVEL-UP MOVES

LV.	NAME	TYPE	KIND	POW.	ACC.	PP	RANGE
1	Light Screen	Psychic	Status	—	—	30	Your Side
1	Sonic Boom	Normal	Special	—	90	20	Normal
1	Tackle	Normal	Physical	40	100	35	Normal
1	Thunder Shock	Electric	Special	40	100	30	Normal
3	Light Screen	Psychic	Status	—	—	30	Your Side
6	Sonic Boom	Normal	Special	—	90	20	Normal
9	Thunder Shock	Electric	Special	40	100	30	Normal
14	Swift	Normal	Special	60	—	20	Many Others
19	Self-Destruct	Normal	Physical	200	100	5	All Others
24	Screech	Normal	Status	—	85	40	Normal
36	Thunderbolt	Electric	Special	90	100	15	Normal
48	Mirror Coat	Psychic	Special	—	100	20	Varies
60	Explosion	Normal	Physical	250	100	5	All Others

TM MOVES

NO.	NAME	TYPE	KIND	POW.	ACC.	PP	RANGE
TM01	Headbutt	Normal	Physical	70	100	15	Normal
TM02	Taunt	Dark	Status	—	100	20	Normal
TM04	Teleport	Psychic	Status	—	—	20	Self
TM05	Rest	Psychic	Status	—	—	10	Self
TM06	Light Screen	Psychic	Status	—	—	30	Your Side
TM07	Protect	Normal	Status	—	—	10	Self
TM08	Substitute	Normal	Status	—	—	10	Self
TM09	Reflect	Psychic	Status	—	—	20	Your Side
TM12	Facade	Normal	Physical	70	100	20	Normal
TM16	Thunder Wave	Electric	Status	—	90	20	Normal
TM21	Foul Play	Dark	Physical	95	100	15	Normal
TM27	Toxic	Poison	Status	—	90	10	Normal
TM36	Thunderbolt	Electric	Special	90	100	15	Normal
TM38	Thunder	Electric	Special	110	70	10	Normal
TM42	Self-Destruct	Normal	Physical	200	100	5	All Others
TM48	Hyper Beam	Normal	Special	150	90	5	Normal

EVOLUTION MOVES

NAME	TYPE	KIND	POW.	ACC.	PP	RANGE

Exeggcute

✓ **102** Egg Pokémon | Average height: 1'04" | Average weight: 5.5 lbs.

♂ ♀ | Same form for male/female

SPECIES STRENGTHS

HP	▰▰▰
ATTACK	▰▰▰
DEFENSE	▰▰▰▰▰
SP. ATK	▰▰▰
SP. DEF	▰▰▰
SPEED	▰▰▰

DAMAGE TAKEN IN BATTLES

◎	×1	🍃	×2
🔥	×2	🌀	×0.5
💧	×0.5	👊	×4
🍃	×0.5	🦋	×1
⚡	×0.5	⬤	×2
❄	×2	☾	×1
🧱	×0.5	◑	×2
☠	×2	⬟	×1
🔺	×0.5	✦	×1

POKÉDEX ENTRY

The heads attract each other and spin around. There must be six heads for it to maintain balance.

MAIN WAY TO OBTAIN

Catch one when it appears on Route 23 (South).

Where to catch

EVOLUTION

Use Leaf Stone
→ → →

Exeggcute   **Exeggutor**

LEVEL-UP MOVES

LV.	NAME	TYPE	KIND	POW.	ACC.	PP	RANGE
1	Barrage	Normal	Physical	15	85	20	Normal
7	Hypnosis	Psychic	Status	—	60	20	Normal
14	Confusion	Psychic	Special	50	100	25	Normal
16	Stun Spore	Grass	Status	—	75	30	Normal
18	Poison Powder	Poison	Status	—	75	35	Normal
20	Sleep Powder	Grass	Status	—	75	15	Normal
27	Psybeam	Psychic	Special	65	100	20	Normal
34	Leech Seed	Grass	Status	—	90	10	Normal
41	Reflect	Psychic	Status	—	—	20	Your Side
48	Solar Beam	Grass	Special	200	100	10	Normal

TM MOVES

NO.	NAME	TYPE	KIND	POW.	ACC.	PP	RANGE
TM01	Headbutt	Normal	Physical	70	100	15	Normal
TM04	Teleport	Psychic	Status	—	—	20	Self
TM05	Rest	Psychic	Status	—	—	10	Self
TM06	Light Screen	Psychic	Status	—	—	30	Your Side
TM07	Protect	Normal	Status	—	—	10	Self
TM08	Substitute	Normal	Status	—	—	10	Self
TM09	Reflect	Psychic	Status	—	—	20	Your Side
TM12	Facade	Normal	Physical	70	100	20	Normal
TM27	Toxic	Poison	Status	—	90	10	Normal
TM40	Psychic	Psychic	Special	90	100	10	Normal
TM42	Self-Destruct	Normal	Physical	200	100	5	All Others
TM45	Solar Beam	Grass	Special	200	100	10	Normal
TM52	Sludge Bomb	Poison	Special	90	100	10	Normal
TM53	Mega Drain	Grass	Special	75	100	10	Normal
TM59	Dream Eater	Psychic	Special	100	100	15	Normal

EVOLUTION MOVES

NAME	TYPE	KIND	POW.	ACC.	PP	RANGE

POKÉMON EXPRESSIONS

HAPPY

UNHAPPY

ATTACKING

Exeggutor

♂ ♀ | Same form for male/female

SPECIES STRENGTHS

HP
ATTACK
DEFENSE
SP. ATK
SP. DEF
SPEED

DAMAGE TAKEN IN BATTLES

◉ ×1		🪶 ×2	
🔥 ×2		◎ ×0.5	
💧 ×0.5		🍃 ×4	
⚡ ×0.5		🌪 ×1	
🍂 ×0.5		🧠 ×2	
❄ ×2		👊 ×1	
🪨 ×0.5		🌙 ×2	
👻 ×2		⭕ ×1	
🔩 ×0.5		✴ ×1	

POKÉDEX ENTRY

Its cries are very noisy. This is because each of the three heads thinks about whatever it likes.

MAIN WAY TO OBTAIN

Catch one when it appears on Route 23 (South). Or obtain an Exeggcute, then use a Leaf Stone on it to evolve it into Exeggutor.

Where to catch

EVOLUTION

Use Leaf Stone
→→→

Exeggcute **Exeggutor**

POKÉMON EXPRESSIONS

HAPPY

UNHAPPY

ATTACKING

LEVEL-UP MOVES

LV.	NAME	TYPE	KIND	POW.	ACC.	PP	RANGE
1	Barrage	Normal	Physical	15	85	20	Normal
1	Confusion	Psychic	Special	50	100	25	Normal
1	Egg Bomb	Normal	Physical	100	75	10	Normal
1	Hypnosis	Psychic	Status	—	60	20	Normal
1	Power Whip	Grass	Physical	120	85	10	Normal
1	Stomp	Normal	Physical	65	100	20	Normal
1	Stun Spore	Grass	Status	—	75	30	Normal

TM MOVES

NO.	NAME	TYPE	KIND	POW.	ACC.	PP	RANGE
TM01	Headbutt	Normal	Physical	70	100	15	Normal
TM04	Teleport	Psychic	Status	—	—	20	Self
TM05	Rest	Psychic	Status	—	—	10	Self
TM06	Light Screen	Psychic	Status	—	—	30	Your Side
TM07	Protect	Normal	Status	—	—	10	Self
TM08	Substitute	Normal	Status	—	—	10	Self
TM09	Reflect	Psychic	Status	—	—	20	Your Side
TM12	Facade	Normal	Physical	70	100	20	Normal
TM27	Toxic	Poison	Status	—	90	10	Normal
TM40	Psychic	Psychic	Special	90	100	10	Normal
TM42	Self-Destruct	Normal	Physical	200	100	5	All Others
TM45	Solar Beam	Grass	Special	200	100	10	Normal
TM48	Hyper Beam	Normal	Special	150	90	5	Normal
TM52	Sludge Bomb	Poison	Special	90	100	10	Normal
TM53	Mega Drain	Grass	Special	75	100	10	Normal
TM59	Dream Eater	Psychic	Special	100	100	15	Normal

EVOLUTION MOVES

NAME	TYPE	KIND	POW.	ACC.	PP	RANGE
Stomp	Normal	Physical	65	100	20	Normal

✓ **103** Coconut Pokémon — Average height: 35'09" — Average weight: 916.2 lbs.

Exeggutor

ALOLA FORM

♂ ♀ | Same form for male/female

SPECIES STRENGTHS

HP	▬▬▬▬▬
ATTACK	▬▬▬▬▬▬
DEFENSE	▬▬▬▬
SP. ATK	▬▬▬▬▬▬▬
SP. DEF	▬▬▬
SPEED	▬▬

DAMAGE TAKEN IN BATTLES

◎	×1	◔	×2
◔	×1	◎	×1
◔	×0.25	◎	×2
◔	×0.25	◔	×1
◔	×0.25	◎	×1
❄	×4	◔	×2
▥	×1	◑	×1
◎	×2	◎	×1
◣	×0.5	✦	×2

POKÉDEX ENTRY

The strong sunlight of the Alola region has awakened the power hidden within Exeggcute. This is the result.

MAIN WAY TO OBTAIN

Trade an Exeggutor for one in the Pokémon League on the Indigo Plateau (p. 103).

Where to catch

Habitat Unknown

EVOLUTION

(DOES NOT EVOLVE)

LEVEL-UP MOVES

LV.	NAME	TYPE	KIND	POW.	ACC.	PP	RANGE
1	Barrage	Normal	Physical	15	85	20	Normal
1	Confusion	Psychic	Special	50	100	25	Normal
1	Dragon Pulse	Dragon	Special	85	100	10	Normal
1	Egg Bomb	Normal	Physical	100	75	10	Normal
1	Hypnosis	Psychic	Status	—	60	20	Normal
1	Power Whip	Grass	Physical	120	85	10	Normal
1	Stun Spore	Grass	Status	—	75	30	Normal

TM MOVES

NO.	NAME	TYPE	KIND	POW.	ACC.	PP	RANGE
TM01	Headbutt	Normal	Physical	70	100	15	Normal
TM04	Teleport	Psychic	Status	—	—	20	Self
TM05	Rest	Psychic	Status	—	—	10	Self
TM06	Light Screen	Psychic	Status	—	—	30	Your Side
TM07	Protect	Normal	Status	—	—	10	Self
TM08	Substitute	Normal	Status	—	—	10	Self
TM09	Reflect	Psychic	Status	—	—	20	Your Side
TM12	Facade	Normal	Physical	70	100	20	Normal
TM13	Brick Break	Fighting	Physical	75	100	15	Normal
TM17	Dragon Tail	Dragon	Physical	60	90	10	Normal
TM19	Iron Tail	Steel	Physical	100	75	15	Normal
TM27	Toxic	Poison	Status	—	90	10	Normal
TM34	Dragon Pulse	Dragon	Special	85	100	10	Normal
TM37	Flamethrower	Fire	Special	90	100	15	Normal
TM39	Outrage	Dragon	Physical	120	100	10	1 Random
TM40	Psychic	Psychic	Special	90	100	10	Normal
TM41	Earthquake	Ground	Physical	100	100	10	All Others
TM42	Self-Destruct	Normal	Physical	200	100	5	All Others
TM45	Solar Beam	Grass	Special	200	100	10	Normal
TM48	Hyper Beam	Normal	Special	150	90	5	Normal
TM49	Superpower	Fighting	Physical	120	100	5	Normal
TM52	Sludge Bomb	Poison	Special	90	100	10	Normal
TM53	Mega Drain	Grass	Special	75	100	10	Normal
TM59	Dream Eater	Psychic	Special	100	100	15	Normal

POKÉMON EXPRESSIONS

HAPPY

UNHAPPY

ATTACKING

EVOLUTION MOVES

NAME	TYPE	KIND	POW.	ACC.	PP	RANGE

Cubone

♂ ♀ | Same form for male/female

SPECIES STRENGTHS

HP ▮▮▮
ATTACK ▮▮▮
DEFENSE ▮▮▮▮▮▮
SP. ATK ▮▮▮
SP. DEF ▮▮▮
SPEED ▮▮▮

DAMAGE TAKEN IN BATTLES

 ×1   ×1
 ×1   ×1
 ×2   ×1
 ×2   ×0.5
 ×0   ×1
 ×2   ×1
 ×1   ×1
 ×0.5   ×1
 ×1   ×1

POKÉDEX ENTRY

Wears the skull of its deceased mother. Its cries echo inside the skull and come out as a sad melody.

MAIN WAY TO OBTAIN

Catch one when it appears in the Rock Tunnel or the Pokémon Tower (3F through 6F).

Where to catch

EVOLUTION

 Cubone → Lv. 28 → Marowak

POKÉMON EXPRESSIONS

HAPPY

UNHAPPY

ATTACKING

LEVEL-UP MOVES

LV.	NAME	TYPE	KIND	POW.	ACC.	PP	RANGE
1	Growl	Normal	Status	—	100	40	Many Others
2	Tail Whip	Normal	Status	—	100	30	Many Others
6	Leer	Normal	Status	—	100	30	Many Others
12	Bone Club	Ground	Physical	65	85	20	Normal
14	Headbutt	Normal	Physical	70	100	15	Normal
18	Rage	Normal	Physical	20	100	20	Normal
24	Focus Energy	Normal	Status	—	—	30	Self
26	Bonemerang	Ground	Physical	50	90	10	Normal
30	Thrash	Normal	Physical	120	100	10	1 Random
36	Double-Edge	Normal	Physical	120	100	15	Normal

TM MOVES

NO.	NAME	TYPE	KIND	POW.	ACC.	PP	RANGE
TM01	Headbutt	Normal	Physical	70	100	15	Normal
TM05	Rest	Psychic	Status	—	—	10	Self
TM07	Protect	Normal	Status	—	—	10	Self
TM08	Substitute	Normal	Status	—	—	10	Self
TM10	Dig	Ground	Physical	80	100	10	Normal
TM12	Facade	Normal	Physical	70	100	20	Normal
TM13	Brick Break	Fighting	Physical	75	100	15	Normal
TM15	Seismic Toss	Fighting	Physical	—	100	20	Normal
TM19	Iron Tail	Steel	Physical	100	75	15	Normal
TM22	Rock Slide	Rock	Physical	75	90	10	Many Others
TM23	Thunder Punch	Electric	Physical	75	100	15	Normal
TM27	Toxic	Poison	Status	—	90	10	Normal
TM31	Fire Punch	Fire	Physical	75	100	15	Normal
TM37	Flamethrower	Fire	Special	90	100	15	Normal
TM41	Earthquake	Ground	Physical	100	100	10	All Others
TM46	Fire Blast	Fire	Special	110	85	5	Normal
TM51	Blizzard	Ice	Special	110	70	5	Many Others
TM55	Ice Beam	Ice	Special	90	100	10	Normal
TM56	Stealth Rock	Rock	Status	—	—	20	Other Side

EVOLUTION MOVES

NAME	TYPE	KIND	POW.	ACC.	PP	RANGE

☑ **105** Bone Keeper Pokémon | Average height: 3'03" | Average weight: 99.2 lbs.

Marowak

♂ ♀ | Same form for male/female

SPECIES STRENGTHS

HP	▬▬▬
ATTACK	▬▬▬▬
DEFENSE	▬▬▬▬▬▬▬
SP. ATK	▬▬▬
SP. DEF	▬▬▬▬
SPEED	▬▬▬

DAMAGE TAKEN IN BATTLES

◎	×1	🕊	×1
🔥	×1	🌀	×1
💧	×2	⬤	×1
🌿	×2	◆	×0.5
⚡	×0	◑	×1
❄	×2	↻	×1
▥	×1	◐	×1
◒	×0.5	◉	×1
◢	×1	✧	×1

POKÉDEX ENTRY

Small and weak, this Pokémon is adept with its bone club. It has grown more vicious over the ages.

MAIN WAY TO OBTAIN

Obtain a Cubone, then level it up to Lv. 28 or higher to evolve it into Marowak.

Where to catch

Habitat Unknown

EVOLUTION

Lv. 28
→ → →

Cubone   **Marowak**

LEVEL-UP MOVES

LV.	NAME	TYPE	KIND	POW.	ACC.	PP	RANGE
1	Bone Club	Ground	Physical	65	85	20	Normal
1	Growl	Normal	Status	—	100	40	Many Others
1	Leer	Normal	Status	—	100	30	Many Others
1	Screech	Normal	Status	—	85	40	Normal
1	Swords Dance	Normal	Status	—	—	20	Self
1	Tail Whip	Normal	Status	—	100	30	Many Others
2	Tail Whip	Normal	Status	—	100	30	Many Others
6	Leer	Normal	Status	—	100	30	Many Others
12	Bone Club	Ground	Physical	65	85	20	Normal
14	Headbutt	Normal	Physical	70	100	15	Normal
18	Rage	Normal	Physical	20	100	20	Normal
24	Focus Energy	Normal	Status	—	—	30	Self
26	Bonemerang	Ground	Physical	50	90	10	Normal
36	Thrash	Normal	Physical	120	100	10	1 Random
48	Double-Edge	Normal	Physical	120	100	15	Normal

TM MOVES

NO.	NAME	TYPE	KIND	POW.	ACC.	PP	RANGE
TM01	Headbutt	Normal	Physical	70	100	15	Normal
TM05	Rest	Psychic	Status	—	—	10	Self
TM07	Protect	Normal	Status	—	—	10	Self
TM08	Substitute	Normal	Status	—	—	10	Self
TM10	Dig	Ground	Physical	80	100	10	Normal
TM12	Facade	Normal	Physical	70	100	20	Normal
TM13	Brick Break	Fighting	Physical	75	100	15	Normal
TM15	Seismic Toss	Fighting	Physical	—	100	20	Normal
TM19	Iron Tail	Steel	Physical	100	75	15	Normal
TM22	Rock Slide	Rock	Physical	75	90	10	Many Others
TM23	Thunder Punch	Electric	Physical	75	100	15	Normal
TM27	Toxic	Poison	Status	—	90	10	Normal
TM31	Fire Punch	Fire	Physical	75	100	15	Normal
TM37	Flamethrower	Fire	Special	90	100	15	Normal
TM39	Outrage	Dragon	Physical	120	100	10	1 Random
TM41	Earthquake	Ground	Physical	100	100	10	All Others
TM46	Fire Blast	Fire	Special	110	85	5	Normal
TM48	Hyper Beam	Normal	Special	150	90	5	Normal
TM51	Blizzard	Ice	Special	110	70	5	Many Others
TM55	Ice Beam	Ice	Special	90	100	10	Normal
TM56	Stealth Rock	Rock	Status	—	—	20	Other Side

EVOLUTION MOVES

NAME	TYPE	KIND	POW.	ACC.	PP	RANGE
Swords Dance	Normal	Status	—	—	20	Self

POKÉMON EXPRESSIONS

HAPPY

UNHAPPY

ATTACKING

Marowak

♂ ♀ | Same form for male/female

SPECIES STRENGTHS

HP	▰▰▰▱▱
ATTACK	▰▰▰▰▱
DEFENSE	▰▰▰▰▰▰▰
SP. ATK	▰▰▱
SP. DEF	▰▰▰▰▱
SPEED	▰▰▱

DAMAGE TAKEN IN BATTLES

◉	×0	🕊	×1
🔥	×0.5	🌀	×1
💧	×2	☯	×0.25
🍃	×0.5	⚔	×2
⚡	×1	👁	×2
❄	×0.5	👊	×1
🪨	×0	🌙	×2
💠	×0.5	⊙	×0.5
🔺	×2	✦	×0.5

POKÉDEX ENTRY

It has transformed the spirit of its dear departed mother into flames, and tonight it will once again dance in mourning of others of its kind.

MAIN WAY TO OBTAIN

Trade a Marowak for one in the Pokémon Center in Fuchsia City (p. 72).

Where to catch
Habitat Unknown

ALOLA FORM

EVOLUTION

(DOES NOT EVOLVE)

POKÉMON EXPRESSIONS

HAPPY

UNHAPPY

ATTACKING

LEVEL-UP MOVES

LV.	NAME	TYPE	KIND	POW.	ACC.	PP	RANGE
1	Bone Club	Ground	Physical	65	85	20	Normal
1	Growl	Normal	Status	—	100	40	Many Others
1	Leer	Normal	Status	—	100	30	Many Others
1	Screech	Normal	Status	—	85	40	Normal
1	Swords Dance	Normal	Status	—	—	20	Self
1	Tail Whip	Normal	Status	—	100	30	Many Others
2	Tail Whip	Normal	Status	—	100	30	Many Others
6	Leer	Normal	Status	—	100	30	Many Others
12	Bone Club	Ground	Physical	65	85	20	Normal
14	Fire Spin	Fire	Special	35	85	15	Normal
18	Rage	Normal	Physical	20	100	20	Normal
24	Will-O-Wisp	Fire	Status	—	85	15	Normal
26	Bonemerang	Ground	Physical	50	90	10	Normal
36	Thrash	Normal	Physical	120	100	10	1 Random
48	Flare Blitz	Fire	Physical	120	100	15	Normal

TM MOVES

NO.	NAME	TYPE	KIND	POW.	ACC.	PP	RANGE
TM01	Headbutt	Normal	Physical	70	100	15	Normal
TM05	Rest	Psychic	Status	—	—	10	Self
TM07	Protect	Normal	Status	—	—	10	Self
TM08	Substitute	Normal	Status	—	—	10	Self
TM10	Dig	Ground	Physical	80	100	10	Normal
TM11	Will-O-Wisp	Fire	Status	—	85	15	Normal
TM12	Facade	Normal	Physical	70	100	20	Normal
TM13	Brick Break	Fighting	Physical	75	100	15	Normal
TM15	Seismic Toss	Fighting	Physical	—	100	20	Normal
TM19	Iron Tail	Steel	Physical	100	75	15	Normal
TM20	Dark Pulse	Dark	Special	80	100	15	Normal
TM22	Rock Slide	Rock	Physical	75	90	10	Many Others
TM23	Thunder Punch	Electric	Physical	75	100	15	Normal
TM27	Toxic	Poison	Status	—	90	10	Normal
TM31	Fire Punch	Fire	Physical	75	100	15	Normal
TM36	Thunderbolt	Electric	Special	90	100	15	Normal
TM37	Flamethrower	Fire	Special	90	100	15	Normal
TM38	Thunder	Electric	Special	110	70	10	Normal
TM39	Outrage	Dragon	Physical	120	100	10	1 Random
TM41	Earthquake	Ground	Physical	100	100	10	All Others
TM43	Shadow Ball	Ghost	Special	80	100	15	Normal
TM46	Fire Blast	Fire	Special	110	85	5	Normal
TM48	Hyper Beam	Normal	Special	150	90	5	Normal
TM51	Blizzard	Ice	Special	110	70	5	Many Others
TM55	Ice Beam	Ice	Special	90	100	10	Normal
TM56	Stealth Rock	Rock	Status	—	—	20	Other Side
TM59	Dream Eater	Psychic	Special	100	100	15	Normal

EVOLUTION MOVES

NAME	TYPE	KIND	POW.	ACC.	PP	RANGE

106 Kicking Pokémon | Average height: 4'11" | Average weight: 109.8 lbs.

Hitmonlee

HITMONLEE 106

♂ | Male only

SPECIES STRENGTHS

HP
ATTACK
DEFENSE
SP. ATK
SP. DEF
SPEED

DAMAGE TAKEN IN BATTLES

⊙	×1		×2
🔥	×1		×2
💧	×1		×0.5
🌿	×1		×0.5
⚡	×1		×1
❄	×1		×1
👊	×1		×0.5
☣	×1		×1
⛰	×1		×2

POKÉDEX ENTRY

When kicking, the sole of its foot turns as hard as a diamond on impact and destroys its enemy.

MAIN WAY TO OBTAIN

Choose Hitmonlee after defeating the Karate Master in the Saffron City Fighting Dojo (p. 80). Or catch one when it appears as an unusual encounter during a Catch Combo (p. 117) on Victory Road (2F).

Where to catch
Unusual Encounter

EVOLUTION

(DOES NOT EVOLVE)

LEVEL-UP MOVES

LV.	NAME	TYPE	KIND	POW.	ACC.	PP	RANGE
1	Rolling Kick	Fighting	Physical	60	85	15	Normal
5	Meditate	Psychic	Status	—	—	40	Self
10	Double Kick	Fighting	Physical	30	100	30	Normal
15	Feint	Normal	Physical	30	100	10	Normal
20	Brick Break	Fighting	Physical	75	100	15	Normal
25	Facade	Normal	Physical	70	100	20	Normal
30	Jump Kick	Fighting	Physical	100	95	10	Normal
35	Focus Energy	Normal	Status	—	—	30	Self
40	Mega Kick	Normal	Physical	120	75	5	Normal
45	High Jump Kick	Fighting	Physical	130	90	10	Normal

TM MOVES

NO.	NAME	TYPE	KIND	POW.	ACC.	PP	RANGE
TM01	Headbutt	Normal	Physical	70	100	15	Normal
TM03	Helping Hand	Normal	Status	—	—	20	1 Ally
TM05	Rest	Psychic	Status	—	—	10	Self
TM07	Protect	Normal	Status	—	—	10	Self
TM08	Substitute	Normal	Status	—	—	10	Self
TM12	Facade	Normal	Physical	70	100	20	Normal
TM13	Brick Break	Fighting	Physical	75	100	15	Normal
TM15	Seismic Toss	Fighting	Physical	—	100	20	Normal
TM22	Rock Slide	Rock	Physical	75	90	10	Many Others
TM26	Poison Jab	Poison	Physical	80	100	20	Normal
TM27	Toxic	Poison	Status	—	90	10	Normal
TM30	Bulk Up	Fighting	Status	—	—	20	Self
TM41	Earthquake	Ground	Physical	100	100	10	All Others
TM49	Superpower	Fighting	Physical	120	100	5	Normal

EVOLUTION MOVES

NAME	TYPE	KIND	POW.	ACC.	PP	RANGE

POKÉMON EXPRESSIONS

HAPPY

UNHAPPY

ATTACKING

Hitmonchan

♂ | Male only

SPECIES STRENGTHS

HP	▮▮▮
ATTACK	▮▮▮▮▮▮▮
DEFENSE	▮▮▮▮▮
SP. ATK	▮▮▮
SP. DEF	▮▮▮▮▮▮
SPEED	▮▮▮▮▮

DAMAGE TAKEN IN BATTLES

◎	×1	🪽	×2
🔥	×1	🌀	×2
💧	×1	🍃	×0.5
⚡	×1	🔮	×0.5
🗡	×1	🔴	×1
❄	×1	🐉	×1
👊	×1	🌙	×0.5
☠	×1	⚙	×1
⛰	×1	✨	×2

POKÉDEX ENTRY

Punches in corkscrew fashion. It can punch its way through a concrete wall like a drill.

MAIN WAY TO OBTAIN

Choose Hitmonchan after defeating the Karate Master in the Saffron City Fighting Dojo (p. 80). Or catch one when it appears as an unusual encounter during a Catch Combo (p. 117) on Victory Road (3F).

Where to catch
Unusual Encounter

EVOLUTION

(DOES NOT EVOLVE)

POKÉMON EXPRESSIONS

HAPPY

UNHAPPY

ATTACKING

LEVEL-UP MOVES

LV.	NAME	TYPE	KIND	POW.	ACC.	PP	RANGE
1	Comet Punch	Normal	Physical	18	85	15	Normal
5	Leer	Normal	Status	—	100	30	Many Others
10	Agility	Psychic	Status	—	—	30	Self
15	Feint	Normal	Physical	30	100	10	Normal
20	Swift	Normal	Special	60	—	20	Many Others
25	Dizzy Punch	Normal	Physical	70	100	10	Normal
30	Fire Punch	Fire	Physical	75	100	15	Normal
30	Ice Punch	Ice	Physical	75	100	15	Normal
30	Thunder Punch	Electric	Physical	75	100	15	Normal
35	Focus Energy	Normal	Status	—	—	30	Self
40	Mega Punch	Normal	Physical	80	85	20	Normal
45	Counter	Fighting	Physical	—	100	20	Varies

TM MOVES

NO.	NAME	TYPE	KIND	POW.	ACC.	PP	RANGE
TM01	Headbutt	Normal	Physical	70	100	15	Normal
TM03	Helping Hand	Normal	Status	—	—	20	1 Ally
TM05	Rest	Psychic	Status	—	—	10	Self
TM07	Protect	Normal	Status	—	—	10	Self
TM08	Substitute	Normal	Status	—	—	10	Self
TM12	Facade	Normal	Physical	70	100	20	Normal
TM13	Brick Break	Fighting	Physical	75	100	15	Normal
TM15	Seismic Toss	Fighting	Physical	—	100	20	Normal
TM22	Rock Slide	Rock	Physical	75	90	10	Many Others
TM23	Thunder Punch	Electric	Physical	75	100	15	Normal
TM27	Toxic	Poison	Status	—	90	10	Normal
TM30	Bulk Up	Fighting	Status	—	—	20	Self
TM31	Fire Punch	Fire	Physical	75	100	15	Normal
TM35	Ice Punch	Ice	Physical	75	100	15	Normal
TM41	Earthquake	Ground	Physical	100	100	10	All Others

EVOLUTION MOVES

NAME	TYPE	KIND	POW.	ACC.	PP	RANGE

Lickitung

LICKITUNG 108

♂ ♀ | Same form for male/female

SPECIES STRENGTHS

HP	▰▰▰▰▰
ATTACK	▰▰▰
DEFENSE	▰▰▰▰
SP. ATK	▰▰▰
SP. DEF	▰▰▰▰
SPEED	▰

DAMAGE TAKEN IN BATTLES

×1		×1	
×1		×1	
×1		×1	
×1		×1	
×1		×0	
×1		×1	
×2		×1	
×1		×1	
×1		×1	

POKÉDEX ENTRY

Its tongue spans almost seven feet and moves more freely than its forelegs. Its licks can cause paralysis.

MAIN WAY TO OBTAIN

Catch one when it appears in the Cerulean Cave.

Where to catch

EVOLUTION

(DOES NOT EVOLVE)

LEVEL-UP MOVES

LV.	NAME	TYPE	KIND	POW.	ACC.	PP	RANGE
1	Lick	Ghost	Physical	30	100	30	Normal
5	Wrap	Normal	Physical	15	90	20	Normal
10	Acid	Poison	Special	40	100	30	Many Others
15	Stomp	Normal	Physical	65	100	20	Normal
20	Disable	Normal	Status	—	100	20	Normal
25	Bind	Normal	Physical	15	85	20	Normal
30	Slam	Normal	Physical	80	75	20	Normal
35	Screech	Normal	Status	—	85	40	Normal
40	Thrash	Normal	Physical	120	100	10	1 Random
45	Power Whip	Grass	Physical	120	85	10	Normal

TM MOVES

NO.	NAME	TYPE	KIND	POW.	ACC.	PP	RANGE
TM01	Headbutt	Normal	Physical	70	100	15	Normal
TM03	Helping Hand	Normal	Status	—	—	20	1 Ally
TM05	Rest	Psychic	Status	—	—	10	Self
TM07	Protect	Normal	Status	—	—	10	Self
TM08	Substitute	Normal	Status	—	—	10	Self
TM10	Dig	Ground	Physical	80	100	10	Normal
TM12	Facade	Normal	Physical	70	100	20	Normal
TM13	Brick Break	Fighting	Physical	75	100	15	Normal
TM15	Seismic Toss	Fighting	Physical	—	100	20	Normal
TM17	Dragon Tail	Dragon	Physical	60	90	10	Normal
TM19	Iron Tail	Steel	Physical	100	75	15	Normal
TM22	Rock Slide	Rock	Physical	75	90	10	Many Others
TM23	Thunder Punch	Electric	Physical	75	100	15	Normal
TM27	Toxic	Poison	Status	—	90	10	Normal
TM31	Fire Punch	Fire	Physical	75	100	15	Normal
TM35	Ice Punch	Ice	Physical	75	100	15	Normal
TM36	Thunderbolt	Electric	Special	90	100	15	Normal
TM37	Flamethrower	Fire	Special	90	100	15	Normal
TM38	Thunder	Electric	Special	110	70	10	Normal
TM41	Earthquake	Ground	Physical	100	100	10	All Others
TM43	Shadow Ball	Ghost	Special	80	100	15	Normal
TM45	Solar Beam	Grass	Special	200	100	10	Normal
TM46	Fire Blast	Fire	Special	110	85	5	Normal
TM47	Surf	Water	Special	90	100	15	All Others
TM48	Hyper Beam	Normal	Special	150	90	5	Normal
TM51	Blizzard	Ice	Special	110	70	5	Many Others
TM55	Ice Beam	Ice	Special	90	100	10	Normal
TM59	Dream Eater	Psychic	Special	100	100	15	Normal

EVOLUTION MOVES

NAME	TYPE	KIND	POW.	ACC.	PP	RANGE

POKÉMON EXPRESSIONS

HAPPY

UNHAPPY

ATTACKING

Koffing

♂ ♀ | Same form for male/female

SPECIES STRENGTHS

HP	■■■
ATTACK	■■■
DEFENSE	■■■■■
SP. ATK	■■■
SP. DEF	■■
SPEED	■■

DAMAGE TAKEN IN BATTLES

⊚	×1	🍃	×1
🔥	×1	◎	×2
💧	×1	🦋	×0.5
⚡	×0.5	❄	×1
🌿	×1	👁	×1
❄	×1	🔥	×1
👊	×0.5	🌙	×1
👁	×0.5	⊙	×1
◢	×2	✦	×0.5

POKÉDEX ENTRY

In hot places, its internal gases could expand and explode without any warning. Be very careful!

MAIN WAY TO OBTAIN

Obtain one in a trade if you are playing *Pokémon: Let's Go, Pikachu!*, as it does not appear in that game. Catch one when it appears in the Power Plant or the Pokémon Mansion in *Pokémon: Let's Go, Eevee!*

Where to catch

EVOLUTION

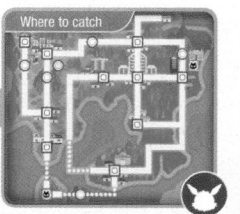

Koffing

Lv. 35
→→→

Weezing

POKÉMON EXPRESSIONS

HAPPY

UNHAPPY

ATTACKING

LEVEL-UP MOVES

LV.	NAME	TYPE	KIND	POW.	ACC.	PP	RANGE
1	Poison Gas	Poison	Status	—	90	40	Many Others
1	Tackle	Normal	Physical	40	100	35	Normal
6	Smog	Poison	Special	30	70	20	Normal
12	Clear Smog	Poison	Special	50	—	15	Normal
18	Sludge	Poison	Special	65	100	20	Normal
24	Self-Destruct	Normal	Physical	200	100	5	All Others
30	Toxic	Poison	Status	—	90	10	Normal
36	Haze	Ice	Status	—	—	30	Both Sides
42	Sludge Bomb	Poison	Special	90	100	10	Normal
48	Explosion	Normal	Physical	250	100	5	All Others

TM MOVES

NO.	NAME	TYPE	KIND	POW.	ACC.	PP	RANGE
TM01	Headbutt	Normal	Physical	70	100	15	Normal
TM02	Taunt	Dark	Status	—	100	20	Normal
TM05	Rest	Psychic	Status	—	—	10	Self
TM07	Protect	Normal	Status	—	—	10	Self
TM08	Substitute	Normal	Status	—	—	10	Self
TM11	Will-O-Wisp	Fire	Status	—	85	15	Normal
TM12	Facade	Normal	Physical	70	100	20	Normal
TM20	Dark Pulse	Dark	Special	80	100	15	Normal
TM27	Toxic	Poison	Status	—	90	10	Normal
TM36	Thunderbolt	Electric	Special	90	100	15	Normal
TM37	Flamethrower	Fire	Special	90	100	15	Normal
TM38	Thunder	Electric	Special	110	70	10	Normal
TM42	Self-Destruct	Normal	Physical	200	100	5	All Others
TM43	Shadow Ball	Ghost	Special	80	100	15	Normal
TM46	Fire Blast	Fire	Special	110	85	5	Normal
TM52	Sludge Bomb	Poison	Special	90	100	10	Normal

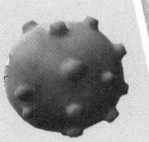

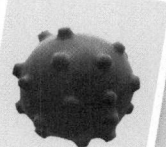

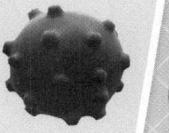

EVOLUTION MOVES

NAME	TYPE	KIND	POW.	ACC.	PP	RANGE

✓ **110** Poison Gas Pokémon   Average height: 3'11"   Average weight: 20.9 lbs.

Weezing

♂ ♀ | Same form for male/female

SPECIES STRENGTHS

HP	▬▬▬
ATTACK	▬▬▬▬
DEFENSE	▬▬▬▬▬▬
SP. ATK	▬▬▬
SP. DEF	▬▬▬
SPEED	▬▬▬

DAMAGE TAKEN IN BATTLES

◎	×1		×1
	×1		×2
	×1		×0.5
	×0.5		×1
	×1		×1
	×1		×1
	×0.5		×1
	×0.5		×1
	×2		×0.5

POKÉDEX ENTRY

This Pokémon lives and grows by absorbing poison gas, dust, and germs that exist inside garbage.

MAIN WAY TO OBTAIN

Catch one when it appears in the Power Plant or the Pokémon Mansion, especially on B1F, in *Pokémon: Let's Go, Eevee!* Or obtain a Koffing, then level it up to Lv. 35 or higher to evolve it into Weezing.

Where to catch

EVOLUTION

Lv. 35
→ → →

Koffing   **Weezing**

LEVEL-UP MOVES

LV.	NAME	TYPE	KIND	POW.	ACC.	PP	RANGE
1	Clear Smog	Poison	Special	50	—	15	Normal
1	Poison Gas	Poison	Status	—	90	40	Many Others
1	Psybeam	Psychic	Special	65	100	20	Normal
1	Screech	Normal	Status	—	85	40	Normal
1	Smog	Poison	Special	30	70	20	Normal
1	Tackle	Normal	Physical	40	100	35	Normal
6	Smog	Poison	Special	30	70	20	Normal
12	Clear Smog	Poison	Special	50	—	15	Normal
18	Sludge	Poison	Special	65	100	20	Normal
24	Self-Destruct	Normal	Physical	200	100	5	All Others
30	Toxic	Poison	Status	—	90	10	Normal
40	Haze	Ice	Status	—	—	30	Both Sides
50	Sludge Bomb	Poison	Special	90	100	10	Normal
60	Explosion	Normal	Physical	250	100	5	All Others

TM MOVES

NO.	NAME	TYPE	KIND	POW.	ACC.	PP	RANGE
TM01	Headbutt	Normal	Physical	70	100	15	Normal
TM02	Taunt	Dark	Status	—	100	20	Normal
TM05	Rest	Psychic	Status	—	—	10	Self
TM07	Protect	Normal	Status	—	—	10	Self
TM08	Substitute	Normal	Status	—	—	10	Self
TM11	Will-O-Wisp	Fire	Status	—	85	15	Normal
TM12	Facade	Normal	Physical	70	100	20	Normal
TM20	Dark Pulse	Dark	Special	80	100	15	Normal
TM27	Toxic	Poison	Status	—	90	10	Normal
TM36	Thunderbolt	Electric	Special	90	100	15	Normal
TM37	Flamethrower	Fire	Special	90	100	15	Normal
TM38	Thunder	Electric	Special	110	70	10	Normal
TM42	Self-Destruct	Normal	Physical	200	100	5	All Others
TM43	Shadow Ball	Ghost	Special	80	100	15	Normal
TM46	Fire Blast	Fire	Special	110	85	5	Normal
TM48	Hyper Beam	Normal	Special	150	90	5	Normal
TM52	Sludge Bomb	Poison	Special	90	100	10	Normal

EVOLUTION MOVES

NAME	TYPE	KIND	POW.	ACC.	PP	RANGE

POKÉMON EXPRESSIONS

HAPPY

UNHAPPY

ATTACKING

Rhyhorn

♂ ♀ | The female has a shorter horn on its face than the male.

♂　　♀

SPECIES STRENGTHS

- HP
- ATTACK
- DEFENSE
- SP. ATK
- SP. DEF
- SPEED

DAMAGE TAKEN IN BATTLES

◎	×0.5	🕊	×0.5
🔥	×0.5	💧	×1
💧	×4	🌿	×1
⚡	×4	🍃	×0.5
🧊	×0	☆	×1
❄	×2	🌀	×1
👊	×2	🌙	×1
👁	×0.25	⭕	×2
🪨	×2	✴	×1

POKÉDEX ENTRY

A Pokémon with a one-track mind. Once it charges, it won't stop running until it falls asleep.

MAIN WAY TO OBTAIN

Catch one when it appears in the Rock Tunnel, on Victory Road, or in the Cerulean Cave.

Where to catch

EVOLUTION

Rhyhorn

Lv. 42
→→→

Rhydon

LEVEL-UP MOVES

LV.	NAME	TYPE	KIND	POW.	ACC.	PP	RANGE
1	Horn Attack	Normal	Physical	65	100	25	Normal
1	Sand Attack	Ground	Status	—	100	15	Normal
1	Tail Whip	Normal	Status	—	100	30	Many Others
7	Fury Attack	Normal	Physical	15	85	20	Normal
12	Stomp	Normal	Physical	65	100	20	Normal
19	Rock Throw	Rock	Physical	50	90	15	Normal
24	Drill Run	Ground	Physical	80	95	10	Normal
31	Take Down	Normal	Physical	90	85	20	Normal
36	Megahorn	Bug	Physical	120	85	10	Normal
43	Rock Slide	Rock	Physical	75	90	10	Many Others
48	Earthquake	Ground	Physical	100	100	10	All Others
55	Horn Drill	Normal	Physical	—	30	5	Normal

TM MOVES

NO.	NAME	TYPE	KIND	POW.	ACC.	PP	RANGE
TM01	Headbutt	Normal	Physical	70	100	15	Normal
TM05	Rest	Psychic	Status	—	—	10	Self
TM07	Protect	Normal	Status	—	—	10	Self
TM08	Substitute	Normal	Status	—	—	10	Self
TM10	Dig	Ground	Physical	80	100	10	Normal
TM12	Facade	Normal	Physical	70	100	20	Normal
TM19	Iron Tail	Steel	Physical	100	75	15	Normal
TM22	Rock Slide	Rock	Physical	75	90	10	Many Others
TM26	Poison Jab	Poison	Physical	80	100	20	Normal
TM27	Toxic	Poison	Status	—	90	10	Normal
TM34	Dragon Pulse	Dragon	Special	85	100	10	Normal
TM36	Thunderbolt	Electric	Special	90	100	15	Normal
TM37	Flamethrower	Fire	Special	90	100	15	Normal
TM38	Thunder	Electric	Special	110	70	10	Normal
TM41	Earthquake	Ground	Physical	100	100	10	All Others
TM46	Fire Blast	Fire	Special	110	85	5	Normal
TM49	Superpower	Fighting	Physical	120	100	5	Normal
TM51	Blizzard	Ice	Special	110	70	5	Many Others
TM55	Ice Beam	Ice	Special	90	100	10	Normal
TM56	Stealth Rock	Rock	Status	—	—	20	Other Side
TM58	Drill Run	Ground	Physical	80	95	10	Normal
TM60	Megahorn	Bug	Physical	120	85	10	Normal

EVOLUTION MOVES

NAME	TYPE	KIND	POW.	ACC.	PP	RANGE

☑ **112** Drill Pokémon Average height: 6'03" Average weight: 264.6 lbs.

Rhydon

♂ ♀ | The female has a shorter horn on its face than the male.

♂   ♀

SPECIES STRENGTHS

HP	▰▰▰▰▰▱▱
ATTACK	▰▰▰▰▰▰▱
DEFENSE	▰▰▰▰▰▰▰
SP. ATK	▰▰▰
SP. DEF	▰▰▰
SPEED	▰▰▰

DAMAGE TAKEN IN BATTLES

⊙	×0.5	🍃	×0.5
🔥	×0.5	⊛	×1
💧	×4	🌱	×1
🍂	×4	✦	×0.5
⚡	×0	◔	×1
❄	×2	🜂	×1
🥊	×2	◐	×1
☠	×0.25	◎	×2
▲	×2	✴	×1

POKÉDEX ENTRY

Its brain developed when it began walking on its hind legs. Its armor-like hide even repels molten lava.

MAIN WAY TO OBTAIN

Catch one when it appears on Victory Road or in the Cerulean Cave, especially on 2F. Or obtain a Rhyhorn, then level it up to Lv. 42 or higher to evolve it into Rhydon.

Where to catch

EVOLUTION

Lv. 42
→ → →

Rhyhorn **Rhydon**

LEVEL-UP MOVES

IV.	NAME	TYPE	KIND	POW.	ACC.	PP	RANGE
1	Counter	Fighting	Physical	—	100	20	Varies
1	Crunch	Dark	Physical	80	100	15	Normal
1	Fury Attack	Normal	Physical	15	85	20	Normal
1	Horn Attack	Normal	Physical	65	100	25	Normal
1	Sand Attack	Ground	Status	—	100	15	Normal
1	Tail Whip	Normal	Status	—	100	30	Many Others
7	Fury Attack	Normal	Physical	15	85	20	Normal
12	Stomp	Normal	Physical	65	100	20	Normal
19	Rock Throw	Rock	Physical	50	90	15	Normal
24	Drill Run	Ground	Physical	80	95	10	Normal
31	Take Down	Normal	Physical	90	85	20	Normal
36	Megahorn	Bug	Physical	120	85	10	Normal
48	Rock Slide	Rock	Physical	75	90	10	Normal
54	Earthquake	Ground	Physical	100	100	10	All Others
67	Horn Drill	Normal	Physical	—	30	5	Normal

TM MOVES

NO.	NAME	TYPE	KIND	POW.	ACC.	PP	RANGE
TM01	Headbutt	Normal	Physical	70	100	15	Normal
TM03	Helping Hand	Normal	Status	—	—	20	1 Ally
TM05	Rest	Psychic	Status	—	—	10	Self
TM07	Protect	Normal	Status	—	—	10	Self
TM08	Substitute	Normal	Status	—	—	10	Self
TM10	Dig	Ground	Physical	80	100	10	Normal
TM12	Facade	Normal	Physical	70	100	20	Normal
TM13	Brick Break	Fighting	Physical	75	100	15	Normal
TM15	Seismic Toss	Fighting	Physical	—	100	20	Normal
TM17	Dragon Tail	Dragon	Physical	60	90	10	Normal
TM19	Iron Tail	Steel	Physical	100	75	15	Normal
TM22	Rock Slide	Rock	Physical	75	90	10	Many Others
TM23	Thunder Punch	Electric	Physical	75	100	15	Normal
TM26	Poison Jab	Poison	Physical	80	100	20	Normal
TM27	Toxic	Poison	Status	—	90	10	Normal
TM31	Fire Punch	Fire	Physical	75	100	15	Normal
TM34	Dragon Pulse	Dragon	Special	85	100	10	Normal
TM35	Ice Punch	Ice	Physical	75	100	15	Normal
TM36	Thunderbolt	Electric	Special	90	100	15	Normal
TM37	Flamethrower	Fire	Special	90	100	15	Normal
TM38	Thunder	Electric	Special	110	70	10	Normal
TM39	Outrage	Dragon	Physical	120	100	10	1 Random
TM41	Earthquake	Ground	Physical	100	100	10	All Others
TM46	Fire Blast	Fire	Special	110	85	5	Normal
TM47	Surf	Water	Special	90	100	15	All Others
TM48	Hyper Beam	Normal	Special	150	90	5	Normal
TM49	Superpower	Fighting	Physical	120	100	5	Normal
TM51	Blizzard	Ice	Special	110	70	5	Many Others
TM55	Ice Beam	Ice	Special	90	100	10	Normal
TM56	Stealth Rock	Rock	Status	—	—	20	Other Side
TM57	Pay Day	Normal	Physical	40	100	20	Normal
TM58	Drill Run	Ground	Physical	80	95	10	Normal
TM60	Megahorn	Bug	Physical	120	85	10	Normal

EVOLUTION MOVES

NAME	TYPE	KIND	POW.	ACC.	PP	RANGE

Chansey

♀ | Female only

SPECIES STRENGTHS

HP	██████████████
ATTACK	█
DEFENSE	█
SP. ATK	███
SP. DEF	████████
SPEED	███

DAMAGE TAKEN IN BATTLES

◎	×1	🪽	×1
🔥	×1	◉	×1
💧	×1	🍃	×1
⚡	×1	👁	×1
🗡	×1	⦿	×0
❄	×1	☾	×1
🧱	×2	☾	×1
⬤	×1	◉	×1
🔺	×1	✦	×1

POKÉDEX ENTRY

A gentle and kindhearted Pokémon that shares its nutritious eggs if it sees an injured Pokémon.

MAIN WAY TO OBTAIN

Catch one when it appears as an unusual encounter during a Catch Combo (p. 117) on Route 5, Route 6, or elsewhere. Or catch one when it appears in the Cerulean Cave (2F).

Where to catch

Unusual Encounter

EVOLUTION

(DOES NOT EVOLVE)

POKÉMON EXPRESSIONS

HAPPY

UNHAPPY

ATTACKING

LEVEL-UP MOVES

LV.	NAME	TYPE	KIND	POW.	ACC.	PP	RANGE
1	Growl	Normal	Status	—	100	40	Many Others
1	Pound	Normal	Physical	40	100	35	Normal
4	Defense Curl	Normal	Status	—	—	40	Self
8	Tail Whip	Normal	Status	—	100	30	Many Others
12	Double Slap	Normal	Physical	15	85	10	Normal
16	Soft-Boiled	Normal	Status	—	—	10	Self
20	Minimize	Normal	Status	—	—	10	Self
25	Take Down	Normal	Physical	90	85	20	Normal
30	Sing	Normal	Status	—	55	15	Normal
35	Egg Bomb	Normal	Physical	100	75	10	Normal
40	Light Screen	Psychic	Status	—	—	30	Your Side
45	Double-Edge	Normal	Physical	120	100	15	Normal

TM MOVES

NO.	NAME	TYPE	KIND	POW.	ACC.	PP	RANGE
TM01	Headbutt	Normal	Physical	70	100	15	Normal
TM03	Helping Hand	Normal	Status	—	—	20	1 Ally
TM04	Teleport	Psychic	Status	—	—	20	Self
TM05	Rest	Psychic	Status	—	—	10	Self
TM06	Light Screen	Psychic	Status	—	—	30	Your Side
TM07	Protect	Normal	Status	—	—	10	Self
TM08	Substitute	Normal	Status	—	—	10	Self
TM09	Reflect	Psychic	Status	—	—	20	Your Side
TM12	Facade	Normal	Physical	70	100	20	Normal
TM13	Brick Break	Fighting	Physical	75	100	15	Normal
TM15	Seismic Toss	Fighting	Physical	—	100	20	Normal
TM16	Thunder Wave	Electric	Status	—	90	20	Normal
TM19	Iron Tail	Steel	Physical	100	75	15	Normal
TM22	Rock Slide	Rock	Physical	75	90	10	Many Others
TM23	Thunder Punch	Electric	Physical	75	100	15	Normal
TM27	Toxic	Poison	Status	—	90	10	Normal
TM28	Tri Attack	Normal	Special	80	100	10	Normal
TM31	Fire Punch	Fire	Physical	75	100	15	Normal
TM32	Dazzling Gleam	Fairy	Special	80	100	10	Many Others
TM33	Calm Mind	Psychic	Status	—	—	20	Self
TM35	Ice Punch	Ice	Physical	75	100	15	Normal
TM36	Thunderbolt	Electric	Special	90	100	15	Normal
TM37	Flamethrower	Fire	Special	90	100	15	Normal
TM38	Thunder	Electric	Special	110	70	10	Normal
TM40	Psychic	Psychic	Special	90	100	10	Normal
TM41	Earthquake	Ground	Physical	100	100	10	All Others
TM43	Shadow Ball	Ghost	Special	80	100	15	Normal
TM45	Solar Beam	Grass	Special	200	100	10	Normal
TM46	Fire Blast	Fire	Special	110	85	5	Normal
TM48	Hyper Beam	Normal	Special	150	90	5	Normal
TM51	Blizzard	Ice	Special	110	70	5	Many Others
TM55	Ice Beam	Ice	Special	90	100	10	Normal
TM56	Stealth Rock	Rock	Status	—	—	20	Other Side
TM59	Dream Eater	Psychic	Special	100	100	15	Normal

EVOLUTION MOVES

NAME	TYPE	KIND	POW.	ACC.	PP	RANGE

☑ **114** Vine Pokémon   Average height: 3'03"   Average weight: 77.2 lbs.

Tangela

TANGELA | 114

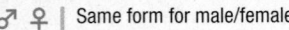

♂ ♀ | Same form for male/female

SPECIES STRENGTHS

HP	▪▪▪
ATTACK	▪▪▪
DEFENSE	▪▪▪▪▪▪▪
SP. ATK	▪▪▪▪▪
SP. DEF	▪▪
SPEED	▪▪▪

DAMAGE TAKEN IN BATTLES

◎ ×1		×2
×2		×1
×0.5		×2
×0.5		×1
×0.5		×1
×2		×1
×1		×1
×2		×1
×0.5		×1

POKÉDEX ENTRY

Its identity is obscured by masses of thick blue vines. The vines are said to never stop growing.

MAIN WAY TO OBTAIN

Catch one when it appears on Route 21.

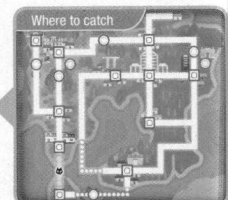
Where to catch

EVOLUTION

(DOES NOT EVOLVE)

LEVEL-UP MOVES

LV.	NAME	TYPE	KIND	POW.	ACC.	PP	RANGE
1	Absorb	Grass	Special	40	100	15	Normal
1	Constrict	Normal	Physical	10	100	35	Normal
5	Sleep Powder	Grass	Status	—	75	15	Normal
10	Confusion	Psychic	Special	50	100	25	Normal
15	Vine Whip	Grass	Physical	45	100	25	Normal
17	Poison Powder	Poison	Status	—	75	35	Normal
22	Bind	Normal	Physical	15	85	20	Normal
27	Growth	Normal	Status	—	—	20	Self
29	Stun Spore	Grass	Status	—	75	30	Normal
34	Mega Drain	Grass	Special	75	100	10	Normal
39	Leech Seed	Grass	Status	—	90	10	Normal
44	Slam	Normal	Physical	80	75	20	Normal
49	Amnesia	Psychic	Status	—	—	20	Self
54	Power Whip	Grass	Physical	120	85	10	Normal

TM MOVES

NO.	NAME	TYPE	KIND	POW.	ACC.	PP	RANGE
TM01	Headbutt	Normal	Physical	70	100	15	Normal
TM05	Rest	Psychic	Status	—	—	10	Self
TM07	Protect	Normal	Status	—	—	10	Self
TM08	Substitute	Normal	Status	—	—	10	Self
TM09	Reflect	Psychic	Status	—	—	20	Your Side
TM12	Facade	Normal	Physical	70	100	20	Normal
TM27	Toxic	Poison	Status	—	90	10	Normal
TM45	Solar Beam	Grass	Special	200	100	10	Normal
TM48	Hyper Beam	Normal	Special	150	90	5	Normal
TM52	Sludge Bomb	Poison	Special	90	100	10	Normal
TM53	Mega Drain	Grass	Special	75	100	10	Normal

POKÉMON EXPRESSIONS

HAPPY

UNHAPPY

ATTACKING

EVOLUTION MOVES

NAME	TYPE	KIND	POW.	ACC.	PP	RANGE

Kangaskhan

♀ | Female only

SPECIES STRENGTHS

HP
ATTACK
DEFENSE
SP. ATK
SP. DEF
SPEED

DAMAGE TAKEN IN BATTLES

◎ ×1   ✦ ×1
🔥 ×1   ◉ ×1
💧 ×1   🌿 ×1
✊ ×1   ❄ ×1
☠ ×1   👁 ×0
❄ ×1   🌀 ×1
🏔 ×2   🌙 ×1
⚙ ×1   ◉ ×1
🌊 ×1   ✹ ×1

POKÉDEX ENTRY

Raises its young in its belly pouch. Won't run from any fight to keep its young protected.

MAIN WAY TO OBTAIN

Catch one when it appears in the Rock Tunnel.

Where to catch

EVOLUTION

(DOES NOT EVOLVE)

LEVEL-UP MOVES

LV.	NAME	TYPE	KIND	POW.	ACC.	PP	RANGE
1	Comet Punch	Normal	Physical	18	85	15	Normal
1	Leer	Normal	Status	—	100	30	Many Others
6	Fake Out	Normal	Physical	40	100	10	Normal
11	Tail Whip	Normal	Status	—	100	30	Many Others
17	Bite	Dark	Physical	60	100	25	Normal
22	Rage	Normal	Physical	20	100	20	Normal
28	Mega Punch	Normal	Physical	80	85	20	Normal
33	Dizzy Punch	Normal	Physical	70	100	10	Normal
39	Crunch	Dark	Physical	80	100	15	Normal
44	Outrage	Dragon	Physical	120	100	10	1 Random
50	Sucker Punch	Dark	Physical	70	100	5	Normal

TM MOVES

NO.	NAME	TYPE	KIND	POW.	ACC.	PP	RANGE
TM01	Headbutt	Normal	Physical	70	100	15	Normal
TM03	Helping Hand	Normal	Status	—	—	20	1 Ally
TM05	Rest	Psychic	Status	—	—	10	Self
TM07	Protect	Normal	Status	—	—	10	Self
TM08	Substitute	Normal	Status	—	—	10	Self
TM10	Dig	Ground	Physical	80	100	10	Normal
TM12	Facade	Normal	Physical	70	100	20	Normal
TM13	Brick Break	Fighting	Physical	75	100	15	Normal
TM15	Seismic Toss	Fighting	Physical	—	100	20	Normal
TM19	Iron Tail	Steel	Physical	100	75	15	Normal
TM22	Rock Slide	Rock	Physical	75	90	10	Many Others
TM23	Thunder Punch	Electric	Physical	75	100	15	Normal
TM27	Toxic	Poison	Status	—	90	10	Normal
TM31	Fire Punch	Fire	Physical	75	100	15	Normal
TM35	Ice Punch	Ice	Physical	75	100	15	Normal
TM36	Thunderbolt	Electric	Special	90	100	15	Normal
TM37	Flamethrower	Fire	Special	90	100	15	Normal
TM38	Thunder	Electric	Special	110	70	10	Normal
TM39	Outrage	Dragon	Physical	120	100	10	1 Random
TM41	Earthquake	Ground	Physical	100	100	10	All Others
TM43	Shadow Ball	Ghost	Special	80	100	15	Normal
TM45	Solar Beam	Grass	Special	200	100	10	Normal
TM46	Fire Blast	Fire	Special	110	85	5	Normal
TM47	Surf	Water	Special	90	100	15	All Others
TM48	Hyper Beam	Normal	Special	150	90	5	Normal
TM51	Blizzard	Ice	Special	110	70	5	Many Others
TM55	Ice Beam	Ice	Special	90	100	10	Normal

EVOLUTION MOVES

NAME	TYPE	KIND	POW.	ACC.	PP	RANGE

☑ **115** Parent Pokémon — Average height: 7'03" — Average weight: 220.5 lbs.

Mega Kangaskhan

MEGA EVOLUTION

Kangaskhan

→ → →

Buy a Kangaskhanite, then Mega Evolve Kangaskhan during battle.

Mega Kangaskhan

SPECIES STRENGTHS

HP	
ATTACK	
DEFENSE	
SP. ATK	
SP. DEF	
SPEED	

DAMAGE TAKEN IN BATTLES

⊙	×1		×1
	×1		×1
	×1		×1
	×1		×1
	×1		×0
	×1		×1
	×2		×1
	×1		×1
	×1		×1

REQUIRED MEGA STONE: KANGASKHANITE

Buy it from a seller who appears at the Pokémon League once you have become Champion (p. 103).

Horsea

♂ ♀ | Same form for male/female

SPECIES STRENGTHS

HP	▮▮
ATTACK	▮▮▮
DEFENSE	▮▮▮▮▮
SP. ATK	▮▮▮▮
SP. DEF	▮▮
SPEED	▮▮▮▮

DAMAGE TAKEN IN BATTLES

×1		×1
×0.5		×1
×0.5		×1
×2		×1
×2		×1
×0.5		×1
×1		×1
×1		×0.5
×1		×1

POKÉDEX ENTRY

If it senses any danger, it will vigorously spray water or a special type of ink from its mouth.

MAIN WAY TO OBTAIN

Catch one when it appears on the water's surface on Route 11, Route 12, or Route 13.

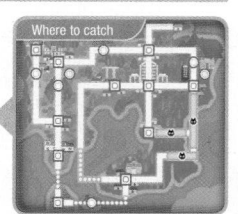
Where to catch

EVOLUTION

Horsea   Lv. 32 →→→   **Seadra**

POKÉMON EXPRESSIONS

HAPPY

UNHAPPY

ATTACKING
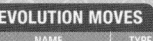

LEVEL-UP MOVES

LV.	NAME	TYPE	KIND	POW.	ACC.	PP	RANGE
1	Bubble	Water	Special	40	100	30	Many Others
6	Smokescreen	Normal	Status	—	100	20	Normal
9	Water Gun	Water	Special	40	100	25	Normal
15	Leer	Normal	Status	—	100	30	Many Others
18	Bubble Beam	Water	Special	65	100	20	Normal
24	Focus Energy	Normal	Status	—	—	30	Self
27	Waterfall	Water	Physical	80	100	15	Normal
33	Agility	Psychic	Status	—	—	30	Self
36	Dragon Pulse	Dragon	Special	85	100	10	Normal
42	Hydro Pump	Water	Special	110	80	5	Normal

TM MOVES

NO.	NAME	TYPE	KIND	POW.	ACC.	PP	RANGE
TM01	Headbutt	Normal	Physical	70	100	15	Normal
TM05	Rest	Psychic	Status	—	—	10	Self
TM07	Protect	Normal	Status	—	—	10	Self
TM08	Substitute	Normal	Status	—	—	10	Self
TM12	Facade	Normal	Physical	70	100	20	Normal
TM25	Waterfall	Water	Physical	80	100	15	Normal
TM27	Toxic	Poison	Status	—	90	10	Normal
TM29	Scald	Water	Special	80	100	15	Normal
TM34	Dragon Pulse	Dragon	Special	85	100	10	Normal
TM39	Outrage	Dragon	Physical	120	100	10	1 Random
TM47	Surf	Water	Special	90	100	15	All Others
TM51	Blizzard	Ice	Special	110	70	5	Many Others
TM54	Flash Cannon	Steel	Special	80	100	10	Normal
TM55	Ice Beam	Ice	Special	90	100	10	Normal

EVOLUTION MOVES

NAME	TYPE	KIND	POW.	ACC.	PP	RANGE

Average height: 3'11" Average weight: 55.1 lbs.

Seadra

♂ ♀ | Same form for male/female

SPECIES STRENGTHS

HP	▪▪▪
ATTACK	▪▪▪
DEFENSE	▪▪▪▪▪▪
SP. ATK	▪▪▪▪▪
SP. DEF	▪▪▪
SPEED	▪▪▪▪

DAMAGE TAKEN IN BATTLES

◎	×1		×1
	×0.5		×1
	×0.5		×1
	×2		×1
	×2		×1
	×0.5		×1
	×1		×1
	×1		×0.5
	×1		×1

POKÉDEX ENTRY

Touching the back fin causes numbness. It hooks its tail to coral to stay in place while sleeping.

MAIN WAY TO OBTAIN

Catch one when it appears on the water's surface on Route 11, Route 12, or Route 13. Or obtain a Horsea, then level it up to Lv. 32 or higher to evolve it into Seadra.

Where to catch

EVOLUTION

Horsea

Lv. 32
→ → →

Seadra

LEVEL-UP MOVES

LV.	NAME	TYPE	KIND	POW.	ACC.	PP	RANGE
1	Bubble	Water	Special	40	100	30	Many Others
1	Clear Smog	Poison	Special	50	—	15	Normal
1	Disable	Normal	Status	—	100	20	Normal
1	Leer	Normal	Status	—	100	30	Many Others
1	Smokescreen	Normal	Status	—	100	20	Normal
1	Water Gun	Water	Special	40	100	25	Normal
6	Smokescreen	Normal	Status	—	100	20	Normal
9	Water Gun	Water	Special	40	100	25	Normal
15	Leer	Normal	Status	—	100	30	Many Others
18	Bubble Beam	Water	Special	65	100	20	Normal
24	Focus Energy	Normal	Status	—	—	30	Self
27	Waterfall	Water	Physical	80	100	15	Normal
36	Agility	Psychic	Status	—	—	30	Self
42	Dragon Pulse	Dragon	Special	85	100	10	Normal
51	Hydro Pump	Water	Special	110	80	5	Normal

TM MOVES

NO.	NAME	TYPE	KIND	POW.	ACC.	PP	RANGE
TM01	Headbutt	Normal	Physical	70	100	15	Normal
TM05	Rest	Psychic	Status	—	—	10	Self
TM07	Protect	Normal	Status	—	—	10	Self
TM08	Substitute	Normal	Status	—	—	10	Self
TM12	Facade	Normal	Physical	70	100	20	Normal
TM25	Waterfall	Water	Physical	80	100	15	Normal
TM27	Toxic	Poison	Status	—	90	10	Normal
TM29	Scald	Water	Special	80	100	15	Normal
TM34	Dragon Pulse	Dragon	Special	85	100	10	Normal
TM39	Outrage	Dragon	Special	120	100	10	1 Random
TM47	Surf	Water	Special	90	100	15	All Others
TM48	Hyper Beam	Normal	Special	150	90	5	Normal
TM51	Blizzard	Ice	Special	110	70	5	Many Others
TM54	Flash Cannon	Steel	Special	80	100	10	Normal
TM55	Ice Beam	Ice	Special	90	100	10	Normal

EVOLUTION MOVES

NAME	TYPE	KIND	POW.	ACC.	PP	RANGE

POKÉMON EXPRESSIONS

HAPPY

UNHAPPY

ATTACKING

Goldeen

♂ ♀ | The female has a shorter horn on its head than the male.

♂ ♀

SPECIES STRENGTHS

HP	▪▪▪
ATTACK	▪▪▪▪
DEFENSE	▪▪▪▪
SP. ATK	▪▪▪
SP. DEF	▪▪▪
SPEED	▪▪▪▪

DAMAGE TAKEN IN BATTLES

⊙	×1	🪽	×1
🔥	×0.5	🌀	×1
💧	×0.5	⬤	×1
🌿	×2	◗	×1
⚡	×2	◉	×1
❄	×0.5	☯	×1
🥊	×1	☾	×1
☣	×1	⬡	×0.5
⛰	×1	✦	×1

POKÉDEX ENTRY

When it is time for them to lay eggs, they can be seen swimming up rivers and falls in large groups.

MAIN WAY TO OBTAIN

Catch one when it appears on the water's surface on Route 6.

Where to catch

EVOLUTION

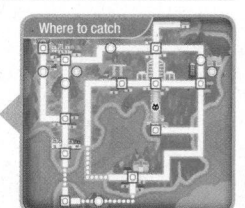

Goldeen

Lv. 33
→→→

Seaking

POKÉMON EXPRESSIONS

HAPPY

UNHAPPY

ATTACKING

LEVEL-UP MOVES

LV.	NAME	TYPE	KIND	POW.	ACC.	PP	RANGE
1	Peck	Flying	Physical	35	100	35	Normal
1	Tail Whip	Normal	Status	—	100	30	Many Others
4	Supersonic	Normal	Status	—	55	20	Normal
10	Quick Attack	Normal	Physical	40	100	30	Normal
14	Horn Attack	Normal	Physical	65	100	25	Normal
20	Fury Attack	Normal	Physical	15	85	20	Normal
24	Waterfall	Water	Physical	80	100	15	Normal
30	Agility	Psychic	Status	—	—	30	Self
34	Horn Drill	Normal	Physical	—	30	5	Normal
40	Megahorn	Bug	Physical	120	85	10	Normal

TM MOVES

NO.	NAME	TYPE	KIND	POW.	ACC.	PP	RANGE
TM01	Headbutt	Normal	Physical	70	100	15	Normal
TM05	Rest	Psychic	Status	—	—	10	Self
TM07	Protect	Normal	Status	—	—	10	Self
TM08	Substitute	Normal	Status	—	—	10	Self
TM12	Facade	Normal	Physical	70	100	20	Normal
TM25	Waterfall	Water	Physical	80	100	15	Normal
TM26	Poison Jab	Poison	Physical	80	100	20	Normal
TM27	Toxic	Poison	Status	—	90	10	Normal
TM29	Scald	Water	Special	80	100	15	Normal
TM47	Surf	Water	Special	90	100	15	All Others
TM51	Blizzard	Ice	Special	110	70	5	Many Others
TM55	Ice Beam	Ice	Special	90	100	10	Normal
TM58	Drill Run	Ground	Physical	80	95	10	Normal
TM60	Megahorn	Bug	Physical	120	85	10	Normal

EVOLUTION MOVES

NAME	TYPE	KIND	POW.	ACC.	PP	RANGE

☑ **119** Goldfish Pokémon | Average height: 4'03" | Average weight: 86.0 lbs.

Seaking

♂ ♀ | The female has a shorter horn on its head than the male.

SPECIES STRENGTHS

HP	▰▰▰▱▱
ATTACK	▰▰▰▰▱
DEFENSE	▰▰▱▱▱
SP. ATK	▰▰▱▱▱
SP. DEF	▰▰▰▱▱
SPEED	▰▰▱▱▱

DAMAGE TAKEN IN BATTLES

◉	×1	🪶	×1
🔥	×0.5	⊙	×1
💧	×0.5	✊	×1
🍃	×2	☠	×1
⚡	×2	🌀	×1
❄	×0.5	🪨	×1
👊	×1	🌙	×1
🐛	×1	⚙	×0.5
⛰	×1	✦	×1

POKÉDEX ENTRY

It is the male's job to make a nest by carving out boulders in a stream using the horn on its head.

MAIN WAY TO OBTAIN

Catch one when it appears on the water's surface on Route 6. Or obtain a Goldeen, then level it up to Lv. 33 or higher to evolve it into Seaking.

Where to catch

EVOLUTION

Lv. 33 →→→

Goldeen →→→ Seaking

LEVEL-UP MOVES

LV.	NAME	TYPE	KIND	POW.	ACC.	PP	RANGE
1	Peck	Flying	Physical	35	100	35	Normal
1	Psybeam	Psychic	Special	65	100	20	Normal
1	Quick Attack	Normal	Physical	40	100	30	Normal
1	Skull Bash	Normal	Physical	130	100	10	Normal
1	Supersonic	Normal	Status	—	55	20	Normal
1	Tail Whip	Normal	Status	—	100	30	Many Others
4	Supersonic	Normal	Status	—	55	20	Normal
10	Quick Attack	Normal	Physical	40	100	30	Normal
14	Horn Attack	Normal	Physical	65	100	25	Normal
20	Fury Attack	Normal	Physical	15	85	20	Normal
24	Waterfall	Water	Physical	80	100	15	Normal
30	Agility	Psychic	Status	—	—	30	Self
39	Horn Drill	Normal	Physical	—	30	5	Normal
50	Megahorn	Bug	Physical	120	85	10	Normal

TM MOVES

NO.	NAME	TYPE	KIND	POW.	ACC.	PP	RANGE
TM01	Headbutt	Normal	Physical	70	100	15	Normal
TM05	Rest	Psychic	Status	—	—	10	Self
TM07	Protect	Normal	Status	—	—	10	Self
TM08	Substitute	Normal	Status	—	—	10	Self
TM12	Facade	Normal	Physical	70	100	20	Normal
TM25	Waterfall	Water	Physical	80	100	15	Normal
TM26	Poison Jab	Poison	Physical	80	100	20	Normal
TM27	Toxic	Poison	Status	—	90	10	Normal
TM29	Scald	Water	Special	80	100	15	Normal
TM47	Surf	Water	Special	90	100	15	All Others
TM48	Hyper Beam	Normal	Special	150	90	5	Normal
TM51	Blizzard	Ice	Special	110	70	5	Many Others
TM55	Ice Beam	Ice	Special	90	100	10	Normal
TM58	Drill Run	Ground	Physical	80	95	10	Normal
TM60	Megahorn	Bug	Physical	120	85	10	Normal

POKÉMON EXPRESSIONS

HAPPY

UNHAPPY

ATTACKING

EVOLUTION MOVES

NAME	TYPE	KIND	POW.	ACC.	PP	RANGE

Staryu

— | Gender unknown

SPECIES STRENGTHS

HP
ATTACK
DEFENSE
SP. ATK
SP. DEF
SPEED

DAMAGE TAKEN IN BATTLES

⊙ ×1		🪶 ×1	
🔥 ×0.5		🌀 ×1	
💧 ×0.5		● ×1	
🍃 ×2		◈ ×1	
⚡ ×2		◐ ×1	
❄ ×0.5		↻ ×1	
▦ ×1		☾ ×1	
● ×1		◉ ×0.5	
◢ ×1		✦ ×1	

POKÉDEX ENTRY

As long as the center section is unharmed, this Pokémon can grow back fully even if it is chopped to bits.

MAIN WAY TO OBTAIN

Catch one when it appears on the water's surface on Route 18 (West), Route 19, or Route 21.

Where to catch

EVOLUTION

Staryu

Use Water Stone
→→→

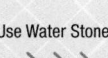

Starmie

POKÉMON EXPRESSIONS

HAPPY

UNHAPPY

ATTACKING

LEVEL-UP MOVES

LV.	NAME	TYPE	KIND	POW.	ACC.	PP	RANGE
1	Harden	Normal	Status	—	—	30	Self
1	Tackle	Normal	Physical	40	100	35	Normal
4	Psywave	Psychic	Special	—	100	15	Normal
9	Water Gun	Water	Special	40	100	25	Normal
13	Swift	Normal	Special	60	—	20	Many Others
18	Minimize	Normal	Status	—	—	10	Self
22	Confuse Ray	Ghost	Status	—	100	10	Normal
27	Bubble Beam	Water	Special	65	100	20	Normal
31	Light Screen	Psychic	Status	—	—	30	Your Side
36	Psychic	Psychic	Special	90	100	10	Normal
40	Recover	Normal	Status	—	—	10	Self
45	Hydro Pump	Water	Special	110	80	5	Normal

TM MOVES

NO.	NAME	TYPE	KIND	POW.	ACC.	PP	RANGE
TM01	Headbutt	Normal	Physical	70	100	15	Normal
TM04	Teleport	Psychic	Status	—	—	20	Self
TM05	Rest	Psychic	Status	—	—	10	Self
TM06	Light Screen	Psychic	Status	—	—	30	Your Side
TM07	Protect	Normal	Status	—	—	10	Self
TM08	Substitute	Normal	Status	—	—	10	Self
TM09	Reflect	Psychic	Status	—	—	20	Your Side
TM12	Facade	Normal	Physical	70	100	20	Normal
TM16	Thunder Wave	Electric	Status	—	90	20	Normal
TM25	Waterfall	Water	Physical	80	100	15	Normal
TM27	Toxic	Poison	Status	—	90	10	Normal
TM28	Tri Attack	Normal	Special	80	100	10	Normal
TM29	Scald	Water	Special	80	100	15	Normal
TM32	Dazzling Gleam	Fairy	Special	80	100	10	Many Others
TM36	Thunderbolt	Electric	Special	90	100	15	Normal
TM38	Thunder	Electric	Special	110	70	10	Normal
TM40	Psychic	Psychic	Special	90	100	10	Normal
TM47	Surf	Water	Special	90	100	15	All Others
TM51	Blizzard	Ice	Special	110	70	5	Many Others
TM54	Flash Cannon	Steel	Special	80	100	10	Normal
TM55	Ice Beam	Ice	Special	90	100	10	Normal

EVOLUTION MOVES

NAME	TYPE	KIND	POW.	ACC.	PP	RANGE

Starmie

— | Gender unknown

SPECIES STRENGTHS

HP	▮▮▮
ATTACK	▮▮▮▮
DEFENSE	▮▮▮▮
SP. ATK	▮▮▮▮▮
SP. DEF	▮▮▮▮
SPEED	▮▮▮▮▮▮

DAMAGE TAKEN IN BATTLES

×1		×1	
×0.5		×0.5	
×0.5		×2	
×2		×1	
×2		×2	
×0.5		×1	
×0.5		×2	
×1		×0.5	
×1		×1	

POKÉDEX ENTRY

The center section is named the core. People think it is communicating when it glows in seven colors.

MAIN WAY TO OBTAIN

Catch one when it appears on the water's surface on Route 18 (West), Route 19, or Route 21. Or obtain a Staryu, then use a Water Stone on it to evolve it into Starmie.

Where to catch

EVOLUTION

Staryu →→→ Use Water Stone →→→ **Starmie**

LEVEL-UP MOVES

LV.	NAME	TYPE	KIND	POW.	ACC.	PP	RANGE
1	Harden	Normal	Status	—	—	30	Self
1	Psywave	Psychic	Special	—	100	15	Normal
1	Tackle	Normal	Physical	40	100	35	Normal
1	Water Gun	Water	Special	40	100	25	Normal

TM MOVES

NO.	NAME	TYPE	KIND	POW.	ACC.	PP	RANGE
TM01	Headbutt	Normal	Physical	70	100	15	Normal
TM04	Teleport	Psychic	Status	—	—	20	Self
TM05	Rest	Psychic	Status	—	—	10	Self
TM06	Light Screen	Psychic	Status	—	—	30	Your Side
TM07	Protect	Normal	Status	—	—	10	Self
TM08	Substitute	Normal	Status	—	—	10	Self
TM09	Reflect	Psychic	Status	—	—	20	Your Side
TM12	Facade	Normal	Physical	70	100	20	Normal
TM16	Thunder Wave	Electric	Status	—	90	20	Normal
TM25	Waterfall	Water	Physical	80	100	15	Normal
TM27	Toxic	Poison	Status	—	90	10	Normal
TM28	Tri Attack	Normal	Special	80	100	10	Normal
TM29	Scald	Water	Special	80	100	15	Normal
TM32	Dazzling Gleam	Fairy	Special	80	100	10	Many Others
TM36	Thunderbolt	Electric	Special	90	100	15	Normal
TM38	Thunder	Electric	Special	110	70	10	Normal
TM40	Psychic	Psychic	Special	90	100	10	Normal
TM47	Surf	Water	Special	90	100	15	All Others
TM48	Hyper Beam	Normal	Special	150	90	5	Normal
TM51	Blizzard	Ice	Special	110	70	5	Many Others
TM54	Flash Cannon	Steel	Special	80	100	10	Normal
TM55	Ice Beam	Ice	Special	90	100	10	Normal
TM59	Dream Eater	Psychic	Special	100	100	15	Normal

EVOLUTION MOVES

NAME	TYPE	KIND	POW.	ACC.	PP	RANGE

Mr. Mime

♂ ♀ | Same form for male/female

SPECIES STRENGTHS

HP
ATTACK
DEFENSE
SP. ATK
SP. DEF
SPEED

DAMAGE TAKEN IN BATTLES

⬤ ×1		⬤ ×1	
⬤ ×1		⬤ ×0.5	
⬤ ×1		⬤ ×1	
⬤ ×1		⬤ ×1	
⬤ ×1		⬤ ×2	
⬤ ×1		⬤ ×0	
⬤ ×0.25		⬤ ×1	
⬤ ×2		⬤ ×2	
⬤ ×1		⬤ ×1	

POKÉDEX ENTRY

Always practicing its pantomime act. It makes enemies believe something exists that really doesn't.

MAIN WAY TO OBTAIN

Catch one when it appears on Route 11.

Where to catch

EVOLUTION

(DOES NOT EVOLVE)

POKÉMON EXPRESSIONS

HAPPY

UNHAPPY

ATTACKING

LEVEL-UP MOVES

LV.	NAME	TYPE	KIND	POW.	ACC.	PP	RANGE
1	Barrier	Psychic	Status	—	—	20	Self
1	Confusion	Psychic	Special	50	100	25	Normal
1	Pound	Normal	Physical	40	100	35	Normal
6	Meditate	Psychic	Status	—	—	40	Self
10	Double Slap	Normal	Physical	15	85	10	Normal
16	Mimic	Normal	Status	—	—	10	Normal
20	Psywave	Psychic	Special	—	100	15	Normal
26	Encore	Normal	Status	—	100	5	Normal
30	Psybeam	Psychic	Special	65	100	20	Normal
36	Light Screen	Psychic	Status	—	—	30	Your Side
36	Reflect	Psychic	Status	—	—	20	Your Side
40	Substitute	Normal	Status	—	—	10	Self
46	Psychic	Psychic	Special	90	100	10	Normal

TM MOVES

NO.	NAME	TYPE	KIND	POW.	ACC.	PP	RANGE
TM01	Headbutt	Normal	Physical	70	100	15	Normal
TM02	Taunt	Dark	Status	—	100	20	Normal
TM03	Helping Hand	Normal	Status	—	—	20	1 Ally
TM04	Teleport	Psychic	Status	—	—	20	Self
TM05	Rest	Psychic	Status	—	—	10	Self
TM06	Light Screen	Psychic	Status	—	—	30	Your Side
TM07	Protect	Normal	Status	—	—	10	Self
TM08	Substitute	Normal	Status	—	—	10	Self
TM09	Reflect	Psychic	Status	—	—	20	Your Side
TM12	Facade	Normal	Physical	70	100	20	Normal
TM13	Brick Break	Fighting	Physical	75	100	15	Normal
TM15	Seismic Toss	Fighting	Physical	—	100	20	Normal
TM16	Thunder Wave	Electric	Status	—	90	20	Normal
TM21	Foul Play	Dark	Physical	95	100	15	Normal
TM23	Thunder Punch	Electric	Physical	75	100	15	Normal
TM27	Toxic	Poison	Status	—	90	10	Normal
TM31	Fire Punch	Fire	Physical	75	100	15	Normal
TM32	Dazzling Gleam	Fairy	Special	80	100	10	Many Others
TM33	Calm Mind	Psychic	Status	—	—	20	Self
TM35	Ice Punch	Ice	Physical	75	100	15	Normal
TM36	Thunderbolt	Electric	Special	90	100	15	Normal
TM38	Thunder	Electric	Special	110	70	10	Normal
TM40	Psychic	Psychic	Special	90	100	10	Normal
TM43	Shadow Ball	Ghost	Special	80	100	15	Normal
TM45	Solar Beam	Grass	Special	200	100	10	Normal
TM48	Hyper Beam	Normal	Special	150	90	5	Normal
TM59	Dream Eater	Psychic	Special	100	100	15	Normal

EVOLUTION MOVES

NAME	TYPE	KIND	POW.	ACC.	PP	RANGE

✓ **123** Mantis Pokémon　　Average height: 4'11"　　Average weight: 123.5 lbs.

Scyther

♂ ♀ | The female has a longer abdomen than the male.

SPECIES STRENGTHS

HP	▪▪▪▫▫
ATTACK	▪▪▪▪▪▫
DEFENSE	▪▪▪▫▫
SP. ATK	▪▪▫▫▫
SP. DEF	▪▪▪▫▫
SPEED	▪▪▪▪▫

DAMAGE TAKEN IN BATTLES

⊙	×1	🪽	×2
🔥	×2	◎	×1
💧	×1	🔮	×0.5
🍃	×0.25	✦	×4
⚡	×2		×1
❄	×2		×1
👊	×0.25	🌙	×1
☠	×1	⊙	×1
⛰	×0	✧	×1

POKÉDEX ENTRY

Leaps out of tall grass and slices prey with its scythes. The movement looks like that of a ninja.

MAIN WAY TO OBTAIN

Catch one when it appears on Route 14 or Route 15 in *Pokémon: Let's Go, Pikachu!* Obtain one in a trade if you are playing *Pokémon: Let's Go, Eevee!*, as it does not appear in that game.

Where to catch

EVOLUTION

(DOES NOT EVOLVE)

LEVEL-UP MOVES

LV.	NAME	TYPE	KIND	POW.	ACC.	PP	RANGE
1	Leer	Normal	Status	—	100	30	Many Others
1	Quick Attack	Normal	Physical	40	100	30	Normal
4	Focus Energy	Normal	Status	—	—	30	Self
8	Double Team	Normal	Status	—	—	15	Self
12	Feint	Normal	Physical	30	100	10	Normal
16	Wing Attack	Flying	Physical	60	100	35	Normal
20	Agility	Psychic	Status	—	—	30	Self
26	Slash	Normal	Physical	70	100	20	Normal
32	Razor Wind	Normal	Special	80	100	10	Many Others
38	Air Slash	Flying	Special	75	95	15	Normal
44	Swords Dance	Normal	Status	—	—	20	Self
50	X-Scissor	Bug	Physical	80	100	15	Normal

TM MOVES

NO.	NAME	TYPE	KIND	POW.	ACC.	PP	RANGE
TM01	Headbutt	Normal	Physical	70	100	15	Normal
TM05	Rest	Psychic	Status	—	—	10	Self
TM06	Light Screen	Psychic	Status	—	—	30	Your Side
TM07	Protect	Normal	Status	—	—	10	Self
TM08	Substitute	Normal	Status	—	—	10	Self
TM12	Facade	Normal	Physical	70	100	20	Normal
TM13	Brick Break	Fighting	Physical	75	100	15	Normal
TM18	U-turn	Bug	Physical	70	100	20	Normal
TM24	X-Scissor	Bug	Physical	80	100	15	Normal
TM27	Toxic	Poison	Status	—	90	10	Normal
TM48	Hyper Beam	Normal	Special	150	90	5	Normal
TM50	Roost	Flying	Status	—	—	10	Self

EVOLUTION MOVES

NAME	TYPE	KIND	POW.	ACC.	PP	RANGE

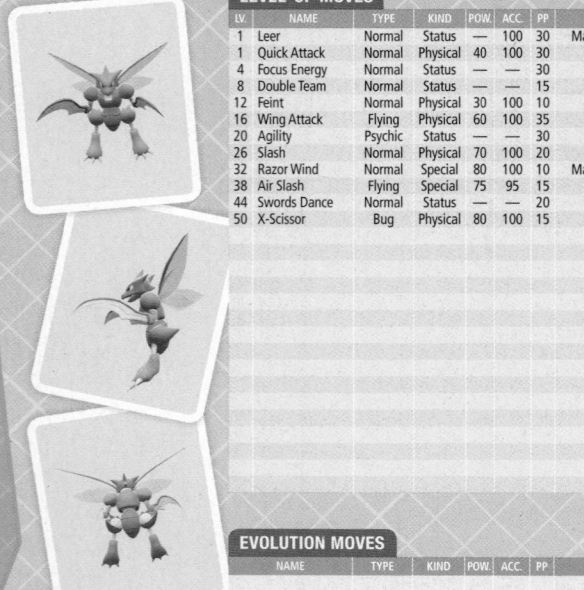

POKÉMON EXPRESSIONS

HAPPY

UNHAPPY

ATTACKING

Jynx

♀ | Female only

SPECIES STRENGTHS

HP
ATTACK
DEFENSE
SP. ATK
SP. DEF
SPEED

DAMAGE TAKEN IN BATTLES

◎ ×1		🍃 ×1	
🔥 ×2		⊚ ×0.5	
💧 ×1		🌀 ×2	
⚡ ×1		🗡 ×2	
🌿 ×1		👁 ×2	
❄ ×0.5		🪨 ×1	
👊 ×1		🌙 ×2	
☠ ×1		⭘ ×2	
🗻 ×1		✦ ×1	

POKÉDEX ENTRY

Appears to move to a rhythm of
its own, as if it were dancing. It
wiggles its hips as it walks.

MAIN WAY TO OBTAIN

Catch one when it appears in the
Seafoam Islands.

Where to catch

EVOLUTION

(DOES NOT EVOLVE)

POKÉMON EXPRESSIONS

HAPPY

UNHAPPY

ATTACKING

LEVEL-UP MOVES

LV.	NAME	TYPE	KIND	POW.	ACC.	PP	RANGE
1	Pound	Normal	Physical	40	100	35	Normal
6	Lick	Ghost	Physical	30	100	30	Normal
12	Confusion	Psychic	Special	50	100	25	Normal
18	Screech	Normal	Status	—	85	40	Normal
22	Double Slap	Normal	Physical	15	85	10	Normal
26	Ice Punch	Ice	Physical	75	100	15	Normal
30	Body Slam	Normal	Physical	85	100	15	Normal
35	Lovely Kiss	Normal	Status	—	75	10	Normal
40	Psychic	Psychic	Special	90	100	10	Normal
45	Blizzard	Ice	Special	110	70	5	Many Others

TM MOVES

NO.	NAME	TYPE	KIND	POW.	ACC.	PP	RANGE
TM01	Headbutt	Normal	Physical	70	100	15	Normal
TM02	Taunt	Dark	Status	—	100	20	Normal
TM03	Helping Hand	Normal	Status	—	—	20	1 Ally
TM04	Teleport	Psychic	Status	—	—	20	Self
TM05	Rest	Psychic	Status	—	—	10	Self
TM06	Light Screen	Psychic	Status	—	—	30	Your Side
TM07	Protect	Normal	Status	—	—	10	Self
TM08	Substitute	Normal	Status	—	—	10	Self
TM09	Reflect	Psychic	Status	—	—	20	Your Side
TM12	Facade	Normal	Physical	70	100	20	Normal
TM13	Brick Break	Fighting	Physical	75	100	15	Normal
TM15	Seismic Toss	Fighting	Physical	—	100	20	Normal
TM27	Toxic	Poison	Status	—	90	10	Normal
TM33	Calm Mind	Psychic	Status	—	—	20	Self
TM35	Ice Punch	Ice	Physical	75	100	15	Normal
TM40	Psychic	Psychic	Special	90	100	10	Normal
TM43	Shadow Ball	Ghost	Special	80	100	15	Normal
TM48	Hyper Beam	Normal	Special	150	90	5	Normal
TM51	Blizzard	Ice	Special	110	70	5	Many Others
TM55	Ice Beam	Ice	Special	90	100	10	Normal
TM59	Dream Eater	Psychic	Special	100	100	15	Normal

EVOLUTION MOVES

NAME	TYPE	KIND	POW.	ACC.	PP	RANGE

☑ **125** Electric Pokémon Average height: 3'07" Average weight: 66.1 lbs.

Electabuzz

♂ ♀ | Same form for male/female

SPECIES STRENGTHS

HP	▉▉▉
ATTACK	▉▉▉▉
DEFENSE	▉▉▉
SP. ATK	▉▉▉▉▉
SP. DEF	▉▉▉▉
SPEED	▉▉▉▉▉▉

DAMAGE TAKEN IN BATTLES

◎ ×1		×0.5
×1		×1
×1		×1
×1		×1
×0.5		×1
×1		×1
×1		×1
×1		×0.5
×2		×1

POKÉDEX ENTRY

If a major power outage occurs, it is certain that this Pokémon has eaten electricity at a power plant.

MAIN WAY TO OBTAIN

Catch one when it appears in the Power Plant.

Where to catch

EVOLUTION

(DOES NOT EVOLVE)

LEVEL-UP MOVES

LV.	NAME	TYPE	KIND	POW.	ACC.	PP	RANGE
1	Leer	Normal	Status	—	100	30	Many Others
1	Thunder Shock	Electric	Special	40	100	30	Normal
6	Quick Attack	Normal	Physical	40	100	30	Normal
11	Thunder Wave	Electric	Status	—	90	20	Normal
17	Swift	Normal	Special	60	—	20	Many Others
22	Low Kick	Fighting	Physical	—	100	20	Normal
28	Light Screen	Psychic	Status	—	—	30	Your Side
33	Thunder Punch	Electric	Physical	75	100	15	Normal
39	Screech	Normal	Status	—	85	40	Normal
44	Thunderbolt	Electric	Special	90	100	15	Normal
50	Thunder	Electric	Special	110	70	10	Normal

TM MOVES

NO.	NAME	TYPE	KIND	POW.	ACC.	PP	RANGE
TM01	Headbutt	Normal	Physical	70	100	15	Normal
TM02	Taunt	Dark	Status	—	100	20	Normal
TM03	Helping Hand	Normal	Status	—	—	20	1 Ally
TM04	Teleport	Psychic	Status	—	—	20	Self
TM05	Rest	Psychic	Status	—	—	10	Self
TM06	Light Screen	Psychic	Status	—	—	30	Your Side
TM07	Protect	Normal	Status	—	—	10	Self
TM08	Substitute	Normal	Status	—	—	10	Self
TM09	Reflect	Psychic	Status	—	—	20	Your Side
TM12	Facade	Normal	Physical	70	100	20	Normal
TM13	Brick Break	Fighting	Physical	75	100	15	Normal
TM15	Seismic Toss	Fighting	Physical	—	100	20	Normal
TM16	Thunder Wave	Electric	Status	—	90	20	Normal
TM19	Iron Tail	Steel	Physical	100	75	15	Normal
TM23	Thunder Punch	Electric	Physical	75	100	15	Normal
TM27	Toxic	Poison	Status	—	90	10	Normal
TM31	Fire Punch	Fire	Physical	75	100	15	Normal
TM35	Ice Punch	Ice	Physical	75	100	15	Normal
TM36	Thunderbolt	Electric	Special	90	100	15	Normal
TM38	Thunder	Electric	Special	110	70	10	Normal
TM40	Psychic	Psychic	Special	90	100	10	Normal
TM48	Hyper Beam	Normal	Special	150	90	5	Normal

EVOLUTION MOVES

NAME	TYPE	KIND	POW.	ACC.	PP	RANGE

POKÉMON EXPRESSIONS

HAPPY

UNHAPPY

ATTACKING

Magmar

♂ ♀ | Same form for male/female

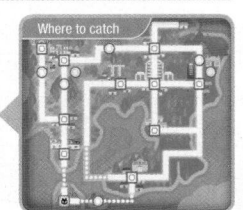

SPECIES STRENGTHS

HP
ATTACK
DEFENSE
SP. ATK
SP. DEF
SPEED

DAMAGE TAKEN IN BATTLES

×1		×1	
×0.5		×1	
×2		×0.5	
×0.5		×2	
×1		×1	
×0.5		×1	
×1		×1	
×1		×0.5	
×2		×0.5	

POKÉDEX ENTRY

Born in an active volcano. Its body is always cloaked in flames, so it looks like a big ball of fire.

MAIN WAY TO OBTAIN

Catch one when it appears in the Pokémon Mansion.

Where to catch

EVOLUTION

(DOES NOT EVOLVE)

POKÉMON EXPRESSIONS

HAPPY

UNHAPPY

ATTACKING

LEVEL-UP MOVES

LV.	NAME	TYPE	KIND	POW.	ACC.	PP	RANGE
1	Ember	Fire	Special	40	100	25	Normal
1	Leer	Normal	Status	—	100	30	Many Others
6	Smog	Poison	Special	30	70	20	Normal
11	Smokescreen	Normal	Status	—	100	20	Normal
17	Clear Smog	Poison	Special	50	—	15	Normal
22	Low Kick	Fighting	Physical	—	100	20	Normal
28	Fire Spin	Fire	Special	35	85	15	Normal
33	Fire Punch	Fire	Physical	75	100	15	Normal
39	Confuse Ray	Ghost	Status	—	100	10	Normal
44	Flamethrower	Fire	Special	90	100	15	Normal
50	Fire Blast	Fire	Special	110	85	5	Normal

TM MOVES

NO.	NAME	TYPE	KIND	POW.	ACC.	PP	RANGE
TM01	Headbutt	Normal	Physical	70	100	15	Normal
TM02	Taunt	Dark	Status	—	100	20	Normal
TM03	Helping Hand	Normal	Status	—	—	20	1 Ally
TM04	Teleport	Psychic	Status	—	—	20	Self
TM05	Rest	Psychic	Status	—	—	10	Self
TM07	Protect	Normal	Status	—	—	10	Self
TM08	Substitute	Normal	Status	—	—	10	Self
TM11	Will-O-Wisp	Fire	Status	—	85	15	Normal
TM12	Facade	Normal	Physical	70	100	20	Normal
TM13	Brick Break	Fighting	Physical	75	100	15	Normal
TM15	Seismic Toss	Fighting	Physical	—	100	20	Normal
TM19	Iron Tail	Steel	Physical	100	75	15	Normal
TM23	Thunder Punch	Electric	Physical	75	100	15	Normal
TM27	Toxic	Poison	Status	—	90	10	Normal
TM31	Fire Punch	Fire	Physical	75	100	15	Normal
TM37	Flamethrower	Fire	Special	90	100	15	Normal
TM40	Psychic	Psychic	Special	90	100	10	Normal
TM46	Fire Blast	Fire	Special	110	85	5	Normal
TM48	Hyper Beam	Normal	Special	150	90	5	Normal

EVOLUTION MOVES

NAME	TYPE	KIND	POW.	ACC.	PP	RANGE

☑ **127** Stag Beetle Pokémon Average height: 4'11" Average weight: 121.3 lbs.

Pinsir

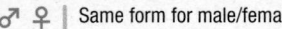

♂ ♀ | Same form for male/female

SPECIES STRENGTHS

HP	▰▰▰
ATTACK	▰▰▰▰▰▰
DEFENSE	▰▰▰▰▰
SP. ATK	▰▰▰
SP. DEF	▰▰▰▰
SPEED	▰▰▰▰

DAMAGE TAKEN IN BATTLES

◎	×1		×2
	×2		×1
	×1		×1
	×0.5		×2
	×1		×1
	×1		×1
	×0.5		×1
	×0.5		×1

POKÉDEX ENTRY

Grips its prey in its pincers and squeezes hard! It can't move if it's cold out, so it lives in warm places.

MAIN WAY TO OBTAIN

Obtain one in a trade if you are playing *Pokémon: Let's Go, Pikachu!*, as it does not appear in that game. Catch one when it appears on Route 14 or Route 15 in *Pokémon: Let's Go, Eevee!*

Where to catch

EVOLUTION

(DOES NOT EVOLVE)

LEVEL-UP MOVES

LV.	NAME	TYPE	KIND	POW.	ACC.	PP	RANGE
1	Focus Energy	Normal	Status	—	—	30	Self
1	Vice Grip	Normal	Physical	55	100	30	Normal
4	Bind	Normal	Physical	15	85	20	Normal
8	Seismic Toss	Fighting	Physical	—	100	20	Normal
12	Harden	Normal	Status	—	—	30	Self
16	Brick Break	Fighting	Physical	75	100	15	Normal
20	X-Scissor	Bug	Physical	80	100	15	Normal
26	Submission	Fighting	Physical	80	80	20	Normal
32	Swords Dance	Normal	Status	—	—	20	Self
38	Thrash	Normal	Physical	120	100	10	1 Random
44	Superpower	Fighting	Physical	120	100	5	Normal
50	Guillotine	Normal	Physical	—	30	5	Normal

TM MOVES

NO.	NAME	TYPE	KIND	POW.	ACC.	PP	RANGE
TM01	Headbutt	Normal	Physical	70	100	15	Normal
TM03	Helping Hand	Normal	Status	—	—	20	1 Ally
TM05	Rest	Psychic	Status	—	—	10	Self
TM07	Protect	Normal	Status	—	—	10	Self
TM08	Substitute	Normal	Status	—	—	10	Self
TM10	Dig	Ground	Physical	80	100	10	Normal
TM12	Facade	Normal	Physical	70	100	20	Normal
TM13	Brick Break	Fighting	Physical	75	100	15	Normal
TM15	Seismic Toss	Fighting	Physical	—	100	20	Normal
TM22	Rock Slide	Rock	Physical	75	90	10	Many Others
TM24	X-Scissor	Bug	Physical	80	100	15	Normal
TM27	Toxic	Poison	Status	—	90	10	Normal
TM30	Bulk Up	Fighting	Status	—	—	20	Self
TM39	Outrage	Dragon	Physical	120	100	10	1 Random
TM41	Earthquake	Ground	Physical	100	100	10	All Others
TM48	Hyper Beam	Normal	Special	150	90	5	Normal
TM49	Superpower	Fighting	Physical	120	100	5	Normal
TM56	Stealth Rock	Rock	Status	—	—	20	Other Side

EVOLUTION MOVES

NAME	TYPE	KIND	POW.	ACC.	PP	RANGE

POKÉMON EXPRESSIONS

HAPPY

UNHAPPY

ATTACKING

Mega Pinsir

MEGA EVOLUTION

Pinsir

Buy a Pinsirite, then Mega Evolve Pinsir during battle.

→ → →

Mega Pinsir

SPECIES STRENGTHS

HP	
ATTACK	
DEFENSE	
SP. ATK	
SP. DEF	
SPEED	

DAMAGE TAKEN IN BATTLES

◎	×1	〰	×2
🔥	×2	◎	×1
💧	×1	👁	×0.5
🍃	×0.25	🔥	×4
⚡	×2	◎	×1
❄	×2	☯	×1
👊	×0.25	◐	×1
◉	×1	◎	×1
▲	×0	✦	×1

 REQUIRED MEGA STONE: PINSIRITE

Buy it from a seller who appears at the Pokémon League once you have become Champion (p. 103).

Tauros

♂ | Male only

SPECIES STRENGTHS

HP	
ATTACK	
DEFENSE	
SP. ATK	
SP. DEF	
SPEED	

DAMAGE TAKEN IN BATTLES

◉ ×1		◎ ×1	
◉ ×1		◎ ×1	
◉ ×1		◉ ×1	
◉ ×1		◎ ×1	
◉ ×1		◉ ×0	
❄ ×1		◉ ×1	
▦ ×2		◑ ×1	
◉ ×1		◉ ×1	
◬ ×1		✦ ×1	

POKÉDEX ENTRY

A rowdy Pokémon with a lot of stamina. Once running, it won't stop until it hits something.

MAIN WAY TO OBTAIN

Catch one when it appears on Route 14 or Route 15.

Where to catch

EVOLUTION

(DOES NOT EVOLVE)

LEVEL-UP MOVES

LV.	NAME	TYPE	KIND	POW.	ACC.	PP	RANGE
1	Tackle	Normal	Physical	40	100	35	Normal
6	Tail Whip	Normal	Status	—	100	30	Many Others
12	Rage	Normal	Physical	20	100	20	Normal
18	Horn Attack	Normal	Physical	65	100	25	Normal
24	Leer	Normal	Status	—	100	30	Many Others
30	Rest	Psychic	Status	—	—	10	Self
34	Take Down	Normal	Physical	90	85	20	Normal
38	Focus Energy	Normal	Status	—	—	30	Self
42	Thrash	Normal	Physical	120	100	10	1 Random
46	Double-Edge	Normal	Physical	120	100	15	Normal
50	Outrage	Dragon	Physical	120	100	10	1 Random

TM MOVES

NO.	NAME	TYPE	KIND	POW.	ACC.	PP	RANGE
TM01	Headbutt	Normal	Physical	70	100	15	Normal
TM03	Helping Hand	Normal	Status	—	—	20	1 Ally
TM05	Rest	Psychic	Status	—	—	10	Self
TM07	Protect	Normal	Status	—	—	10	Self
TM08	Substitute	Normal	Status	—	—	10	Self
TM12	Facade	Normal	Physical	70	100	20	Normal
TM19	Iron Tail	Steel	Physical	100	75	15	Normal
TM22	Rock Slide	Rock	Physical	75	90	10	Many Others
TM27	Toxic	Poison	Status	—	90	10	Normal
TM36	Thunderbolt	Electric	Special	90	100	15	Normal
TM37	Flamethrower	Fire	Special	90	100	15	Normal
TM38	Thunder	Electric	Special	110	70	10	Normal
TM39	Outrage	Dragon	Physical	120	100	10	1 Random
TM41	Earthquake	Ground	Physical	100	100	10	All Others
TM45	Solar Beam	Grass	Special	200	100	10	Normal
TM46	Fire Blast	Fire	Special	110	85	5	Normal
TM47	Surf	Water	Special	90	100	15	All Others
TM48	Hyper Beam	Normal	Special	150	90	5	Normal
TM51	Blizzard	Ice	Special	110	70	5	Many Others
TM55	Ice Beam	Ice	Special	90	100	10	Normal

EVOLUTION MOVES

NAME	TYPE	KIND	POW.	ACC.	PP	RANGE

Magikarp

♂ ♀ | The female has white whiskers, whereas the male has yellow whiskers.

♂   ♀

SPECIES STRENGTHS

HP	▪▪
ATTACK	▪
DEFENSE	▪▪▪▪
SP. ATK	▪
SP. DEF	▪▪
SPEED	▪▪▪▪▪

DAMAGE TAKEN IN BATTLES

◉	×1	✋	×1
🔥	×0.5	🌀	×1
💧	×0.5	🍃	×1
⚡	×2	🔮	×1
🌱	×2	●	×1
❄	×0.5	🌙	×1
👊	×1	☾	×1
☠	×1	◎	×0.5
⛰	×1	✦	×1

POKÉDEX ENTRY

Famous for being very unreliable. It can be found swimming in seas, lakes, rivers, and shallow puddles.

MAIN WAY TO OBTAIN

Catch one when it appears on the water's surface on Route 4 (East), Route 24, or elsewhere.

Where to catch

EVOLUTION

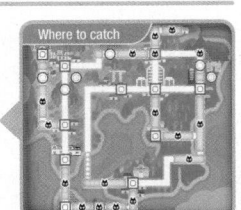

Magikarp   Lv. 20 →→→   Gyarados

POKÉMON EXPRESSIONS

HAPPY

UNHAPPY

ATTACKING

LEVEL-UP MOVES

LV.	NAME	TYPE	KIND	POW.	ACC.	PP	RANGE
1	Splash	Normal	Status	—	—	40	Self
15	Tackle	Normal	Physical	40	100	35	Normal

TM MOVES

NO.	NAME	TYPE	KIND	POW.	ACC.	PP	RANGE

EVOLUTION MOVES

NAME	TYPE	KIND	POW.	ACC.	PP	RANGE

✓ **130** Atrocious Pokémon   Average height: 21'04"   Average weight: 518.1 lbs.

Gyarados

♂ ♀ | The female has white whiskers, whereas the male has blue whiskers.

SPECIES STRENGTHS

HP	
ATTACK	
DEFENSE	
SP. ATK	
SP. DEF	
SPEED	

DAMAGE TAKEN IN BATTLES

×1		×1	
×0.5		×1	
×0.5		×0.5	
×1		×2	
×4		×1	
×1		×1	
×0.5		×1	
×1		×0.5	
×0		×1	

POKÉDEX ENTRY

Brutally vicious and enormously destructive. Known for totally destroying cities in ancient times.

MAIN WAY TO OBTAIN

Catch one when it appears on the water's surface on Route 20. Or obtain a Magikarp, then level it up to Lv. 20 or higher to evolve it into Gyarados.

Where to catch

EVOLUTION

Lv. 20
→→→

Magikarp   **Gyarados**

LEVEL-UP MOVES

LV.	NAME	TYPE	KIND	POW.	ACC.	PP	RANGE
1	Bind	Normal	Physical	15	85	20	Normal
1	Bite	Dark	Physical	60	100	25	Normal
1	Dragon Rage	Dragon	Special	—	100	10	Normal
1	Leer	Normal	Status	—	100	30	Many Others
1	Thrash	Normal	Physical	120	100	10	1 Random
6	Leer	Normal	Status	—	100	30	Many Others
11	Dragon Rage	Dragon	Special	—	100	10	Normal
16	Bind	Normal	Physical	15	85	20	Normal
21	Rage	Normal	Physical	20	100	20	Normal
26	Dragon Tail	Dragon	Physical	60	90	10	Normal
31	Waterfall	Water	Physical	80	100	15	Normal
36	Crunch	Dark	Physical	80	100	15	Normal
41	Outrage	Dragon	Physical	120	100	10	1 Random
46	Hydro Pump	Water	Special	110	80	5	Normal
51	Hyper Beam	Normal	Special	150	90	5	Normal

TM MOVES

NO.	NAME	TYPE	KIND	POW.	ACC.	PP	RANGE
TM01	Headbutt	Normal	Physical	70	100	15	Normal
TM02	Taunt	Dark	Status	—	100	20	Normal
TM05	Rest	Psychic	Status	—	—	10	Self
TM07	Protect	Normal	Status	—	—	10	Self
TM08	Substitute	Normal	Status	—	—	10	Self
TM09	Reflect	Psychic	Status	—	—	20	Your Side
TM12	Facade	Normal	Physical	70	100	20	Normal
TM16	Thunder Wave	Electric	Status	—	90	20	Normal
TM17	Dragon Tail	Dragon	Physical	60	90	10	Normal
TM19	Iron Tail	Steel	Physical	100	75	15	Normal
TM20	Dark Pulse	Dark	Special	80	100	15	Normal
TM25	Waterfall	Water	Physical	80	100	15	Normal
TM27	Toxic	Poison	Status	—	90	10	Normal
TM29	Scald	Water	Special	80	100	15	Normal
TM34	Dragon Pulse	Dragon	Special	85	100	10	Normal
TM36	Thunderbolt	Electric	Special	90	100	15	Normal
TM37	Flamethrower	Fire	Special	90	100	15	Normal
TM38	Thunder	Electric	Special	110	70	10	Normal
TM39	Outrage	Dragon	Physical	120	100	10	1 Random
TM41	Earthquake	Ground	Physical	100	100	10	All Others
TM46	Fire Blast	Fire	Special	110	85	5	Normal
TM47	Surf	Water	Special	90	100	15	All Others
TM48	Hyper Beam	Normal	Special	150	90	5	Normal
TM51	Blizzard	Ice	Special	110	70	5	Many Others
TM55	Ice Beam	Ice	Special	90	100	10	Normal

EVOLUTION MOVES

NAME	TYPE	KIND	POW.	ACC.	PP	RANGE
Bite	Dark	Physical	60	100	25	Normal

Mega Gyarados

MEGA EVOLUTION

Gyarados

Buy a Gyaradosite, then Mega Evolve Gyarados during battle.

→ → →

Mega Gyarados

SPECIES STRENGTHS

HP	
ATTACK	
DEFENSE	
SP. ATK	
SP. DEF	
SPEED	

DAMAGE TAKEN IN BATTLES

⊙	×1	🍃	×1
🔥	×0.5	⊚	×0
💧	×0.5	🐛	×2
🍂	×2	🦋	×1
⚡	×2	👻	×0.5
❄	×0.5	🐉	×1
👊	×2	◐	×0.5
☣	×1	⊙	×0.5
⛰	×1	✦	×2

REQUIRED MEGA STONE: GYARADOSITE

Buy it from a seller who appears at the Pokémon League once you have become Champion (p. 103).

✓ **131** Transport Pokémon · Average height: 8'02" · Average weight: 485.0 lbs.

Lapras

LAPRAS 131

♂ ♀ | Same form for male/female

SPECIES STRENGTHS

HP	▨▨▨▨▨▨▨
ATTACK	▨▨▨▨
DEFENSE	▨▨▨▨▨
SP. ATK	▨▨▨▨▨
SP. DEF	▨▨▨▨▨▨
SPEED	▨▨▨

DAMAGE TAKEN IN BATTLES

×1		×1	
×1		×1	
×0.5		×1	
×2		×2	
×2		×1	
×0.25		×1	
×2		×1	
×1		×1	
×1		×1	

POKÉDEX ENTRY

A gentle soul that can understand human speech. It can ferry people across the sea on its back.

MAIN WAY TO OBTAIN

Receive one from an employee in Silph Co. (p. 84). Or catch one when it appears as an unusual encounter during a Catch Combo (p. 117) on Route 20.

Where to catch

Unusual Encounter

EVOLUTION

(DOES NOT EVOLVE)

LEVEL-UP MOVES

LV.	NAME	TYPE	KIND	POW.	ACC.	PP	RANGE
1	Sing	Normal	Status	—	55	15	Normal
1	Water Gun	Water	Special	40	100	25	Normal
6	Growl	Normal	Status	—	100	40	Many Others
13	Mist	Ice	Status	—	—	30	Your Side
19	Ice Shard	Ice	Physical	40	100	30	Normal
26	Confuse Ray	Ghost	Status	—	100	10	Normal
32	Body Slam	Normal	Physical	85	100	15	Normal
39	Ice Beam	Ice	Special	90	100	10	Normal
45	Surf	Water	Special	90	100	15	All Others
52	Dragon Pulse	Dragon	Special	85	100	10	Normal
58	Blizzard	Ice	Special	110	70	5	Many Others
65	Hydro Pump	Water	Special	110	80	5	Normal

TM MOVES

NO.	NAME	TYPE	KIND	POW.	ACC.	PP	RANGE
TM01	Headbutt	Normal	Physical	70	100	15	Normal
TM05	Rest	Psychic	Status	—	—	10	Self
TM07	Protect	Normal	Status	—	—	10	Self
TM08	Substitute	Normal	Status	—	—	10	Self
TM09	Reflect	Psychic	Status	—	—	20	Your Side
TM12	Facade	Normal	Physical	70	100	20	Normal
TM19	Iron Tail	Steel	Physical	100	75	15	Normal
TM25	Waterfall	Water	Physical	80	100	15	Normal
TM27	Toxic	Poison	Status	—	90	10	Normal
TM34	Dragon Pulse	Dragon	Special	85	100	10	Normal
TM36	Thunderbolt	Electric	Special	90	100	15	Normal
TM38	Thunder	Electric	Special	110	70	10	Normal
TM39	Outrage	Dragon	Physical	120	100	10	1 Random
TM40	Psychic	Psychic	Special	90	100	10	Normal
TM45	Solar Beam	Grass	Special	200	100	10	Normal
TM47	Surf	Water	Special	90	100	15	All Others
TM48	Hyper Beam	Normal	Special	150	90	5	Normal
TM51	Blizzard	Ice	Special	110	70	5	Many Others
TM55	Ice Beam	Ice	Special	90	100	10	Normal
TM58	Drill Run	Ground	Physical	80	95	10	Normal
TM59	Dream Eater	Psychic	Special	100	100	15	Normal
TM60	Megahorn	Bug	Physical	120	85	10	Normal

EVOLUTION MOVES

NAME	TYPE	KIND	POW.	ACC.	PP	RANGE

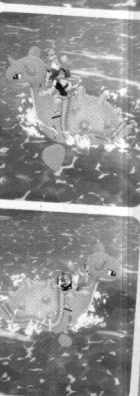

Ditto

— | Gender unknown

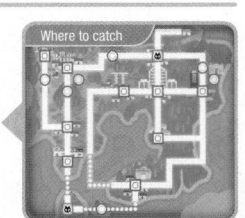

SPECIES STRENGTHS

HP	▪▪▪
ATTACK	▪▪▪
DEFENSE	▪▪▪
SP. ATK	▪▪▪
SP. DEF	▪▪▪
SPEED	▪▪▪

DAMAGE TAKEN IN BATTLES

⦿	×1	🍃	×1
🔥	×1	🌀	×1
💧	×1	🍄	×1
⚡	×1	🌙	×1
⚡	×1	👻	×0
❄	×1	🐉	×1
👊	×2	🌑	×1
☠	×1	⚙	×1
⛰	×1	✦	×1

POKÉDEX ENTRY

When it spots an enemy, its body transfigures into an almost-perfect copy of its opponent.

MAIN WAY TO OBTAIN

Catch one when it appears in the Pokémon Mansion, especially on B1F, or in the Cerulean Cave.

Where to catch

EVOLUTION

(DOES NOT EVOLVE)

POKÉMON EXPRESSIONS

HAPPY

UNHAPPY

ATTACKING

LEVEL-UP MOVES

LV.	NAME	TYPE	KIND	POW.	ACC.	PP	RANGE
1	Transform	Normal	Status	—	—	10	Normal

TM MOVES

NO.	NAME	TYPE	KIND	POW.	ACC.	PP	RANGE

EVOLUTION MOVES

NAME	TYPE	KIND	POW.	ACC.	PP	RANGE

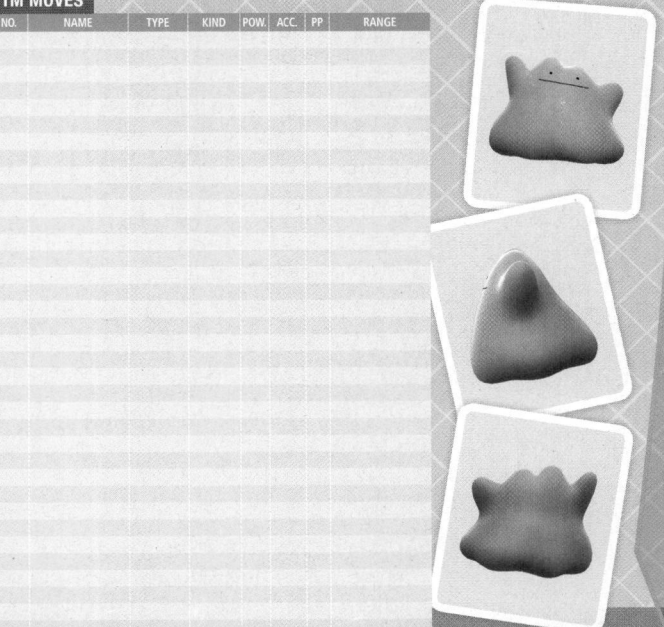

133 Evolution Pokémon | Average height: 1'00" | Average weight: 14.3 lbs.

Eevee

♂ ♀ | Same form for male/female

SPECIES STRENGTHS

HP	▰▰▰
ATTACK	▰▰▰
DEFENSE	▰▰
SP. ATK	▰▰
SP. DEF	▰▰▰
SPEED	▰▰▰

DAMAGE TAKEN IN BATTLES

Type	Mult	Type	Mult
Normal	×1	Flying	×1
Fire	×1	Psychic	×1
Water	×1	Bug	×1
Grass	×1	Rock	×1
Electric	×1	Ghost	×0
Ice	×1	Dragon	×1
Fighting	×2	Dark	×1
Poison	×1	Steel	×1
Ground	×1	Fairy	×1

POKÉDEX ENTRY

It can evolve into a variety of forms. Eevee's genes are the key to solving the mysteries of Pokémon evolution.

MAIN WAY TO OBTAIN

Catch one when it appears on Route 17.

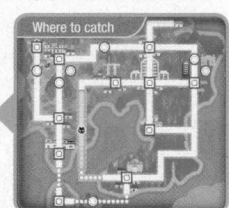

Where to catch

EVOLUTION

 →→→

Eevee	Vaporeon	Jolteon	Flareon
	Use Water Stone	Use Thunder Stone	Use Fire Stone

LEVEL-UP MOVES

LV.	NAME	TYPE	KIND	POW.	ACC.	PP	RANGE
1	Growl	Normal	Status	—	100	40	Many Others
1	Tackle	Normal	Physical	40	100	35	Normal
3	Tail Whip	Normal	Status	—	100	30	Many Others
6	Quick Attack	Normal	Physical	40	100	30	Normal
10	Double Kick	Fighting	Physical	30	100	30	Normal
14	Sand Attack	Ground	Status	—	100	15	Normal
17	Bite	Dark	Physical	60	100	25	Normal
21	Swift	Normal	Special	60	—	20	Many Others
24	Take Down	Normal	Physical	90	85	20	Normal
28	Double-Edge	Normal	Physical	120	100	15	Normal
31	Helping Hand	Normal	Status	—	—	20	1 Ally

TM MOVES

NO.	NAME	TYPE	KIND	POW.	ACC.	PP	RANGE
TM01	Headbutt	Normal	Physical	70	100	15	Normal
TM03	Helping Hand	Normal	Status	—	—	20	1 Ally
TM05	Rest	Psychic	Status	—	—	10	Self
TM07	Protect	Normal	Status	—	—	10	Self
TM08	Substitute	Normal	Status	—	—	10	Self
TM09	Reflect	Psychic	Status	—	—	20	Your Side
TM10	Dig	Ground	Physical	80	100	10	Normal
TM12	Facade	Normal	Physical	70	100	20	Normal
TM19	Iron Tail	Steel	Physical	100	75	15	Normal
TM27	Toxic	Poison	Status	—	90	10	Normal
TM43	Shadow Ball	Ghost	Special	80	100	15	Normal
TM57	Pay Day	Normal	Physical	40	100	20	Normal

EVOLUTION MOVES

NAME	TYPE	KIND	POW.	ACC.	PP	RANGE

POKÉMON EXPRESSIONS

HAPPY

UNHAPPY

ATTACKING

Vaporeon

♂ ♀ | Same form for male/female

SPECIES STRENGTHS

HP	▨▨▨▨▨▨▨
ATTACK	▨▨▨
DEFENSE	▨▨▨
SP. ATK	▨▨▨▨▨▨
SP. DEF	▨▨▨▨▨
SPEED	▨▨▨

DAMAGE TAKEN IN BATTLES

⊙ ×1		🪶 ×1	
🔥 ×0.5		🌀 ×1	
💧 ×0.5		👁 ×1	
🍃 ×2		✴ ×1	
⚡ ×2		🌑 ×1	
❄ ×0.5		🜚 ×1	
👊 ×1		◐ ×1	
☠ ×1		⬡ ×0.5	
⛰ ×1		✦ ×1	

POKÉDEX ENTRY

Its cell structure is similar to water molecules. It melts into the water and becomes invisible.

MAIN WAY TO OBTAIN

Obtain an Eevee, then use a Water Stone on it to evolve it into Vaporeon. Note that your partner Eevee will not evolve into Vaporeon if you are playing *Pokémon: Let's Go, Eevee!*

Where to catch

Habitat Unknown

EVOLUTION

Use Water Stone
→→→→

Eevee   **Vaporeon**

POKÉMON EXPRESSIONS

HAPPY

UNHAPPY

ATTACKING

LEVEL-UP MOVES

LV.	NAME	TYPE	KIND	POW.	ACC.	PP	RANGE
1	Growl	Normal	Status	—	100	40	Many Others
1	Sand Attack	Ground	Status	—	100	15	Normal
1	Tackle	Normal	Physical	40	100	35	Normal
1	Tail Whip	Normal	Status	—	100	30	Many Others
1	Water Gun	Water	Special	40	100	25	Normal
1	Yawn	Normal	Status	—	—	10	Normal
3	Tail Whip	Normal	Status	—	100	30	Many Others
6	Quick Attack	Normal	Physical	40	100	30	Normal
10	Double Kick	Fighting	Physical	30	100	30	Normal
14	Sand Attack	Ground	Status	—	100	15	Normal
17	Aurora Beam	Ice	Special	65	100	20	Normal
21	Haze	Ice	Status	—	—	30	Both Sides
24	Acid Armor	Poison	Status	—	—	20	Self
28	Helping Hand	Normal	Status	—	—	20	1 Ally
31	Hydro Pump	Water	Special	110	80	5	Normal

TM MOVES

NO.	NAME	TYPE	KIND	POW.	ACC.	PP	RANGE
TM01	Headbutt	Normal	Physical	70	100	15	Normal
TM03	Helping Hand	Normal	Status	—	—	20	1 Ally
TM05	Rest	Psychic	Status	—	—	10	Self
TM07	Protect	Normal	Status	—	—	10	Self
TM08	Substitute	Normal	Status	—	—	10	Self
TM09	Reflect	Psychic	Status	—	—	20	Your Side
TM10	Dig	Ground	Physical	80	100	10	Normal
TM12	Facade	Normal	Physical	70	100	20	Normal
TM19	Iron Tail	Steel	Physical	100	75	15	Normal
TM25	Waterfall	Water	Physical	80	100	15	Normal
TM27	Toxic	Poison	Status	—	90	10	Normal
TM29	Scald	Water	Special	80	100	15	Normal
TM43	Shadow Ball	Ghost	Special	80	100	15	Normal
TM47	Surf	Water	Special	90	100	15	All Others
TM48	Hyper Beam	Normal	Special	150	90	5	Normal
TM51	Blizzard	Ice	Special	110	70	5	Many Others
TM55	Ice Beam	Ice	Special	90	100	10	Normal
TM57	Pay Day	Normal	Physical	40	100	20	Normal

EVOLUTION MOVES

NAME	TYPE	KIND	POW.	ACC.	PP	RANGE
Water Gun	Water	Special	40	100	25	Normal

Jolteon

JOLTEON 135

♂ ♀ | Same form for male/female

SPECIES STRENGTHS

HP	▩▩▩
ATTACK	▩▩▩
DEFENSE	▩▩▩
SP. ATK	▩▩▩▩▩
SP. DEF	▩▩▩▩▩
SPEED	▩▩▩▩▩▩

DAMAGE TAKEN IN BATTLES

⊙ ×1		🍃 ×0.5	
🔥 ×1		🌀 ×1	
💧 ×1		◉ ×1	
🍂 ×1		◐ ×1	
⚡ ×0.5		◑ ×1	
❄ ×1		♦ ×1	
🥊 ×1		☾ ×1	
◎ ×1		◯ ×0.5	
🪨 ×2		✦ ×1	

POKÉDEX ENTRY

A sensitive Pokémon that easily becomes sad or angry. Every time its mood changes, it charges power.

MAIN WAY TO OBTAIN

Obtain an Eevee, then use a Thunder Stone on it to evolve it into Jolteon. Note that your partner Eevee will not evolve into Jolteon if you are playing *Pokémon: Let's Go, Eevee!*

Where to catch

Habitat Unknown

EVOLUTION

Use Thunder Stone
→ → →

Eevee   **Jolteon**

LEVEL-UP MOVES

LV.	NAME	TYPE	KIND	POW.	ACC.	PP	RANGE
1	Growl	Normal	Status	—	100	40	Many Others
1	Sand Attack	Ground	Status	—	100	15	Normal
1	Tackle	Normal	Physical	40	100	35	Normal
1	Tail Whip	Normal	Status	—	100	30	Many Others
1	Thunder Shock	Electric	Special	40	100	30	Normal
1	Yawn	Normal	Status	—	—	10	Normal
3	Tail Whip	Normal	Status	—	100	30	Many Others
6	Quick Attack	Normal	Physical	40	100	30	Normal
10	Double Kick	Fighting	Physical	30	100	30	Normal
14	Sand Attack	Ground	Status	—	100	15	Normal
17	Pin Missile	Bug	Physical	25	95	20	Normal
21	Thunder Wave	Electric	Status	—	90	20	Normal
24	Agility	Psychic	Status	—	—	30	Self
28	Helping Hand	Normal	Status	—	—	20	1 Ally
31	Thunder	Electric	Special	110	70	10	Normal

TM MOVES

NO.	NAME	TYPE	KIND	POW.	ACC.	PP	RANGE
TM01	Headbutt	Normal	Physical	70	100	15	Normal
TM03	Helping Hand	Normal	Status	—	—	20	1 Ally
TM05	Rest	Psychic	Status	—	—	10	Self
TM06	Light Screen	Psychic	Status	—	—	30	Your Side
TM07	Protect	Normal	Status	—	—	10	Self
TM08	Substitute	Normal	Status	—	—	10	Self
TM09	Reflect	Psychic	Status	—	—	20	Your Side
TM10	Dig	Ground	Physical	80	100	10	Normal
TM12	Facade	Normal	Physical	70	100	20	Normal
TM16	Thunder Wave	Electric	Status	—	90	20	Normal
TM19	Iron Tail	Steel	Physical	100	75	15	Normal
TM27	Toxic	Poison	Status	—	90	10	Normal
TM36	Thunderbolt	Electric	Special	90	100	15	Normal
TM38	Thunder	Electric	Special	110	70	10	Normal
TM43	Shadow Ball	Ghost	Special	80	100	15	Normal
TM48	Hyper Beam	Normal	Special	150	90	5	Normal
TM57	Pay Day	Normal	Physical	40	100	20	Normal

POKÉMON EXPRESSIONS

HAPPY

UNHAPPY

ATTACKING

EVOLUTION MOVES

NAME	TYPE	KIND	POW.	ACC.	PP	RANGE
Thunder Shock	Electric	Special	40	100	30	Normal

Flareon

♂ ♀ | Same form for male/female

SPECIES STRENGTHS

HP	
ATTACK	
DEFENSE	
SP. ATK	
SP. DEF	
SPEED	

DAMAGE TAKEN IN BATTLES

◎	×1		×1
	×0.5	◎	×1
	×2		×0.5
	×0.5		×2
	×1		×1
✳	×0.5		×1
	×1	☾	×1
	×1	◎	×0.5
	×2	✷	×0.5

POKÉDEX ENTRY

It has a flame chamber inside its body. It inhales, then breathes out fire that is over 3,000 degrees Fahrenheit.

MAIN WAY TO OBTAIN

Obtain an Eevee, then use a Fire Stone on it to evolve it into Flareon. Note that your partner Eevee will not evolve into Flareon if you are playing *Pokémon: Let's Go, Eevee!*

Where to catch
Habitat Unknown

EVOLUTION

Eevee

Use Fire Stone
→→→

Flareon

POKÉMON EXPRESSIONS

HAPPY

UNHAPPY

ATTACKING

LEVEL-UP MOVES

LV.	NAME	TYPE	KIND	POW.	ACC.	PP	RANGE
1	Ember	Fire	Special	40	100	25	Normal
1	Growl	Normal	Status	—	100	40	Many Others
1	Sand Attack	Ground	Status	—	100	15	Normal
1	Tackle	Normal	Physical	40	100	35	Normal
1	Tail Whip	Normal	Status	—	100	30	Many Others
1	Yawn	Normal	Status	—	—	10	Normal
3	Tail Whip	Normal	Status	—	100	30	Many Others
6	Quick Attack	Normal	Physical	40	100	30	Normal
10	Double Kick	Fighting	Physical	30	100	30	Normal
14	Sand Attack	Ground	Status	—	100	15	Normal
17	Fire Spin	Fire	Special	35	85	15	Normal
21	Smog	Poison	Special	30	70	20	Normal
24	Focus Energy	Normal	Status	—	—	30	Self
28	Helping Hand	Normal	Status	—	—	20	1 Ally
31	Flare Blitz	Fire	Physical	120	100	15	Normal

TM MOVES

NO.	NAME	TYPE	KIND	POW.	ACC.	PP	RANGE
TM01	Headbutt	Normal	Physical	70	100	15	Normal
TM03	Helping Hand	Normal	Status	—	—	20	1 Ally
TM05	Rest	Psychic	Status	—	—	10	Self
TM07	Protect	Normal	Status	—	—	10	Self
TM08	Substitute	Normal	Status	—	—	10	Self
TM09	Reflect	Psychic	Status	—	—	20	Your Side
TM10	Dig	Ground	Physical	80	100	10	Normal
TM11	Will-O-Wisp	Fire	Status	—	85	15	Normal
TM12	Facade	Normal	Physical	70	100	20	Normal
TM19	Iron Tail	Steel	Physical	100	75	15	Normal
TM27	Toxic	Poison	Status	—	90	10	Normal
TM37	Flamethrower	Fire	Special	90	100	15	Normal
TM43	Shadow Ball	Ghost	Special	80	100	15	Normal
TM46	Fire Blast	Fire	Special	110	85	5	Normal
TM48	Hyper Beam	Normal	Special	150	90	5	Normal
TM49	Superpower	Fighting	Physical	120	100	5	Normal
TM57	Pay Day	Normal	Physical	40	100	20	Normal

EVOLUTION MOVES

NAME	TYPE	KIND	POW.	ACC.	PP	RANGE
Ember	Fire	Special	40	100	25	Normal

PORYGON 137

Porygon

— | Gender unknown

SPECIES STRENGTHS

HP	▰▰▰
ATTACK	▰▰▰
DEFENSE	▰▰▰▰
SP. ATK	▰▰▰▰
SP. DEF	▰▰▰▰
SPEED	▰▰

DAMAGE TAKEN IN BATTLES

◉	×1	🪶	×1
🔥	×1	◎	×1
💧	×1	🌿	×1
🍃	×1	🪨	×1
⚡	×1	👁	×0
❄	×1	☯	×1
👊	×2	🌙	×1
☠	×1	⭕	×1
⛰	×1	✦	×1

POKÉDEX ENTRY

The only Pokémon that people anticipate can fly into space. None has managed the feat yet, however.

MAIN WAY TO OBTAIN

Receive one from a Silph Co. employee in Saffron City after freeing Silph Co. from Team Rocket (p. 86). Or catch one when it appears as an unusual encounter during a Catch Combo (p. 117) on Route 7.

Where to catch

Unusual Encounter

EVOLUTION

(DOES NOT EVOLVE)

LEVEL-UP MOVES

LV.	NAME	TYPE	KIND	POW.	ACC.	PP	RANGE
1	Tackle	Normal	Physical	40	100	35	Normal
4	Sharpen	Normal	Status	—	—	30	Self
9	Psybeam	Psychic	Special	65	100	20	Normal
13	Agility	Psychic	Status	—	—	30	Self
18	Barrier	Psychic	Status	—	—	20	Self
22	Tri Attack	Normal	Special	80	100	10	Normal
27	Thunder Wave	Electric	Status	—	90	20	Normal
31	Conversion	Normal	Status	—	—	30	Self
36	Recover	Normal	Status	—	—	10	Self
40	Hyper Beam	Normal	Special	150	90	5	Normal

EVOLUTION MOVES

NAME	TYPE	KIND	POW.	ACC.	PP	RANGE

TM MOVES

NO.	NAME	TYPE	KIND	POW.	ACC.	PP	RANGE
TM01	Headbutt	Normal	Physical	70	100	15	Normal
TM04	Teleport	Psychic	Status	—	—	20	Self
TM05	Rest	Psychic	Status	—	—	10	Self
TM07	Protect	Normal	Status	—	—	10	Self
TM08	Substitute	Normal	Status	—	—	10	Self
TM09	Reflect	Psychic	Status	—	—	20	Your Side
TM12	Facade	Normal	Physical	70	100	20	Normal
TM16	Thunder Wave	Electric	Status	—	90	20	Normal
TM19	Iron Tail	Steel	Physical	100	75	15	Normal
TM21	Foul Play	Dark	Physical	95	100	15	Normal
TM27	Toxic	Poison	Status	—	90	10	Normal
TM28	Tri Attack	Normal	Special	80	100	10	Normal
TM36	Thunderbolt	Electric	Special	90	100	15	Normal
TM38	Thunder	Electric	Special	110	70	10	Normal
TM40	Psychic	Psychic	Special	90	100	10	Normal
TM43	Shadow Ball	Ghost	Special	80	100	15	Normal
TM45	Solar Beam	Grass	Special	200	100	10	Normal
TM48	Hyper Beam	Normal	Special	150	90	5	Normal
TM51	Blizzard	Ice	Special	110	70	5	Many Others
TM55	Ice Beam	Ice	Special	90	100	10	Normal
TM59	Dream Eater	Psychic	Special	100	100	15	Normal

POKÉMON EXPRESSIONS

HAPPY

UNHAPPY

ATTACKING

Omanyte

♂ ♀ | Same form for male/female

SPECIES STRENGTHS

HP	▰▰▱
ATTACK	▰▰▱
DEFENSE	▰▰▰▰▰▱
SP. ATK	▰▰▰▰▱
SP. DEF	▰▰▱
SPEED	▰▰▱

DAMAGE TAKEN IN BATTLES

⊙	×0.5	🖐	×0.5
🔥	×0.25	🌀	×1
💧	×1	☯	×1
🍃	×4	✦	×1
⚡	×2	👁	×1
❄	×0.5	↻	×1
👊	×2	☾	×1
☣	×0.5	⊙	×1
🪨	×2	✧	×1

POKÉDEX ENTRY

An ancient Pokémon that was recovered from a fossil. It swam by cleverly twisting its 10 tentacles about.

MAIN WAY TO OBTAIN

Choose the Helix Fossil in Mt. Moon, or find one in the Cerulean Cave, then have it restored to Omanyte on Cinnabar Island (p. 92).

Where to catch

Habitat Unknown

EVOLUTION

Omanyte

Lv. 40
→→→

Omastar

POKÉMON EXPRESSIONS

HAPPY

UNHAPPY

ATTACKING

LEVEL-UP MOVES

LV.	NAME	TYPE	KIND	POW.	ACC.	PP	RANGE
1	Constrict	Normal	Physical	10	100	35	Normal
4	Withdraw	Water	Status	—	—	40	Self
11	Leer	Normal	Status	—	100	30	Many Others
15	Water Gun	Water	Special	40	100	25	Normal
22	Bite	Dark	Physical	60	100	25	Normal
26	Rock Throw	Rock	Physical	50	90	15	Normal
33	Protect	Normal	Status	—	—	10	Self
37	Rock Slide	Rock	Physical	75	90	10	Many Others
44	Hydro Pump	Water	Special	110	80	5	Normal
48	Shell Smash	Normal	Status	—	—	15	Self

TM MOVES

NO.	NAME	TYPE	KIND	POW.	ACC.	PP	RANGE
TM01	Headbutt	Normal	Physical	70	100	15	Normal
TM05	Rest	Psychic	Status	—	—	10	Self
TM07	Protect	Normal	Status	—	—	10	Self
TM08	Substitute	Normal	Status	—	—	10	Self
TM09	Reflect	Psychic	Status	—	—	20	Your Side
TM12	Facade	Normal	Physical	70	100	20	Normal
TM22	Rock Slide	Rock	Physical	75	90	10	Many Others
TM25	Waterfall	Water	Physical	80	100	15	Normal
TM27	Toxic	Poison	Status	—	90	10	Normal
TM29	Scald	Water	Special	80	100	15	Normal
TM47	Surf	Water	Special	90	100	15	All Others
TM51	Blizzard	Ice	Special	110	70	5	Many Others
TM55	Ice Beam	Ice	Special	90	100	10	Normal
TM56	Stealth Rock	Rock	Status	—	—	20	Other Side

EVOLUTION MOVES

NAME	TYPE	KIND	POW.	ACC.	PP	RANGE

✓ **139** Spiral Pokémon · Average height: 3'03" · Average weight: 77.2 lbs.

Omastar

OMASTAR 139

♂ ♀ | Same form for male/female

SPECIES STRENGTHS

HP	▰▰▰
ATTACK	▰▰▰▰
DEFENSE	▰▰▰▰▰▰▰▰
SP. ATK	▰▰▰▰▰▰
SP. DEF	▰▰▰▰
SPEED	▰▰▰

DAMAGE TAKEN IN BATTLES

×0.5		×0.5	
×0.25		×1	
×1		×1	
×4		×1	
×2		×1	
×0.5		×1	
×2		×1	
×0.5		×1	
×2		×1	

POKÉDEX ENTRY

Its sharp beak rings its mouth. Its shell was too big for it to move freely, so it became extinct.

MAIN WAY TO OBTAIN

Obtain an Omanyte, then level it up to Lv. 40 or higher to evolve it into Omastar.

Where to catch

Habitat Unknown

EVOLUTION

Lv. 40
→→→

Omanyte   **Omastar**

LEVEL-UP MOVES

LV.	NAME	TYPE	KIND	POW.	ACC.	PP	RANGE
1	Bide	Normal	Physical	—	—	10	Self
1	Constrict	Normal	Physical	10	100	35	Normal
1	Leer	Normal	Status	—	100	30	Many Others
1	Spike Cannon	Normal	Physical	20	100	15	Normal
1	Supersonic	Normal	Status	—	55	20	Normal
1	Water Gun	Water	Special	40	100	25	Normal
1	Withdraw	Water	Status	—	—	40	Self
4	Withdraw	Water	Status	—	—	40	Self
11	Leer	Normal	Status	—	100	30	Many Others
15	Water Gun	Water	Special	40	100	25	Normal
22	Bite	Dark	Physical	60	100	25	Normal
26	Rock Throw	Rock	Physical	50	90	15	Normal
33	Protect	Normal	Status	—	—	10	Self
37	Rock Slide	Rock	Physical	75	90	10	Many Others
50	Hydro Pump	Water	Special	110	80	5	Normal
60	Shell Smash	Normal	Status	—	—	15	Self

TM MOVES

NO.	NAME	TYPE	KIND	POW.	ACC.	PP	RANGE
TM01	Headbutt	Normal	Physical	70	100	15	Normal
TM05	Rest	Psychic	Status	—	—	10	Self
TM07	Protect	Normal	Status	—	—	10	Self
TM08	Substitute	Normal	Status	—	—	10	Self
TM09	Reflect	Psychic	Status	—	—	20	Your Side
TM12	Facade	Normal	Physical	70	100	20	Normal
TM15	Seismic Toss	Fighting	Physical	—	100	20	Normal
TM22	Rock Slide	Rock	Physical	75	90	10	Many Others
TM25	Waterfall	Water	Physical	80	100	15	Normal
TM27	Toxic	Poison	Status	—	90	10	Normal
TM29	Scald	Water	Special	80	100	15	Normal
TM47	Surf	Water	Special	90	100	15	All Others
TM48	Hyper Beam	Normal	Special	150	90	5	Normal
TM51	Blizzard	Ice	Special	110	70	5	Many Others
TM55	Ice Beam	Ice	Special	90	100	10	Normal
TM56	Stealth Rock	Rock	Status	—	—	20	Other Side

EVOLUTION MOVES

NAME	TYPE	KIND	POW.	ACC.	PP	RANGE
Spike Cannon	Normal	Physical	20	100	15	Normal

POKÉMON EXPRESSIONS

HAPPY

UNHAPPY

ATTACKING

Kabuto

♂ ♀ | Same form for male/female

SPECIES STRENGTHS

HP	▪▪
ATTACK	▪▪▪▪
DEFENSE	▪▪▪▪▪
SP. ATK	▪▪▪
SP. DEF	▪▪▪
SPEED	▪▪▪▪

DAMAGE TAKEN IN BATTLES

◉	×0.5	💧	×0.5
🔥	×0.25	⊙	×1
💧	×1	⦿	×1
⚡	×4	◈	×1
⚡	×2	●	×1
❄	×0.5	↻	×1
✊	×2	☾	×1
☁	×0.5	◉	×1
◣	×2	✦	×1

POKÉDEX ENTRY

A Pokémon that was recovered from a fossil. It used the eyes on its back while hiding on the seafloor.

MAIN WAY TO OBTAIN

Choose the Dome Fossil in Mt. Moon, or find one in the Cerulean Cave, then have it restored to Kabuto on Cinnabar Island (p. 92).

Where to catch

Habitat Unknown

EVOLUTION

Kabuto

Lv. 40
→→→

Kabutops

POKÉMON EXPRESSIONS

HAPPY

UNHAPPY

ATTACKING

LEVEL-UP MOVES

LV.	NAME	TYPE	KIND	POW.	ACC.	PP	RANGE
1	Scratch	Normal	Physical	40	100	35	Normal
6	Harden	Normal	Status	—	—	30	Self
12	Leer	Normal	Status	—	100	30	Many Others
18	Absorb	Grass	Special	40	100	15	Normal
24	Aqua Jet	Water	Physical	40	100	20	Normal
30	Rock Throw	Rock	Physical	50	90	15	Normal
36	Sand Attack	Ground	Status	—	100	15	Normal
42	Rock Slide	Rock	Physical	75	90	10	Many Others
48	Leech Life	Bug	Physical	80	100	10	Normal

TM MOVES

NO.	NAME	TYPE	KIND	POW.	ACC.	PP	RANGE
TM01	Headbutt	Normal	Physical	70	100	15	Normal
TM05	Rest	Psychic	Status	—	—	10	Self
TM07	Protect	Normal	Status	—	—	10	Self
TM08	Substitute	Normal	Status	—	—	10	Self
TM09	Reflect	Psychic	Status	—	—	20	Your Side
TM10	Dig	Ground	Physical	80	100	10	Normal
TM12	Facade	Normal	Physical	70	100	20	Normal
TM22	Rock Slide	Rock	Physical	75	90	10	Many Others
TM25	Waterfall	Water	Physical	80	100	15	Normal
TM27	Toxic	Poison	Status	—	90	10	Normal
TM29	Scald	Water	Special	80	100	15	Normal
TM47	Surf	Water	Special	90	100	15	All Others
TM51	Blizzard	Ice	Special	110	70	5	Many Others
TM53	Mega Drain	Grass	Special	75	100	10	Normal
TM55	Ice Beam	Ice	Special	90	100	10	Normal
TM56	Stealth Rock	Rock	Status	—	—	20	Other Side

EVOLUTION MOVES

NAME	TYPE	KIND	POW.	ACC.	PP	RANGE

141 · Shellfish Pokémon · Average height: 4'03" · Average weight: 89.3 lbs.

Kabutops

♂ ♀ | Same form for male/female

SPECIES STRENGTHS

HP	▬▬
ATTACK	▬▬▬▬▬
DEFENSE	▬▬▬▬▬▬
SP. ATK	▬▬▬
SP. DEF	▬▬▬▬
SPEED	▬▬▬▬

DAMAGE TAKEN IN BATTLES

×0.5		×0.5	
×0.25		×1	
×1		×1	
×4		×1	
×2		×1	
×0.5		×1	
×2		×1	
×0.5		×1	
×2		×1	

POKÉDEX ENTRY

A slim and fast swimmer. It sliced its prey with its sharp sickles and drank the body fluids.

MAIN WAY TO OBTAIN

Obtain a Kabuto, then level it up to Lv. 40 or higher to evolve it into Kabutops.

Where to catch

Habitat Unknown

EVOLUTION

Kabuto → Lv. 40 → → → Kabutops

Kabuto **Kabutops**

LEVEL-UP MOVES

LV.	NAME	TYPE	KIND	POW.	ACC.	PP	RANGE
1	Absorb	Grass	Special	40	100	15	Normal
1	Confuse Ray	Ghost	Status	—	100	10	Normal
1	Feint	Normal	Physical	30	100	10	Normal
1	Harden	Normal	Status	—	—	30	Self
1	Leer	Normal	Status	—	100	30	Many Others
1	Scratch	Normal	Physical	40	100	35	Normal
1	Screech	Normal	Status	—	85	40	Normal
1	Slash	Normal	Physical	70	100	20	Normal
6	Harden	Normal	Status	—	—	30	Self
12	Leer	Normal	Status	—	100	30	Many Others
18	Absorb	Grass	Special	40	100	15	Normal
24	Aqua Jet	Water	Physical	40	100	20	Normal
30	Rock Throw	Rock	Physical	50	90	15	Normal
36	Sand Attack	Ground	Status	—	100	15	Normal
45	Rock Slide	Rock	Physical	75	90	10	Many Others
54	Leech Life	Bug	Physical	80	100	10	Normal
63	Swords Dance	Normal	Status	—	—	20	Self

TM MOVES

NO.	NAME	TYPE	KIND	POW.	ACC.	PP	RANGE
TM01	Headbutt	Normal	Physical	70	100	15	Normal
TM05	Rest	Psychic	Status	—	—	10	Self
TM07	Protect	Normal	Status	—	—	10	Self
TM08	Substitute	Normal	Status	—	—	10	Self
TM09	Reflect	Psychic	Status	—	—	20	Your Side
TM10	Dig	Ground	Physical	80	100	10	Normal
TM12	Facade	Normal	Physical	70	100	20	Normal
TM13	Brick Break	Fighting	Physical	75	100	15	Normal
TM15	Seismic Toss	Fighting	Physical	—	100	20	Normal
TM22	Rock Slide	Rock	Physical	75	90	10	Many Others
TM24	X-Scissor	Bug	Physical	80	100	15	Normal
TM25	Waterfall	Water	Physical	80	100	15	Normal
TM27	Toxic	Poison	Status	—	90	10	Normal
TM29	Scald	Water	Special	80	100	15	Normal
TM47	Surf	Water	Special	90	100	15	All Others
TM48	Hyper Beam	Normal	Special	150	90	5	Normal
TM49	Superpower	Fighting	Physical	120	100	5	Normal
TM51	Blizzard	Ice	Special	110	70	5	Many Others
TM53	Mega Drain	Grass	Special	75	100	10	Normal
TM55	Ice Beam	Ice	Special	90	100	10	Normal
TM56	Stealth Rock	Rock	Status	—	—	20	Other Side

EVOLUTION MOVES

NAME	TYPE	KIND	POW.	ACC.	PP	RANGE
Slash	Normal	Physical	70	100	20	Normal

POKÉMON EXPRESSIONS

HAPPY

UNHAPPY

ATTACKING

Aerodactyl

♂ ♀ | Same form for male/female

SPECIES STRENGTHS

HP	▰▰▰
ATTACK	▰▰▰▰▰
DEFENSE	▰▰▰
SP. ATK	▰▰▰
SP. DEF	▰▰▰
SPEED	▰▰▰▰▰▰

DAMAGE TAKEN IN BATTLES

◎	×0.5		×0.5
🔥	×0.5	◎	×1
💧	×2		×0.5
	×1		×2
⚡	×2		×1
❄	×2		×1
👊	×1	☾	×1
◎	×0.5	◎	×2
▲	×0	✦	×1

POKÉDEX ENTRY

A savage Pokémon that died out in ancient times. It was resurrected using DNA taken from amber.

MAIN WAY TO OBTAIN

Receive an Old Amber in Pewter City (p. 53), or find one in the Cerulean Cave, then have it restored to Aerodactyl on Cinnabar Island (p. 92).

Where to catch

Habitat Unknown

EVOLUTION

(DOES NOT EVOLVE)

LEVEL-UP MOVES

LV.	NAME	TYPE	KIND	POW.	ACC.	PP	RANGE
1	Bite	Dark	Physical	60	100	25	Normal
1	Wing Attack	Flying	Physical	60	100	35	Normal
7	Roar	Normal	Status	—	—	20	Normal
14	Supersonic	Normal	Status	—	55	20	Normal
21	Rock Throw	Rock	Physical	50	90	15	Normal
28	Agility	Psychic	Status	—	—	30	Self
35	Crunch	Dark	Physical	80	100	15	Normal
42	Rock Slide	Rock	Physical	75	90	10	Many Others
49	Fly	Flying	Physical	90	95	15	Normal
56	Take Down	Normal	Physical	90	85	20	Normal
63	Hyper Beam	Normal	Special	150	90	5	Normal

TM MOVES

NO.	NAME	TYPE	KIND	POW.	ACC.	PP	RANGE
TM01	Headbutt	Normal	Physical	70	100	15	Normal
TM02	Taunt	Dark	Status	—	100	20	Normal
TM05	Rest	Psychic	Status	—	—	10	Self
TM07	Protect	Normal	Status	—	—	10	Self
TM08	Substitute	Normal	Status	—	—	10	Self
TM09	Reflect	Psychic	Status	—	—	20	Your Side
TM12	Facade	Normal	Physical	70	100	20	Normal
TM14	Fly	Flying	Physical	90	95	15	Normal
TM19	Iron Tail	Steel	Physical	100	75	15	Normal
TM22	Rock Slide	Rock	Physical	75	90	10	Many Others
TM27	Toxic	Poison	Status	—	90	10	Normal
TM34	Dragon Pulse	Dragon	Special	85	100	10	Normal
TM37	Flamethrower	Fire	Special	90	100	15	Normal
TM41	Earthquake	Ground	Physical	100	100	10	All Others
TM46	Fire Blast	Fire	Special	110	85	5	Normal
TM48	Hyper Beam	Normal	Special	150	90	5	Normal
TM50	Roost	Flying	Status	—	—	10	Self
TM56	Stealth Rock	Rock	Status	—	—	20	Other Side

EVOLUTION MOVES

NAME	TYPE	KIND	POW.	ACC.	PP	RANGE

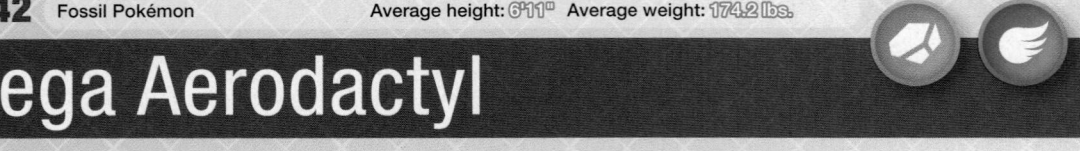

✓ **142** Fossil Pokémon   Average height: 6'11"   Average weight: 174.2 lbs.

Mega Aerodactyl

MEGA EVOLUTION

Aerodactyl

Buy an Aerodactylite, then Mega Evolve Aerodactyl during battle.

Mega Aerodactyl

SPECIES STRENGTHS

HP	▰▰▰▱▱
ATTACK	▰▰▰▰▰▰▰
DEFENSE	▰▰▰▱▱
SP. ATK	▰▰▰▱▱
SP. DEF	▰▰▰▰▱
SPEED	▰▰▰▰▰▰▰

DAMAGE TAKEN IN BATTLES

⊙	×0.5	🌀	×0.5
🔥	×0.5	🌀	×1
💧	×2		×0.5
⚡	×1		×2
🍃	×2		×1
❄	×2		×1
👊	×1	☽	×1
☠	×0.5		×2
🗿	×0	✦	×1

REQUIRED MEGA STONE: AERODACTYLITE

Buy it from a seller who appears at the Pokémon League once you have become Champion (p. 103).

Snorlax

♂ ♀ | Same form for male/female

SPECIES STRENGTHS

HP
ATTACK
DEFENSE
SP. ATK
SP. DEF
SPEED

DAMAGE TAKEN IN BATTLES

◎ ×1	🔥 ×1
🔥 ×1	◎ ×1
💧 ×1	🍃 ×1
⚡ ×1	🍂 ×1
⚡ ×1	👻 ×0
❄ ×1	🌙 ×1
👊 ×2	🌑 ×1
☠ ×1	⭘ ×1
⛰ ×1	✦ ×1

POKÉDEX ENTRY

Will eat anything, even if the food happens to be a little moldy. It never gets an upset stomach.

MAIN WAY TO OBTAIN

Wake the Snorlax on Route 12 or Route 16, and catch it after defeating it in battle. Or catch one when it appears as an unusual encounter during a Catch Combo (p. 117) in the Cerulean Cave.

Where to catch
Unusual Encounter

EVOLUTION

(DOES NOT EVOLVE)

LEVEL-UP MOVES

LV.	NAME	TYPE	KIND	POW.	ACC.	PP	RANGE
1	Tackle	Normal	Physical	40	100	35	Normal
6	Defense Curl	Normal	Status	—	—	40	Self
13	Yawn	Normal	Status	—	—	10	Normal
19	Lick	Ghost	Physical	30	100	30	Normal
26	Headbutt	Normal	Physical	70	100	15	Normal
32	Rest	Psychic	Status	—	—	10	Self
39	Screech	Normal	Status	—	85	40	Normal
45	Amnesia	Psychic	Status	—	—	20	Self
52	Body Slam	Normal	Physical	85	100	15	Normal
58	Crunch	Dark	Physical	80	100	15	Normal
65	Superpower	Fighting	Physical	120	100	5	Normal

TM MOVES

NO.	NAME	TYPE	KIND	POW.	ACC.	PP	RANGE
TM01	Headbutt	Normal	Physical	70	100	15	Normal
TM05	Rest	Psychic	Status	—	—	10	Self
TM07	Protect	Normal	Status	—	—	10	Self
TM08	Substitute	Normal	Status	—	—	10	Self
TM09	Reflect	Psychic	Status	—	—	20	Your Side
TM12	Facade	Normal	Physical	70	100	20	Normal
TM13	Brick Break	Fighting	Physical	75	100	15	Normal
TM15	Seismic Toss	Fighting	Physical	—	100	20	Normal
TM22	Rock Slide	Rock	Physical	75	90	10	Many Others
TM23	Thunder Punch	Electric	Physical	75	100	15	Normal
TM27	Toxic	Poison	Status	—	90	10	Normal
TM31	Fire Punch	Fire	Physical	75	100	15	Normal
TM35	Ice Punch	Ice	Physical	75	100	15	Normal
TM36	Thunderbolt	Electric	Special	90	100	15	Normal
TM37	Flamethrower	Fire	Special	90	100	15	Normal
TM38	Thunder	Electric	Special	110	70	10	Normal
TM39	Outrage	Dragon	Physical	120	100	10	1 Random
TM40	Psychic	Psychic	Special	90	100	10	Normal
TM41	Earthquake	Ground	Physical	100	100	10	All Others
TM42	Self-Destruct	Normal	Physical	200	100	5	All Others
TM43	Shadow Ball	Ghost	Special	80	100	15	Normal
TM45	Solar Beam	Grass	Special	200	100	10	Normal
TM46	Fire Blast	Fire	Special	110	85	5	Normal
TM47	Surf	Water	Special	90	100	15	All Others
TM48	Hyper Beam	Normal	Special	150	90	5	Normal
TM49	Superpower	Fighting	Physical	120	100	5	Normal
TM51	Blizzard	Ice	Special	110	70	5	Many Others
TM55	Ice Beam	Ice	Special	90	100	10	Normal
TM57	Pay Day	Normal	Physical	40	100	20	Normal

EVOLUTION MOVES

NAME	TYPE	KIND	POW.	ACC.	PP	RANGE

Average height: 5'07"　Average weight: 122.1 lbs.

Articuno

— | Gender unknown

SPECIES STRENGTHS

HP	▪▪▪▪▪▫
ATTACK	▪▪▪▪▫
DEFENSE	▪▪▪▪▪▪
SP. ATK	▪▪▪▪▪▫
SP. DEF	▪▪▪▪▪▪▪
SPEED	▪▪▪▪▫

DAMAGE TAKEN IN BATTLES

×1		×1	
×2		×1	
×1		×0.5	
×0.5		×4	
×2		×1	
×1		×1	
×1		×1	
×1		×2	
×0		×1	

POKÉDEX ENTRY

A legendary bird Pokémon. It freezes water that is contained in winter air and makes it snow.

MAIN WAY TO OBTAIN

Catch Articuno after you defeat it in battle in the Seafoam Islands.

Where to catch

Habitat Unknown

EVOLUTION

(DOES NOT EVOLVE)

LEVEL-UP MOVES

LV.	NAME	TYPE	KIND	POW.	ACC.	PP	RANGE
1	Gust	Flying	Special	40	100	35	Normal
1	Ice Shard	Ice	Physical	40	100	30	Normal
8	Mist	Ice	Status	—	—	30	Your Side
16	Leer	Normal	Status	—	100	30	Many Others
24	Mirror Coat	Psychic	Special	—	100	20	Varies
32	Ice Beam	Ice	Special	90	100	10	Normal
40	Agility	Psychic	Status	—	—	30	Self
48	Reflect	Psychic	Status	—	—	20	Your Side
56	Roost	Flying	Status	—	—	10	Self
64	Blizzard	Ice	Special	110	70	5	Many Others
72	Sky Attack	Flying	Physical	200	90	5	Normal

TM MOVES

NO.	NAME	TYPE	KIND	POW.	ACC.	PP	RANGE
TM01	Headbutt	Normal	Physical	70	100	15	Normal
TM05	Rest	Psychic	Status	—	—	10	Self
TM07	Protect	Normal	Status	—	—	10	Self
TM08	Substitute	Normal	Status	—	—	10	Self
TM09	Reflect	Psychic	Status	—	—	20	Your Side
TM12	Facade	Normal	Physical	70	100	20	Normal
TM14	Fly	Flying	Physical	90	95	15	Normal
TM18	U-turn	Bug	Physical	70	100	20	Normal
TM27	Toxic	Poison	Status	—	90	10	Normal
TM48	Hyper Beam	Normal	Special	150	90	5	Normal
TM50	Roost	Flying	Status	—	—	10	Self
TM51	Blizzard	Ice	Special	110	70	5	Many Others
TM55	Ice Beam	Ice	Special	90	100	10	Normal

POKÉMON EXPRESSIONS

HAPPY

UNHAPPY

ATTACKING

EVOLUTION MOVES

NAME	TYPE	KIND	POW.	ACC.	PP	RANGE

Zapdos

— | Gender unknown

SPECIES STRENGTHS

HP ▪▪▪▪▫▫
ATTACK ▪▪▪▪▫▫
DEFENSE ▪▪▪▫▫▫
SP. ATK ▪▪▪▪▪▪▪▫
SP. DEF ▪▪▪▪▫▫
SPEED ▪▪▪▪▫▫

DAMAGE TAKEN IN BATTLES

◉ ×1		🪶 ×0.5
🔥 ×1		⊚ ×1
💧 ×1		❋ ×0.5
⚡ ×0.5		⚔ ×2
🍃 ×1		● ×1
❄ ×2		◐ ×1
👊 ×0.5		☾ ×1
☠ ×1		◎ ×0.5
⛰ ×0		✦ ×1

POKÉDEX ENTRY

This legendary bird Pokémon is said to appear when the sky turns dark and lightning showers down.

MAIN WAY TO OBTAIN

Catch Zapdos after you defeat it in battle in the Power Plant.

Where to catch

Habitat Unknown

EVOLUTION

(DOES NOT EVOLVE)

POKÉMON EXPRESSIONS

HAPPY

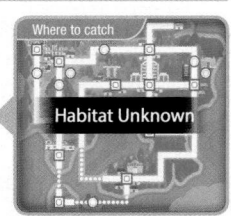

UNHAPPY

ATTACKING

LEVEL-UP MOVES

LV.	NAME	TYPE	KIND	POW.	ACC.	PP	RANGE
1	Peck	Flying	Physical	35	100	35	Normal
1	Thunder Shock	Electric	Special	40	100	30	Normal
8	Thunder Wave	Electric	Status	—	90	20	Normal
16	Leer	Normal	Status	—	100	30	Many Others
24	Drill Peck	Flying	Physical	80	100	20	Normal
32	Thunderbolt	Electric	Special	90	100	15	Normal
40	Agility	Psychic	Status	—	—	30	Self
48	Light Screen	Psychic	Status	—	—	30	Your Side
56	Roost	Flying	Status	—	—	10	Self
64	Thunder	Electric	Special	110	70	10	Normal
72	Sky Attack	Flying	Physical	200	90	5	Normal

TM MOVES

NO.	NAME	TYPE	KIND	POW.	ACC.	PP	RANGE
TM01	Headbutt	Normal	Physical	70	100	15	Normal
TM05	Rest	Psychic	Status	—	—	10	Self
TM06	Light Screen	Psychic	Status	—	—	30	Your Side
TM07	Protect	Normal	Status	—	—	10	Self
TM08	Substitute	Normal	Status	—	—	10	Self
TM09	Reflect	Psychic	Status	—	—	20	Your Side
TM12	Facade	Normal	Physical	70	100	20	Normal
TM14	Fly	Flying	Physical	90	95	15	Normal
TM16	Thunder Wave	Electric	Status	—	90	20	Normal
TM18	U-turn	Bug	Physical	70	100	20	Normal
TM27	Toxic	Poison	Status	—	90	10	Normal
TM36	Thunderbolt	Electric	Special	90	100	15	Normal
TM38	Thunder	Electric	Special	110	70	10	Normal
TM48	Hyper Beam	Normal	Special	150	90	5	Normal
TM50	Roost	Flying	Status	—	—	10	Self

EVOLUTION MOVES

NAME	TYPE	KIND	POW.	ACC.	PP	RANGE

MOLTRES 146

| ✓ **146** | Flame Pokémon | Average height: 6'07" | Average weight: 132.3 lbs. |

Moltres

— | Gender unknown

SPECIES STRENGTHS

HP	▬▬▬▬
ATTACK	▬▬▬▬
DEFENSE	▬▬▬▬
SP. ATK	▬▬▬▬▬▬
SP. DEF	▬▬▬▬
SPEED	▬▬▬▬

DAMAGE TAKEN IN BATTLES

◎ ×1		🪶 ×1	
🔥 ×0.5		🌀 ×1	
💧 ×2		🧊 ×0.25	
🍃 ×0.25		🦴 ×4	
⚡ ×2		👻 ×1	
❄ ×1		🐉 ×1	
👊 ×0.5		🌑 ×1	
☣ ×1		⚙ ×0.5	
🏔 ×0		✨ ×0.5	

POKÉDEX ENTRY

A legendary bird Pokémon. As it flaps its flaming wings, even the night sky will turn red.

MAIN WAY TO OBTAIN

Catch Moltres after you defeat it in battle on Victory Road.

Where to catch

Habitat Unknown

EVOLUTION

(DOES NOT EVOLVE)

LEVEL-UP MOVES

LV.	NAME	TYPE	KIND	POW.	ACC.	PP	RANGE
1	Ember	Fire	Special	40	100	25	Normal
1	Wing Attack	Flying	Physical	60	100	35	Normal
8	Fire Spin	Fire	Special	35	85	15	Normal
16	Leer	Normal	Status	—	100	30	Many Others
24	Air Slash	Flying	Special	75	95	15	Normal
32	Flamethrower	Fire	Special	90	100	15	Normal
40	Agility	Psychic	Status	—	—	30	Self
48	Heat Wave	Fire	Special	95	90	10	Many Others
56	Roost	Flying	Status	—	—	10	Self
64	Solar Beam	Grass	Special	200	100	10	Normal
72	Sky Attack	Flying	Physical	200	90	5	Normal

TM MOVES

NO.	NAME	TYPE	KIND	POW.	ACC.	PP	RANGE
TM01	Headbutt	Normal	Physical	70	100	15	Normal
TM05	Rest	Psychic	Status	—	—	10	Self
TM07	Protect	Normal	Status	—	—	10	Self
TM08	Substitute	Normal	Status	—	—	10	Self
TM09	Reflect	Psychic	Status	—	—	20	Your Side
TM11	Will-O-Wisp	Fire	Status	—	85	15	Normal
TM12	Facade	Normal	Physical	70	100	20	Normal
TM14	Fly	Flying	Physical	90	95	15	Normal
TM18	U-turn	Bug	Physical	70	100	20	Normal
TM27	Toxic	Poison	Status	—	90	10	Normal
TM37	Flamethrower	Fire	Special	90	100	15	Normal
TM45	Solar Beam	Grass	Special	200	100	10	Normal
TM46	Fire Blast	Fire	Special	110	85	5	Normal
TM48	Hyper Beam	Normal	Special	150	90	5	Normal
TM50	Roost	Flying	Status	—	—	10	Self

EVOLUTION MOVES

NAME	TYPE	KIND	POW.	ACC.	PP	RANGE

POKÉMON EXPRESSIONS

HAPPY

UNHAPPY

ATTACKING

Dratini

♂ ♀ | Same form for male/female

SPECIES STRENGTHS

HP	▪▪▪
ATTACK	▪▪▪▪
DEFENSE	▪▪▪
SP. ATK	▪▪▪
SP. DEF	▪▪▪
SPEED	▪▪▪

DAMAGE TAKEN IN BATTLES

⬤	×1	🪽	×1
🔥	×0.5	⚪	×1
💧	×0.5	🌀	×1
⚡	×0.5	🔮	×1
🍃	×0.5	⚫	×1
❄	×2	🔴	×2
👊	×1	🌙	×1
☠	×1	⚙	×1
🪨	×1	✦	×2

POKÉDEX ENTRY

Long thought to be a myth, this Pokémon's existence was only recently confirmed by a fisherman who caught one.

MAIN WAY TO OBTAIN

Catch one when it appears on the water's surface on Route 10 (North).

Where to catch

EVOLUTION

Lv. 30 →→→   Lv. 55 →→→

Dratini   **Dragonair**   **Dragonite**

POKÉMON EXPRESSIONS

HAPPY

UNHAPPY

ATTACKING

LEVEL-UP MOVES

LV.	NAME	TYPE	KIND	POW.	ACC.	PP	RANGE
1	Leer	Normal	Status	—	100	30	Many Others
1	Wrap	Normal	Physical	15	90	20	Normal
7	Thunder Wave	Electric	Status	—	90	20	Normal
14	Dragon Rage	Dragon	Special	—	100	10	Normal
21	Agility	Psychic	Status	—	—	30	Self
28	Dragon Tail	Dragon	Physical	60	90	10	Normal
35	Slam	Normal	Physical	80	75	20	Normal
42	Outrage	Dragon	Physical	120	100	10	1 Random
49	Hyper Beam	Normal	Special	150	90	5	Normal

TM MOVES

NO.	NAME	TYPE	KIND	POW.	ACC.	PP	RANGE
TM01	Headbutt	Normal	Physical	70	100	15	Normal
TM05	Rest	Psychic	Status	—	—	10	Self
TM06	Light Screen	Psychic	Status	—	—	30	Your Side
TM07	Protect	Normal	Status	—	—	10	Self
TM08	Substitute	Normal	Status	—	—	10	Self
TM09	Reflect	Psychic	Status	—	—	20	Your Side
TM12	Facade	Normal	Physical	70	100	20	Normal
TM16	Thunder Wave	Electric	Status	—	90	20	Normal
TM17	Dragon Tail	Dragon	Physical	60	90	10	Normal
TM19	Iron Tail	Steel	Physical	100	75	15	Normal
TM25	Waterfall	Water	Physical	80	100	15	Normal
TM27	Toxic	Poison	Status	—	90	10	Normal
TM34	Dragon Pulse	Dragon	Special	85	100	10	Normal
TM36	Thunderbolt	Electric	Special	90	100	15	Normal
TM37	Flamethrower	Fire	Special	90	100	15	Normal
TM38	Thunder	Electric	Special	110	70	10	Normal
TM39	Outrage	Dragon	Physical	120	100	10	1 Random
TM46	Fire Blast	Fire	Special	110	85	5	Normal
TM47	Surf	Water	Special	90	100	15	All Others
TM48	Hyper Beam	Normal	Special	150	90	5	Normal
TM51	Blizzard	Ice	Special	110	70	5	Many Others
TM55	Ice Beam	Ice	Special	90	100	10	Normal

EVOLUTION MOVES

NAME	TYPE	KIND	POW.	ACC.	PP	RANGE

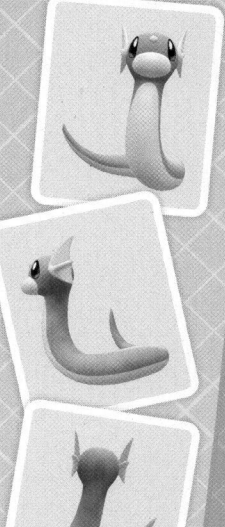

✓ 148 Dragon Pokémon | Average height: 13'01" | Average weight: 36.4 lbs.

Dragonair

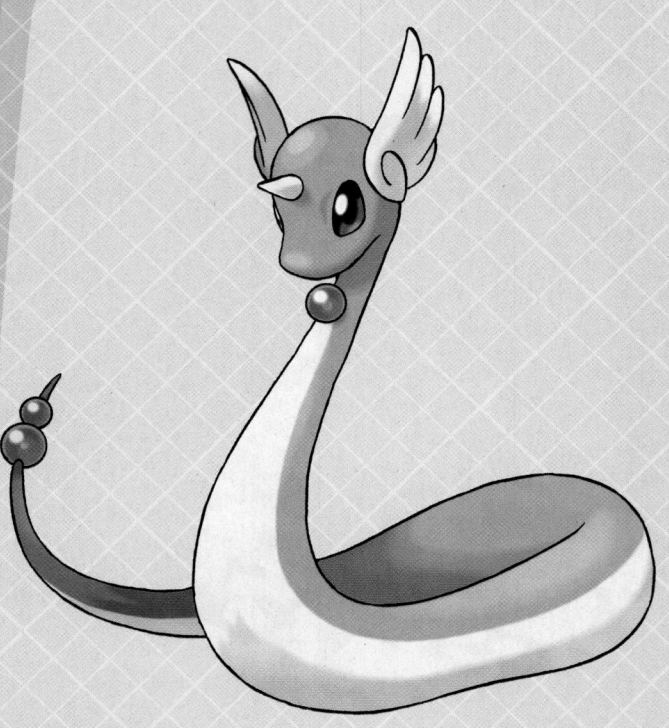

♂ ♀ | Same form for male/female

SPECIES STRENGTHS

HP	▪▪▪
ATTACK	▪▪▪▪
DEFENSE	▪▪▪
SP. ATK	▪▪▪▪
SP. DEF	▪▪▪▪
SPEED	▪▪▪▪

DAMAGE TAKEN IN BATTLES

◉	×1	🪽	×1
🔥	×0.5	⭕	×1
💧	×0.5	🟣	×1
🍃	×0.5	✴	×1
⚡	×0.5	⬤	×1
❄	×2	👊	×2
🗡	×1	🌙	×1
💠	×1	◎	×1
🪨	×1	✦	×2

POKÉDEX ENTRY

According to a witness, its body was surrounded by a strange aura that gave it a mystical look.

MAIN WAY TO OBTAIN

Catch one when it appears on the water's surface on Route 10 (North). Or obtain a Dratini, then level it up to Lv. 30 or higher to evolve it into Dragonair.

Where to catch

EVOLUTION

Dratini

Lv. 30 →→→

Dragonair

Lv. 55 →→→

Dragonite

LEVEL-UP MOVES

LV.	NAME	TYPE	KIND	POW.	ACC.	PP	RANGE
1	Dragon Rage	Dragon	Special	—	100	10	Normal
1	Leer	Normal	Status	—	100	30	Many Others
1	Thunder Wave	Electric	Status	—	90	20	Normal
1	Wrap	Normal	Physical	15	90	20	Normal
7	Thunder Wave	Electric	Status	—	90	20	Normal
14	Dragon Rage	Dragon	Special	—	100	10	Normal
21	Agility	Psychic	Status	—	—	30	Self
28	Dragon Tail	Dragon	Physical	60	90	10	Normal
40	Slam	Normal	Physical	80	75	20	Normal
52	Outrage	Dragon	Physical	120	100	10	1 Random
64	Hyper Beam	Normal	Special	150	90	5	Normal

TM MOVES

NO.	NAME	TYPE	KIND	POW.	ACC.	PP	RANGE
TM01	Headbutt	Normal	Physical	70	100	15	Normal
TM05	Rest	Psychic	Status	—	—	10	Self
TM06	Light Screen	Psychic	Status	—	—	30	Your Side
TM07	Protect	Normal	Status	—	—	10	Self
TM08	Substitute	Normal	Status	—	—	10	Self
TM09	Reflect	Psychic	Status	—	—	20	Your Side
TM12	Facade	Normal	Physical	70	100	20	Normal
TM16	Thunder Wave	Electric	Status	—	90	20	Normal
TM17	Dragon Tail	Dragon	Physical	60	90	10	Normal
TM19	Iron Tail	Steel	Physical	100	75	15	Normal
TM25	Waterfall	Water	Physical	80	100	15	Normal
TM27	Toxic	Poison	Status	—	90	10	Normal
TM34	Dragon Pulse	Dragon	Special	85	100	10	Normal
TM36	Thunderbolt	Electric	Special	90	100	15	Normal
TM37	Flamethrower	Fire	Special	90	100	15	Normal
TM38	Thunder	Electric	Special	110	70	10	Normal
TM39	Outrage	Dragon	Physical	120	100	10	1 Random
TM46	Fire Blast	Fire	Special	110	85	5	Normal
TM47	Surf	Water	Special	90	100	15	All Others
TM48	Hyper Beam	Normal	Special	150	90	5	Normal
TM51	Blizzard	Ice	Special	110	70	5	Many Others
TM55	Ice Beam	Ice	Special	90	100	10	Normal

EVOLUTION MOVES

NAME	TYPE	KIND	POW.	ACC.	PP	RANGE

POKÉMON EXPRESSIONS

HAPPY

UNHAPPY

ATTACKING

Dragonite

♂ ♀ | Same form for male/female

SPECIES STRENGTHS

HP	▰▰▰▰▰▱▱
ATTACK	▰▰▰▰▰▰▰▰
DEFENSE	▰▰▰▰▱▱▱
SP. ATK	▰▰▰▰▱▱▱
SP. DEF	▰▰▰▰▱▱▱
SPEED	▰▰▰▱▱▱▱

DAMAGE TAKEN IN BATTLES

⊙ ×1		🪶 ×1	
🔥 ×0.5		⊚ ×1	
💧 ×0.5		⊛ ×0.5	
🍃 ×0.25		🌿 ×2	
⚡ ×1		👁 ×1	
❄ ×4		🥊 ×2	
🪨 ×0.5		☾ ×1	
⬤ ×1		◎ ×1	
⛰ ×0		✦ ×2	

POKÉDEX ENTRY

It is said that this Pokémon lives somewhere in the sea and that it flies. However, these are only rumors.

MAIN WAY TO OBTAIN

Obtain a Dragonair, then level it up to Lv. 55 or higher to evolve it into Dragonite. Or catch one when it appears in the sky as an unusual encounter during a Catch Combo after becoming Champion (p. 107).

Where to catch
Unusual Encounter

EVOLUTION

Dratini → Lv. 30 →→→ **Dragonair** → Lv. 55 →→→ **Dragonite**

LEVEL-UP MOVES

LV.	NAME	TYPE	KIND	POW.	ACC.	PP	RANGE
1	Aqua Jet	Water	Physical	40	100	20	Normal
1	Dragon Rage	Dragon	Special	—	100	10	Normal
1	Fire Punch	Fire	Physical	75	100	15	Normal
1	Leer	Normal	Status	—	100	30	Many Others
1	Mist	Ice	Status	—	—	30	Your Side
1	Thunder Punch	Electric	Physical	75	100	15	Normal
1	Thunder Wave	Electric	Status	—	90	20	Normal
1	Wing Attack	Flying	Physical	60	100	35	Normal
1	Wrap	Normal	Physical	15	90	20	Normal
7	Thunder Wave	Electric	Status	—	90	20	Normal
14	Dragon Rage	Dragon	Special	—	100	10	Normal
21	Agility	Psychic	Status	—	—	30	Self
28	Dragon Tail	Dragon	Physical	60	90	10	Normal
40	Slam	Normal	Physical	80	75	20	Normal
52	Outrage	Dragon	Physical	120	100	10	1 Random
70	Hyper Beam	Normal	Special	150	90	5	Normal
88	Roost	Flying	Status	—	—	10	Self

TM MOVES

NO.	NAME	TYPE	KIND	POW.	ACC.	PP	RANGE
TM01	Headbutt	Normal	Physical	70	100	15	Normal
TM05	Rest	Psychic	Status	—	—	10	Self
TM06	Light Screen	Psychic	Status	—	—	30	Your Side
TM07	Protect	Normal	Status	—	—	10	Self
TM08	Substitute	Normal	Status	—	—	10	Self
TM09	Reflect	Psychic	Status	—	—	20	Your Side
TM12	Facade	Normal	Physical	70	100	20	Normal
TM13	Brick Break	Fighting	Physical	75	100	15	Normal
TM14	Fly	Flying	Physical	90	95	15	Normal
TM16	Thunder Wave	Electric	Status	—	90	20	Normal
TM17	Dragon Tail	Dragon	Physical	60	90	10	Normal
TM19	Iron Tail	Steel	Physical	100	75	15	Normal
TM22	Rock Slide	Rock	Physical	75	90	10	Many Others
TM23	Thunder Punch	Electric	Physical	75	100	15	Normal
TM25	Waterfall	Water	Physical	80	100	15	Normal
TM27	Toxic	Poison	Status	—	90	10	Normal
TM31	Fire Punch	Fire	Physical	75	100	15	Normal
TM34	Dragon Pulse	Dragon	Special	85	100	10	Normal
TM35	Ice Punch	Ice	Physical	75	100	15	Normal
TM36	Thunderbolt	Electric	Special	90	100	15	Normal
TM37	Flamethrower	Fire	Special	90	100	15	Normal
TM38	Thunder	Electric	Special	110	70	10	Normal
TM39	Outrage	Dragon	Physical	120	100	10	1 Random
TM41	Earthquake	Ground	Physical	100	100	10	All Others
TM46	Fire Blast	Fire	Special	110	85	5	Normal
TM47	Surf	Water	Special	90	100	15	All Others
TM48	Hyper Beam	Normal	Special	150	90	5	Normal
TM49	Superpower	Fighting	Physical	120	100	5	Normal
TM50	Roost	Flying	Status	—	—	10	Self
TM51	Blizzard	Ice	Special	110	70	5	Many Others
TM55	Ice Beam	Ice	Special	90	100	10	Normal

EVOLUTION MOVES

NAME	TYPE	KIND	POW.	ACC.	PP	RANGE
Wing Attack	Flying	Physical	60	100	35	Normal

☑ **150** Genetic Pokémon Average height: 6'07" Average weight: 269.0 lbs.

Mewtwo

— | Gender unknown

SPECIES STRENGTHS

HP	▬▬▬▬▬▬
ATTACK	▬▬▬▬▬▬
DEFENSE	▬▬▬▬▬
SP. ATK	▬▬▬▬▬▬▬▬
SP. DEF	▬▬▬▬▬
SPEED	▬▬▬▬▬▬▬

DAMAGE TAKEN IN BATTLES

⊙ ×1		🍃 ×1	
🔥 ×1		⚪ ×0.5	
💧 ×1		✴ ×2	
🍃 ×1		✦ ×1	
⚡ ×1		👻 ×2	
❄ ×1		☆ ×1	
🥊 ×0.5		🌙 ×2	
☁ ×1		⊙ ×1	
🔔 ×1		✧ ×1	

POKÉDEX ENTRY

Its DNA is almost the same as Mew's. However, its size and disposition are vastly different.

MAIN WAY TO OBTAIN

Catch Mewtwo after defeating it in battle in the Cerulean Cave (p. 108).

Where to catch

Habitat Unknown

EVOLUTION

(DOES NOT EVOLVE)

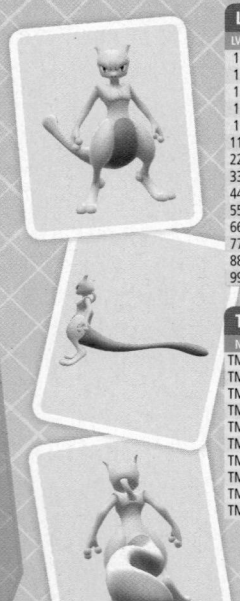

LEVEL-UP MOVES

LV.	NAME	TYPE	KIND	POW.	ACC.	PP	RANGE
1	Confuse Ray	Ghost	Status	—	100	10	Normal
1	Confusion	Psychic	Special	50	100	25	Normal
1	Disable	Normal	Status	—	100	20	Normal
1	Psywave	Psychic	Special	—	100	15	Normal
1	Teleport	Psychic	Status	—	—	20	Self
11	Mist	Ice	Status	—	—	30	Your Side
22	Psybeam	Psychic	Special	65	100	20	Normal
33	Swift	Normal	Special	60	—	20	Many Others
44	Amnesia	Psychic	Status	—	—	20	Self
55	Recover	Normal	Status	—	—	10	Self
66	Psychic	Psychic	Special	90	100	10	Normal
77	Barrier	Psychic	Status	—	—	20	Self
88	Agility	Psychic	Status	—	—	30	Self
99	Calm Mind	Psychic	Status	—	—	20	Self

TM MOVES

NO.	NAME	TYPE	KIND	POW.	ACC.	PP	RANGE
TM01	Headbutt	Normal	Physical	70	100	15	Normal
TM02	Taunt	Dark	Status	—	100	20	Normal
TM04	Teleport	Psychic	Status	—	—	20	Self
TM05	Rest	Psychic	Status	—	—	10	Self
TM06	Light Screen	Psychic	Status	—	—	30	Your Side
TM07	Protect	Normal	Status	—	—	10	Self
TM08	Substitute	Normal	Status	—	—	10	Self
TM09	Reflect	Psychic	Status	—	—	20	Your Side
TM11	Will-O-Wisp	Fire	Status	—	85	15	Normal
TM12	Facade	Normal	Physical	70	100	20	Normal

TM MOVES

NO.	NAME	TYPE	KIND	POW.	ACC.	PP	RANGE
TM13	Brick Break	Fighting	Physical	75	100	15	Normal
TM15	Seismic Toss	Fighting	Physical	—	100	20	Normal
TM16	Thunder Wave	Electric	Status	—	90	20	Normal
TM19	Iron Tail	Steel	Physical	100	75	15	Normal
TM21	Foul Play	Dark	Physical	95	100	15	Normal
TM22	Rock Slide	Rock	Physical	75	90	10	Many Others
TM23	Thunder Punch	Electric	Physical	75	100	15	Normal
TM26	Poison Jab	Poison	Physical	80	100	20	Normal
TM27	Toxic	Poison	Status	—	90	10	Normal
TM28	Tri Attack	Normal	Special	80	100	10	Normal
TM30	Bulk Up	Fighting	Status	—	—	20	Self
TM31	Fire Punch	Fire	Physical	75	100	15	Normal
TM33	Calm Mind	Psychic	Status	—	—	20	Self
TM35	Ice Punch	Ice	Physical	75	100	15	Normal
TM36	Thunderbolt	Electric	Special	90	100	15	Normal
TM37	Flamethrower	Fire	Special	90	100	15	Normal
TM38	Thunder	Electric	Special	110	70	10	Normal
TM40	Psychic	Psychic	Special	90	100	10	Normal
TM41	Earthquake	Ground	Physical	100	100	10	All Others
TM42	Self-Destruct	Normal	Physical	200	100	5	All Others
TM43	Shadow Ball	Ghost	Special	80	100	15	Normal
TM45	Solar Beam	Grass	Special	200	100	10	Normal
TM46	Fire Blast	Fire	Special	110	85	5	Normal
TM48	Hyper Beam	Normal	Special	150	90	5	Normal
TM51	Blizzard	Ice	Special	110	70	5	Many Others
TM55	Ice Beam	Ice	Special	90	100	10	Normal
TM57	Pay Day	Normal	Physical	40	100	20	Normal
TM59	Dream Eater	Psychic	Special	100	100	15	Normal

POKÉMON EXPRESSIONS

HAPPY

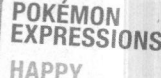

UNHAPPY

ATTACKING

Mega Mewtwo X

MEGA EVOLUTION

Mewtwo

Get a Mewtwonite X from Green, then Mega Evolve Mewtwo during battle by selecting the X icon.

→ → →

Mega Mewtwo X

SPECIES STRENGTHS

HP	▰▰▰▰▰▱▱▱▱▱
ATTACK	▰▰▰▰▰▰▰▰▰▱
DEFENSE	▰▰▰▰▰▱▱▱▱▱
SP. ATK	▰▰▰▰▰▰▰▰▰▱
SP. DEF	▰▰▰▰▱▱▱▱▱▱
SPEED	▰▰▰▰▰▰▰▱▱▱

DAMAGE TAKEN IN BATTLES

⊙	×1	🪶	×2
🔥	×1	⊛	×1
💧	×1	🌸	×1
🍃	×1	◓	×0.5
⚡	×1	☯	×2
❄	×1	🐉	×1
👊	×0.5	◑	×1
☠	×1	◉	×1
⛰	×1	✦	×2

REQUIRED MEGA STONE: MEWTWONITE X

Receive it from Green when you defeat her in battle after catching Mewtwo (p. 110).

Mega Mewtwo Y

MEGA EVOLUTION

Mewtwo

Get a Mewtwonite Y from Green, then Mega Evolve Mewtwo during battle by selecting the Y icon.

→→→

Mega Mewtwo Y

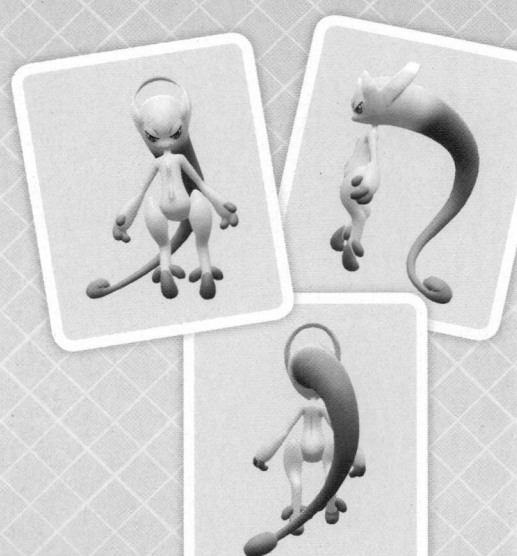

SPECIES STRENGTHS

HP

ATTACK

DEFENSE

SP. ATK

SP. DEF

SPEED

DAMAGE TAKEN IN BATTLES

◎	×1		×1
	×1		×0.5
	×1		×2
	×1		×1
	×1		×2
	×1		×1
	×0.5		×2
	×1		×1
	×1		×1

**REQUIRED MEGA STONE:
MEWTWONITE Y**

Receive it from Green when you defeat her in battle after catching Mewtwo (p. 110).

Mew

— | Gender unknown

SPECIES STRENGTHS

HP	▰▰▰▰▱
ATTACK	▰▰▰▰▱
DEFENSE	▰▰▰▰▱
SP. ATK	▰▰▰▰▱
SP. DEF	▰▰▰▰▱
SPEED	▰▰▰▰▱

DAMAGE TAKEN IN BATTLES

◉	×1	🌿	×1
🔥	×1	◎	×0.5
💧	×1	🦋	×2
⚡	×1	🪨	×1
❄	×1	👻	×2
❄	×1	🐉	×1
👊	×0.5	🌙	×2
☠	×1	◉	×1
🏔	×1	✦	×1

POKÉDEX ENTRY

When viewed through a microscope, this Pokémon's short, fine, delicate hair can be seen.

MAIN WAY TO OBTAIN

Receive Mew as a Mystery Gift (p. 158) if you have a Poké Ball Plus and pair it with your game.

Where to catch

Habitat Unknown

EVOLUTION

(DOES NOT EVOLVE)

POKÉMON EXPRESSIONS

HAPPY

UNHAPPY

ATTACKING

LEVEL-UP MOVES

LV.	NAME	TYPE	KIND	POW.	ACC.	PP	RANGE
1	Confusion	Psychic	Special	50	100	25	Normal
1	Mimic	Normal	Status	—	—	10	Normal
1	Pound	Normal	Physical	40	100	35	Normal
11	Swift	Normal	Special	60	—	20	Many Others
22	Amnesia	Psychic	Status	—	—	20	Self
33	Psywave	Psychic	Special	—	100	15	Normal
44	Barrier	Psychic	Status	—	—	20	Self
55	Mega Punch	Normal	Physical	80	85	20	Normal
66	Metronome	Normal	Status	—	—	10	Self
77	Psychic	Psychic	Special	90	100	10	Normal
88	Nasty Plot	Dark	Status	—	—	20	Self
99	Transform	Normal	Status	—	—	10	Normal

TM MOVES

NO.	NAME	TYPE	KIND	POW.	ACC.	PP	RANGE
TM01	Headbutt	Normal	Physical	70	100	15	Normal
TM02	Taunt	Dark	Status	—	100	20	Normal
TM03	Helping Hand	Normal	Status	—	—	20	1 Ally
TM04	Teleport	Psychic	Status	—	—	20	Self
TM05	Rest	Psychic	Status	—	—	10	Self
TM06	Light Screen	Psychic	Status	—	—	30	Your Side
TM07	Protect	Normal	Status	—	—	10	Self
TM08	Substitute	Normal	Status	—	—	10	Self
TM09	Reflect	Psychic	Status	—	—	20	Your Side
TM10	Dig	Ground	Physical	80	100	10	Normal
TM11	Will-O-Wisp	Fire	Status	—	85	15	Normal
TM12	Facade	Normal	Physical	70	100	20	Normal
TM13	Brick Break	Fighting	Physical	75	100	15	Normal
TM14	Fly	Flying	Physical	90	95	15	Normal
TM15	Seismic Toss	Fighting	Physical	—	100	20	Normal
TM16	Thunder Wave	Electric	Status	—	90	20	Normal
TM17	Dragon Tail	Dragon	Physical	60	90	10	Normal
TM18	U-turn	Bug	Physical	70	100	20	Normal
TM19	Iron Tail	Steel	Physical	100	75	15	Normal
TM20	Dark Pulse	Dark	Special	80	100	15	Normal
TM21	Foul Play	Dark	Physical	95	100	15	Normal
TM22	Rock Slide	Rock	Physical	75	90	10	Many Others

TM MOVES

NO.	NAME	TYPE	KIND	POW.	ACC.	PP	RANGE
TM23	Thunder Punch	Electric	Physical	75	100	15	Normal
TM24	X-Scissor	Bug	Physical	80	100	15	Normal
TM25	Waterfall	Water	Physical	80	100	15	Normal
TM26	Poison Jab	Poison	Physical	80	100	20	Normal
TM27	Toxic	Poison	Status	—	90	10	Normal
TM28	Tri Attack	Normal	Special	80	100	10	Normal
TM29	Scald	Water	Special	80	100	15	Normal
TM30	Bulk Up	Fighting	Status	—	—	20	Self
TM31	Fire Punch	Fire	Physical	75	100	15	Normal
TM32	Dazzling Gleam	Fairy	Special	80	100	10	Many Others
TM33	Calm Mind	Psychic	Status	—	—	20	Self
TM34	Dragon Pulse	Dragon	Special	85	100	10	Normal
TM35	Ice Punch	Ice	Physical	75	100	15	Normal
TM36	Thunderbolt	Electric	Special	90	100	15	Normal
TM37	Flamethrower	Fire	Special	90	100	15	Normal
TM38	Thunder	Electric	Special	110	70	10	Normal
TM39	Outrage	Dragon	Physical	120	100	10	1 Random
TM40	Psychic	Psychic	Special	90	100	10	Normal
TM41	Earthquake	Ground	Physical	100	100	10	All Others
TM42	Self-Destruct	Normal	Physical	200	100	5	All Others
TM43	Shadow Ball	Ghost	Special	80	100	15	Normal
TM44	Play Rough	Fairy	Physical	90	90	10	Normal
TM45	Solar Beam	Grass	Special	200	100	10	Normal
TM46	Fire Blast	Fire	Special	110	85	5	Normal
TM47	Surf	Water	Special	90	100	15	All Others
TM48	Hyper Beam	Normal	Special	150	90	5	Normal
TM49	Superpower	Fighting	Physical	120	100	5	Normal
TM50	Roost	Flying	Status	—	—	10	Self
TM51	Blizzard	Ice	Special	110	70	5	Many Others
TM52	Sludge Bomb	Poison	Special	90	100	10	Normal
TM53	Mega Drain	Grass	Special	75	100	10	Normal
TM54	Flash Cannon	Steel	Special	80	100	10	Normal
TM55	Ice Beam	Ice	Special	90	100	10	Normal
TM56	Stealth Rock	Rock	Status	—	—	20	Other Side
TM57	Pay Day	Normal	Physical	40	100	20	Normal
TM58	Drill Run	Ground	Physical	80	95	10	Normal
TM59	Dream Eater	Psychic	Special	100	100	15	Normal
TM60	Megahorn	Bug	Physical	120	85	10	Normal

Meltan ☑ 152

Hex Nut Pokémon   Average height: 0'08"   Average weight: 17.6 lbs.

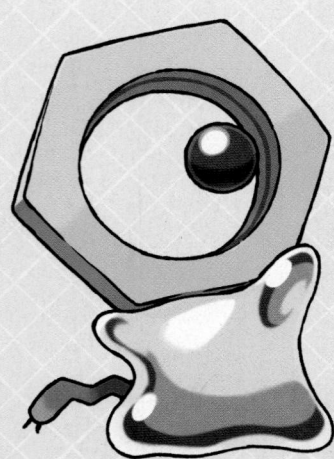

POKÉDEX ENTRY

It melts particles of iron and other metals found in the subsoil, so it can absorb them into its body of molten steel.

SPECIES STRENGTHS

HP ▮▮▮
ATTACK ▮▮▮▮
DEFENSE ▮▮▮▮
SP. ATK ▮▮▮▮
SP. DEF ▮▮▮
SPEED ▮▮

DAMAGE TAKEN IN BATTLES

×0.5		×0.5	
×2		×0.5	
×1		×0.5	
×0.5		×0.5	
×1		×1	
×0.5		×0.5	
×2		×1	
×0		×0.5	
×2		×0.5	

HOW TO OBTAIN

Send Pokémon from Pokémon GO to *Pokémon: Let's Go, Pikachu!* or *Pokémon: Let's Go, Eevee!* (p. 159) to receive a Mystery Box in Pokémon GO. Use the Mystery Box for the chance to encounter Meltan in Pokémon GO, then catch one. Or take part in Special Research for the chance to encounter Meltan in Pokémon GO, then catch one. Once you've caught a Meltan in Pokémon GO, send it to your game.

EVOLUTION

Use Meltan Candies to evolve Meltan in Pokémon GO
→→→

Meltan   **Melmetal**

Melmetal ☑ 153

Hex Nut Pokémon   Average height: 8'02"   Average weight: 1763.7 lbs.

POKÉDEX ENTRY

Revered long ago for its capacity to create iron from nothing, for some reason it has come back to life after 3,000 years.

SPECIES STRENGTHS

HP ▮▮▮▮▮▮▮
ATTACK ▮▮▮▮▮▮▮▮
DEFENSE ▮▮▮▮▮▮▮▮
SP. ATK ▮▮▮▮▮
SP. DEF ▮▮▮▮
SPEED ▮▮

DAMAGE TAKEN IN BATTLES

Same as Meltan

HOW TO OBTAIN

Collect enough Meltan Candies to Evolve Meltan in Pokémon GO, then send it to *Pokémon: Let's Go, Pikachu!* or *Pokémon: Let's Go, Eevee!*

SIGNATURE MOVE: DOUBLE IRON BASH

The user rotates, centering its hex nut in its chest, and then strikes with its arms twice in a row. This may also make the target flinch.

Special
Content

Pokémon: Let's Go, Pikachu!
& Pokémon: Let's Go, Eevee!

Official Creator Interview

Junichi Masuda

Junichi Masuda

Director of GAME FREAK inc.

Director of *Pokémon: Let's Go, Pikachu!* *& Pokémon: Let's Go, Eevee!*

Interview conducted by Shusuke Motomiya (ONEUP Inc.)

GAMES FILLED WITH AS MANY WAYS TO PLAY AS POSSIBLE

When it comes to the development of Pokémon series titles, each entry has a keyword that serves as a core idea. That keyword is shared with the many creators contributing to the project as the development drives forward. Tell us what the keyword was for this pair of games.

MASUDA

We have always decided a keyword for our projects, but the truth is that we didn't have a single definitive keyword this time. Instead we had the idea of creating a game that wouldn't be frightening and that everyone could play together in their living room. That's because these games started off from the desire to rebuild the Pokémon series for the new home gaming console—Nintendo Switch—based on the 1999 Game Boy title *Pokémon Yellow: Special Pikachu Edition*. If we simply brought *Pokémon Yellow* to Nintendo Switch as it was, though, we would only see a limited number of people play the game. That's why we forged ahead with adding Pokémon-catching mechanics from Pokémon GO and the two-player Support Play feature, and we really included as many new ways to play as we could manage. The major concern we had when development first started was how well Nintendo Switch would sell. After all, we were working on development before the hardware had even been released, so we really couldn't predict at all whether the console was going to sell well or not. Of course, we were all quite relieved to see it hit record sales figures after its release! *(Laughs.)*

SPECIAL CONTENT

What made you consider making a game for Nintendo Switch based on *Pokémon Yellow* in the first place?

◁═══⟨ **MASUDA** ⟩═══▷

Pokémon Yellow is the one title in the Pokémon series that has the closest ties to the animated TV series. That TV series is broadcast in over 80 countries around the world. There are quite likely people who watch the TV series even though they've never played a Pokémon game—including Pokémon GO. I felt it would be important to include elements of the TV series to try to get those fans to feel like they would want to play the core Pokémon series, too. In *Pokémon Yellow*, the player had Pikachu following behind him, right? When we were wondering whether we could depict that in some new fashion, we decided we could have it ride on the player's shoulder, just like how Ash's Pikachu does in the TV series. I thought that seeing your Pokémon riding right there on your shoulder would make it feel more like a partner in your adventure—really promoting that sense of closeness. "*You* can become Ash!" That idea was the real starting line for our development.

> **"I felt it would be important to include elements of the TV series to try to get those fans to feel like they would want to play the core Pokémon series, too."**

IT'S BECAUSE OF THE FANS THAT EEVEE HAS A MAJOR ROLE

So at the heart of it all, when people see these games, you want to inspire as many people as possible to feel like they are games they would want to try playing for themselves.

MASUDA

Pikachu is well recognized by people all around the world, and there are a lot of fans of the TV show out there. Team Rocket is pretty popular, too. And Pokémon GO has an amazing number of players. But a lot of young kids don't have their own smartphones, so they can't play Pokémon GO. I thought that I'd like to make *Pokémon: Let's Go, Pikachu!* and *Pokémon: Let's Go, Eevee!* games that could target people who had never played a Pokémon series game, including those small kids. I wanted to make them games that act as an entry to the Pokémon series—the first games you might play.

Why did you pick Eevee to serve as a partner Pokémon alongside Pikachu?

MASUDA

One of the new gameplay features born when *Pokémon Red* and *Pokémon Blue* came out in 1998 was the ability to trade Pokémon with other players. Even with a game on Nintendo Switch, we wanted to release two versions to be able to have players trade their Pokémon. To achieve that, though, we'd need a popular Pokémon that could stand on the same level as Pikachu. So, I decided that Eevee would be the one to face this challenge. There are really a lot of people out there who love Eevee, and I get all kinds of amazing fan art of Eevee sent to my Twitter account. People had a ball when we declared November 21 as Eevee Day in Japan, and Pokémon fans refer to all the Pokémon that evolve from Eevee with the fond nickname "Eeveelutions." When I felt just how much love those fans had for Eevee, that's what made me start considering Eevee as a candidate. It made me notice all over again the charms of Eevee. It's cute in some of the ways a dog is and some of the ways a cat is—plus it's also got a babyish appeal to it. "Eevee, of all Pokémon, could stand beside Pikachu." Once I felt sure of that, I decided to make a game with Eevee playing the central role, too.

Go! Pikachu!

Go! Pikachu!

When you see images of these games, the first thing you notice is how different they look. I was surprised to see the high-quality graphics, scaled up from the small Nintendo 3DS screen to something suited for a large TV screen.

MASUDA

At the root of the visual direction was the idea we had of people playing these games at home in their living room. Like if an eight- or nine-year-old kid is playing games in their living room and their mom glances out from the kitchen while cooking dinner and catches sight of the TV screen. Then if she sees something weird on it, she shouts, "Stop that! What d'you think you're doing, playing a game like that?!" I wanted to look at it from the perspective of those moms and dads. I took care in every detail, aware that I didn't want to make it a game that would cause parents to feel mistrustful of our games. And we kept in mind that we wanted them to be games that would let parents jump in and help out with Support Play whenever their kids might beg, "Help me out!" Same for friends being able to jump in and help, too. We wanted people to come together thanks to these games, with everyone having fun in the living room together. That's why we didn't want it to look scary. We've built it up as a fantasy world. We set up the proportions of the player character to look a bit childish, too.

I never get tired of watching the way Pikachu or Eevee runs down your arm to leap into action when a battle begins. It's so good! How did you think of a scene like that?

MASUDA

The members of our motion design team thought that up for us. The first time I noticed it, it was pretty much already finished and in the games! *(Laughs.)* And I was just like, "This is *awesome*!" *(Huge laugh.)*

Go! Pikachu!

Go! Pikachu!

THE CATCHING SCREEN IS LIKE POKÉMON GO—AND ALSO NOT LIKE POKÉMON GO

You can choose a number of a different ways to play these games, but it seems like playing by holding a Joy-Con in one hand is what's being recommended. Is that right?

◆ MASUDA ◆

Personally, I feel that playing while holding a Joy-Con in one hand is what fits the best. My impression is that it's easier to play when using a single Joy-Con than in handheld mode. And the fact that we developed the Pokémon-catching mechanics based on those in Pokémon GO is also another reason for that. You can experience controls where you actually throw the Poké Balls yourself, and playing with the Joy-Con matches

> **"Wouldn't it be cool if you could play together with someone at the same time?"**

perfectly with that. Now you can easily throw out balls with one hand and really get into that experience. And of course, there's one more Joy-Con with the system—that's what allowed us to achieve Support Play. Our reasoning for this was pretty simple—basically, "Hey, wouldn't it be cool if you could play together with someone at the same time?"

These games use the same kind of catching screen as you see in Pokémon GO, so why does the play experience feel so different?

◆ MASUDA ◆

We put our first priority on the physicality of being able to wave your Joy-Con and throw Poké Balls to catch Pokémon in these games. The screen might bring to mind the catching screen in Pokémon GO, but I think that the play experience is something entirely new. Catching is really about getting that Pokémon. So we made it something simple, like the way you use a net to catch bugs in the wild. And since your Pokémon can get more Exp. Points from catching and Trainer battles, they can keep growing stronger.

What are the biggest changes when you look back at how the Pokémon series has continued these past twenty-plus years?

MASUDA

The biggest evolution in these games was having the Pokémon appear in the field. It's a point that lets us convey how the Pokémon move and act as vibrant living creatures and lets players feel how big they each are. Of course, there are examples like Onix, but even Pokémon like Venomoth and Nidoran♂ might surprise you when you're confronted with how large they are.

> **"The biggest evolution in these games was having the Pokémon appear in the field. ...Players feel how big they each are."**

Tell us about the battles in these games. Why did you make the partner Pikachu or Eevee so strong—strong enough that you can really make significant progress in the game with just your partner alone?

◆──◆ **MASUDA** ◆──◆

We really had it in mind to make your partner Pikachu or Eevee special for the player. You can go on this adventure relying just on the strength of your Pikachu or Eevee, or you can choose to lean on the strength of the Pokémon in your party. We worked on the balance so that players could enjoy either play style. The most important factors were thinking of the tendency for kids to give up partway through a game if it gets too hard and also thinking about how long children can play games. Like we were talking about before about kids playing in the living room, right? Kids can't always play games for long stretches at a time. It's common that kids are told they can play for one hour a day or some other limited time. I had a wish to allow those kids to enjoy their adventure at their own pace while catching all kinds of different Pokémon along the way. So their partner should really be someone they can rely on for those times.

GAME DESIGN BASED ON
THE WAY PEOPLE LIVE

Why did you decide to include the feature that allows another Pokémon to travel together with the player, in addition to the partner?

The total play time needed to reach the Hall of Fame in these games isn't all that long compared to recent RPGs—wouldn't you agree?

MASUDA

We want players to love their partner Pikachu or Eevee, of course, but in the end, we want them to treasure the other Pokémon in their party, too. When we thought about that, we thought up the idea of having these Pokémon that travel with you finding helpful items for you on your journey. I think you end up loving the Pokémon that travel with you in a slightly different way than you might love your partner Pikachu or Eevee.

MASUDA

When you consider how people live in this day and age, I think it's safe to say everyone's pretty busy. The way we spend our time is different now from how it was 20 years ago. Thanks to smartphones, you're constantly bombarded with information, and it's natural that you end up thinking you want to play some other games, too. So I felt like perhaps the time you spend on your adventures in these games didn't need to dominate all your free time. We sped up the walking speed for the player and kept the playtime needed to reach the Hall of Fame on the shorter side. For the people who want to play more, I'd like them to enjoy cuddling their partner Pikachu or Eevee and giving them Berries, having fun with outfits, and building up their bonds with their partner. And after they reach the Hall of Fame, I hope they might also enjoy battling the Master Trainers, who can give you special titles to boast about.

Tell us about why you added the Candy feature that's used in Pokémon GO.

MASUDA

I was thinking of a way to motivate players to want to catch tons of Pokémon. You catch Pokémon, send them to Professor Oak, get Candies, and then you can make the Pokémon in your party stronger. The Pokémon series has long had an item called Rare Candy that could be used to raise your Pokémon's level. So rather than saying that we were thinking of Pokémon GO, I think that this system is more the result of really wanting to make something that would be easy to understand.

Tell us why there are new Pokémon— Meltan and Melmetal—appearing in these games.

MASUDA

Those two were born from our desire to build a bridge between players of the core Pokémon series and players of Pokémon GO. We wanted something that would make both groups happy.

Meltan

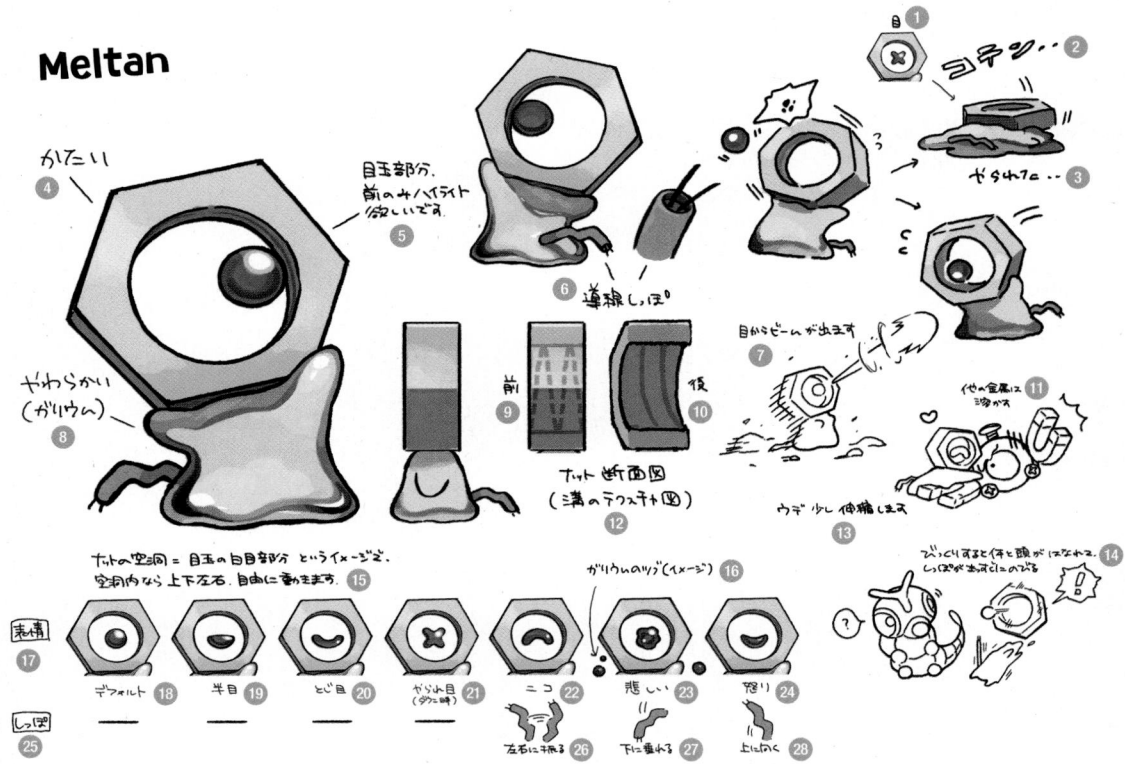

1. Eye 2. Clunk 3. Defeated... 4. Hard 5. Eye part (would like a highlight just on the front) 6. Wire tail 7. Shoots a beam from its eye 8. Soft (gallium) 9. Front 10. Back 11. It melts other metals. 12. Cross section of the nut (showing where the texture of the threads should go) 13. Its arms can stretch to be a bit longer or shorter. 14. When it's shocked, its head and body separate and its tail sticks straight up. 15. The hole in the nut is like the white of the eye. The eye can move freely up, down, left, or right within the hole in the nut. 16. Imagine they're droplets of gallium. 17. Expressions 18. Default 19. Half-closed eye 20. Closed eye 21. Defeated eye (when it faints) 22. Smiling 23. Sad 24. Angry 25. Tail 26. Wagging right and left 27. Drooping down 28. Pointing up

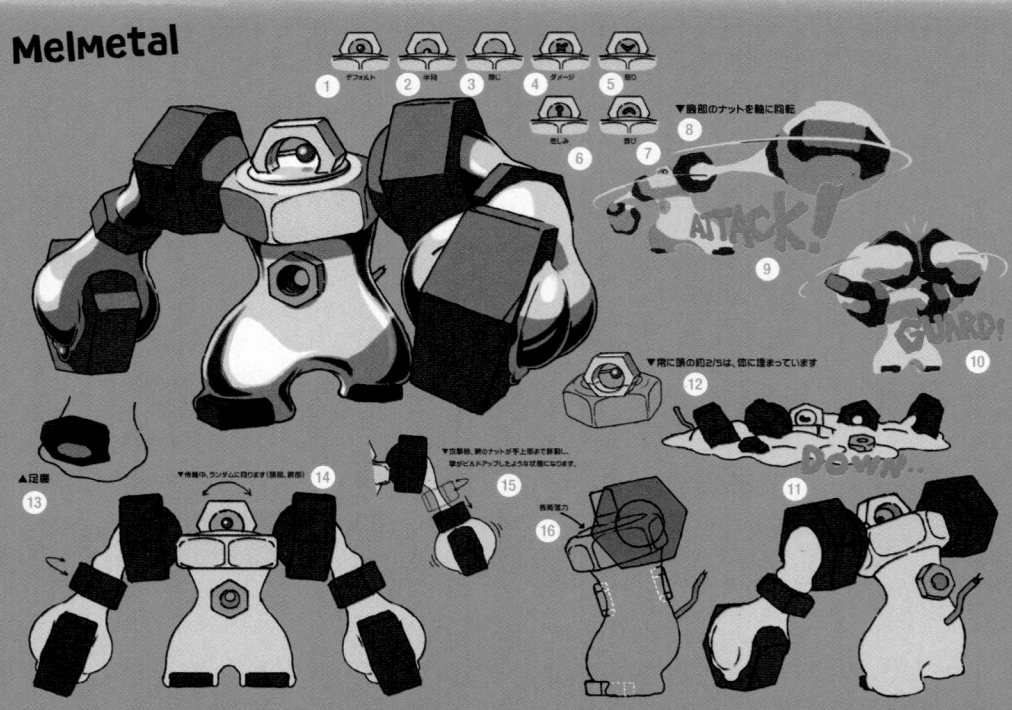

Melmetal

1 デフォルト 2 半段 3 閉じ 4 ダメージ 5 怒り 6 悲しみ 7 喜び

8 ▼胸部のナットを軸に回転

9 ATTACK!

10 GUARD!

11 DOWN...

12 ▼常に頭の約2/5は、体に埋まっています

13 ▲足裏

14 ▼待機中、ランダムに回ります（頭部、腕部）

15 ▼攻撃時、腕のナットが手上部まで移動し、腕がビルドアップしたような拳になります。

16 重心落力

1. Default 2. Half-closed eye 3. Closed eye 4. Took damage 5. Angry 6. Sad 7. Happy 8. Rotates around, using the nut in its chest like an axle 9. Attack!
10. Guard! 11. Down... 12. About 2/5 of its head is always sunk within its body. 13. Underside of foot 14. Randomly spins when it's idle (head part and arm parts)
15. When it attacks, the nuts in its arms slide down as if to bulk up its fists. 16. Surface tension

What was most important to you when it came to making the Poké Ball Plus? And how do you recommend playing with it?

◀ MASUDA ▶

When you catch Pokémon using the Poké Ball Plus, the light on it will flash like the Poké Ball you can see on your TV screen and you can hear their unique cries—but that's just the start of it. If you press the button on it when you have a Pokémon inside, it will light up with a color matching the Pokémon

you've taken for a stroll. And as you try things like shaking it or rolling it on a table and hear all kinds of different cries, I hope players will imagine how their Pokémon might be enjoying the experience from inside.

Are *Pokémon: Let's Go, Pikachu!* and *Pokémon: Let's Go, Eevee!* spin-offs? And would you consider making other games that could connect to Pokémon GO?

◀ MASUDA ▶

These games aren't spin-offs. These are core Pokémon titles. As for whether we would make other games that could connect to Pokémon GO, that will depend on how the games are received. If we hear a lot of people saying that they enjoyed being able to bring Pokémon to these games from Pokémon GO, then we'll think about maybe having future titles also be able to connect to it.

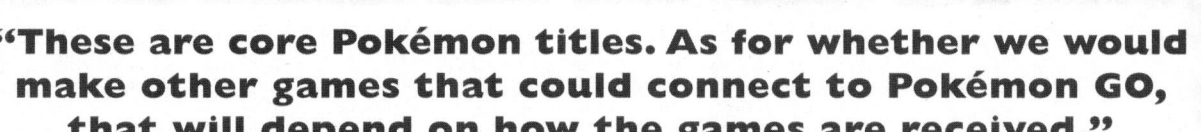

"These are core Pokémon titles. As for whether we would make other games that could connect to Pokémon GO, that will depend on how the games are received."

What is your favorite new feature in these games, Mr. Masuda?

MASUDA

It's gotta be the catching. Being able to throw a Poké Ball by swinging my own arm and actually experience being able to catch Pokémon—I think it's a lot of fun. I can tell you, I've done it a fair number of times—but no matter how many times I try it, it's still fun. *(Mimes throwing a ball.)* Imagine people around the world doing this. Doesn't that make you happy? *(Laughs.)*

How do you want players to experience these games?

MASUDA

My wish for these games is that I want everyone to enjoy it together. Maybe you bought *Pokémon: Let's Go, Pikachu!* but you don't play Pokémon GO. For someone like that, try getting Pokémon from a friend playing Pokémon GO or maybe from a parent. I think it's amazing that two friends could get seriously into playing together with Support Play or that people might build new relationships playing together in the living room. And as people's relationships grow in new ways, then so too does the world of Pokémon grow. That's really what these games are all about.

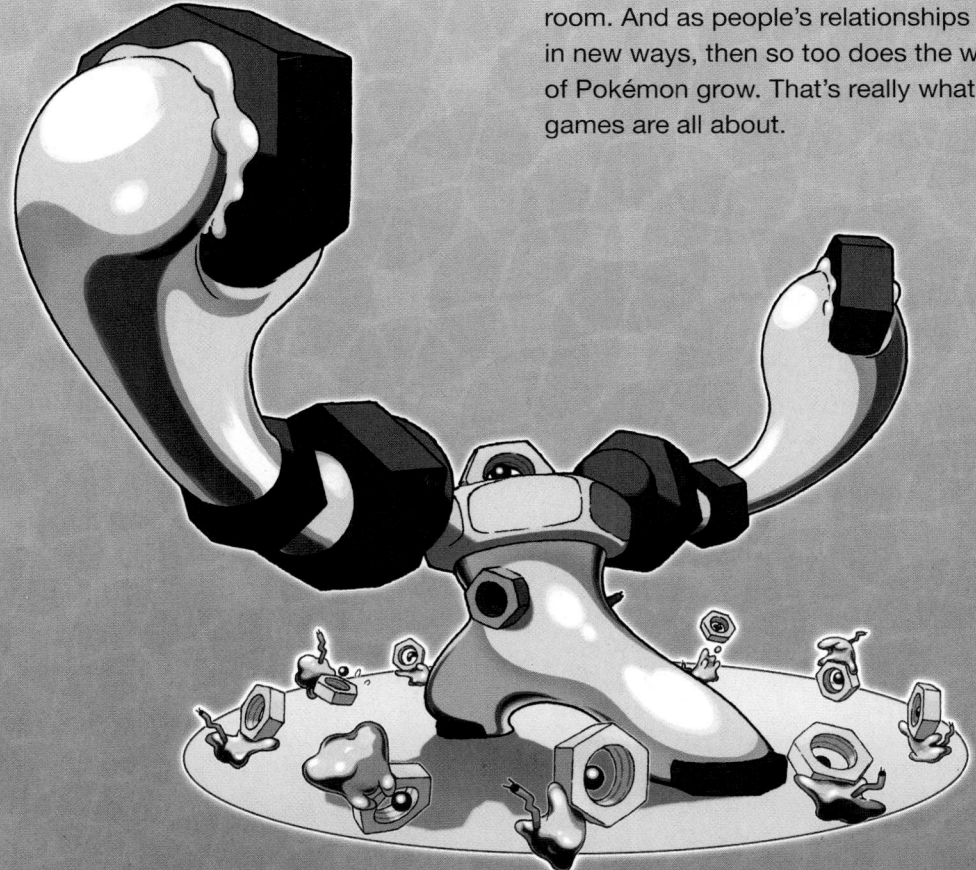

This interview is a reproduction of an original article written by Shusuke Motomiya (the author of the official Japanese strategy guide) and published by OVERLAP, Inc.

Pokémon: Let's Go, Pikachu! & Pokémon: Let's Go, Eevee! Concept Art

On the following pages, you'll find a rare selection of concept art used in the making of *Pokémon: Let's Go, Pikachu!* and *Pokémon: Let's Go, Eevee!* This is your exclusive chance to get a peek into the thought that goes into building up the detailed world of Pokémon, straight from the developers at GAME FREAK. Learn more about the people you meet on your adventure with images you won't see anywhere else, and pore over the details of some of the towns, buildings, and tools you see in the Kanto region.

Main Character (Male/Female)

Professor Oak

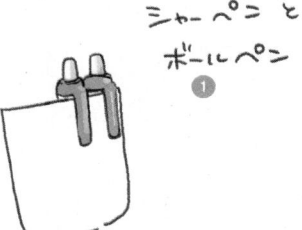

シャーペン と
ボールペン
①

1. A mechanical pencil and a ballpoint pen

Rival

1. Falls forward a bit **2.** Right-handed **3.** On the road **4.** Were you always... **5.** ...this strong? **6.** Surprised to have lost **7.** Champion **8.** No backpack
9. Like he's ready to face you head on—fair and square

SPECIAL CONTENT

Blue

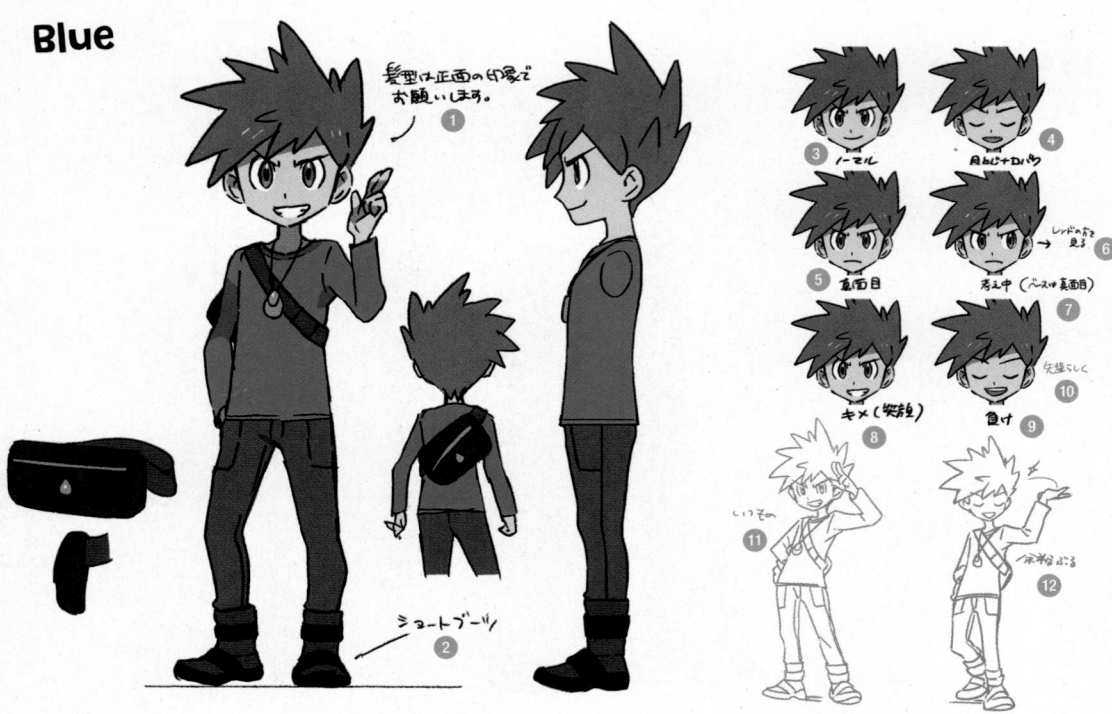

1. Please make his hair as you see it from the front. **2.** Short boots **3.** Normal **4.** Eyes closed, mouth open **5.** Serious **6.** Looking over at Red **7.** Thinking (based on a serious expression) **8.** Determined (smiling) **9.** Defeated **10.** Like an experienced role model **11.** His usual pose **12.** Pretending to be confident

Green

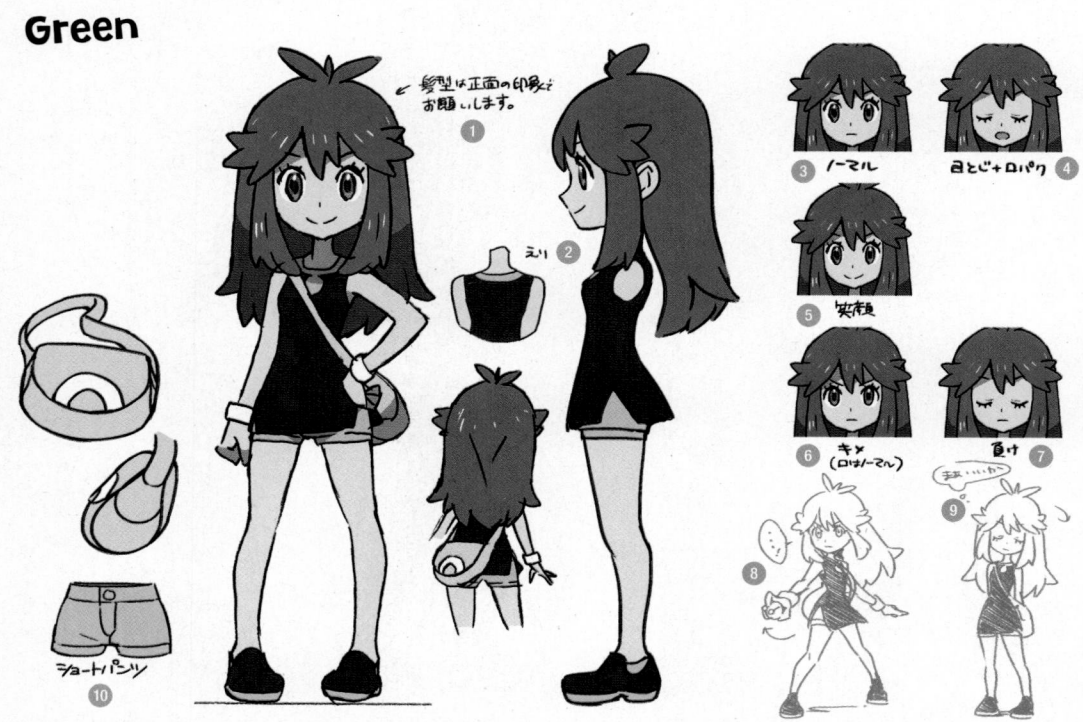

1. Please make the hairstyle follow her appearance from the front. **2.** Collar **3.** Normal **4.** Eyes closed, mouth open **5.** Smiling **6.** Determined (normal mouth) **7.** Lost **8.** ...! **9.** Oh well. **10.** Shorts

SPECIAL CONTENT

Red

1. The badge has a certain thickness. **2.** High-top sneakers **3.** Normal **4.** Eyes closed, mouth open **5.** Smiling **6.** Determined (normal mouth) **7.** Defeated **8.** Wants to hide his face as much as possible **9.** ...!

Mina

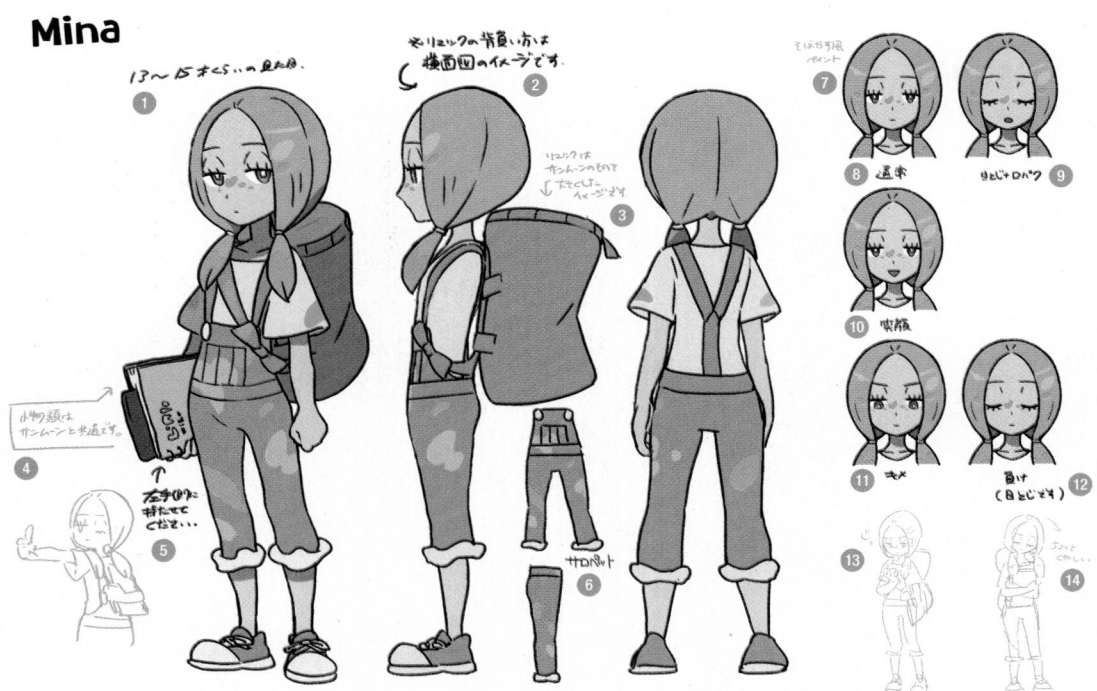

1. Looks to be about 13 to 15 years old **2.** The way her bag hangs on her back should be as you see here from the side. **3.** Her bag should look like the one in *Pokémon Sun* and *Pokémon Moon*, only bigger. **4.** Her belongings should be the same as in *Pokémon Sun* and *Pokémon Moon*. **5.** Please have her carry them in her left hand. **6.** Overalls **7.** Paint is splattered on her face like freckles. **8.** Normal **9.** Eyes closed, mouth open **10.** Smiling **11.** Determined **12.** Defeated (eyes closed) **13.** Staring **14.** This kinda sucks...

Brock

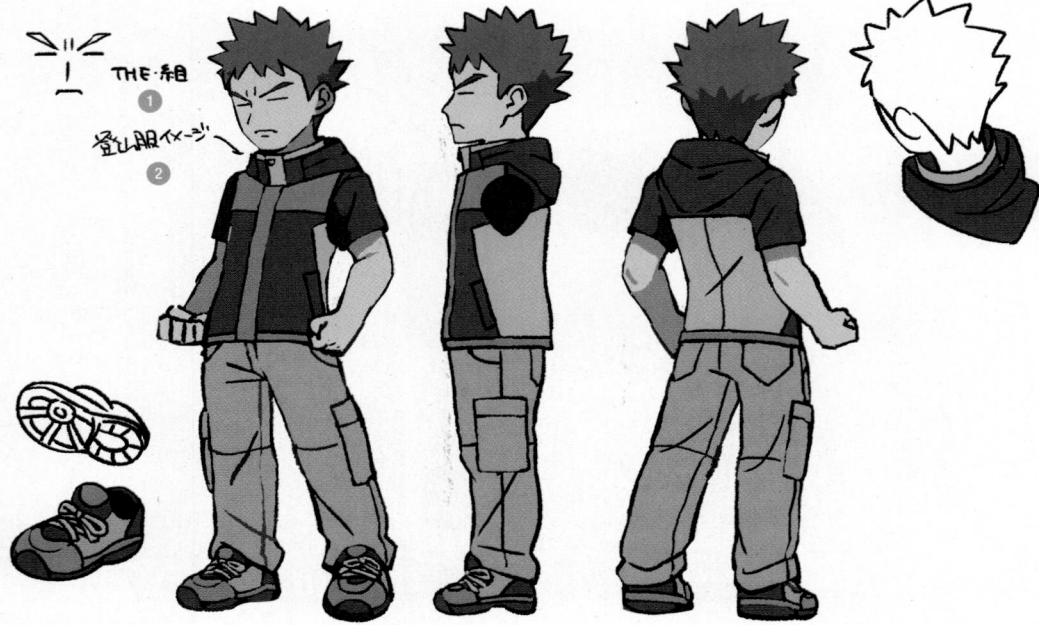

THE·組

登山服イメージ

1. The signature Brock look **2.** Like hiking wear

Misty

インナーは初代風
水着です。

彼はまっすぐ

水面のような
イメージの
ジーンズ。

水着イメージ→

口は小さめ

1. Underneath is a swimsuit in the style of the first generation. **2.** Lines are straight **3.** Shadow **4.** Jeans have a pattern like the water's surface **5.** Like a swimsuit
6. Mouth is on the smaller side

Lt. Surge

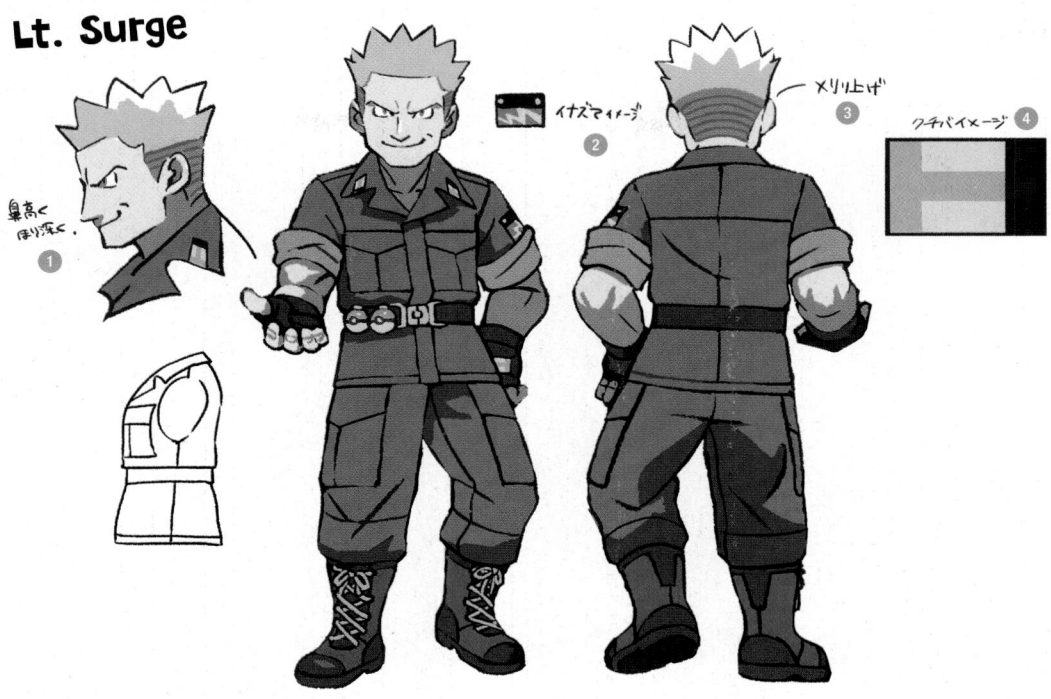

鼻高く
ほり深く
①

イナズマイメージ
②

メリハリ上げ
③

クチバイメージ
④

1. Prominent nose and deep furrow in his brow 2. Lightning pattern 3. Buzz cut on the back 4. Vermilion image

Erika

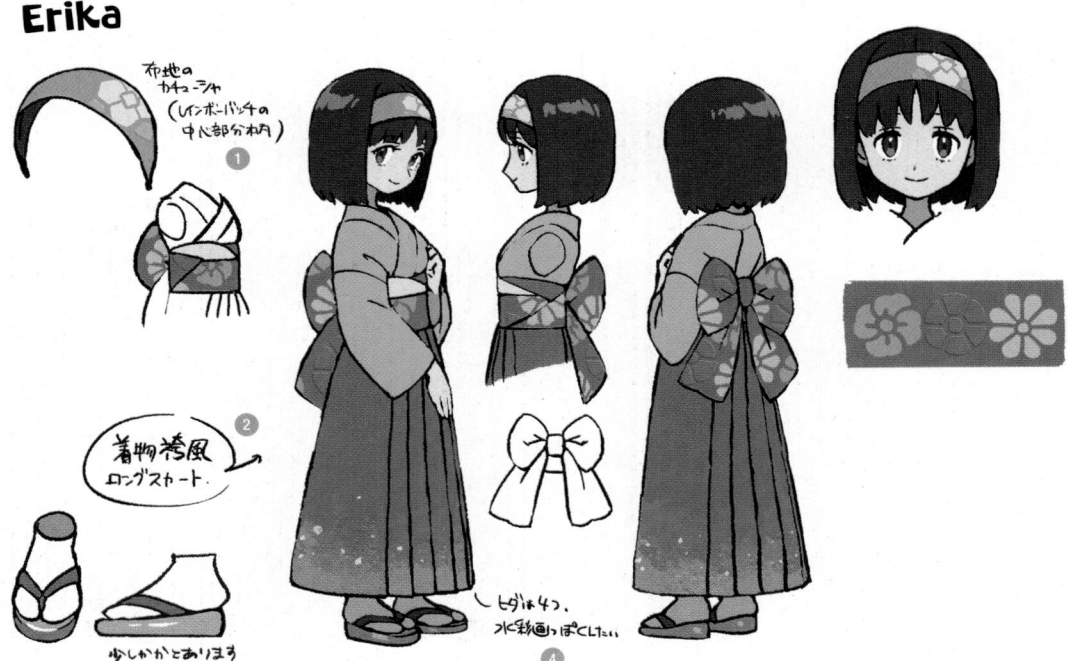

布地の
カチューシャ
（レインボーバッチの
中心部分内）
①

着物袴風
ロングスカート
②

少しかかとあります
③

ヒダは4つ
水彩画っぽくしたい
④

1. Cloth headband (pattern like the center of a Rainbow Badge) 2. Kimono-style long skirt 3. Heels have a bit of height 4. Four folds: want it to look like a watercolor painting

Koga

1. Father! 2. Face 3. Like a gas mask

Sabrina

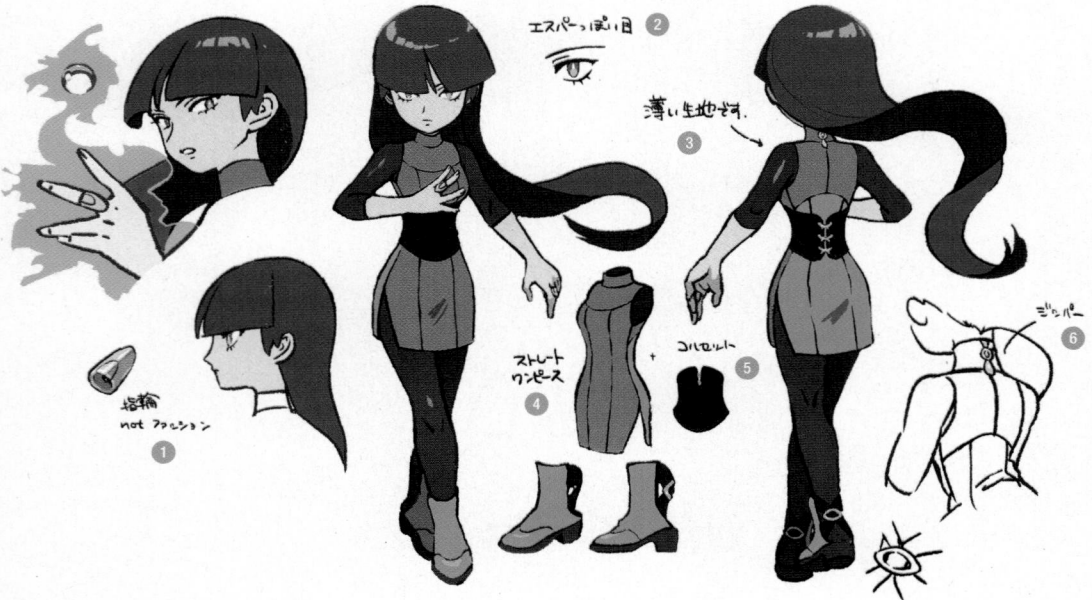

1. Ring: not a fashion statement 2. Psychic-looking eyes 3. Thin material 4. Formfitting dress 5. Corset 6. Zipper

Blaine

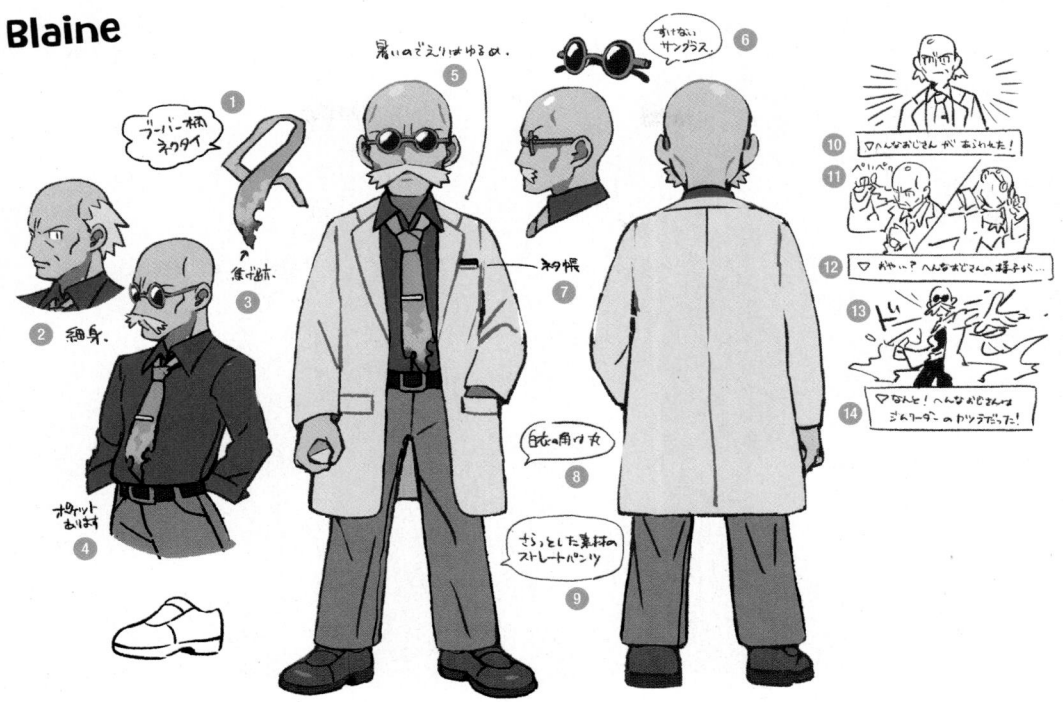

1. Magmar-patterned necktie **2.** Slender body type **3.** Singed **4.** Pants have pockets **5.** His collar is a bit loose in response to the heat. **6.** Mirrored sunglasses
7. Notebook for his lines **8.** The hem of his lab coat is rounded at the corners. **9.** Straight-leg pants made of a smooth material **10.** A strange old man appeared!
11. Peel **12.** What's this? The old man seems to be— **13.** Ta-da! **14.** Oh my! The strange old man was actually Gym Leader Blaine!

Giovanni

1. A bit of lift at the front **2.** Round at the back **3.** An embroidered patch...?

Lorelei

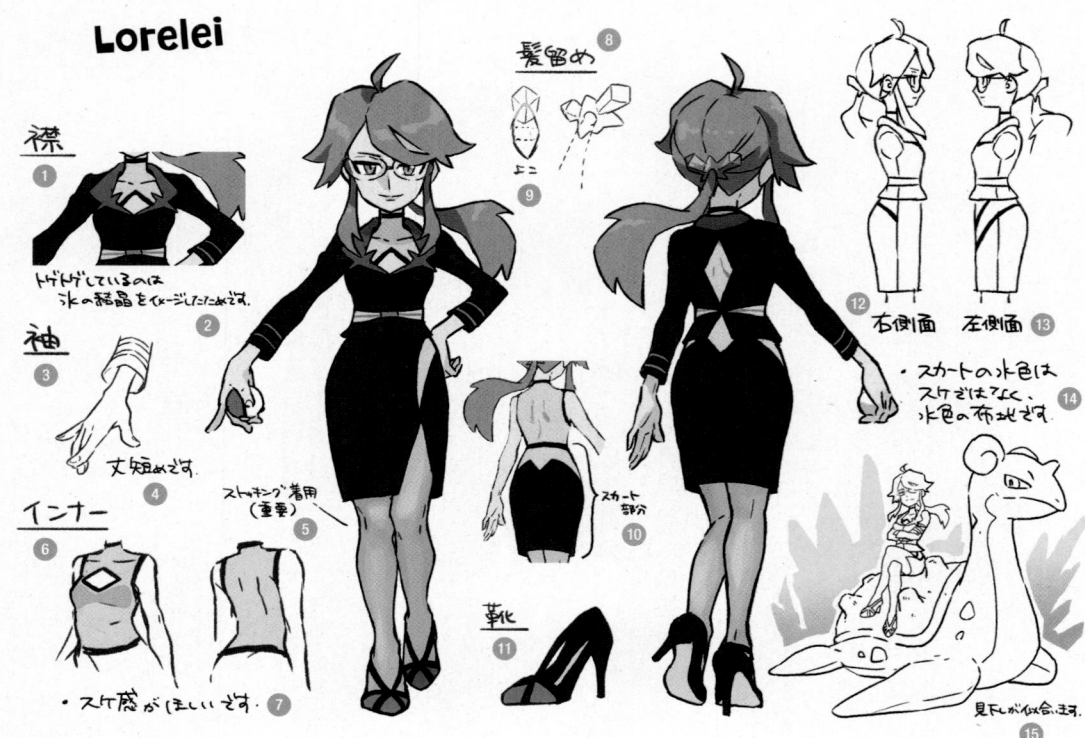

1. Collar 2. The sharp points are based on the image of ice crystals. 3. Sleeve 4. Slightly cropped at the wrists 5. Wearing stockings (this is key) 6. Inner shirt 7. Want it to be somewhat transparent 8. Hair tie 9. Side view 10. Skirt portion 11. Shoes 12. Right side view 13. Left side view 14. The blue area on the skirt isn't transparent but simply blue-colored cloth. 15. She looks good looking down on people.

Bruno

1. The shadow beneath his brow is always there. 2. Legs come to here. Pants are loose. 3. Belt 4. Looks used 5. Nine in total 6. Accessories' motif: chains 7. (To restrain his excessive strength...) 8. Bracelet 9. Seven in total 10. Anklet 11. Five in total 12. Hoo hah! 13. Each pant leg has a cut on both sides.

Agatha

ブローチと
ビジューシャツ ①

ロープなし ②

レースは
ドクロモチーフです ③
(×5)

呪！ ④

ロープ ⑤
キクの葉と
人型イメージです ⑥

AHAHAHAHAHAHAH

光ほす ⑧

ゲンガー杖 ⑦

両端の叶形
ちがいます ⑨

靴化 ⑩

1. Brooch and shirt design 2. Without her shawl 3. The lace's design is based on a skull. 4. Cursed! 5. Shawl 6. Design is based on chrysanthemum leaves and humanoid shapes (note: Agatha's name in Japanese includes "chrysanthemum") 7. Gengar cane 8. Lights up 9. The ends of each side have a different shape. 10. Shoes

Lance

腕 おろした時の
シルエット ①

目 ②

真剣 ③

④

ふむ… ⑤

集 ⑤

なかなか
やるな…！ ⑥

マントは
ドラゴン使いに
欠かせない！ ⑦

段あり ⑧

段なし ⑨

マントの様からうしろへ
つながり 真っすぐです ⑩

柄のイメージは
ドラゴンの翼です ⑪

1. Silhouette when he has his arms lowered 2. Eye 3. Serious 4. Hmm... 5. Flustered 6. You're quite formidable... 7. Any Dragon-type user worth his salt needs a cape! 8. Layered 9. Flat 10. The line is straight where the cape wraps around the shoulders to the back. 11. The design is inspired by a dragon's wings.

Pokédex

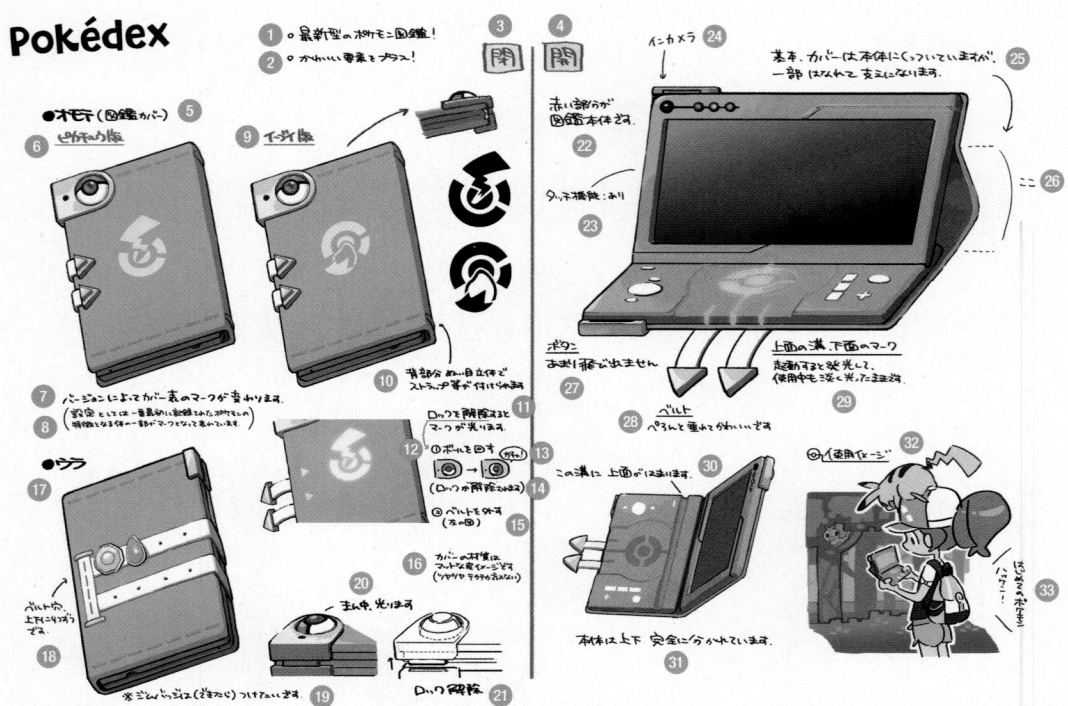

1. The latest Pokédex! 2. Cute new elements added! 3. Closed 4. Open 5. Front (Pokédex cover) 6. Pikachu version 7. The mark on the cover will change designs based on the game version. 8. (Setting-wise, the most characteristic part of the Pokémon that is first recorded will be displayed as a mark.) 9. Eevee version 10. The stitching stands out on the spine, so you can attach a strap or something. 11. The mark lights up when you unlock the Pokédex. 12. (1) Turn the ball. 13. Click! 14. (Now it's unlocked.) 15. (2) Undo the belts (as shown on the left). 16. The cover material should be something like a matte leather (not shiny or textured). 17. Back 18. There are four holes on each belt (upper and lower). 19. Want the Gym Badges to attach (if possible) 20. The middle glows. 21. Unlocked 22. The red part is the body of the Pokédex. 23. Touch-screen function: yes 24. Inward-facing camera 25. The cover is basically attached to the body, but a section of it detaches and acts as a stand. 26. Here 27. Buttons are pretty flat. 28. Belts look cute when they're just flopping out. 29. The lines on the top screen and the mark on the bottom screen light up when the Pokédex is turned on. They continue to glow faintly while the device is in use. 30. The top screen fits into this recess here. 31. The top and bottom parts of the body are completely separate. 32. In use 33. Found my first Pokémon!

Ghost

1. Stopper ghost 2. Like the horns on a Marowak 3. Hands like Haunter's, floating in the air 4. Different in terms of size, color, expression, and horns
5. Following ghosts

Pokémon Box

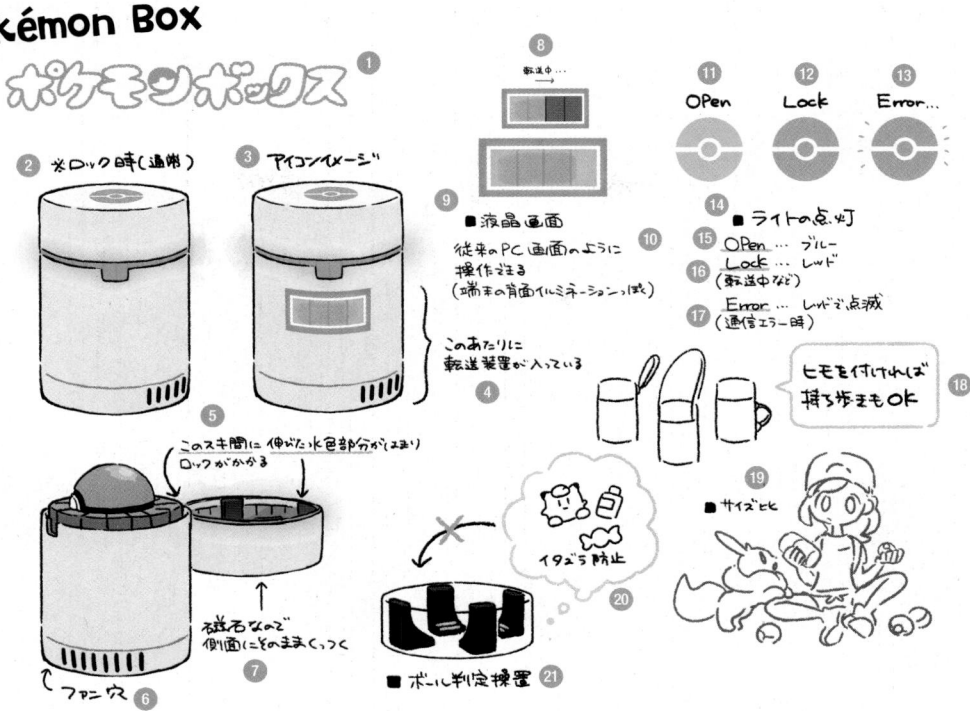

1. The Pokémon Box 2. When locked (normal state) 3. Icon image 4. The device for sending Pokémon is down inside here. 5. The blue parts that extend between these areas will slot into place and lock the top on. 6. Fan vents 7. It's magnetic, so it sticks to the side on its own. 8. Now sending... 9. LCD screen 10. Can be used to control the box just like the conventional PC screen (looks like an illuminated screen on a console) 11. Open 12. Lock 13. Error... 14. Lights 15. Open: blue 16. Locked: red (when sending Pokémon, etc.) 17. Error: flashing red (when there's a connection error) 18. You can also attach a strap to it and carry it around. 19. Scale image 20. To prevent misuse 21. Ball verification device

Silph Scope

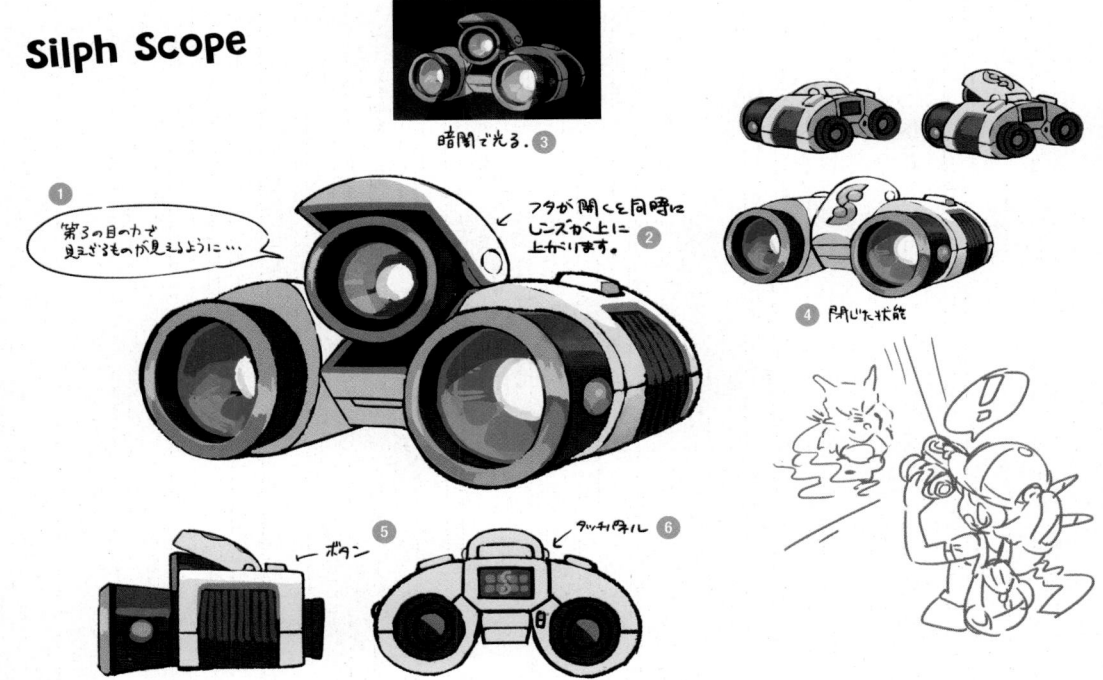

1. Like you can see the unseen with the power of the third eye... 2. When you open this top, the lens rises up. 3. Glows in the dark 4. When it's closed 5. Button 6. Touch-screen panel

Pokémon Center Exterior

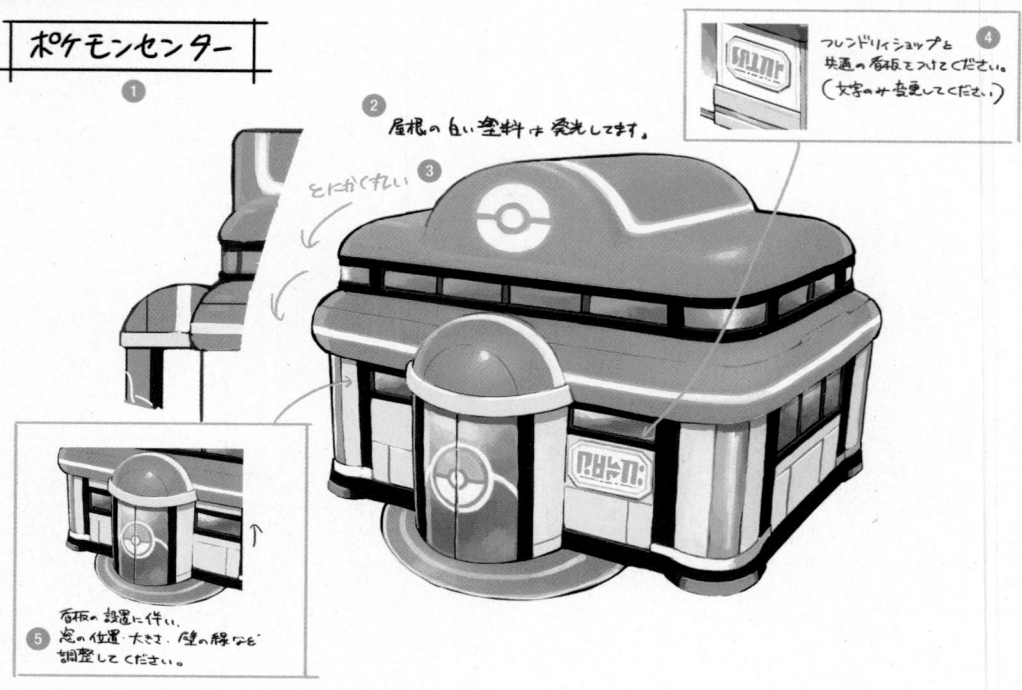

ポケモンセンター ①

② 屋根の白い塗料は発光してます。

とにかくまるい

③

④ フレンドリィショップと
共通の看板を入れてください。
（文字のみ変更してください。）

⑤ 看板の 設置に伴い、
窓の 位置・大きさ・壁の線 など
調整してください。

1. Pokémon Center **2.** The white parts of the roof light up. **3.** Just make it round. **4.** Add the same sign as on the Poké Mart. (But replace the characters, please.)
5. Adjust the size and placement of the windows and trim of the walls as needed to place the sign on the front.

Poké Mart Exterior

フレンドリィ ショップ ①

② 外観

③ 白い溝2本は発光してます。

④ 全体的に角丸イメージです。

⑤ Yes 窓。
反対側は窓なしです。

⑥ Not窓。青いガラスです。

1. Poké Mart **2.** Exterior **3.** The Poké Ball mark and the two white lines both light up. **4.** All of the corners should be a bit rounded. **5.** Yes, this is a window. The other side doesn't have windows, though. **6.** Not windows, just blue glass

Pokémon Center Interior

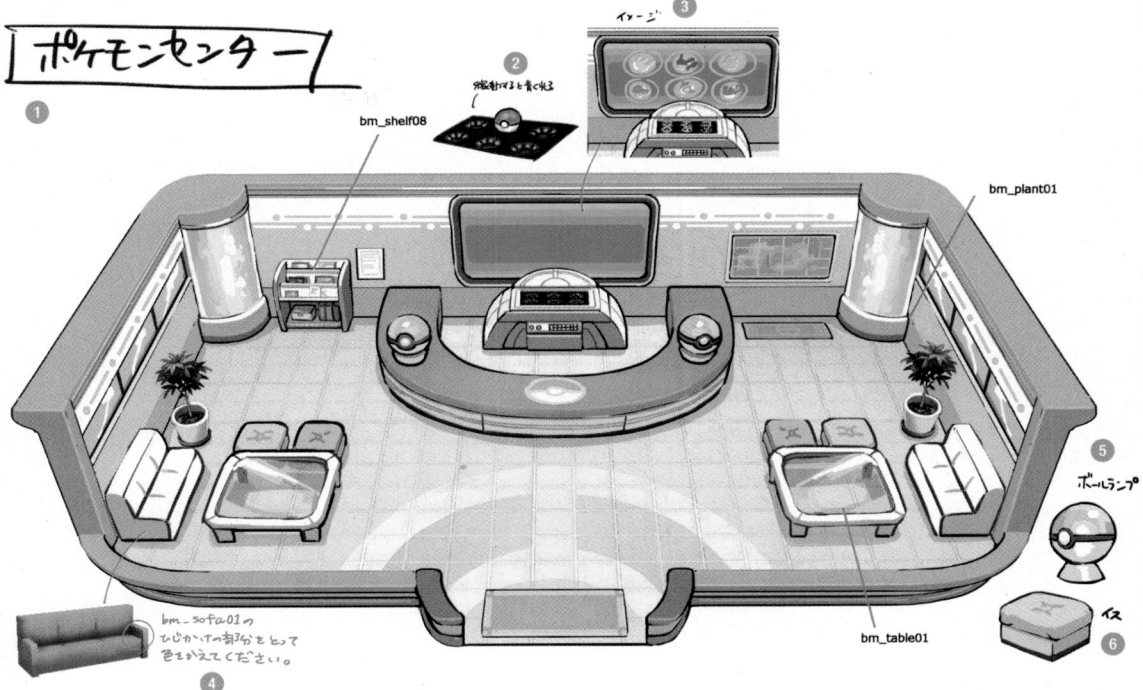

ポケモンセンター

イメージ

穴が動くと青く光る

bm_shelf08

bm_plant01

ボールランプ

bm_sofa01の
ひじかけの部分をとって
色をかえてください。

bm_table01

イス

1. Pokémon Center **2.** Glows blue when activated **3.** Image **4.** Take the arms off of "bm_sofa01" and change the color. **5.** Poké Ball lamp **6.** Chair

Poké Mart Interior

フレンドリィ ショップ

内観

おきゃくのイメージです

窓あります.

1. Poké Mart **2.** Interior **3.** The idea is that they're TMs. **4.** Has a window here

Pokémon Gym Exterior

ポケモンジム・外観 ①

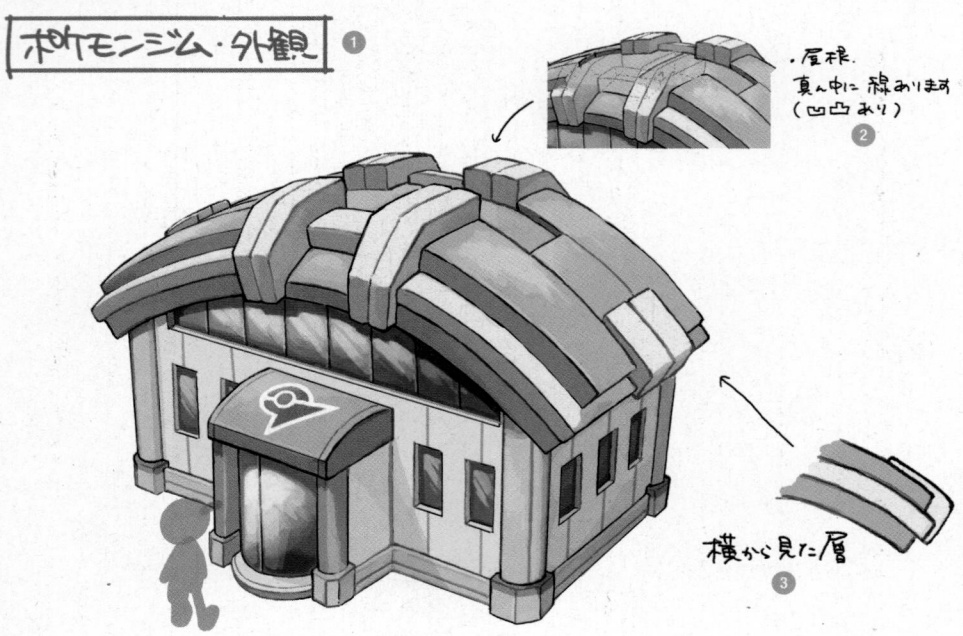

・屋根.
真ん中に 線あります
(凹凸 あり) ②

横から見た層 ③

1. Pokémon Gym: Exterior **2.** Roof. There's a line in the middle. (Some areas are higher and some are recessed.) **3.** The layers when you look at them from the side

Cerulean City Pokémon Gym Interior

ハナダジム ①

にぎやかし達 ②

色かえ ③

色かえ ④

カスミ 背後のガラス ⑤

ガラス質感はいいな
(ヒトデマン窓を同様に) ⑥

にぎやかしを置く場所を
増やしたいです. ⑦

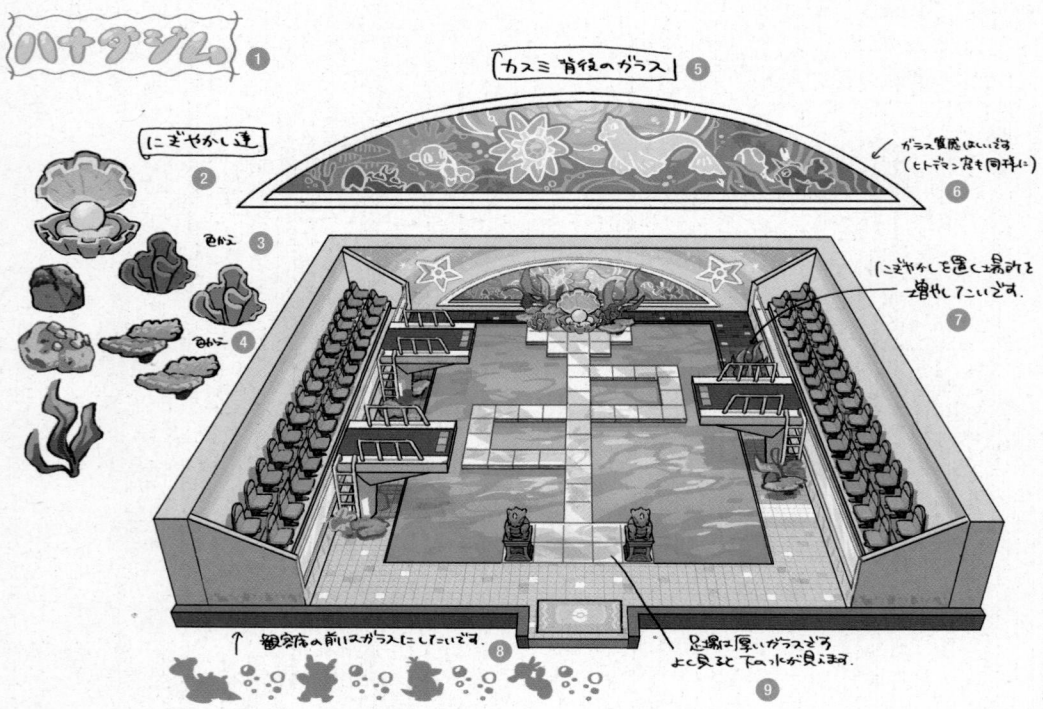

↑ 観客席の前はガラスにしています. ⑧

足場は厚いガラスなので
よく見ると 下の水が見えます. ⑨

1. Cerulean City Pokémon Gym **2.** Decorations **3.** Color swap **4.** Color swap **5.** The glass art behind Misty **6.** The glass should have texture (as well as the Staryu windows). **7.** Want to have more places to put decorations to liven things up **8.** Want to put glass in front of the spectators' seats **9.** The walkways are made of thick glass. If you look carefully, you can see the water below.

Pallet Town

1. Pallet Town map art direction 2. Fence style 3. Height comparison of the weeds and fences 4. Player character

Pewter City

1. Pewter City map art direction 2. Stone tiles and borders (want to adjust the size of the tiles for balance) 3. Something like this

Sky Dash

1. You can adjust the length of the balloons' strings and more from within this part. **2.** Can control the energy within the belt using the steering wheel **3.** Saddle
4. Eevee will put its paws on top to steer. **5.** Balloon stopper

Present from Your Partner

1. Like a plant vine

Adventure
Data

Moves

The following pages give details on the many moves that Pokémon can learn. Most moves are learned by your Pokémon leveling up or evolving, but your partner Pikachu or Eevee can also learn some unique moves from the Partner Move Tutor. Learn more about him on page 387. Plus, there are moves that many different Pokémon can learn from TMs. You'll find the list of all TMs and where to find them on page 387. These tables include information about each move, such as power and accuracy. To understand what the information in each column means, refer to the key below!

Key to the Move Tables

Move	The move's name
Type	The move's type
Kind	Whether the move is a physical, special, or status move
	Physical moves do more damage the higher the Attack stat is. Damage is lessened when the target has a high Defense stat.
	Special moves do more damage the higher the Sp. Atk stat is. Damage is lessened when the target has a high Sp. Def stat.
	Status moves affect stats or inflict status conditions on the target(s)—or have various other effects.
Pow.	The move's power
Acc.	The move's accuracy (out of a max of 100)
PP	How many times the move can be used before the Pokémon must have its PP restored with an item or at a Pokémon Center
Range	The number and range of targets the move can affect

Range Guide

Normal	The move affects the selected target. If the move is used by a Pokémon during a Double Battle, the move can target any of the three other Pokémon (including your ally).
Self	The move targets the user.
1 Ally	The move affects your ally Pokémon during a Double Battle or Support Battle. It has no effect in a Single Battle.
1 Random	The move affects one of the opposing Pokémon at random in a Double Battle. It affects the opposing Pokémon in a Single Battle.
Many Others	If the move is used by a Pokémon during a Double Battle, the move will affect both opposing Pokémon. Otherwise, it affects the opposing Pokémon in a Single Battle.
All Others	The move affects all surrounding Pokémon at the same time. If the move is used by a Pokémon during a Double Battle, the move will affect all three of the other Pokémon (including your ally) simultaneously.
Your Side	The move affects your side of the field. In a Double Battle, these effects will be felt by the user and any ally Pokémon. Since the move affects the field, the move's effects continue even if the Pokémon are swapped out.
Other Side	The move affects the opponent's side of the field. Since the move affects the field, the move's effects continue even if the targeted Pokémon are swapped out.
Both Sides	The move affects the entire field and all Pokémon on it. Since the move affects the field, the move's effects continue even if Pokémon are swapped out.
Varies	The move is influenced by things such as the opposing Pokémon using a move, so the effect and range are not fixed.

Remember that there are also some universal rules when it comes to moves. For example, when two Pokémon use a move with the same priority, the Pokémon with the higher Speed stat will get to use its move first. And then there are the ways that Pokémon's types affect what the move does, such as Fire-type Pokémon being immune to the burned status condition and Ghost-type Pokémon being immune to Normal- and Fighting-type moves. These type-based immunities are summed up in the table on page 399. There are also some oddities, such as frozen Pokémon thawing out after they are hit with a Fire-type move. You'll learn a lot as you play, so keep at it, and you'll become a battle expert in time!

Move	Type	Kind	Pow.	Acc.	PP	Range	Battle effects
Absorb	Grass	Special	40	100	15	Normal	Restores the user's HP by an amount equal to half of the damage dealt to the target.
Acid	Poison	Special	40	100	30	Many Others	Has a 10% chance of lowering the targets' Sp. Def by 1 stage. Its power is reduced by 25% when it hits multiple Pokémon in a Double Battle.
Acid Armor	Poison	Status	—	—	20	Self	Raises the user's Defense by 2 stages.
Agility	Psychic	Status	—	—	30	Self	Raises the user's Speed by 2 stages.
Air Slash	Flying	Special	75	95	15	Normal	Has a 30% chance of making the target flinch (unable to use moves on that turn).
Amnesia	Psychic	Status	—	—	20	Self	Raises the user's Sp. Def by 2 stages.
Aqua Jet	Water	Physical	40	100	20	Normal	Strikes with high priority.
Aurora Beam	Ice	Special	65	100	20	Normal	Has a 10% chance of lowering the target's Attack by 1 stage.

Move	Type	Kind	Pow.	Acc.	PP	Range	Battle effects
Baddy Bad	Dark	Special	90	100	15	Normal	After attacking, the move will trigger the same effect as Reflect.
Barrage	Normal	Physical	15	85	20	Normal	Attacks 2–5 times in a row in a single turn.
Barrier	Psychic	Status	—	—	20	Self	Raises the user's Defense by 2 stages.
Bide	Normal	Physical	—	—	10	Self	Strikes with high priority. Inflicts twice the damage received during the next 2 turns. Cannot choose moves during those 2 turns.
Bind	Normal	Physical	15	85	20	Normal	Inflicts damage equal to 1/8 the target's max HP at the end of each turn for 4–5 turns. The target cannot be switched out of battle during that time.
Bite	Dark	Physical	60	100	25	Normal	Has a 30% chance of making the target flinch (unable to use moves on that turn).
Blizzard	Ice	Special	110	70	5	Many Others	Has a 10% chance of inflicting the frozen status condition on the targets. Its power is reduced by 25% when it hits multiple Pokémon in a Double Battle.
Body Slam	Normal	Physical	85	100	15	Normal	Has a 30% chance of inflicting the paralysis status condition on the target. If the target has used Minimize, this move will be a sure hit and its power will be doubled.
Bone Club	Ground	Physical	65	85	20	Normal	Has a 10% chance of making the target flinch (unable to use moves on that turn).
Bonemerang	Ground	Physical	50	90	10	Normal	Attacks twice in a row in a single turn.
Bouncy Bubble	Water	Special	90	100	15	Normal	Restores the user's HP by an amount equal to half of the damage dealt to the target.
Brick Break	Fighting	Physical	75	100	15	Normal	This move is not affected by Reflect. It removes the effects of Light Screen and Reflect.
Bubble	Water	Special	40	100	30	Many Others	Has a 10% chance of lowering the targets' Speed by 1 stage. Its power is reduced by 25% when it hits multiple Pokémon in a Double Battle.
Bubble Beam	Water	Special	65	100	20	Normal	Has a 10% chance of lowering the target's Speed by 1 stage.
Bug Buzz	Bug	Special	90	100	10	Normal	Has a 10% chance of lowering the target's Sp. Def by 1 stage. Strikes the target even if it is using Substitute.
Bulk Up	Fighting	Status	—	—	20	Self	Raises the user's Attack and Defense by 1 stage.
Buzzy Buzz	Electric	Special	90	100	15	Normal	Inflicts the paralysis status condition on the target.
Calm Mind	Psychic	Status	—	—	20	Self	Raises the user's Sp. Atk and Sp. Def by 1 stage.
Clamp	Water	Physical	35	85	15	Normal	Inflicts damage equal to 1/8 the target's max HP at the end of each turn for 4–5 turns. The target cannot be switched out of battle during that time.
Clear Smog	Poison	Special	50	—	15	Normal	Eliminates every stat change of the target.
Comet Punch	Normal	Physical	18	85	15	Normal	Attacks 2–5 times in a row in a single turn.
Confuse Ray	Ghost	Status	—	100	10	Normal	Makes the target confused.
Confusion	Psychic	Special	50	100	25	Normal	Has a 10% chance of making the target confused.
Constrict	Normal	Physical	10	100	35	Normal	Has a 10% chance of lowering the target's Speed by 1 stage.
Conversion	Normal	Status	—	—	30	Self	Changes the user's type to the same type as the move at the top of the list of moves it knows.
Counter	Fighting	Physical	—	100	20	Varies	Strikes with low priority. If the user is attacked physically, this move inflicts twice the damage done to the user.
Crabhammer	Water	Physical	100	90	10	Normal	This move is more likely to be a critical hit.
Crunch	Dark	Physical	80	100	15	Normal	Has a 20% chance of lowering the target's Defense by 1 stage.
Cut	Normal	Physical	50	95	30	Normal	A regular attack.
Dark Pulse	Dark	Special	80	100	15	Normal	Has a 20% chance of making the target flinch (unable to use moves on that turn).
Dazzling Gleam	Fairy	Special	80	100	10	Many Others	Its power is reduced by 25% when it hits multiple Pokémon in a Double Battle.
Defense Curl	Normal	Status	—	—	40	Self	Raises the user's Defense by 1 stage.
Dig	Ground	Physical	80	100	10	Normal	The user burrows underground on the first turn and attacks on the second.
Disable	Normal	Status	—	100	20	Normal	The target can't use the move it just used for 4 turns.
Dizzy Punch	Normal	Physical	70	100	10	Normal	Has a 20% chance of making the target confused.
Double Iron Bash	Steel	Physical	60	100	5	Normal	Attacks twice in a row in a single turn. Has a 30% chance of making the target flinch (unable to use moves on that turn).
Double Kick	Fighting	Physical	30	100	30	Normal	Attacks twice in a row in a single turn.
Double Slap	Normal	Physical	15	85	10	Normal	Attacks 2–5 times in a row in a single turn.
Double Team	Normal	Status	—	—	15	Self	Raises the user's evasion by 1 stage.
Double-Edge	Normal	Physical	120	100	15	Normal	The user takes 1/3 of the damage inflicted.
Dragon Pulse	Dragon	Special	85	100	10	Normal	A regular attack.
Dragon Rage	Dragon	Special	—	100	10	Normal	Deals a fixed amount of damage, reducing the target's HP by 40 points.
Dragon Tail	Dragon	Physical	60	90	10	Normal	Strikes with the lowest priority. Forces another Pokémon to switch in. If there is no Pokémon to switch in, no additional effect takes place.
Dream Eater	Psychic	Special	100	100	15	Normal	Only works when the target is asleep. Restores the user's HP by an amount equal to half of the damage dealt to the target.
Drill Peck	Flying	Physical	80	100	20	Normal	A regular attack.
Drill Run	Ground	Physical	80	95	10	Normal	This move is more likely to be a critical hit.
Earthquake	Ground	Physical	100	100	10	All Others	Does twice the damage if targets are underground due to using Dig. Its power is reduced by 25% when it hits multiple Pokémon in a Double Battle.
Egg Bomb	Normal	Physical	100	75	10	Normal	A regular attack.
Ember	Fire	Special	40	100	25	Normal	Has a 10% chance of inflicting the burned status condition on the target.
Encore	Normal	Status	—	100	5	Normal	The target is forced to keep using the last move it used. This effect lasts 3 turns.
Explosion	Normal	Physical	250	100	5	All Others	The user faints after using it. Its power is reduced by 25% when it hits multiple Pokémon in a Double Battle.
Facade	Normal	Physical	70	100	20	Normal	This move's power is doubled if the user has been paralyzed, poisoned, or burned.
Fake Out	Normal	Physical	40	100	10	Normal	Strikes with the highest priority and makes the target flinch (unable to use moves on that turn). Only works on the first turn after the user is sent out.

Move	Type	Kind	Pow.	Acc.	PP	Range	Battle effects
Feint	Normal	Physical	30	100	10	Normal	Strikes with very high priority. Strikes the target even if it is using Protect.
Fire Blast	Fire	Special	110	85	5	Normal	Has a 10% chance of inflicting the burned status condition on the target.
Fire Punch	Fire	Physical	75	100	15	Normal	Has a 10% chance of inflicting the burned status condition on the target.
Fire Spin	Fire	Special	35	85	15	Normal	Inflicts damage equal to 1/8 the target's max HP at the end of each turn for 4–5 turns. The target cannot be switched out of battle during that time.
Fissure	Ground	Physical	—	30	5	Normal	The target faints with one hit. The higher the user's level is compared to the target's, the more accurate the move becomes. If the target's level is higher than the user's, this move fails.
Flamethrower	Fire	Special	90	100	15	Normal	Has a 10% chance of inflicting the burned status condition on the target.
Flare Blitz	Fire	Physical	120	100	15	Normal	User takes 1/3 of the damage done to the target. Has a 10% chance of inflicting the burned status condition on the target. This move can be used even if the user is frozen. If the user is frozen, this also thaws the user.
Flash	Normal	Status	—	100	20	Normal	Lowers the target's accuracy by 1 stage.
Flash Cannon	Steel	Special	80	100	10	Normal	Has a 10% chance of lowering the target's Sp. Def by 1 stage.
Floaty Fall	Flying	Physical	90	95	15	Normal	Has a 30% chance of making the target flinch (unable to use moves on that turn).
Fly	Flying	Physical	90	95	15	Normal	The user flies into the air on the first turn and attacks on the second.
Focus Energy	Normal	Status	—	—	30	Self	Heightens the critical-hit ratio of the user's subsequent moves.
Foul Play	Dark	Physical	95	100	15	Normal	The user turns the target's strength against it. Damage dealt by this move is calculated using the target's Attack rather than the user's Attack.
Freezy Frost	Ice	Special	90	100	15	Normal	Eliminates stat changes of all Pokémon in battle.
Fury Attack	Normal	Physical	15	85	20	Normal	Attacks 2–5 times in a row in a single turn.
Fury Swipes	Normal	Physical	18	80	15	Normal	Attacks 2–5 times in a row in a single turn.
Glare	Normal	Status	—	100	30	Normal	Inflicts the paralysis status condition on the target.
Glitzy Glow	Psychic	Special	90	100	15	Normal	After attacking, the move will trigger the same effect as Light Screen.
Growl	Normal	Status	—	100	40	Many Others	Lowers the targets' Attack by 1 stage. Strikes the targets even if they are using Substitute.
Growth	Normal	Status	—	—	20	Self	Raises the user's Attack and Sp. Atk by 1 stage.
Guillotine	Normal	Physical	—	30	5	Normal	The target faints with one hit. The higher the user's level is compared to the target's, the more accurate the move becomes. If the target's level is higher than the user's, this move fails.
Gust	Flying	Special	40	100	35	Normal	Does twice the damage if the target is in the sky due to using Fly.
Harden	Normal	Status	—	—	30	Self	Raises the user's Defense by 1 stage.
Haze	Ice	Status	—	—	30	Both Sides	Eliminates stat changes of all Pokémon in battle.
Headbutt	Normal	Physical	70	100	15	Normal	Has a 30% chance of making the target flinch (unable to use moves on that turn).
Heat Wave	Fire	Special	95	90	10	Many Others	Has a 10% chance of inflicting the burned status condition on the targets. Its power is reduced by 25% when it hits multiple Pokémon in a Double Battle.
Helping Hand	Normal	Status	—	—	20	1 Ally	Acts before all other moves that turn. Strengthens the attack power of one ally's moves by 50%.
High Jump Kick	Fighting	Physical	130	90	10	Normal	If this move misses or otherwise fails, the user loses half of its maximum HP.
Horn Attack	Normal	Physical	65	100	25	Normal	A regular attack.
Horn Drill	Normal	Physical	—	30	5	Normal	The target faints with one hit. The higher the user's level is compared to the target's, the more accurate the move becomes. If the target's level is higher than the user's, this move fails.
Hydro Pump	Water	Special	110	80	5	Normal	A regular attack.
Hyper Beam	Normal	Special	150	90	5	Normal	The user can't move during the next turn.
Hyper Fang	Normal	Physical	80	90	15	Normal	Has a 10% chance of making the target flinch (unable to use moves on that turn).
Hypnosis	Psychic	Status	—	60	20	Normal	Inflicts the asleep status condition on the target.
Ice Beam	Ice	Special	90	100	10	Normal	Has a 10% chance of inflicting the frozen status condition on the target.
Ice Punch	Ice	Physical	75	100	15	Normal	Has a 10% chance of inflicting the frozen status condition on the target.
Ice Shard	Ice	Physical	40	100	30	Normal	Strikes with high priority.
Iron Tail	Steel	Physical	100	75	15	Normal	Has a 30% chance of lowering the target's Defense by 1 stage.
Jump Kick	Fighting	Physical	100	95	10	Normal	If this move misses or otherwise fails, the user loses half of its maximum HP.
Karate Chop	Fighting	Physical	50	100	25	Normal	This move is more likely to be a critical hit.
Kinesis	Psychic	Status	—	80	15	Normal	Lowers the target's accuracy by 1 stage.
Leech Life	Bug	Physical	80	100	10	Normal	Restores the user's HP by an amount equal to half of the damage dealt to the target.
Leech Seed	Grass	Status	—	90	10	Normal	Steals 1/8 of the target's max HP every turn and absorbs it to restore the user. Keeps working even after the user switches out.
Leer	Normal	Status	—	100	30	Many Others	Lowers the targets' Defense by 1 stage.
Lick	Ghost	Physical	30	100	30	Normal	Has a 30% chance of inflicting the paralysis status condition on the target.
Light Screen	Psychic	Status	—	—	30	Your Side	Halves the damage to the Pokémon on your side from special moves. Effect lasts 5 turns even if the user is switched out. Effect is weaker in Double Battles.
Lovely Kiss	Normal	Status	—	75	10	Normal	Inflicts the asleep status condition on the target.
Low Kick	Fighting	Physical	—	100	20	Normal	The heavier the target is, the greater the move's power becomes (max 120).
Meditate	Psychic	Status	—	—	40	Self	Raises the user's Attack by 1 stage.
Mega Drain	Grass	Special	75	100	10	Normal	Restores the user's HP by an amount equal to half of the damage dealt to the target.
Mega Kick	Normal	Physical	120	75	5	Normal	A regular attack.
Mega Punch	Normal	Physical	80	85	20	Normal	A regular attack.
Megahorn	Bug	Physical	120	85	10	Normal	A regular attack.

Move	Type	Kind	Pow.	Acc.	PP	Range	Battle effects
Metronome	Normal	Status	—	—	10	Self	Uses one move randomly chosen from nearly all moves Pokémon can learn.
Mimic	Normal	Status	—	—	10	Normal	Copies the target's last-used move (copied move has its max original PP). Fails if used before the opposing Pokémon uses a move or if it copies a move that the user already knows. The copied move will be retained until the battle ends or the user is switched out.
Minimize	Normal	Status	—	—	10	Self	Raises the user's evasion by 2 stages. The user will take twice the usual damage, however, if hit by Body Slam or Stomp.
Mirror Coat	Psychic	Special	—	100	20	Varies	Strikes with low priority. If the user is attacked with a special move, this move inflicts twice the damage done to the user.
Mirror Move	Flying	Status	—	—	20	Normal	Uses the last move that the target used.
Mist	Ice	Status	—	—	30	Your Side	Protects against stat-lowering moves and additional effects for 5 turns.
Moonblast	Fairy	Special	95	100	15	Normal	Has a 30% chance of lowering the target's Sp. Atk by 1 stage.
Nasty Plot	Dark	Status	—	—	20	Self	Raises the user's Sp. Atk by 2 stages.
Night Shade	Ghost	Special	—	100	15	Normal	Deals a fixed amount of damage equal to the user's level.
Outrage	Dragon	Physical	120	100	10	1 Random	Attacks consecutively over 2–3 turns. Cannot choose other moves during this time. The user becomes confused after using this move.
Pay Day	Normal	Physical	40	100	20	Normal	Increases the amount of prize money received after battle, paying out ₽5 multiplied by the user's level and the number of times the move was used.
Peck	Flying	Physical	35	100	35	Normal	A regular attack.
Petal Dance	Grass	Special	120	100	10	1 Random	Attacks consecutively over 2–3 turns. Cannot choose other moves during this time. The user becomes confused after using this move.
Pika Papow*	Electric	Special	—	—	—	1 Random	A sure hit. Its power is determined by how much your partner loves you (max 148).
Pin Missile	Bug	Physical	25	95	20	Normal	Attacks 2–5 times in a row in a single turn.
Play Rough	Fairy	Physical	90	90	10	Normal	Has a 10% chance of lowering the target's Attack by 1 stage.
Poison Gas	Poison	Status	—	90	40	Many Others	Inflicts the poisoned status condition on the targets.
Poison Jab	Poison	Physical	80	100	20	Normal	Has a 30% chance of inflicting the poisoned status condition on the target.
Poison Powder	Poison	Status	—	75	35	Normal	Inflicts the poisoned status condition on the target.
Poison Sting	Poison	Physical	15	100	35	Normal	Has a 30% chance of inflicting the poisoned status condition on the target.
Pound	Normal	Physical	40	100	35	Normal	A regular attack.
Power Whip	Grass	Physical	120	85	10	Normal	A regular attack.
Protect	Normal	Status	—	—	10	Self	The user evades all moves that turn. If used in succession, its chance of failing rises.
Psybeam	Psychic	Special	65	100	20	Normal	Has a 10% chance of making the target confused.
Psychic	Psychic	Special	90	100	10	Normal	Has a 10% chance of lowering the target's Sp. Def by 1 stage.
Psywave	Psychic	Special	—	100	15	Normal	Inflicts damage equal to the user's level multiplied by a random value between 0.5 and 1.5.
Quick Attack	Normal	Physical	40	100	30	Normal	Strikes with high priority.
Quiver Dance	Bug	Status	—	—	20	Self	Raises the user's Sp. Atk, Sp. Def, and Speed by 1 stage.
Rage	Normal	Physical	20	100	20	Normal	Attack rises by 1 stage with each hit the user takes.
Razor Leaf	Grass	Physical	55	95	25	Many Others	This move is more likely to be a critical hit. Its power is reduced by 25% when it hits multiple Pokémon in a Double Battle.
Razor Wind	Normal	Special	80	100	10	Many Others	The user stores power on the first turn and attacks on the second. This move is more likely to be a critical hit. Its power is reduced by 25% when it hits multiple Pokémon in a Double Battle.
Recover	Normal	Status	—	—	10	Self	Restores the user's HP by half of the user's maximum HP.
Reflect	Psychic	Status	—	—	20	Your Side	Halves the damage to the Pokémon on your side from physical moves. Effect lasts 5 turns even if the user is switched out. Effect is weaker in Double Battles.
Rest	Psychic	Status	—	—	10	Self	Fully restores HP and cures status conditions of the user, but makes the user asleep for 2 turns.
Roar	Normal	Status	—	—	20	Normal	Strikes with the lowest priority. Forces the opposing Trainer to switch Pokémon. When there are no Pokémon to switch in, this move fails. Strikes the target even if it is using Protect or Substitute.
Rock Slide	Rock	Physical	75	90	10	Many Others	Has a 30% chance of making the targets flinch (unable to use moves on that turn). Its power is reduced by 25% when it hits multiple Pokémon in a Double Battle.
Rock Throw	Rock	Physical	50	90	15	Normal	A regular attack.
Rolling Kick	Fighting	Physical	60	85	15	Normal	Has a 30% chance of making the target flinch (unable to use moves on that turn).
Roost	Flying	Status	—	—	10	Self	Restores the user's HP by half of the user's maximum HP, but takes away the Flying type from the user for that turn.
Sand Attack	Ground	Status	—	100	15	Normal	Lowers the target's accuracy by 1 stage.
Sappy Seed	Grass	Physical	90	100	15	Normal	After attacking, the move will trigger the same effect as Leech Seed.
Scald	Water	Special	80	100	15	Normal	Has a 30% chance of inflicting the burned status condition on the target. This move can be used even when the user is frozen. Using this move will thaw the user, relieving the frozen status condition.
Scratch	Normal	Physical	40	100	35	Normal	A regular attack.
Screech	Normal	Status	—	85	40	Normal	Lowers the target's Defense by 2 stages. Strikes the target even if it is using Substitute.
Seismic Toss	Fighting	Physical	—	100	20	Normal	Deals a fixed amount of damage equal to the user's level.
Self-Destruct	Normal	Physical	200	100	5	All Others	The user faints after using it. Its power is reduced by 25% when it hits multiple Pokémon in a Double Battle.
Shadow Ball	Ghost	Special	80	100	15	Normal	Has a 20% chance of lowering the target's Sp. Def by 1 stage.
Sharpen	Normal	Status	—	—	30	Self	Raises the user's Attack by 1 stage.
Shell Smash	Normal	Status	—	—	15	Self	Lowers the user's Defense and Sp. Def by 1 stage and raises the user's Attack, Sp. Atk, and Speed by 2 stages.
Sing	Normal	Status	—	55	15	Normal	Inflicts the asleep status condition on the target. Strikes the target even if it is using Substitute.
Sizzly Slide	Fire	Physical	90	100	15	Normal	Inflicts the burned status condition on the target.

*Pika Papow is an exclusive move that your partner can only use when you activate its partner powers while it's in battle. To find out more, head to page 142!

Move	Type	Kind	Pow.	Acc.	PP	Range	Battle effects
Skull Bash	Normal	Physical	130	100	10	Normal	Builds power on the first turn and attacks on the second. It raises the user's Defense stat by 1 stage on the first turn.
Sky Attack	Flying	Physical	200	90	5	Normal	Builds power on the first turn and attacks on the second. This move is more likely to be a critical hit. Has a 30% chance of making the target flinch (unable to use moves on that turn).
Slam	Normal	Physical	80	75	20	Normal	A regular attack.
Slash	Normal	Physical	70	100	20	Normal	This move is more likely to be a critical hit.
Sleep Powder	Grass	Status	—	75	15	Normal	Inflicts the asleep status condition on the target.
Sludge	Poison	Special	65	100	20	Normal	Has a 30% chance of inflicting the poisoned status condition on the target.
Sludge Bomb	Poison	Special	90	100	10	Normal	Has a 30% chance of inflicting the poisoned status condition on the target.
Smog	Poison	Special	30	70	20	Normal	Has a 40% chance of inflicting the poisoned status condition on the target.
Smokescreen	Normal	Status	—	100	20	Normal	Lowers the target's accuracy by 1 stage.
Soft-Boiled	Normal	Status	—	—	10	Self	Restores the user's HP by half of the user's maximum HP.
Solar Beam	Grass	Special	200	100	10	Normal	Builds power on the first turn and attacks on the second.
Sonic Boom	Normal	Special	—	90	20	Normal	Deals a fixed amount of damage, reducing the target's HP by 20 points.
Sparkly Swirl	Fairy	Special	90	100	15	Normal	Heals any status conditions for all the Pokémon in your party.
Spike Cannon	Normal	Physical	20	100	15	Normal	Attacks 2–5 times in a row in a single turn.
Splash	Normal	Status	—	—	40	Self	Has no effect.
Splishy Splash	Water	Special	90	100	15	Many Others	Has a 30% chance of inflicting the paralysis status condition on the targets.
Spore	Grass	Status	—	100	15	Normal	Inflicts the asleep status condition on the target.
Stealth Rock	Rock	Status	—	—	20	Other Side	Damages Pokémon as they are sent out to the opposing side. Damage is subject to type matchups.
Stomp	Normal	Physical	65	100	20	Normal	Has a 30% chance of making the target flinch (unable to use moves on that turn). If the target has used Minimize, this move will be a sure hit and its power will be doubled.
Strength	Normal	Physical	80	100	15	Normal	A regular attack.
String Shot	Bug	Status	—	95	40	Many Others	Lowers the targets' Speed by 2 stages.
Struggle	Normal	Physical	50	—	1	1 Random	This move becomes available when all other moves are out of PP. The user takes damage equal to 1/4 of its maximum HP. Inflicts damage regardless of type matchup.
Stun Spore	Grass	Status	—	75	30	Normal	Inflicts the paralysis status condition on the target.
Submission	Fighting	Physical	80	80	20	Normal	The user takes 1/4 of the damage inflicted.
Substitute	Normal	Status	—	—	10	Self	Uses 1/4 of maximum HP to create a copy of the user.
Sucker Punch	Dark	Physical	70	100	5	Normal	Strikes with high priority. Deals damage only if the target's chosen move is an attack move.
Super Fang	Normal	Physical	—	90	10	Normal	Halves the target's HP.
Superpower	Fighting	Physical	120	100	5	Normal	Lowers the user's Attack and Defense by 1 stage.
Supersonic	Normal	Status	—	55	20	Normal	Makes the target confused. Strikes the target even if it is using Substitute.
Surf	Water	Special	90	100	15	All Others	Its power is reduced by 25% when it hits multiple Pokémon in a Double Battle.
Swift	Normal	Special	60	—	20	Many Others	A sure hit. Its power is reduced by 25% when it hits multiple Pokémon in a Double Battle.
Swords Dance	Normal	Status	—	—	20	Self	Raises the user's Attack by 2 stages.
Tackle	Normal	Physical	40	100	35	Normal	A regular attack.
Tail Whip	Normal	Status	—	100	30	Many Others	Lowers the targets' Defense by 1 stage.
Take Down	Normal	Physical	90	85	20	Normal	The user takes 1/4 of the damage inflicted.
Taunt	Dark	Status	—	100	20	Normal	Prevents the target from using anything other than attack moves for 3 turns.
Teleport	Psychic	Status	—	—	20	Self	Strikes with the lowest priority. The user teleports out of battle, and another Pokémon from the party is brought onto the field.
Thrash	Normal	Physical	120	100	10	1 Random	Attacks consecutively over 2–3 turns. Cannot choose other moves during this time. The user becomes confused after using this move.
Thunder	Electric	Special	110	70	10	Normal	Has a 30% chance of inflicting the paralysis status condition on the target. It hits even Pokémon that are in the sky due to using Fly.
Thunder Punch	Electric	Physical	75	100	15	Normal	Has a 10% chance of inflicting the paralysis status condition on the target.
Thunder Shock	Electric	Special	40	100	30	Normal	Has a 10% chance of inflicting the paralysis status condition on the target.
Thunder Wave	Electric	Status	—	90	20	Normal	Inflicts the paralysis status condition on the target.
Thunderbolt	Electric	Special	90	100	15	Normal	Has a 10% chance of inflicting the paralysis status condition on the target.
Toxic	Poison	Status	—	90	10	Normal	Inflicts the badly poisoned status condition on the target. Damage from being badly poisoned increases with every turn. This move never misses if used by a Poison-type Pokémon.
Transform	Normal	Status	—	—	10	Normal	The user transforms into the target. The user has the same moves as the target. (All moves have 5 PP.)
Tri Attack	Normal	Special	80	100	10	Normal	Has a 20% chance of inflicting the paralysis, burned, or frozen status condition on the target.
Twineedle	Bug	Physical	25	100	20	Normal	Attacks twice in a row in a single turn. Has a 20% chance of inflicting the poisoned status condition on the target.
U-turn	Bug	Physical	70	100	20	Normal	After attacking, the user switches out with another Pokémon in the party.
Veevee Volley*	Normal	Physical	—	—	—	1 Random	A sure hit. Its power is determined by how much your partner loves you (max 148).
Vice Grip	Normal	Physical	55	100	30	Normal	A regular attack.
Vine Whip	Grass	Physical	45	100	25	Normal	A regular attack.
Water Gun	Water	Special	40	100	25	Normal	A regular attack.
Waterfall	Water	Physical	80	100	15	Normal	Has a 20% chance of making the target flinch (unable to use moves on that turn).

*Veevee Volley is an exclusive move that your partner can only use when you activate its partner powers while it's in battle. To find out more, head to page 142!

ADVENTURE DATA

Move	Type	Kind	Pow.	Acc.	PP	Range	Battle effects
Whirlwind	Normal	Status	—	—	20	Normal	Strikes with the lowest priority. Forces the opposing Trainer to switch Pokémon. When there are no Pokémon to switch in, this move fails. Strikes the target even if it is using Protect or Substitute.
Will-O-Wisp	Fire	Status	—	85	15	Normal	Inflicts the burned status condition on the target.
Wing Attack	Flying	Physical	60	100	35	Normal	A regular attack.
Withdraw	Water	Status	—	—	40	Self	Raises the user's Defense by 1 stage.
Wrap	Normal	Physical	15	90	20	Normal	Inflicts damage equal to 1/8 the target's max HP at the end of each turn for 4–5 turns. The target cannot be switched out of battle during that time.
X-Scissor	Bug	Physical	80	100	15	Normal	A regular attack.
Yawn	Normal	Status	—	—	10	Normal	Inflicts the asleep status condition on the target at the end of the next turn unless the target switches out.
Zippy Zap	Electric	Physical	50	100	15	Normal	Strikes with very high priority. Will always be a critical hit.

The **Partner Move Tutor** hangs around in the Pokémon Centers listed to the right. He'll teach your partner Pikachu or Eevee exclusive moves, and more moves are added as you progress in the game. He'll do this for free, as many times as you like, so try them all out!

Location	Moves Pikachu can learn	Moves Eevee can learn
Cerulean City	Zippy Zap	Bouncy Bubble, Buzzy Buzz, and Sizzly Slide
Celadon City	The above, plus Floaty Fall	The above, plus Glitzy Glow and Baddy Bad
Fuchsia City	The above, plus Splishy Splash	The above, plus Sappy Seed, Freezy Frost, and Sparkly Swirl

How to obtain TMs

Below is a list of all the TMs you can obtain in these games to teach your Pokémon new moves.

Move name	Type	How to obtain
TM01 Headbutt	Normal	Defeat Gym Leader Brock in Pewter City
TM02 Taunt	Dark	Receive from a researcher in the Cinnabar Lab
TM03 Helping Hand	Normal	Receive from a clerk in the Celadon Department Store (3F)
TM04 Teleport	Psychic	Find in the Pokémon Tower (4F)
TM05 Rest	Psychic	Find in the Team Rocket Hideout (B2F)
TM06 Light Screen	Psychic	Receive from the girl on the rooftop of the Celadon Department Store (after giving her Fresh Water)
TM07 Protect	Normal	Receive from the girl on the rooftop of the Celadon Department Store (after giving her Lemonade)
TM08 Substitute	Normal	Receive from the Copycat on the second floor of a house in Saffron City by showing her a Clefairy
TM09 Reflect	Psychic	Receive from the girl on the rooftop of the Celadon Department Store (after giving her Soda Pop)
TM10 Dig	Ground	Defeat the Team Rocket Grunt outside of the burgled house in Cerulean City
TM11 Will-O-Wisp	Fire	Receive from the man next to the pond in Viridian City (requires Chop Down)
TM12 Facade	Normal	Defeat Coach Trainer Alpesh on Route 7
TM13 Brick Break	Fighting	Defeat Coach Trainer Tasha on Route 10
TM14 Fly	Flying	Receive from the girl in the house on Route 16 (requires Chop Down)
TM15 Seismic Toss	Fighting	Defeat Coach Trainer Amala on Route 25
TM16 Thunder Wave	Electric	Find on Route 25 (may require Chop Down)
TM17 Dragon Tail	Dragon	Buy at the Celadon Department Store (2F) for ₽20,000
TM18 U-turn	Bug	Buy at the Celadon Department Store (2F) for ₽20,000
TM19 Iron Tail	Steel	Buy at the Celadon Department Store (2F) for ₽50,000
TM20 Dark Pulse	Dark	Find in the Team Rocket Hideout (B3F)
TM21 Foul Play	Dark	Find in the Pokémon Mansion (3F)
TM22 Rock Slide	Rock	Defeat Coach Trainer Rita in the Pokémon Mansion (2F)
TM23 Thunder Punch	Electric	Defeat Coach Trainer Leona in the Fighting Dojo in Saffron City
TM24 X-Scissor	Bug	Find on Route 12 (requires Sea Skim)
TM25 Waterfall	Water	Buy at the Celadon Department Store (2F) for ₽30,000
TM26 Poison Jab	Poison	Receive from the man in front of the house next to the Rocket Game Corner (requires Sea Skim)
TM27 Toxic	Poison	Defeat Gym Leader Koga in Fuchsia City
TM28 Tri Attack	Normal	Buy at the Celadon Department Store (2F) for ₽30,000
TM29 Scald	Water	Defeat Gym Leader Misty in Cerulean City
TM30 Bulk Up	Fighting	Buy at the Celadon Department Store (2F) for ₽10,000

Move name	Type	How to obtain
TM31 Fire Punch	Fire	Defeat Coach Trainer Midge on Route 15 (requires Chop Down)
TM32 Dazzling Gleam	Fairy	Receive from Mr. Dazzling in the house on Route 12
TM33 Calm Mind	Psychic	Defeat Gym Leader Sabrina in Saffron City
TM34 Dragon Pulse	Dragon	Find in Silph Co. (7F)
TM35 Ice Punch	Ice	Defeat Coach Trainer Pam on Route 21 (requires Sea Skim)
TM36 Thunderbolt	Electric	Defeat Gym Leader Lt. Surge in Vermilion City
TM37 Flamethrower	Fire	Find in Silph Co. (10F)
TM38 Thunder	Electric	Find in the abandoned Power Plant
TM39 Outrage	Dragon	Defeat Coach Trainer Ryan on Victory Road (3F)
TM40 Psychic	Psychic	Receive from Mr. Psychic in a house in Saffron City
TM41 Earthquake	Ground	Defeat Gym Leader Giovanni in Viridian City
TM42 Self-Destruct	Normal	Receive from an employee in Silph Co. (2F)
TM43 Shadow Ball	Ghost	Buy at the Celadon Department Store (2F) for ₽30,000
TM44 Play Rough	Fairy	Find in the Celadon Condominiums (4F), accessible through rear entrance
TM45 Solar Beam	Grass	Find on Victory Road (2F)
TM46 Fire Blast	Fire	Defeat Gym Leader Blaine on Cinnabar Island
TM47 Surf	Water	Find on Route 15 (requires Chop Down)
TM48 Hyper Beam	Normal	Buy at the Celadon Department Store (2F) for ₽100,000
TM49 Superpower	Fighting	Find on Victory Road (2F)
TM50 Roost	Flying	Receive from a girl in the Route 12 gate (2F)
TM51 Blizzard	Ice	Find on Victory Road (3F)
TM52 Sludge Bomb	Poison	Find in the Pokémon Mansion (B1F)
TM53 Mega Drain	Grass	Defeat Gym Leader Erika in Celadon City
TM54 Flash Cannon	Steel	Find in Silph Co. (5F)
TM55 Ice Beam	Ice	Find in the Seafoam Islands (B2F)
TM56 Stealth Rock	Rock	Find on Victory Road (1F)
TM57 Pay Day	Normal	Defeat Coach Trainer Oberon on Route 4 (West)
TM58 Drill Run	Ground	Defeat Coach Trainer Grantley on Route 17
TM59 Dream Eater	Psychic	Defeat Coach Trainer Priya on Route 12 (south of junction with Route 11)
TM60 Megahorn	Bug	Defeat Coach Trainer Harjit in front of the Cerulean Cave (after entering the Hall of Fame)

Pokémon Natures & Characteristics

Pokémon Natures

Each individual Pokémon has a Nature (p. 125), which affects how its stats grow when it levels up. Most Natures will cause one stat to develop better and one stat to develop worse than usual. A few Natures, however, provide no benefit and no liability.

Nature	Increased stat	Decreased stat
Adamant	Attack	Sp. Atk
Bashful	—	—
Bold	Defense	Attack
Brave	Attack	Speed
Calm	Sp. Def	Attack
Careful	Sp. Def	Sp. Atk
Docile	—	—
Gentle	Sp. Def	Defense
Hardy	—	—

Nature	Increased stat	Decreased stat
Hasty	Speed	Defense
Impish	Defense	Sp. Atk
Jolly	Speed	Sp. Atk
Lax	Defense	Sp. Def
Lonely	Attack	Defense
Mild	Sp. Atk	Defense
Modest	Sp. Atk	Attack
Naive	Speed	Sp. Def
Naughty	Attack	Sp. Def

Nature	Increased stat	Decreased stat
Quiet	Sp. Atk	Speed
Quirky	—	—
Rash	Sp. Atk	Sp. Def
Relaxed	Defense	Speed
Sassy	Sp. Def	Speed
Serious	—	—
Timid	Speed	Attack

Madam Celadon

Madam Celadon, the fortune teller in Celadon City's Pokémon Center (p. 62), can help you encounter Pokémon with the Nature you are seeking. If you pay her fee, the Pokémon you encounter for the rest of the day will have the Nature predicted by your answers. This effect will end at midnight or when you choose to have her tell your fortune once again—whichever comes first!

Which flower will you thin out?	Which flower do you water?				
	RED	**YELLOW**	**BLUE**	**GREEN**	**PINK**
RED	Hardy	Bold	Modest	Calm	Timid
YELLOW	Lonely	Docile	Mild	Gentle	Hasty
BLUE	Adamant	Impish	Bashful	Careful	Jolly
GREEN	Naughty	Lax	Rash	Quirky	Naive
PINK	Brave	Relaxed	Quiet	Sassy	Serious

Pokémon Characteristics

On top of having a Nature, each individual Pokémon has a Characteristic. Characteristics hint at which of the Pokémon's stats likely has the highest individual strength (p. 125).

Stat that grows easily	Characteristic				
HP	Loves to eat	Scatters things often	Takes plenty of siestas	Likes to relax	Nods off a lot
Attack	Proud of its power	Likes to fight	Likes to thrash about	Quick tempered	A little quick tempered
Defense	Sturdy body	Good endurance	Capable of taking hits	Good perseverance	Highly persistent
Sp. Atk	Highly curious	Often lost in thought	Mischievous	Very finicky	Thoroughly cunning
Sp. Def	Strong willed	Hates to lose	Somewhat vain	Somewhat stubborn	Strongly defiant
Speed	Likes to run	Somewhat of a clown	Alert to sounds	Quick to flee	Impetuous and silly

The following tables tell you about the many different items you can collect and use during your adventure in Kanto. They list the main ways that you can obtain these items, but note that many of them can also be found elsewhere in this vast region! Plus, hidden items will keep reappearing daily, or even more often, so take note of spots where you've found items you want more of. And remember that locations like the Underground Paths (p. 46 and p. 61) are great spots to keep revisiting to find a variety of hidden items. If an item can be found in shops, you'll find its price listed in the table below, too.

Item	Description	Main way to obtain	Price
Aerodactylite	Allows Aerodactyl to Mega Evolve into Mega Aerodactyl.	Buy from the Mega Stone seller in the Pokémon League after entering the Hall of Fame	₽30,000
Alakazite	Allows Alakazam to Mega Evolve into Mega Alakazam.	Buy from the Mega Stone seller in the Pokémon League after entering the Hall of Fame	₽30,000
Antidote	Cures the poisoned and badly poisoned status conditions.	Buy at any Poké Mart or the Celadon Department Store (no Gym Badges required)	₽200
Autograph	An autograph from Lt. Surge. Show it off!	Receive from Lt. Surge in the Vermilion City Pokémon Gym	—
Awakening	Cures the asleep status condition.	Buy at any Poké Mart or the Celadon Department Store (no Gym Badges required)	₽100
Beach Glass	A piece of colored glass. It's a gift from your partner.	Receive from your partner Pokémon in Partner Play	—
Beedrillite	Allows Beedrill to Mega Evolve into Mega Beedrill.	Buy from the Mega Stone seller in the Pokémon League after entering the Hall of Fame	₽30,000
Big Mushroom	A big mushroom. It can be sold at shops for a high price.	Find as a hidden item in Mt. Moon (B1F)	—
Big Pearl	A big pearl. It can be sold at shops for a high price.	Receive once per day for watching the Slowpoke by the Pewter Museum of Science / Find as a hidden item in Vermilion City and the Pokémon Tower (5F)	—
Blastoisinite	Allows Blastoise to Mega Evolve into Mega Blastoise.	Receive from Blue in the Oak Pokémon Research Lab	—
Bottle Cap	A beautiful bottle cap that gives off a silver gleam. Give one to Mr. Hyper to have a Lv. 100 Pokémon max out one stat via Hyper Training.	Receive once per day after defeating Mina in Vermilion City / Find as a hidden item in the Rocket Game Corner	—
Burn Heal	Cures the burned status condition.	Buy at any Poké Mart or the Celadon Department Store (no Gym Badges required)	₽300
Card Key	Opens the locked doors in Silph Co.	Receive from your rival in Silph Co. after defeating Archer	—
Chalky Stone	A small whitish stone. It's a gift from your partner.	Receive from your partner Pokémon in Partner Play	—
Charizardite X	Allows Charizard to Mega Evolve into Mega Charizard X.	Receive from Blue in the Oak Pokémon Research Lab	—
Charizardite Y	Allows Charizard to Mega Evolve into Mega Charizard Y.	Receive from Blue in the Oak Pokémon Research Lab	—
Courage Candy	Increases a Pokémon's Sp. Def by 1. The number of Candies you need increases as your Pokémon's Go Power rises.	Receive after catching Pokémon or sending Pokémon to Professor Oak / Find as a hidden item in the Rocket Game Corner, in the Pokémon Mansion, and on Victory Road	—
Courage Candy L	Increases a Pokémon's Sp. Def by 1. Can only be used on Pokémon at Lv. 30 or higher. The number of Candies you need increases as your Pokémon's Go Power rises.	Receive after catching Pokémon or sending Pokémon to Professor Oak / Find as a hidden item in the Rocket Game Corner	—
Courage Candy XL	Increases a Pokémon's Sp. Def by 1. Can only be used on Pokémon at Lv. 60 or higher. The number of Candies you need increases as your Pokémon's Go Power rises.	Receive after catching Pokémon or sending Pokémon to Professor Oak / Find as a hidden item in the Rocket Game Corner	—
Dire Hit	Significantly raises the critical-hit ratio of a Pokémon during battle. Cannot be used again on the same Pokémon until the effect wears off.	Buy at any Poké Mart or the Celadon Department Store (after earning one Gym Badge)	₽650
Dome Fossil	A Pokémon Fossil. When restored, it becomes Kabuto.	Receive it in Mt. Moon (B2F) / Find as a hidden item in the Cerulean Cave (B1F, 2F)	—
Elixir	Restores the PP of all of a Pokémon's moves by 10 points.	Find as a hidden item in Silph Co. (9F)	—
Escape Rope	Use it to escape instantly from a cave or a dungeon.	Buy at any Poké Mart or the Celadon Department Store (after earning one Gym Badge)	₽300
Ether	Restores the PP of a Pokémon's move by 10 points.	Find in Mt. Moon (1F) and on Route 25, Route 5, and Route 9	—
Fire Stone	Evolves Vulpix, Growlithe, and Eevee when used on them. Does not work on partner Eevee.	Buy at the Celadon Department Store	₽5,000
Fresh Water	Restores the HP of a Pokémon by 30 points.	Buy at vending machines at the Celadon Department Store and the Rocket Game Corner	₽200
Full Heal	Cures all status conditions and confusion.	Buy at any Poké Mart or the Celadon Department Store (after earning three Gym Badges)	₽400
Full Restore	Completely restores the HP of a Pokémon and cures any status conditions and confusion.	Buy at any Poké Mart or the Celadon Department Store (after earning eight Gym Badges)	₽3,000
Gengarite	Allows Gengar to Mega Evolve into Mega Gengar.	Buy from the Mega Stone seller in the Pokémon League after entering the Hall of Fame	₽30,000
Gold Bottle Cap	A beautiful bottle cap that gives off a golden gleam. Give one to Mr. Hyper to have a Lv. 100 Pokémon max out all six stats via Hyper Training.	Find as a hidden item in the Rocket Game Corner	—
Gold Leaf	A mysterious gold leaf. It's a gift from your partner.	Receive from your partner Pokémon in Partner Play	—
Gold Teeth	Give to the warden in Fuchsia City to learn the Secret Technique Strong Push.	Receive from Jessie on Route 19	—
Golden Nanab Berry	A Berry that drastically calms wild Pokémon you're trying to catch when given to them.	Receive after catching Pokémon / Find as a hidden item on Route 15 and in the Cerulean Cave (2F)	—
Golden Pinap Berry	A Berry that makes you drastically more likely to get an item when given to Pokémon you're trying to catch.	Receive after catching Pokémon / Find as a hidden item on Route 13 and in the Cerulean Cave (2F)	—
Golden Razz Berry	A Berry that makes it drastically easier to catch Pokémon when given to them.	Receive after catching Pokémon / Find as a hidden item on Route 14 and in the Cerulean Cave (2F)	—
Guard Spec.	Prevents stat reduction among the Trainer's party Pokémon for five turns. Cannot be used again until the effect wears off.	Buy at any Poké Mart or the Celadon Department Store (after earning one Gym Badge)	₽700
Gyaradosite	Allows Gyarados to Mega Evolve into Mega Gyarados.	Buy from the Mega Stone seller in the Pokémon League after entering the Hall of Fame	₽30,000
Health Candy	Increases a Pokémon's HP by 1. The number of Candies you need increases as your Pokémon's Go Power rises.	Receive after catching Pokémon or sending Pokémon to Professor Oak / Find as a hidden item in the Rocket Game Corner, in the Pokémon Mansion, and on Victory Road	—
Health Candy L	Increases a Pokémon's HP by 1. Can only be used on Pokémon at Lv. 30 or higher. The number of Candies you need increases as your Pokémon's Go Power rises.	Receive after catching Pokémon or sending Pokémon to Professor Oak / Find as a hidden item in the Rocket Game Corner	—

Item	Description	Main way to obtain	Price
Health Candy XL	Increases a Pokémon's HP by 1. Can only be used on Pokémon at Lv. 60 or higher. The number of Candies you need increases as your Pokémon's Go Power rises.	Receive after catching Pokémon or sending Pokémon to Professor Oak / Find as a hidden item in the Rocket Game Corner	–
Heart Scale	A pretty, heart-shaped scale that is extremely rare. Give one to Madam Memorial to remind your Pokémon of a move it forgot or to teach it a move it did not learn.	Receive from your partner Pokémon in Partner Play / Find as a hidden item in the Seafoam Islands (B2F, 1F)	–
Helix Fossil	A Pokémon Fossil. When restored, it becomes Omanyte.	Receive it in Mt. Moon (B2F) / Find as a hidden item in the Cerulean Cave (B1F, 2F)	–
Hyper Potion	Restores the HP of a Pokémon by 120 points.	Buy at any Poké Mart or the Celadon Department Store (after earning four Gym Badges)	₽1,500
Ice Heal	Cures the frozen status condition.	Buy at any Poké Mart or the Celadon Department Store (no Gym Badges required)	₽100
Ice Stone	Evolves Alolan Sandshrew and Alolan Vulpix when used on them.	Buy at the Celadon Department Store	₽5,000
Kangaskhanite	Allows Kangaskhan to Mega Evolve into Mega Kangaskhan.	Buy from the Mega Stone seller in the Pokémon League after entering the Hall of Fame	₽30,000
Key Stone	A stone filled with an unexplained power. It allows a Pokémon to Mega Evolve if you have the corresponding Mega Stone for that Pokémon.	Receive from Blue in the Oak Pokémon Research Lab	–
Leaf Letter	A letter written on a leaf. It's a gift from your partner.	Receive from your partner Pokémon in Partner Play	–
Leaf Stone	Evolves Gloom, Weepinbell, and Exeggcute when used on them.	Buy at the Celadon Department Store	₽5,000
Lemonade	Restores the HP of a Pokémon by 70 points.	Buy at vending machines at the Celadon Department Store	₽350
Lift Key	Allows you to operate the elevator in the Team Rocket Hideout.	Receive from your partner Pokémon in the Team Rocket Hideout	–
Lone Earring	A single earring that somebody dropped. It's a gift from your partner.	Receive from your partner Pokémon in Partner Play	–
Lure	Makes rare Pokémon more likely to appear for a while after its use.	Buy at any Poké Mart or the Celadon Department Store (after earning two Gym Badges)	₽400
Marble	A round glass marble. It's a gift from your partner.	Receive from your partner Pokémon in Partner Play	–
Max Elixir	Completely restores the PP of all of a Pokémon's moves.	Find in Silph Co. (11F), the Pokémon Mansion (B1F, 1F), and the Cerulean Cave (B1F)	–
Max Ether	Completely restores the PP of a Pokémon's move.	Find in Silph Co. (5F) and the Pokémon Mansion (2F)	–
Max Lure	Makes rare Pokémon more likely to appear for a very long while after its use.	Buy at any Poké Mart or the Celadon Department Store (after earning six Gym Badges)	₽900
Max Potion	Completely restores the HP of a Pokémon.	Buy at any Poké Mart or the Celadon Department Store (after earning six Gym Badges)	₽2,500
Max Repel	Prevents wild Pokémon from appearing for a very long while after its use.	Buy at any Poké Mart or the Celadon Department Store (after earning five Gym Badges)	₽900
Max Revive	Revives a fainted Pokémon and fully restores its HP.	Find as a hidden item in the Team Rocket Hideout (B4F), the Seafoam Islands (B1F), and the Cerulean Cave (B1F, 2F)	–
Mewtwonite X	Allows Mewtwo to Mega Evolve into Mega Mewtwo X.	Receive from Green in the Cerulean Cave	–
Mewtwonite Y	Allows Mewtwo to Mega Evolve into Mega Mewtwo Y.	Receive from Green in the Cerulean Cave	–
Mighty Candy	Increases a Pokémon's Attack by 1. The number of Candies you need increases as your Pokémon's Go Power rises.	Receive after catching Pokémon or sending Pokémon to Professor Oak / Find as a hidden item in the Rocket Game Corner, in the Pokémon Mansion, and on Victory Road	–
Mighty Candy L	Increases a Pokémon's Attack by 1. Can only be used on Pokémon at Lv. 30 or higher. The number of Candies you need increases as your Pokémon's Go Power rises.	Receive after catching Pokémon or sending Pokémon to Professor Oak / Find as a hidden item in the Rocket Game Corner	–
Mighty Candy XL	Increases a Pokémon's Attack by 1. Can only be used on Pokémon at Lv. 60 or higher. The number of Candies you need increases as your Pokémon's Go Power rises.	Receive after catching Pokémon or sending Pokémon to Professor Oak / Find as a hidden item in the Rocket Game Corner	–
Moon Stone	Evolves Nidorina, Nidorino, Clefairy, and Jigglypuff when used on them.	Find as a hidden item in Mt. Moon (B2F) and Saffron City	–
Nanab Berry	A Berry that slightly calms wild Pokémon you're trying to catch when given to them.	Receive after catching Pokémon / Find as a hidden item on Route 25 and Route 10 (South)	–
Nugget	A nugget of pure gold. It can be sold at shops for a high price.	Receive once per day from the Diglett in the warden's house in Fuchsia City / Find in Mt. Moon (B2F), Celadon City, Silph Co. (5F), and elsewhere	–
Old Amber	A piece of amber with Pokémon DNA trapped inside. When restored, it becomes Aerodactyl.	Receive it in the Pewter Museum of Science / Find as a hidden item in the Cerulean Cave (B1F, 2F)	–
Paralyze Heal	Cures the paralysis status condition.	Buy at any Poké Mart or the Celadon Department Store (no Gym Badges required)	₽300
Parcel	Deliver to Professor Oak to get a reward.	Receive from a Poké Mart clerk in Viridian City	–
Pearl	A pretty pearl. It can be sold at shops for a low price.	Find as a hidden item in the Pokémon Tower (2F) and the Seafoam Islands (B2F)	–
Pewter Crunchies	Pewter City's famous snack. It can be used once to cure all the status conditions and confusion of a Pokémon.	Buy once per day at the Pewter City Pokémon Center	₽500
Pidgeotite	Allows Pidgeot to Mega Evolve into Mega Pidgeot.	Buy from the Mega Stone seller in the Pokémon League after entering the Hall of Fame	₽30,000
Pinap Berry	A Berry that makes you slightly more likely to get an item when given to Pokémon you're trying to catch.	Receive after catching Pokémon / Find as a hidden item on Route 7 and Route 9	–
Pinsirite	Allows Pinsir to Mega Evolve into Mega Pinsir.	Buy from the Mega Stone seller in the Pokémon League after entering the Hall of Fame	₽30,000
Poké Flute	A flute that will wake up certain sleeping Pokémon that block your path.	Receive from Mr. Fuji in the Pokémon House in Lavender Town	–
Polished Mud Ball	A ball made of mud. It's a gift from your partner.	Receive from your partner Pokémon in Partner Play	–
Potion	Restores the HP of a Pokémon by 20 points.	Buy at any Poké Mart or the Celadon Department Store (no Gym Badges required)	₽200
PP Max	Increases the maximum PP of a move as high as it will go.	Find as a hidden item in the Cerulean Cave (B1F)	–
PP Up	Increases the maximum PP of a move by a small amount.	Find as a hidden item on Route 4 (East) and in the Pokémon Tower (6F)	–
Pretty Wing	A beautiful feather. It can be sold at shops for a low price.	Receive from your partner Pokémon in Partner Play / Find as a hidden item in the Power Plant, in the Seafoam Islands (B4F), and on Victory Road (2F)	–
Quick Candy	Increases a Pokémon's Speed by 1. The number of Candies you need increases as your Pokémon's Go Power rises.	Receive after catching Pokémon or sending Pokémon to Professor Oak / Find as a hidden item in the Rocket Game Corner, in the Pokémon Mansion, and on Victory Road	–
Quick Candy L	Increases a Pokémon's Speed by 1. Can only be used on Pokémon at Lv. 30 or higher. The number of Candies you need increases as your Pokémon's Go Power rises.	Receive after catching Pokémon or sending Pokémon to Professor Oak / Find as a hidden item in the Rocket Game Corner	–
Quick Candy XL	Increases a Pokémon's Speed by 1. Can only be used on Pokémon at Lv. 60 or higher. The number of Candies you need increases as your Pokémon's Go Power rises.	Receive after catching Pokémon or sending Pokémon to Professor Oak / Find as a hidden item in the Rocket Game Corner	–
Rare Candy	Raises a Pokémon's level by 1.	Find in Cerulean City, Celadon City, Silph Co. (7F), and elsewhere / Find as a hidden item on Route 6 and in the Cerulean Cave (2F)	–

Item	Description	Main way to obtain	Price
Razz Berry	A Berry that makes it slightly easier to catch Pokémon when given to them.	Receive after catching Pokémon / Find as a hidden item on Route 5 and in Celadon City	–
Repel	Prevents wild Pokémon from appearing for a while after its use.	Buy at any Poké Mart or the Celadon Department Store (after earning one Gym Badge)	₽400
Revive	Revives a fainted Pokémon and restores half of its HP.	Buy at any Poké Mart or the Celadon Department Store (after earning three Gym Badges)	₽2,000
S.S. Ticket	A ticket to board the luxury cruise liner S.S. Anne.	Receive from Bill in Bill's house on Route 25	–
Secret Key	The key that unlocks the entrance to the Cinnabar Island Pokémon Gym.	Find in the Pokémon Mansion	–
Shalour Sable	The Kalos region's famous shortbread. It can be used once to cure all the status conditions and confusion of a Pokémon.	Receive from Blue aboard the S.S. Anne	–
Shiny Charm	A shiny charm said to increase the chance of finding a Shiny Pokémon in the wild.	Receive from the game director in the GAME FREAK Development Office after completing your Pokédex	–
Silph Scope	Allows you to see the true identities of the ghosts in the Pokémon Tower.	Receive from Giovanni in the Team Rocket Hideout	–
Silver Leaf	A mysterious silver leaf. It's a gift from your partner.	Receive from your partner Pokémon in Partner Play	–
Silver Nanab Berry	A Berry that calms wild Pokémon you're trying to catch when given to them.	Receive after catching Pokémon / Find as a hidden item on Route 13 and in Silph Co. (5F)	–
Silver Pinap Berry	A Berry that makes you more likely to get an item when given to Pokémon you're trying to catch.	Receive after catching Pokémon / Find as a hidden item on Route 8 and Route 12	–
Silver Razz Berry	A Berry that makes it easier to catch Pokémon when given to them.	Receive after catching Pokémon / Find as a hidden item on Route 18 (West) and in Silph Co. (3F, 8F)	–
Slowbronite	Allows Slowbro to Mega Evolve into Mega Slowbro.	Buy from the Mega Stone seller in the Pokémon League after entering the Hall of Fame	₽30,000
Small Bouquet	A small bouquet. It's a very special gift from your partner.	Receive from your partner Pokémon in Partner Play	–
Smart Candy	Increases a Pokémon's Sp. Atk by 1. The number of Candies you need increases as your Pokémon's Go Power rises.	Receive after catching Pokémon or sending Pokémon to Professor Oak / Find as a hidden item in the Rocket Game Corner, in the Pokémon Mansion, and on Victory Road	–
Smart Candy L	Increases a Pokémon's Sp. Atk by 1. Can only be used on Pokémon at Lv. 30 or higher. The number of Candies you need increases as your Pokémon's Go Power rises.	Receive after catching Pokémon or sending Pokémon to Professor Oak / Find as a hidden item in the Rocket Game Corner	–
Smart Candy XL	Increases a Pokémon's Sp. Atk by 1. Can only be used on Pokémon at Lv. 60 or higher. The number of Candies you need increases as your Pokémon's Go Power rises.	Receive after catching Pokémon or sending Pokémon to Professor Oak / Find as a hidden item in the Rocket Game Corner	–
Soda Pop	Restores the HP of a Pokémon by 50 points.	Buy at vending machines at the Celadon Department Store and the Rocket Game Corner	₽300
Star Piece	A red gem. It can be sold at shops for a high price.	Find as a hidden item in the Pokémon Tower (3F)	–
Stardust	Lovely, red-colored sand. It can be sold at shops for a low price.	Receive from your partner Pokémon in Partner Play / Find as a hidden item in Mt. Moon (1F), on Route 20, and on Route 21	–
Stretchy Spring	A thin small spring. It's a gift from your partner.	Receive from your partner Pokémon in Partner Play	–
Super Lure	Makes rare Pokémon more likely to appear for a long while after its use.	Buy at any Poké Mart or the Celadon Department Store (after earning four Gym Badges)	₽700
Super Potion	Restores the HP of a Pokémon by 60 points.	Buy at any Poké Mart or the Celadon Department Store (after earning two Gym Badges)	₽700
Super Repel	Prevents wild Pokémon from appearing for a long while after its use.	Buy at any Poké Mart or the Celadon Department Store (after earning three Gym Badges)	₽700
Tea	Give to one of the guards in the gates leading to Saffron City to be allowed to pass through.	Receive from Brock in Celadon City	–
Thunder Stone	Evolves Pikachu and Eevee when used on them. Does not work on partner Pikachu or Eevee.	Buy at the Celadon Department Store	₽5,000
Tiny Mushroom	A tiny mushroom. It can be sold at shops for a low price.	Receive from your partner Pokémon in Partner Play / Find as a hidden item in the kitchen of the S.S. Anne	–
Tough Candy	Increases a Pokémon's Defense by 1. The number of Candies you need increases as your Pokémon's Go Power rises.	Receive after catching Pokémon or sending Pokémon to Professor Oak / Find as a hidden item in the Rocket Game Corner, in the Pokémon Mansion, and on Victory Road	–
Tough Candy L	Increases a Pokémon's Defense by 1. Can only be used on Pokémon at Lv. 30 or higher. The number of Candies you need increases as your Pokémon's Go Power rises.	Receive after catching Pokémon or sending Pokémon to Professor Oak / Find as a hidden item in the Rocket Game Corner	–
Tough Candy XL	Increases a Pokémon's Defense by 1. Can only be used on Pokémon at Lv. 60 or higher. The number of Candies you need increases as your Pokémon's Go Power rises.	Receive after catching Pokémon or sending Pokémon to Professor Oak / Find as a hidden item in the Rocket Game Corner	–
Town Map	A map of the Kanto region.	Receive from your mom in Pallet Town	–
Tropical Shell	A beautiful white shell. It's a gift from your partner.	Receive from your partner Pokémon in Partner Play	–
Venusaurite	Allows Venusaur to Mega Evolve into Mega Venusaur.	Receive from Blue in the Oak Pokémon Research Lab	–
Water Stone	Evolves Poliwhirl, Shellder, Staryu, and Eevee when used on them. Does not work on partner Eevee.	Buy at the Celadon Department Store	₽5,000
X Accuracy	Raises the accuracy of a Pokémon by 2 stages during battle.	Buy at any Poké Mart or the Celadon Department Store (after earning one Gym Badge)	₽950
X Attack	Raises the Attack stat of a Pokémon by 2 stages during battle.	Buy at any Poké Mart or the Celadon Department Store (after earning one Gym Badge)	₽550
X Defense	Raises the Defense stat of a Pokémon by 2 stages during battle.	Buy at any Poké Mart or the Celadon Department Store (after earning one Gym Badge)	₽500
X Sp. Atk	Raises the Sp. Atk stat of a Pokémon by 2 stages during battle.	Buy at any Poké Mart or the Celadon Department Store (after earning one Gym Badge)	₽350
X Sp. Def	Raises the Sp. Def stat of a Pokémon by 2 stages during battle.	Buy at any Poké Mart or the Celadon Department Store (after earning one Gym Badge)	₽350
X Speed	Raises the Speed stat of a Pokémon by 2 stages during battle.	Buy at any Poké Mart or the Celadon Department Store (after earning one Gym Badge)	₽350

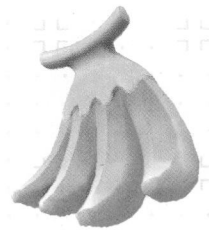

Poké Balls

Different Poké Balls can be more or less effective at catching Pokémon, so use them wisely when trying to catch 'em all!

	Name	Description	Main way to obtain	Price
	Poké Ball	Basic Poké Ball with a decent success rate.	Purchase at any Poké Mart, or receive as a reward for defeating most other Trainers in battle.	₽100
	Great Ball	A more advanced Poké Ball with a higher success rate.	Purchase at any Poké Mart after earning your first Gym Badge, or receive as a reward for defeating Campers and Picnickers in battle.	₽300
	Ultra Ball	The best Poké Ball that can be found in shops, with a very high success rate.	Purchase at any Poké Mart after earning four Gym Badges, or receive as a reward for defeating Ace Trainers in battle.	₽500
	Master Ball	A very rare Poké Ball that is guaranteed to catch any wild Pokémon.	Receive one from the president of Silph Co. after saving his company from Team Rocket, or find one as a hidden item in the Cerulean Cave if you are incredibly lucky.	–
	Premier Ball	A special Poké Ball made to celebrate an event of some sort. About as effective as a normal Poké Ball.	Receive one as a bonus each time you buy 10 of any type of Poké Ball at a Poké Mart.	–

Generic Candies each species gives

When you catch Pokémon or send them to Professor Oak, you'll receive generic Candies most of the time. The kind of Candy you get will depend on the species of the Pokémon, so refer to the handy table below to make your Candy hunt that much easier, and remember the tips on pages 126 and 127, too! (Regional variants may give different Candies!)

Health Candy (Raises HP)	Mighty Candy (Raises Attack)	Tough Candy (Raises Defense)	Smart Candy (Raises Sp. Atk)	Courage Candy (Raises Sp. Def)	Quick Candy (Raises Speed)
010 Caterpie	047 Parasect*	007 Squirtle	001 Bulbasaur	002 Ivysaur*	019 Rattata
029 Nidoran ♀	056 Mankey	008 Wartortle*	002 Ivysaur*	003 Venusaur*	020 Raticate
030 Nidorina	057 Primeape	011 Metapod	003 Venusaur*	008 Wartortle*	021 Spearow
031 Nidoqueen	058 Growlithe	014 Kakuna	005 Charmeleon*	009 Blastoise	022 Fearow
035 Clefairy	059 Arcanine	027 Sandshrew	006 Charizard	012 Butterfree*	025 Pikachu
036 Clefable	066 Machop	028 Sandslash	012 Butterfree*	015 Beedrill*	026 Raichu
039 Jigglypuff	067 Machoke	047 Parasect*	043 Oddish	038 Ninetales*	037 Vulpix
040 Wigglytuff	068 Machamp	062 Poliwrath	044 Gloom	048 Venonat	038 Ninetales*
079 Slowpoke	069 Bellsprout	074 Geodude	045 Vileplume	072 Tentacool	041 Zubat
088 Grimer	070 Weepinbell	075 Graveler	049 Venomoth*	073 Tentacruel	042 Golbat
089 Muk*	071 Victreebel	076 Golem	054 Psyduck	086 Seel	049 Venomoth*
108 Lickitung	083 Farfetch'd	080 Slowbro	055 Golduck	087 Dewgong	050 Diglett
113 Chansey	084 Doduo	090 Shellder	063 Abra	096 Drowzee	051 Dugtrio
115 Kangaskhan	085 Dodrio	091 Cloyster	064 Kadabra	097 Hypno	052 Meowth
131 Lapras	089 Muk*	095 Onix	065 Alakazam	107 Hitmonchan	053 Persian
132 Ditto	098 Krabby	102 Exeggcute	081 Magnemite	122 Mr. Mime	060 Poliwag
134 Vaporeon	099 Kingler	104 Cubone	082 Magneton	133 Eevee	061 Poliwhirl
143 Snorlax	106 Hitmonlee	105 Marowak	092 Gastly	144 Articuno	077 Ponyta
151 Mew	112 Rhydon	109 Koffing	093 Haunter		078 Rapidash
	118 Goldeen	110 Weezing	094 Gengar		100 Voltorb
	119 Seaking	111 Rhyhorn	103 Exeggutor		101 Electrode
	123 Scyther	114 Tangela	116 Horsea		120 Staryu
	127 Pinsir	117 Seadra*	117 Seadra*		121 Starmie
Mighty Candy (Raises Attack)	128 Tauros*	138 Omanyte	124 Jynx	**Quick Candy (Raises Speed)**	125 Electabuzz
	130 Gyarados	139 Omastar	126 Magmar		128 Tauros*
015 Beedrill*	136 Flareon	140 Kabuto	137 Porygon	004 Charmander	129 Magikarp
023 Ekans	141 Kabutops	152 Meltan*	145 Zapdos	005 Charmeleon*	135 Jolteon
024 Arbok	147 Dratini	153 Melmetal*	146 Moltres	013 Weedle	142 Aerodactyl
032 Nidoran♂	148 Dragonair		150 Mewtwo	016 Pidgey	
033 Nidorino	149 Dragonite			017 Pidgeotto	
034 Nidoking	152 Meltan*			018 Pidgeot	
046 Paras	153 Melmetal*				

*Note that entries marked with an asterisk show Pokémon that can yield more than one kind of Candy, so your chance of getting the kind listed at the head of the table is a bit lower than with Pokémon who can only yield that one kind!

Species-specific Candies

The table below lists up all of the species-specific Candies (p. 126) that can be obtained in these games. Use them to help raise all of the stats for your Pokémon in one go!

Item	Description
Abra Candy	Can be used on Abra, Kadabra, and Alakazam to raise all stats by 1 point.
Aerodactyl Candy	Can be used on Aerodactyl to raise all stats by 1 point.
Articuno Candy	Can be used on Articuno to raise all stats by 1 point.
Bellsprout Candy	Can be used on Bellsprout, Weepinbell, and Victreebel to raise all stats by 1 point.
Bulbasaur Candy	Can be used on Bulbasaur, Ivysaur, and Venusaur to raise all stats by 1 point.
Caterpie Candy	Can be used on Caterpie, Metapod, and Butterfree to raise all stats by 1 point.
Chansey Candy	Can be used on Chansey to raise all stats by 1 point.
Charmander Candy	Can be used on Charmander, Charmeleon, and Charizard to raise all stats by 1 point.
Clefairy Candy	Can be used on Clefairy and Clefable to raise all stats by 1 point.
Cubone Candy	Can be used on Cubone, Marowak, and Alolan Marowak to raise all stats by 1 point.
Diglett Candy	Can be used on Diglett, Dugtrio, Alolan Diglett, and Alolan Dugtrio to raise all stats by 1 point.
Ditto Candy	Can be used on Ditto to raise all stats by 1 point.
Doduo Candy	Can be used on Doduo and Dodrio to raise all stats by 1 point.
Dratini Candy	Can be used on Dratini, Dragonair, and Dragonite to raise all stats by 1 point.
Drowzee Candy	Can be used on Drowzee and Hypno to raise all stats by 1 point.
Eevee Candy	Can be used on Eevee, Vaporeon, Jolteon, and Flareon to raise all stats by 1 point.
Ekans Candy	Can be used on Ekans and Arbok to raise all stats by 1 point.
Electabuzz Candy	Can be used on Electabuzz to raise all stats by 1 point.
Exeggcute Candy	Can be used on Exeggcute, Exeggutor, and Alolan Exeggutor to raise all stats by 1 point.
Farfetch'd Candy	Can be used on Farfetch'd to raise all stats by 1 point.
Gastly Candy	Can be used on Gastly, Haunter, and Gengar to raise all stats by 1 point.
Geodude Candy	Can be used on Geodude, Graveler, Golem, Alolan Geodude, Alolan Graveler, and Alolan Golem to raise all stats by 1 point.
Goldeen Candy	Can be used on Goldeen and Seaking to raise all stats by 1 point.
Grimer Candy	Can be used on Grimer, Muk, Alolan Grimer, and Alolan Muk to raise all stats by 1 point.
Growlithe Candy	Can be used on Growlithe and Arcanine to raise all stats by 1 point.
Hitmonchan Candy	Can be used on Hitmonchan to raise all stats by 1 point.
Hitmonlee Candy	Can be used on Hitmonlee to raise all stats by 1 point.
Horsea Candy	Can be used on Horsea and Seadra to raise all stats by 1 point.
Jigglypuff Candy	Can be used on Jigglypuff and Wigglytuff to raise all stats by 1 point.
Jynx Candy	Can be used on Jynx to raise all stats by 1 point.
Kabuto Candy	Can be used on Kabuto and Kabutops to raise all stats by 1 point.
Kangaskhan Candy	Can be used on Kangaskhan to raise all stats by 1 point.
Koffing Candy	Can be used on Koffing and Weezing to raise all stats by 1 point.
Krabby Candy	Can be used on Krabby and Kingler to raise all stats by 1 point.
Lapras Candy	Can be used on Lapras to raise all stats by 1 point.
Lickitung Candy	Can be used on Lickitung to raise all stats by 1 point.
Machop Candy	Can be used on Machop, Machoke, and Machamp to raise all stats by 1 point.
Magikarp Candy	Can be used on Magikarp and Gyarados to raise all stats by 1 point.
Magmar Candy	Can be used on Magmar to raise all stats by 1 point.
Magnemite Candy	Can be used on Magnemite and Magneton to raise all stats by 1 point.

Item	Description
Mankey Candy	Can be used on Mankey and Primeape to raise all stats by 1 point.
Meltan Candy	Can be used on Meltan and Melmetal to raise all stats by 1 point.
Meowth Candy	Can be used on Meowth, Persian, Alolan Meowth, and Alolan Persian to raise all stats by 1 point.
Mew Candy	Can be used on Mew to raise all stats by 1 point.
Mewtwo Candy	Can be used on Mewtwo to raise all stats by 1 point.
Moltres Candy	Can be used on Moltres to raise all stats by 1 point.
Mr. Mime Candy	Can be used on Mr. Mime to raise all stats by 1 point.
Nidoran ♀ Candy	Can be used on Nidoran ♀, Nidorina, and Nidoqueen to raise all stats by 1 point.
Nidoran ♂ Candy	Can be used on Nidoran ♂, Nidorino, and Nidoking to raise all stats by 1 point.
Oddish Candy	Can be used on Oddish, Gloom, and Vileplume to raise all stats by 1 point.
Omanyte Candy	Can be used on Omanyte and Omastar to raise all stats by 1 point.
Onix Candy	Can be used on Onix to raise all stats by 1 point.
Paras Candy	Can be used on Paras and Parasect to raise all stats by 1 point.
Pidgey Candy	Can be used on Pidgey, Pidgeotto, and Pidgeot to raise all stats by 1 point.
Pikachu Candy	Can be used on Pikachu, Raichu, and Alolan Raichu to raise all stats by 1 point.
Pinsir Candy	Can be used on Pinsir to raise all stats by 1 point.
Poliwag Candy	Can be used on Poliwag, Poliwhirl, and Poliwrath to raise all stats by 1 point.
Ponyta Candy	Can be used on Ponyta and Rapidash to raise all stats by 1 point.
Porygon Candy	Can be used on Porygon to raise all stats by 1 point.
Psyduck Candy	Can be used on Psyduck and Golduck to raise all stats by 1 point.
Rattata Candy	Can be used on Rattata, Raticate, Alolan Rattata, and Alolan Raticate to raise all stats by 1 point.
Rhyhorn Candy	Can be used on Rhyhorn and Rhydon to raise all stats by 1 point.
Sandshrew Candy	Can be used on Sandshrew, Sandslash, Alolan Sandshrew, and Alolan Sandslash to raise all stats by 1 point.
Scyther Candy	Can be used on Scyther to raise all stats by 1 point.
Seel Candy	Can be used on Seel and Dewgong to raise all stats by 1 point.
Shellder Candy	Can be used on Shellder and Cloyster to raise all stats by 1 point.
Slowpoke Candy	Can be used on Slowpoke and Slowbro to raise all stats by 1 point.
Snorlax Candy	Can be used on Snorlax to raise all stats by 1 point.
Spearow Candy	Can be used on Spearow and Fearow to raise all stats by 1 point.
Squirtle Candy	Can be used on Squirtle, Wartortle, and Blastoise to raise all stats by 1 point.
Staryu Candy	Can be used on Staryu and Starmie to raise all stats by 1 point.
Tangela Candy	Can be used on Tangela to raise all stats by 1 point.
Tauros Candy	Can be used on Tauros to raise all stats by 1 point.
Tentacool Candy	Can be used on Tentacool and Tentacruel to raise all stats by 1 point.
Venonat Candy	Can be used on Venonat and Venomoth to raise all stats by 1 point.
Voltorb Candy	Can be used on Voltorb and Electrode to raise all stats by 1 point.
Vulpix Candy	Can be used on Vulpix, Ninetales, Alolan Vulpix, and Alolan Ninetales to raise all stats by 1 point.
Weedle Candy	Can be used on Weedle, Kakuna, and Beedrill to raise all stats by 1 point.
Zapdos Candy	Can be used on Zapdos to raise all stats by 1 point.
Zubat Candy	Can be used on Zubat and Golbat to raise all stats by 1 point.

How to obtain species-specific Candies

Here's a handy summary of all the ways you can obtain the rare species-specific Candies listed in the table above!

- Once you've caught at least 120 Pokémon in total, you may get a species-specific Candy after a successful Pokémon catch (p. 126).
- You may get species-specific Candies when your Pokémon come back from a stroll in your Poké Ball Plus (p. 158).
- Each time you've sent 50 of a particular species to Professor Oak, you can get one of the species-specific Candies it can use (p. 127).
- When you send a Pokémon to the professor that's seen its Go Power increase a lot during its time with you, either because of leveling up or having Candies used on it, you may get a small number of species-specific Candies back (p. 127).
- You can receive Pikachu Candies or Eevee Candies after defeating certain Coach Trainers (p. 136).
- Find Voltorb Candies as hidden items in the Power Plant (p. 77).

Items found by the Pokémon traveling with you

As you can read about on page 144, the Pokémon traveling with you may sometimes find items in the field. All items that can be found by your Pokémon are listed in the table below, along with the locations where you might find them. These items can reappear, too, as soon as the clock on your Nintendo Switch turns to a new day after midnight. You might want to revisit some of these spots to collect more of these items!

TIP The items highlighted in red are items the Pokémon traveling with you might just give you sometimes without spotting them in the field. Make sure to talk to them often to see what they might have for you!

Item	Where to find
Razz Berry	Any type of Pokémon has a chance to find this on Route 1, Route 3, and elsewhere.
Nanab Berry	Any type of Pokémon has a chance to find this on Route 3, Route 4, and elsewhere.
Pinap Berry	Any type of Pokémon has a chance to find this on Route 15, Route 17, and elsewhere.
Silver Razz Berry	Any type of Pokémon has a chance to find this on Route 25 and elsewhere.
Silver Nanab Berry	Any type of Pokémon has a chance to find this on Route 7, Route 14, and elsewhere.
Silver Pinap Berry	Any type of Pokémon has a chance to find this on Route 17 and elsewhere.
Golden Razz Berry	Any type of Pokémon has a chance to find this on Route 11 and elsewhere.
Golden Nanab Berry	Any type of Pokémon has a chance to find this on Route 17 and elsewhere.
Golden Pinap Berry	Any type of Pokémon has a chance to find this on Route 8 and elsewhere.
Tiny Mushroom	Paras or Parasect have a chance to find this in Mt. Moon. Rock-type Pokémon have a chance to find this in the Rock Tunnel or on Victory Road.
Big Mushroom	Paras or Parasect have a chance to find this in Mt. Moon. Rock-type Pokémon have a chance to find this in the Rock Tunnel or on Victory Road.
Nugget	Fighting-type Pokémon have a chance to find this in Mt. Moon, in the Rock Tunnel, or on Victory Road.
Stardust	Fighting-type Pokémon have a chance to find this in Mt. Moon or on Victory Road. Fighting- or Ground-type Pokémon have a chance to find this in the Rock Tunnel. Any type of Pokémon has a chance to find this in the Cerulean Cave.

Item	Where to find
Star Piece	Fighting-type Pokémon have a chance to find this in Mt. Moon or on Victory Road. Fighting- or Ground-type Pokémon have a chance to find this in the Rock Tunnel. Any type of Pokémon has a chance to find this in the Cerulean Cave.
Fire Stone	Rock-type Pokémon have a chance to find this in the Rock Tunnel or on Victory Road.
Thunder Stone	Rock-type Pokémon have a chance to find this in the Rock Tunnel.
Water Stone	Rock-type Pokémon have a chance to find this in the Rock Tunnel.
Ice Stone	Ice-type Pokémon have a chance to find this in the Seafoam Islands.
Pearl	Water-type Pokémon have a chance to find this in Viridian City, on Route 25, and on Route 12. Ground-type Pokémon have a chance to find this on Route 19. Ice-type Pokémon have a chance to find this in the Seafoam Islands. Any type of Pokémon has a chance to find this in the Cerulean Cave.
Big Pearl	Water-type Pokémon have a chance to find this in Viridian City, on Route 25, and on Route 12. Ground-type Pokémon have a chance to find this on Route 19. Ice-type Pokémon have a chance to find this in the Seafoam Islands. Any type of Pokémon has a chance to find this in the Cerulean Cave.
Heart Scale	Water-type Pokémon have a chance to find this on Route 12 or in the Cerulean Cave.
Pretty Wing	Grass-type Pokémon have a chance to find this in Viridian City, Cerulean City, Vermilion City, Lavender Town, Celadon City and Saffron City.

The tables below list all the items you can buy from various shops, sellers, and vending machines in the Kanto region.

Poké Marts & Trainers' Market (2F) in the Celadon Department Store

Item	Price
Poké Ball	₽100
Potion	₽200
Antidote	₽200
Burn Heal	₽300
Ice Heal	₽100
Awakening	₽100
Paralyze Heal	₽300
After earning one Gym Badge	
Great Ball	₽300
Escape Rope	₽300
Repel	₽400
X Attack	₽550
X Defense	₽500
X Sp. Atk	₽350
X Sp. Def	₽350
X Speed	₽350
X Accuracy	₽950
Dire Hit	₽650
Guard Spec.	₽700
After earning two Gym Badges	
Super Potion	₽700
Lure	₽400
After earning three Gym Badges	
Full Heal	₽400
Revive	₽2,000
Super Repel	₽700
After earning four Gym Badges	
Ultra Ball	₽500
Hyper Potion	₽1,500
Super Lure	₽700
After earning five Gym Badges	
Max Repel	₽900
After earning six Gym Badges	
Max Potion	₽2,500
Max Lure	₽900
After earning seven Gym Badges	
(No additional items are unlocked.)	
After earning eight Gym Badges	
Full Restore	₽3,000

Pewter City Pokémon Center

Pewter Crunchies seller	
Pewter Crunchies	₽500

Celadon Department Store

Technical Machine shop (2F)	
TM17 Dragon Tail	₽20,000
TM18 U-turn	₽20,000
TM19 Iron Tail	₽50,000
TM25 Waterfall	₽30,000
TM28 Tri Attack	₽30,000
TM30 Bulk Up	₽10,000
TM43 Shadow Ball	₽30,000
TM48 Hyper Beam	₽100,000
Wiseman Gifts (4F)	
Fire Stone	₽5,000
Thunder Stone	₽5,000
Water Stone	₽5,000
Leaf Stone	₽5,000
Ice Stone	₽5,000
Accessory Market (5F)	
Hat table	
Straw Hat	₽10,000
Sweet Hat	₽20,000
Elegant Hat	₽20,000
Crown	₽999,999
Diglett table	
Diglett Cap	₽50
Accessories table	
Little Red Bow	₽1,000
Little Green Bow	₽1,000
Little Blue Bow	₽1,000
Little Black Bow	₽1,000
Little Plaid Bow	₽1,000
Little Formal Bow	₽1,000
Little Polka-Dot Bow	₽1,000
Little Bow	₽1,000
Fancy Red Bow	₽2,000
Fancy Green Bow	₽2,000
Fancy Blue Bow	₽2,000
Fancy Black Bow	₽2,000
Fancy Plaid Bow	₽2,000
Fancy Polka-Dot Bow	₽2,000
Fancy Cute Bow	₽2,000
Fancy Frilly Bow	₽2,000
Sailor Bandanna	₽3,000
Safari Bandanna	₽3,000
Polka-Dot Bandanna	₽3,000
Ruby Bandanna	₽3,000
Sapphire Bandanna	₽3,000
Emerald Bandanna	₽3,000
Black Bandanna	₽3,000
White Bandanna	₽3,000
Red Flowers	₽5,000
Pink Flowers	₽5,000
Blue Flowers	₽5,000
White Flowers	₽5,000
Orange Flowers	₽5,000
Purple Flowers	₽5,000
Pale Blue Flowers	₽5,000
Green Flowers	₽5,000
Glasses table	
Black Framed Glasses	₽8,000
Red Framed Glasses	₽8,000
Green Framed Glasses	₽8,000
Brown Framed Glasses	₽12,000
Thick Glasses	₽5,000
Blue Sky Sunglasses	₽10,000
Dawn Sunglasses	₽10,000
Dusk Sunglasses	₽10,000
Midnight Sunglasses	₽10,000
Rooftop vending machines	
Fresh Water	₽200
Soda Pop	₽300
Lemonade	₽350

Rocket Game Corner vending machines

Item	Price
Fresh Water	₽200
Soda Pop	₽300

Pokémon League

Mega Stone seller (after entering Hall of Fame)	
Beedrillite	₽30,000
Pidgeotite	₽30,000
Alakazite	₽30,000
Slowbronite	₽30,000
Gengarite	₽30,000
Kangaskhanite	₽30,000
Pinsirite	₽30,000
Gyaradosite	₽30,000
Aerodactylite	₽30,000

TIP

In addition to all the items above, you can also buy a Magikarp for ₽500 from the man in the Pokémon Center on Route 4 (West)!

Don't know your Attack from your Sp. Attack? Not sure how a status condition is different from a stat? Use this glossary of common Pokémon terms whenever you need to look something up in a jiffy.

Accuracy: Accuracy is a variable that shows how likely it is that a move will hit the target. The closer a move's accuracy is to 100, the more likely the move will hit. Accuracy can be boosted or lowered in battle.

Asleep: When a Pokémon is asleep, it can't use moves. The Pokémon will wake up after several turns, or it can be woken up with an item.

Attack: The Attack stat influences how much damage a Pokémon's physical moves will do.

Battle: A battle is a competition between Pokémon Trainers, where they have their Pokémon engage in battle against each other. Each Trainer directs their Pokémon to use moves to try to best their opponents.

Battle Item: A battle item can be used to temporarily increase a Pokémon's performance during a battle. Battle items include those such as X Attacks, which boost a Pokémon's Attack stat, and Dire Hits, which raise the Pokémon's chance to land a critical hit.

Berry: A Berry can be used to help catch wild Pokémon or to increase the chance of getting items after a successful catch.

Boosting Stats: Stats can be temporarily boosted during battle by using certain moves or items. These effects don't last after the battle ends. For permanent increases, see Go Power.

Burned: The burned status condition lowers the power of physical moves and reduces the Pokémon's HP at the end of each turn. The condition does not go away on its own after the battle ends.

Candy: A Candy can be used to boost your Pokémon's stats. Each type of Candy increases a specific stat, such as Mighty Candy increasing Attack. The exception is Candies with a Pokémon's name, such as Bulbasaur Candy. These will increase all stats of that specific Pokémon or its Evolutions by 1.

Coach Trainer: A Coach Trainer is a Pokémon Trainer whose aim is to help you hone your skills in battle. They are stronger than the average Pokémon Trainer in their area and will give you useful items, such as a TM or Candies, if you manage to defeat them.

Confused: Being confused may cause a Pokémon to damage itself instead of using its intended move. The Pokémon will recover after several turns, when the Pokémon is switched out, or when the battle ends.

Critical Hit: A critical hit is when a move deals extra damage to an opponent. Each damage-dealing move has a chance to score a critical hit, but some moves, such as Slash, are especially likely to land critical hits.

Defense: The Defense stat influences how well a Pokémon can defend against physical moves.

Effectiveness: The damage dealt with an attack changes based on the type of the move used by the attacking Pokémon and the type of the targeted Pokémon. Attacks can be effective, super effective, not very effective, or have no effect, depending on how these types match up.

Elite Four: The Elite Four are four very skilled Trainers you have to defeat to prove yourself a Pokémon League Champion.

Encounter: You encounter wild Pokémon when walking around in the world of Pokémon. Pokémon can be found in all kinds of environments, such as patches of grass or dark caves. You can catch wild Pokémon in these encounters to add them to your team.

Evasiveness: Evasiveness is a variable that determines whether your Pokémon can evade an attack or not. It is not one of the six main stats (HP, Attack, Defense, Sp. Atk, Sp. Def, Speed), but it can be boosted or lowered during battle by using specific items or moves.

Evolution: The process of a Pokémon becoming a different Pokémon is known as Evolution. Evolved Pokémon are usually stronger than their predecessors, and they can often learn moves that are more powerful. Conditions for Evolution depend on the Pokémon species, but leveling up is a common way to evolve a Pokémon.

Experience Points: Pokémon earn Experience Points (Exp. Points) through battling. Earning enough Exp. Points will cause a Pokémon to level up.

Fainting: When a Pokémon's HP has been reduced to zero, it faints. A Pokémon that has fainted cannot take part in battle. If all the Pokémon on a Trainer's team faint, that Trainer loses the battle.

Flinching: The target Pokémon may flinch when hit by certain moves, causing its own move to fail on the current turn. The effect lasts only for the turn in which the Pokémon flinches.

Frozen: When a Pokémon is frozen, it cannot use most moves. The Pokémon will recover from this status condition after several turns pass. Being hit by a Fire-type move—or using certain Fire-type moves—will cause a frozen Pokémon to thaw and recover from this status condition.

Gender: The gender of a Pokémon is designated as male, female, or unknown. Some Pokémon have different appearances depending on their gender.

ADVENTURE DATA

Go Power: With Go Power, your Pokémon's stats can be permanently increased. Your Pokémon will get a dose of Go Power each time they level up, causing one of their stats to increase by one point. You can also use Candies to affect your Pokémon's Go Power and increase their stats at any time.

HP: HP (Hit Points) shows how healthy a Pokémon is, indicating how much damage it can take before it faints.

Hyper Training: Pokémon that have reached Lv. 100 may undergo Hyper Training to boost their individual strengths to the maximum. Trainers must pay the old man at the Pokémon Day Care (Route 5) for this service using Bottle Caps. Trainers with a Bottle Cap can use Hyper Training on one of their Pokémon's stats—or, with a Gold Bottle Cap, maximize them all! See also Individual Strengths.

Individual Strengths: Individual strengths are the innate gifts of an individual Pokémon that help determine each of its stats. A Pokémon with a higher individual strength for Attack will see its Attack stat grow faster and have a higher maximum Attack stat than a Pokémon of the same species with a lower individual strength for Attack. See also Hyper Training.

Item: An item is an object that can be used or consumed and can often be bought, sold, or traded. Key items, such as the Town Map, perform unique functions and cannot be bought or sold.

Judge: One of Professor Oak's assistants in the Route 11 gate (2F) will give you access to this function if you've caught enough Pokémon. The Judge function allows you to see the potential for each of your Pokémon's individual strengths in each stat—and see an evaluation of your Pokémon's overall potential. Stats that display Best have maximum individual strengths.

Level: The experience level of a Pokémon is indicated by a number from 1 to 100. As it levels up, a Pokémon may gain stat increases and learn new moves. Leveling up is achieved by gaining set amounts of Exp. Points or using a Rare Candy.

Love: Love is the level of affection a Pokémon feels toward you. It increases by having the Pokémon in your party for a long time, having it travel with you, using items on it, leveling it up, etc. A Pokémon with lots of love will get benefits in battle, such as a higher chance of scoring a critical hit or evading an attack.

Medicine: Medicine refers to items that you'll find in the Medicine Pocket of your Bag. These include items to restore HP or PP, such as Potions and Elixirs, and items that help Pokémon recover from status conditions or fainting, such as Antidotes and Revives. Using a medicine item on your Pokémon in battle will take up a turn, preventing your Pokémon from using a move that turn.

Mega Evolution: Mega Evolution is a powerful transformation that some Pokémon can undergo during battle. You must possess the correct Mega Stone as well as a Key Stone that can resonate with Mega Stones. The Pokémon's types and stats may change upon Mega Evolution.

Move: A move is the primary action a Pokémon can take during a battle to either damage an opponent or help itself or an ally in some way. A Pokémon can know up to four moves at a time. If a Pokémon already knows four moves, then it must forget an old move before it can learn a new move.

Nature: A permanent, unchangeable quality that each Pokémon has, Nature affects the growth of a Pokémon's stats, typically making one stat grow faster than average and another grow slower than average. The stat whose name appears in blue on the stat graph on the Summary screen is the one that has a decreased maximum value due to your Pokémon's Nature, and the one in pink has an increased maximum value. There are 25 different Natures, such as Adamant, Jolly, and Timid.

Original Trainer: The Trainer who first caught a Pokémon is known as its original Trainer—or OT. Pokémon traded away from their original Trainer will gain extra experience, but they might not obey a Trainer in battle if the Trainer hasn't gathered enough Gym Badges.

Paralysis: Paralysis lowers the Pokémon's Speed and causes moves to fail 25 percent of the time. This status condition does not go away on its own after the battle ends.

Partner Move Tutor: The Partner Move Tutor teaches moves that only your partner Pikachu or Eevee can learn.

Partner Power: A partner power is a special power your partner Pokémon can use during battle. It will trigger a special move (Pika Papow for Pikachu or Veevee Volley for Eevee) if your partner is the one battling—or raise all the stats of the battling Pokémon if your partner's just watching. Partner powers can only be used when your partner is feeling motivated—feed it Berries or play with it to increase the chances of your partner helping you with its special power.

Physical Move: Like a special move, a physical move deals damage. The damage dealt by a physical move is influenced by the Attack stat of the attacking Pokémon and the Defense stat of the defending Pokémon.

Poisoned: Being poisoned or badly poisoned reduces the Pokémon's HP at the end of each turn. The poisoned status condition does not go away on its own after the battle ends.

Poké Ball: A Poké Ball is an item used to catch wild Pokémon. There are different kinds of Poké Balls, such as Great Balls and Ultra Balls, and they vary in effectiveness. Poké Balls cannot be used in Trainer battles.

Pokédex: The Pokédex records every Pokémon a Trainer has seen, caught, or traded during an adventure. It may also refer to a printed guide containing data about each Pokémon.

Poké Mart: This blue-roofed type of shop can be found in most cities. They sell items useful for battle and for catching Pokémon. The number of items they carry will increase as you gather Gym Badges from Pokémon Gyms.

Pokémon Center: This red-roofed type of facility can be found in most cities. You can come here to have your Pokémon healed—restoring their HP, allowing them to recover from fainting, and removing any status conditions.

Pokémon Day Care: The Pokémon Day Care (Route 5) is a facility where you can drop off your Pokémon to be cared for. They'll gain Exp. Points and may level up.

Pokémon Gym: Pokémon Gyms are facilities where aspiring Trainers go to test their skills. If you can impress a Gym Leader by defeating them in battle, they will give you a Gym Badge that indicates to others that you've been found worthy. With eight Gym Badges, you can challenge the Pokémon League.

Pokémon League: The Pokémon League is an organization that recognizes the most powerful Trainers in a region. You can become a Pokémon League Champion if you overcome certain challenges decided by the Pokémon League, including defeating the Elite Four.

PP: PP (Power Points) represents the number of times a Pokémon can use a particular move. If no PP remains for any of a Pokémon's moves, that Pokémon will use the move Struggle when it attacks. The items PP Max and PP Up can permanently increase the max PP of a move. During regular gameplay, PP can be restored by using items or when a Pokémon is healed at a Pokémon Center.

Range: Range describes the potential distance and scope that a move will target. The range for most attacks is to target a single Pokémon. Some moves, such as Surf, will target all Pokémon but the user, if used in a Double Battle, for example.

Same-Type Attack Bonus: The additional damage done when a Pokémon uses a damage-dealing move that matches its type—for example, a Fire-type Pokémon using the Fire-type move Ember—is known as a same-type attack bonus.

Secret Technique: A Secret Technique is a skill that your partner will learn at some point during your adventure. Each will help you along your adventure by allowing you to do something new, such as chop down thin trees, light up dark caves, etc.

Shiny Pokémon: Scarce and sought after, Pokémon with alternative coloration are known as Shiny. Whether a Pokémon is Shiny or not has no effect in battle.

Sp. Atk: The Sp. Atk (Special Attack) stat influences how much damage a Pokémon's special moves will do.

Sp. Def: The Sp. Def (Special Defense) stat influences how well a Pokémon can defend against special moves.

Special Move: Like physical moves, special moves deal damage. The damage dealt by a special move is influenced by the Sp. Atk stat of the attacking Pokémon and the Sp. Def stat of the defending Pokémon.

Species Strengths: Species strengths are the unique strengths of each species of Pokémon that determine the general range of stats for that species. A Pokémon's species strengths cannot be changed, but its stats will be affected further by its Go Power, individual strengths, and Nature.

Speed: The Speed stat influences which Pokémon acts first in battle.

Stat: A stat is any of the six primary factors that determine how a Pokémon will perform in battle. These six are HP, Attack, Defense, Special Attack (Sp. Atk), Special Defense (Sp. Def), and Speed.

Status Condition: A status condition is a temporary condition that affects how a Pokémon performs in battle. Some status conditions will go away on their own, while others must be healed with items or at a Pokémon Center.

Status Move: A status move is one that does not inflict direct damage but instead causes status conditions or other effects, such as boosting or lowering the stats of a targeted Pokémon.

Summary: The summary screen is an in-game feature that shows data on a Pokémon, including its stats, moves, level, original Trainer, Nature, and more.

TM: A TM (Technical Machine) is an item that can be used to teach moves to Pokémon. TMs can be used multiple times.

Turn: Each period in a battle where you or your Pokémon performs an action (performing a move, using an item, swapping Pokémon, etc.) is called a turn. For example, if a move says it has an effect for five turns, that means you or your Pokémon can act five times without the effect wearing off.

Type: Types interact like rock-paper-scissors, where certain types are stronger against other types. For example, Electric-type moves are strong against Flying-type Pokémon. A move usually has a single type. Pokémon may have one or two types.

Type Matchup Chart: A handy table—like the one to the right!—that shows the effectiveness of different types of moves against each Pokémon type.

Type Matchup Chart

Knowing the types of Pokémon is vital during battles. All Pokémon—and their moves—have types, and each type has its own strengths and weaknesses, as well as types it will simply deal regular damage to. This regular damage will be calculated using the Pokémon's stats and the move's power. These matchups are all shown in the table below.

As you continue on your adventure, you may notice that some Pokémon have two types. If a Pokémon has two types, the strengths and weaknesses of the types are both taken into account. They might multiply the damage the Pokémon takes, or they might cancel each other out. Turn back to page 123 if you need a review of how type matchups work!

Type	Effect
◉	• Immune to damage-dealing Ghost-type moves.
◉	• Cannot be burned.
◉	• Immune to Leech Seed. • Immune to powder and spore moves.
◉	• Cannot be paralyzed.
✳	• Cannot be frozen.
◉	• Cannot be poisoned or badly poisoned.
◉	• Immune to Electric-type moves (including non-damaging moves, such as Thunder Wave).
◉	• Immune to Ground-type moves (including non-damaging moves, such as Sand Attack).
◉	• Immune to Fighting-type moves and damage-dealing Normal-type moves.
◉	• Immune to damage-dealing Psychic-type moves.
◉	• Immune to Poison-type moves. • Cannot be poisoned or badly poisoned.
◈	• Immune to Dragon-type moves.

Defending Pokémon's Type

Attacking Pokémon's Move Type

	NORMAL	FIRE	WATER	GRASS	ELECTRIC	ICE	FIGHTING	POISON	GROUND	FLYING	PSYCHIC	BUG	ROCK	GHOST	DRAGON	DARK	STEEL	FAIRY
NORMAL													△	✕			△	
FIRE	△	△	◎		◎							◎	△		△		◎	
WATER	◎	△	△					◎					◎		△			
GRASS	△	◎	△					△	◎	△		△	◎		△		△	
ELECTRIC		◎	△	△					✕	◎					△			
ICE	△	△	◎		△				◎	◎					◎		△	
FIGHTING	◎					◎		△		△	△	△	◎	✕		◎	◎	△
POISON			◎					△	△				△	△			✕	◎
GROUND	◎		△	◎			◎		✕			△	◎				◎	
FLYING			◎	△			◎					◎	△				△	
PSYCHIC					◎	◎					△					✕	△	
BUG		△		◎			△	△		△	◎			△		◎	△	△
ROCK		◎				◎	△		△	◎		◎					△	
GHOST	✕										◎			◎	△			
DRAGON															◎		△	✕
DARK							△				◎			◎		△		△
STEEL		△	△		△	◎							◎				△	◎
FAIRY		△					◎	△							◎	◎	△	

Key

Super effective Moves will do 2× damage.	No weakness or resistance Moves will do the regular amount of damage.	Not very effective Moves will do ½ damage.	No effect Moves will do no damage.
◎	No icon	△	✕

◉ NORMAL	◉ GRASS	◉ FIGHTING	◉ FLYING	◉ ROCK	◉ DARK	
◉ FIRE	◉ ELECTRIC	◉ POISON	◉ PSYCHIC	◉ GHOST	◉ STEEL	
◉ WATER	✳ ICE	◉ GROUND	◉ BUG	◉ DRAGON	◈ FAIRY	

Credits

Content and Writing
Jillian Nonaka
Jordan Blanco

Writing Support
Sayuri Munday
Shawn Williams-Brown

Editing
Kellyn Ballard
Rei Nakazawa
Isaac Nickerson

Additional Research & Fact Checking
Matthieu Béthencourt
Olivier Hagué (JAC Recruitment)
Yuriko Iwasaki
Sophie Jueterbock
Kathleen Kalms

Diego Luque de la Campa
Irene Mascaró Genestar
Valentina Menale
Juliana Niederwanger
Bryan Olsson

Screenshots
Jeff Hines
Robert Colling
Steve Stratton (AltaSource Group)
Marvin Andrews
Peter Bagley

Design
Chris Franc
Kevin Lalli
Hiromi Kimura
Mark Pedini
Elisabeth Lariviere
Jane Kusuma

Acknowledgments
Heather Dalgleish
Yasuhiro Usui
Mikiko Ryu
Anja Weinbach
Elena Nardo
Hisato Yamamori
Blaise Selby
Mayu Todo
Bertrand Lecocq
Cyril Schultz
Pierre Gauthier
Emanuel Turchetta
Daniel Anscomb
Mark Hughes (Prima Games)
Shaida Boroumand (Prima Games)

Project Management
Yohei Sugiyama
Terry Mihashi
Hannah Vassallo
Owen Preece

Special Thanks
GAME FREAK inc.
The Pokémon Company

Pokémon: Let's Go, Pikachu! & *Pokémon: Let's Go, Eevee!*
Official Trainer's Guide & Pokédex

©2018 The Pokémon Company International
ISBN: 978-0744019-81-0
Published in the United States by

The Pokémon Company International
10400 NE 4th Street, Suite 2800
Bellevue, WA 98004 USA

3rd Floor Building 10, Chiswick Park
566 Chiswick High Road
London, W4 5XS United Kingdom

Printed in the United States of America.

Australian Warranty Statement

This product comes with guarantees that cannot be excluded under the Australian Consumer Law. You are entitled to a replacement or refund for a major failure and for compensation for any other reasonably foreseeable loss or damage. You are also entitled to have the goods repaired or replaced if the goods fail to be of acceptable quality and the failure does not amount to a major failure. This product comes with a one-year warranty from date of purchase. Defects in the product must have appeared within one year from date of purchase in order to claim the warranty. All warranty claims must be facilitated back through the retailer of purchase, in accordance with the retailer's returns policies and procedures. Any cost incurred as a result of returning the product to the retailer of purchase are the full responsibility of the consumer.

AU wholesale distributor:
Bluemouth Interactive Pty Ltd,
Suite 1502, 9 Yarra Street, South Yarra
Victoria, 3141 Australia
+613 9646 4011
Email: support@bluemouth.com.au